Joe Wright

P9-ECR-285

Less managing. More teaching. Greater learning.

 INSTRUCTORS...

Would you like your **students** to show up for class more **prepared**? *(Let's face it, class is much more fun if everyone is engaged and prepared...)*

Want ready-made application-level **interactive assignments,** student progress reporting, and auto-assignment grading? *(Less time grading means more time teaching...)*

Want an **instant view of student or class performance** relative to learning objectives? *(No more wondering if students understand...)*

Need to **collect data and generate reports** required for administration or accreditation? *(Say goodbye to manually tracking student learning outcomes...)*

Want to **record and post your lectures** for students to view online?

 With **McGraw-Hill's *Connect*™ *Plus* Management,**

INSTRUCTORS GET:

- Interactive Applications – **book-specific interactive assignments** that require students to APPLY what they've learned.

- Simple **assignment management,** allowing you to spend more time teaching.

- **Auto-graded** assignments, quizzes, and tests.

- **Detailed Visual Reporting** where student and section results can be viewed and analyzed.

- Sophisticated **online testing** capability.

- A **filtering and reporting** function that allows you to easily assign and report on materials that are correlated to accreditation standards, learning outcomes, and Bloom's taxonomy.

- An easy-to-use **lecture capture** tool.

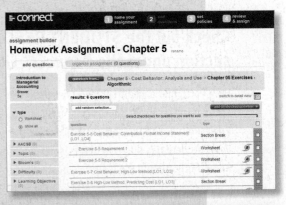

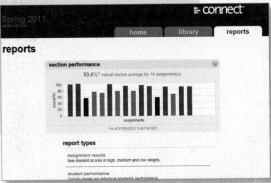

Want an online, **searchable version** of your textbook?

Wish your textbook could be **available online** while you're doing your assignments?

 ### *Connect™ Plus Management* eBook

If you choose to use *Connect™ Plus Management*, you have an affordable and searchable online version of your book integrated with your other online tools.

Connect™ Plus Management eBook offers features like:

- Topic search
- Direct links from assignments
- Adjustable text size
- Jump to page number
- Print by section

 Want to get more **value** from your textbook purchase?

Think learning organizational behavior should be a bit more **interesting**?

 ### Check out the STUDENT RESOURCES section under the *Connect™* Library tab.

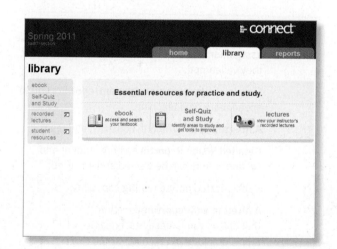

Here you'll find a wealth of resources designed to help you achieve your goals in the course. You'll find things like **quizzes, PowerPoints, and Internet activities** to help you study. Every student has different needs, so explore the STUDENT RESOURCES to find the materials best suited to you.

organizational
behavior

Steven L. McShane
University of Western Australia

Mary Ann Von Glinow
Florida International University

The McGraw-Hill Companies

McGraw-Hill
Irwin

organizational
behavior

VICE PRESIDENT AND EDITOR-IN-CHIEF **BRENT GORDON**

EDITORIAL DIRECTOR **PAUL DUCHAM**

EXECUTIVE EDITOR **MICHAEL ABLASSMEIR**

EXECUTIVE DIRECTOR OF DEVELOPMENT **ANN TORBERT**

DEVELOPMENT EDITOR **KELLY I. PEKELDER**

EDITORIAL ASSISTANT **ANDREA HEIRENDT**

VICE PRESIDENT AND DIRECTOR OF MARKETING **ROBIN J. ZWETTLER**

MARKETING DIRECTOR **AMEE MOSLEY**

EXECUTIVE MARKETING MANAGER **ANKE BRAUN WEEKES**

MARKETING SPECIALIST **ANNIE FERRO**

VICE PRESIDENT OF EDITING, DESIGN, AND PRODUCTION **SESHA BOLISETTY**

PROJECT MANAGER **DANA M. PAULEY**

SENIOR BUYER **MICHAEL R. MCCORMICK**

SENIOR DESIGNER **MARY KAZAK SANDER**

SENIOR PHOTO RESEARCH COORDINATOR **KERI JOHNSON**

PHOTO RESEARCH COORDINATOR **JOANNE MENNEMEIER**

PHOTO RESEARCHER **ALLISON GRIMES**

SENIOR MEDIA PROJECT MANAGER **GREG BATES**

MEDIA PROJECT MANAGER **JOYCE J. CHAPPETTO**

TYPEFACE **10/12 MINION PRO REGULAR**

COMPOSITOR **APTARA®, INC.**

PRINTER **QUAD/GRAPHICS**

COVER IMAGE **FUSE**

ORGANIZATIONAL BEHAVIOR

Published by McGraw-Hill/Irwin, a business unit of The McGraw-Hill Companies, Inc., 1221 Avenue of the Americas, New York, NY, 10020.

Copyright © 2012 by The McGraw-Hill Companies, Inc. All rights reserved. No part of this publication may be reproduced or distributed in any form or by any means, or stored in a database or retrieval system, without the prior written consent of The McGraw-Hill Companies, Inc., including, but not limited to, in any network or other electronic storage or transmission, or broadcast for distance learning.

Some ancillaries, including electronic and print components, may not be available to customers outside the United States.

This book is printed on acid-free paper.

1 2 3 4 5 6 7 8 9 0 QDB/QDB 1 0 9 8 7 6 5 4 3 2 1

ISBN 978-0-07-802941-7
MHID 0-07-802941-4

Library of Congress Control Number: 2010939740

brief contents

contents

CHAPTER 4   WORKPLACE EMOTIONS, ATTITUDES, AND STRESS   68

CHAPTER 3   PERCEPTION AND LEARNING IN ORGANIZATIONS   48

part three   TEAM PROCESSES

part four   ORGANIZATIONAL PROCESSES

organizational
behavior

chapter one

Introduction to the Field of
Organizational Behavior

Apple Inc. and Google Inc. are the two most admired companies in the world, according to *Fortune* magazine's annual list.[1] This is not surprising news to most of us. Both firms are trusted brands with groundbreaking products and services. They lead their industries in innovation, invest in and support their employees, and have top-class visionary leaders. Apple designs stylish and user-friendly computers with cool software

The World's Most Admired Companies[2]

1. Apple
2. Google
3. Berkshire Hathaway
4. Johnson & Johnson
5. Amazon.com
6. Procter & Gamble
7. Toyota Motor
8. Goldman Sachs Group
9. Walmart Stores
10. Coca-Cola

(Garageband, iMovie) and has quickly become a leader or major competitor in portable music players, online music sales, smart phones, and electronic tablets (iPad). Google has reignited the Internet through its powerful search engine, innovative advertising relationships, interactive and customizable maps, and online software. Gmail became the third most popular Web e-mail service (after Yahoo! and Hotmail) before it was out of beta

continued on p. 4

LEARNING OBJECTIVES

After studying Chapter 1, you should be able to

LO1 Define *organizational behavior* and *organizations*, and discuss the importance of this field of inquiry.

LO2 Compare and contrast the four perspectives of organizational effectiveness.

LO3 Summarize the five types of individual behavior in organizations.

LO4 Debate the organizational opportunities and challenges of globalization, workforce diversity, and emerging employment relations.

LO5 Discuss the anchors on which organizational behavior knowledge is based.

continued from p. 3

testing. Google has also become famous for its cool workplaces, free-wheeling culture of creativity, and selection and development of talented people to expand the Internet universe.

What is surprising about Apple and Google being the world's most admired companies is that neither company was on anyone's radar screen a dozen years ago. Apple was on life support in the late 1990s, barely clinging to a few percentage points of market share in the computer industry. Google wasn't even registered as a company. It was just a computer project by two Stanford PhD students that was quickly outgrowing the dorm room where their equipment was housed. Leading the most admired list in the late 1990s were General Electric, Coca-Cola, Microsoft, and Walt Disney. All of these are still ranked among the most admired, but they are further down the list. Other companies that were most admired in the late 1990s, such as Dell and Merck, have completely disappeared from the list because they failed to innovate or fell into trouble with unethical conduct. ■

WELCOME TO THE FIELD OF ORGANIZATIONAL BEHAVIOR!

Fortune magazine's list of most admired companies may be a crude measure of company success or even reputation, but it reveals some important truths about organizations that succeed and fail in today's turbulent environment. In almost every sector of the economy (including not-for-profit), organizations need to adapt quickly, be innovative, have leaders with vision and foresight, and employ people who can collaborate, coordinate, and continuously learn. In other words, the best companies succeed through the concepts and practices that we discuss in this book about organizational behavior.

The purpose of this book is to help you understand what goes on in organizations, including the thoughts and behavior of employees and teams. We examine the factors that make companies effective, that improve employee well-being, and that drive successful teams. We look at organizations from numerous and diverse perspectives, from the deepest foundations of employee thoughts and behavior (personality, self-concept, commitment, and so on) to the complex interplay between the organization's structure and culture and its external

environment. Along this journey, we emphasize why things happen and what you can do to predict and manage organizational events.

We begin in this chapter by introducing you to the field of organizational behavior and why it is important to your career and to organizations. Next this chapter describes the "ultimate dependent variable" in this field by presenting the four main perspectives of organizational effectiveness. This is followed by an overview of the five types of individual behaviors that are most often studied as dependent variables in organizational behavior. This chapter also introduces three challenges facing organizations—globalization, increasing workforce diversity, and emerging employment relationships—and highlights the anchors that guide organizational behavior knowledge development.

Learning Objectives

After reading the next section, you should be able to

LO1 Define *organizational behavior* and *organizations,* and discuss the importance of this field of inquiry.

THE FIELD OF ORGANIZATIONAL BEHAVIOR

Organizational behavior (OB) is the study of what people think, feel, and do in and around organizations. It looks at employee behavior, decisions, perceptions, and emotional responses. It examines how individuals and teams in organizations relate to each other and to their counterparts in other organizations. OB also encompasses the study of how organizations interact with their external environments, particularly in the context of employee behavior and decisions. OB researchers systematically study these topics at multiple levels of analysis—namely the individual, the team (including interpersonal), and the organization.[4]

The definition of organizational behavior begs this question: What are organizations? **Organizations** are groups of people who work interdependently toward some purpose.[5] Notice that organizations are not buildings or government-registered entities. In fact, many organizations exist without either physical walls or government documentation to confer their legal status. Organizations have existed for as long as people have worked together.[6] Massive temples dating back to 3500 BC were constructed through the organized actions of multitudes of people. Craftspeople and merchants in ancient Rome formed guilds, complete with elected managers. More than 1,000 years ago, Chinese factories were producing 125,000 tons of iron each year. We have equally impressive examples of contemporary

with each other to achieve common objectives.

One key feature of organizations is that they are collective entities. They consist of human beings (typically, but not necessarily, employees), and these people interact with each other in an *organized* way. This organized relationship requires some minimal level of communication, coordination, and collaboration to achieve organizational objectives. As such, all organizational members have degrees of interdependence with each other; they accomplish goals by sharing materials, information, or expertise with coworkers.

A second key feature of organizations is that their members have a collective sense of purpose. There is some debate among

organizational behavior (OB)
The study of what people think, feel, and do in and around organizations.

organizations
Groups of people who work interdependently toward some purpose.

> ## A COMPANY IS ONE OF HUMANITY'S MOST AMAZING INVENTIONS. . . . [IT'S] THIS ABSTRACT CONSTRUCT WE'VE INVENTED, AND IT'S INCREDIBLY POWERFUL.
> —STEVE JOBS[3]

organizations, some of which employ more than a million people around the globe. Throughout history, organizations have consisted of people who communicate, coordinate, and collaborate

it's a FACT.

World's Largest Employers by Number of Employees[7]

Organization	Number of Employees	Country
Walmart	2.1 million	United States
China National Petroleum	1.61 million	People's Republic of China
State Grid	1.53 million	People's Republic of China
Indian State Railways	1.42 million	India
National Health Service	1.3 million	United Kingdom

Note: This list excludes governments but includes government agencies. This list is likely imprecise because it is difficult to identify all of the largest employers in the world, due to limited statistics in some countries.

OB experts about whether everyone who works for a company has a common vision or agreed upon goals. The collective purpose isn't always well defined or agreed on. Furthermore, although most companies have vision and mission statements, these documents are sometimes out of date or don't describe what employees and leaders try to achieve in reality. These arguments may be true, but imagine an organization without goals: It would consist of a mass of people wandering aimlessly without any sense of direction. So whether it's selling fresh food at Whole Foods or maintaining huge electrical infrastructure at China's State Grid, people working in organizations do have some sense of collective purpose. "A business is just a registered name on a piece of paper," explains Grahame Maher, head of Vodafone in Qatar. "It's nothing more than that unless there's a group of people who care about a common purpose for why they are, where they are going, how they are going to be when they are there."[8]

Why Study Organizational Behavior?

Organizational behavior instructors face a challenge: Students who have not yet begun their careers tend to value courses related to specific jobs, such as accounting and marketing.[9] However, OB doesn't have a specific career path—there is no "vice president of OB"—so students sometimes have difficulty recognizing the value that OB knowledge can offer to their future. Meanwhile,

> ## In theory there's no difference between theory and practice. In practice there is.
> ### —Yogi Berra

students with several years of work experience place OB near the top of their list of important courses. Why? Because they have directly observed that OB *does make a difference* to their career success. OB theories help people make sense of the workplace. These theories also give them the opportunity to question and rebuild their personal mental models that have developed through observation and experience. Thus OB is important because it helps to fulfill the need to understand and predict the world in which we live.[10]

But the main reason why people with work experience value OB knowledge is that they have discovered how it helps them get things done in organizations. This practical side of organizational behavior is, according to some experts, a critical feature of the best OB theories.[11] Everyone in the organization needs to work with other people, and OB provides the knowledge and tools for working with and through others. Building a high-performance team, motivating coworkers, handling workplace conflicts, influencing your boss, and changing employee behavior are just a few of the areas of knowledge and skills offered in organizational behavior. No matter what career path you choose, you'll find that OB concepts play an important role in performing your job and working more effectively within organizations.

Organizational Behavior Is for Everyone Our explanation of why organizational behavior is important for your career success does not assume that you are, or intend to be, a manager. In fact, this book pioneered the notion that OB knowledge is for everyone. Whether you are a geologist, financial analyst, customer service representative, or chief executive officer, you need to understand and apply the many organizational behavior topics that are discussed in this book. Yes, organizations will continue to have managers; but their roles have changed, and the rest of us are increasingly expected to manage ourselves in the workplace. In the words of one forward-thinking OB writer many years ago, everyone is a manager.[12]

OB and the Bottom Line Up to this point, our answer to the question "Why study OB?" has focused on how organizational behavior knowledge benefits you as an individual. However, OB knowledge is just as important for the organization's financial health. Apple and Google have flourished because they emphasize creativity, innovation, employee development, and (for Apple) clever design and corporate culture, leadership, involvement, and other OB practices. Several studies report that a company's performance increases with employee involvement, training and development, performance-based rewards, high-quality leadership, employee communication, and other OB practices.[13] For example, one investigation found that hospitals with higher levels of specific OB activities (such as training, staff involvement, rewards, and recognition) have lower patient mortality rates. Another study found that companies receiving "the best place to work" awards have significantly higher financial and long-term stock market performance.

The bottom-line value of organizational behavior is also supported by investment portfolio studies. These investigations suggest that specific OB characteristics (employee attitudes, work/life balance, performance-based rewards, leadership, employee training and development, and so forth) are important "positive screens" for selecting companies with the best long-term share appreciation.[14]

After reading the next two sections, you should be able to

LO2 Compare and contrast the four perspectives of organizational effectiveness.

LO3 Summarize the five types of individual behavior in organizations.

PERSPECTIVES OF ORGANIZATIONAL EFFECTIVENESS

Almost all organizational behavior theories have the implicit or explicit objective of making organizations more effective.[15] In fact, **organizational effectiveness** is considered the "ultimate dependent variable" in organizational behavior.[16] One problem though, is that the concept is burdened with too many labels, such as organizational performance, success, goodness, health, competitiveness, and excellence. Another significant issue is that there is a lot of unresolved debate about what an effective organization looks like.

Long ago, companies were considered effective if they achieved their stated goals.[17] If drugstore chain Walgreens meets or exceeds its annual sales and profit targets, then it must be effective, according to this definition. But this goal attainment view of organizational effectiveness has some inherent flaws. One flaw is that some leaders set easy goals for their companies, yet we wouldn't consider achievement of those easy goals an indication of effectiveness, particularly compared to another company that achieves more difficult goals.

A second flaw with the goal attainment view is that some goals are so abstract that it is difficult to know how well the organization has achieved them. For example, many companies have established goals to become more environmentally friendly, but it is difficult to determine the extent to which they really are becoming more "green" or are mainly engaging in "greenwashing"—creating an environmentally friendly image (often through considerable marketing expense) but not coming close to achieving the environmental goal implied by that image.[18]

A third flaw with the goal attainment definition is that a company's stated objectives might threaten its long-term survival. Consider incidents in which chief executives have been motivated by incentives and pressure from the board of directors to increase the company's short-term profits. Dutifully, the CEOs achieved those tough targets by drastically cutting expenditures on infrastructure renewal, product development, and employee training. The resulting lower cost increased profits for a few years. But the underfunding of infrastructure, research, and employee development soon undermined the company's ability to compete. In an extreme case a company achieves its short-term targets but eventually goes out of business.

If goal attainment is not a good measure of organizational effectiveness, what is the correct yardstick? The answer is that there are several perspectives of organizational effectiveness, each of which has some unique value, so we need to consider *all of these perspectives together.*[19] Organizations are considered effective when they have a good fit with their external environment, when their internal subsystems are efficient and effective (that is, they use high-performance work practices), when they are learning organizations, and when they satisfy the needs of key stakeholders. Over the next few pages we will discuss each of these four perspectives of organizational effectiveness in some detail.

> " Organizations are considered effective when they have a good fit with their external environment, when their internal subsystems are efficient and effective, when they are learning organizations, and when they satisfy the needs of key stakeholders. "

Open Systems Perspective

The **open systems** perspective of organizational effectiveness is one of the earliest and most deeply embedded ways of thinking about organizations. In fact, the other major organizational effectiveness perspectives might be considered detailed extensions of the open systems model.[20] The open systems perspective views organizations as complex organisms that "live" within an external environment, rather like the illustration in Exhibit 1.1. The word *open* describes this permeable relationship, whereas *closed systems* can exist without dependence on an external environment.

As open systems, organizations depend on the external environment for resources, including raw materials, employees, financial resources, information, and equipment. Inside the organization are numerous subsystems, such as processes (communication and reward systems), task activities (production, marketing), and

organizational effectiveness
A broad concept represented by several perspectives, including the organization's fit with the external environment, internal subsystems configuration for high-performance, emphasis on organizational learning, and ability to satisfy the needs of key stakeholders.

open systems
A perspective that organizations depend on the external environment for resources, affect that environment through their output, and consist of internal subsystems that transform inputs to outputs.

▼ EXHIBIT 1.1 Open Systems Perspective of Organizations

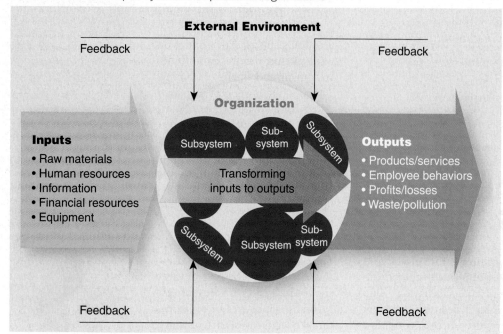

social dynamics (informal groups, power relationships). With the aid of technology (such as equipment, work methods, and information), these subsystems transform inputs into various outputs. Some outputs (such as products and services) may be valued by the external environment, whereas other outputs (like employee layoffs or pollution) have adverse effects. The organization receives feedback from the external environment regarding the value of its outputs and the availability of future inputs.

According to the open systems perspective, successful organizations monitor their environments and are able to maintain a close "fit" with those changing conditions.[21] One way they do this is by finding new opportunities to secure essential inputs. For instance, McDonald's restaurants have developed innovative ways to maintain an adequate supply of people. Years ago, the company was among the first to recruit retirees as employees. Recently, McDonald's UK introduced the Family Contract, an employment arrangement that allows members of the employee's family (spouses, grandparents, and children over the age of 16) to swap shifts without notifying management.[22] Successful organizations also redesign outputs so they remain compatible with needs in the external environment. Food manufacturers have changed their ingredients to satisfy more health-conscious consumers. Grocery stores have added more ethnically diverse foods to reflect the increasing ethnic diversity of shoppers.

Internal Subsystems Effectiveness The open systems perspective considers more than an organization's fit with the external environment. It also considers how well it operates internally—that is, how well the company transforms inputs into outputs. The most common

indicator of this internal transformation process is **organizational efficiency** (also called *productivity*), which is the ratio of inputs to outcomes.[23] Companies that produce more goods or services with less labor, material, and energy are more efficient. However, successful organizations not only have efficient transformation processes; they also have more *adaptive* and *innovative* transformation processes.[24] The shift from mass production to mass customization illustrates this point. Mass production typically makes a large number of the same product, which results in low costs per unit. Mass customization, on the other hand, produces small batches. This results in somewhat higher costs, but it also allows the product to be customized for specific clients, which results in higher client satisfaction.

Organizational Learning Perspective

The open systems perspective has traditionally focused on physical resources that enter the organization and are processed into physical goods (outputs). This was representative of the industrial

Soaring
Farm Efficiency[25]

35–40
Labor-hours required to produce 100 bushels of wheat in the United States in **1890**.

15–20
Labor-hours required to produce 100 bushels of wheat in the United States in **1930**.

3
Labor-hours required to produce 100 bushels of wheat in the United States **today**.

250–300
Labor-hours required to produce 100 bushels of wheat in the United States in **1830**.

8 PART 1 | Introduction

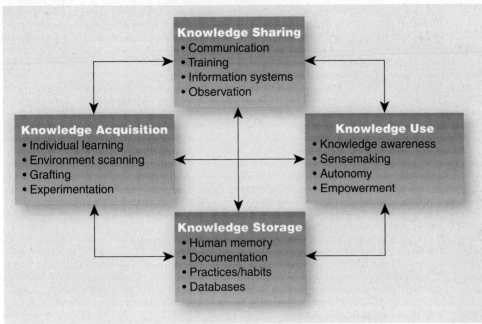

Knowledge Sharing
- Communication
- Training
- Information systems
- Observation

Knowledge Acquisition
- Individual learning
- Environment scanning
- Grafting
- Experimentation

Knowledge Use
- Knowledge awareness
- Sensemaking
- Autonomy
- Empowerment

Knowledge Storage
- Human memory
- Documentation
- Practices/habits
- Databases

organizational efficiency The amount of outputs relative to inputs in the organization's transformation process.

organizational learning A perspective that organizational effectiveness depends on the organization's capacity to acquire, share, use, and store valuable knowledge.

learning (such as observation, experience, training, practice).[28]

- *Knowledge use:* The competitive advantage of knowledge comes from applying it in ways that add value to the organization and its stakeholders. To do this, employees must realize that the

economy but not the "new economy," where the most valued input is knowledge. The **organizational learning** perspective (also called *knowledge management*) emphasizes knowledge as a key driver of competitive advantage. Through this lens, organizational effectiveness depends on the organization's capacity to acquire, share, use, and store valuable knowledge (see Exhibit 1.2).[26] A growing body of research supports the idea that successful companies are better than others at these knowledge processes.[27]

- *Knowledge acquisition:* This includes extracting information and ideas from the external environment as well as through insight. One of the fastest and most powerful ways to acquire knowledge is by hiring individuals or acquiring entire companies. Knowledge also enters the organization when employees learn from external sources, such as by discovering new resources from suppliers or becoming aware of new trends from clients. A third knowledge acquisition strategy is experimentation. Companies receive knowledge through insight as a result of research and other creative processes.

- *Knowledge sharing:* This aspect of organizational learning involves distributing knowledge to others across the organization. Although typically associated with computer intranets and digital repositories of knowledge, knowledge sharing occurs mainly through communication as well as various forms of

FACT. **Google's Learning Organization Strategies**[29]

Google Inc. is a master at organizational learning. The Internet technology company applies knowledge acquisition by hiring the best talent, buying entire companies (such as Keyhole Inc., whose knowledge created Google Earth), and giving staff 20 percent of their time to discover new knowledge and try out their ideas. The company has many practices that encourage or facilitate knowledge sharing. Its campus-like environment (called the Googleplex) increases the chance that employees from different parts of the organization will mingle and casually share information. It organizes employees into teams so they share information as part of their job. Google also relies on sophisticated information technologies to support knowledge sharing. Google encourages knowledge use by giving employees the freedom to apply their newfound knowledge and encouraging them to experiment with that knowledge. Given the value of knowledge within the Googleplex and other sites around the world, Google actively stores knowledge. Employee turnover is minimal because Google is one of the world's most enjoyable places to work. Its wikis, intranet repositories, and other technologies also encourage documentation and storage of information. "Google is truly a learning organization," says a senior Google executive.

knowledge is available and that they have enough freedom to apply it. This requires a culture that supports the learning process.

- *Knowledge storage:* This process includes any means by which knowledge is held for later retrieval. It is the process that creates organizational memory. Human memory plays a critical role here, as do the many forms of documentation and database systems that exist in organizations. Individual practices and habits hold less explicit (more tacit) knowledge.

An interesting dilemma in organizational learning is that the ability to acquire, share, and use new knowledge is limited by the

potential of this marketing channel. Many countries also suffer from a lack of absorptive capacity. Without sufficient knowledge, a society is slow or completely unable to adopt new information that may improve social and economic conditions.[31]

Intellectual Capital: The Stock of Organizational Knowledge Knowledge acquisition, sharing, and use represent the flow of knowledge. The organizational learning perspective also considers the company's stock of knowledge, called its **intellectual capital**.[32] The most obvious form of intellectual capital is **human capital**—the knowledge, skills, and

> " An organization's ability to learn, and translate that learning into action rapidly, is the ultimate competitive advantage.
>
> —Jack Welch "

company's existing body of knowledge. To recognize the value of new information, assimilate it, and use it for value-added activities, organizations require sufficient **absorptive capacity**.[30] For example, many companies were slow to develop online marketing practices because no one in the organizations knew enough about the Internet to fathom its potential or apply that knowledge to the companies' business. In some cases companies had to acquire entire teams of people with the requisite knowledge to realize the

abilities that employees carry around in their heads. This is an important part of a company's stock of knowledge, and it is a huge risk in companies where knowledge is the main competitive advantage. When key people leave, they take with them some of the knowledge that makes the company effective.

Even if every employee left the organization, intellectual capital would still remain as *structural capital*. This includes the

absorptive capacity	intellectual capital	human capital	organizational memory
The ability to recognize the value of new information, assimilate it, and use it for value-added activities.	Company's stock of knowledge, including human capital, structural capital, and relationship capital.	The stock of knowledge, skills, and abilities among employees that provide economic value to the organization.	The storage and preservation of intellectual capital.

knowledge captured and retained in an organization's systems and structures, such as the documentation of work procedures and the physical layout of the production line. Structural capital also includes the organization's finished products because knowledge can be extracted by taking them apart to discover how they work and are constructed (reverse engineering).

Finally, intellectual capital includes *relationship capital,* which is the value derived from an organization's relationships with customers, suppliers, and others who provide added mutual value for the organization.

Organizational Memory and Unlearning

Corporate leaders need to recognize that they are the keepers of an **organizational memory**.[33] This unusual metaphor refers to the storage and preservation of intellectual capital. It includes knowledge that employees possess as well as knowledge embedded in the organization's systems and structures. It includes documents, objects, and anything else that provides meaningful information about how the organization should operate.

How do organizations retain intellectual capital? One way is by keeping good employees. Progressive companies achieve this by adapting their employment practices to become more compatible with emerging workforce expectations, including work/life balance, an egalitarian hierarchy, and a workspace that generates more fun. A second organizational memory strategy is to systematically transfer knowledge to other employees. This occurs when newcomers apprentice with skilled employees, thereby acquiring knowledge that is not documented. A third strategy is to transfer knowledge into structural capital. This includes bringing out hidden knowledge, organizing it, and putting it in a form that can be available to others. Reliance Industries, India's largest business enterprise, applies this strategy by encouraging employees to document their successes and failures through a special intranet knowledge portal. One of these reports alone provided information that allowed others to prevent a costly plant shutdown.[34]

The organizational learning perspective states not only that effective organizations learn but also that they unlearn routines and patterns of behavior that are no longer appropriate.[35] Unlearning removes knowledge that no longer adds value and, in fact, may undermine the organization's effectiveness. Some forms of unlearning involve replacing dysfunctional policies, procedures, and routines. Other forms of unlearning erase

FACT. The Information Explosion[36]

Researchers at the University of California at Berkeley estimated that between 2.1 and 3.2 exebytes* of new information** were recorded worldwide in 1999. They completed a second calculation in 2002 and found that between 3.4 and 5.4 exebytes of new information were recorded in that year. These data suggest that the global stock of information is growing about 30 percent annually (without taking into account information lost during that time). Ninety-two percent of recorded information is stored electronically (hard disks, tapes, and so on) and 7 percent is recorded on film. Only .01 percent is stored on paper. Let's put this volume of information in context. The U.S. Library of Congress is the world's largest repository of printed knowledge; it holds 142 million items and 32 million cataloged books and other print collections. If digitized, these sources would be about 17 terabytes of information. Using the 2002 data, the UC Berkeley researchers estimated that the world annually produces 57,000 times the volume of information found in the Library of Congress.

*One exebyte is 10^{18} bytes (1 billion billion bytes).

**Information differs from knowledge. Knowledge represents information that has been structured and integrated with the person's experience, intuition, and judgment so the information has meaning.

attitudes, beliefs, and assumptions. For instance, employees rethink the "best way" to perform a task and how to serve clients.

High-Performance Work Practices (HPWP) Perspective

The open systems perspective described earlier states that successful companies are good at transforming inputs to outputs, but it does not explain how effective organizations accomplish this. Consequently an entire field of research has blossomed around the objective of determining specific "bundles" of organizational practices that offer competitive advantage. This research has had various labels over the years, but it is now most commonly known as **high-performance work practices (HPWP)**.[37]

The HPWP perspective begins with the idea that *human capital*—the knowledge, skills, and abilities that employees possess—is an important source of competitive advantage for organizations.[38] Human capital helps the organization realize opportunities or minimize threats in the external environment. Furthermore, human capital is neither widely available nor easily duplicated. For instance, a new company cannot quickly acquire a workforce with the same capabilities as those of the workforce at an established company. Nor can technology replace the capabilities that employees bring to the workplace. In short, human capital is valuable, rare, difficult to imitate, and nonsubstitutable.[39] Therefore, organizations excel by introducing a bundle of systems and structures that leverage the potential of their workforce.

Researchers have investigated numerous potential high-performance work practices, but a few subsystem characteristics are recognized in most studies.[40] Two widely recognized high-performance practices are employee involvement and job autonomy. Both activities tend to strengthen employee motivation as well as improve decision making, organizational responsiveness, and commitment to change. In high-performance workplaces, employee involvement and job autonomy often take the form of self-directed teams (see Chapter 7).

Another key variable in the HPWP model is employee competence. Specifically, organizations are more effective when they recruit and select people with relevant skills, knowledge, values, and other personal characteristics. Furthermore, successful companies invest in employee training and development. A fourth characteristic of high-performance organizations is that they link performance and skill development to various forms of financial and nonfinancial rewards valued by employees.

The HPWP perspective is currently popular among OB experts and practitioners, but it also has its share of critics. One concern is that many studies try to find out which practices predict

> " *Researchers have identified several high-performance work practices, including involvement, autonomy, rewards, and employee competence.* "

organizational performance without understanding *why* those practices should have this effect.[41] In other words, some of the practices identified as HPWPs lack theoretical foundation; the causal connection between work practices and organizational effectiveness is missing. Without this explanation, it is difficult to be confident that the practice will be valuable in the future and in other situations.

A second concern with the HPWP perspective is that it may satisfy shareholder and customer needs at the expense of employee well-being.[42] Some experts point out that HPWPs increase work stress and that management is reluctant to delegate power or share the financial benefits of productivity improvements. If high-performance work practices improve organizational performance at a cost to employee well-being, then this perspective (along with the open systems and organizational learning perspectives) offers an incomplete picture of organizational effectiveness. The remaining gaps are mostly filled by the stakeholder perspective of organizational effectiveness.

Stakeholder Perspective

The three organizational effectiveness perspectives described so far mainly consider processes and resources, yet they only minimally recognize the importance of relations with **stakeholders**. Stakeholders include individuals, organizations, and other entities that affect, or are affected by, the organization's objectives and actions (see Exhibit 1.3). They include anyone with a stake in the

▼**EXHIBIT 1.3** Organizational Stakeholders

Note: This exhibit does not show the complete set of possible stakeholders.

company—employees, shareholders, suppliers, labor unions, government, communities, consumer and environmental interest groups, and so on. The essence of the stakeholder perspective is that companies must take into account how their actions affect others, and this requires that they understand, manage, and satisfy the interests of their stakeholders.[43] The stakeholder perspective personalizes the open systems perspective; it identifies specific people and social entities in the external and internal environment. It also recognizes that stakeholder relations are dynamic; they can be negotiated and managed, not just taken as a fixed condition.[44]

Consider Walmart's evolving relationships with its stakeholders.[45] For decades, the world's largest retailer concentrated on customers by providing the lowest possible prices and on shareholders by generating healthy financial returns. Yet emphasizing these two stakeholders exposed the company to increasing hostility from other groups in society. Some interest groups accused Walmart of destroying America's manufacturing base and tacitly allowing unethical business practices (such as child labor) in countries where it purchased goods. Other groups pointed out that Walmart had a poor record of environmental and social responsibility. Still other groups lobbied to keep Walmart out of their communities because the giant retailer typically built in outlying suburbs where land is cheap, thereby fading the vibrancy of the community's downtown area. These stakeholder pressure points existed for some time, but Walmart mostly ignored them until they became serious threats. In fact, Walmart recently created the position "senior director of stakeholder engagement" to ensure that it pays more attention to its stakeholders and to proactively manage stakeholder relationships.

perspective—namely, that it incorporates values, ethics, and corporate social responsibility into the organizational effectiveness equation.[47] The stakeholder perspective states that to manage the interests of diverse stakeholders, leaders ultimately need to rely on their personal and organizational values for guidance. **Values** are relatively stable, evaluative beliefs that guide our preferences for outcomes or courses of action in a variety of situations.[48] Values help us to know what is right or wrong, or good or bad, in the world. Chapter 2 explains how values are an important part of our self-concept and, as such, motivate our actions. Although values exist within individuals, groups of people often hold similar values, so we tend to ascribe these *shared values* to the team, department, organization, profession, or entire society. For example, Chapter 13 discusses the importance and dynamics of organizational culture, which includes shared values across the company or within subsystems.

high-performance work practices (HPWP) A perspective that effective organizations incorporate several workplace practices that leverage the potential human capital.

stakeholders Individuals, organizations, or other entities who affect, or are affected by, the organization's objectives and actions.

values Relatively stable, evaluative beliefs that guide a person's preferences for outcomes or courses of action in a variety of situations.

ethics The study of moral principles or values that determine whether actions are right or wrong and outcomes are good or bad.

> ## It's not hard to make decisions when you know what your values are.
> —Roy Disney

Understanding, managing, and satisfying the interests of stakeholders is more challenging than it sounds because stakeholders have conflicting interests, and organizations don't have the resources to completely satisfy every stakeholder. Therefore, organizational leaders need to decide how much priority to give to each group. One commonly cited factor is to favor stakeholders with the most power.[46] This makes sense when one considers that the most powerful stakeholders hold the greatest threat to and opportunity for the company's survival. Yet stakeholder power should not be the only criterion for determining organizational strategy and resource allocation. Ignoring less powerful stakeholders might motivate them to become more powerful by forming coalitions or seeking government support. It might also irritate more powerful stakeholders if ignoring weaker interests violates the norms and standards of society.

Values, Ethics, and Corporate Social Responsibility

This brings us to one of the key strengths of the stakeholder

Values have become a popular topic in corporate boardrooms because the values-driven organizational approach to guiding employee behavior is potentially more effective, as well as more popular, than the old command-and-control approach (which consists of top-down decisions with close supervision of employees). Several governments around the world have also made values the foundation of employee decisions and behavior. As one government report proclaimed, "Values are essentially the link between the daily work of public servants and the broad aims of democratic governance."[49] In a recent global survey of MBA students, almost 80 percent felt that a well-run company operates according to its values and code of ethics.[50]

By incorporating values into organizational effectiveness, the stakeholder perspective also provides the strongest case for ethics and corporate social responsibility. In fact, the stakeholder perspective emerged out of earlier writing about ethics and corporate social responsibility. **Ethics** refers to the study of moral

Organizational activities intended to benefit society and the environment beyond the firm's immediate financial interests or legal obligations.

principles or values that determine whether actions are right or wrong and outcomes are good or bad. We rely on our ethical values to determine "the right thing to do." Ethical behavior is driven by the moral principles we use to make decisions. These moral principles represent fundamental values. Chapter 2 provides more detail about ethical principles and related influences on moral reasoning.

Corporate social responsibility (CSR) consists of organizational activities intended to benefit society and the environment beyond the firm's immediate financial interests or legal obligations.[51] It is the view that companies have a contract with society, in which they must serve stakeholders beyond shareholders and customers. In some situations, the interests of the firm's shareholders should be secondary to those of other stakeholders.[52] As part of CSR, many companies have adopted the triple-bottom-line philosophy: They try to support or "earn positive returns" in the economic, social, and environmental spheres of sustainability. Firms that adopt the triple bottom line aim to survive and be profitable in the marketplace (economic), but they also intend to maintain or improve conditions for society (social) as well as the physical environment.[53] Companies are particularly keen on become "greener"—that is, minimizing any negative effect they have on the physical environment.

Not everyone agrees with the idea that organizations are more effective when they cater to a wide variety of stakeholders. More than 30 years ago, economist Milton Friedman pronounced that "there is one and only one social responsibility of business—to use its resources and engage in activities designed to increase its profits." Although few writers take this extreme view today, some point out that companies can benefit other stakeholders only if those with financial interests in the company receive first priority. Yet four out of five people in an American survey said that a company's commitment to a social issue is an important factor in deciding whether to work for the company and whether to buy its products or services. In another survey, more than two-thirds of North American

FACT. The Greenest Big Companies in America[54]

Rank	Company	Green Score	Environmental Practices
1	Hewlett-Packard	100.00	• Several practices to reduce greenhouse gas (GHG) emissions. • First major IT firm to report GHG emissions related to its supply chain. • Efforts to remove toxic substances from its products.
2	Dell	98.87	• One of the top corporate users of renewable energy; headquarters uses 100% renewable energy. • Efforts to reduce energy consumption in its computers. • Became carbon neutral in 2008. • Leads the industry in product take-back and recycling programs.
3	Johnson & Johnson	98.56	• Has largest fleet of hybrid vehicles in the world. • Strong commitment to climate change and has strong environmental management in place (but not carbon neutral).
4	Intel	95.12	• Largest corporate purchaser of renewable energy in the United States. • Product development focuses on energy efficiency. • Industry leader in programs to reduce waste and toxins.
5	IBM	94.08	• Early adopter of environmental policies (1971). • Environmental awareness training for new staff. • Ultra carbon-conscious (only company to receive EPA's Climate Protection Award twice). • Heavy investment to double data center capacity without increasing power consumption.

As part of its corporate social responsibility initiative, Aviva Hong Kong involves employees in planting trees (shown here). The British-based insurance company also sponsors energy research and was the first insurer to carbon-neutralize its worldwide operations.

students said they would not apply for a job at a company that is considered irresponsible. Most American and European MBA students also claim they would accept lower pay and benefits to work for an organization with a better ethical/CSR reputation. However, a recent global survey indicated that while most MBA students believe socially responsible companies have a better reputation, fewer than half of these respondents believe CSR improves revenue, employee loyalty, customer satisfaction, community well-being, or the company's long-term viability. Another large survey reported that about half of the employees polled think their company should do more to be environmentally friendly, but only one-third would be more inclined to work for a "green" company.[55]

Capgemini recently discovered the importance of corporate social responsibility when the Netherlands-based information technology (IT) consulting firm tried to fill 800 IT and management consulting positions in that country. Rather than offering a T-shirt for completing the 30-minute online survey about recruitment issues, Capgemini advised respondents (IT and management consultants) that for each completed survey it would provide funding for a street kid in

Kolkata, India, to have one week of schooling and accommodation. The survey included an option for respondents to find out more about employment with the consulting firm. Far beyond its expectations, Capgemini received more than 10,000 completed surveys and 2,000 job inquiries from qualified respondents. The company filled its 800 jobs and developed a waiting list of future prospects. Furthermore, media attention about this initiative raised Capgemini's brand reputation for corporate social responsibility. The consulting firm supported 10,400 weeks of housing and education for children in Kolkata.[56]

TYPES OF INDIVIDUAL BEHAVIOR

The four perspectives described over the past few pages—open systems, organizational learning, high-performance work practices, and stakeholders—provide a multidimensional view of what makes companies effective. Within these models, however, are numerous behaviors that employees need to perform that

▼EXHIBIT 1.4 Five Types of Individual Behavior in the Workplace

enable companies to interact with their environments; acquire, share, and use knowledge to the best advantage; process inputs to outputs efficiently and responsively; and meet the needs of various stakeholders. While organizational effectiveness is the ultimate dependent variable, these behaviors are the individual-level dependent variables found in most OB research. The five types of employee behavior are task performance, organizational citizenship, counterproductive work behaviors, joining and staying with the organization, and work attendance (Exhibit 1.4).

Task Performance

Task performance refers to goal-directed behaviors under the individual's control that support organizational objectives. Task performance behaviors transform raw materials into goods and services or support and maintain the technical activities.[57] For example, foreign exchange traders make decisions and take actions to exchange currencies.

Employees in most jobs have more than one performance dimension. Foreign exchange traders must be able to identify profitable trades, work cooperatively with clients and co-workers in a stressful environment, assist in training new staff, and work on special telecommunications equipment without error. Some of these performance dimensions are more important than others, but only by considering all of them can we fully evaluate an employee's contribution to the organization.

Organizational Citizenship

Companies could not effectively compete, transform resources, or serve the needs of their stakeholders if employees performed only their formal job duties. They also need to engage in **organizational citizenship behaviors (OCBs)**—various forms of cooperation and helpfulness to others that support the organization's social and psychological context.[58] In other words, companies require contextual performance (that is, OCBs) along with task performance.

Organizational citizenship behaviors take many forms. Some are directed toward individuals, such as assisting coworkers with their work problems, adjusting your work schedule to accommodate coworkers, showing genuine courtesy toward coworkers, and sharing your work resources (supplies, technology, staff) with coworkers. Other OCBs represent cooperation and helpfulness toward the organization in general. These include supporting the company's public image, taking discretionary action to help the organization avoid potential problems, offering ideas beyond those required for your own job, attending voluntary functions that support the organization, and keeping up with new developments in the organization.[59]

Counterproductive Work Behaviors

Organizational behavior is interested in all workplace behaviors, including those on the "dark side," collectively known as **counterproductive work behaviors (CWBs)**. CWBs are voluntary behaviors that have the potential to directly or indirectly harm the organization. These CWBs can be organized into five categories: abuse of others (such as insults and nasty comments), threats (threatening harm), work avoidance (such as tardiness), work sabotage (doing work incorrectly), and overt acts (theft). CWBs are not minor concerns; research suggests that they can substantially undermine an organization's effectiveness.[60]

Joining and Staying with the Organization

Task performance, organizational citizenship, and the lack of counterproductive work behaviors are obviously important; but if qualified people don't join and stay with the organization, none of these performance-related behaviors will occur. Attracting and retaining talented people are particularly important as worries about skills shortages heat up. Companies survive and thrive not just by hiring people with talent or potential; they also need to ensure that these employees stay with the company. Companies with high turnover suffer because of the high cost of replacing people who leave. More important, as was mentioned earlier in this chapter, much of an organization's intellectual capital is the knowledge carried around in employees' heads. When people leave, some of this vital knowledge is lost, often resulting in inefficiencies, poorer customer service, and so forth. This threat is not trivial: between one-third and one-half of employees say they would change companies if offered a comparable job.[61]

Maintaining Work Attendance

Along with attracting and retaining employees, organizations need everyone to show up for work at scheduled times. In some situations, chronic absenteeism is responsible for undermining the health and educational development of entire countries. Situational factors—such as a snowstorm or car breakdown—explain some work absences. Motivation is another factor. Employees who experience job dissatisfaction or work-related stress are more likely to be absent or late for work because taking time off is a way to temporarily withdraw from stressful or dissatisfying conditions. Absenteeism is also higher in organizations with generous sick leave because this benefit limits the negative financial impact of taking time

organizational citizenship behaviors (OCBs) Various forms of cooperation and helpfulness to others that support the organization's social and psychological context.

counterproductive work behaviors (CWBs) Voluntary behaviors that have the potential to directly or indirectly harm the organization.

FACT. The U.S. Army Is Game for Recruiting[62]

America's Army, an online first-person action video game, is making it much easier for the U.S. Army to hire thousands of new recruits. Millions of people have downloaded the game, now in its third edition, which is free after users submit information about themselves to the U.S. Army recruitment Web site. The site also offers profiles and video testimonials from real soldiers about why they joined the army. Critics complain that video games are a misleading form of recruitment because they cannot depict the true harshness of warfare. However, military organizations have used games for many centuries to train soldiers, and the U.S. Army claims that *America's Army* is very realistic, such as showing how the equipment works, how training is conducted, and how teamwork is emphasized. Researchers at the Massachusetts Institute of Technology reported that "30 percent of all Americans age 16 to 24 had a more positive impression of the army because of the game." They also concluded that "the game had more impact on recruits than all other forms of army advertising combined."

globalization
Economic, social, and cultural connectivity with people in other parts of the world.

surface-level diversity
The observable demographic or physiological differences in people, such as their race, ethnicity, gender, age, and physical disabilities.

deep-level diversity Differences in the psychological characteristics of employees, including personalities, beliefs, values, and attitudes.

some changes, over the past decade and in the decade to come, are more profound than others. These changes require that corporate leaders and all other employees adjust to new realities. In this section we highlight three of the major challenges facing organizations: globalization, increasing workforce diversity, and emerging employment relationships.

away from work. One recent global study found that 15 percent of employees admitted taking sick leave when they were not genuinely sick. This percentage was much higher in some countries, such as Malaysia, where 27 percent admitted taking sick leave for reasons other than sickness.[63] Studies have found that absenteeism is also higher in teams with strong absence norms, meaning that team members tolerate and even expect coworkers to take time off.[64]

Globalization

Globalization refers to economic, social, and cultural connectivity with people in other parts of the world. Organizations globalize when they actively participate in other countries and cultures. Although businesses have traded goods across borders for centuries, the degree of globalization today is unprecedented because information technology and transportation systems

> " Globalization has changed us into a company that searches the world, not just to sell or to source, but to find intellectual capital—the world's best talents and greatest ideas.
>
> —Jack Welch "

Learning Objectives

After reading the next two sections, you should be able to

LO4 Debate the organizational opportunities and challenges of globalization, workforce diversity, and emerging employment relationships.

LO5 Discuss the anchors on which organizational behavior knowledge is based.

CONTEMPORARY CHALLENGES FOR ORGANIZATIONS

Earlier in this chapter we learned that organizations are affected by their external environment. Effective organizations therefore anticipate and continually adapt so they maintain a good fit with their environment. This external environment is continuously changing; but

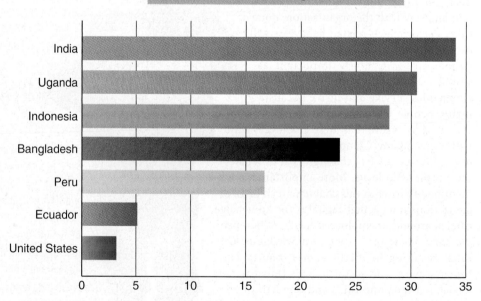

Chronic Teacher Absenteeism in Selected Developing Countries[65]

Average teacher absenteeism in selected developing countries. U.S. teacher absenteeism statistic is included for comparison. Data were collected from two or three random checks of up to two dozen primary schools in each country.

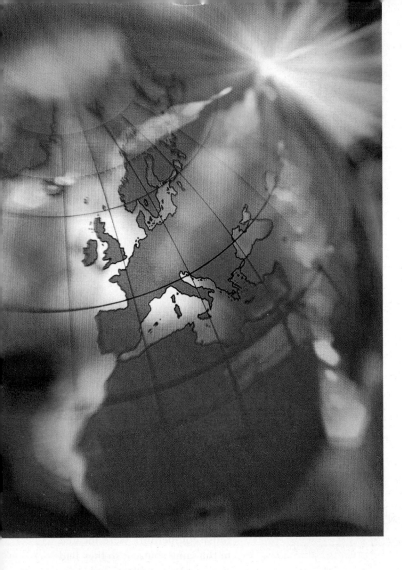

discovering human resource management practices based on companies around the globe.[69]

Increasing Workforce Diversity

Walk into the offices of Verizon Communications and you can quickly see that the communications service giant reflects the communities it serves. Minorities make up 35 percent of Verizon's 230,000 workforce and 29 percent of management positions. Women represent 42 percent of its workforce and 38 percent of management positions. Verizon's inclusive culture has won awards from numerous organizations and publications representing Hispanic Americans, African Americans, gays and lesbians, people with disabilities, and other groups. "A commitment to diversity is as much about good business as it is about doing the right thing," says Magda Yrizarry, vice president of workplace culture, diversity, and compliance for Verizon. "As a company, we serve some of the most diverse markets; so from our leadership to our frontline employees, we understand and value diversity."[70]

Verizon Communications is a model employer and a reflection of the increasing diversity of people living in the United States and in many other countries. The description of Verizon's diversity refers to **surface-level diversity**—the observable demographic and other overt differences in people, such as their race, ethnicity, gender, age, and physical capabilities. Surface-level diversity has changed considerably in the United States over the past few decades. People with nonwhite or Hispanic origins represent one-third of the American population, and this is projected to increase substantially over the next few decades. Within the next 50 years, one in four Americans will be Hispanic, 14 percent will be African American, and 8 percent will be of Asian descent. By 2060 people with European non-Hispanic ethnicity will be a minority.[71] Many other countries are also experiencing increasing levels of racial and ethnic diversification.

Diversity also includes differences in the psychological characteristics of employees, including personalities, beliefs, values, and attitudes.[72] We can't directly see this **deep-level diversity**, but it is evident in a person's decisions, statements, and actions. One illustration of deep-level diversity is the different attitudes and expectations held by employees across generational cohorts.[73] *Baby boomers*—people born between 1946 and 1964—seem to expect and desire more job security, and are more intent on improving their economic and social status. In contrast, *Generation-X* employees—those born between 1965 and 1979—expect less job security and are motivated more by

allow a much more intense level of connectivity and interdependence around the planet.[66]

Globalization offers numerous benefits to organizations in terms of larger markets, lower costs, and greater access to knowledge and innovation. At the same time, there is considerable debate about whether globalization benefits developing nations, and whether it is primarily responsible for increasing work intensification, as well as reducing job security and work/life balance in developed countries.[67] Globalization is now well entrenched, so the real issue in organizational behavior is how corporate leaders and employees alike can lead and work effectively in this emerging reality[68] OB researchers are turning their attention to this topic. In Project GLOBE, dozens of experts are studying leadership and organizational practices across dozens of countries. Another consortium, called the Best Practices Project, is

work/life balance The degree to which a person minimizes conflict between work and nonwork demands.

virtual work Work performed away from the traditional physical workplace using information technology.

workplace flexibility, the opportunity to learn (particularly new technology), and working in an egalitarian and "fun" organization. Meanwhile, some observers suggest that *Millennial* (also called *Generation-Y*) employees (those born from 1980 to 1990) are noticeably self-confident, optimistic, multitasking, and more independent than even Gen-X coworkers. These statements certainly don't apply to everyone in each cohort, but they do reflect the dynamics of deep-level diversity and shifting values and expectations across generations.

Consequences of Diversity

Diversity presents both opportunities and challenges in organizations.[75] In some circumstances and to some degree, diversity can become a competitive advantage by improving decision making and team performance on complex tasks. Studies suggest that teams with some forms of diversity (particularly occupational diversity) make better decisions about complex problems than do teams whose members have similar backgrounds. A few studies also report that companies that win diversity awards have higher financial returns, at least in the short run.[76] This is consistent with anecdotal evidence from many corporate leaders—namely that having a diverse workforce improves customer service and creativity. For instance, PepsiCo estimates that one-eighth of revenue growth is directly attributable to new products inspired by diversity efforts.[77]

Based on this information, the popular refrain is that workforce diversity is a sound business proposition. Unfortunately, it's not that simple. There is growing evidence that most forms of diversity offer both advantages and disadvantages.[78] Teams with diverse employees usually take longer to perform effectively. Diversity brings numerous communication problems as well as "fault lines" in informal group dynamics. Diversity is also a source of conflict, which can lead to lack of information sharing and, in extreme cases, morale problems and higher turnover.

Whether or not workforce diversity is a business advantage,

companies need to make it a priority because surface-level diversity is a moral and legal imperative. Ethically, companies that offer an inclusive workplace are, in essence, making fair and just decisions regarding employment, promotions, rewards, and so on. Fairness is a well-established influence on employee loyalty and satisfaction. "Diversity is about fairness; we use the term inclusive meritocracy," says a Bank of America New Jersey executive. "What it does for our workforce is build trust and assures that individual differences are valued."[79] Our main point here is that workforce diversity is the new reality, and that organizations need to adjust to this reality both to survive and to experience its potential benefits for organizational success.

Emerging Employment Relationships

Combine globalization with emerging workforce diversity, and add in new information technology. The resulting concoction has created incredible changes in employment relationships. A few decades ago, most (although not all) employees in the United States and similar cultures would finish their workday after eight or nine hours and could separate their personal time from the workday. There were no Blackberrys and no Internet connections to keep staff tethered to work on a 24/7 schedule. Even business travel was more of an exception due to its high cost. Most competitors were located in the same country, so they had similar work practices and labor costs. Today work hours are longer (although arguably less than 100 years ago), employees experience more work-related stress, and there is growing evidence that family and personal relations are suffering. Little wonder that one of the emerging issues in this new century is for more **work/life balance**—minimizing conflict between work and nonwork demands.[80]

Another employment relationship trend is **virtual work**, whereby employees use information technology to perform their jobs away from the traditional physical workplace. The most common form of virtual work, called *telecommuting* or *teleworking*, involves working at home rather than commuting to

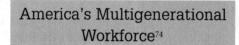

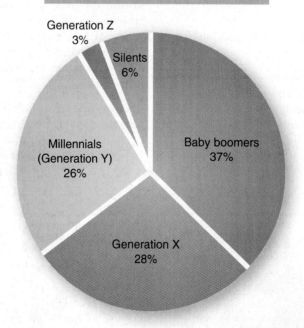

America's Multigenerational Workforce[74]

Generation Z 3%

Silents 6%

Baby boomers 37%

Millennials (Generation Y) 26%

Generation X 28%

Percentage of U.S. workforce by age group, based on 2009 data from the U.S. Bureau of Labor Statistics. "Silents" represent the generation of employees born before 1946. Generation Z employees were born after 1990, although some sources consider this age group part of the Millennials.

the office. Virtual work also includes employees connected to the office while on the road or at clients' offices. For instance, nearly 50 percent of employees at Sun Microsystems complete some of their work from home, cafés, drop-in centers, or clients' offices. More than two-thirds of the employees at Agilent Technologies engage in virtual work some or all of the time.[81]

Some research suggests that virtual work, particularly telecommuting, potentially reduces employee stress by offering better work/life balance and dramatically reducing time lost by commuting to the office. AT&T estimates that its telecommuters reduce pollution and are about 10 percent more productive than before they started working from home.[83] Against these potential benefits, virtual workers face a number of real and potential challenges. For example, family relations may suffer rather than improve if employees lack sufficient space and resources for a home office. Some virtual workers complain of social isolation and reduced promotion opportunities. We've all heard the phrase "out of sight, out of mind"; some remote employees have found themselves furloughed or even let go in economically difficult times. Virtual work is clearly better suited to people who are self-motivated and organized, can work effectively with broadband and other technology, and have sufficient fulfillment of social needs elsewhere in their life. It also works better in organizations that evaluate employees by their performance outcomes rather than face time.[84]

> "Companies that offer an inclusive workplace are, in essence, making fair and just decisions."

ANCHORS OF ORGANIZATIONAL BEHAVIOR KNOWLEDGE

Globalization, increasing workforce diversity, and emerging employment relationships are just a few of the trends that challenge organizations and make OB theories and practices more relevant than ever before. To understand these and other topics, the field of organizational behavior relies on a set of basic beliefs or knowledge structures (see Exhibit 1.5). These conceptual anchors represent the principles on which OB knowledge is developed and refined.

The Multidisciplinary Anchor

Organizational behavior is anchored around the idea that the field should develop from knowledge in other disciplines, not just from its own isolated research base. For instance, psychological research has aided our understanding of individual and interpersonal behavior. Sociologists have contributed to our knowledge of team dynamics, organizational socialization, organizational power, and other aspects of the social system. OB knowledge has also benefited from knowledge in emerging fields such as communications, marketing, and information systems. Some OB experts have recently argued that the field suffers from a "trade deficit"—importing far more knowledge from other disciplines than is exported to other disciplines. While this is a possible concern, organizational behavior has thrived through its diversity of knowledge from other fields of study.[85]

The Systematic Research Anchor

A critical feature of OB knowledge is that it should be based on systematic research, which typically involves forming research questions, systematically collecting data, and testing hypotheses against those data. The result is *evidence-based management*, which involves making decisions and taking actions based on this research evidence. This makes perfect sense, doesn't it? Yet many OB scholars are amazed at how

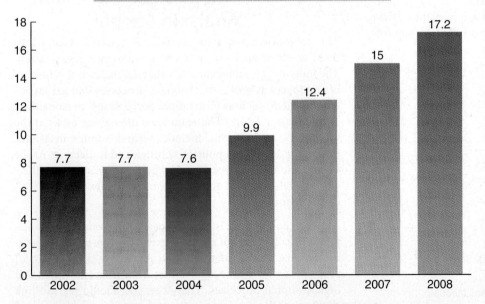

Telecommuting Is Gaining Popularity[82]

Number of full-time or part-time employees in the United States who work at home or remotely at least one day per month for their employer. Numbers are in millions (e.g., 7.7 = 7,700,000 people).

Multidisciplinary anchor	OB should import knowledge from many disciplines.
Systematic research anchor	OB should study organizations using systematic research methods.
Contingency anchor	OB theory should recognize that the effects of actions often vary with the situation.
Multiple levels of analysis anchor	OB knowledge should include three levels of analysis: individual, team, and organization.

and popular book writers are rewarded for marketing their concepts and theories, not for testing to see if they actually work. Indeed, some management concepts have become popular—they are even found in some OB textbooks!—because of heavy marketing, not because of any evidence that they are valid. Finally, as we will learn in Chapter 3, people form perceptions and beliefs quickly and tend to ignore evidence that their beliefs are inaccurate.

often corporate leaders embrace fads, consulting models, and their own pet beliefs without bothering to find out if they actually work![86]

There are many reasons why people have difficulty applying evidence-based management. Leaders and other decision makers are bombarded with so many ideas from newspapers, books, consultant reports, and other sources that it is a challenge to figure out which ones are based on good evidence. Another problem is that good OB research is necessarily generic; it is rarely described in the context of a specific problem in a specific organization. Managers therefore have the difficult task of figuring out which theories are relevant to their unique situation. A third problem is that many consultants

> " A critical feature of OB knowledge is that it should be based on systematic research. "

The Contingency Anchor

People and their work environments are complex, and the field of organizational behavior recognizes this by stating that a particular action may have different consequences in different situations. In other words, no single solution is best in all circumstances.[88] Of course it would be so much simpler if we could rely on "one best way" theories, in which a particular concept or practice has the same results in every situation. OB experts do search for simpler theories, but they also remain skeptical about surefire recommendations; an exception is somewhere around the corner. Thus, when faced with a particular problem or opportunity, we need to understand and diagnose the situation and select the strategy most appropriate *under those conditions.*[89]

The Multiple Levels of Analysis Anchor

This textbook divides organizational behavior topics into three levels of analysis: individual, team, and organization. The individual level includes the characteristics and behaviors of employees as well as the thought processes that are attributed to them, such as motivation, perceptions, personalities, attitudes, and values. The team level of analysis looks at the way people interact. This includes team dynamics, decisions, power, organizational politics, conflict, and leadership. At the organizational level, we focus on how people structure their working relationships and on how organizations interact with their environments.

Although an OB topic is typically pegged into one level of analysis, it usually relates to multiple levels.[90] For instance, communication is located in this book as a team (interpersonal) process, but we also recognize that it includes individual and organizational processes. Therefore, you should try to think about each OB topic at the individual, team, and organizational levels, not just at one of these levels.

Creating an Evidence-Based Management Organization[87]

1. Stop treating old ideas as if they are brand-new.
2. Be suspicious of "breakthrough" ideas and studies.
3. Celebrate and develop collective brilliance.
4. Emphasize drawbacks as well as virtues.
5. Use success (and failure) stories to illustrate sound practices, but not in place of a valid research method.
6. Adopt a neutral stance toward ideologies and theories.

THE JOURNEY BEGINS

This chapter gives you some background about the field of organizational behavior. But it's only the beginning of our journey. Throughout this book, we will challenge you to learn new ways of thinking about how people work in and around organizations. We begin this process in Chapter 2 by presenting a basic model of individual behavior, then introducing over the next few chapters various stable and mercurial characteristics of individuals that relate to elements of the individual behavior model. Next this book moves to the team level of analysis. We examine a model of team effectiveness and specific features of high-performance teams. We also look at decision making and creativity, communication, power and influence, conflict, and leadership. Finally we shift our focus to the organizational level of analysis, where the topics of organizational structure, organizational culture, and organizational change are examined in detail. ■

CHECK IT OUT!

mhhe.com/McShaneM

for study materials
including quizzes
and Internet resources

individual behavior, personality, and **values**

The Metropolitan Area Transit Authority in Washington, DC, (WMATA) has been plagued by a series of collisions, accidents, and train derailments.[1] Most of these can be traced to human factors. Several investigations have reported that track walkers—employees who monitor tracks for unsafe conditions—failed to discover unsafe track because they lacked sufficient training or time to test track, or weren't motivated to adequately perform their job. A panel of experts from other transit systems concluded that some WMATA track walkers are "apathetic." In one recent incident, two track walkers were killed because they didn't bother to observe or move safely away from a train approaching from behind, even after the conductor had twice sounded the train's horn.

continued on p. 26

LEARNING OBJECTIVES

After studying Chapter 2, you should be able to

LO1 Describe the four factors that directly influence voluntary individual behavior and performance.

LO2 Describe personality, the "Big Five" personality traits, and the MBTI types.

LO3 Describe self-concept and explain how social identity theory relates to a person's self-concept.

LO4 Describe Schwartz's model of individual values as well as five values commonly studied across cultures, and identify the conditions under which values influence behavior.

LO5 Discuss three factors that influence ethical behavior.

"people" problems associated with Washington's system. As Washington's metro transit woes reveal, there are several reasons why employees perform poorly or act unsafely. Some people lack skill or knowledge; others lack motivation. Occasionally employees aren't even aware that a task is part of their job duties or a behavior is considered risky. In turn, these direct causes of behavior and performance are affected by a variety of personal characteristics, such as attitude, self-concept, personality, mood, perceptions, learning, and stress.

This chapter concentrates our attention on the role of individual differences in organizations. We begin by presenting the MARS model, which outlines the four direct drivers of individual behavior and results. Next we introduce the most stable aspect of individuals—personality—including personality development, personality traits, and how personality relates to behavior in organizational settings. We then look at the individual's self-concept, including self-enhancement, self-verification, self-evaluation, and social identity. The latter part of this chapter examines another relatively stable characteristic of individuals: their personal values. We look at types of values, issues of values congruence in organizations, cross-cultural values, and ethical values and practices. ■

Learning Objectives

After reading this section, you should be able to

LO1 Describe the four factors that directly influence voluntary individual behavior and performance.

MARS MODEL OF INDIVIDUAL BEHAVIOR AND PERFORMANCE

For most of the past century, experts have investigated the direct predictors of individual behavior and performance.[2] One of the earliest formulas was *performance = person × situation*, where *person* includes individual characteristics and *situation* represents external influences on the individual's behavior. Another frequently mentioned formula is *performance = ability × motivation*. Sometimes known as the "skill-and-will" model, this formula elaborates two specific characteristics within the person that influence individual performance. Ability, motivation, and situation are by far the most commonly mentioned direct

continued from p. 25

Another investigation learned that WMATA trains were derailing due to lack of lubricant on the tight curves of track. Apparently no one in the track department knew that lubricating these tracks was part of their job duties. Staff who were aware of the lubrication task had retired, and the responsibility had never been documented. WMATA's most serious accident, which recently claimed the lives of nine people and injured dozens of other passengers, may have been caused by a faulty electronic sensor that prevents trains from crashing into each other (the accident is still under investigation). Staff knew that several sensors (including this one) had been unreliable, yet operators were not notified of these risks.

In contrast, Japan's high-speed bullet trains and China's new fast trains boast state-of-the-art construction, with none of the predictors of individual behavior and performance, but in the 1960s researchers identified a fourth key factor: role perceptions (the individual's expected role obligations).[3] Pulling these all together, Exhibit 2.1 illustrates the four variables—motivation, ability, role perceptions, and situational factors—which are represented by the acronym *MARS*.[4] All four factors are critical influences on an individual's voluntary behavior and performance; if any one of them is low in a given situation, the employee would perform the task poorly. For example, motivated salespeople with clear role perceptions and sufficient resources (situational factors) will not perform their jobs well if they lack sales skills and related knowledge (ability). Motivation, ability, and role perceptions are clustered together in the model because they are located within the person. Situational factors are external to the individual but still affect his or her behavior and performance.[5] Let's look at each of the four factors in more detail.

Employee Motivation

Motivation represents the forces within a person that affect his or her direction, intensity, and persistence of voluntary behavior.[6] *Direction* refers to the path along which people engage their effort. People have choices about where they put their effort; they have a sense of what they are trying to achieve and at what level of quality, quantity, and so forth. In other words, motivation is goal-directed, not random. People are motivated to arrive at work on time, finish a project a few hours early, or aim for many other targets. The second element of motivation, called *intensity,* is the amount of effort allocated to the goal. Intensity is how much people push themselves to complete a task. For example, two employees

motivation
The forces within a person that affect his or her direction, intensity, and persistence of voluntary behavior.

> " I believe the real difference between success and failure in a corporation can be very often traced to the question of how well the organization brings out the great energies and talents of its people.[7] "
>
> —Thomas J. Watson, Jr.

▼ **EXHIBIT 2.1** MARS Model of Individual Behavior and Results

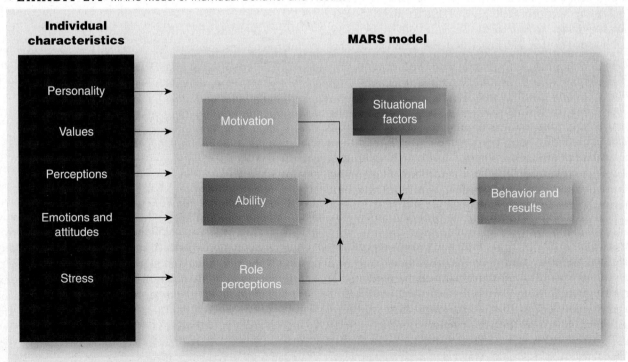

might be motivated to finish their project a few hours early (direction), but only one of them puts forth enough effort (intensity) to achieve this goal.

Finally, motivation involves varying levels of *persistence*—that is, continuing the effort for a certain amount of time. Employees sustain their effort until they reach their goal or give up beforehand. Remember that motivation exists within individuals; it is not their actual behavior. Thus direction, intensity, and persistence are cognitive and emotional conditions that directly cause us to move.

Ability

Employee abilities also make a difference in behavior and task performance. **Ability** includes both the natural aptitudes and the learned capabilities required to successfully complete a task. *Aptitudes* are the natural talents that help employees learn specific tasks more quickly and perform them better. There are many physical and mental aptitudes, and our ability to acquire skills is affected by these aptitudes. For example, finger dexterity is an aptitude by which individuals learn more quickly and potentially achieve higher performance at picking up and handling small objects with their fingers. Employees with high finger dexterity are not necessarily better than others at first; rather, their learning tends to be faster, and their performance potential tends to be higher. *Learned capabilities* are the skills and knowledge that you currently possess. These capabilities include the physical and mental skills and knowledge you have acquired. Learned capabilities tend to wane over time when not in use. This includes language facility; if you don't regularly use a language you learned as a child, it atrophies, but it can be "relearned" with extensive use over time.

Aptitudes and learned capabilities are closely related to *competencies*—a term now used frequently in business. **Competencies** are characteristics of a person that result in superior performance.[8] Many experts describe these characteristics as personal capabilities, such as knowledge, skills, aptitudes, and behaviors. Others also include personality and values. Still others suggest that competencies are action-oriented results of these characteristics, such as serving customers, coping with

heavy workloads, and providing creative ideas. With any of these interpretations, the challenge is to match a person's competencies with the job's task requirements. A good person–job match not only produces higher performance; it also tends to increase the employee's well-being.

One way to match a person's competencies with the job's task requirements is to select applicants who already demonstrate the required competencies. For example, companies ask applicants to perform work samples, provide references for checking their past performance, and complete various selection tests. A second strategy is to provide training so employees develop required skills and knowledge. Research indicates that training has a strong influence on individual performance and organizational effectiveness.[10] The third person–job matching strategy is to redesign the job so employees are given tasks only within their current learned capabilities. For example, a complex task might be simplified—some aspects of the work are transferred to others—so a new employee performs only tasks he or she is currently able to perform. As the employee becomes more competent at these tasks, other tasks are added back into the job.

Core Competencies at the U.S. Department of Health and Human Services[9]

Competency	Description
Results driven	Focuses on desired results, and sets and achieves challenging goals.
Customer service	Commits to satisfying internal and external customers.
Decision making	Makes decisions in a timely manner.
Collaboration/partnering	Establishes and maintains relationships for the purpose of achieving business goals.
Problem solving	Accurately assesses problems and effectively and efficiently arrives at excellent solutions.
Written communication	Express oneself clearly in business writing.
Oral communication	Delivers clear, effective communication and takes responsibility for understanding others.
Continuous development	Builds professional skills and competencies and improves work processes.
Diversity	The ability to recognize each person's differences and utilize those differences to increase the organization's effectiveness.
Integrity	Gains the trust of others by taking responsibility for own actions and telling the truth.

This list of competencies is required of all employees at the U.S. Department of Health and Human Services. The department also has technical competencies for each job group and four sets of competencies for various levels of supervision, management, and leadership.

Do Managers Develop Their Employees?

The Corporate Leadership Council reports that 54 percent of people surveyed thought it was vital for managers to develop people on the job, but only 24 percent said that senior managers do this well.[11]

Role Perceptions

Motivation and ability are important influences on individual behavior and performance, but employees also require accurate **role perceptions** to perform their jobs well. Role perceptions are the extent to which people understand the job duties (roles) assigned to them or expected of them. These perceptions are critical because they guide the employee's direction of effort and improve coordination with coworkers, suppliers, and other stakeholders. Unfortunately many employees do not have clear role perceptions.

There are three forms of role perceptions. First, employees have accurate role perceptions when they *understand* the specific tasks assigned to them—that is, when they know the specific duties or consequences for which they are accountable. This may seem obvious, but recall that some train derailments at the Washington metro transit system occurred because track department employees didn't know that lubricating the curved tracks was part of their job. Second, people have accurate role perceptions when they understand the *priority* of their various tasks and performance expectations. This includes the quantity versus quality dilemma, such as how many customers to serve in an hour (quantity) versus how well the employee should serve each customer (quality). It also refers to properly allocating time and resources to various tasks, such as how much time a manager should spend coaching employees in a typical week. The third form of role perceptions is understanding the *preferred behaviors* or procedures for accomplishing the assigned tasks. This refers to situations in which more than one method could be followed to perform the work. Employees with clear role perceptions know which of these methods is preferred by the organization.

ability The natural aptitudes and learned capabilities required to successfully complete a task.

competencies Skills, knowledge, aptitudes, and other personal characteristics that lead to superior performance.

role perceptions The extent to which a person accurately understands the job duties (roles) assigned to or are expected of him or her.

Falling Short on Role Clarity[12]

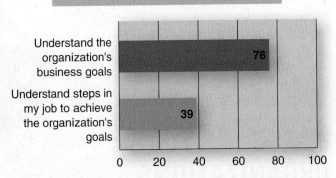

Percentage of Canadian employees who say they understand their organization's business goals and percentage saying they understand the steps in their own jobs to achieve the company's goals.

personality The relatively enduring pattern of thoughts, emotions, and behaviors that characterize a person, along with the psychological processes behind those characteristics.

five-factor model (FFM) The five abstract dimensions representing most personality traits: conscientiousness, emotional stability, openness to experience, agreeableness, and extroversion.

conscientiousness A personality dimension describing people who are careful, dependable, and self-disciplined.

neuroticism A personality dimension describing people with high levels of anxiety, hostility, depression, and self-consciousness.

Situational Factors

Employees' behavior and performance also depend on how much the situation supports or interferes with their task goals. Situational factors include conditions beyond the employee's immediate control that constrain or facilitate behavior and performance.[13] Some situational characteristics—such as consumer preferences and economic conditions—originate from the external environment and consequently are beyond the employee's and organization's control. However, other situational factors—such as time, people, budget, and physical work facilities—are controlled by people within the organization. Therefore, corporate leaders need to carefully arrange these conditions so employees can achieve their performance potential.

Corporate leaders are also interested in personality, so much so that many firms try to estimate the personality profiles of job applicants and employees. **Personality** is the relatively enduring pattern of thoughts, emotions, and behaviors that characterizes a person, along with the psychological processes behind those characteristics.[14] It is, in essence, the bundle of characteristics that makes us similar to or different from other people. We estimate an individual's personality by what they say and do, and we infer the person's internal states—including thoughts and emotions—from these observable behaviors.

A basic premise of personality theory is that people have inherent characteristics or traits that can be identified by the consis-

> Personality is to a man/woman what perfume is to a flower.[15]
>
> —Charles M. Schwab

The four elements of the MARS model—motivation, ability, role perceptions, and situational factors—affect all voluntary workplace behaviors and their performance outcomes. These elements are themselves influenced by other individual differences. In the remainder of this chapter, we introduce three of the most stable individual characteristics: personality, self-concept, and values.

Learning Objectives

After reading the next two sections, you should be able to

LO2 Describe personality, the "Big Five" personality traits, and the MBTI types.

LO3 Describe self-concept and explain how social identity theory relates to a person's self-concept.

PERSONALITY IN ORGANIZATIONS

Personality is an important individual characteristic. Think about how often you refer to someone's personality or attribute their behavior to a personality trait.

tency or stability of their behavior across time and situations.[16] For example, you probably have some friends who are more talkative than others. You might know some people who like to take risks and others who are risk-averse. This consistency is an essential requirement for personality theory because it attributes a person's behavior to something within them—the individual's personality—rather than to purely environmental influences.

Of course people do not act the same way in all situations; in fact, such consistency would be considered abnormal because it indicates a person's insensitivity to social norms, reward systems, and other external conditions.[17] People vary their behavior to suit the situation, even if the behavior is at odds with their personality. For example, talkative people remain relatively quiet in a library where "no talking" rules are explicit. People typically exhibit a wide range of behaviors, yet within that variety are discernible patterns that we refer to as *personality traits*. Traits are broad concepts that allow us to label and understand individual differences. Furthermore, traits predict an individual's behavior far into the future. For example, studies report that an individual's

FACT. Living Apart with Parallel Personalities[20]

Jim Springer and Jim Lewis are twins who were separated when only four weeks old and didn't meet each other until age 39. Despite being raised in different families and communities in Ohio, the "Jim twins" held similar jobs, smoked the same type of cigarettes, drove the same make and color of car, spent their vacations on the same Florida beach, had the same woodworking hobby, gave their first sons almost identical names, and had been married twice. Both their first and second wives also had the same first names!

personality in childhood predicts various behaviors and outcomes in adulthood, including educational attainment, employment success, marital relationships, illegal activities, and health risk behaviors.[18]

Personality Determinants: Nature versus Nurture

What determines an individual's personality? Most experts agree that personality is shaped by both nature and nurture, although the relative importance of each continues to be debated and studied. *Nature* refers to our genetic or hereditary origins—the genes we inherit from our parents. Studies of identical twins, particularly those separated at birth, reveal that heredity has a large effect on personality; up to 50 percent of variation in behavior and 30 percent of temperament preferences can be attributed to a person's genetic characteristics.[19] In other words, genetic code not only determines our eye color, skin tone, and physical shape; it also significantly affects our attitudes, decisions, and behavior.

Although personality is heavily influenced by heredity, it is also affected to some degree by *nurture*—the person's socialization, life experiences, and other forms of interaction with the environment. Studies have found that the stability of an individual's personality increases up to at least age 30 and possibly to age 50, indicating that some personality development and change occurs when people are young.[21] The main explanation of why personality becomes more stable over time is that people form clearer and more rigid self-concepts as they get older. The executive function—the part of the brain that manages goal-directed behavior—tries to keep our behavior consistent with our self-concept.[22] As self-concept becomes clearer and more

stable with age, behavior and personality also become more stable and consistent. We discuss self-concept in more detail later in this chapter. The main point here is that personality is not completely determined by heredity; life experiences, particularly early in life, also shape each individual's personality traits.

Five-Factor Model of Personality

One of the most important elements of personality theory is that people possess specific personality traits. Traits such as sociable, depressed, cautious, and talkative represent clusters of thoughts, feelings, and behaviors that allow us to identify, differentiate, and understand people.[23] The most widely respected model of personality traits is the **five-factor model (FFM)**. Several decades ago, personality experts identified more than 17,000 words in Roget's thesaurus and Webster's dictionary that describe an individual's personality. These words were aggregated into 171 clusters and then further reduced to five abstract personality dimensions. Using more sophisticated techniques, recent investigations identified the same five personality dimensions. Analyses of trait words in several other languages have produced strikingly similar results, although they also lend support for the notion of six or possibly seven dimensions of personality. Generally, though, the five-factor model is fairly robust across cultures.[24] These "Big Five" dimensions, represented by the handy acronym *CANOE*, are outlined in Exhibit 2.2 and described here:

- *Conscientiousness:* **Conscientiousness** characterizes people who are careful, dependable, and self-disciplined. Some scholars argue that this dimension also includes the will to achieve. People with low conscientiousness tend to be careless, less thorough, more disorganized, and irresponsible.

- *Agreeableness:* This dimension includes the traits of being courteous, good-natured, empathic, and caring. Some scholars prefer the label "friendly compliance" for this dimension, with its opposite being "hostile noncompliance." People with low agreeableness tend to be uncooperative, short-tempered, and irritable.

- *Neuroticism:* **Neuroticism** characterizes people with high levels of anxiety, hostility, depression, and self-consciousness. In contrast, people with low neuroticism (high emotional stability) are poised, secure, and calm.

- *Openness to experience:* This dimension is the most complex and has the least agreement among scholars. It generally refers to the extent to which people are imaginative, creative, curious, and aesthetically sensitive. Those who score low on this dimension tend to be more resistant to change, less open to new ideas, and more conventional and fixed in their ways.

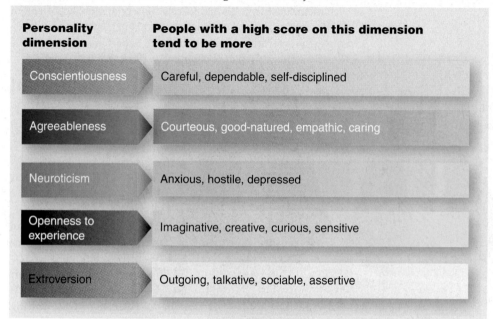

Personality dimension	People with a high score on this dimension tend to be more
Conscientiousness	Careful, dependable, self-disciplined
Agreeableness	Courteous, good-natured, empathic, caring
Neuroticism	Anxious, hostile, depressed
Openness to experience	Imaginative, creative, curious, sensitive
Extroversion	Outgoing, talkative, sociable, assertive

Estimated Personality Profiles of U.S. Presidents[25]

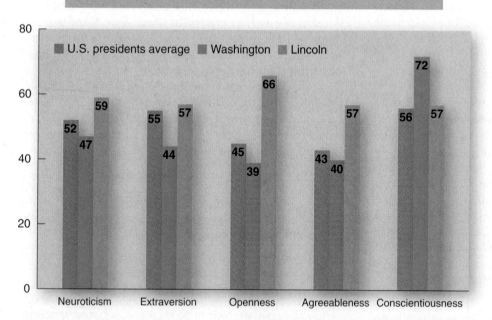

Forty-one authors who had written biographies of one or more U.S. presidents completed a validated five-factor personality measure of one or more presidents. The number of raters per president ranged from 1 to 13, with a mean of 4.2. These data show T-scores, where 50 is the mean score for today's general population (not necessarily when the presidents were living) and 10 points represent one standard deviation from the mean. The average personality scores for all presidents are displayed as well as those for George Washington and Abraham Lincoln. These results support previous evidence that George Washington had very high conscientiousness and that Abraham Lincoln had relatively high neuroticism (specifically depression and anxiety) as well as high openness to experience (specifically openness to feelings).

- *Extraversion:* **Extraversion** characterizes people who are outgoing, talkative, sociable, and assertive. The opposite is *introversion,* which characterizes those who are quiet, shy,

and cautious. Extraverts get their energy from the outer world (people and things around them), whereas introverts get their energy from the internal world, such as personal reflection on concepts and ideas. Introverts do not necessarily lack social skills. Rather, they are more inclined to direct their interests to ideas than to social events. Introverts feel quite comfortable being alone, whereas extraverts do not.

These five personality dimensions are not independent of each other. Some experts suggest that conscientiousness, agreeableness, and low neuroticism (high emotional stability) represent a common underlying characteristic broadly described as "getting along"; people with these traits are aware of and more likely to abide by rules and norms of society. The other two dimensions share the common underlying factor called "getting ahead"; people with high scores on extraversion and openness to experience exhibit more behaviors aimed at achieving goals, managing their environment, and advancing themselves in teams.[26] However, conscientiousness is also associated with job performance, so it likely crosses both categories.

Studies report fairly strong associations between personality and several workplace behaviors and outcomes, even when employee ability and other factors are taken into account. Conscientiousness and emotional stability (low neuroticism) stand out as the personality traits that best predict individual performance in almost every job group.[28] Both are motivational components of personality because they energize a willingness to fulfill work obligations within established rules (conscientiousness) and to allocate resources to accomplish those tasks (emotional stability). Various studies have reported that conscientious employees set higher personal goals for themselves, are more motivated, and have higher performance expectations than do employees with low levels of conscientiousness. They also tend to have higher

extraversion
A personality dimension describing people who are outgoing, talkative, sociable, and assertive.

Myers-Briggs Type Indicator (MBTI)®
An instrument designed to measure the elements of Jungian personality theory, particularly preferences regarding perceiving and judging information.

employees are expected to be cooperative and helpful, such as working in teams, customer relations, and other conflict-handling situations. People high on the openness-to-experience personality dimension tend to be more creative and adaptable to change. Finally, personality influences employee well-being in various ways. Studies report that personality influences a person's general emotional reactions to her or his job, how well the person copes with stress, and what type of career paths make that person happiest.[30]

levels of organizational citizenship and work better in organizations that give employees more freedom than is found in traditional command-and-control workplaces.[29]

The other three personality dimensions predict more specific types of employee behavior and performance. Extraversion is associated with performance in sales and management jobs, where employees must interact with and influence people. Agreeableness is associated with performance in jobs where

Jungian Personality Theory and the Myers-Briggs Type Indicator

The five-factor model of personality is the most respected and supported in research, but it is not the most popular in practice. That distinction goes to Jungian personality theory, which is

> " Conscientiousness and emotional stability (low neuroticism) stand out as the personality traits that best predict individual performance in almost every job group. "

The Right Personality for Lengthy Arctic/Antarctic Expeditions[27]

Personality Dimension	Preferred Characteristic for Polar Expeditioners
Neuroticism	Moderately below population average (i.e., moderately high emotional stability)
Extraversion	Somewhat introverted but socially adept (i.e., low need for social interaction and support)
Conscientiousness	Neutral (but lower need for order or achievement)
Openness to experience	Moderately high (but not easily bored)
Agreeableness	Neutral or slightly above average (particularly for those motivated to return)

measured through the **Myers-Briggs Type Indicator (MBTI)** (see Exhibit 2.3). Nearly a century ago, Swiss psychiatrist Carl Jung proposed that personality is represented primarily by the individual's preferences regarding perceiving and judging information.[31] Jung explained that perceiving, which involves how people prefer to gather information or perceive the world around them, occurs through two competing orientations: *sensing (S)* and *intuition (N)*. Sensing involves perceiving information directly through the five senses; it relies on an organized structure to acquire factual and preferably quantitative details. Intuition, on the other hand, relies more on insight and subjective experience to see relationships among variables. Sensing types focus on the here and now, whereas intuitive types focus more on future possibilities.

Jung also proposed that judging—how people process information or make decisions based on what they have perceived—consists of two

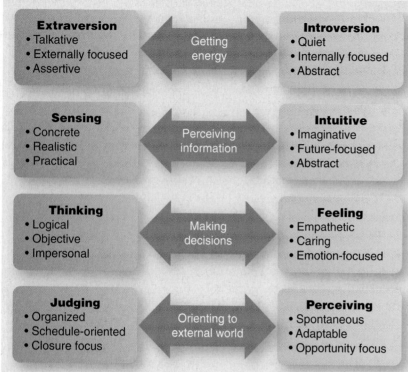

Extraversion		Introversion
• Talkative	Getting energy	• Quiet
• Externally focused		• Internally focused
• Assertive		• Abstract

Sensing		Intuitive
• Concrete	Perceiving information	• Imaginative
• Realistic		• Future-focused
• Practical		• Abstract

Thinking		Feeling
• Logical	Making decisions	• Empathetic
• Objective		• Caring
• Impersonal		• Emotion-focused

Judging		Perceiving
• Organized	Orienting to external world	• Spontaneous
• Schedule-oriented		• Adaptable
• Closure focus		• Opportunity focus

competing processes: *thinking (T)* and *feeling (F)*. People with a thinking orientation rely on rational cause–effect logic and systematic data collection to make decisions. Those with a strong feeling orientation, on the other hand, rely on their emotional responses to the options presented, as well as to how those choices affect others. Jung noted that along with differing in the four core processes of sensing, intuition, thinking, and feeling, people also differ in their degrees of extraversion–introversion, which was introduced earlier as one of the Big Five personality traits.

Along with measuring the personality traits identified by Jung, the MBTI measures Jung's broader categories of *perceiving* and *judging*, which represent a person's attitude toward the external world. People with a perceiving orientation are open, curious, and flexible; prefer to adapt spontaneously to events as they unfold; and prefer to keep their options open. Judging types prefer order and structure and want to resolve problems quickly.

The MBTI is one of the most widely used personality tests in work settings as well as in career counseling and executive coaching.[33] For example, many staff at Southwest Airlines post their Myers-Briggs Type Indicator (MBTI) results in their offices. "You can walk by and see someone's four-letter [MBTI type] posted up in their cube," says Elizabeth Bryant, Southwest's director of leadership development. Southwest began using the MBTI a decade ago to help staff understand and

respect coworkers' different personalities and thinking styles. It also helps leaders to work more effectively with individuals and teams. For example, Bryant recalls a session where employees and the manager in one department developed more trust and empathy by discovering their MBTI scores. "We saw a lot of 'aha' moments," Bryant recalls about employee reactions when they saw each other's MBTI scores. "Behaviors that might have once caused misunderstanding and frustration now are viewed through a different filter."[34]

Despite this popularity, evidence regarding the effectiveness of the MBTI and Jung's psychological types is mixed.[35] On one hand, the MBTI does a reasonably good job of measuring Jung's psychological types and seems to improve self-awareness for career development and mutual understanding. On the other hand, it poorly predicts job performance and is generally not recommended for employment selection or promotion decisions. Furthermore, the MBTI overlaps with the five-factor personality model, yet it does so less satisfactorily than existing measures of the Big Five personality dimensions.[36]

Caveats about Personality Testing in Organizations

Personality is clearly an important concept for understanding, predicting, and changing behavior in organizational settings. However, a few problems continue to hound personality testing.[37] One concern is that most tests are self-report scales, which allow applicants or employees to fake their answers. Rather than measuring a person's personality, many test results might identify the traits that people believe the company values. This concern is compounded by the fact that test takers often don't know what personality traits the company is looking for and may not know which statements are relevant to each trait. Thus the test scores might not represent the individual's personality or anything else meaningful.

A second issue is that personality is a relatively weak predictor of a person's performance. Some experts point to strong associations between a few personality traits and specific types of performance, but personality generally doesn't predict a person's behavior and performance as well as more immediate indicators (such as recent past performance). Thus personality testing could cause companies to wrongly reject applicants who would have performed well. Finally, some companies have discovered that personality testing does not convey a favorable image of the company. For example, the British operations of PricewaterhouseCoopers (PwC) required that applicants complete an online personality test early in the

Swiss psychiatrist Carl Gustav Jung developed his psychological types model in 1921; this later became the basis of the Myers-Briggs Type Indicator, the most popular psychological test in the world.

its a
FACT.

Getting Personality at Air New Zealand[38]

Air New Zealand discovered which personality traits predicted high-performing staff in various job functions. "We sampled a high-performing group of cabin crew, call centre agents, and corporate Air NZers," explains Simon Pomeroy, Air New Zealand's head of recruitment. "That gave us a group of items that created a model Air NZer." Pomeroy emphasizes that the personality test does not screen out applicants. Instead it helps to identify questions that the applicant would be asked in the job interview. He also suggests that the test results help applicants to decide whether the company fits their work preferences.

FLY!

BOARDING PASS

Originating Flight # — *Gate*
Connecting Flight # — *Gate* — *Destination* — *Seat #*
Destination — *Seat #*

concept has not received much attention in organizational behavior research, but scholars in psychology, social psychology, and other disciplines have discovered that it is critically important for understanding individual perceptions, attitudes, decisions, and behavior.

People do not have a single unitary self-concept (see Exhibit 2.4).[40] Rather, they think of themselves in several ways in various situations. For example, you might think of yourself as a creative employee, a health-conscious vegetarian, and an aggressive skier. A person's self-concept has higher *complexity* when it consists of many categories. Along with varying in complexity, self-concept varies in the degree of its *consistency*. People have high consistency when similar personality traits and values are required across all aspects of self-concept. Low consistency occurs when some aspects of self require personal characteristics that conflict with the characteristics required for other aspects of self. A third structural feature of self-concept is *clarity*—that is, the degree to which a person's self-conceptions are clearly and confidently described, internally consistent, and stable across time. A clear self-concept necessarily requires a consistent self-concept. Generally people develop clearer self-concepts as they get older.

selection process. The accounting firm learned that the test discouraged female applicants from applying because the process was impersonal and the test could be faked. "Our personality test was seen to alienate women and so we had to respond to that," says PwC's head of

[**People function better when their self-concept has many elements (high complexity) that are compatible with each other (high consistency) and are relatively clear.**]

diversity.[39] Overall, we need to understand personality in the workplace but also to be cautious about measuring and applying it too precisely.

SELF-CONCEPT: THE "I" IN ORGANIZATIONAL BEHAVIOR

People value organizations that recognize, support, and are aligned with their own self-concepts. **Self-concept** refers to an individual's self-beliefs and self-evaluations. It is the "Who am I?" and "How do I feel about myself?" that people ask themselves and that guide their decisions and actions. Self-

These three conceptual dimensions of self-concept—complexity, consistency, and clarity—influence an individual's adaptability and well-being. People function better when their self-concepts have many elements (high complexity) that are compatible with each other (high consistency) and are relatively clear. In contrast, people are more rigid and inflexible, and therefore less adaptable, when their self-views consist of only a few similar characteristics (low complexity). People also have poorer psychological adjustment when their self-concepts are less clear and include conflicting elements.

self-concept
An individual's self-beliefs and self-evaluations.

▼ **EXHIBIT 2.4** Conceptual Dimensions of Self-Concept

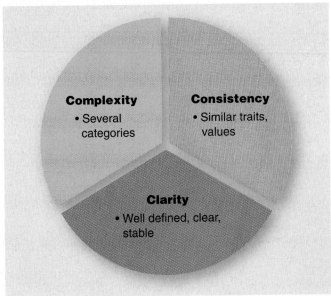

Complexity
• Several categories

Consistency
• Similar traits, values

Clarity
• Well defined, clear, stable

Self-Enhancement

A key ingredient in self-concept is the desire to feel valued. People are inherently motivated to promote and protect a self-view of being competent, attractive, lucky, ethical, and important.[41] This *self-enhancement* is observed in many ways. Individuals tend to rate themselves above average, selectively recall positive feedback while forgetting negative feedback, attribute their successes to personal motivation or ability while blaming the situation for their mistakes, and believe that they have a better than average probability of success. People don't see themselves as above average in all circumstances, but this bias is apparent for conditions that are common rather than rare and that are important to them.[42]

Self-enhancement has both positive and negative consequences in organizational settings.[43] On the positive side, research has found that individuals have better personal adjustment and experience better mental and physical health when they view their self-concepts in a positive light. On the negative side, self-enhancement can result in bad decisions. For example, studies report that self-enhancement causes managers to overestimate the probability of success in investment decisions.[44] Generally, though, successful companies strive to help employees feel they are valued and integral members of the organization.

Self-Verification

Along with being motivated by self-enhancement, people are motivated to verify and maintain their existing self-concepts.[46] *Self-verification* stabilizes an individual's self-concept, which, in turn, provides an important anchor that guides his or her thoughts and actions. Self-verification differs from self-enhancement because people usually prefer feedback that is consistent with their self-concepts even when that feedback is unflattering. Self-verification has several implications for organizational behavior.[47] First, it affects the perceptual process because employees are more likely to remember information that is consistent with their self-concepts. Second, the more confident employees are in their self-concepts, the less they will accept feedback—positive or negative—that is at odds with their self-concepts. Third, employees are motivated to interact with others who affirm their self-concepts, and this affects how well they get along with their boss and with coworkers in teams.

Self-Evaluation

Almost everyone strives to have a positive self-concept, but some people have a more positive evaluation of themselves than do others. This self-evaluation is mostly defined by three concepts: self-esteem, self-efficacy, and locus of control.[48]

Self-Esteem *Self-esteem*—the extent to which people like, respect, and are satisfied with themselves—represents a global self-evaluation. People with high self-esteem are less influenced by others, tend to persist in spite of failure, and think more rationally. Self-esteem regarding specific aspects of self (such as being a good student, a good driver, or a good parent) predicts specific thoughts and behaviors, whereas a person's overall self-esteem predicts only large bundles of thoughts and behaviors.[49]

Many Recognition Programs,
But Few Employees Feel Valued[45]

35%
of employees polled who say they received any recognition at all from their employer in the previous year.

89%
of human resources executives polled who say they have employee recognition programs.

79%
of employees polled who say that lack of recognition is a key reason why they quit their jobs.

Self-Efficacy

Self-efficacy refers to a person's belief that he or she can successfully complete a task.[50] Those with high self-efficacy have a "can do" attitude. They believe they possess the energy (motivation), resources (situational factors), understanding of the correct course of action (role perceptions), and competencies (ability) to perform the task. In other words, self-efficacy is an individual's perception regarding the MARS model in a specific situation. Although originally defined in terms of specific tasks, self-efficacy is also a general trait related to self-concept.[51] General self-efficacy is a perception of one's competence to perform across a variety of situations. The higher the person's general self-efficacy, the higher is his or her overall self-evaluation.

Locus of Control

Locus of control, the third concept related to self-evaluation, is defined as a person's general belief about the amount of control he or she has over personal life events. Individuals with more of an internal locus of control believe their personal characteristics (motivation and competencies) mainly influence life's outcomes. Those with more of an external locus of control believe that events in their lives are due mainly to fate, luck, or conditions in the external environment. Locus of control is a generalized belief, so people with an external locus can feel in control in familiar situations (such as performing common tasks). However, their underlying locus of control would be apparent in new situations in which control over events is uncertain.

People with a more internal locus of control have a more positive self-evaluation. They also tend to perform better in most employment situations, are more successful in their careers, earn more money, and are better suited for leadership positions. Internals are also more satisfied with their jobs, cope better in stressful situations, and are more motivated by performance-based reward systems.[52]

The Social Self

A person's self-concept can be organized into two fairly distinct categories: personal identity characteristics and social identity characteristics.[53] *Personal identity* consists of characteristics that make us unique and distinct from people in the social groups to which we have a connection. For instance, an unusual achievement that distinguishes you from other people typically becomes a personal identity characteristic. Personal identity refers to something about you as an individual without reference to a larger group. At the same time, human beings are social animals; they have an inherent drive to be associated with others and to be recognized as part of social communities. This drive to belong is reflected in self-concept by the fact that all individuals define themselves to some degree by their association with others.[54]

This social element of self-concept is described by **social identity theory**. According to social identity theory, people define themselves by the groups to which they belong or have an emotional attachment. For instance, someone might have a social identity as an American, a graduate of the University of Dallas, and an employee at IBM (see Exhibit 2.5). Social identity is a complex combination of many memberships arranged in a hierarchy of importance. One factor determining importance is how easily we are identified as a member of the reference group, such as by our gender, age, and ethnicity. It is difficult to ignore your gender in a class where most other students are the opposite gender, for example. In that context, gender tends to become a stronger defining feature of your social identity than it is in social settings where there are many people of the same gender.

Along with our demographic characteristics, a group's status is typically an important influence on whether we include the group in our social identity. We identify with groups that have

> "Human beings are social animals, so all individuals define themselves to some degree by their association with others."

self-efficacy
A person's belief that he or she has the ability, motivation, correct role perceptions, and favorable situation to complete a task successfully.

locus of control
A person's general belief about the amount of control he or she has over personal life events.

social identity theory A theory that explains self-concept in terms of the person's unique characteristics (personal identity) and membership in various social groups (social identity).

high status or respect because this aids the self-enhancement of our self-concept. Medical doctors usually define themselves by their profession because of its high status, whereas people in low-status jobs tend to define themselves by nonjob groups. Some people define themselves in terms of where they work because their employer has a positive reputation in the community. In contrast, other people never mention where they work because their employer is noted for poor relations with employees and has a poor reputation in the community.[55]

Self-Concept and Organizational Behavior

We began this section by stating that self-concept is an important topic for understanding individual perceptions, attitudes, decisions, and behavior. In fact, self-concept may eventually be recognized as one of the more useful ways to understand and improve an employee's performance and well-being. Some aspects of self-concept, such as self-efficacy and locus of control, are already known to have powerful influences on job performance. Self-concept also affects how people select and interpret information, as well as their biases in judgments (such as probability of success). Furthermore, as you will learn in future chapters, the social identity component of self-concept influences team dynamics, organizational commitment, and other OB concepts.

▼**EXHIBIT 2.5** Social Identity Theory Example

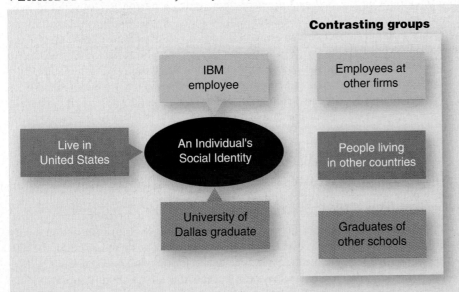

Learning Objectives

After reading the next three sections, you should be able to

LO4 Describe Schwartz's model of individual values as well as five values commonly studied across cultures, and identify the conditions under which values influence behavior.

LO5 Discuss three factors that influence ethical behavior.

VALUES IN THE WORKPLACE

Related to self-concept are the individual's personal values.[56] *Values* are stable, evaluative beliefs that guide our preferences for outcomes or courses of action in a variety of situations. They are perceptions about what is good or bad, right or wrong. Values tell us to what we "ought" to do. They serve as a moral compass that directs our motivation and, potentially, our decisions and actions. Values are related to self-concept because they partly define who we are as individuals and as members of groups with similar values.

> ## [The more choices you have, the more your values matter.]
> —Michael Schrage

People arrange values into a hierarchy of preferences, called a *value system*. Some individuals value new challenges more than they value conformity. Others value generosity more than frugality. Each person's unique value system is developed and reinforced through socialization from parents, religious institutions, friends, personal experiences, and the society in which he or she lives. As such, a person's hierarchy of values is stable and long-lasting. For example, one study found that value systems of a sample of adolescents were remarkably similar 20 years later when they were adults.[57]

Notice that our description of values has focused on individuals, whereas executives often describe values as though they belong to the organization. In reality, values exist only within individuals—we call them *personal values*. However, groups of people might hold the same or similar values, so we tend to ascribe these *shared values* to the team, department, organization, profession, or entire society. The values shared by people throughout an organization (*organizational values*) receive fuller discussion in Chapter 13 because they are a key part of corporate culture. The values shared across a society (*cultural values*) receive attention later in this chapter.

Types of Values

Values come in many forms, and experts on this topic have devoted considerable attention to organizing them into clusters. Several decades ago, social psychologist Milton Rokeach developed two lists of values, distinguishing means (instrumental values) from end goals (terminal values). Although Rokeach's lists are still mentioned in some organizational behavior sources, they are no longer considered acceptable representations of personal values. The instrumental–terminal values distinction was neither accurate nor useful, and experts have more recently identified values that were excluded from Rokeach's lists.

Today by far the most respected and widely studied set of values is the model developed and tested by social psychologist Shalom Schwartz and his colleagues.[58] Schwartz's list of 57 values builds on Rokeach's earlier work but does not distinguish instrumental from terminal values. Instead, through painstaking empirical research, Schwartz reported that human values are organized into the circular model (circumplex) shown in Exhibit 2.6.[59] The model organizes values into 10 broad categories, each representing several specific values. For example, conformity consists of four values: politeness, honoring parents, self-discipline, and obedience.

These 10 categories of values are further reduced to two bipolar dimensions. One dimension has the opposing value domains of openness to change and conservation. *Openness to change* refers to the extent to which a person is motivated to pursue innovative ways. It includes the value domains of self-direction (creativity, independent thought) and stimulation (excitement and challenge). *Conservation* is the extent to which a person is motivated to preserve the status quo. This dimension includes the value clusters of conformity (adherence to social norms and expectations), security (safety and stability), and tradition (moderation and preservation of the status quo).

The other bipolar dimension in Schwartz's model has the opposing value domains of self-enhancement and self-transcendence. *Self-enhancement*—how much a person is motivated by self-interest—includes the value categories of achievement (pursuit of personal success) and power (dominance over others). The opposite of self-enhancement is *self-transcendence*, which refers to motivation to promote the welfare of others and nature. Self-transcendence includes the values of benevolence (concern for others in one's life) and universalism (concern for the welfare of all people and nature).

Values and Individual Behavior

Personal values guide our decisions and actions to some extent, but this connection isn't always as strong as some would like to believe. Habitual behavior tends to be consistent with our values, but our everyday conscious decisions and actions apply our values much less consistently. The main reason for the disconnect between personal values and individual behavior is that values are abstract concepts that sound good in theory but are less easily followed in practice.

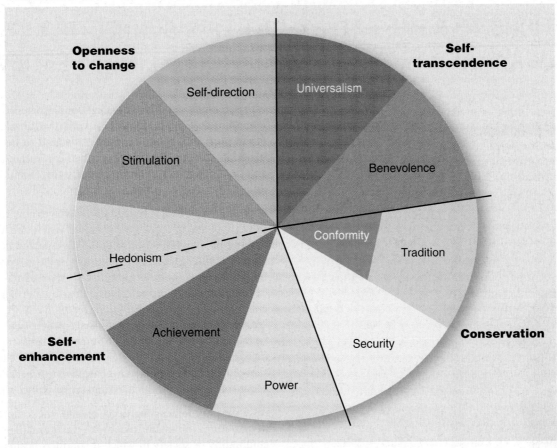

Source: Schwartz, "Universals in the Content and Structure of Values: Theoretical Advances and Empirical Tests in 20 Countries,";
Schwartz and Boehnke, "Evaluating the Structure of Human Values with Confirmatory Factor Analysis."

Three conditions strengthen the linkage between personal values and behavior.[61] First, we tend to apply our values only when we can think of specific reasons for doing so. In other words, we need logical reasons for applying a specific value in a specific situation. Second, we tend to apply our values in situations that facilitate doing so. Work environments shape our behavior, at least in the short term, so they necessarily encourage or discourage values-consistent behavior. Third, we are more likely to apply values when we actively think about them (that is, when they are salient). For example, people are more likely to apply their dominant values when they are reminded of them.

Consider the following study, which illustrates how making values salient affects a person's behavior: Students were given a math test in which they were paid for each correct answer. It wasn't possible to cheat under one condition (the results were scored by the experimenter), but it was possible to cheat under another condition where students kept their results and told the experimenter how well they scored. Students did cheat under this second condition. However, the experimenters also created a third condition where cheating was possible but the test form

had the following statement at the top of the page: "I understand that this short survey falls under (the university's) honor system." The university had no such honor code, but students who received that version of the test were required to sign their names to the statement. The researchers found that none of the students who received the "honor system" form cheated on the test. Similar results were reported in another study in which some students were asked to list as many of the Ten Commandments as they could remember. In each study, students who were reminded of their obligation to be ethical were more likely to apply those values.[62]

Values Congruence

Personal values not only define an individual's self-concept; they also affect how comfortable that person feels about their relationship to the organization and to other people. The key concept here is *values congruence,* which refers to how similar a person's values hierarchy is to the values hierarchy of the organization, a coworker, or another source of comparison. *Person–organization value congruence* occurs when the employee's and organization's dominant values are similar. Values are guideposts, so employees whose

for the reasons just noted, organizations also benefit from some level of incongruence. Employees with diverse values offer different perspectives, which potentially lead to better decision making. Also, too much congruence can create a "corporate cult" that potentially undermines creativity, organizational flexibility, and business ethics.

A second type of values congruence involves how consistent the values apparent in our actions (enacted values) are with what we say we believe in (espoused values). This *espoused–enacted values congruence* is especially important for people in leadership positions because any obvious gap between espoused and enacted values undermines their perceived integrity, a critical feature of effective leaders. One global survey reported recently that 55 percent of employees believe senior management behaves consistently with the company's core values.[65] Some companies try to maintain high levels of espoused–enacted values congruence by surveying subordinates and peers about whether the manager's decisions and actions are consistent with the company's espoused values.

A third type of values congruence involves the compatibility of an organization's dominant values with the prevailing values of the community or society in which it conducts business.[66] For example, an organization headquartered in one country that tries to impose its value system on employees and other stakeholders located in another culture may experience higher employee turnover and have more difficult relations with the communities in which the company operates. Thus globalization calls for a delicate balancing act: companies depend on shared values to maintain consistent standards and behaviors, yet they need to operate within the values of different cultures around the world. Let's look more closely at how values vary across cultures.

VALUES ACROSS CULTURES

Sean Billing had been working as director of rooms at Fairmont Hotels in Chicago when he casually asked his boss whether the hotel chain could use his skills and knowledge elsewhere. Soon after, the economics graduate was offered a position in Kenya, bringing Fairmont's new properties in the African country up to world-class standards through training and technology without losing the distinctive Kenyan character. Billing jumped at the opportunity, but he also soon discovered the challenge of inculcating Fairmont's deep values of customer service, environmentalism, and empowerment into another culture. "It's a little bit of hotel culture shock . . . things are quite different here," admitted Billing.[67]

values are similar to the dominant organizational values are more likely to make decisions compatible with the organization's values-based mission and objectives. Person–organization values congruence also leads to higher job satisfaction, loyalty, and organizational citizenship as well as lower stress and turnover. "The most difficult but rewarding accomplishment in any career is 'living true' to your values and finding companies where you can contribute at the highest level while being your authentic self," says an executive at Japanese biopharmaceutical company Eisai Co. Ltd. "There is nothing more important in my estimation."[63]

Do the most successful organizations have the highest possible levels of person–organization values congruence? Not at all! While a comfortable degree of values congruence is necessary

individualism
A cross-cultural value describing the degree to which people in a culture emphasize independence and personal uniqueness.

collectivism
A cross-cultural value describing the degree to which people in a culture emphasize duty to groups to which people belong, and to group harmony.

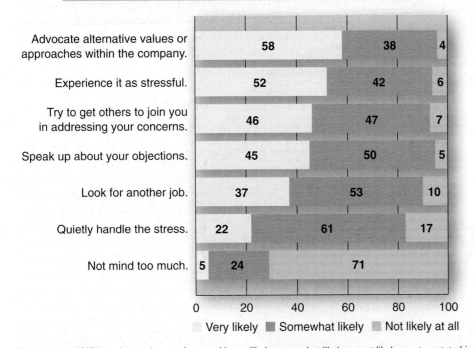

How MBA Students Say They Would React to Personal–Organizational Values Incongruence[64]

Advocate alternative values or approaches within the company. — Very likely 58, Somewhat likely 38, Not likely at all 4

Experience it as stressful. — Very likely 52, Somewhat likely 42, Not likely at all 6

Try to get others to join you in addressing your concerns. — Very likely 46, Somewhat likely 47, Not likely at all 7

Speak up about your objections. — Very likely 45, Somewhat likely 50, Not likely at all 5

Look for another job. — Very likely 37, Somewhat likely 53, Not likely at all 10

Quietly handle the stress. — Very likely 22, Somewhat likely 61, Not likely at all 17

Not mind too much. — Very likely 5, Somewhat likely 24, Not likely at all 71

■ Very likely   ■ Somewhat likely   ■ Not likely at all

Percentage of MBA students who say they would very likely, somewhat likely, or not likely react as stated in situations where their personal values conflict with the organization's values. Most students (71 percent) would very likely mind values incongruence situations, and 52 percent say they would very likely experience stress from these conflicts. Many would very likely speak up about the issue (45 percent), form a coalition to address the incongruence (46 percent), or advocate different values or approaches for the company (58 percent). This sample consisted of 1,943 MBA students at 15 top-ranked business schools in the United States, Canada, and Britain. Eighty-three percent predicted that they will experience conflict between their personal values and what they are asked to do in business.

Fairmont Hotels & Resorts operates world-class hotels in several countries and is eager to help Sean Billing and other employees develop and strengthen their cross-cultural competence. As Billing learned, people think and act differently across cultures, and these differences are due to unique norms of behavior as well as emphasis on different values. The next few pages describes the five values most widely studied across cultures.

Individualism and Collectivism

Many values have been studied in the context of cross-cultural differences, but the two most commonly mentioned are individualism and collectivism. **Individualism** is the extent to which we value independence and personal uniqueness. Highly individualist people value personal freedom, self-sufficiency, control over their own lives, and appreciation of the unique qualities that distinguish them from others. As shown in Exhibit 2.7, Americans and Italians generally exhibit high individualism, whereas Taiwanese tend to have low individualism. **Collectivism** is the extent to which we value our duty to groups to which we belong and to group harmony. Highly collectivist people define themselves by their group memberships and value harmonious relationships within those groups.[69] Americans generally have low collectivism, whereas Italians and Taiwanese have relatively high collectivism.

Contrary to popular belief, individualism is not the opposite of collectivism. In fact, an analysis of most previous studies

▼**EXHIBIT 2.7** Five Cross-Cultural Values in Selected Countries

Country	Individualism	Collectivism	Power Distance	Uncertainty Avoidance	Achievement Orientation
United States	High	Low	Medium low	Medium low	Medium high
Denmark	Medium	Medium low	Low	Low	Low
India	Medium high	Medium	High	Medium low	Medium high
Italy	High	High	Medium	High	High
Japan	Medium high	Low	Medium	High	High
Taiwan	Low	High	Medium	High	Medium

Sources: Individualism and collectivism results are from the meta-analysis reported in D. Oyserman, H. M. Coon, and M. Kemmelmeier, "Rethinking Individualism and Collectivism: Evaluation of Theoretical Assumptions and Meta-Analyses," *Psychological Bulletin*, 128 (2002), pp. 3–72. The other results are from G. Hofstede, *Culture's Consequences,* 2nd ed. (Thousand Oaks, CA: Sage, 2001).

FACT. **We're Not in Bentonville Anymore!**[68]

Walmart is established in many countries, but the retailer's capabilities in this globalized world haven't always been up to expectations. In the late 1990s Walmart established a European beachhead in Germany by opening 85 stores from two acquisitions. The decision may have been astute— if Walmart executives had realized that they weren't in the United States anymore. The first CEO of the German operations spoke no German, so he required all direct reports to speak English at all times. The company naïvely imported the daily morning cheer and required greeters and staff to ask customers, "How are you today?" The morning cheer offended German managers, who felt a loss of their hierarchical position when required to cheer along with frontline employees (who were also somewhat ambivalent to the ritual). The friendly greeting was an affront to German customers because such signs of friendliness are reserved for friends and family. Walmart also banned coworkers from dating each other—yet another sign that Walmart had much to learn about the world beyond America. Less than a decade later, Walmart closed down its German operations, taking a $1 billion loss.

reported that the two concepts are unrelated.[70] Some cultures that highly value duty to one's group do not necessarily give a low priority to personal freedom and self-sufficiency. The distinction between individualism and collectivism makes sense when we realize that people across all cultures define themselves by both their uniqueness (personal identity) and their relationship to others (social identity). Some cultures clearly emphasize one more than the other, but both have a place in a person's values and self-concept.

Power Distance

Power distance refers to the extent to which people accept unequal distribution of power in a society.[71] On average, employees in Thailand, Malaysia, and most (but not all) other Asian countries have high power distance. They accept and value unequal power. They also value obedience to authority, are comfortable receiving commands from their superiors without consultation or debate, and prefer to resolve differences indirectly through formal procedures rather than directly.

In contrast, people with low power distance expect relatively equal power sharing. They view the relationship with their boss as one of interdependence, not dependence; that is, they believe their boss is also dependent on them, so they expect power sharing and consultation before decisions affecting them are made. People in India tend to have high power distance, whereas people in Denmark generally have low power distance.

Uncertainty Avoidance

Uncertainty avoidance is the degree to which people tolerate ambiguity (low uncertainty avoidance) or feel threatened by ambiguity and uncertainty (high uncertainty avoidance). Employees with high uncertainty avoidance value structured situations in which rules of conduct and decision making are clearly documented. They usually prefer direct rather than indirect or ambiguous communications. Uncertainty avoidance tends to be high in Italy and Taiwan and very high in Japan. It is generally low in Denmark.

Achievement–Nurturing Orientation

Achievement–nurturing orientation reflects a competitive versus cooperative view of relations with other people.[72] People with a high achievement orientation value assertiveness, competitiveness, and materialism. They appreciate people who are tough, and they favor the acquisition of money and material goods. In contrast, people in nurturing-oriented cultures emphasize relationships and the well-being of others. They focus on human interaction and caring rather than competition and personal success. People in Sweden, Norway, and Denmark score very low on achievement orientation (they have a high nurturing orientation). In contrast, very high achievement orientation scores have been reported in Japan and Hungary, with fairly high scores in the United States and Italy.

Before leaving this topic, we need to point out two concerns about this information on cross-cultural values.[73] One concern is that country scores on power distance, uncertainty avoidance, and achievement–nurturing orientation are based on a survey of IBM staff worldwide more than a quarter century ago. More than 100,000 IBM employees in dozens of countries completed that survey, but IBM employees might not represent the general population. Indeed, there is evidence that values have since changed considerably in some countries. For example, studies report that value systems are converging across Asia as people in these countries interact more frequently with each other and as globalization results in more standardized business practices at both the corporate and national levels.[74]

power distance
A cross-cultural value describing the degree to which people in a culture accept unequal distribution of power in a society.

uncertainty avoidance
A cross-cultural value describing the degree to which people in a culture tolerate ambiguity (low uncertainty avoidance) or feel threatened by ambiguity and uncertainty (high uncertainty avoidance).

achievement–nurturing orientation
A cross-cultural value describing the degree to which people in a culture emphasize competitive versus cooperative relations with other people.

moral intensity
The degree to which an issue demands the application of ethical principles.

ethical sensitivity
A personal characteristic that enables people to recognize the presence and determine the relative importance of an ethical issue.

A second concern is the assumption that everyone in a society has similar cultural values. This may be true in a few countries, but *multiculturalism*—in which several microcultures coexist in the same country—is becoming the more common trend. For example, one study reported significantly different values among Japanese and Chinese Indonesians, yet cross-cultural studies tend to lump these diverse groups together into one culture. By attributing specific values to an entire society, we are engaging in a form of stereotyping that limits our ability to understand the more complex reality of that society.[75]

ETHICAL VALUES AND BEHAVIOR

When employees are asked to rank the most important characteristics they look for in a leader, honesty and ethics are near the top of the list.[76] The term *ethics* refers to the study of moral principles or values that determine whether actions are right or wrong and outcomes are good or bad. People rely on their ethical values to determine the right thing to do. The importance of ethical corporate conduct is almost constantly in the news, yet there doesn't seem to be any noticeable decline in wrongdoing. Almost half of the 2,800 employees recently surveyed said they had witnessed misconduct on the job, such as abuse of company resources, abusive behavior, lying to employees, e-mail or Internet abuse, conflicts of interest, discrimination, and lying to outside stakeholders.[77]

Three Ethical Principles

To better understand business ethics, we need to consider three distinct types of ethical principles: utilitarianism, individual rights, and distributive justice.[78] While your personal values might sway you more toward one principle than the others, all three should be actively considered to put important ethical issues to the test.

- *Utilitarianism:* This principle advises us to seek the greatest good for the greatest number of people. In other words, we should choose the option that provides the highest degree of satisfaction to those affected. This is sometimes known as a *consequential principle* because it focuses on the consequences of our actions, not on how we achieve those consequences. One problem with utilitarianism is that it is almost impossible to evaluate the benefits or costs of many decisions, particularly when many stakeholders have wide-ranging needs and values. Another problem is that most of us are uncomfortable engaging in behaviors that seem, well, unethical to attain results that are ethical.

- *Individual rights:* This principle reflects the belief that everyone has entitlements that let her or him act in a certain way. Some of the most widely cited rights are freedom of movement, physical security, freedom of speech, fair trial, and freedom from torture. The individual rights principle includes more than legal rights; it also includes human rights that everyone is granted as a moral norm of society. One problem with individual rights is that certain individual rights may conflict with others. The shareholders' right to be informed about corporate activities may ultimately conflict with an executive's right to privacy, for example.

- *Distributive justice:* This principle suggests that people who are similar to each other should receive similar benefits and burdens; those who are dissimilar should receive different benefits and burdens in proportion to their dissimilarity. For example, we expect that two employees who contribute equally in their work should receive similar rewards, whereas those who make a lesser contribution should receive less. A variation of the distributive justice principle says that inequalities are acceptable when they benefit the least well off in society. Thus employees in risky jobs should be paid more if their work benefits others who are less well off. One problem with the distributive justice principle is that it is difficult to agree on who is similar and what factors are relevant.

Moral Intensity, Ethical Sensitivity, and Situational Influences

Along with ethical principles and their underlying values, three other factors influence ethical conduct in the workplace: the moral intensity of an issue, the individual's ethical sensitivity, and situational factors. **Moral intensity** is the degree to which an issue demands the application of ethical principles. Decisions with high moral intensity are more important, so the decision maker needs to more carefully apply ethical principles to resolve them. Several factors influence the moral intensity of an issue, including those listed in Exhibit 2.8. Keep in mind that this list represents the factors people tend to think about; some of them might not be considered morally acceptable when people are formally making ethical decisions.[79]

Even if an issue has high moral intensity, some employees might not recognize its ethical importance because they have low **ethical sensitivity.** Ethical sensitivity is a personal characteristic that enables people to recognize the presence of

Moral Intensity Factor	Moral Intensity Question	Moral Intensity Is Higher When
Magnitude of consequences	How much harm or benefit will occur to others as a result of this action?	The harm or benefit is larger.
Social consensus	How many other people agree that this action is ethically good or bad?	Many people agree.
Probability of effect	(a) What is the chance that this action will actually occur? (b) What is the chance that this action will actually cause good or bad consequences?	The probability is higher.
Temporal immediacy	How long after the action will the consequences occur?	The time delay is shorter.
Proximity	How socially, culturally, psychologically, and/or physically close to me are the people affected by this decision?	Those affected are close rather than distant.
Concentration of effect	(a) How many people are affected by this action? (b) Are the people affected by this action easily identifiable as a group?	Many people are affected. Those affected are easily identifiable as a group.

*These are factors people tend to ask themselves about when determining the moral intensity of an issue. Whether some of these questions should be relevant is itself an ethical question.

Source: Based on information in T. J. Jones, "Ethical Decision Making by Individuals in Organizations: An Issue Contingent Model," *Academy of Management Review* 16 (1991), pp. 366–95.

an ethical issue and determine its relative importance.[80] Ethically sensitive people are not necessarily more ethical. Rather, they are more likely to sense whether an issue requires ethical consideration; that is, they can more accurately estimate the moral intensity of the issue. Ethically sensitive people tend to have higher empathy. They also have more information about the specific situation. For example, accountants would be more ethically sensitive regarding the appropriateness of specific accounting procedures than would someone who has not received training in this profession.

The third important factor explaining why good people engage in unethical decisions and behavior is the situation in which the conduct occurs. Employees say they regularly experience pressure from top management that motivates them to lie to customers, breach regulations, or otherwise act unethically. According to a global survey of managers and human resource managers, pressure from top management or the board to meet unrealistic deadlines and business objectives is the leading cause of unethical corporate behavior.[81] Situational factors do not justify unethical conduct. Rather, we need to be aware of these factors so organizations can reduce their influence in the future.

Supporting Ethical Behavior

FACT. **Is a Company's Ethical Reputation Important to Job Applicants?**[82]

Two-thirds of surveyed British university and polytechnic students said they would need to feel happy with a prospective employer's ethical record to work there. This rose to 82 percent of students when referring to charity organizations. Similarly, 73 percent of Irish university and polytechnic students indicated that the prospective employer's ethical reputation was important (51 percent) or extremely important (22 percent). Yet ethical reputation was far down the list (8th place out of 16th factors) in the Irish study. This parallels a major survey of MBA students at top-ranked U.S., Canadian, and British universities; only 15 percent of them placed a company's high ethical standards in the top three factors they would consider when choosing a job.

Most large and medium-size organizations in the United States, United Kingdom, and several other countries apply one or more strategies to improve ethical conduct. Creating ethical codes of conduct is the most common. Almost all *Fortune* 500 companies in the United States and the majority of the 500 largest U.K. companies now have codes of ethics. These statements communicate the organization's ethical standards and signal to employees that the company takes ethical conduct seriously. However, critics point out that ethics codes alone do little to reduce unethical conduct. A glaring illustration is that

Enron had a well-developed 64-page code of ethics, but that document didn't prevent senior executives from engaging in wholesale accounting fraud, resulting in the energy company's bankruptcy.[83]

To supplement ethics codes, many firms provide ethics training. At Texas Instruments, employees learn to consider the following ideas as their moral compass:

> Is the action legal? Does it comply with our values? If you do it, will you feel bad? How would it look in the newspaper? If you know it's wrong, don't do it! If you're not sure, ask. Keep asking until you get an answer.

Molson Coors developed an award-winning online training program set up as an expedition: Employees must resolve ethics violations at each "camp" as they ascend a mountain. The first few camps present real scenarios with fairly clear ethical violations of the company's ethics code; later camps present much fuzzier dilemmas requiring more careful thought about the company's underlying values.[84]

Some companies have also introduced procedures whereby employees can communicate possible ethical violations in confidence. Food manufacturer H. J. Heinz Co. has an ethics hotline that operates around the clock and in 150 languages for its global workforce. Heinz's director of ethics says that the hotline "has provided an early warning signal of problems we were not aware of." Rogers Cable Communications Inc. also has an anonymous "star hotline" as well as a Web link that employees can use to raise ethical issues or concerns about ethical conduct.

Rogers employees can even call back to find out what actions have been taken to resolve an ethical issue.[85]

These additional measures support ethical conduct to some extent, but the most powerful foundation is a set of shared values that reinforce ethical conduct. "If you don't have a culture of ethical decision making to begin with, all the controls and compliance regulations you care to deploy won't necessarily prevent ethical misconduct," warns a senior executive at British communications giant Vodafone. This culture is supported by the ethical conduct and vigilance of corporate leaders. By acting with the highest standards of moral conduct, leaders not only gain support and trust from followers; they model the ethical standards that employees are more likely to follow.[87] ■

CHECK IT OUT!

mhhe.com/McShaneM

for study materials
including quizzes
and Internet resources

Growing an Ethical Culture[86]

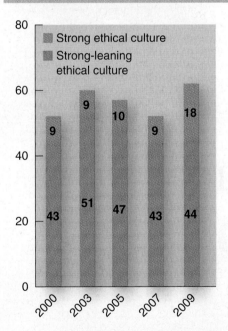

Legend:
- Strong ethical culture
- Strong-leaning ethical culture

Year	Strong-leaning	Strong
2000	9	43
2003	9	51
2005	10	47
2007	9	43
2009	18	44

Percentage of American employees in for-profit companies who believe their company has a strong or strong-leaning ethical culture. An ethical culture consists of ethical leadership, accountability, and values, not just rules or a written ethics code. Sample size in 2009 survey was 2,852 people.

perception and learning
in organizations

chapter three

"It is a capital mistake to theorize before you have all the evidence," warned the mythical detective Sherlock Holmes in the story "A Study in Scarlet." "It biases the judgment." Law enforcement agencies around the world have been following Holmes's advice to reduce the risk of wrongful conviction. Rather than test theories about a crime, detectives do their best to *avoid* forming any theories too early in the investigation. "We're very careful to let the evidence drive the investigation, not theories," explains U.S. Federal Bureau of Investigation (FBI) special agent Mark MacKizer. Vernon Geberth echoes this view. "At times, investigators may close their minds to other possibilities once they've developed a theory," says the retired lieutenant commander of the New York City police department's homicide division. "Then they begin to try to make the evidence fit their theory instead of allowing the evidence to lead you to the suspect."[1] ■

LEARNING OBJECTIVES

After reading this chapter, you should be able to

LO1 Outline the perceptual process.

LO2 Discuss the effects of stereotyping, attribution, self-fulfilling prophecy, halo, primacy, recency, and false-consensus effects on the perceptual process.

LO3 Discuss three ways to improve social perception, with specific application to organizational situations.

LO4 Describe the three features of social learning theory.

Whether as a crime investigator, a forensic accountant, or a senior executive, everyone needs to pay attention to how they perceive the world around them, including the conditions that challenge the accuracy of those perceptions. The Greek philosopher Plato wrote long ago that we see reality only as shadows reflecting against the rough wall of a cave.[3] This metaphor may suggest that we will never perceive things with complete accuracy. Fortunately, we now have a better understanding about perceptual biases and ways to develop more accurate perceptions.

The first part of this chapter focuses on perceptions in organizational settings, including conditions that make it difficult to perceive things and strategies to minimize perceptual biases. We begin by describing the perceptual process—that is, the dynamics of selecting, organizing, and interpreting external stimuli. Next we examine the perceptual processes of social identity and stereotyping, attribution, and self-fulfilling prophecy, including biases created within these processes. Four other perceptual biases—halo, primacy, recency, and false consensus—are also briefly introduced. We then identify potentially effective

you will learn in this chapter, but it generally follows the steps shown in Exhibit 3.1. Perception begins when environmental stimuli are received through our senses. Most stimuli that bombard our senses are screened out; the rest are organized and interpreted.

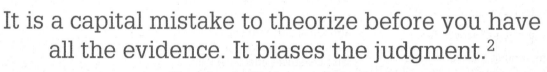

[It is a capital mistake to theorize before you have all the evidence. It biases the judgment.[2]]
—Sherlock Holmes (Sir Arthur Conan Doyle)

ways to improve perceptions, including practices similar to corporate volunteering. The latter part of this chapter looks at three perspectives of learning: behavior modification, social learning theory, and experiential learning.

Learning Objectives

After reading the next two sections, you should be able to

LO1 Outline the perceptual process.

LO2 Discuss the effects of stereotyping, attribution, self-fulfilling prophecy, halo, primacy, recency, and false-consensus effects on the perceptual process.

THE PERCEPTUAL PROCESS

Perception is the process of receiving information about and making sense of the world around us. It entails determining which information to notice, how to categorize this information, and how to interpret it within the framework of our existing knowledge. This perceptual process is far from perfect, as

The process of attending to some information received by our senses and ignoring other information is called **selective attention**. Selective attention is influenced by characteristics of the person or object being perceived, particularly size, intensity, motion, repetition, and novelty. For example, a small, flashing red light on a nurse station console is immediately noticed because it is bright (intensity), flashing (motion), and a rare event (novelty), and it has symbolic meaning that a patient's vital signs are failing. Notice that selective attention is also influenced by the context in which the target is perceived. The selective attention process is triggered by things or people who might be out of context, such as hearing someone with a foreign accent in a setting where most people have American accents.

Characteristics of the perceiver play an important role in selection attention, much of it without the perceiver's awareness.[4] When information is received through the senses, our brain quickly and nonconsciously assesses whether it is relevant or irrelevant to us and then attaches emotional markers (worry, happiness, boredom) to that information. The emotional markers help us to store information in memory; they also reproduce the same emotions when we are subsequently thinking about this information.[5]

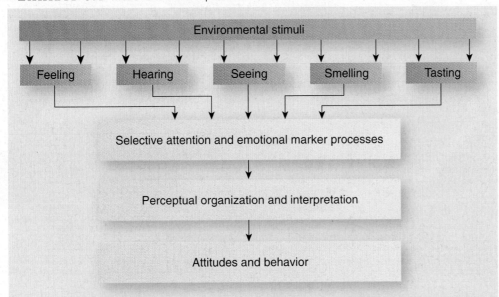

▼ **EXHIBIT 3.1** Model of the Perceptual Process

Environmental stimuli

Feeling · Hearing · Seeing · Smelling · Tasting

Selective attention and emotional marker processes

Perceptual organization and interpretation

Attitudes and behavior

perception
The process of receiving information about and making sense of the world around us.

selective attention
The process of attending to some information received by our senses and ignoring other information.

confirmation bias
The process of screening out information that is contrary to our values and assumptions.

> ❝ We don't see things as they are. We see them as we are.
> —Anais Nin ❞

The selective attention process is far from perfect. As mentioned in Chapter 2, we have a natural tendency to seek out information that supports our self-concept or puts us in a favorable light and to ignore or undervalue information that is contrary to our self-concept. This **confirmation bias** also screens out information that is contrary to our values and assumptions.[6] Several studies have found that people fail to perceive (or soon forget) statements and events that undermine political parties that they support. One study examined how people perceived and accepted stories during the first weeks of the Iraq war that were subsequently retracted (acknowledged by the media as false stories). The investigation found that most of the Germans and Australians surveyed dismissed the retracted events, whereas a significantly large percentage of Americans continued to believe these false stories, even though many of them recalled that the stories had been retracted by the media. In essence, many (but not all) of the Americans perceptually ignored the retractions that supported their beliefs about the Iraq war.[7]

Finally, selective attention is influenced by our assumptions and conscious anticipation of future events. You are more likely to notice a coworker's e-mail among the daily bombardment of messages when you expect to receive that e-mail (particularly when it is important to you). Unfortunately, expectations and assumptions also cause us to screen out

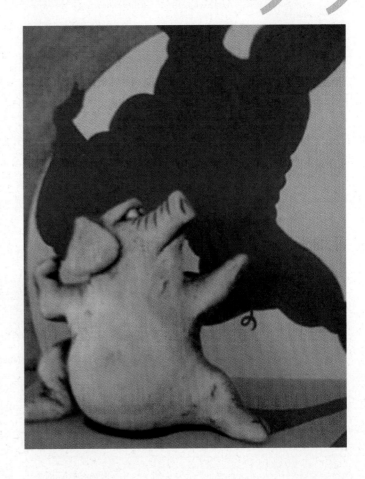

Manager–Employee Perceptual Misalignments[9]

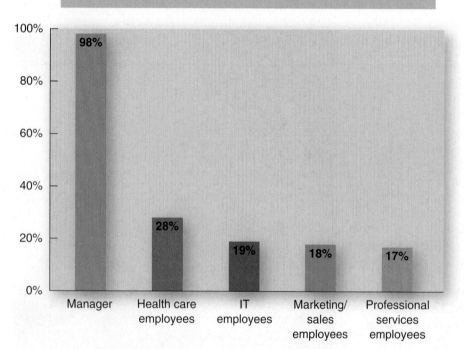

Percentage of British managers who believe they "know their people well" compared with percentage of employees (by occupation) who believe that their bosses know them well.

instructed just to watch the video clip easily noticed someone dressed in a gorilla suit walking among the players for nine seconds and stopping to thump his or her chest. But only half of the students who were asked to carefully count the number of times one basketball was passed around noticed the intruding gorilla.[8]

This perceptual blindness also occurs when we form an opinion or theory about something, such as a consumer trend or an employee's potential. The preconception causes us to select information that is consistent with the theory and to ignore contrary or seemingly irrelevant information. Studies have reported that this faulty selective attention occurs when police detectives and other forensic experts quickly form theories about what happened.[10] As we mentioned at the beginning of this chapter, these experts are now increasingly aware of the need to avoid selective attention traps by keeping an open mind, absorbing as much information as possible, and avoiding theories too early in an investigation.

potentially important information. In one study, students were asked to watch a 30-second video clip in which several people passed around two basketballs. Students who were

Perceptual Organization and Interpretation

People make sense of information even before they become aware of it. This sense making partly includes **categorical thinking**—the mostly nonconscious process of organizing people and objects into preconceived categories that are stored in our long-term memory.[11] Categorical thinking relies on a variety of automatic perceptual grouping principles. Things are often grouped together based on their similarity or proximity to others. If you notice that a group of similar-looking people includes several professors, for instance, you will likely assume that other members of the group are also professors. Another form of perceptual grouping is based on the need for cognitive closure, such as filling in missing information about what happened at a meeting that you didn't attend (such as who was there and where it was held). A third form of grouping occurs when we think we see trends in otherwise ambiguous information. Several studies have found that people have a natural tendency to see patterns that really are random events, such as presumed winning streaks among sports stars or in gambling.[12]

The process of "making sense" of the world around us also involves interpreting incoming information. This happens as quickly as selecting and organizing because the previously mentioned emotional markers are tagged to incoming stimuli, which are essentially quick judgments about whether that information is good or bad for us. To give you an idea of how quickly and systematically this nonconscious perceptual interpretation process occurs, consider the following study:[13] After viewing video clips of university instructors teaching an undergraduate class, eight observers rated the instructors on several personal characteristics (optimistic, likable, anxious, active, and so on). The observers assigned similar ratings to each instructor, even though the observers did not communicate with each other and had never seen the instructors before. Equally important, these ratings were very similar to the ratings completed by students who attended the actual class.

These results may be interesting, but they become extraordinary when you realize that the observers formed their perceptions from as little as *six seconds* of video—three segments of two seconds each selected randomly from the one-hour class! Furthermore, the video had no sound. In other words, people form similar perceptions and judgments based on very thin slices of information. How often have you heard it said that "you never have a second chance to make a first impression?" Other studies have reported similar findings for observations of high school teachers, courtroom judges, and physicians.

Collectively, these "thin slice" or first impression studies reveal that selective attention, as well as perceptual organization and interpretation, operates very quickly and to a large extent without our awareness.

Mental Models

To achieve our goals with some degree of predictability and sanity, we need road maps of the environments in which we live. These road maps, called **mental models**, are internal representations of the external world.[14] They consist of visual or relational images in our minds, such as what the classroom looks like or, conceptually, what happens when we submit an assignment late. We rely on mental models to make sense of our environment through perceptual grouping; the models fill in the missing pieces, including the causal connections among events. For example, you have a mental model about attending a class lecture or seminar, including assumptions or expectations about where the instructor and students arrange themselves in the room, how they ask and answer questions, and so forth. We can create a mental image of a class in progress.

Mental models play an important role in sense making, yet they also make it difficult to see the world in different ways. For

> " We need mental models— road maps of the environments in which we live—to achieve our goals with some degree of predictability and sanity. "

categorical thinking
Organizing people and objects into preconceived categories that are stored in our long-term memory.

mental models
Visuals or relational images in our mind representing the external world.

SOCIAL IDENTITY AND STEREOTYPING

The previous chapter explained that social identity is an important component of a person's self-concept. We define ourselves to a large extent by the groups to which we belong or have an emotional attachment. Along with shaping our self-concept, social identity theory explains the dynamics of *social perception*—how we perceive others.[15] Social perception is influenced by three activities in the process of forming and maintaining our social identity: categorization, homogenization, and differentiation.

- *Categorization:* Social identity is a comparative process, and the comparison begins by categorizing people into distinct

example, accounting professionals tend to see corporate problems from an accounting perspective, whereas marketing professionals see the same problems from a marketing perspective. Mental models also block our recognition of new opportunities. How do we change mental models? That's a tough challenge. After all, we developed models from several years of experience and reinforcement. The most important way to minimize the perceptual problems with mental models is to constantly question them. We need to ask ourselves about the assumptions we make. Working with people from diverse backgrounds is another way to break out of existing mental models. Colleagues from different cultures and areas of expertise tend to have different mental models, so working with them makes our own assumptions more obvious.

groups. By viewing someone (including yourself) as a Texan, for example, you remove that person's individuality and, instead, see him or her as a prototypical representative of the group "Texans." This categorization then allows you to distinguish Texans from people who live in, say, California or New Hampshire.

- *Homogenization:* To simplify the comparison process, we tend to think that people within each group are similar to each other. For instance, we think Texans collectively have similar attitudes and characteristics, whereas Californians collectively have their own set of characteristics. Of course every individual is unique, but we tend to lose sight of this fact when thinking about our social identity and how we compare to people in other social groups.

- *Differentiation:* Social identity fulfills our inherent need to have a distinct and positive self-concept. To achieve this, we do more than categorize and homogenize people; we also differentiate groups by assigning more favorable characteristics to people in our groups than to people in other groups. This differentiation is often subtle, but it can escalate into a "good guy–bad guy" contrast when groups are in conflict with each other.[16]

Stereotyping in Organizations

Stereotyping is an extension of social identity theory and a product of our natural process of organizing information through categorical thinking.[17] Stereotyping has three elements. First, we develop categories of identifiable groups (age, race, gender, occupation, nationality, and the like) and assign traits to those groups. Some assigned traits are observable, but most are nonobservable characteristics such as intelligence, personality, and values. For instance, students might form the stereotype that professors are both intelligent and absentminded. These clusters of traits (stereotypes) are formed from personal experience to some extent, but they are provided to us mainly through media images (such as movie characters) and other cultural prototypes. Second, we assign people to one or more social categories based on easily observable information about them, such as their gender, appearance, or physical location. Third, people who seem to belong to the stereotyped group are assigned nonobservable traits associated with the group. For example, if we learn that someone is a professor, we implicitly tend to assume the person is also intelligent and absentminded.

One reason why people engage in stereotyping is that, as a form of categorical thinking, it is a natural and mostly nonconscious "energy-saving" process that simplifies our understanding of the world. It is easier to remember features of a stereotype than the constellation of characteristics unique to everyone we meet.[18] A second

reason is that we have an innate need to understand and anticipate how others will behave. We don't have much information when first meeting someone, so we rely heavily on stereotypes to fill in the missing pieces. People with a strong need for cognitive closure have a higher tendency to rely on stereotypes. A third reason is that stereotyping enhances our self-concept. As mentioned earlier, the social identity process includes differentiation—we have more favorable views of members of our own groups than we do of people in other groups. When out-group members threaten our self-concept, we are particularly motivated (often without our awareness) to assign negative stereotypes to them.[19]

Problems with Stereotyping

Stereotypes are not completely fictional, but neither do they accurately describe every person in a social category. For instance, the widespread "bean counter" stereotype of accountants

stereotyping
The process of assigning traits to people based on their membership in a social category.

FACT. **Emergence of a More Favorable Accountant Stereotype?[20]**

Everyone seems to have a stereotype of accountants, but what does that stereotype look like? Several studies over the past three decades have identified consistent traits (mostly negative) of accountant characters in literature, film, advertising, and other cultural sources. The most common traits identified are boring, monotonous, cautious, unromantic, obtuse, antisocial, shy, dysfunctional, devious, calculating, and malicious. There may be good news for accounting stereotypes, however. One recent study reported that fewer than one-third of the 168 accountant characters in feature films represented negative traits, particularly when professional accountants were distinguished from bookkeepers. Most characters portraying professional accountants were "more sympathetic stereotypes," including everyday heroes (an ordinary person who rises to the challenge). Another recent study similarly reported both positive and negative characteristics of accountants portrayed in 73 German advertisements. The positive traits were conscientious, exacting, and high identification with (loyalty to) the company. The negative traits of accountants depicted in the German ads were unimaginative, passive, and inflexible.

Same Qualifications, Different Names, Different Success[23]

In France researchers submitted two nearly identical job applications to 2,323 help wanted ads. The main difference between the applications was that the candidate in one application had a French-sounding name whereas the individual in the other application had a North African or sub-Saharan African name. Almost 80 percent of employers preferred the applicant with the French-sounding name. Furthermore, when applicants personally visited human resource staff, those who had foreign names seldom received job interviews; instead they were often told that the job had been filled or that the company would not be hiring after all. The report concluded that "almost 90 percent of overall discrimination occurred before the employer had even bothered to interview both test candidates."

views people in this profession as "single-mindedly preoccupied with precision and form, methodical and conservative, and a boring joyless character."[21] Although this may be true of some accountants, it is certainly not characteristic of all—or even most—people in this profession. Even so, once we categorize someone as an accountant, the features of accountants in general rather than the features of the specific person get recalled, even when the person does not possess many of the stereotypical traits.

Another problem with stereotyping is that it lays the foundation for discriminatory attitudes and behavior. Most of this perceptual bias occurs as *unintentional (systemic) discrimination,* whereby decision makers rely on stereotypes to establish notions of the "ideal" person in specific roles. A person who doesn't fit the ideal tends to receive a less favorable evaluation. This subtle discrimination often shows up in age discrimination claims, such as the case in which Ryanair's recruitment advertising said it was looking for "young dynamic" employees. Recruiters at the Irish discount airline probably didn't intentionally discriminate against older people, but the tribunal concluded that systemic discrimination did occur because none of the job applicants were over 40 years old.[22]

The more serious form of stereotype bias is *intentional discrimination* or *prejudice,* in which people hold unfounded negative attitudes toward people belonging to a particular stereotyped group.[24] Is overt prejudice less common today? Perhaps, but there is still evidence that it exists. More than one-quarter of Americans say they have overheard racial slurs in the workplace.[25] In one recent case, three female advisers in California successfully sued their employer, Smith Barney, on the grounds that their male coworkers were deliberately assigned more lucrative clients (and therefore received higher pay) and more administrative support. These complaints were raised less than a decade after Smith Barney was ordered to correct discriminatory practices in its New York offices, where female employees complained of sexist and discriminatory behavior. A tribunal in Quebec, Canada, was shocked to discover in 2005 that one of Canada's largest vegetable farms required black employees to eat in a "blacks only" eating area that lacked heat, running water, proper toilets, and refrigeration.[26]

If stereotyping is such a problem, shouldn't we try to avoid this process altogether? Unfortunately, it's not that simple. Most experts agree that categorical thinking (including stereotyping) is an automatic and nonconscious process. Intensive training can minimize stereotype activation to some extent, but for the most part the process is hardwired in our brain cells.[28] Also remember that stereotyping helps us in several valuable (although fallible) ways described earlier: minimizing mental effort, filling in missing information, and supporting our social identity. The good news is that while it is difficult to prevent the *activation* of stereotypes, we can minimize the *application* of stereotypical information. Later in this chapter we identify ways to minimize stereotyping and other perceptual biases.

ATTRIBUTION THEORY

The **attribution process** involves deciding whether an observed behavior or event is caused mainly by the person (internal factors) or by the environment (external factors).[29] Internal factors include the person's ability or motivation, whereas external factors include lack of resources, other people, or just luck. If a coworker doesn't show up for an

Employment Discrimination Charge Filings with the U.S. Equal Employment Opportunity Commission[27]

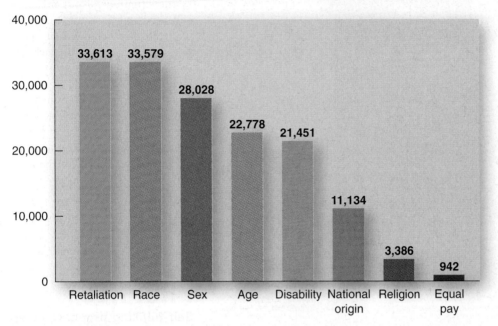

Number of individual charge filings with the U.S. Equal Employment Opportunity Commission in 2009. Category numbers add up to more than the total number of charges filed (93,266) because some charges claimed two or more types of discrimination. Retaliation refers to charges where the individual believes he or she was retaliated against for filing charges of discrimination.

important meeting, for instance, we infer either internal attributions (the coworker is forgetful or lacks motivation) or external attributions (traffic, a family emergency, or other circumstances prevented the coworker from attending).

People rely on the three attribution rules shown in Exhibit 3.2 to determine whether someone's behavior has mainly an internal or external attribution. Internal attributions are made when the observed individual behaved this way in the past (high consistency), he or she behaves like this toward other people or in different situations (low distinctiveness), and other people do not behave this way in similar situations (low consensus). On the other hand, an external attribution is made when there are low consistency, high distinctiveness, and high consensus.

To illustrate how these three attribution rules operate, suppose an employee is making poor-quality products one day on a particular machine. We would probably conclude that there is something wrong with the machine (an external attribution) if the employee has made good-quality products on this machine in the past (low consistency), the employee makes good-quality products on other machines (high distinctiveness), and other employees have recently had quality problems on this machine (high consensus). We would make an internal attribution, on the other hand, if the employee usually makes poor-quality products on this machine (high consistency), other employees produce good-quality products on this machine (low consensus), and the employee also makes poor-quality products on other machines (low distinctiveness).[30]

Attribution is a necessary process; we need to form cause–effect relationships to interact effectively with our environment. How we react to a coworker's poor performance depends on our internal or external attribution of that performance. Students who make internal attributions about their poor performance are more likely to drop out of their programs, for

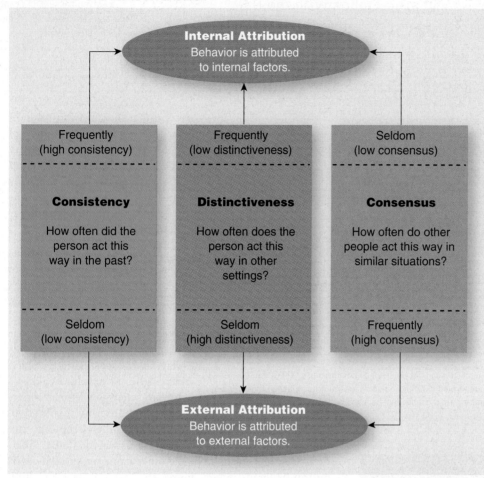

Internal Attribution
Behavior is attributed to internal factors.

Frequently (high consistency)	Frequently (low distinctiveness)	Seldom (low consensus)
Consistency	**Distinctiveness**	**Consensus**
How often did the person act this way in the past?	How often does the person act this way in other settings?	How often do other people act this way in similar situations?
Seldom (low consistency)	Seldom (high distinctiveness)	Frequently (high consensus)

External Attribution
Behavior is attributed to external factors.

instance.[31] However, as we see next, people are subject to various attribution errors.

Attribution Errors

Researchers have identified a variety of attribution errors. One common bias, called **fundamental attribution error**, refers to our tendency to see the person rather than the situation as the main cause of that person's behavior.[32] If an employee is late for work, observers are more likely to conclude that the person is lazy than to realize that external factors may have caused this behavior. Fundamental attribution error occurs because observers can't easily see the external factors that constrain the person's behavior. We didn't see the traffic jam that caused the person to be late, for instance. Research suggests that fundamental attribution error is more common in Western countries than in Asian cultures, where people are taught from an early age to pay attention to the context in interpersonal relations and to see everything as being connected in a holistic way.[33]

Another attribution error, known as **self-serving bias**, is the tendency to attribute our favorable outcomes to internal factors and our failures to external factors. Simply put, we take credit for our successes and blame others or the situation for our mistakes. Self-serving bias is one of several related biases that maintain a positive self-concept, particularly engaging in self-enhancement to maintain a positive self-evaluation. In annual reports, for example, executives mainly refer to their personal qualities as reasons for the company's successes and to external factors as reasons for the company's failures.[34]

SELF-FULFILLING PROPHECY

Self-fulfilling prophecy occurs when our expectations about another person cause that person to act in a way that is consistent with those expectations. In other words, our perceptions can influence reality. Exhibit 3.3 illustrates the four steps in the self-fulfilling-prophecy process using the example of a supervisor and a subordinate.[35] The process begins when the supervisor forms expectations about the employee's future behavior and performance. These expectations are sometimes inaccurate because first impressions are usually formed from limited information. The supervisor's expectations influence his or her treatment of employees. Specifically, high-expectancy employees (those expected to do well) receive more emotional support through nonverbal cues (such as more smiling and eye contact), more frequent and valuable feedback and reinforcement, more challenging goals, better training, and more opportunities to demonstrate good performance.

The third step in self-fulfilling prophecy includes two effects of the supervisor's behavior on the employee. First, through better training and more practice opportunities, a high-expectancy employee learns more skills and knowledge than a low-expectancy employee. Second, the employee becomes more self-confident, which results in higher motivation and willingness to set more challenging goals.[36] In the final step, high-expectancy employees have higher motivation and better skills, resulting in better performance, while the opposite is true of low-expectancy employees.

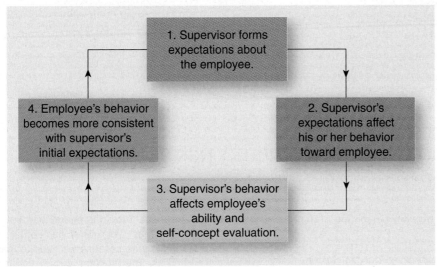

▼ **EXHIBIT 3.3** The Self-Fulfilling-Prophecy Cycle

1. Supervisor forms expectations about the employee.

2. Supervisor's expectations affect his or her behavior toward employee.

3. Supervisor's behavior affects employee's ability and self-concept evaluation.

4. Employee's behavior becomes more consistent with supervisor's initial expectations.

There are many examples of self-fulfilling prophecies in work and school settings.[37] Research has found that women perform less well on math tests after being informed that men tend to perform better on them. Women perform better on these tests when they are not exposed to this negative self-fulfilling prophecy. Similarly, people over 65 years of age receive lower results on memory tests after hearing that mental ability declines with age. Another study reported that the performance of Israeli Defense Force trainees was influenced by their instructor's expectations regarding the trainee's potential in the program. Self-fulfilling prophecy was at work here because the instructor's expectations were based on a list provided by researchers showing which recruits had high and low potential, even though the researchers had actually listed these trainees randomly.

Contingencies of Self-Fulfilling Prophecy

Self-fulfilling prophecies are more powerful under some conditions than others. The self-fulfilling-prophecy effect is stronger at the beginning of a relationship, such as when employees are first hired. It is also stronger when several people (rather than just one person) hold the same expectations of the individual. In other words, we might be able to ignore one person's doubts about our potential but not the collective doubts of several people. The self-fulfilling-prophecy effect is also stronger among people with a history of low achievement. High achievers can draw on their past successes to offset low expectations, whereas low achievers do not have past successes to support their self-confidence. Fortunately, the opposite is also true: Low achievers respond more favorably than high achievers to positive self-fulfilling prophecy.

> " The self-fulfilling-prophecy effect is stronger when employees are first hired, when several people hold the same expectations of the employee, and when the employee is a low achiever. "

Low achievers don't often receive this positive encouragement, so it probably has a stronger effect on their motivation to excel.[38]

The main lesson from the self-fulfilling-prophecy literature is that leaders need to develop and maintain a positive, yet realistic, expectation toward all employees. This recommendation is consistent with the emerging philosophy of **positive organizational behavior**, which suggests that focusing on the positive rather than negative aspects of life will improve organizational success and individual well-being. Communicating hope and optimism is so important that it is identified as one of the critical success factors for physicians and surgeons. Training programs that make leaders aware of the power of positive expectations seem to have minimal effect, however. Instead, generating positive expectations and hope depends on a corporate culture of support and learning. Hiring supervisors who are inherently optimistic toward their staff is another way of increasing the incidence of positive self-fulfilling prophecies.

OTHER PERCEPTUAL ERRORS

Self-fulfilling prophecy, attribution, and stereotyping are among the most common perceptual processes and biases in organizational settings, but there are many others. Four others are briefly

fundamental attribution error The tendency to see the person rather than the situation as the main cause of that person's behavior.

self-serving bias The tendency to attribute our favorable outcomes to internal factors and our failures to external factors.

self-fulfilling prophecy Occurs when our expectations about another person cause that person to act in a way that is consistent with those expectations.

positive organizational behavior A perspective of organizational behavior that focuses on building positive qualities and traits within individuals or institutions as opposed to focusing on what is wrong with them.

halo effect A perceptual error whereby our general impression of a person, usually based on one prominent characteristic, colors our perception of other characteristics of that person.

primacy effect A perceptual error in which we quickly form an opinion of people based on the first information we receive about them.

recency effect A perceptual error in which the most recent information dominates our perception of others.

false consensus effect A perceptual error in which we overestimate the extent to which others have beliefs and characteristics similar to our own.

[Awareness of perceptual biases can reduce these biases to some extent by making people more mindful of their thoughts and actions.]

described here because they can also bias our perception of the world around us:

- *Halo effect:* The **halo effect** occurs when our general impression of a person, usually based on one prominent characteristic, distorts our perception of other characteristics of that person.[39] If a supervisor who values punctuality notices that an employee is sometimes late for work, the supervisor might form a negative image of the employee and evaluate that person's other traits unfavorably as well. The halo effect is most likely to occur when concrete information about the perceived target is missing or we are not sufficiently motivated to search for it. Instead we use our general impression of the person to fill in the missing information.

- *Primacy effect:* The **primacy effect** is our tendency to quickly form an opinion of people on the basis of the first information

we receive about them.[40] It is the notion that first impressions are lasting impressions. This rapid perceptual organization and interpretation occurs because we need to make sense of the world around us. The problem is that first impressions—particularly negative first impressions—are difficult to change. After categorizing someone, we tend to select subsequent information that supports our first impression and screen out information that opposes that impression.

- *Recency effect:* The **recency effect** occurs when the most recent information dominates our perceptions.[42] This perceptual bias is most common when people (especially those with limited experience) are making an evaluation involving complex information. For instance, auditors must digest large volumes of information in their judgments about financial documents, and the most recent information received prior to the decision tends to get weighted more heavily than information received at the beginning of the audit. Similarly, when supervisors evaluate the performance of employees over the previous year, the most recent performance information dominates the evaluation because it is the most easily recalled.

- *False consensus effect:* Sometimes called the *similar-to-me effect,* the **false consensus effect** is a widely observed bias in which we overestimate the extent to which others have beliefs and characteristics similar to our own.[43] Employees who are thinking of quitting their jobs believe that a large percentage of their coworkers are also thinking about quitting. This bias occurs to some extent because we associate with others who are similar to us, and we selectively remember information that is consistent with our own views. We also believe "everyone does it" to reinforce our self-concept regarding behaviors that do not have a positive image (quitting, parking illegally, or the like).

First Impressions
Count in Job Applications[41]

72%

of executives who say it is somewhat or very common for applicants with promising résumés not to live up to expectations during the interview.

Résumé Bloopers
"Hope to hear from you, **shorty**"
"Have a keen eye for **derail**"
"I'm **attacking** my resume for you to review"
"INTERESTS: **Exorcising** my sense of humor every day."
"Fluent in both English and **Spinach**."
"Dear Sir or **Madman**."

40%

of executives who say that applicants with just one typo in their résumé are removed from further consideration.

76%

of executives who say that applicants with just one or two typos in their résumé are removed from further consideration.

Survey consisted of telephone interviews with 150 senior executives at America's top 1,000 companies. Résumé gaffs were identified in documents received by Accountemps or parent company Robert Half.

Learning Objectives

After reading this section, you should be able to

LO3 Discuss three ways to improve social perception, with specific application to organizational situations.

IMPROVING PERCEPTIONS

We can't bypass the perceptual process, but we should try to minimize perceptual biases and distortions. Three potentially effective ways to improve perceptions include awareness of perceptual biases, self-awareness, and meaningful interaction.

Awareness of Perceptual Biases

One of the most obvious and widely practiced ways to reduce perceptual biases is knowing that they exist. For example, diversity awareness training tries to minimize discrimination by making people aware of systemic discrimination as well as prejudices that occur through stereotyping. This training also attempts to dispel myths about people from various cultural and demographic groups. Awareness of perceptual biases can reduce these biases to some extent by making people more mindful of their thoughts and actions. However, awareness has only a limited effect.[44] For example, trying to correct misinformation about demographic groups has limited effect on people with deeply held prejudices against those groups. Also, self-fulfilling-prophecy training informs managers about this perceptual bias and encourages them to engage in more positive rather than negative self-fulfilling prophecies, yet research has found that managers continue to

> Self-awareness is an essential prerequisite to becoming more openminded and nonjudgmental toward others.

engage in negative self-fulfilling prophecies after they complete the training program.

Improving Self-Awareness

A more powerful way to minimize perceptual biases is to help people become more aware of biases in their own decisions and behavior.[45] In fact, self-awareness of one's beliefs, values, and attitudes is an essential prerequisite to becoming more openminded and nonjudgmental toward others. Self-awareness is equally important in other ways. For instance, the emerging concept of authentic leadership emphasizes self-awareness as the first step in a person's ability to effectively lead others (see Chapter 11).[46]

But how do we become more self-aware? One approach is to complete formal tests that indicate any implicit biases we might have toward others. One such test (the accuracy of which is hotly debated by scholars) is the Implicit Association Test (IAT). The IAT attempts to detect subtle race, age, and gender bias by associating positive and negative words with specific demographic groups.[47] Many people are much more cautious about their stereotypes and prejudices after discovering that their test results show a personal bias against older people or individuals from different ethnic backgrounds.[48]

Johari Window
A model of mutual understanding that encourages disclosure and feedback to increase our own open area and reduce the blind, hidden, and unknown areas.

contact hypothesis
A theory stating that the more we interact with someone, the less prejudiced or perceptually biased we will be against that person.

empathy
A person's understanding of and sensitivity to the feelings, thoughts, and situations of others.

learning
A relatively permanent change in behavior (behavior tendency) that occurs as a result of a person's interaction with the environment.

tacit knowledge
Knowledge embedded in our actions and ways of thinking, and transmitted only through observation and experience.

Another way to increase self-awareness (and thereby reduce perceptual biases) is by applying the **Johari Window**.[49] Developed by Joseph Luft and Harry Ingram (hence the name "Johari"), this model of self-awareness and mutual understanding divides information about you into four "windows"—open, blind, hidden, and unknown—based on whether your own values, beliefs, and experiences are known to you and to others (see Exhibit 3.4). The *open area* includes information about you that is known both to you and to others. The *blind area* refers to information that is known to others but not to you. For example, your colleagues might notice that you are self-conscious and awkward when meeting the company chief executive, but you are unaware of this fact. Information known to you but unknown to others is found in the *hidden area*. Finally, the *unknown area* includes your values, beliefs, and experiences that aren't known to you or others.

> The main objective of the Johari Window is to increase the size of the open area so both you and colleagues are aware of your perceptual limitations.

The main objective of the Johari Window is to increase the size of the open area so both you and colleagues are aware of your perceptual limitations. This is partly accomplished by reducing the hidden area through *disclosure*—informing others of your beliefs, feelings, and experiences that may influence the work relationship.[50] The open area also increases through *feedback* from others about your behavior. This information helps you to reduce your blind area because coworkers often see things in you that you do not see. Finally, the combination of disclosure and feedback occasionally produces revelations about information in the unknown area.

Meaningful Interaction

While the Johari Window relies on dialogue, self-awareness and mutual understanding can also improve through *meaningful interaction*.[51] This statement is based on the **contact hypothesis**, which states that, under certain conditions, people who interact with each other will be less prejudiced or perceptually biased against each other. Consider IBM's practice of sending employees from diverse parts of the company to developing countries for a month, where they work together with local citizens on

▼ **EXHIBIT 3.4** Johari Window Model of Self-Awareness and Mutual Understanding

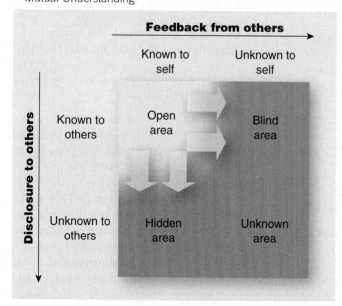

Source: Based on J. Luft, *Group Processes* (Palo Alto, CA: Mayfield, 1984).

> ## THE ILLITERATE OF THE 21ST CENTURY WILL NOT BE THOSE WHO CANNOT READ AND WRITE, BUT THOSE WHO CANNOT LEARN, UNLEARN, AND RELEARN.
>
> —ALVIN TOFFLER

community development projects. Jennifer Vickery, an IBM employee who completed a month of community work in Romania, explains how the project enabled her to develop more accurate perceptions and understanding with coworkers and local people: "I've learned that the more you get to know someone on a personal level, the easier it is to overcome time zones and differences—and work together," says Vickery.[52]

Meaningful interaction typically involves more than close and frequent interaction. It also includes working toward a shared goal on a meaningful task in which you and the other people need to rely on each other (that is, you must cooperate rather than compete with each other). It also includes the condition that you and the others have equal status in that context. IBM's month-long community project work is an ideal example of these conditions. In these programs, professionals from developed countries work alongside people from developing countries. Although the volunteers have expertise (and therefore status), they often perform work outside that expertise and in unfamiliar environments requiring the expertise of people in the local community. The projects are also meaningful with specific goals.

Another potential application of the contact hypothesis occurs when senior executives and other staff from headquarters work in frontline jobs frequently or for an extended time. Everyone at Domino's head office in Ann Arbor, Michigan, attends Pizza Prep School, where they learn how to make pizzas and run a pizza store. Every month, Air New Zealand executives serve as flight attendants, check-in counter staff, or baggage handlers to give them a reality check while working alongside employees. Every new hire at 1-800-GOT-JUNK? (North America's largest rubbish removal company) spends an entire week on a junk removal truck to better understand how the business works. "How can you possibly empathize with someone out in the field unless you've been on the truck yourself?" asks CEO and founder Brian Scudamore.[53]

Meaningful interaction does more than reduce our reliance on stereotypes. It also potentially improves **empathy** toward others—that is, the extent to which we understand and are sensitive to the feelings, thoughts, and situations of others.[54] You have empathy when actively visualizing the other person's situation and feeling that person's emotions in that situation. Empathizing with others improves our sensitivity to the external causes of another person's performance and behavior, thereby reducing

fundamental attribution error. A supervisor who imagines what it's like to be a single mother, for example, would become more sensitive to the external causes of lateness and other events among such employees.

The perceptual process represents the filter through which information passes from the external environment to our memory. As such, it is really the beginning of the learning process, which we discuss next.

Learning Objectives

After reading the next two sections, you should be able to

LO4 Describe and compare three perspectives of learning in organizations.

LEARNING IN ORGANIZATIONS

Learning is a relatively permanent change in behavior (or behavioral tendency) that occurs as a result of a person's interaction with the environment. Learning occurs when the learner behaves differently. For example, you have "learned" computer skills when you operate the keyboard and software more quickly than before. Learning occurs when interaction with the environment leads to behavior change. This means that we learn through our senses, such as through study, observation, and experience.

Some of what we learn is *explicit knowledge*, such as reading the information in this book. However, explicit knowledge is only the tip of the knowledge iceberg. Most of what we know is **tacit knowledge**.[55] Tacit knowledge is not documented; rather, it is acquired through observation and direct experience. For example, airline pilots learn to operate commercial jets more by watching experts and practicing on flight simulators than by attending lectures. They acquire tacit knowledge by directly experiencing the complex interaction of behavior with the machine's response.

Three perspectives of learning tacit and explicit knowledge are reinforcement, social learning, and direct experience. Each perspective offers a different angle for understanding the dynamics of learning.

behavior modification
A theory that explains learning in terms of the antecedents and consequences of behavior.

Behavior Modification: Learning through Reinforcement

One of the oldest perspectives on learning, called **behavior modification** (also known as *operant conditioning* and *reinforcement theory*), takes the rather extreme view that learning is completely dependent on the environment. Behavior modification does not question the notion that thinking is part of the learning process, but it views human thoughts as unimportant intermediate stages between behavior and the environment. The environment teaches us to alter our behaviors so that we maximize positive consequences and minimize adverse consequences.[56]

A–B–C's of Behavior Modification The central objective of behavior modification is to change behavior (B) by managing its antecedents (A) and consequences (C). This process is nicely illustrated in the A–B–C model of behavior modification, shown in Exhibit 3.5.[57]

Antecedents are events preceding the behavior, informing employees that certain behaviors will have particular consequences. An antecedent may be a sound from your computer signaling that an e-mail message has arrived or a request from your supervisor asking you to complete a specific task by tomorrow. Such antecedents let employees know that a particular action will produce specific consequences. Notice that antecedents do not cause behaviors. The computer sound doesn't cause us to open our e-mail. Rather, the sound is a cue telling us that certain consequences are likely to occur if we engage in certain behaviors. In behavior modification, *consequences* are events following a particular behavior that influence its future occurrence. Generally speaking, people tend to repeat behaviors that are followed by pleasant consequences and are less likely to repeat behaviors that are followed by unpleasant consequences or no consequences at all.

Contingencies of Reinforcement Behavior modification identifies four types of consequences, called the *contingencies of reinforcement*, that increase, maintain, or reduce the probability that behavior will be repeated (see Exhibit 3.6):[58]

- *Positive reinforcement* occurs when the *introduction* of a consequence *increases or maintains* the frequency or future probability of a specific behavior. Receiving a bonus after successfully completing an important project is considered positive reinforcement because it typically increases the probability that you will use that behavior in the future.

- *Punishment* occurs when a consequence decreases the frequency or future probability of a behavior. This consequence typically involves introducing something that employees try to avoid. For instance, most of us would consider being demoted or being ostracized by our coworkers as forms of punishment.[59]

- *Negative reinforcement* occurs when the removal or avoidance of a consequence increases or maintains the frequency or future probability of a specific behavior. Supervisors apply negative reinforcement when they stop criticizing employees whose substandard performance has improved. When the

▼ **EXHIBIT 3.5** A–B–Cs of Behavior Modification

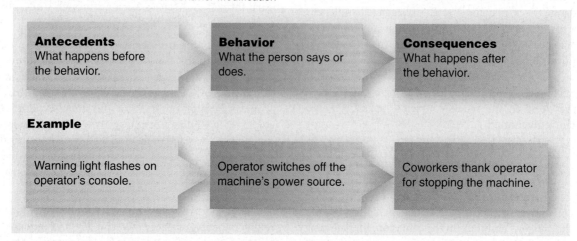

Antecedents	Behavior	Consequences
What happens before the behavior.	What the person says or does.	What happens after the behavior.

Example

Warning light flashes on operator's console.	Operator switches off the machine's power source.	Coworkers thank operator for stopping the machine.

Sources: Adapted from T. K. Connellan, *How to Improve Human Performance* (New York: Harper & Row, 1978), p. 50; and F. Luthans and R. Kreitner, *Organizational Behavior Modification and Beyond* (Glenview, IL: Scott Foresman, 1985), pp. 85–88.

	Positive Consequence	No Consequence	Negative Consequence
Behavior Increases or Is Maintained	Positive reinforcement Example: Coworkers praise you for helping complete a project on time.		Negative reinforcement Example: Boss stops criticizing the quality of your work.
Behavior Decreases		Extinction Example: You no longer receive praise for work well done.	Punishment Example: Boss warns you to speed up production or face dismissal.

criticism is withheld, employees are more likely to repeat behaviors that improved their performance. Notice that negative reinforcement is not punishment. Whereas punishment extinguishes behavior by introducing a negative consequence, negative reinforcement actually reinforces behavior by removing the negative consequence.

- *Extinction* occurs when the target behavior decreases because no consequence follows it. In this respect, extinction is a do-nothing strategy. Generally, behavior that is no longer reinforced tends to disappear; it becomes extinct. For instance, research suggests that performance tends to decline when managers stop congratulating employees for their good work.[60]

Which contingency of reinforcement should be used in the learning process? In most situations, positive reinforcement should follow desired behaviors and extinction (do nothing) should follow undesirable behaviors. This approach is preferred because punishment and negative reinforcement generate negative emotions and attitudes toward the punisher (such as the supervisor) and organization. However, some form of punishment (dismissal, suspension, demotion, and the like) may be necessary for extreme behaviors, such as deliberately hurting a coworker or stealing inventory. Indeed, research suggests that under certain conditions, punishment maintains a sense of fairness.[61]

Schedules of Reinforcement
Along with the types of reinforcement, the frequency and timing of the reinforcers also influence employee behaviors.[62] These reinforcement schedules can be continuous or intermittent. The most effective reinforcement schedule for learning new tasks is *continuous reinforcement*—providing positive reinforcement after every occurrence of the desired behavior. Employees learn desired behaviors quickly, and when the reinforcer is removed, extinction also occurs quickly.

The best schedule for reinforcing learned behavior is a *variable ratio schedule* in which employee behavior is reinforced after a variable number of times. Salespeople experience

> "The best schedule for reinforcing learned behavior is a variable ratio schedule in which employee behavior is reinforced after a variable number of times."

variable ratio reinforcement because they make a successful sale (the reinforcer) after a varying number of client calls. They might make four unsuccessful calls before receiving an order on the fifth one, then make 10 more calls before receiving the next order, and so on. The variable ratio schedule makes behavior highly resistant to extinction because the reinforcer is never expected at a particular time or after a fixed number of accomplishments.

Behavior Modification in Practice Everyone practices behavior modification in one form or another. We thank people for a job well done, are silent when displeased, and sometimes try to punish those who go against our wishes. Behavior modification also occurs in various formal programs to reduce absenteeism, improve task performance, encourage safe work behaviors, and have a more healthful lifestyle. In Arkansas, for example, the North Little Rock School Board introduced an absenteeism reduction plan in which teachers can earn $300 after every six months with perfect attendance. Those with no more than one day of absence receive $100. ExxonMobil's Fawley refinery in the United Kingdom introduced a "Behave Safely Challenge" program in which supervisors rewarded employees and contractors on the spot when they exhibited good safety behavior or intervened to improve the safe behavior of coworkers. These rewards were a form of

FACT.

Humana Inc. reinforces long and healthful walks by encouraging its employees to monitor and record the number of steps they take each day (using a pedometer). The more steps employees take, the higher the rewards they can receive as cash cards that can be used at popular retail stores.[64]

social learning theory

A theory stating that much learning occurs by observing others and then modeling the behaviors that lead to favorable outcomes and avoiding behaviors that lead to punishing consequences.

self-reinforcement

Occurs whenever an employee has control over a reinforcer but doesn't "take" it until completing a self-set goal.

learning orientation

An individual attitude and organizational culture in which people welcome new learning opportunities, actively experiment with new ideas and practices, view reasonable mistakes as a natural part of the learning process, and continuously question past practices.

positive reinforcement using a variable ratio schedule (safe work behaviors were reinforced after a variable number of times that they occurred).[63]

Although a natural part of human interaction, behavior modification has a number of limitations when applied strategically in organizational settings. One limitation is "reward inflation," in which the reinforcer is eventually considered an entitlement. For this reason, most behavior modification programs must run infrequently and for a short duration. Another concern is that the variable ratio schedule of reinforcement tends to create a lottery-style reward system, which is unpopular to people who dislike gambling. Probably the most significant problem is behavior modification's radical view that behavior is learned only through personal interaction with the environment.[65] This view is no longer accepted; instead learning experts recognize that people also learn by observing others and thinking logically about possible consequences. This learning-through-observation process is explained by social learning theory.

Creating Jobs with High Learning Potential[71]

Not all jobs are the same when it comes to real-time learning. Some offer employees more opportunity to learn on the job. Here are action plans to help employees engage in more on-the-job learning:

1. Design jobs that have complex tasks with plenty of variety.
2. Ensure that jobs offer opportunities for feedback, evaluation, and reflection.
3. Give employees opportunities to participate in problem handling and developmental activities.
4. Give employees objective learning resources, such as time to reflect on what has been learned.

because tacit knowledge and skills are mainly acquired through observation and practice. As an example, it is difficult to document or explain in a conversation all the steps necessary to bake professional-quality bread. Student chefs also need to observe the master baker's subtle behaviors. Behavioral modeling also increases self-efficacy because people gain more self-confidence after seeing someone else perform the task. This is particularly true when observers identify with the model, such as someone who is similar in age, experience, gender, and related features.

- *Learning behavior consequences:* People learn the consequences of behavior through logic and observation, not just through direct experience. They logically anticipate consequences after completing a task well or poorly. They also learn behavioral consequences by observing the experiences

> " Organizations develop and maintain a learning orientation culture by supporting experimentation, acknowledging reasonable mistakes without penalty, and supporting the mindset that employees should engage in continuous learning. "

Social Learning Theory: Learning by Observing

Social learning theory states that much learning occurs when people observe others and then model the behaviors that lead to favorable outcomes and avoid behaviors that lead to punishing consequences.[66] This form of learning occurs in three ways: behavior modeling, learning behavior consequences, and self-reinforcement.

- *Behavior modeling:* People learn by observing the behaviors of a role model on a critical task, remembering the important elements of the observed behaviors, and then practicing those behaviors.[67] This is a valuable form of learning

of other people. Consider the employee who observes a coworker receiving a stern warning for working in an unsafe manner. This event would reduce the observer's likelihood of engaging in unsafe behaviors because he or she has learned to anticipate a similar reprimand following those behaviors.[68]

- *Self-reinforcement:* **Self-reinforcement** occurs whenever an employee has control over a reinforcer but doesn't "take" it until completing a self-set goal.[69] For example, you might be thinking about having a snack after you finish reading the rest of this chapter. Raiding the refrigerator is a form of self-induced positive reinforcement for completing this reading assignment. Self-reinforcement has many forms, such as taking a short walk, watching a movie, or simply congratulating yourself for completing a task.

> Making mistakes simply means you are learning faster.
>
> —Weston H. Agor[74]

Learning through Experience

Along with behavior modification and social learning, another way that employees learn is through direct experience. In fact, most tacit knowledge and skills are acquired through experience as well as observation. Generally, experiential learning begins when we engage with the environment; then we reflect on that experience and form theories about how the world around us works. This is followed by experimentation, in which we find out how well the newly formed theories work.[70] Experiential learning requires all these steps, although people tend to prefer one step more than the others.

One of the most important ingredients for learning through experience is that the organization and its employees should possess a strong **learning orientation**.[72] A strong learning orientation means employees welcome new learning opportunities, actively experiment with new ideas and practices, view reasonable mistakes as a natural part of the learning process, and continuously question past practices. This individual orientation becomes part of the organization's culture when it is held by many people throughout the organization.

Organizations develop and maintain a learning orientation culture by supporting experimentation, acknowledging reasonable mistakes without penalty, and supporting the mind-set that employees should engage in continuous learning. They encourage employees to question long-held assumptions or mental models and to actively "unlearn" practices that are no longer ideal. Without a learning orientation, mistakes are hidden and problems are more likely to escalate or reemerge later. It's not surprising, then, that one of the most frequently mentioned lessons from the best-performing manufacturers is to expect mistakes. "At CIMB we have learned to admit our mistakes openly," says Datuk Nazir Razak, chief executive of CIMB Group, Malaysia's second-largest financial services company. "Some of these mistakes cost us a lot of money," he adds, but "each mistake is a learning opportunity."[73]

This chapter has introduced two fundamental activities in human behavior in the workplace: perceptions and learning. These activities involve receiving information from the environment, organizing it, and acting on it as a learning process. Our knowledge about perceptions and learning in the workplace lays the foundation for the next chapter, which looks at workplace emotions and attitudes. ▪

CHECK IT OUT!

mhhe.com/McShaneM

for study materials

including quizzes

and Internet resources

workplace emotions, attitudes, and stress

chapter four

A few years ago, the contact (call) center of Clydesdale Bank, one of Scotland's largest banks, suffered from 10 percent absenteeism and 56 percent annual employee turnover. Customer service suffered, operating costs were well above the industry average, and employee productivity was below average. Kevin Page, then head of Clydesdale's contact center (now Clydesdale's operations director), believed that the best way to improve customer satisfaction and productivity would be to improve employees' satisfaction and pride in their work. Page and his management team listened to and acted on employee concerns, spruced up the work environment, introduced career development programs, provided better coaching, and gave staff more freedom to decide how to serve clients. Within two years, job satisfaction and customer satisfaction improved substantially; both absenteeism and turnover fell to half their previous levels. More recently, Clydesdale Bank's contact center was named the best large contact center in the world, beating 1,000 entrants across all industries.[1]

continued on p. 70

LEARNING OBJECTIVES

After reading this chapter, you should be able to

LO1 Explain how emotions and cognition (conscious reasoning) influence attitudes and behavior.

LO2 Discuss the dynamics of emotional labor and the role of emotional intelligence in the workplace.

LO3 Summarize the consequences of job dissatisfaction as well as strategies to increase organizational (affective) commitment.

LO4 Describe the stress experience and review three major stressors.

LO5 Identify five ways to manage workplace stress.

continued from p. 69

Clydesdale Bank's dramatic turnaround illustrates that emotions and attitudes make a difference in individual behavior and well-being, as well as in the organization's performance and customer service. Over the past decade, the field of organizational behavior has experienced a sea change in thinking about workplace emotions, so this chapter begins by introducing the concept and explaining why researchers are so eager to discover how emotions influence attitudes and behavior. Next we consider the dynamics of emotional labor, followed by the popular topic of emotional intelligence. The specific work attitudes of job satisfaction and organizational commitment are then discussed, including their association with various employee behaviors and work performance. The final section looks at work-related stress, including the stress experience, three prominent stressors, individual differences in stress, and ways to combat excessive stress. ■

Learning Objectives

After reading this section, you should be able to

LO1 Explain how emotions and cognition (conscious reasoning) influence attitudes and behavior.

EMOTIONS IN THE WORKPLACE

Emotions influence almost everything we do in the workplace. This is a strong statement, and one that you would rarely find a decade ago in organizational behavior research or textbooks. Until recently OB experts assumed that a person's thoughts and actions are governed primarily by conscious reasoning (called *cognition*). Yet groundbreaking neuroscience discoveries have revealed that our perceptions, attitudes, decisions, and behavior are influenced by both cognition and emotion.[2] In fact, emotions may have a greater influence because emotional processes often occur before cognitive processes and, consequently, influence the latter. By ignoring emotionality, many theories have overlooked a large piece of the puzzle about human behavior in the workplace.

Emotions are physiological, behavioral, and psychological episodes experienced toward an object, person, or event that create a state of readiness.[3] These "episodes" are very brief events that typically subside or occur in waves lasting from milliseconds to a few minutes. Emotions are directed toward someone or something. For example, we experience joy, fear, anger, and other emotional episodes toward tasks, customers, or a software program we are using. This differs from *moods,* which are less intense and longer-term emotional states that are not directed toward anything in particular.[4]

Emotions are experiences. They represent changes in our physiological state (such as blood pressure and heart rate), psychological state (including the ability to think clearly), and behavior (facial expressions, for example). Most of these emotional reactions are subtle and occur without our awareness.

This is a particularly important point because people often think about "getting emotional" when the subject of emotions is mentioned. In reality, you experience emotions every minute but aren't even aware of most of them. Finally, emotions put us in a state of readiness. When we get worried, for example, our heart rate and blood pressure increase to make our body better prepared to engage in fight or flight. Strong emotions also trigger our conscious awareness of a threat or opportunity in the external environment.[5]

People experience many emotions as well as various combinations of emotions, but all of them have two common features.

emotions
Physiological, behavioral, and psychological episdoes experienced toward an object, person, or event that create a state of readiness.

attitudes The cluster of beliefs, assessed feelings, and behavioral intentions toward a person, object, or event (called an *attitude object*).

[**Let's not forget that the little emotions are the great captains of our lives and we obey them without realizing it.**]
—Vincent Van Gogh

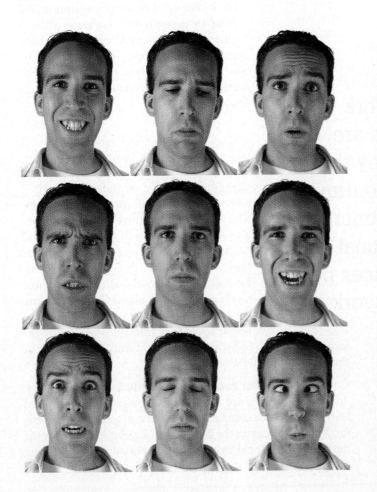

First, emotions generate a global evaluation (called *core affect*) that something is good or bad, helpful or harmful, to be approached or to be avoided. Second, all emotions produce some level of activation. However, they vary considerably in this activation—that is, in how much they demand our attention and motivate us to act.[6] Distressed is a negative emotion that generates a high level of activation, whereas relaxed is a pleasant emotion that has fairly low activation.

Emotions, Attitudes, and Behavior

To understand how emotions influence our thoughts and behavior in the workplace, we first need to know about attitudes. **Attitudes** represent the cluster of beliefs, assessed feelings, and behavioral intentions toward a person, object, or event (called an *attitude object*).[7] Attitudes are *judgments,* whereas emotions are *experiences.* In other words, attitudes involve conscious logical reasoning, whereas emotions operate as events, usually without our awareness. We also experience most emotions briefly, whereas our attitude toward someone or something is more stable over time.

Until recently, experts believed that attitudes could be understood just by the three cognitive components illustrated on the left side of Exhibit 4.1: beliefs, feelings, and behavioral intentions. Now evidence suggests that a parallel emotional process is also at work, shown on the right side of the exhibit.[8] Using

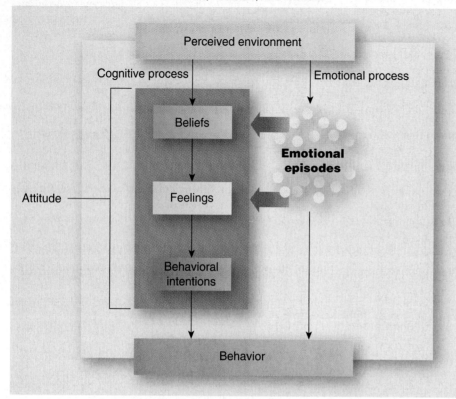

attitude toward mergers as an example, let's look more closely at this model, beginning with the traditional cognitive perspective of attitudes:

- *Beliefs:* These are your established perceptions about the attitude object—what you believe to be true. For example, you might believe that mergers reduce job security for employees in the merged firms, or you might believe that mergers increase the company's competitiveness in this era of globalization. These beliefs are perceived facts that you acquire from experience and other forms of learning.

- *Feelings:* Feelings represent your positive or negative evaluations of the attitude object. Some people think mergers are good; others think they are bad. Your like or dislike of mergers represents your assessed feelings. According to the traditional cognitive perspective of attitudes (left side of the model), feelings are calculated from your beliefs about mergers. If you believe that mergers typically have negative consequences such as layoffs and organizational politics, you will form negative feelings toward mergers in general or about a specific planned merger in your organization.

" Work attitudes are shaped by the almost continuous bombardment of emotional experiences people have at work. "

- *Behavioral intentions:* Intentions represent your motivation to engage in a particular behavior regarding the attitude object.[9] Upon hearing that the company will merge with another organization, you might become motivated to look for a job elsewhere or possibly to complain to management about the merger decision. Your feelings toward mergers motivate your behavioral intentions, and which actions you choose depends on your past experience, self-concept (values, personality), and social norms of appropriate behavior.

Exhibit 4.1 also illustrates that behavioral intentions directly predict behavior. You are more likely to quit your job (behavior) if you intend to do so (behavioral intention). However, whether your intentions translate into behavior depends on all four elements of the MARS model, such as opportunity and ability to act. Many people harbor intentions to quit their jobs, but many do not because of lack of alternative employment opportunities. Furthermore, the influence of behavioral intentions on behavior depends on the strength of those attitudes and associated emotions. Sudden negative events create strong emotions, which are more likely to trigger a person to act than if the negative emotions and feelings remain subtle.

How Emotions Influence Attitudes and Behavior As we mentioned, emotions play a central role in forming and changing employee attitudes.[10] The right side of Exhibit 4.1 illustrates this process, which (like the cognitive process) also begins with perceptions of the world around us. As soon as we receive sensory information, we nonconsciously tag some of that information with emotional markers. These markers are not calculated feelings; they are innate and nonconscious emotional responses to very thin slices of sensory information, triggered by whether that information supports or threatens our innate drives.[11]

Consider our earlier example about attitude toward mergers. You might experience worry, mild unease, or relief upon learning that your company intends to merge with a competitor. The fuzzy dots on the right side of Exhibit 4.1 illustrate the numerous emotional episodes you experience upon hearing

FACT.

Best Employers to Work for in America, Europe, and India[14]

	Top Five in America	Top Five in Europe	Top Five in India
1	SAS	Microsoft (several countries)	RMSI Private Limited
2	Edward Jones	Impuls Finanzmanagement (Germany)	Intel Technology India Pvt Ltd.
3	Wegmans Food Markets	Google (three countries)	Federal Express Corporation
4	Google	Cisco (several countries)	Aviva Life Insurance Co India Ltd
5	Nugget Market	Fater (Italy)	Google India Pvt Ltd.

Neither of the major "best employer" survey firms rank order companies across Asia. They rank order only for specific countries, so India is shown here as a representation. Companies in India also dominated an alphabetical list of the best 25 employers in Asia. The top five list in Europe represents only large companies. There is a separate list for small and midsized firms.

the merger announcement, subsequently thinking about the merger, discussing the merger with coworkers, and so on. These emotions are transmitted to the reasoning process, where they are logically analyzed along with other information about the attitude object.[12] Thus, while you are consciously evaluating whether the merger is good or bad, your emotions have already formed an opinion. These emotional responses influence your conscious logical evaluation of the situation. In fact, we often deliberately "listen in" on our emotions to help us consciously decide whether to support or oppose something.[13] You might visualize working in the merged organization and pay attention to the emotions generated by that visualization. The positive or negative emotions you experience are then incorporated into your logical reasoning regarding your attitude toward the merger.

This dual cognitive–emotional attitude process explains how employees form positive or negative attitudes toward their job, coworkers, and other aspects of work. Work attitudes are shaped by the almost continuous bombardment of emotional experiences people have at work. Those who experience more positive emotions tend to have more favorable attitudes toward their jobs and organizations, even when they aren't consciously aware of many of these emotional experiences. And when they do think about how they feel about their jobs, they listen in on the emotions generated from past positive or negative events in the workplace.

This emotional influence on employee attitudes explains why many companies try to create positive experiences at work. Google is renowned for providing employees with a comfortable workplace at its Googleplexes around the world. At Dixon Schwabl, the Rochester-based marketing and public relations firm, employees are encouraged to bring their water guns to meetings, where anyone who utters a negative comment gets blasted. And at Razer, the Singapore-based gaming peripherals company, employees zoom around on scooters and pit their gaming skills against each other on the state-of-the-art online gaming console. "Sometimes I can't believe that I have been here for seven months already," admits one Razer employee. "I guess you don't feel the time passing when you are having so much fun."[15]

When Cognitions and Emotions Collide The influence of both cognitive reasoning and emotions on attitudes is most

Having Fun across the Generations[16]

GenY	41
GenX	32
Baby boomers	32

Percentage of American employees surveyed who say it is extremely important that a prospective employer offers a "fun place to work." Another study reported that these three generations regard fun in different ways, but baby boomers are not as opposed to workplace fun as was hypothesized.

apparent when they disagree with each other. People occasionally experience this mental tug-of-war, sensing that something isn't right even though they can't think of any logical reason to be concerned. This conflicting experience indicates that the person's logical analysis of the situation (left side of Exhibit 4.1) can't identify reasons to support the automatic emotional reaction (right side of Exhibit 4.1).[17]

Should we pay attention to our emotional response or our logical analysis? This question is not easy to answer, but some studies indicate that while executives tend to make quick decisions based on their gut feelings (emotional response), the best decisions tend to occur when executives spend time logically evaluating situations.[18] Thus we should pay attention to both the cognitive and emotional sides of the attitude model—and hope they agree with each other most of the time!

> How much we are expected to hide or reveal our true emotions in public depends to some extent on the culture in which we live.

One last comment about Exhibit 4.1: Notice the arrow from the emotional episodes to behavior. It indicates that emotions directly (without conscious thinking) influence a person's behavior. This occurs when we jump suddenly if someone sneaks up on us. It also occurs in everyday situations because even low-intensity emotions automatically change our facial expressions. These actions are not carefully thought out. They are automatic emotional responses that are learned or hardwired by heredity for particular situations.[19]

Cognitive Dissonance

Emotions and attitudes usually lead to behavior, but the opposite sometimes occurs through the process of **cognitive dissonance**.[20] Cognitive dissonance occurs when we perceive an inconsistency between our beliefs, feelings, and behavior. When this inconsistency violates our self-concept, it generates emotions that motivate us to change one or more of these elements. For example, let's say that you agreed to accept a foreign posting, even though it didn't interest you, because you believed it might be necessary for promotion into senior management. However, you later learn that many people become senior managers in the firm without spending any time on foreign assignment. In this situation you will likely experience cognitive dissonance because of the inconsistency between your beliefs and feelings (dislike foreign assignments) and behavior (accepted a foreign posting).

Behavior is usually more difficult to change than beliefs and feelings. This is particularly true when the dissonant behavior has been observed by others, was done voluntarily, and can't be undone. In the foreign assignment example, you experience cognitive dissonance because others know you accepted the assignment, it was accepted voluntarily (you weren't threatened with dismissal if you refused the assignment), and working overseas can't be undone (although you might be able to change your mind beforehand). Thus people usually change their beliefs and feelings to reduce the inconsistency. For example, you might convince yourself that the foreign posting is not so bad after all because it will develop your management skills. Alternatively, you might downplay the features that previously made the foreign posting less desirable. Over time, a somewhat negative attitude toward foreign assignments can become a more favorable one.

Emotions and Personality

Our coverage of the dynamics of workplace emotions wouldn't be complete unless we mentioned that emotions are also partly determined by a person's personality, not just by workplace experiences.[21] Some people experience positive emotions as a natural trait. These people tend to have higher emotional stability (low neuroticism) and higher extraversion (outgoing, talkative, sociable, and assertive); see Chapter 2. In contrast, other people have a personality with a tendency to experience more negative emotions. Positive and negative emotional traits affect a person's attendance, turnover, and long-term work attitudes. For example, several studies report that people with a negative emotional trait have lower levels of job satisfaction and higher levels of job burnout.[22] While positive and negative personality traits have some effect, other research concludes that the actual situation in which people work has a noticeably stronger influence on their attitudes and behavior.[23]

Learning Objectives

After reading the next two sections, you should be able to

LO2 Discuss the dynamics of emotional labor and the role of emotional intelligence in the workplace.

MANAGING EMOTIONS AT WORK

People are expected to manage their emotions in the workplace. They must conceal their frustration when serving an irritating customer, display compassion to an ill patient, and hide their boredom in a long meeting with senior management. These are all forms of **emotional labor**—the effort, planning, and control needed to express organizationally desired emotions during interpersonal transactions.[24] Almost everyone is expected to abide by *display rules*—norms requiring us to display specific emotions and to hide other emotions.

Emotional labor is higher in jobs requiring a variety of emotions (such as both anger and joy) and more intense emotions (such as showing delight rather than smiling weakly), as well as in jobs where interaction with clients is frequent and has a longer duration. Emotional labor also increases when employees must precisely rather than casually abide by the display rules.[25] This particularly occurs in the service industries, where employees have frequent face-to-face interaction with clients.

Emotional Display Norms across Cultures

How much we are expected to hide or reveal our true emotions in public depends to some extent on the culture in which we live. Cultural values in some countries—particularly Ethiopia, Korea, Japan, and Austria—expect people to subdue their emotional expression and minimize physical contact with others. Even voice intonation tends to be monotonic. In other countries—notably Kuwait, Egypt, Spain, and Russia—cultural values allow

cognitive dissonance
Occurs when we perceive an inconsistency between our beliefs, feelings, and behavior.

emotional labor
The effort, planning, and control needed to express organizationally desired emotions during interpersonal transactions.

FACT.

Learning to Show Correct Emotions at Malaysia Airlines[26]

Malaysia Airlines flight attendants receive extensive training on the essentials of safety and medical emergencies, but they also learn how to remain composed and pleasant even in difficult conditions. "Are they presentable? Respectable? Do they make you feel comfortable? Do they seem approachable?" asks Madam Choong Lee Fong, Malaysia Airlines' cabin crew training and standards manager. Students at the Malaysia Airlines Academy in Petalign Jaya learn the fine art of smiling, making eye contact, and keeping their chin up at a level that displays confidence without arrogance. The academy even has mirrors on every wall so students constantly see how their facial expressions appear to others. Students receive training in voice enrichment and public speaking. They also learn about personal grooming as well as different formalities of behavior in countries where the airline flies.

or encourage open display of one's true emotions. People are expected to be transparent in revealing their thoughts and feelings, dramatic in their conversational tones, and animated in their use of nonverbal behaviors to get their message across.

These cultural variations in emotional display can be quite noticeable. One major study a decade ago reported that 74 percent of Japanese believe it is inappropriate to openly show their emotions, compared with 43 percent of Americans, 30 percent of French, and only 19 percent of Spaniards. In other words, people in Spain are generally more likely to accept or tolerate people who openly display their true emotions,

whereas acting this way in Japan would be considered rude or embarrassing.[27]

Emotional Dissonance

Emotional labor can be challenging for most of us because it is difficult to conceal true emotions and to display the emotions required by the job. Joy, sadness, worry, and other emotions automatically activate a complex set of facial muscle responses that are difficult to prevent and equally difficult to fake. Pretending to be cheerful or concerned requires adjustment and cordination of several specific facial muscles and body positions. Meanwhile, our true emotions tend to reveal themselves as subtle gestures, usually without our awareness. More often than not, observers see when we are faking and sense that we feel a different emotion.[29]

Emotional labor also creates conflict between required and true emotions, which is called **emotional dissonance**. The larger the gap between the required and true emotions, the more employees tend to experience stress, job burnout, and psychological separation from self.[30] Hiring people with a natural tendency to display the emotions required for the job can minimize emotional dissonance.

Emotional dissonance is also minimized through deep acting rather than surface acting.[31] People engage in *surface acting* when they try to modify their behavior to be consistent with required emotions but continue to hold different internal feelings. For instance, we force a smile while greeting a customer whom we consider rude. *Deep acting* involves changing true emotions to match the required emotions. Rather than feeling irritated by a rude customer, you might view your next interaction with that person as an opportunity to test your sales skills. This change in perspective can potentially generate more positive emotions next time you meet that difficult customer, thereby producing friendlier displays of emotion. However, deep acting also requires considerable emotional intelligence, which we discuss next.

FACT.

No Fun Here, Please; We're British![28]

A survey of 4,000 employees across Europe reported that 37 percent of employees in the United Kingdom said they suppressed any feeling of fun when they arrived at work. This was the highest percentage among countries across Europe. In contrast, only 13 percent of employees surveyed in Holland and 19 percent in France said they suppressed any feeling of fun at work.

emotional dissonance
The conflict between required and true emotions.

emotional intelligence (EI)
A set of abilities to perceive and express emotion, assimilate emotion in thought, understand and reason with emotion, and regulate emotion in oneself and others.

EMOTIONAL INTELLIGENCE

Emotional intelligence (EI) refers to a set of *abilities* to perceive and express emotion, assimilate emotion in thought, understand and reason with emotion, and regulate emotion in oneself and others.[32] One popular model, shown in Exhibit 4.2, organizes EI into four dimensions representing the recognition of emotions in ourselves and in others, as well as the regulation of emotions in ourselves and in others.[33]

- *Self-awareness:* Self-awareness is the ability to perceive and understand the meaning of your own emotions. You are more sensitive to subtle emotional responses to events and understand their message. Self-aware people are better able to eavesdrop on their emotional responses to specific situations and to use this awareness as conscious information.[34]

- *Self-management:* Self-management is the ability to manage your own emotions, something that we all do to some extent. We keep disruptive impulses in check. We try not to feel angry or frustrated when events go against us. We try to feel and express joy and happiness toward others when the occasion calls for these emotional displays. We try to create a second wind of motivation late in the workday. Notice that self-management goes beyond displaying behaviors that represent desired emotions in a particular situation. It includes generating or suppressing emotions. In other words, the deep acting described earlier requires high levels of the self-management component of emotional intelligence.

- *Social awareness:* Social awareness is the ability to perceive and understand the emotions of other people. To a large extent, this ability is represented by *empathy*—having an understanding of and sensitivity to the feelings, thoughts, and situations of others (see Chapter 3). Empathy includes understanding another person's situation, experiencing the other person's emotions, and knowing his or her needs even though unstated. Social awareness extends beyond empathy to include being organizationally aware, such as sensing office politics and understanding social networks.

- *Relationship management:* This dimension of EI involves managing other people's emotions. This includes consoling people who feel sad, emotionally inspiring your team members to complete a class project on time, getting strangers to feel comfortable working with you, and managing dysfunctional emotions among staff who experience conflict with customers or other employees.

These four dimensions of emotional intelligence form a hierarchy.[35] Self-awareness is the lowest level of EI because it is a prerequisite for the other three dimensions but does not require the other dimensions. Self-management and social awareness are necessarily above self-awareness in the EI hierarchy. You can't manage your own emotions (self-management) if you aren't good at knowing your own emotions (self-awareness). Relationship management is the highest level of EI because it

▼**EXHIBIT 4.2** Dimensions of Emotional Intelligence

	Yourself	Other people
Recognition of emotions	**Self-awareness**	**Social awareness**
Regulation of emotions	**Self-management**	**Relationship management**

Sources: D. Goleman, R. Boyatzis, and A. McKee, *Primal Leadership* (Boston: Harvard Business School Press, 2002), Chap. 3; D. Goleman, "An EI-Based Theory of Performance," in *The Emotionally Intelligent Workplace*, ed. C. Cherniss and D. Goleman (San Francisco: Jossey-Bass, 2001), p. 28.

FACT. Testing Pilots for Emotional Intelligence

All new pilots at Air Canada are tested for their emotional intelligence. Pilots are team leaders of the onboard crew and need to work effectively with staff on the ground, so they must have the ability to understand and manage their own emotions as well as the emotions of others. "If you have to interact well with other people, these [emotional intelligence tests] are instruments that we can use during the selection process to identify people that have these enhanced skills," says Captain Dave Legge, Air Canada's senior vice president of operations. "At the end of the day, we want to have a better idea of who we're hiring."[39]

requires all three other dimensions. In other words, we require a high degree of emotional intelligence to master relationship management because this set of competencies requires sufficiently high levels of self-awareness, self-management, and social awareness.

Research indicates that people with high EI are better at interpersonal relations, perform better in jobs requiring emotional labour, are superior leaders, make better decisions involving social exchanges, are more successful in many aspects of job interviews, and are better at organizational learning activities. Teams whose members have high emotional intelligence initially perform better than teams with low EI.[36] Emotional intelligence is particularly important for managers because their work requires management of their own emotions and the emotions of others. "(Managers) need to use EQ (EI) to influence and convince their peers to foster effective collaboration," explains Elaine Luey Kit Ling, Greater China regional director for Marriott International.[37] Emotional intelligence does not seem to improve some forms of performance, however, such as work that requires minimal social interaction.[38]

Improving Emotional Intelligence

Emotional intelligence is associated with some personality traits, but it is not completely hardwired or socialized at an early age. It can also be learned, which is why many companies invest in developing EI skills in employees and future leaders.[40] Sony Europe incorporates EI training in its executive development program, including an exercise in which leaders keep a journal of their emotional experiences throughout a week of work. One study reported that business students scored higher on emotional intelligence after taking an undergraduate interpersonal skills course. Emotional intelligence training also improved interpersonal relations among employees at GM Holden's new manufacturing facility in Australia.[41] Personal coaching, plenty of practice, and frequent feedback are particularly effective at developing EI. Emotional intelligence also increases with age; it is part of the process called maturity. Overall, emotional intelligence offers considerable potential, but we also have a lot to learn about its measurement and effects on people in the workplace.

So far this chapter has introduced the model of emotions and attitudes, as well as emotional intelligence as the means by which we manage emotions in the workplace. The next two sections of this chapter introduce the topics of job satisfaction and organizational commitment. These two attitudes are so important in our understanding of workplace behavior that some experts suggest the two combined should be called "overall job attitude."[42]

Learning Objectives

After reading the next two sections, you should be able to

LO3 Summarize the consequences of job dissatisfaction as well as strategies to increase organizational (affective) commitment.

JOB SATISFACTION

Job satisfaction, a person's evaluation of his or her job and work context, is probably the most studied attitude in organizational behavior.[43] It is an *appraisal* of the perceived job characteristics, work environment, and emotional experiences at work. Satisfied employees have favorable evaluations of their jobs, based on their observations and emotional experiences. Job satisfaction is best viewed as a collection of attitudes about different aspects of the job and work context.

You might like your coworkers but be less satisfied with your workload, for instance.

How satisfied are employees at work? The answer depends on the person and the workplace, but it also depends on the country. Global surveys indicate with some consistency that job satisfaction tends to be highest in the Nordic countries (Denmark, Sweden, Norway, and Finland), as well as in India and the United States. The lowest levels of overall job satisfaction are usually recorded in several Asian countries (such as mainland China, Hong Kong, and South Korea) as well as a few European countries (such as Hungary). Historically Americans have shown consistent happiness at work. Even the recent global financial crisis and subsequent recession didn't put much of a dent into the percentage of employees who say they are somewhat or very satisfied with their jobs.

It's probably fair to conclude that employees in India and the United States are more satisfied than those in some other parts of the world, but we also need to be somewhat cautious about these and other job satisfaction surveys. One problem is that surveys often use a single direct question, such as "How satisfied are you with your job?" Many dissatisfied employees are reluctant to reveal their feelings in a direct question because this is tantamount to admitting that they made a poor job choice and are not enjoying life. A second problem is that cultural values make it difficult to compare job satisfaction across countries. People in China, South Korea, and Japan tend to subdue their emotions in public, so they probably avoid extreme survey ratings such as "very satisfied."[44]

> " Job satisfaction and organizational commitment are so important in our understanding of workplace behavior that some experts suggest the two combined should be called "overall job attitude." "

job satisfaction
A person's evaluation of his or her job and work context.

exit–voice–loyalty–neglect (EVLN) model
The four ways, as indicated in the name, that employees respond to job dissatisfaction.

Job Satisfaction and Work Behavior

Brad Bird pays a lot of attention to job satisfaction. "In my experience, the thing that has the most significant impact on a budget—but never shows up in a budget—is morale," advises Bird, who directed *Ratatouille* and other award-winning films at Pixar Animation Studios. "If you have low morale, for every dollar your spend, you get 25 cents of value. If you have high morale, for every dollar your spend, you get about $3 of value."[46] Brad Bird's opinion about the importance of job satisfaction is reflected in the increasing competition to win best-workplace awards. In some firms, executive bonuses depend partly on employee satisfaction ratings. The reason for this attention is simple: Job satisfaction affects many of the individual behaviors introduced in Chapter 1. A useful template for organizing and understanding the consequences of job dissatisfaction is the **exit–voice–loyalty–neglect (EVLN) model**. As the name suggests, the EVLN model identifies four ways that employees respond to dissatisfaction:[47]

- *Exit:* Exit includes leaving the organization, transferring to another work unit, or at least trying to get away from the dissatisfying situation. The general theory is that job dissatisfaction builds over time

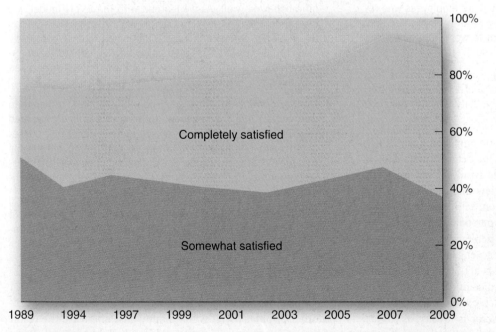

Still Satisfied after All These Years[45]

Completely satisfied

Somewhat satisfied

100%
80%
60%
40%
20%
0%

1989   1994   1997   1999   2001   2003   2005   2007   2009

Percentage of American employees who say they are somewhat or completely satisfied with their jobs, for selected years from 1989 to 2009. These data by Gallup Inc. are similar to those reported by NORC at the University of Chicago.

> ## "IT JUST SEEMS COMMON SENSE TO ME THAT IF YOU START WITH A HAPPY, WELL-MOTIVATED WORKFORCE, YOU'RE MUCH MORE LIKELY TO HAVE HAPPY CUSTOMERS.
>
> —SIR RICHARD BRANSON[57]

and is eventually strong enough to motivate employees to search for better work opportunities elsewhere. This may be true to some extent, but emerging research suggests that "shock events" energize employees to think about and engage in exit behavior. For example, the emotional reaction you experience to an unfair management decision or a conflict episode with a coworker motivates you to look at job ads and speak to friends about job opportunities where they work. This begins the process of realigning your self-concept more with another company than with your current employer.[48]

- *Voice:* Voice is any attempt to change, rather than escape from, the dissatisfying situation. Voice can be a constructive response, such as recommending ways for management to improve the situation, or it can be more confrontational, such as filing formal grievances or forming a coalition to oppose a decision.[49] In the extreme, some employees might engage in counterproductive behaviors to get attention and force changes in the organization.

- *Loyalty:* In the original version of this model, loyalty was not an outcome of dissatisfaction. Rather, it determined whether people chose exit or voice (high loyalty resulted in voice; low loyalty produced exit).[50] More recent writers describe loyalty as an outcome, but in various and somewhat unclear ways. Generally they suggest that "loyalists" are employees who respond to dissatisfaction by patiently waiting—some say they "suffer in silence"—for the problem to work itself out or be resolved by others.[51]

- *Neglect:* Neglect includes reducing work effort, paying less attention to quality, and increasing absenteeism and lateness. It is generally considered a passive activity that has negative consequences for the organization.

Which of the four EVLN alternatives do employees use? It depends on the person and situation.[52] One determining factor is the person's self-concept. Some people avoid the self-image of being a complainer, whereas others view themselves as taking action when they dislike a work situation. Self-concept relates to personal and cultural values as well as personality. For example, people with a high-conscientiousness personality are less likely to engage in neglect and more likely to engage in voice. Past experience also influences which EVLN action is applied. Employees who were unsuccessful with voice in the past are more likely to engage in exit or neglect when experiencing job dissatisfaction in the future. Another factor is loyalty, as it was originally intended in the EVLN model. Specifically, employees are more likely to quit when they have low loyalty to the

company, and they are more likely to engage in voice when they have high loyalty. Finally, the response to dissatisfaction depends on the situation. Employees are less likely to use the exit option when there are few alternative job prospects, for example.

Job Satisfaction and Performance

"A happy worker is a more productive worker!" This popular saying has encouraged many corporate leaders to pay attention to employee morale. Yet for most of the past century, organizational behavior scholars have challenged this belief, concluding that job satisfaction minimally affects job performance. Now the evidence suggests that the popular saying may be correct after all: there is a moderate relationship between job satisfaction and job performance. In other words, happy workers really are more productive workers to some extent.[53]

Even with a moderate association between job satisfaction and performance, there are a few underlying reasons why the relationship isn't stronger:

- General attitudes (such as job satisfaction) don't predict specific behaviors well. As we learned with the EVLN model, job dissatisfaction can lead to a variety of outcomes other than lower job performance (neglect). Some employees continue to work productively while they complain (voice), look for another job (exit), or patiently wait for the problem to be fixed (loyalty).

- Job performance might lead to job satisfaction (rather than vice versa), but only when performance is linked to valued rewards. Higher performers receive more rewards and consequently are more satisfied than low-performing employees who receive fewer rewards. The connection between job satisfaction and performance isn't stronger because many organizations do not reward good performance.

- Job satisfaction influences employee motivation but doesn't affect performance in jobs where employees have little control over their job output (such as assembly-line work).

Job Satisfaction and Customer Satisfaction

Another popular belief is that happy customers are the result of happy employees. This view is clearly held by Kevin Page, the Clydesdale Bank manager described in the opening story to this chapter. Page improved customer satisfaction levels by ensuring that the bank's contact center employees are satisfied and feel valued. This strategy relates to the *service profit chain model*, which proposes that increasing employee satisfaction and loyalty results in higher customer perceptions of value, thereby improving the company's profitability (see Exhibit 4.3). In other words, job satisfaction has a positive effect on customer service, which flows on to shareholder financial returns.[54]

There are two main reasons why job satisfaction should predict customer satisfaction. First, employees are usually in a more positive mood when they feel satisfied with their jobs and working conditions. Employees in a good mood display friendliness and positive emotions more naturally and frequently, and this causes customers to experience positive emotions. Second, satisfied employees are less likely to quit their jobs, so they have better knowledge and skills to serve clients. Lower turnover also enables customers to have the same employees serve them, so there is more consistent service. Some evidence indicates that customers build their loyalty to specific employees, not to the organization, so keeping employee turnover low tends to build customer loyalty.[56]

Job Satisfaction and Business Ethics

Before leaving the topic of job satisfaction, we should mention that job satisfaction does more than improve work behaviors and customer satisfaction. Job satisfaction is also an ethical issue that influences the organization's reputation in the community. People spend a large portion of their time working in organizations, and many societies now expect companies to provide

> "Job satisfaction does more than improve work behaviors and customer satisfaction; it is also an ethical issue that influences the organization's reputation."

work environments that are safe and enjoyable. Indeed, employees in several countries closely monitor ratings of the best companies to work for—an indication that employee satisfaction is a virtue worth considerable goodwill to employers. This virtue is apparent when an organization has low job satisfaction. The company tries to hide this fact, and when morale problems become public, corporate leaders are usually quick to improve the situation.

ORGANIZATIONAL COMMITMENT

Organizational commitment represents the other half (with job satisfaction) of what some experts call "overall job attitude." **Organizational commitment**—more specifically called **affective commitment**—is the employee's emotional attachment to, identification with, and involvement in a particular organization.[58] Affective commitment is an emotional attachment to the organization—a person's feeling of loyalty.

Affective commitment differs from **continuance commitment**, which is a calculative attachment.[59] Employees have high continuance commitment when they do not particularly identify with the organization where they work

---

organizational (affective) commitment
The employee's emotional attachment to, identification with, and involvement in a particular organization.

continuance commitment
An employee's calculative attachment to the organization, whereby an employee is motivated to stay only because leaving would be costly.

▼**EXHIBIT 4.3** Service Profit Chain Model[55]

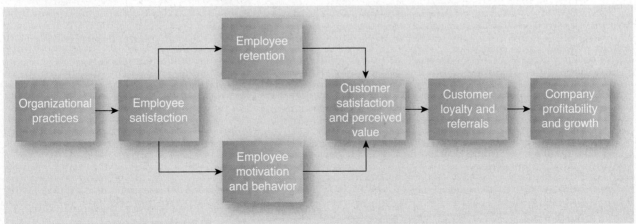

trust Positive expectations one person has toward another person in situations involving risk.

stress An adaptive response to a situation that is perceived as challenging or threatening to the person's well-being.

but feel bound to remain there because it would be too costly to quit. In other words, they choose to stay because the calculated (typically financial) value of staying is higher than the value of working somewhere else. You can tell an employee has high calculative commitment when he or she says, "I hate this place but can't afford to quit!" This reluctance to quit may exist because the employee might lose a large bonus by leaving early or is well established in the community where he or she works.[60]

Consequences of Organizational Commitment

Affective commitment can be a significant competitive advantage.[61] Loyal employees are less likely to quit their jobs and be absent from work. They also have higher work motivation and organizational citizenship, as well as somewhat higher job performance. Affective commitment also improves customer satisfaction because long-tenure employees have better knowledge of work practices and because clients like to do business with the same employees. One warning is that employees with very high loyalty tend to have high conformity, which results in lower creativity. There are also cases of dedicated employees who violated laws to defend the organi-

zation. However, most companies suffer from too little rather than too much employee loyalty.

Although affective commitment is beneficial, research suggests that continuance commitment can be dysfunctional. Research has found that employees with high levels of continuance commitment tend to have *lower* performance ratings and are *less* likely to engage in organizational citizenship behaviors. Furthermore, unionized employees with high continuance commitment are more likely to use formal grievances, whereas employees with high affective commitment engage in more constructive problem solving when employee–employer relations sour.[62] Although some level of financial connection may be necessary, employers should not confuse continuance commitment with employee loyalty. Employers still need to win employees' hearts (affective commitment) beyond tying them financially to the organization (continuance commitment).

Building Affective Commitment

There are almost as many ways to build organizational loyalty as there are topics in this book, but the following list is most prominent in the literature:

- *Justice and support:* Affective commitment is higher when employees believe the company abides by high standards of organizational justice, which we discuss in the next chapter. It is also higher when employees believe the organization supports

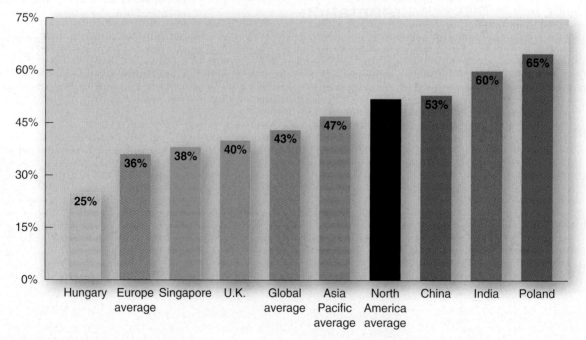

Totally Committed: Loyalty around the Planet[63]

Percentage of employees surveyed in selected countries who say they feel "totally committed" to their employers. Survey conducted on 134,000 people in 29 countries from October 2009 to January 2010.

them. This perceived support improves relations with management, but it also generates a sense of reciprocity, whereby employees become more willing to support the organization.[64]

- *Shared values:* Affective commitment is partly defined as a person's identification with the organization. That sense of identification is highest when employees believe their values are congruent with the organization's dominant values. Also, employees experience more comfort and predictability when they agree with the values underlying corporate decisions. This comfort increases their motivation to stay with the organization.[65]

- *Trust:* **Trust** refers to positive expectations one person has toward another person in situations involving risk.[66] Trust means putting faith in the other person or group. It is also a reciprocal activity: to receive trust, you must demonstrate trust. Employees identify with and feel obliged to work for an organization only when they trust its leaders. This explains why layoffs are one of the greatest blows to employee loyalty: by reducing job security, companies reduce the trust employees have in their employer and the employment relationship.[67]

- *Organizational comprehension:* Organizational comprehension refers to how well employees understand the organization, including its strategic direction, social dynamics, and physical layout. In other words, it refers to how well employees have formed a mental map of their organization. This awareness is a necessary prerequisite to affective commitment because it is difficult to identify with something that you don't know well. The practical implication here is to ensure that employees are able to develop a reasonably clear and complete mental picture of the organization. This occurs by giving staff information and opportunities to keep up to date about organizational events, interact with coworkers, discover what goes on in different parts of the organization, and learn about the organization's history and future plans.[68]

- *Employee involvement:* Employee involvement increases affective commitment by strengthening the employee's social identity with the organization. Employees feel that they are part of the organization when they participate in decisions that guide the organization's future. Employee involvement also builds loyalty because giving this power demonstrates the company's trust in its employees.

Organizational commitment and job satisfaction represent two of the most often studied and discussed attitudes in the workplace. Each is linked to emotional episodes and cognitive judgments about the workplace and relationship with the company. Emotions also play an important role in another concept that is on everyone's mind these days: stress. The final section of this chapter provides an overview of work-related stress and how it can be managed.

Learning Objectives

After reading the next section, you should be able to

LO4 Describe the stress experience and review three major stressors.

LO5 Identify five ways to manage workplace stress.

WORK-RELATED STRESS AND ITS MANAGEMENT

The past few years have been rough on many employees at France Telecom. The former state-owned company was privatized and restructured, resulting in 22,000 job cuts (about 20 percent of the company's workforce). Management developed a "time to move" doctrine of regularly shifting people around to new locations and different types of jobs. Several telephone engineers have been transferred to call centers, for example. The stress has been overwhelming for some staff. During the most recent two years, more than two dozen France Telecom employees committed suicide and another dozen attempted suicide. Several left notes saying they couldn't stand the pressure any longer or blamed management for terrorizing them. The CEO who led the transition resigned over this matter. Stephane Richard, France Telecom's incoming CEO, claims he will be more sensitive to employee stress. "The former management needed to change the nature of peoples' jobs due to technological change and increased competition, but the company underestimated the consequences," Richard acknowledges.[69]

Experts have trouble defining **stress**, but it is most often described as an adaptive response to a situation that is perceived as challenging or threatening to the person's well-being.[70] Stress is a physiological and psychological condition that prepares us to adapt to hostile or noxious environmental conditions. Our heart rate increases, muscles tighten, breathing speeds up, and perspiration increases. Our body also moves more blood to the brain, releases adrenaline and other hormones, fuels the system by releasing more glucose and fatty acids, activates systems that sharpen our senses, and conserves resources by limiting our immune system. One school of thought suggests that stress is a negative evaluation of the external environment. However, critics of this cognitive appraisal perspective point out that the stress experience is an emotional experience, which may occur before or after a conscious evaluation of the situation.[71]

general adaptation syndrome A model of the stress experience, consisting of three stages: alarm reaction, resistance, and exhaustion.

job burnout The process of emotional exhaustion, cynicism, and reduced personal accomplishment resulting from prolonged exposure to stressors.

stressors Any environmental condition that places a physical or emotional demand on the person.

psychological harassment Repeated and hostile or unwanted conduct, verbal comments, actions or gestures that affect an employee's dignity or psychological or physical integrity and that result in harmful work environment for the employee.

sexual harassment Unwelcome conduct of a sexual nature that detrimentally affects the work environment or leads to adverse job-related consequences for its victims.

As the France Telecom situation suggests, stress is typically described as a negative experience. This is known as *distress*—the degree of physiological, psychological, and behavioral deviation from healthy functioning. However, some level of stress—called *eustress*—is a necessary part of life because it activates and motivates people to achieve goals, change their environments, and succeed in life's challenges.[72] Our focus is on the causes and management of distress because it has become a chronic problem in many societies.

General Adaptation Syndrome

More than 500 years ago, people began using the word *stress* to describe the human response to harsh environmental conditions. However, it wasn't until the 1930s that Hans Selye (often described as the father of stress research) first documented the stress experience, called the **general adaptation syndrome**. Selye determined (initially

> " Stress is a physiological and psychological condition that prepares us to adapt to hostile or noxious environmental conditions. "

by studying rats) that people have a fairly consistent and automatic physiological response to stressful situations, which helps them cope with environmental demands.

The general adaptation syndrome consists of the three stages shown in Exhibit 4.4.[74] The *alarm reaction* stage occurs when a threat or challenge activates the physiological stress responses that were just noted. The individual's energy level and coping effectiveness decrease in response to the initial shock. The second stage, *resistance*, activates various biochemical, psychological, and behavioral mechanisms that give the individual more energy and activate coping mechanisms to overcome or remove the source of stress. To focus energy on the source of the stress, the body reduces resources to the immune system during this stage. This explains why people are more likely to catch a cold or some other illness when they experience prolonged stress. People have a limited resistance capacity, and if the source of stress persists, the individual will eventually move into the third stage, *exhaustion*. Most of us are able to remove the source of stress or remove ourselves from that source before becoming too exhausted. However, people who frequently reach exhaustion have increased risk of long-term physiological and psychological damage.[75]

Consequences of Distress

Stress takes its toll on the human body.[76] Many people experience tension headaches, muscle pain, and related problems due mainly to muscle contractions from the stress response. Studies have found that high stress levels also contribute to cardiovascular disease, including heart attacks and strokes, and may be associated with some forms of cancer. Stress also produces various psychological consequences, such as job dissatisfaction, moodiness, depression, and lower organizational commitment. Furthermore, various behavioral outcomes have been linked to high or persistent stress, including lower job performance, poor decision making, and increased workplace accidents and aggressive behavior. Most people react to stress through "fight or flight," so increased absenteeism is another outcome because it is a form of flight.[77]

good vs bad
STRESS vs STRESS[73]

69% of 1,000 American employees surveyed who are completely or somewhat satisfied with the amount of on-the-job stress.

69% of 42,000 American employees polled who report they are neutral or energized by on-the-job stress.

27% of 1,000 American employees surveyed who had an "excessive" score in a Rutgers University anxieties index.

13% of 115,000 employees polled globally who say their work is so stressful it makes it hard for them to sleep at night.

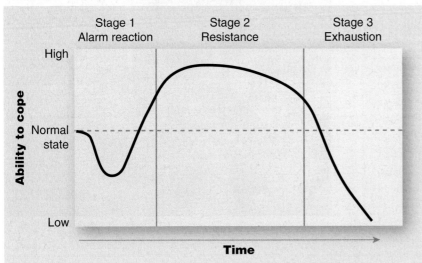

▼ **EXHIBIT 4.4** General Adaptation Syndrome

Stage 1
Alarm reaction

Stage 2
Resistance

Stage 3
Exhaustion

High

Ability to cope

Normal
state

Low

Time

Source: Adapted from H. Selye, *The Stress of Life* (New York: McGraw-Hill, 1956).

Job Burnout **Job burnout** is a particular stress consequence that refers to the process of emotional exhaustion, cynicism, and reduced feelings of personal accomplishment.[78] *Emotional exhaustion,* the first stage, is characterized by a lack of energy, tiredness, and a feeling that one's emotional resources are depleted. This is followed by *cynicism* (also called *depersonalization*), which is characterized by an indifferent attitude toward work, emotional detachment from clients, a cynical view of the organization, and a tendency to strictly follow rules and regulations rather than adapt to the needs of others. The final stage of burnout, called *reduced personal accomplishment,* entails feelings of diminished confidence in one's ability to perform the job well. In such situations, employees develop a sense of learned helplessness as they no longer believe that their efforts make a difference.

Stressors: The Causes of Stress

Before identifying ways to manage work-related stress, we must first understand its causes, known as stressors. **Stressors** include any environmental conditions that place a physical or emotional demand on a person.[79] There are numerous stressors in the workplace and in life in general. In this section, we'll highlight three of the most common workplace stressors: harassment and incivility, workload, and lack of task control.

Harassment and Incivility One of the fastest-growing sources of workplace stress is **psychological harassment**.

" For many, toiling away far beyond the normal workweek is a badge of honor, a symbol of their superhuman capacity to perform above others. "

Psychological harassment includes repeated hostile or unwanted conduct, verbal comments, actions, and gestures that undermine an employee's dignity or psychological or physical integrity. This covers a broad landscape of behaviors, from threats and bullying to subtle yet persistent forms of incivility.[80] Psychological harassment permeates throughout many workplaces. Two-thirds of Americans think people are less civil today than 20 years ago; 10 percent say they witness incivility daily in their workplaces and are targets of that abuse at least once each week. A survey of more than 100,000 employees in Asia reported that between 19 percent (China) and 46 percent (Korea) of employees experience incivility monthly or more often.[81]

Sexual harassment is a type of harassment in which a person's employment or job performance is conditional and depends on unwanted sexual relations (called *quid pro quo* harassment) or the person experiences sexual conduct from others (such as posting pornographic material) that unreasonably interferes with work performance or creates an intimidating, hostile, or offensive working environment (called *hostile work environment* harassment).[82]

Work Overload A half century ago, social scientists predicted that by 2030 technology would allow employees to enjoy a 15-hour workweek at full pay. So far, it hasn't turned out that way.[83] Many employees around the world are experiencing stress due to *work overload*—working more hours, and more intensely during those hours, than they can reasonably manage. Why do employees work such long hours? One explanation is the combined effect of technology and globalization. "Everyone in this industry is working harder now because of e-mail, wireless access, and globalization," says one marketing executive in California. "You can't even get a rest on the weekend."[84]

A second cause of work overload is that many people are caught up in consumerism; they want to buy more goods and services, and doing so requires more income through longer work hours. A third reason, called the "ideal worker norm," is that professionals expect themselves and others to work longer work hours. For many, toiling away far beyond the normal workweek is a badge of honor, a symbol of their superhuman capacity to perform above others.[85] This badge of honor is particularly serious in several (but not all) Asian countries, to the point where "death from

Japanese Professionals Are Dying to Get Ahead

Kenichi Uchino worked long hours as a Toyota quality control inspector in Japan. After each regular shift, he would stay to complete paperwork, perform unpaid "voluntary" activities such as leading quality circle meetings, and complete additional administrative duties. After about 14 hours at the Toyota plant, Uchino would go home, sleep for a few hours, then return to work. At 4:20 a.m. one morning, after working for 13 hours, Uchino collapsed and died on the factory floor from sudden heart failure. He was just 30 years old.[87]

overwork" is now part of the common language (*karoshi* in Japanese and *guolaosi* in Chinese). Officially the karoshi death toll in Japan is 300 to 500 annually, but these numbers consider only employees whose families have claimed damages. The actual death toll from overwork is many times higher.[86]

Low Task Control   An increasingly popular model of job burnout suggests that emotional exhaustion depends on both job demands and job resources.[88] *Job demands* are aspects of work that require sustained physical or psychological effort. High workload is one of the more significant job demands in the contemporary workplace. At the same time, the effect of job demands on burnout (or stress in general) depends on the individual's job resources. *Job resources* represent aspects of the job that help employees to achieve work goals, reduce job demands, and stimulate personal growth and development.

An important job resource is autonomy or control over the pace of work. Low task control increases employee exposure to the risk of burnout because they face high workloads without the ability to adjust the pace of the load to their own energy, attention span, and other resources. Furthermore, the degree to which low task control is a stressor increases with the burden of responsibility the employee must carry.[89] Assembly-line workers have low task control, but their stress can be fairly low if their level of responsibility is also low. In contrast, sports coaches are under immense pressure to win games (high responsibility), yet they have little control over what happens on the playing field (low task control).

Individual Differences in Stress

Because of unique personal characteristics, people have different stress experiences when exposed to the same stressor. One

SIX JOBS WITH HIGH STRESS RISK[90]

Ambulance paramedics

Teachers

Social services caregivers

Call center employees

Prison officers

Police officers

These jobs were identified based on job incumbent scores regarding physical health, psychological well-being, and job satisfaction.

reason for this is that people have different threshold levels of resistance to the stressor. Those who exercise and have healthful lifestyles have a larger store of energy to cope with high stress levels. A second reason for different stress responses is that people use different coping strategies, some of which are more effective than others. Research suggests that employees who try to ignore or deny the existence of a stressor suffer more in the long run than those who try to find ways to weaken the stressor and seek social support.[91]

A third reason why some people experience less stress than others is that some have higher resilience.[92] **Resilience** is the capability of individuals to cope successfully in the face of significant change, adversity, or risk. Those with high resilience are able to withstand adversity as well as recover more quickly from it. Resilient people possess personality traits (such as high extroversion and low neuroticism) that generate more optimism, confidence, and positive emotions. Resilience also involves specific competencies and behaviors for responding and adapting more effectively to stressors. Research indicates that resilient people have higher emotional intelligence and good problem-solving skills. They also apply productive coping strategies, such as analyzing the sources of stress and finding ways to neutralize these problems.[93]

While resilience helps people to withstand stress, another personal characteristic—workaholism—attracts more stressors and weakens the capacity to cope with them. The classic **workaholic** (also called *work addict*) is highly involved in work, feels compelled or driven to work because of inner pressures, and has a low enjoyment of work. Workaholics are compulsive and preoccupied with work, often to the exclusion and detriment of personal health, intimate relationships, and family.[94] Classic workaholics are more prone to job stress and have significantly higher scores on depression, anxiety, and anger.[95]

Managing Work-Related Stress

Some degree of stress is good (eustress), but much of the stress discussed in this chapter is dysfunctional for employee well-being and organizational performance. In this final section, we examine five types of strategies to minimize stress in the workplace: remove the stressor, withdraw from the stressor, change stress perceptions, control stress consequences, and receive social support.

Remove the Stressor Removing the stressor usually begins by identifying areas of high stress and determining the main causes of the stress. By identifying the specific stressors that adversely affect specific areas of the organization, such "stress audits" recognize that a one-size-fits-all approach to stress management is ineffective. For example, Unisys Asia-Pacific conducted this diagnosis through a survey in which employees were asked where they were struggling with work and how well they took care of their physical and mental health. These results gave the information technology services company some direction on how to help combat employee stress. In particular, the company introduced a health and well-being program called "Living Wellness@Unisys." Unisys Asia-Pacific estimates that employee stress fell by 11 percent and employee health levels improved significantly.[96]

Some of the more common actions to remove stressors involve assigning employees to jobs that match their skills and preferences, reducing excessive workplace noise, having a complaint system and taking corrective action against harassment, and giving employees more control over the work process. Another important way that companies can remove stressors is by facilitating better work/life balance. Work/life balance initiatives minimize conflict between the employee's work and nonwork demands. Five of the most common work/life balance initiatives are flexible and limited work time, job sharing, telecommuting, personal leave, and child care support.[97]

- *Flexible and restricted work hours:* An important way to improve work/life balance is restricting the number of hours that employees are expected to work and giving them flexibility in scheduling those hours. Electronics retailer Best Buy has become a role model in work/life balance by giving employees very flexible work hours through its results-only work environment (ROWE) initiative.

- *Job sharing:* Job sharing splits a career position between two people so that they experience less time-based stress between work and family. They typically work different parts of the week, with some overlapping work time in the weekly schedule to coordinate activities. This strategy gives employees the ability to work part-time in jobs that are naturally designed for full-time responsibilities.

- *Telecommuting:* Telecommuting reduces the time and stress of commuting to work and makes it easier to fulfill family obligations, such as temporarily leaving the home office to pick the kids up from school. Research suggests that telecommuters tend to experience better work/life balance.[99] However, telecommuting may increase stress for those who

resilience
The capability of individuals to cope successfully in the face of significant change, adversity, or risk.

workaholic
A person who is highly involved in work, feels compelled to work, and has a low enjoyment of work.

FACT. Best Buy Work/Life Balance through ROWE

A few years ago, Best Buy decided to ditch the age-old standard of rewarding people for their face time—how many hours its office staff were in the office. Instead it created a results-only work environment (ROWE) in which office staff are encouraged to get their work completed at times and places that work best for them. E-learning specialist Mark Wells was away 42 days one year, mostly attending concerts. Wells is shown in this photo (center) attending one of those concerts. Best Buy management didn't mind because Wells's productivity increased markedly. ROWE not only improves employee satisfaction and loyalty; it also reduces work-related stress. "ROWE has helped me to find the right balance in my work and home life, and now I actually have a life," says Best Buy strengths coach Christy Runningen. "I know my family would tell you that I am a lot less stressed out overall than I used to be."[98]

crave social interaction and who lack the space and privacy necessary to work at home.

- *Personal leave:* Employers with strong work/life values offer extended maternity, paternity, and personal leave for employees to care for a new family or take advantage of a personal experience. Most countries provide 12 to 16 weeks of paid leave, with some offering one year or more of fully or partially paid maternity leave.[100]

- *Child care support:* According to one estimate, almost one-quarter of large American employers provide on-site or subsidized child care facilities. Child care support reduces stress because employees are less rushed to drop off children and less worried during the day about how well their children are doing.[101]

Withdraw from the Stressor

Removing the stressor may be the ideal solution, but it is often not feasible. An alternative strategy is to permanently or temporarily remove employees from the stressor. Permanent withdrawal occurs when employees are transferred to jobs that better fit their competencies and values. Temporarily withdrawing from stressors is the most frequent way that employees manage stress. Vacations and holidays are important opportunities for employees to recover from stress and reenergize for future challenges. A very small number of organizations offer sabbaticals for long-service employees.[102] On a daily basis, many companies offer quiet retreats at the office, such as the live lunchtime piano recitals at SAS Institute in Cary, North Carolina.

Change Stress Perceptions

Earlier we learned that employees experience different stress levels because they have different levels of resilience, including self-confidence and optimism. Consequently another way to manage stress is to help employees improve their self-concepts so that job challenges are not perceived as threatening. One study reported that personal goal setting and self-reinforcement can also reduce the stress that people experience when they enter new work settings. Other research suggests that some (but not all) forms of humor can improve optimism and create positive emotions by taking some psychological weight off the situation.[103]

Control Stress Consequences

Coping with workplace stress also involves controlling its consequences. For this reason, many companies have fitness centers or subsidize the cost of membership at off-site centers. Research indicates that physical exercise reduces the physiological consequences of stress by helping employees moderate their breathing and heart rate, muscle tension, and stomach acidity.[104] A few firms, such as AstraZeneca, encourage employees to practice relaxation and meditation techniques during the workday. Research has found that various forms of meditation reduce anxiety, reduce blood pressure and muscle tension, and moderate breathing and heart rate.[105]

Along with fitness, relaxation, and meditation, wellness programs can also help control the consequences of stress. These programs educate and support employees in regard to better

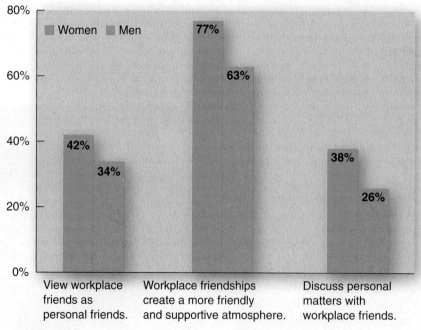

Gender Differences: Tending and Befriending[107]

Percentage of 1,000 employed U.S. adults who agreed with each of these statements, by gender.

nutrition and fitness, regular sleep, and other good health habits. Many large employers offer *employee assistance programs (EAPs)*—counseling services that help employees resolve marital, financial, or work-related troubles; but some counseling varies with the industry.

Receive Social Support Social support occurs when co-workers, supervisors, family members, friends, and others provide emotional and informational support to buffer an individual's stress experience. It potentially improves the person's resilience (particularly her or his optimism and self-confidence) because support makes people feel valued and worthy. Social support also provides information to help the person interpret, comprehend, and possibly remove the stressor. For instance, to reduce a new employee's stress, co-workers could describe ways to handle difficult customers. Seeking social support is called a "tend and befriend" response to stress, and research suggests that women often follow this route rather than the "fight-or-flight" response mentioned earlier.[106]

Employee emotions, attitudes, and stress influence employee behavior mainly through motivation. Recall, for instance, that behavioral intentions are judgments or expectations about the motivation to engage in a particular behavior. The next chapter introduces the prominent employee motivation theories and practices. ■

CHECK IT OUT!

mhhe.com/McShaneM

for study materials

including quizzes

and Internet resources

90

chapter five

employee
motivation

Rackspace Hosting, Inc., was founded in the late 1990s but has already become one of the world's largest and most successful companies in the enterprise-level Web hosting and information technology services industry. A key reason for this success is a highly motivated and engaged workforce. Rackspace's 2,600 employees—called "Rackers"—receive quarterly bonuses based on meeting companywide goals. Free restaurant dinners, weekend vacations, and other perks are awarded to those who receive special commendation from customers or otherwise demonstrate exemplary performance. Rackers with the most fanatical motivation and

performance get a special treat: they are tied up in a straitjacket and have a photograph of them in the outfit hung on the Wall of Fanatics. Rackers are organized into teams, so there is the extra motivation of meeting coworker expectations. Rackers receive plenty of training and career development opportunities. The company also emphasizes the strengths rather than the weaknesses of each employee. Little wonder that 85 percent of Rackers say that work fulfills their need for personal growth.[1]

Recognition, rewards, strengths-based feedback, and various forms of team support and motivation are

continued on p. 92

After reading this chapter, you should be able to

LO1 Explain how human drives result in employee motivation, and describe the three drive/need-based theories of motivation (needs hierarchy, learned needs, and four-drive theories).

LO2 Explain employee motivation using expectancy, organizational justice, and goal setting/feedback theories.

LO3 Compare and contrast job design approaches that increase work efficiency versus work motivation, and describe three strategies for improving employee motivation through job design.

LO4 Define *empowerment* and identify strategies that support empowerment.

motivation
The forces within a person that affect the direction, intensity, and persistence of voluntary behavior.

employee engagement The employee's emotional and cognitive motivation, self-efficacy to perform the job, perceived clarity of the organization's vision and their specific role in that vision, and a belief that they have the resources to get their job done.

drives Hardwired characteristics of the brain that correct deficiencies or maintain an internal equilibrium by producing emotions to energize individuals.

continued from p. 91

designed to maintain and improve employee motivation at Rackspace hosting in San Antonio, Texas, and at its other locations worldwide. This motivation has catapulted the company's performance over the past decade and raised its employer brand, making it easier to attract top-quality talent. Recall from Chapter 2 that **motivation** refers to the forces within a person that affect the direction, intensity, and persistence of voluntary behavior.[2] Motivated employees are willing to exert a particular level of effort (intensity) for a certain amount of time (persistence) toward a particular goal (direction). Motivation is one of the four essential drivers of individual behavior and performance.

This chapter reviews both the theories and several practices of employee motivation. We begin by introducing employee engagement, an increasingly popular concept associated with motivation. Next we distinguish drives and needs and review three needs-based theories: Maslow's needs hierarchy, McClelland's learned needs theory, and four-drive theory. Two popular rational theories of employee motivation—expectancy theory and organizational justice (including equity theory)—are discussed. The latter part of this chapter describes three applied performance practices: goal setting and feedback, job design, and empowerment. ∎

EMPLOYEE ENGAGEMENT

When Rackspace Hosting executives discuss employee motivation, they are just as likely to use the phrase *employee engagement*. Employee engagement is closely connected to employee motivation and has become so popular in everyday business language that we introduce it here. Although its definition is still being debated,[3] **employee engagement** can be cautiously defined as an individual's emotional and cognitive (rational) motivation—particularly a focused, intense, persistent,

and purposive effort toward work-related goals. It is typically described as an emotional involvement in, commitment to, and satisfaction with the work. Additionally, employee engagement includes a high level of absorption in the work—the experience of "getting carried away" while working. Finally, employee engagement is often described as (and is often measured by) the individual's perceived ability to perform the job, a clear understanding of the organization's vision, clarity of one's own role in that vision, and a belief of having sufficient resources to get the job done. In other words, employee engagement incorporates a strong self-efficacy (see Chapter 2) because the individual perceives alignment from all four cornerstones of the MARS model: motivation, ability, role perceptions, and situational factors.

However employee engagement is defined, only a small percentage of the workforce seems to be fully engaged at work. Several consulting reports estimate that only about one-quarter of American employees are highly engaged, which is slightly above the global average. Fewer than 60 percent are somewhat engaged, and approximately one-fifth have low engagement or are actively disengaged. Actively disengaged employees tend to be disruptive at work, not just disconnected from work. Globally, employees in Mexico and Brazil seem to have the

Value of an Engaged Workforce: Company Evidence[4]

- Standard Chartered Bank: Bank branches with highly engaged employees produce 20 percent higher returns than branches with lower engagement scores.

- Marks & Spencer: A 1 percent improvement in employee engagement levels produces a 2.9 percent increase in sales per square foot.

- Best Buy: A 0.1 increase (on a 5.0-point scale) in a retail outlet's employee engagement score is associated with a $100,000 increase in that store's profitability for the year.

- JCPenney: Stores with the top-quartile engagement scores generate about 10 percent more sales per square foot and 36 percent greater operating income than similar size stores in the lowest quartile.

Corporate interest in employee engagement is so great that one report estimates that a quarter of large organizations have a formal employee engagement program and three out of five intend to develop plans to improve employee engagement.[6] Some companies even have employee engagement departments or managers. The popularity of employee engagement is partly due to preliminary evidence that it improves customer service, sales, company profits, employee retention (low turnover), and other indicators of organizational effectiveness.

This leads to the following question: What are the drivers of employee engagement? Goal setting, empowerment, employee involvement, fairness (organizational justice), communication about the business (organizational comprehension), employee development opportunities, sufficient resources, and an appealing company vision are some of the more commonly mentioned influences on employee engagement.[7] In other words, building an engaged workforce calls on most topics in this book, such as the MARS model (Chapter 2), the ways to build affective commitment (Chapter 4), motivation practices (Chapter 5), and leadership (Chapter 11).

highest levels of engagement, whereas several Asian countries (notably Japan, China, and South Korea) and a few European countries (notably Italy, the Netherlands, and France) have the lowest levels.[5]

JCPenney executives are counting on an engaged workforce to help the retailer remain competitive in a hypercompetitive industry. "We feel strongly there's a correlation between engaged associates and store profitability," says Myron "Mike" Ullman, CEO of the Plano, Texas, retailer.[8]

Learning Objectives

After reading this section, you should be able to

LO1 Explain how human drives result in employee motivation, and describe the three drive/need-based theories of motivation (needs hierarchy, learned needs, and four-drive theories).

EMPLOYEE DRIVES AND NEEDS

To figure out how to create a more engaged and motivated workforce, we first need to understand the motivational forces or prime movers of employee behavior.[9] Our starting point is innate **drives** (also called *primary needs*), which represent a universal and innate brain function that produces emotions that energize individuals to act on their environment.[10] Although there is no clear list of human drives, several are consistently identified in research, such as the drives for social interaction, for knowing what goes on around you, for competence or status, and for defending against physiological and psychological harm or loss.[11] Drives are innate and universal, meaning that we are born with them and everyone has them. Furthermore, drives are the prime movers of behavior because they generate emotions, and these emotions put people in a state of readiness to change their situation (see Chapter 4).[12]

As Exhibit 5.1 illustrates, drives (and in particular the emotions produced by these drives) generate human needs. **Needs** are goal-directed forces that people experience; they are emotions channeled toward particular goals to correct deficiencies or imbalances. Suppose you arrive at work and discover a stranger sitting at your desk. Seeing this situation produces emotions that motivate you to act. You channel these emotions toward specific goals, such as finding out who that person is and possibly seeking reassurance from coworkers

that your job is still safe. In this case you have a need to know or understand what is going on. Notice that your emotional reaction to seeing the stranger sitting at your desk represents the force that moves you, but you channel those emotions toward specific goals.

Individual Differences in Needs

Everyone has the same drives; they are hardwired in us through evolution. However, the type and intensity of emotions formed in a particular situation vary from one person to the next. Exhibit 5.1 explains why this difference occurs. The model shows that the individual's self-concept (including personality and values), social norms, and past experience amplify or suppress drive-based emotions, thereby resulting in stronger or weaker needs.[13] People who define themselves as very sociable typically experience a strong need for social interaction if alone for a while, whereas people who view themselves as less sociable would experience a less intense need to socialize over that time. These individual differences also explain, as will be discussed later

▼ **EXHIBIT 5.1** Drives, Needs, and Behavior

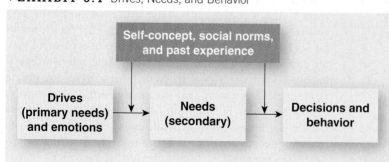

in this section of the chapter, why needs can be learned to some extent. Socialization and reinforcement may cause people to alter their self-concepts somewhat, resulting in stronger or weaker needs for social interaction, achievement, and so on.

Self-concept, social norms, and past experience also regulate a person's motivated decisions and behavior, as Exhibit 5.1 illustrates. Consider the earlier example of the stranger sitting at your desk. You probably wouldn't walk up to the person and demand that he or she immediately get away from your desk because such blunt behavior is contrary to social norms in most cultures. To varying degrees, self-concept, social norms, and past experience translate our needs into goal-directed behavior. Employees who view themselves as forthright would more likely approach the stranger directly, whereas those who have a different self-concept or have had negative experiences with direct confrontation in the past are more likely to gather information from coworkers first.

Exhibit 5.1 provides a useful template for understanding how drives and emotions are the prime sources of employee motivation and how drives and needs influence goal-directed behavior. You will see pieces of this theory when we discuss four-drive theory, expectancy theory, goal setting, and

needs
Goal-directed forces that people experience.

Maslow's needs hierarchy theory
A motivation theory of needs arranged in a hierarchy, whereby people are motivated to fulfill a higher need as a lower one becomes gratified.

> ## The difference between a successful person and others is not a lack of strength, not a lack of knowledge, but rather in a lack of will.
>
> —Vince Lombardi[14]

▼ **EXHIBIT 5.2** Maslow's Needs Hierarchy

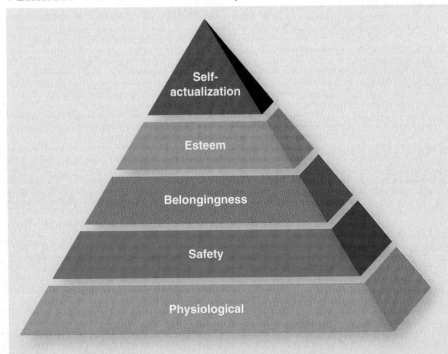

Self-actualization

Esteem

Belongingness

Safety

Physiological

Source: Based on information in A. H. Maslow, "A Theory of Human Motivation," *Psychological Review* 50 (1943), pp. 370–396.

other concepts in this chapter. The remainder of this section describes theories that try to explain the dynamics of drives and needs.

Maslow's Needs Hierarchy Theory

By far the most widely known theory of human motivation is **Maslow's needs hierarchy theory** (see Exhibit 5.2). Developed by psychologist Abraham Maslow in the 1940s, the model condenses and integrates the long list of primary needs (drives) that had been studied previously into a hierarchy of five basic categories (from lowest to highest):[15]

- *Physiological:* The need for food, air, water, shelter, and the like.

- *Safety:* The need for a secure and stable environment and the absence of pain, threat, or illness.

- *Belongingness/love:* The need for love, affection, and interaction with other people.

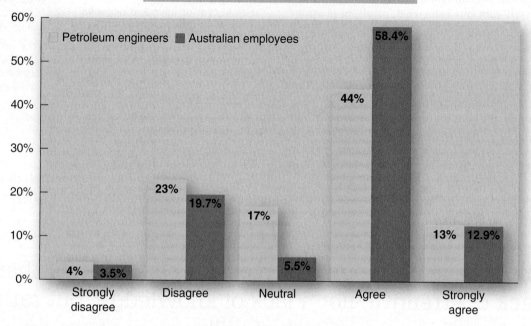

Petroleum engineers ■ **Australian employees**

- 60%
- 50%
- 40%
- 30%
- 20%
- 10%
- 0%

Strongly disagree: 4%, 3.5%
Disagree: 23%, 19.7%
Neutral: 17%, 5.5%
Agree: 44%, 58.4%
Strongly agree: 13%, 12.9%

Percentage of 9,441 petroleum engineers worldwide who agree or disagree that "My job utilizes my full potential," and percentage of 2,928 Australian employees (75 percent in management positions) who agree or disagree that "I am working to my full potential." For comparison purposes, agree/moderately agree and disagree/moderately disagree were combined in the Australian study.

- *Esteem:* The need for self-esteem through personal achievement as well as social esteem through recognition and respect from others.

- *Self-actualization:* The need for self-fulfillment and realization of one's potential.

Along with developing these five categories, Maslow identified the desire to know and the desire for aesthetic beauty as two innate drives that do not fit within the hierarchy.

Maslow describes primary needs (that is, drives) in his model because they are innate and universal. According to Maslow, we are motivated simultaneously by several primary needs, but the strongest source is the lowest unsatisfied need at the time. As a person satisfies a lower-level need, the next higher need in the hierarchy becomes the primary motivator and remains so even if never satisfied. Physiological needs are initially the most important, and people are motivated to satisfy them first. As they become gratified, the desire for safety emerges as the strongest motivator. As safety needs are satisfied, belongingness needs become most important, and so forth. The exception to this need fulfillment process is self-actualization; as people experience self-actualization, they desire more rather than less of this need. Thus while the bottom four groups are *deficiency*

> "Maslow deserves credit for bringing a more holistic, humanistic, and positive approach to the study of human motivation."

needs because they become activated when unfulfilled, self-actualization is known as a *growth need* because it continues to develop even when fulfilled.

Limitations and Contributions of Maslow's Work In spite of its popularity, Maslow's needs hierarchy theory has been dismissed by most motivation experts.[17] Maslow developed the theory from only his professional observations, and he was later surprised that it was so widely accepted before anyone tested it. Empirical studies have concluded that people do not progress through the hierarchy as the theory predicts. For example, some people strive more for self-esteem before their belongingness needs have been satisfied. The theory also assumes that needs priorities shift over a long time, whereas needs priorities rise and fall far more frequently with the situation. A person's needs for status, food, social interaction, and so forth change daily or weekly, not just every few years.

Although needs hierarchy theory has failed the reality test, Maslow deserves credit for bringing a more holistic, humanistic, and positive approach to the study of human motivation:[18]

- *Holistic perspective of motivation:* Maslow argued that motivation research must look at all needs and drives together rather than examining one or two of them apart from others. The reason is that human behavior is typically initiated by more than one need or drive at the same time.[19]

- *Humanistic perspective of motivation:* Higher-order needs are influenced by personal and social influences (such as self-concept and social norms), not just instincts. Previous motivation research had focused almost entirely on instinctive behavior.

- *Positive perspective of motivation:* Maslow refocused attention on need gratification rather than only need deprivation. He popularized the term *self-actualization,* suggesting that people are naturally motivated to reach their potential and that organizations and societies need to be structured to help people continue and develop this motivation.[20] Indeed, Maslow is considered a pioneer in positive organizational behavior (see Chapter 3).[21]

What's Wrong with Needs Hierarchy Models?

Why have Maslow's needs hierarchy theory and other needs hierarchies largely failed to explain the dynamics of employee needs? The most glaring explanation is that people don't fit into a single needs hierarchy. Some people place social status at the top of their personal hierarchy; others consider personal development and growth an ongoing priority over social relations or status. There is increasing evidence that needs hierarchies are unique to each person, not universal, because needs are strongly influenced by each individual's self-concept, including personal values and social identity. If your most important values are stimulation and self-direction, you probably

need for achievement (nAch) A learned need in which people want to accomplish reasonably challenging goals, and desire unambiguous feedback and recognition for their success.

need for affiliation (nAff) A learned need in which people seek approval from others, conform to their wishes and expectations, and avoid conflict and confrontation.

need for power (nPow) A learned need in which people want to control environment, including people and material resources, to benefit either themselves (personalized power) or others (socialized power).

pay more attention to self-actualization needs. If power and achievement are at the top of your value system, status needs will likely be at the top of your needs hierarchy. This connection between values and needs suggests that a needs hierarchy is unique to each person and can possibly change over time, just as values change over a lifetime.[22]

Learned Needs Theory

Earlier in this chapter we said that drives (primary needs) are innate whereas needs are shaped, amplified, or suppressed through self-concept, social norms, and past experience. Maslow noted that individual characteristics influence the strength of higher-order needs, such as the need to belong. Psychologist David McClelland further investigated the idea that need strength can be altered through social influences. In particular, he recognized that a person's needs can be strengthened through reinforcement, learning, and social conditions. McClelland examined three "learned" needs: achievement, power, and affiliation.[23]

Need for Achievement People with a strong **need for achievement (nAch)** want to accomplish reasonably challenging goals through their own effort. They prefer working alone rather than in teams, and they choose tasks with a moderate degree of risk (neither too easy nor impossible to complete). High nAch people also desire unambiguous feedback and recognition for their success. Money is a weak motivator, except when it provides feedback and recognition.[24] In contrast, employees with a low nAch perform their work better when money is used as an incentive. Successful entrepreneurs tend to have a high nAch, possibly because they establish challenging goals for themselves and thrive on competition.[25]

Need for Affiliation **Need for affiliation (nAff)** refers to a desire to seek approval from others, conform to their wishes and expectations, and avoid conflict and confrontation. People with a strong nAff try to project a favorable image of themselves. They tend to actively support others and try to smooth out workplace conflicts. High nAff employees generally work well in coordinating roles to mediate conflicts and in sales positions where the main task is cultivating long-term relations. However, they tend to be less effective at allocating scarce resources and making other decisions that potentially generate conflict. People in decision-making positions must have a relatively low need for affiliation so that their choices and actions are not biased by a personal need for approval.[26]

Need for Power People with a high **need for power (nPow)** want to exercise control over others and are concerned

FACT. **Measuring Achievement Motivation**[27]

David McClelland and his colleagues relied on the Thematic Apperception test (TAT) to measure a person's need for achievement, affiliation, and power. The TAT is a projective technique in which subjects write stories based on photos or drawings provided by the researchers showing people at work (similar to the photo at right). The stories are decoded by looking at specific words and phrases, such as feelings of success, need to overcome obstacles, fear of failure, and so forth.

about maintaining their leadership position. They frequently rely on persuasive communication, make more suggestions in meetings, and tend to publicly evaluate situations more frequently. McClelland pointed out that there are two types of nPow. Individuals who enjoy their power for its own sake, use it to advance personal interests, and wear their power as a status

symbol have *personalized power*. Others mainly have a high need for *socialized power* because they desire power as a means to help others.[28] McClelland argues that effective leaders should have a high need for socialized rather than personalized power. They must have a high degree of altruism and social responsibility and be concerned about the consequences of their own actions on others.

Learning Needs McClelland's research supported his theory that needs can be learned (more accurately, strengthened or weakened), so he developed training programs for this purpose. In his achievement motivation program, trainees wrote achievement-oriented stories and practiced achievement-oriented behaviors in business games. They also completed a detailed achievement plan and formed a reference group with other trainees to support each other's achievement motivation style.[29] In essence, McClelland's programs attempted to alter the individual's self-concept or experiences so that they amplified or suppressed emotions generated by innate drives.

Four-Drive Theory

One of the central messages of this chapter is that emotions play a significant role in employee motivation. This view is supported by a groundswell of research in neuroscience, but it is almost completely absent from contemporary motivation theories in organizational behavior. Also, social scientists in several fields (psychology, anthropology, and the like) increasingly agree that human beings have several hardwired drives, including social interaction, learning, and dominance. One of the few theories to apply this emerging knowledge is **four-drive theory**.[30] Developed by Harvard Business School professors Paul Lawrence and Nitin Nohria, four-drive theory states that everyone has the drive to acquire, bond, learn, and defend:

- *Drive to acquire:* This is the drive to seek, take, control, and retain objects and personal experiences. The drive to acquire extends beyond basic food and water; it includes enhancing one's self-concept through relative status and recognition in society.[31] Thus it is the foundation of competition and the basis of our need for esteem. Four-drive theory states that the drive to acquire is insatiable because the purpose of human motivation is to achieve a higher position than others, not just to fulfill one's physiological needs.

- *Drive to bond:* This is the drive to form social relationships and develop mutual caring commitments with others. It explains why people form social identities by aligning their self-concept with various social groups (see Chapter 2). It may also explain why people who lack social contact are more prone to serious health problems.[32] The drive to bond motivates people to cooperate and consequently is a fundamental ingredient in the success of organizations and the development of societies.

- *Drive to learn:* This is the drive to satisfy our curiosity, to know and understand ourselves and the environment around us.[33] When observing something that is inconsistent with or beyond our current knowledge, we experience a tension that motivates us to close that information gap. In fact, studies have revealed that people who are removed from any novel information will crave even boring information; the drive to learn generated such strong emotions that the study participants eventually craved month-old stock reports![34] The drive to learn is related to the higher-order needs of growth and self-actualization described earlier.

- *Drive to defend:* This is the drive to protect ourselves physically and socially. Probably the first drive to develop, it creates a "fight-or-flight" response in the face of personal danger. The drive to defend goes beyond protecting our physical selves. It includes defending our relationships, our acquisitions, and our belief systems.

These four drives are innate and universal, meaning that they are hardwired in our brains and are found in all human beings. They are also independent of each other. There is no hierarchy of drives, so one drive is neither dependent on nor inherently inferior or superior to another drive. Four-drive theory also states that these four drives are a complete set—there are no fundamental drives excluded from the model. Another key feature is that three of the four drives are proactive—we regularly try to fulfill them. Only the drive to defend is reactive—it is triggered by threat. Thus any notion of fulfilling drives is temporary, at best.

How Drives Influence Employee Motivation

Four-drive theory draws from current neuroscience knowledge to explain how drives translate into goal-directed effort. To begin with, recall from previous chapters that the information we receive is quickly and nonconsciously tagged with emotional markers that subsequently shape our logical analysis of a situation.[35] According to four-drive theory, the four drives determine which emotions are tagged to incoming stimuli. If you arrive at work one day and see a stranger sitting in your office chair, you might quickly experience worry, curiosity, or both. These emotions are automatically created by one or more of the four drives. In this example, the emotions produced are likely strong enough to demand your attention and motivate you to act on this observation.

Most of the time, we aren't aware of our emotional experiences because they are subtle and fleeting. However, emotions become conscious experiences when they are sufficiently strong or when we experience conflicting emotions. Under these circumstances, our mental skill set relies on social norms, past experience, and personal values to direct the motivational force of our emotions to useful and acceptable goals that address the source of those emotions (see Exhibit 5.3). In other words, the emotions generated by the four drives motivate us to act, and our mental skill set chooses courses of action that are acceptable to society and our own moral compass.[36] This is the process described at the beginning of this chapter—namely, that drives produce emotions; our self-concept, social norms, and past experience translate these emotions into goal-directed needs; and these individual characteristics also translate needs into decisions and behavior.

Evaluating Four-Drive Theory

Although four-drive theory was introduced recently, it is based on a deep foundation of research that dates back more than three decades. The drives have

four-drive theory
A motivation theory based on the innate drives to acquire, bond, learn, and defend that incorporates both emotions and rationality.

▼ **EXHIBIT 5.3** Four-Drive Theory of Motivation

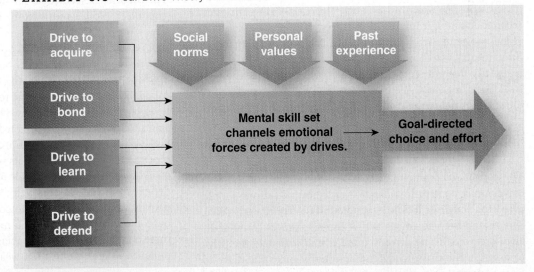

Source: Based on information in P. R. Lawrence and N. Nohria, *Driven: How Human Nature Shapes Our Choices* (San Francisco: Jossey-Bass, 2002).

THE MAIN RECOMMENDATION FROM FOUR-DRIVE THEORY IS TO ENSURE THAT INDIVIDUAL JOBS AND WORKPLACES PROVIDE A BALANCED OPPORTUNITY TO FULFILL THE DRIVES TO ACQUIRE, BOND, LEARN, AND DEFEND. "

been identified from psychological and anthropological studies. The translation of drives into goal-directed behavior originates from considerable research on emotions and neural processes. The theory avoids the assumption that everyone has the same needs hierarchy, and it explains why needs vary from one person to the next. Notice, too, that four-drive theory is both holistic (it relates to all drives, not just one or two) and humanistic (it acknowledges the role of human thought and social influences, not just instinct). Maslow had identified these two principles as important features of an effective motivation theory. Four-drive theory also provides a much clearer understanding of the role of emotional intelligence in employee motivation and behavior. Employees with high emotional intelligence are more sensitive to competing demands from the four drives, are better able to avoid impulsive behavior from those drives, and can judge the best way to act to fulfill those drive demands in a social context.

Even with its well-researched foundations, four-drive theory is far from complete. First, most experts would argue that one or two other drives exist that should be included. Second, social norms, personal values, and past experience probably don't represent the full set of individual characteristics that translate emotions into goal-directed effort. For example, other elements of self-concept beyond personal values, such as personality and social identity, likely play a significant role in translating drives into needs and needs into decisions and behavior.

Practical Implications of Four-Drive Theory

The main recommendation from four-drive theory is to ensure that individual jobs and workplaces provide a balanced opportunity to fulfill the drives to acquire, bond, learn, and defend.[37] There are really two recommendations here. The first is that the best workplaces for employee motivation and well-being offer conditions that help employees fulfill all four drives. Employees continually seek fulfillment of their innate drives, so successful companies provide sufficient rewards, learning opportunities, social interaction, and so forth for all employees.

The second recommendation is that fulfillment of the four drives must be kept in balance; that is, organizations should avoid too much or too little opportunity to fulfill each drive. The reason for this advice is that the four drives counterbalance each other. The drive to bond counterbalances the drive to acquire; the drive to defend counterbalances the drive to learn. An organization that energizes the drive to acquire without the drive to bond may eventually suffer from organizational

politics and dysfunctional conflict. Change and novelty in the workplace will aid the drive to learn, but too much of it will trigger the drive to defend to such an extent that employees become territorial and resistant to change. Thus the workplace should offer enough opportunity to keep all four drives in balance.

These recommendations explain why Rackspace Hosting, described at the beginning of this chapter, has a motivated workforce and is rated as one of the best places to work in America. The company encourages staff to be courageous and creative, yet balances those values with a nurturing environment that emphasizes employee strengths rather than faults. The company likely also minimizes the drive to defend because it is in a growth phase with little probability of layoffs or other risks to personal well-being.

Learning Objectives

After reading the next three sections, you should be able to

LO2 Explain employee motivation using expectancy, organizational justice, and goal setting/feedback theories.

EXPECTANCY THEORY OF MOTIVATION

The theories described so far mainly explain the internal origins of employee motivation. But how do these drives and needs translate into specific effort and behavior? Four-drive theory recognizes that social norms, personal values, and past experience direct our effort, but it doesn't offer more detail. **Expectancy theory**, on the other hand, offers an elegant model based on rational logic to predict the chosen direction, level, and persistence of motivation. Essentially, the theory states that work effort is directed toward behaviors that people believe will lead to desired outcomes. In other words, we are motivated to achieve the goals with the highest expected payoff.[38] As illustrated in Exhibit 5.4, an individual's effort level depends on three factors: effort-to-performance (E-to-P) expectancy, performance-to-outcome (P-to-O) expectancy, and outcome valences. Employee motivation is influenced by all three components of the expectancy theory model. If any component weakens, motivation weakens.

- *E-to-P expectancy:* This is the individual's perception that his or her effort will result in a particular level of performance. In

▼ **EXHIBIT 5.4** Expectancy Theory of Motivation

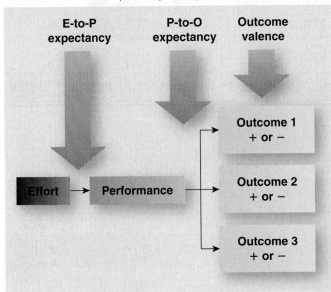

some situations, employees may believe that they can unquestionably accomplish the task (a probability of 1.0). In other situations, they expect that even their highest level of effort will not result in the desired performance level (a probability of 0.0). In most cases, the E-to-P expectancy falls somewhere between these two extremes.

• *P-to-O expectancy:* This is the perceived probability that a specific behavior or performance level will lead to a particular outcome. In extreme cases, employees may believe that

accomplishing a particular task (performance) will definitely result in a particular outcome (a probability of 1.0), or they may believe that successful performance will have no effect on this outcome (a probability of 0.0). More often, the P-to-O expectancy falls somewhere between these two extremes.

• *Outcome valences:* A *valence* is the anticipated satisfaction or dissatisfaction that an individual feels toward an outcome. It ranges from negative to positive. (The actual range doesn't matter; it may be from −1 to +1 or from −100 to +100.) An outcome valence represents a person's anticipated satisfaction with the outcome.[39] Outcomes have a positive valence when they are consistent with our values and satisfy our needs; they have a negative valence when they oppose our values and inhibit need fulfillment.

Expectancy Theory in Practice

One of the appealing characteristics of expectancy theory is that it provides clear guidelines for increasing employee motivation.[40] Several practical applications of expectancy theory are listed in Exhibit 5.5 and described here.

Increasing E-to-P Expectancies
E-to-P expectancies are influenced by the individual's belief that he or she can successfully complete the task. Some companies increase this can-do attitude by ensuring that employees have the necessary competencies, clear role perceptions, and necessary resources to reach the desired levels of performance. An important part of this

▼ **EXHIBIT 5.5** Practical Applications of Expectancy Theory

Expectancy Theory Component	Objective	Applications
E-to-P expectancies	To increase the belief that employees are capable of performing the job successfully.	• Select people with the required skills and knowledge. • Provide required training and clarify job requirements. • Provide sufficient time and resources. • Assign simpler or fewer tasks until employees can master them. • Provide examples of similar employees who have successfully performed the task. • Provide coaching to employees who lack self-confidence.
P-to-O expectancies	To increase the belief that good performance will result in certain (valued) outcomes.	• Measure job performance accurately. • Clearly explain the outcomes that will result from successful performance. • Describe how the employee's rewards were based on past performance. • Provide examples of other employees whose good performance has resulted in higher rewards.
Outcome valences	To increase the expected value of outcomes resulting from desired performance.	• Distribute rewards that employees value. • Individualize rewards. • Minimize the presence of countervalent outcomes.

distributive justice
Perceived fairness in the individual's ratio of outcomes to contributions compared with the other's ratio of outcomes to contributions.

procedural justice
Perceived fairness of the procedures used to decide the distribution of resources.

process involves matching employee competencies to job requirements and clearly communicating the tasks required for the job. Similarly, E-to-P expectancies are learned, so behavioral modeling and supportive feedback (positive reinforcement) typically strengthen the individual's belief that he or she can perform the task.

Increasing P-to-O Expectancies

The most obvious ways to improve P-to-O expectancies are to measure employee performance accurately and distribute more valued rewards to those with higher job performance. P-to-O expectancies are perceptions, so employees need to know that higher performance will result in higher rewards, and they need to know how that connection occurs. Companies satisfy these needs by explaining how specific rewards are connected to specific past performance and by using examples, anecdotes, and public ceremonies to illustrate when behavior has been rewarded.

Increasing Outcome Valences

Everyone has unique values and experiences, which translate into different needs at different times. Consequently, individualizing rather than standardizing rewards and other performance outcomes is an important ingredient in employee motivation. At the same time, leaders need to watch for countervalent outcomes—consequences with negative valences that reduce rather than enhance employee motivation. For example, peer pressure may cause some employees to perform their jobs at the minimum standard even though formal rewards and the job itself would otherwise motivate them to perform at higher levels.

Overall, expectancy theory is a useful model that explains how people rationally figure out the best direction, intensity, and persistence of effort. It has been tested in a variety of situations and predicts employee motivation in different cultures.[42] However, critics have a number of concerns with how the theory has been tested. Another concern is that expectancy theory ignores the central role of emotion in employee effort and behavior. The valence element of expectancy theory captures some of this emotional process, but only peripherally.[43]

Performance-to-Outcome Expectancy: the Missing Link[41]

56%
of American managers polled who say that employees at their company who do a better job get better pay and benefits than those who do a poor job.

27%
of Canadian employees polled who say there is a clear link between their job performance and pay.

32%
of American employees polled who say that employees at their company who do a better job get better pay and benefits than those who do a poor job.

ORGANIZATIONAL JUSTICE

Treating employees fairly is both morally correct and good for employee motivation, loyalty, and well-being. Yet feelings of injustice are regular occurrences in the workplace. To minimize these incidents, we need to first understand that there are two forms of organizational justice: distributive justice and procedural justice.[44] **Distributive justice** refers to perceived fairness in the outcomes we receive compared to our contributions and the outcomes and contributions of others. **Procedural justice**, on the other hand, refers to fairness of the procedures used to decide the distribution of resources. We look at both forms of organizational justice, beginning with distributive justice.

Equity Theory

The first thing we usually think about and experience in situations of injustice is distributive injustice—the belief (and its emotional response) that the pay and other outcomes

equity theory
A theory explaining
how people develop
perceptions of fairness
in the distribution and
exchange of resources.

we receive in the exchange relationship are unfair. What is considered "fair" varies with each person and situation. We apply an *equality principle* when we believe that everyone in the group should receive the same outcomes, such as when everyone gets subsidized meals in the company cafeteria. The *need principle* is applied when we believe that those with the greatest need should receive more outcomes than others with less need. The *equity principle* implies that people should be paid in proportion to their contribution. The equity principle is the most common distributive justice rule in organizational settings, so let's look at it in more detail.

The equity principle is nicely explained by **equity theory**. This theory states that employees determine feelings of equity by comparing their own outcome/input ratio to the outcome/input ratio of some other person.[45] The *outcome/input ratio* is the value of the outcomes you receive divided by the value of the inputs you provide in the exchange relationship. Inputs include such things as skill, effort, reputation, performance, experience, and hours worked. Outcomes are what employees receive from the organization in exchange for the inputs, such as pay, promotions, recognition, preferential treatment, or preferred jobs in the future.

According to equity theory, we compare our outcome/input ratio with that of a *comparison other*.[47] A comparison other is often someone else in a similar position, such as a coworker, but it might also be someone or a group of people in other jobs. For example, many people are interested in how much chief executives earn because we occasionally compare our (typically much lower) salaries to their paychecks. Some research suggests that employees frequently collect information about several referents to form a "generalized" comparison other.[48] For the most part, however, the comparison other varies from one person to the next and is not easily identifiable.

People develop feelings of equity or inequity by comparing their own outcome/input ratio with the comparison other's ratio. Exhibit 5.6 diagrams the three equity evaluations. In the underreward inequity situation, people believe

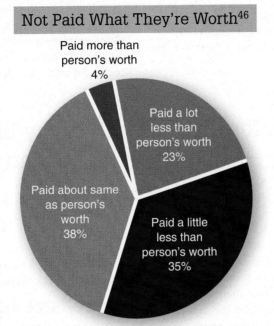

Not Paid What They're Worth[46]

Fifty-eight percent of 1,000 American employees surveyed say they are paid a little or a lot less than they believe they are worth. Only 4 percent believe they are overpaid.

their outcome/input ratio is lower than the comparison other's ratio. In the equity condition, people believe that their outcome/input ratio is similar to the ratio of the comparison other. In the overreward inequity condition, people believe their outcome/input ratio is higher than the comparison other's ratio.

Inequity and Employee Motivation How does the equity evaluation relate to employee motivation? The answer is that perceptions of inequity generate negative emotions, and as we have pointed out throughout this chapter, emotions are the engines of motivation. In the case of inequity, people are motivated to reduce the emotional tension, and researchers have identified many ways that this occurs. The following list refers specifically to responses to underreward inequity, some of which are considered unethical:[49]

- *Reduce our inputs:* Perform the work more slowly, give fewer helpful suggestions, or engage in less organizational citizenship behavior.

- *Increase our outcomes:* Ask for a pay increase directly or through a labor union, or make unauthorized use of company resources.

- *Increase the comparison other's inputs:* Subtly ask the better-off coworker to do a larger share of the work to justify his or her higher pay or other outcomes.

- *Reduce the comparison other's outcomes:* Ask the company to reduce the coworker's pay.

▼**EXHIBIT 5.6** Equity Theory Model

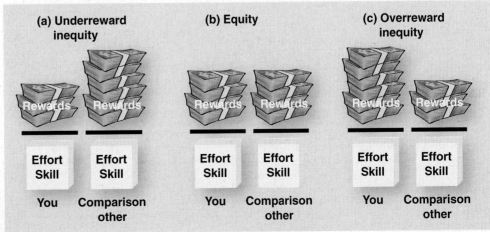

goal setting
The process of motivating employees and clarifying their role perceptions by establishing performance objectives.

- *Change our perceptions:* Believe that the coworker really is doing more (such as working longer hours) or that the higher outcomes (like a better office) he or she receives really aren't so much better than what you get.

- *Change the comparison other:* Compare yourself to someone else closer to your situation (for example, in job duties or pay scale).

- *Leave the field:* Avoid thinking about the inequity by keeping away from the work site where the overpaid coworker is located; take more sick leave; move to another department; or quit your job.

is that the overrewarded employee changes his or her perceptions to justify the more favorable outcomes.

Evaluating Equity Theory

Equity theory is widely studied and quite successful at predicting various situations involving feelings of workplace injustice.[51] However, equity theory isn't so easy to put into practice because it doesn't identify the comparison other and doesn't indicate which inputs or outcomes are most valuable to each employee. The best solution here is for leaders to know their employees well enough to minimize the risk of inequity feelings. Open communication is also a key, enabling employees to let decision makers know when they feel decisions are unfair. A second problem is that equity theory accounts for only some of our feelings of fairness or justice in the

> " I was underpaid for the first half of my life. I don't mind being overpaid for the second half. "
>
> —Pierre Burton[50]

Although the seven responses to inequity remain the same, people who feel overreward inequity would, of course, act differently. Some overrewarded employees reduce their feelings of inequity by working harder, but this might be the exception more than the rule. A common response to overreward inequity

workplace. Experts now say that procedural justice is at least as important as distributive justice.

Procedural Justice

Recall that *procedural justice* refers to fairness of the procedures used to decide the distribution of resources. How do companies improve procedural justice?[53] A good way to start is by giving employees a voice in the process: encourage them to present their facts and perspectives on the issue. Voice also provides a value-expressive function because employees tend to feel better after having an opportunity to speak their minds. Procedural justice is also higher when the decision maker is perceived as unbiased, relies on complete and accurate information, applies existing policies consistently, and has listened to all sides of the dispute. If employees still feel unfairness in the allocation of resources, these feelings tend to weaken if the company offers a way for them to appeal decisions to a higher authority.

Finally, people usually feel less inequity when they are given a full explanation of the decision and their concerns are treated with respect. If employees believe a decision is unfair, refusing to explain how the decision was made could fuel their feelings of inequity. For instance, one study found

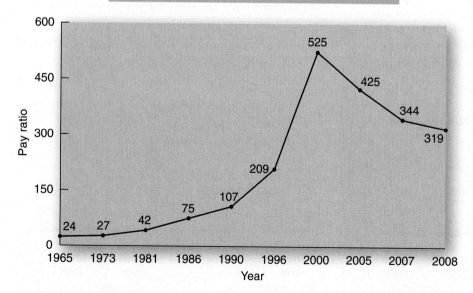

Ratio of CEO/Employee Pay: The Rise of Corporate Royalty?[52]

Ratio of total pay of CEOs in major U.S. companies to total pay of average employees in the United States for selected years. In 1965 CEOs earned an average of 24 times the average wage of American employees. The ratio peaked at 525:1 in 2000 and has since fallen to 319:1.

that nonwhite nurses who experienced racism tended to file grievances only after experiencing disrespectful treatment in their attempt to resolve the racist situation. Another study reported that employees with repetitive strain injuries were more likely to file workers' compensation claims after experiencing disrespectful behavior from management. A third recent study noted that employees have stronger feelings of injustice when a manager has a reputation of treating people unfairly most of the time.[54]

Consequences of Procedural Injustice Procedural justice has a strong influence on a person's emotions and motivation. Employees tend to experience anger toward a source of injustice, which generates various response behaviors that scholars categorize as either withdrawal or aggression.[55] Notice how these response behaviors are similar to the fight-or-flight responses described earlier in the chapter regarding situations that activate our drive to defend. Research suggests that being treated unfairly threatens our self-concept and social status, particularly when others see that we have been unjustly treated. Employees retaliate to restore their self-concept and reinstate their status and power in the relationship with the perpetrator of the injustice. Employees also engage in these counterproductive behaviors to educate the decision maker, thereby trying to minimize the likelihood of future injustices.[56]

GOAL SETTING AND FEEDBACK PRACTICES

Walk into almost any customer contact center (that is, call center)—whether it is Sitel's offices in Albuquerque, New Mexico, or Dell's contact center in Quezon City in the Philippines—and you will notice that work activities are dominated by goal setting and plenty of feedback.[57] Contact center performance is judged on several *key performance indicators (KPIs)*, such as average time to answer a call, length of time per call, and abandon rates (customers who hang up before their calls are handled by a customer service representative). Some contact centers have large electronic boards showing how many customers are waiting, the average time they have been waiting, and the average time before someone talks to them.[58]

Goal setting is the process of motivating employees and clarifying their role perceptions by establishing performance objectives. It potentially improves employee performance in two ways: (1) by amplifying the intensity and persistence of effort and (2) by giving employees clearer role perceptions so their effort is channeled toward behaviors that will improve work performance. Goal setting is more complex than simply telling someone to "do your best." It requires the following six key characteristics:[59]

- *Specific goals:* Employees put more effort into a task when they work toward specific goals rather than "do your best" targets, such as "reduce patient wait time by 25 percent over the next six months." Notice that specific goals are both *measurable* and *time-bound,* so it is possible to determine levels of change over a specific and relatively short time frame. Specific goals are motivational because they communicate precise performance expectations so employees can direct their effort efficiently and reliably.

- *Relevant goals:* Goals must also be relevant to the individual's job and be within his or her control. For example, a goal to reduce waste materials would have little value if employees don't have much control over waste in the production process.

- *Challenging goals:* Challenging goals (rather than easy ones) cause people to raise the intensity and persistence of their work effort and to think through information more actively. They also fulfill a person's achievement or growth needs when the goal is achieved. General Electric, Goldman Sachs, and many other organizations challenge employees with *stretch goals*. These goals don't just stretch a person's abilities and motivation; they are goals that people don't even know how to reach, so they need to be creative to achieve them.

- *Goal commitment:* Challenging goals are effective only if employees are committed to them. As Exhibit 5.7 illustrates, there is an optimal level where goals are difficult (challenging), yet employees remain motivated (committed) to achieving them.[60] This relates to the E-to-P expectancy discussed earlier in the section about expectancy theory. When goals are too challenging, the E-to-P expectancy that the goal can be accomplished decreases, and a lower E-to-P expectancy results in lower employee motivation (commitment) to accomplish the goal.

- *Goal participation* (sometimes): Goal setting is usually (but not always) more effective when employees participate in setting the goals.[61] Participation potentially creates a higher level of goal commitment than is found when goals are set by the supervisor alone. Participation may also improve goal quality because employees have valuable information and knowledge that may not be known to those who initially formed the goal.

strengths-based coaching A positive organizational behavior approach to coaching and feedback that focuses on building and leveraging the employee's strengths rather than trying to correct their weaknesses.

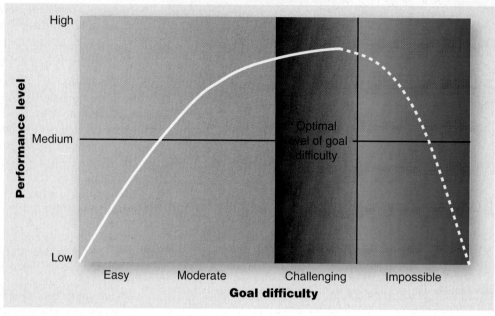

▼ EXHIBIT 5.7 Optimal Level of Goal Challenge and Performance

- *Goal feedback:* Feedback is another necessary condition for effective goal setting.[62] Feedback is any information that lets us know whether we have achieved a goal or are properly directing our effort toward it. Feedback redirects our effort, but it potentially also fulfills our growth needs.

Characteristics of Effective Feedback

Feedback is an important practice in employee motivation and performance, and it is closely tied to goal setting. Along with clarifying role perceptions and improving employee skills and knowledge, feedback motivates when it is constructive and when employees have strong self-efficacy.[63] As with goal setting, feedback should be *specific* and *relevant*. In other words, the information should refer to specific metrics (such as sales having increased by 5 percent last month) and to the individual's behavior or outcomes within his or her control. Feedback should also be *timely;* the information should be available soon after the behavior or results occur so employees see a clear association between their actions and the consequences. Effective feedback is also *credible.* Employees are more likely to accept feedback from trustworthy and credible sources.

The final characteristic of effective feedback is that it should be *sufficiently frequent.* How frequent is "sufficiently"? The answer depends on at least two things. One consideration is the employee's knowledge and experience with the task. Feedback is a form of reinforcement, so employees working on new tasks should receive more frequent feedback because they require more behavior guidance and reinforcement (see Chapter 3). Employees who perform repetitive or familiar tasks can receive less frequent feedback. The second factor is how long it takes to complete the task. Feedback is necessarily less frequent in jobs with a long cycle time (like the jobs of executives and scientists) than in jobs with a short cycle time (grocery store cashiers would be an example).

Feedback through Strengths-Based Coaching Forty
years ago Peter Drucker recognized that leaders are more effective when they focus on strengths rather than weaknesses.

"The effective executive builds on strengths—their own strengths, the strengths of superiors, colleagues, subordinates; and on the strength of the situation," wrote the late management guru.[64] Rackspace Hosting, which was described at the beginning of this chapter, has adopted this positive OB approach. It gives employees opportunities to develop their strengths rather than requiring them to focus on areas where they have limited interest or talent. This is the essence of **strengths-based coaching** (and its variation, called *appreciative coaching*)—maximizing employees' potential by focusing on their strengths rather than their weaknesses.[65] In strengths-based coaching, employees describe areas of work where they excel or demonstrate potential. The coach guides this discussion by asking exploratory questions and by helping to discover ways of leveraging these strengths. For example, the discussion would explore situational barriers to practicing the coachee's strengths as well as aspects of these strengths that require further development.

Strengths-based coaching is a potentially powerful way to motivate because people inherently seek feedback about their strengths, not their flaws. Recall from Chapter 2 that people engage in self-enhancement, at least for those domains of self that are most important. Furthermore, strengths-based coaching maintains that people have relatively stable competencies and interests in adulthood, so trying to develop an employee's weaknesses is more costly and frustrating than developing his or her strengths.[66] Despite these research observations, many coaching or performance feedback sessions analyze the employee's weaknesses, including determining what went wrong and what the employee needs to do to improve. These inquisitions sometimes produce so much negative feedback that

> ACCORDING TO STRENGTHS-BASED COACHING, PEOPLE HAVE RELATIVELY STABLE COMPETENCIES AND INTERESTS IN ADULTHOOD, SO TRYING TO DEVELOP AN EMPLOYEE'S WEAKNESSES IS MORE COSTLY AND FRUSTRATING THAN DEVELOPING HIS OR HER STRENGTHS.

employees become defensive; they can also undermine self-efficacy, thereby making the employee's performance worse rather than better. By focusing on weaknesses, companies fail to realize the full potential of the employee's strengths.[67]

Sources of Feedback

Employees receive feedback about their behavior and performance from many sources—equipment gauges, executive dashboards, customer surveys, feedback from their boss, multisource feedback, and so forth. The preferred feedback source depends on the purpose of the information. Information from nonsocial sources, such as computer charts and electronic gauges, is considered more accurate than information from social sources (from other people), so employees usually prefer nonsocial feedback sources to learn about their progress toward goal accomplishment. Negative feedback is also less damaging to the person's self-esteem when it is received from nonsocial than social sources. In other words, employees are more comfortable discovering from computer data than from a meeting with their boss that they are performing poorly. In contrast, social sources tend to delay negative information, leave some of it out, and distort the bad news in a positive way.[68] When employees want to improve their self-image, on the other hand, they seek out positive feedback from social sources.

Evaluating Goal Setting and Feedback

Goal setting represents one of the tried-and-true theories in organizational behavior—so much so that scholars consider it to be one of the top OB theories in terms of validity and usefulness.[70] In partnership with goal setting, feedback also has an excellent reputation for improving employee motivation and performance. At the same time, putting goal setting into practice can create problems.[71] One concern is that goal setting tends to focus employees on a narrow subset of measurable performance indicators while ignoring aspects of job performance that are difficult to measure. The saying "What gets measured, gets done" applies here. A second problem is that when goal achievement is tied to financial rewards, many employees are motivated to set easy goals (while making the boss think they are difficult) so they have a higher probability of receiving a bonus or pay increase. As a former chief executive at Ford once quipped, "At Ford, we hire very smart people. They quickly learn how to make relatively easy goals look difficult!"[72] A third problem is that setting performance goals is effective in established jobs but seems to interfere with the learning process in new, complex jobs. Thus we need to be careful not to apply goal setting where an intense learning process is occurring.

Nova Chemicals employees receive real-time feedback from a computer screen that monitors the plant's production output and operational capacity. The plant's operations staff uses this feedback to get output closer to the operation's capacity.[69]

Learning Objectives

After reading the next two sections, you should be able to

LO3 Compare and contrast job design approaches that increase work efficiency versus work motivation, and describe three strategies for improving employee motivation through job design.

LO4 Define *empowerment* and identify strategies that support empowerment.

job design
The process of assigning tasks to a job, including the interdependency of those tasks with other jobs.

job specialization
The result of division of labor in which work is subdivided into separate jobs assigned to different people.

scientific management The practice of systematically partitioning work into its smallest elements and standardizing tasks to achieve maximum efficiency.

motivator–hygiene theory Herzberg's theory stating that employees are primarily motivated by growth and esteem needs, not by lower-level needs.

job characteristics model A job design model that relates the motivational properties of jobs to specific personal and organizational consequences of those properties.

JOB DESIGN PRACTICES

How do you build a better job? That question has challenged organizational behavior experts as well as psychologists, engineers, and economists for a few centuries. Some jobs have few tasks and usually require little skill. Other jobs are immensely complex and require years of experience and learning to master them. From one extreme to the other, jobs have different effects on work efficiency and employee motivation. The challenge, at least from the organization's perspective, is to find the right combination so work is performed efficiently but employees are motivated and engaged.[73] This challenge requires careful **job design**—the process of assigning tasks to a job, including the interdependency of those tasks with other jobs. A *job* is a set of tasks performed by one person. To understand this issue more fully, let's begin by describing early job design efforts aimed at increasing work efficiency through job specialization.

Work Efficiency through Job Design

One of the oldest forms of job design is **job specialization**, whereby the required work is subdivided into separate jobs assigned to different people. Each resulting job includes a narrow subset of tasks, usually completed in a short cycle time. *Cycle time* is the time required to complete a task before starting over with a new work unit. A grocery store cashier might have a cycle time of a few minutes—the time it takes to check out a customer. An accounting auditor might have a cycle time of a few days or more. Some factory employees have cycle times of 15–20 seconds, such as painting the eyes on dolls or inserting and removing plastic molds from molding machines.

Why would companies divide work into such tiny bits? The simple answer is that job specialization improves work efficiency. Specialized jobs require fewer physical and mental skills to accomplish the assigned work, so less time and fewer resources are needed for training. Employees practice their tasks more frequently with shorter work cycles, so jobs are mastered quickly. Work efficiency also increases because employees with specific aptitudes or skills can be matched more precisely to the jobs for which they are best suited. Finally,

> " The challenge for organizations is to design jobs in which the work is performed efficiently but employees are motivated and engaged. "

employees have fewer tasks to juggle and therefore need less time to change activities.[74]

Scientific Management

One of the strongest advocates of job specialization was Frederick Winslow Taylor, an American industrial engineer who introduced the principles of **scientific management** in the early 1900s.[75] Scientific management consists of a toolkit of practices, such as training, goal setting, and work incentives. However, scientific management is mainly associated with high levels of job specialization and standardization of tasks to achieve maximum efficiency. According to Taylor, the most effective companies have detailed procedures and work practices developed by engineers, enforced by supervisors, and executed by employees. Taylor and other industrial engineers demonstrated that scientific management significantly improves work efficiency. No doubt some of the increased productivity can be credited to the training, goal setting, and work incentives, but job specialization quickly became popular in its own right.

Problems with Job Specialization

Frederick Taylor and his contemporaries focused on how job specialization reduces labor "waste" by improving the mechanical efficiency of work (by matching skills, faster learning, and less switchover time). Yet they didn't seem to notice how this extreme job specialization adversely affects employee attitudes and motivation. Some jobs are so specialized that they may soon become tedious, trivial, and socially isolating. Employee turnover and absenteeism tend to be higher in specialized jobs with very short time cycles. Companies sometimes have to pay higher wages to attract job applicants to this dissatisfying, narrowly defined work.[76]

Job specialization often reduces work quality because employees see only a small part of the process. As one observer of an automobile assembly line reports, "Often [employees] did not know how their jobs related to the total picture. Not knowing, there was no incentive to strive for quality—what did quality even mean as it related to a bracket whose function you did not understand?"[77] Equally important, job specialization can undermine the motivational potential of jobs. As work becomes specialized, it tends to become easier to perform but less interesting. As jobs become more complex, work motivation increases but the ability to master the job decreases. Maximum job performance occurs somewhere between these two extremes, where most people can eventually perform the job tasks efficiently yet the work is interesting.

Work Motivation through Job Design

Industrial engineers may have overlooked the motivational effect of job characteristics, but this is now the central focus of many job design changes. Organizational behavior researcher Frederick Herzberg is credited with shifting the spotlight when he introduced **motivator–hygiene theory** in the 1950s.[78] Motivator–hygiene theory proposes that employees experience job satisfaction when they fulfill growth and esteem needs (called *motivators*) and they experience dissatisfaction when they have poor working conditions, job security, and other factors categorized as lower-order needs (called *hygienes*). Herzberg argued that only characteristics of the job itself motivate employees, whereas the hygiene factors merely prevent dissatisfaction. It might seem obvious to us today that the job itself is a source of motivation, but the concept was radical when Herzberg proposed the idea.

Motivator–hygiene theory has been soundly rejected due to lack of research support, but Herzberg's ideas generated new thinking about the motivational potential of the job itself.[79] Out of subsequent research emerged the **job characteristics model**, shown in Exhibit 5.8. The job characteristics model identifies five core job dimensions that produce three psychological states. Employees who experience these psychological states tend to have higher levels of internal work motivation (motivation from the work itself), job satisfaction (particularly satisfaction with the work itself), and work effectiveness.[80]

Core Job Characteristics The job characteristics model identifies five core job characteristics. Under the right conditions, employees are more motivated and satisfied when jobs have higher levels of these characteristics:

- *Skill variety:* **Skill variety** refers to the use of different skills and talents to complete a variety of work activities. For example, sales clerks who normally only serve customers might be assigned the additional duties of stocking inventory and changing storefront displays.

- *Task identity:* **Task identity** is the degree to which a job requires completion of a whole or identifiable piece of work, such as assembling an entire broadband modem rather than just soldering in the circuitry.

- *Task significance:* **Task significance** is the degree to which a job affects the organization or the larger society. For instance, many employees at Medtronic, the Minneapolis-based maker of pacemakers and other medical equipment, have high job specialization, yet 86 percent say their work has special meaning and 94 percent feel pride in what they accomplish. The reason for their high task significance is

skill variety The extent to which employees must use different skills and talents to perform tasks within their job.

task identity The degree to which a job requires completion of a whole or an identifiable piece of work.

task significance The degree to which the job has a substantial impact on the organization and/or larger society.

▼**EXHIBIT 5.8** The Job Characteristics Model

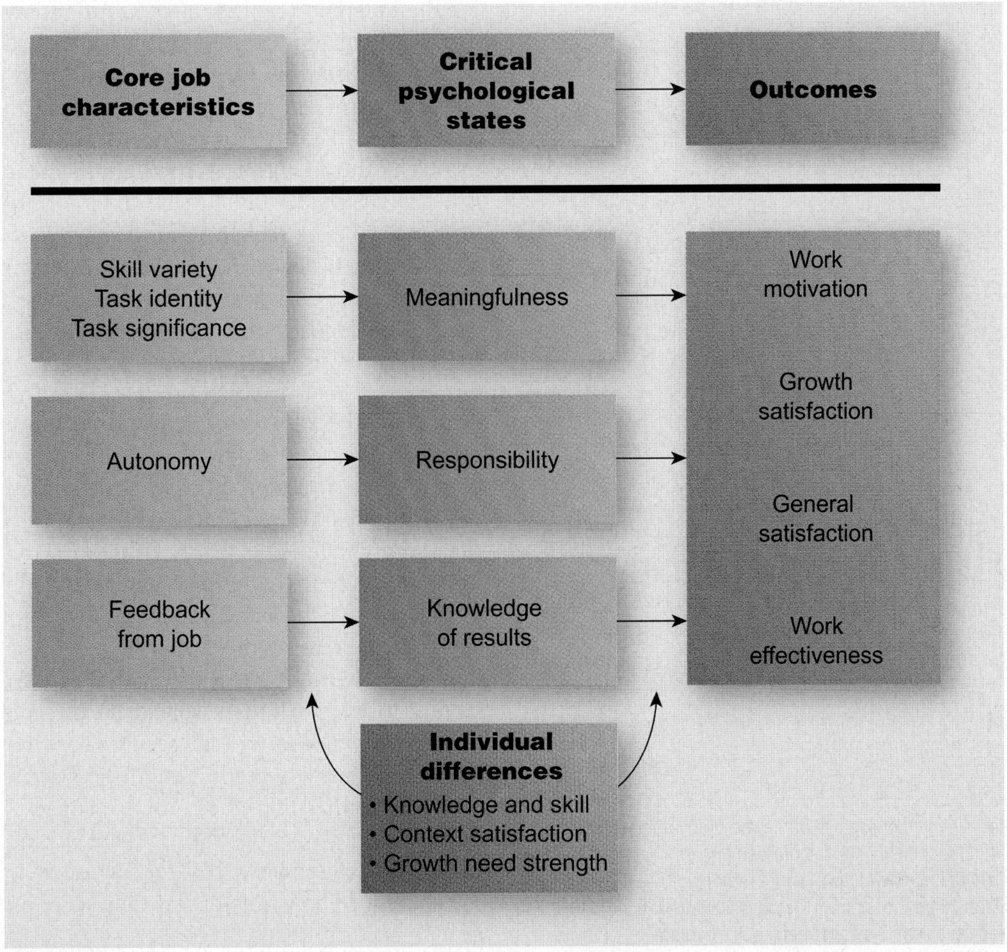

Source: J. R. Hackman and G. Oldham, *Work Redesign* (Reading, MA: Addison-Wesley, 1980), p. 90. Used with permission.

Rolls Royce Engine Services facility in Oakland, California, invited customers to talk to production staff about the importance of their work. These sessions improve task significance because, as one Roll Royce executive noted, they give "employees with relatively repetitive jobs the sense that they're not just working on a part but rather are key in keeping people safe."

that they attend seminars that show how the products they manufacture save lives. "We have patients who come in who would be dead if it wasn't for us," says a Medtronic production supervisor.[81]

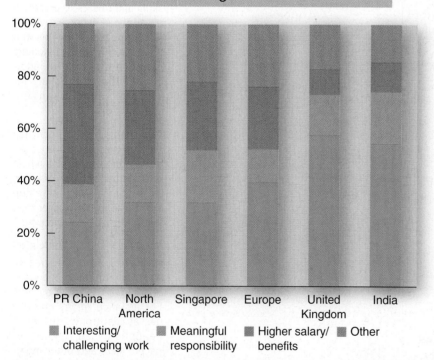

Employees Want Interesting, Challenging, Meaningful Jobs[82]

Legend: Interesting/challenging work; Meaningful responsibility; Higher salary/benefits; Other

Categories: PR China, North America, Singapore, Europe, United Kingdom, India

What is the one thing that would make employees feel more committed or engaged with their job? Almost 75 percent of employees in India and the United Kingdom chose one of the two motivating job characteristics (interesting/challenging work or meaningful responsibility). In contrast, higher salary and benefits were almost as important as motivating work in China as well as in some regions of the United States. The survey was conducted on 134,000 people in 29 countries from October 2009 to January 2010. The United Kingdom is included in the European results as well as separately in this exhibit.

- *Autonomy:* Jobs with high levels of **autonomy** provide freedom, independence, and discretion in scheduling the work and determining the procedures to be used to complete the work. In autonomous jobs, employees make their own decisions rather than relying on detailed instructions from supervisors or procedure manuals.

- *Job feedback:* Job feedback is the degree to which employees can tell how well they are doing on the basis of direct sensory information from the job itself. Airline pilots can tell how well they land their aircraft, and road crews can see how well they have prepared the roadbed and laid the asphalt.

Critical Psychological States

The five core job characteristics affect employee motivation and satisfaction through three critical psychological states, shown in Exhibit 5.8. One of these psychological states is *experienced meaningfulness*—the belief that one's work is worthwhile or important. Skill variety, task identity, and task significance directly contribute to the job's meaningfulness. If the job has high levels of all three characteristics, employees are likely to feel that their jobs are highly meaningful. The meaningfulness of a job drops as one or more of these characteristics declines.

Work motivation and performance increase when employees feel personally accountable for the outcomes of their efforts. Autonomy directly contributes to this feeling of *experienced responsibility*. Employees must be assigned control of their work environment to feel responsible for their successes and failures. The third critical psychological state is *knowledge of results.* Employees want information about the consequences of their work effort. Knowledge of results can originate from coworkers, supervisors, or clients. However, job design focuses on knowledge of results from the work itself.

Individual Differences

Job design doesn't increase work motivation for everyone in every situation. Employees must have the required skills and knowledge to master the more challenging work. Otherwise job design tends to increase stress and reduce job performance. The original model also suggests that increasing the motivational potential of jobs will not motivate employees who are dissatisfied with their work context (such as working conditions or job security) or who have a low growth need strength. However, research findings have been mixed, suggesting that employees might be motivated by job design no matter how they feel about their job context or how high or low they score on growth needs.[83]

autonomy The degree to which a job gives employees the freedom, independence, and discretion to schedule their work and determine the procedures used in completing it.

job rotation The practice of moving employees from one job to another.

job enlargement Occurs when more tasks are added to an existing job.

job enrichment Occurs when employees are given more responsibility for scheduling, coordinating, and planning their own work.

Job Design Practices That Motivate

Three main strategies can increase the motivational potential of jobs: job rotation, job enlargement, and job enrichment. This section also identifies several ways to implement job enrichment.

Job Rotation

Automobile industry leaders are aware of the motivational and physiological problems that repetitive work can create, so they have introduced **job rotation**, whereby employees move to different workstations every few hours. Job rotation has three main benefits. First, it minimizes health risks from repetitive strain and heavy lifting because employees use different muscles and physical positions in the various jobs. Second, it supports multiskilling (employees learn several jobs), which increases workforce flexibility in staffing the production process and in finding replacements for employees on vacation. A third benefit of job rotation is that it potentially reduces the boredom of highly repetitive jobs. However, organizational behavior experts continue to debate whether job rotation really is a form of job redesign because the jobs remain the same; they are still highly specialized. Critics argue that job redesign requires changes within the job, such as job enlargement.

> Job rotation minimizes health risks, supports multiskilling, and potentially reduces the boredom of highly repetitive jobs.

Job Enlargement

Job enlargement adds tasks to an existing job. This might involve combining two or more complete jobs into one or just adding one or two more tasks to an existing job. Either way, skill variety increases because there are more tasks to perform. Video journalists represent a clear example of an enlarged job. As Exhibit 5.9 illustrates, a traditional news team consists of a camera operator, a sound and lighting specialist, and the journalist who writes and presents or narrates the story. One video journalist performs all of these tasks.

Job enlargement significantly improves work efficiency and flexibility. However, research suggests that giving employees more tasks has little effect on motivation, performance, or job satisfaction. These benefits result only when skill variety is combined with more autonomy and job knowledge.[84] In other words, employees are motivated when they perform a variety of tasks *and* have the freedom and knowledge to structure their work to achieve the highest satisfaction and performance. These job characteristics are at the heart of job enrichment.

Job Enrichment

Job enrichment occurs when employees are given more responsibility for scheduling, coordinating, and planning their own work.[85] Generally, people in enriched jobs experience higher job satisfaction and work motivation, along with lower absenteeism and turnover. Productivity is also higher when task identity and job feedback are improved. Product and service quality tend to improve because job enrichment increases the jobholder's felt responsibility and sense of ownership over the product or service.[86]

One way to increase job enrichment is by combining highly interdependent tasks into one job. This *natural grouping* approach is reflected in the video journalist job. Video journalist was just described as an enlarged job, but it is also an example of job enrichment because it naturally groups tasks together to complete an entire product (a news clip). By forming natural work units, jobholders have stronger feelings of responsibility for an identifiable body of work.

▼**EXHIBIT 5.9** Job Enlargement of Video Journalists

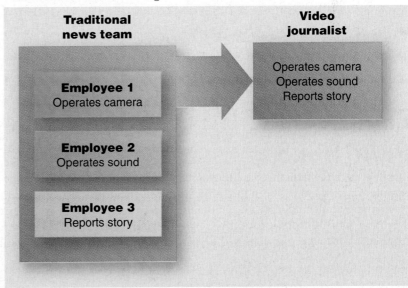

Traditional news team

Employee 1 Operates camera

Employee 2 Operates sound

Employee 3 Reports story

Video journalist

Operates camera
Operates sound
Reports story

empowerment
An individual's feelings of self-determination, meaning, competence, and impact regarding their role in the organization.

They feel a sense of ownership and therefore tend to provide better job quality. Forming natural work units increases task identity and task significance because employees perform a complete product or service and can more readily see how their work affects others.

A second job enrichment strategy, called *establishing client relationships,* involves putting employees in direct contact with their clients rather than using the supervisor as a go-between. By being directly responsible for specific clients, employees have more information and can make decisions affecting those clients.[87] Establishing client relationships also increases task significance because employees see a line-of-sight connection between their work and consequences for customers. This was apparent among medical secretaries at a large regional hospital in Sweden after the hospital reduced its workforce by 10 percent and gave the secretaries expanded job duties. Although these employees experienced more stress from the higher workloads, some of them also felt more motivated and satisfied because they now had direct interaction with patients. "Before, I never saw a patient; now they have a face," says one medical secretary. "I feel satisfied and pleased with myself; you feel someone needs you."[88]

Forming natural task groups and establishing client relationships are common ways to enrich jobs, but the heart of the job enrichment philosophy is to give employees more autonomy over their work. This basic idea is at the core of one of the most widely mentioned—and often misunderstood—practices, known as empowerment.

competence, and impact of the individual's role in the organization. If any dimension weakens, the employee's sense of empowerment will weaken.[89]

- *Self-determination:* Empowered employees feel that they have freedom, independence, and discretion over their work activities.
- *Meaning:* Employees who feel empowered care about their work and believe that what they do is important.
- *Competence:* Empowered people are confident about their ability to perform the work well and have a capacity to grow with new challenges.
- *Impact:* Empowered employees view themselves as active participants in the organization; that is, their decisions and actions influence the company's success.

Supporting Empowerment

Chances are that you have heard leaders say they are "empowering" the workforce. Empowerment is something that employees experience, so what these executives really mean is that they are changing the work environment to support the feeling of empowerment.[90] Numerous individual, job design, and organizational or work context factors support empowerment. At the individual level, employees must possess the necessary competencies to be able to perform the work as well as handle the additional decision-making requirements.[91] Job characteristics clearly influence the degree to which people feel empowered.[92] Employees are much more likely to experience self-determination when working in jobs with a high degree of autonomy and minimal bureaucratic control. They experience more meaningfulness when working in jobs with high levels of task identity and task significance. They experience more self-confidence

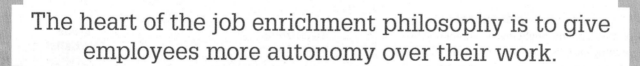

The heart of the job enrichment philosophy is to give employees more autonomy over their work.

EMPOWERMENT PRACTICES

Empowerment is a term that has been loosely tossed around in corporate circles and has been the subject of considerable debate among academics. However, the most widely accepted definition is that **empowerment** is a psychological concept represented by four dimensions: self-determination, meaning,

when working in jobs that allow them to receive feedback about their performance and accomplishments.

Several organizational and work context factors also influence empowerment. Employees experience more empowerment in organizations where information and other resources are easily accessible. Empowerment also requires a learning orientation culture. In other words, empowerment flourishes in organizations that appreciate the value of employee learning and that accept reasonable mistakes as a natural part of the learning process. Furthermore, empowerment requires corporate leaders who trust employees and are willing to take the risks that empowerment creates.[93]

With the right individuals, job characteristics, and organizational environment, empowerment can substantially improve motivation and performance. For instance, a study of bank employees concluded that empowerment improved customer service and tended to reduce conflict between employees and their supervisors. A study of nurses reported that empowerment is associated with higher trust in management, which ultimately influences job satisfaction, belief in and acceptance of organizational goals and values, and effective organizational commitment. Empowerment also tends to increase personal initiative because employees identify with and assume more psychological ownership of their work.[94] ▪

CHECK IT OUT!

mhhe.com/McShaneM

for study materials

including quizzes

and Internet resources

LEARNING OBJECTIVES

After reading this chapter, you should be able to

LO1 Describe the rational choice paradigm.

LO2 Explain why people differ from the rational choice paradigm when identifying problems/opportunities, evaluating/choosing alternatives, and evaluating decision outcomes.

LO3 Discuss the roles of emotions and intuition in decision making.

LO4 Describe the benefits of employee involvement and identify four contingencies that affect the optimal level of employee involvement.

LO5 Describe employee characteristics, workplace conditions, and specific activities that support creativity.

six

decision making
and creativity

"My job as CEO is not to make business decisions—it's to push managers to be leaders," says Sergio Marchionne. In reality, the chief executive of Fiat S.p.A. and Chrysler Group LLC makes more critical decisions in a week than most of us would make in a year. He was one of four people who negotiated the final proposal for Fiat to acquire a controlling share of Chrysler. When the acquisition was approved, he sped up decision making by canceling alliances that Chrysler had with other firms and, instead, ordered executives at Fiat and Chrysler to work cooperatively and intensively on new projects. Marchionne and his 23 direct reports hold two- to three-day weekend meetings where they listen to junior managers present their business plans and then vote on them using majority rule. Marchionne

believes that companies succeed by having the best decision makers, so he is actively involved in choosing new leaders and then judging them on the quality of their decisions.[1]

Decision making is a vital function in an organization's health; it's rather like breathing is to a human being. Indeed, turnaround experts such as Sergio Marchionne sometimes see themselves as physicians who resuscitate organizations by encouraging and teaching employees at all levels to make decisions more quickly and effectively. **Decision making** is the process of making choices among alternatives with the intention of moving toward some desired state of affairs.[2] The decision-making process can be viewed from three paradigms, and this chapter investigates all three of them. The chapter begins by

continued on p. 116

decision making
The conscious process of making choices among alternatives with the intention of moving toward some desired state of affairs.

rational choice paradigm The view in decision making that people should—and typically do—use logic and all available information to choose the alternative with the highest value.

subjective expected utility The probability (expectation) of satisfaction (utility) resulting from choosing a specific alternative in a decision.

continued from p. 115

outlining the rational choice paradigm of decision making. Next the limitations of this paradigm are discussed, including the human limitations of rational choice. We also examine the emerging paradigm that decisions consist of a complex interaction of logic and emotion. Later this chapter explores the role of employee involvement in decision making, including the benefits of involvement and the factors that determine the optimal level of involvement. The final section of this chapter examines the factors that support creativity in decision making, including characteristics of creative people, work environments that support creativity, and creativity activities. ■

decisions use pure logic and all available information to choose the alternative with the highest value—such as highest expected profitability, customer satisfaction, employee well-being, or some combination of these outcomes. These decisions sometimes involve complex calculations of data to produce a formula that points to the best choice.

In its extreme form, this calculative view of decision making represents the **rational choice paradigm**, which has dominated decision making philosophy in Western societies for most of written history.[3] The ultimate principle of the rational choice paradigm is to choose the alternative with the highest **subjective expected utility**.[4] Subjective expected utility is the probability (expectation) of satisfaction (utility) for each alternative. Rational choice assumes that decision makers naturally select the alternative that offers the greatest level of happiness (that is, maximization), such as highest returns for stockholders and highest satisfaction for customers, employees, government, and other stakeholders. The maximum subjective expected utility depends on the value (utility) of outcomes resulting from that choice and the probability of those outcomes occurring. For example, when Sergio Marchionne chooses someone to lead one of Chrysler's brands, he considers several desirable

> ## " Some problems are so complex that you have to be highly intelligent and well-informed just to be undecided about them. "
> —Laurence J. Peter

Learning Objectives

After reading this section, you should be able to

LO1 Describe the rational choice paradigm.

RATIONAL CHOICE PARADIGM OF DECISION MAKING

How should people make decisions in organizations? Most business leaders would likely answer this question by saying that effective decision making involves identifying, selecting, and applying the best possible alternative. In other words, the best

outcomes for that division (innovation, car sales, profitability, talent management, and so forth), the relative importance of each of those outcomes, and the probability that each candidate will deliver those outcomes. The candidate with the highest subjective expected utility has the highest probability of providing those valued outcomes.

Rational Choice Decision Making Process

Along with its principle of making decisions according to subjective expected utility, the rational choice paradigm assumes that decision makers follow the systematic process illustrated in Exhibit 6.1.[6] The first step is to identify the problem or recognize an opportunity. A *problem* is a deviation between the current and the desired situation—the gap between "what is" and "what ought to be." This deviation is a symptom of more

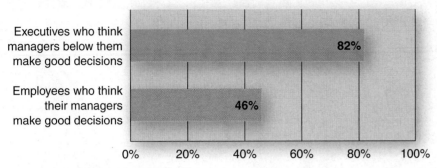

Are Bosses Good Decision Makers?[5]

Executives who think managers below them make good decisions — **82%**

Employees who think their managers make good decisions — **46%**

Employees in the United Kingdom are much less likely than senior executives to think that middle managers in their organization make good decisions. Employees with longer service have less favorable opinions than do employees with less than one year in the company. Results are based on 3,471 U.K. adults.

fundamental root causes that need to be corrected.[7] An *opportunity* is a deviation between current expectations and a potentially better situation that was not previously expected. In other words, decision makers realize that some decisions may produce results beyond current goals or expectations.

The second step involves choosing how to process the decision.[8] One issue is whether the decision maker has enough information or needs to involve others in the process. Later in this chapter, we'll examine the contingencies of employee involvement in the decision. Another issue is

> " The rational choice paradigm seems so logical, yet it is impossible to apply in reality. "

whether the decision is programmed or non-programmed. *Programmed decisions* follow standard operating procedures; they have been resolved in the past, so the optimal solution has already been identified and documented. In contrast, *nonprogrammed decisions* require all steps in the decision model because the problems are new, complex, or ill-defined. The third step is to identify and develop a list of possible solutions. This usually begins by searching for ready-made solutions, such as practices that have worked well for similar problems. If an acceptable solution cannot be found, then decision makers need to design a custom-made solution or modify an existing one.

The fourth step in the rational choice decision process is to choose the alternative with the highest subjective expected utility. This calls for all possible information about all possible alternatives and their outcomes, but the rational choice paradigm assumes this can be accomplished with ease. The fifth step in the rational choice decision process is to implement the selected alternative. Rational choice experts have little to say about this step because they assume implementation occurs without any problems. This is followed by the sixth step—evaluating whether the gap has narrowed between "what is" and "what ought to be." Ideally this information should come from systematic benchmarks so that relevant feedback is objective and easily observed.

Problems with the Rational Choice Paradigm

The rational choice paradigm seems so logical, yet it is impossible to apply in reality. One reason is that the model assumes people are efficient and logical information processing machines. In reality, people have difficulty recognizing problems; they cannot (or will not) simultaneously process the huge volume of information needed to identify the best solution; and they have difficulty recognizing when their choices have failed. The second reason why the rational model doesn't fit reality is that it focuses on logical thinking and completely ignores the fact that emotions also influence—perhaps even dominate—the decision-making process. As we will discover in this chapter, emotions both support and interfere with our quest to make better decisions.[9] With these points in mind, let's look again at each step in the rational choice decision making process, but with more detail about what really happens.

▼ **EXHIBIT 6.1** Rational Choice Decision Making Process

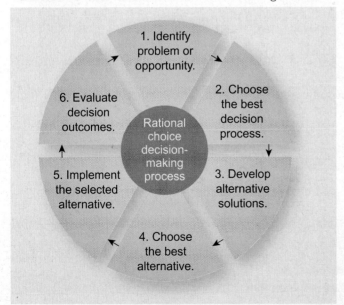

Rational choice decision-making process

1. Identify problem or opportunity.
2. Choose the best decision process.
3. Develop alternative solutions.
4. Choose the best alternative.
5. Implement the selected alternative.
6. Evaluate decision outcomes.

Learning Objectives

After reading the next four sections, you should be able to

LO2 Explain why people differ from the rational choice paradigm when identifying problems/opportunities, evaluating/choosing alternatives, and evaluating decision outcomes.

LO3 Discuss the roles of emotions and intuition in decision making.

IDENTIFYING PROBLEMS AND OPPORTUNITIES

When Albert Einstein was asked how he would save the world in one hour, he replied that the first 55 minutes should be spent defining the problem and the last 5 minutes solving it.[10] Einstein's point is that problem identification is not just the first step in decision making; it is arguably the most important step. But problems and opportunities are not clearly labeled objects that appear on our desks. Instead they are conclusions that we form from ambiguous and conflicting information. Indeed, as Chapter 3 explained, we form preferences as soon as we perceive something.[11] Specifically, we attach emotional markers (anger, caution, delight, and so on) to things we perceive, and these automatic emotional responses shape our attitudes that something is a problem, an opportunity, or irrelevant.

Problems with Problem Identification

The problem identification stage is itself filled with problems. Here are five of the most widely recognized concerns.[12]

Stakeholder Framing One school of management thought states that organizational decisions and actions are influenced mainly by what attracts management's attention, rather than by the objective reality of the external or internal environment.[13] This attention process is subject to a variety of cognitive biases, such as the decision maker's perceptual process, specific circumstances, and deliberate actions of stakeholders. Suppliers, employees, clients, and other stakeholders actively manage information so it becomes more (or less) conspicuous to decision makers. Furthermore, stakeholders present the information in such a way that it triggers the decision maker's emotional response that the information is a problem, an opportunity, or inconsequential.

Mental Models Even if stakeholders don't frame information, our cognitive structure does it through preconceived mental models. Recall from Chapter 3 that mental models are visual or relational images in our mind of the external world. They fill in information that we don't immediately see, thereby helping us to understand and navigate in our surrounding environment.

Many mental images are also prototypes—they represent models of how things should be. Unfortunately these mental models also blind us from seeing unique problems or opportunities because they produce a negative evaluation of things that are dissimilar to the mental model. If an idea doesn't fit the existing mental model of how things should work, the idea is dismissed as unworkable or undesirable.

Decisive Leadership Studies report that employees rate decisive leaders as more effective leaders.[14] Being decisive includes quickly forming an opinion about whether an event signals a problem or opportunity. Consequently, eager to look effective, many leaders quickly announce problems or opportunities before having a chance to logically assess the situation. The result, according to research, is often a poorer decision than would result if more time had been devoted to identifying the problem and evaluating the alternatives.

Solution-Focused Problems Decision makers have a tendency to define problems as veiled solutions.[15] For instance, someone might say, "The problem is that we need more control over our suppliers." This statement doesn't describe the problem; it is really a slightly rephrased presentation of a solution to an ill-defined problem. Decision makers engage in solution-focused problem identification because it provides comforting

solution focus a step further by seeing all problems as solutions that have worked well for them in the past, even though they were applied under different circumstances. Again, the familiarity of past solutions makes the current problem less ambiguous or uncertain.

Perceptual Defense People occasionally block out bad news. Their brain refuses to see information that threatens their self-concept. This phenomenon does not occur in everyone. Some people inherently avoid negative information, whereas others are more sensitive to it. Recent studies also report that people are more likely to disregard danger signals when they have limited control over the situation.[17]

For example, an investigation of the space shuttle *Columbia* disaster in 2003 revealed that NASA managers were in denial that the shuttle and its seven crew members were in trouble. NASA management almost immediately rejected a proposal by a team of engineers to have military satellites take photos of Columbia's exterior to determine if any damage was visible. Managers also criticized tests suggesting that damage could have occurred, yet quickly accepted a faulty test indicating that the shuttle was not damaged. In one meeting, *Columbia*'s lead flight director candidly admitted, "I don't think there is much we can do, so you know it's not really a factor during the flight because there isn't much we can do about it."[18]

> ## When the only tool you have is a hammer, all problems begin to resemble nails.[16]
> —Abraham Maslow

closure to the otherwise ambiguous and uncertain nature of problems. People with a strong need for cognitive closure (those who feel uncomfortable with ambiguity) are particularly prone to solution-focused problems. Some decision makers take this

Action PLAN
Identifying Problems and Opportunities More Effectively

- Be aware of the problem identification biases.
- Resist the temptation to look decisive.
- Develop a norm of divine discontent (an aversion to complacency).
- Discuss the situation with others.

Identifying Problems and Opportunities More Effectively

Recognizing problems and opportunities will always be a challenge, but one way to improve the process is by becoming aware of the five problem identification biases just described. For example, by recognizing that mental models restrict a person's perspective of the world, decision makers are more motivated to consider other perspectives of reality. Along with increasing their awareness of problem identification flaws, leaders require considerable willpower to resist the temptation of looking decisive when a more thoughtful examination of the situation should occur.

A third way to improve problem identification is for leaders to create a norm of "divine discontent." They are never satisfied with the status quo, and this aversion to complacency creates a mind-set that more actively searches for problems and opportunities.[19] Finally, employees can minimize the problems with problem identification by discussing the situation with colleagues. The logic here is that we can reduce blind spots in problem identification by hearing how others perceive that situation.

Opportunities also become apparent when outsiders explore this information from their different mental models.

EVALUATING AND CHOOSING ALTERNATIVES

According to the rational choice paradigm, people rely on logic to evaluate and choose alternatives. It also assumes that decision makers have well-articulated and agreed-on organizational goals, that they efficiently and simultaneously process facts about all alternatives and the consequences of those alternatives, and that they choose the alternative with the highest payoff.

Nobel Prize–winning organizational scholar Herbert Simon questioned these assumptions a half century ago. He argued that people engage in **bounded rationality** because they process limited and imperfect information and rarely select the best choice.[20] Simon and other OB experts demonstrated that how people evaluate and choose alternatives differs from the rational choice paradigm in several ways, as illustrated in Exhibit 6.2. These differences are so significant that many economists are now shifting from rational choice to bounded rationality assumptions in their theories. Let's look at these differences in terms of goals, information processing, and maximization.

Problems with Goals

The rational choice paradigm assumes that organizational goals are clear and agreed on. In fact, these conditions are necessary to identify "what ought to be" and, therefore, provide a standard against which to evaluate each alternative. Unfortunately organizational goals are often ambiguous or in conflict with each other.

Problems with Information Processing

The rational choice paradigm also makes several assumptions about the human capacity to process information. It assumes that decision makers can process information about all alternatives and their consequences, whereas this is not possible in reality. Instead people evaluate only a few alternatives and only some of the main outcomes of those alternatives.[21] For example, there may be dozens of computer brands to choose from and dozens of features to consider, yet people typically evaluate only a few brands and a few features.

> **bounded rationality**
> The view that people are bounded in their decision making capabilities, including access to limited information, limited information processing, and tendency toward satisficing rather than maximizing when making choices.

▼ **EXHIBIT 6.2** Rational Choice Assumptions versus Organizational Behavior Findings about Choosing Alternatives

Rational choice paradigm assumptions	Observations from organizational behavior
Goals are clear, compatible, and agreed upon.	Goals are ambiguous, are in conflict, and lack full support.
Decision makers can calculate all alternatives and their outcomes.	Decision makers have limited information processing abilities.
Decision makers evaluate all alternatives simultaneously.	Decision makers evaluate alternatives sequentially.
Decision makers use absolute standards to evaluate alternatives.	Decision makers evaluate alternatives against an implicit favorite.
Decision makers use factual information to choose alternatives.	Decision makers process perceptually distorted information.
Decision makers choose the alternative with the highest payoff.	Decision makers choose the alternative that is good enough (satisficing).

A related problem is that decision makers typically evaluate alternatives sequentially rather than all at the same time. As a new alternative comes along, it is immediately compared to an **implicit favorite**—an alternative that the decision maker prefers and that is used as a comparison with other choices. When choosing a new computer system, for example, people typically have an implicit favorite brand or model in their heads that they compare with the others. This sequential process of comparing alternatives with an implicit favorite occurs even when decision makers aren't consciously aware that they are doing this.[22]

Although the implicit favorite comparison process seems to be hardwired in human decision making (that is, we naturally compare things), it often undermines effective decision making because people distort information to favor their implicit favorite over the alternative choices. They tend to ignore problems with the implicit favorite and advantages of the alternative. Decision makers also overweight factors on which the implicit favorite is better and underweight areas in which the alternative is superior.[23]

Problems with Maximization

One of the main assumptions of the rational choice paradigm is that people want to (and are able to) choose the alternative with the highest payoff. This highest payoff is the "utility" in subjective expected utility.

> People distort information to favor their implicit favorite over the alternative choices in a decision.

Yet rather than aiming for maximization, people engage in **satisficing**—they choose an alternative that is satisfactory or "good enough."[24] They evaluate alternatives sequentially and select the first one perceived to be above a standard of acceptance for their needs and preferences. One reason why satisficing occurs is that, as mentioned earlier, decision makers have a natural tendency to evaluate alternatives sequentially, not all at the same time. They evaluate each alternative against the implicit favorite and eventually select an option that scores above a subjective minimum point considered to be good enough.

A second reason why people engage in satisficing rather than maximization is that choosing the best alternative demands more information processing capacity than people possess or are willing to apply. Studies have found that people like to have choices, but when exposed to many alternatives, they become cognitive misers by engaging in less optimal decision making.[25] Along with satisficing rather than maximizing, decision makers reduce cognitive effort by quickly discarding alternatives that fail a threshold level on one or two factors (such as color or size) and by evaluating only a few alternatives rather than all choices. Studies also report that making decisions when there are many alternatives can be cognitively and emotionally draining. Finally, there is evidence that as the number of choices increases, people are more likely to avoid making any decision at all!

Evaluating Opportunities

Opportunities are just as important as problems, but what happens when an opportunity is "discovered" is quite different from the process of problem solving. According to a major study of decision failures, decision makers do not evaluate several alternatives when they find an opportunity; after all, the opportunity *is* the solution, so why look for others? An opportunity is usually experienced as an exciting and rare revelation, so decision makers tend to have an emotional attachment to the opportunity. Unfortunately this emotional preference motivates decision makers to apply the opportunity and short-circuit any detailed evaluation of it.[27]

FACT. Too Many Choices

People avoid making choices in decisions that have too many alternatives, particularly when they lack expertise on that decision topic. In one study, consumers in a grocery store were presented with one of two jam-tasting booths. Some consumers saw a booth displaying 6 types of jam; others saw a booth displaying 24 types of jam. Thirty percent of shoppers who stopped at the 6-jam display bought some jam; only 3 percent of shoppers who stopped by the 24-jam display bought jam. The larger number of choices discouraged customers from making any purchase decision. These results are similar to those in other studies where people made decisions about chocolates, term essays, and pension plan investment options.[26]

Emotions and Making Choices

Herbert Simon and many other experts have presented plenty of evidence that people do not evaluate alternatives nearly as well as is assumed by the rational choice paradigm. However, they neglected to mention another glaring weakness with rational choice: it completely ignores the effect of emotions in human decision making. Just as both the rational and emotional brain centers alert us to problems, they also influence our choice of alternatives.[28] Emotions affect the evaluation of alternatives in three ways.

Emotions Form Early Preferences
The emotional marker process described earlier in this chapter as well as in previous chapters (Chapters 3 through 5) determines our preferences for each alternative. Our brain quickly attaches specific emotions to information about each alternative, and our preferred alternative is strongly influenced by those initial emotional markers. Of course logical analysis also influences which alternative we choose, but it requires strong logical evidence to change our initial preferences (initial emotional markers). Yet even logical analysis depends on emotions to sway our decision. Specifically, neuroscientific evidence says that information produced from logical analysis is tagged with emotional markers that then motivate us to choose or avoid a particular alternative. Ultimately emotions, not rational logic, energize us to make the preferred choice. In fact, people with damaged brain emotional centers have difficulty making choices.

Emotions Change the Decision Evaluation Process
A considerable body of literature indicates that moods and specific emotions influence the *process* of evaluating alternatives.[29] For instance, we pay more attention to details when in a negative mood, possibly because a negative mood signals that there is something wrong that requires attention. When in a positive mood, on the other hand, we pay less attention to details and rely on a more programmed decision routine. This phenomenon explains why executive teams in successful companies are often less vigilant about competitors and other environmental threats.[30] Research also suggests that decision makers who experience anger rely on stereotypes and other shortcuts to speed up the choice process. Anger also makes them more optimistic about the success of risky alternatives, whereas the emotion of fear tends to make them less optimistic. Overall, emotions shape *how* we evaluate information, not just which choice we select.

Emotions Serve as Information When We Evaluate Alternatives
The third way that emotions influence the evaluation of alternatives is through a process called "emotions as information." Marketing experts have found that we listen in on our emotions to gain guidance when making choices.[31] This process is similar to having a temporary improvement in emotional intelligence. Most emotional experiences remain below the level of conscious awareness, but people actively try to be more sensitive to these subtle emotions when making a decision.

When buying a new car, for example, you not only logically evaluate each vehicle's features; you also try to gauge your emotions when visualizing what it would be like to own each of the alternative cars on your list of choices. Even if you have solid information about the quality of each vehicle on key features (purchase price, fuel efficiency, maintenance costs, resale value, and so on), you are swayed by your emotional reaction to each vehicle and actively try to sense that emotional response when thinking about it. Some people pay more attention to these gut feelings, and personality tests such as the Myers-Briggs Type Indicator (see Chapter 2) identify individuals who listen in on their emotions more than others.[32] But all of us use our emotions as information to some degree. This phenomenon ties directly into our next topic, intuition.

Intuition and Making Choices

Intuition refers to the ability to know when a problem or opportunity exists and to select the best course of action without conscious reasoning.[33] Intuition is both an emotional experience and a rapid nonconscious analytic process. As mentioned in the previous section, the gut feelings we experience are emotional signals that have enough intensity to make us consciously aware of them. These signals warn us of impending problems, such as interrupted delivery of critical supplies, or motivate us to take advantage of an opportunity. Some intuition also directs us to preferred choices relative to other alternatives in that situation.

All gut feelings are emotional signals, but not all emotional signals are intuition. The key distinction is that intuition involves rapidly comparing our observations with deeply held patterns learned through experience.[35] These templates represent tacit knowledge that has been implicitly acquired over time. They are mental models that help us understand whether a current situation is good or bad, depending on how well that situation fits our mental model. When a template fits or doesn't fit the current

> Emotions shape how we evaluate information, not just which choice we select.

implicit favorite
A preferred alternative that the decision maker uses repeatedly as a comparison with other choices.

satisficing Selecting an alternative that is satisfactory or "good enough," rather than the alternative with the highest value (maximization).

intuition The ability to know when a problem or opportunity exists and to select the best course of action without conscious reasoning.

Using Intuition to Make People Decisions[34]

39%

of line managers **who say they rely on gut instinct as one of the most important factors when making any decisions about their people.**

45%

of employees who say they don't trust their manager's gut instincts on staff decisions relating to them or to others.

situation, emotions are produced that motivate us to act. Studies have found that chess masters receive emotional signals when they sense an opportunity through quick observation of a chessboard. When given the opportunity to think about the situation, chess masters can explain why they see a favorable move on the chessboard. However, their intuition signals the opportunity long before this rational analysis takes place.

As mentioned, some emotional signals are not intuition. As a result, some experts warn that we should not trust our gut feelings. The problem is that emotional responses are not always based on well-grounded mental models. Instead they occur when we compare the current situation to more remote templates, which may or may not be relevant. A new employee might feel confident about relations with a supplier, whereas an experienced employee might sense potential problems. The difference is that the new employee relies on templates from other experiences or industries that might not work well in this situation. Thus whether the emotions we experience in a situation represent intuition depends largely on our level of experience in that situation.

So far we have described intuition as an emotional experience (gut feeling) and a process in which we compare the current situation with well-established templates of the mind. Intuition also relies on *action scripts*—programmed decision routines that speed up our response to pattern matches or mismatches.[36] Action scripts effectively shorten the decision-making process by jumping from problem identification to selection of a solution. In other words, action

scripting is a form of programmed decision making. Action scripts are generic, so we need to consciously adapt them to the specific situation.

Making Choices More Effectively

It is difficult to get around the human limitations of making choices, but a few strategies help minimize these concerns. One important discovery is that decisions tend to have a higher failure rate when leaders are decisive rather than contemplative about the available options. Of course decisions can also be ineffective when leaders take too long to make a choice, but research indicates that a lack of logical evaluation of alternatives is a greater concern. By systematically assessing alternatives against relevant factors, decision makers minimize the implicit favorite and satisficing problems that occur when they rely on general subjective judgments. This recommendation does not suggest that we ignore intuition; rather it suggests that we use it in combination with careful analysis of relevant information.[37]

A second piece of advice is to remember that decisions are influenced by both rational and emotional processes. With this awareness, some decision makers deliberately revisit important issues so they look at the information in different moods and allow their initial emotions to subside. For example, if you sense that your team is feeling somewhat too confident when making an important competitive decision, you might decide to have the team members revisit the decision a few days later when they are thinking more critically. Another strategy is **scenario planning**, which is a disciplined method for imagining possible futures. It typically involves thinking about what would happen if a significant environmental condition changed and what the organization should do to anticipate and react to such an outcome.[38] Scenario planning is useful for choosing the best solutions under possible scenarios long before they occur because alternative actions are evaluated without the pressure and emotions that occur during real emergencies.

Making Choices More Effectively

- Be more contemplative than decisive for complex problems.
- Balance intuition with logical analysis.
- Practice scenario planning.

scenario planning
A systematic process of thinking about alternative futures and what the organization should do to anticipate and react to those environments.

escalation of commitment
Repeating an apparently bad decision or allocating more resources to a failing course of action.

IMPLEMENTING DECISIONS

Most writing about the decision-making process skips over the step describing implementation of the decision. Yet leading business writers and practitioners emphasize that execution—translating decisions into action—is one of the most important and challenging tasks of leaders. "When assessing candidates, the first thing I looked for was energy and enthusiasm for execution," says Larry Bossidy, the former CEO of Honeywell and Allied Signal.[40] Ways to implement decisions are discussed in later chapters, such as those about leadership and organizational change.

EVALUATING DECISION OUTCOMES

Contrary to the rational choice paradigm, decision makers aren't completely honest with themselves when evaluating the effectiveness of their decisions. One problem is *confirmation bias* (also known as *postdecisional justification* in the context of decision evaluation), which is the "unwitting selectivity in the acquisition and use of evidence."[41] When evaluating decisions, people with confirmation bias ignore or downplay the negative features of the selected alternative and overemphasize its positive features. Confirmation bias gives people an excessively optimistic evaluation of their decisions, but only until they receive clear and undeniable information to the contrary. Unfortunately it also inflates the decision maker's initial evaluation of the decision, so reality often comes as a painful shock when objective feedback is finally received.

Escalation of Commitment

Along with confirmation bias, people poorly evaluate their decision outcomes due to **escalation of commitment**—the tendency to repeat an apparently bad decision or allocate more resources to a failing course of action.[42] Why are people led deeper

FACT. What If . . .?[39]

Scenario planning has long been recognized as a potentially effective way to help decision makers figure out the best solutions to crises before those crises occur. Norwegian firm Dreyer Kompetense has created a variation of scenario planning as a board game for shipping, IT security, and other industries. The game teaches employees to make better decisions when facing risky situations. Participants first review several dozen scenarios and collectively determine which of these events pose the greatest risk. For example, one scenario in the shipping exercise is a situation where a fire knocks out all engines, resulting in a collision with another vessel. Next the team examines drills or exercises associated with the highest-risk scenarios. Finally the team determines what actions are required to prepare the company or ship for these high-risk scenarios.

and deeper into failing projects? Organizational behavior scholars have identified several reasons. Four of the main influences include self-justification, prospect theory effect, perceptual blinders, and closing costs.

Self-Justification Individuals are motivated to maintain their course of action when they have a high need to justify their decision. This self-justification is particularly evident when decision makers are personally identified with the project and have staked their reputations to some extent on the project's success.[43]

Prospect Theory Effect You would think that people dislike losing $50 just as much as they like receiving $50, but that isn't true for most of us. The negative emotions we experience when losing a particular amount are stronger than the positive emotions we experience when gaining the same amount. Consequently we are willing to take more risk to avoid losses than to increase our gains. This effect, called **prospect theory**, is a second explanation for escalation of commitment. Stopping a project is a certain loss, which is more painful to most people than the uncertainty of success associated with continuing to fund the project. Given the choice, decision makers choose the less painful option.[44]

Perceptual Blinders Escalation of commitment sometimes occurs because decision makers do not see problems soon enough.[45] They nonconsciously screen out or explain away negative information to protect self-esteem. Serious problems initially look like random errors along the trend line to success. Even when decision makers see that something is wrong, the information is sufficiently ambiguous that it can be misinterpreted or justified.

Closing Costs Even when a project's success is in doubt, decision makers will persist because the costs of ending the project are high or unknown. Stopping a major project before its completion may involve large financial penalties, a bad public image, or personal political costs.

Escalation of commitment may seem irrational. Usually it is, but there are exceptions. Studies suggest that throwing more money into a failing project is sometimes a logical attempt to further understand an ambiguous situation. This strategy is essentially a variation of testing unknown waters. By adding more resources, the decision maker gains new information about the effectiveness of these funds, which provides more feedback about the project's future success. This strategy is particularly common where the project has high closing costs.[47]

Evaluating Decision Outcomes More Effectively

One of the most effective ways to minimize escalation of commitment and confirmation bias is to ensure that the people who made the original decision are not the same people who later evaluate that decision. This separation of roles minimizes the self-justification effect because the person responsible for

FACT. Classics in Escalation of Commitment[46]

- When proposed in 1997, Scotland's new parliament building had an estimated cost of £50 million. The project was completed in 2006, four years behind schedule and at a cost of more than £400 million.

- Planning for the Sydney Opera House began in the 1950s with a projected cost of AUD $7 million. The final scaled-down version cost 10 times more than the original budget, took 17 years to complete, and has never functioned well for its intended purpose. Fortunately it has become a priceless iconic structure for Sydney and Australia.

- In the early 1980s the London Stock Exchange formed a project team called Taurus to build an information technology system that would replace paper-based stock settlement. The original budget of £6 million blew out to more than £400 million before the project was abandoned in 1993.

- In 1994 the provincial government in British Columbia wanted to revive its shipbuilding industry by having three catamaran-style ferries designed and built. The projected cost of CAD $210 million ballooned to nearly $500 million. The ferries were almost unusable due to their damaging wakes, maintenance problems, poor maneuverability, and high fuel costs. The three ferries were eventually auctioned off for $20 million.

- In the mid-1990s executives at health boards across Ireland funded a common payroll system with an estimated cost of US$12 million. The project was officially axed in 2007 with losses somewhere between $250 million and $350 million.

- Denver's International airport was supposed to include a state-of-the-art automated baggage handling system. Instead the project was eventually abandoned in the mid-1990s, causing the airport to open 16 months late and to be $2 billion over budget.

Action PLAN

Evaluating Decision Outcomes More Effectively

- Those who evaluate the success of a decision should be different from those who made the decision.

- Publicly establish a preset level at which the decision is abandoned or reevaluated.

- Seek out sources of systematic and clear feedback for the decision's outcomes.

- Involve several people in the decision evaluation process.

evaluating the decision is not connected to the original decision. A second strategy is to publicly establish a preset level at which the decision is abandoned or reevaluated. This is similar to a stop-loss order in the stock market, whereby the stock is sold if it falls below a certain price. The problem with this solution is that conditions are often so complex that it is difficult to identify an appropriate point to abandon a project.[48]

A third strategy is to find a source of systematic and clear feedback.[49] At some point even the strongest escalation and confirmation bias effects deflate when the evidence highlights the project's failings. A fourth strategy to improve the decision evaluation process is to involve several people in the evaluation. Coworkers continuously monitor each other and might notice problems sooner than someone working alone on the project. Employee involvement offers these and other benefits to the decision-making process, as we discuss next.

Learning Objectives

After reading the next two sections, you should be able to

LO4 Describe the benefits of employee involvement and identify four contingencies that affect the optimal level of employee involvement.

LO5 Describe employee characteristics, workplace conditions, and specific activities that support creativity.

EMPLOYEE INVOLVEMENT IN DECISION MAKING

In this world of rapid change and increasing complexity, leaders rarely have enough information to make the best decisions alone, so organizations rely on the knowledge and multiple perspectives of employees to more effectively solve problems or realize opportunities. "The Information Age has brought us into a democratic age, an age of participation and influence," says Traci Fenton, founder and CEO of WorldBlu, a consulting firm that specializes in employee involvement and organizational democracy.[50]

Employee involvement (also called *participative management*) refers to the degree to which employees influence how their work is organized and carried out.[51] Every organization has some form and various levels of employee involvement. At the lowest level, participation involves asking employees for information. They do not make recommendations and might not even know what the problem is. At a moderate level of involvement, employees are told about the problem and provide recommendations to the decision maker. At the highest level of involvement, the entire decision-making process is handed over to employees. They identify the problem, choose the best alternative, and implement their choice.

Benefits of Employee Involvement

For the past half-century, organizational behavior scholars have advised that employee involvement potentially improves

prospect theory
A natural tendency to feel more dissatisfaction from losing a particular amount than satisfaction from gaining an equal amount.

employee involvement
The degree to which employees influence how their work is organized and carried out.

Mixed
Involvement in Decisions[52]

58%
of American employees polled who say management regularly seeks out and values employees' ideas before making changes.

21%
of American employees polled who say their companies do not encourage employees at all levels to contribute ideas.

26%
of American employees polled in large companies who say lack of value placed on employee input is a major barrier to getting things done.

15%
of American employees who say they're unlikely to share with others in the company their ideas about improving how things get done.

creativity
The development of original ideas that make a socially recognized contribution.

divergent thinking
Reframing the problem in a unique way and generating different approaches to the issue.

decision-making quality and commitment.[53] Involved employees can help improve decision quality by recognizing problems more quickly and defining them more accurately. Employees are, in many respects, the sensors of the organization's environment. When the organization's activities misalign with customer expectations, employees are usually the first to know. Employee involvement ensures that everyone in the organization is quickly alerted to such problems.[54] Employee involvement can also potentially improve the number and quality of solutions generated. In a well-managed meeting, team members create synergy by pooling their knowledge to form new alternatives. In other words, several people working together can potentially generate more and better solutions than the same people working alone.

A third benefit of employee involvement is that, under specific conditions, it improves the evaluation of alternatives. Numerous studies of participative decision making, constructive conflict, and team dynamics have found that involvement brings out more diverse perspectives, tests ideas, and provides more valuable knowledge, all of which help the decision maker to select the best alternative.[55] A mathematical theorem introduced in 1785 by the Marquis de Condorcet states that the alternative selected by the team's majority is more likely to be correct than is the alternative selected by any team member individually.[56]

Along with improving decision quality, employee involvement tends to strengthen employee commitment to the decision. Rather than viewing themselves as agents of someone else's decision, staff members feel personally responsible for its success. Involvement

> ## "Tell me and I'll forget; show me and I may remember; involve me and I'll understand.
> —Chinese proverb

▼ **EXHIBIT 6.3** Model of Employee Involvement in Decision Making

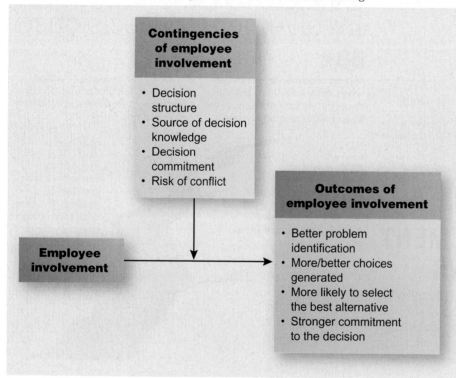

also has positive effects on employee motivation, satisfaction, and turnover. A recent study reported that employee involvement increases skill variety, feelings of autonomy, and task identity, all of which increase job enrichment and potentially employee motivation. Participation is also a critical practice in organizational change because employees are more motivated to implement the decision and less likely to resist changes resulting from the decision.[57]

Contingencies of Employee Involvement

If employee involvement is so wonderful, why don't leaders leave all decisions to employees? The answer is that the optimal level of employee involvement depends on the situation. The employee involvement model shown in Exhibit 6.3 lists four contingencies: decision structure, source of decision knowledge, decision commitment, and risk of conflict in the decision process.

- *Decision structure:* At the beginning of this chapter, we learned that some decisions are programmed, whereas others are nonprogrammed. Programmed decisions are less likely to need employee involvement because the solutions are already worked out from past incidents. In other words, the benefits of employee involvement increase with the novelty and complexity of the problem or opportunity.

- *Source of decision knowledge:* Subordinates should be involved in some level of decision making when the leader lacks sufficient knowledge and subordinates have additional information to improve decision quality. In many cases, employees are closer to customers and production activities, so they often know where the company can save money, improve product or service quality, and realize opportunities. This is particularly true for complex decisions where employees are more likely to possess relevant information.

- *Decision commitment:* Participation tends to improve employee commitment to the decision. If employees are unlikely to accept a decision made without their involvement, some level of participation is usually necessary.

- *Risk of conflict:* Two types of conflict undermine the benefits of employee involvement. First, if employee goals and norms conflict with the organization's goals, only a low level of employee involvement is advisable. Second, the degree of involvement depends on whether employees will agree on the preferred solution. If conflict is likely, high involvement (that is, employees making the decision alone) would be difficult to achieve.

Employee involvement is an important component of the decision-making process. To make the best decisions, we need to involve people who have the most valuable information and who will increase commitment to implement the decision. Another important component of decision making is creativity, which we discuss next.

CREATIVITY

Creativity refers to the development of original ideas that make a socially recognized contribution.[58] Although there are unique conditions for creativity that we discuss over the next few pages, it is really part of the decision-making process described earlier in the chapter. We rely on creativity to find problems, identify alternatives, and implement solutions. Creativity is not something saved for special occasions. It is an integral part of decision making.

Exhibit 6.4 illustrates one of the earliest and most influential models of creativity.[59] Although there are other models of the creative process, many of them overlap with the model presented here. The first stage is *preparation*—the person's or team's effort to acquire knowledge and skills regarding the problem or opportunity. Preparation involves developing a clear understanding of what you are trying to achieve through a novel solution and then actively studying information related to the topic.

The second stage, called *incubation*, is the period of reflective thought. We put the problem aside, but our mind is still working on it in the background.[60] The important condition here is to maintain a low-level awareness by frequently revisiting the problem. Incubation does not mean you forget about the problem or issue. Incubation assists **divergent thinking**—reframing the problem in a unique way and generating different approaches to the issue. This contrasts with *convergent thinking*—calculating the conventionally accepted "right answer" to a logical problem. Divergent thinking breaks us away from existing mental models so we can apply concepts or processes from completely different areas of life. Consider the following classic example: Years ago, the experimental lightbulbs in Thomas Edison's lab kept falling off their fixtures until a technician wondered whether the threaded caps that screwed down tightly on kerosene bottles would work on lightbulbs. They did, and the design remains to this day.[61]

Insight, the third stage of creativity, refers to the experience of suddenly becoming aware of a unique idea.[62] Insight is often visually depicted as a lightbulb, but a better image would be a brief flash of light or perhaps a briefly flickering candle because these bits of inspiration are fleeting and can be quickly lost if

▼**EXHIBIT 6.4** The Creative Process Model

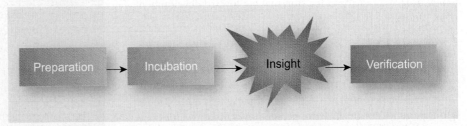

Source: Based on Graham Wallas, The Art of Thought (New York: Harcourt Brace Jovanovich, 1926).

not documented. For this reason, many creative people keep a journal or notebook nearby so they can jot down their ideas before they disappear. Also, flickering ideas don't keep a particular schedule; they might come to you at any time of day or night.

Insights are merely rough ideas. Their usefulness requires verification through detailed logical evaluation, experimentation, and further creative insight. Thus, although *verification* is labeled as the final stage of creativity, it is really the beginning of a long process of creative decision making toward development of an innovative product or service.

Characteristics of Creative People

Everyone is creative, but some people have a higher potential for creativity. Four of the main characteristics that give individuals more creative potential are intelligence, persistence, knowledge and experience, and a cluster of personality traits and values representing independent imagination (see Exhibit 6.5).

- *Cognitive and practical intelligence:* Creative people have above-average intelligence to synthesize information, analyze ideas, and apply their ideas.[63] Like the fictional sleuth Sherlock Holmes, creative people recognize the significance of small bits of information and are able to connect them in ways that no one

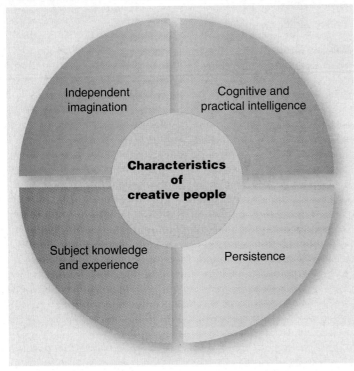

Independent imagination

Cognitive and practical intelligence

Characteristics of creative people

Subject knowledge and experience

Persistence

else could imagine. They also have *practical intelligence*—the capacity to evaluate the potential usefulness of their ideas.

- *Persistence:* Creative people have persistence, which includes a higher need for achievement, a strong motivation from the task itself, and a moderate or high degree of self-esteem. Studies report that inventors have higher levels of confidence and optimism than do people in the general population, and these traits motivate inventors to continue working on and investing in a project after others have urged them to quit.[64]

- *Subject knowledge and experience:* Creative people possess sufficient knowledge about and experience with the subject.[65] Essentially, we require existing knowledge to discover new knowledge. However, knowledge and experience are double-edged swords. They can also undermine creativity by forming mental models that lead to "mindless behavior," whereby people stop questioning their assumptions.[66] This relates to the discussion earlier in this chapter about mental models—namely that they sometimes restrict the decision maker's ability to see different perspectives. To overcome this limitation, some corporate leaders like to hire people from other industries and areas of expertise.

- *Independent imagination:* Creative people possess a cluster of personality traits and values that support an independent imagination: high openness to experience, moderately low need for affiliation, and strong values around self-direction and stimulation.[67] Openness to experience is a Big Five personality dimension representing the extent to which a person is imaginative, curious, sensitive, open-minded, and original (see Chapter 2). Creative people have a moderately low need for affiliation, so they are less embarrassed when making mistakes. Self-direction includes the values of creativity and

independent thought; stimulation includes the values of excitement and challenge. Together these values form openness to change—representing the motivation to pursue innovative ways (see Chapter 2).

Organizational Conditions Supporting Creativity

Intelligence, persistence, knowledge and experience, and independent imagination represent a person's creative potential, but the extent to which this translates into more creative output depends on a work environment that supports the creative process.[68] Several job and workplace characteristics have been identified in the literature, and different combinations of situations can equally support creativity; there isn't one best work environment.[69]

One of the most important conditions that supports creative practice is that the organization has a *learning orientation;* that is, leaders recognize that employees make reasonable mistakes as part of the creative process. "Creativity comes from failure," Samsung Electronics CEO and vice chairman Yun Jong-yong recently advised employees. "We should reform our corporate culture to forgive failure if workers did their best."[71] Motivation from the job itself is another important condition for creativity.[72] Employees tend to be more creative when they believe their work benefits the organization and the larger society (task significance) and when they have the freedom to pursue novel ideas without bureaucratic delays (autonomy). Creativity is about changing things, and change is possible only when employees have the authority to experiment. More generally, jobs encourage creativity when they are challenging and aligned with the employee's competencies.

Along with supporting a learning orientation and intrinsically motivating jobs, companies foster creativity through open communication and sufficient resources. They also provide a comfortable degree of job security, which explains why creativity

Nurturing a Creative Workplace

- Maintain a learning orientation culture (reasonable mistakes are viewed as learning experiences).
- Ensure that jobs have high task significance and autonomy.
- Ensure that jobs are aligned with employee competencies.
- Encourage open communication across the organization.
- Give employees sufficient resources to perform their work.
- Ensure that employees experience a comfortable degree of job security.
- Create nontraditional workspaces.
- Create a culture of mutual support.

Google is a hotbed of creativity, partly because the firm encourages its engineers to use 20 percent of their time to develop projects of their choosing. "Almost everything that is interesting which Google does starts out as a 20 percent time idea," says Google CEO Eric Schmidt.[70]

suffers during times of downsizing and corporate restructuring.[73] Some companies also support creativity by designing nontraditional workspaces, such as unique buildings or unconventional office areas.[74]

To some degree, creativity also improves with support from leaders and coworkers. One study reported that effective product champions provide enthusiastic support for new ideas. Other studies suggest that coworker support can improve creativity in some situations, whereas competition among coworkers improves creativity in other situations.[75] Similarly, it isn't clear how much pressure should be exerted on employees to produce creative ideas. Extreme time pressures are well-known creativity inhibitors, but lack of pressure doesn't seem to produce the highest creativity either.

Activities That Encourage Creativity

Hiring people with strong creative potential and providing a work environment that supports creativity are two cornerstones of a creative workplace. The third cornerstone consists of various activities that help employees think more creatively. One set of activities involves redefining the problem. Employees might be encouraged to revisit old projects that have been set aside. After a few months of neglect, these projects might be seen in new ways.[76] Another strategy involves asking people unfamiliar with the issue (preferably with different expertise) to explore the problem with you. You would state the objectives and give some facts and then let the other person ask questions to further understand the situation. By describing the problem, listening to questions, and hearing what others think, you are more likely to form new perspectives on the issue.[77]

A second set of creativity activities, known as *associative play*, ranges from art classes to impromptu storytelling and acting. For example, British media giant OMD sends employees to two-day retreats in the countryside, where they play grapefruit croquet, chant like medieval monks, and pretend to be dog collars. "Being creative is a bit like an emotion; we need to be stimulated," explains Harriet Frost, one of OMD's specialists in building creativity. "The same is true for our imagination and its ability to come up with new ideas. You can't just sit in a room and devise hundreds of ideas."[78] Another associative play activity, called *morphological analysis,* involves listing different dimensions of a system and the elements of each dimension and then looking at each combination. This encourages people to carefully examine combinations that initially seem nonsensical.

A third set of activities that promote creative thinking falls under the category of *cross-pollination*.[79] Cross-pollination occurs when people from different areas of the organization exchange ideas. Mother, the London-based creative agency, has an unusual policy and workspace to encourage cross-pollination. The company's 100 or so employees perform their daily work around one monster-size table—an 8-foot-wide reinforced concrete slab that extends 300 feet like a skateboard ramp around the entire floor. Every three weeks, employees are asked to relocate their laptops, portable telephones, and trolleys to another area around the table. Why the musical-chairs exercise? "It encourages cross-pollination of ideas," explains Stef Calcraft, one of Mother's founding partners. "You have people working on the same problem from different perspectives. It makes problem solving much more organic."[80]

CHECK IT OUT!

mhhe.com/McShaneM

for study materials

including quizzes

and Internet resources

Cross-pollination highlights the fact that creativity rarely occurs alone. Some creative people may be individualistic, but most creative ideas are generated through teams and informal social interaction. "This whole thing about the solitary tortured artist is nonsense I think," says John Collee, the screenwriter who penned such films as *Happy Feet* and *Master and Commander*. "All the great creative people I know have become great precisely because they know how to get along with people and swim around in the communal unconscious."[81] The next chapter turns our attention to the main concepts in team effectiveness, as well as ways to improve team decision making and creativity. ■

team dynamics

Teams have become an important part of contemporary organizations. More than half of the organizations polled in a recent survey use teams to a high or very high extent to conduct day-to-day business. Furthermore, 77 percent of those firms rely on teams for one-time projects and 67 percent rely on teams for ongoing projects. A decade ago 50 percent of American executives surveyed said their work was done in teams. Only 20 percent of those executives said they worked in teams in the 1980s.[1] Teamwork has also become more important in scientific research. A recent study of almost 20 million research publications reported that the percentage of journal articles written by teams rather than individuals has increased substantially over the past five decades. Team-based articles also had a much higher number of subsequent citations, suggesting that journal articles written by teams are superior to articles written by individuals.[2]

Why are teams becoming so important, and how can organizations

continued on p. 136

LEARNING OBJECTIVES

After reading this chapter, you should be able to

LO1 Discuss the benefits and limitations of teams, and explain why people are motivated to join informal groups.

LO2 Outline the team effectiveness model and discuss how task characteristics, team size, and team composition influence team effectiveness.

LO3 Discuss how the four team processes—team development, norms, cohesion, and trust—influence team effectiveness.

LO4 Discuss the characteristics and factors required for success of self-directed teams and virtual teams.

LO5 Identify four constraints on team decision making and discuss the advantages and disadvantages of four structures aimed at improving team decision making.

continued from p. 135

strengthen their potential for organizational effectiveness? We find the answers to these (and other) questions in this chapter about team dynamics. This chapter begins by defining *teams* and examining the reasons why organizations rely on teams and why people join informal groups in organizational settings. A large segment of this chapter examines a model of team effectiveness, which includes team and organizational environment, team design, and the team processes of development, norms, cohesion, and trust. We then turn our attention to two specific types of teams: self-directed teams and virtual teams. The final section of this chapter looks at the challenges and strategies for making better decisions in teams. ■

Learning Objectives

After reading the next two sections, you should be able to

LO1 Discuss the benefits and limitations of teams, and explain why people are motivated to join informal groups.

TEAMS AND INFORMAL GROUPS

Teams are groups of two or more people who interact and influence each other, are mutually accountable for achieving common goals associated with organizational objectives, and perceive themselves as a social entity within an organization.[3] This definition has a few important components worth repeating. First, all teams exist to fulfill some purpose, such as repairing electric power lines, assembling a product, designing a new social welfare program, making an important decision, or achieving some other goal. Second, team members are held together by their interdependence and need for collaboration to achieve common goals. All teams require some form of communication so members can coordinate and share common objectives. Third, team members influence each other, although some members may be more influential than others regarding the team's goals and activities. Finally, a team exists when its members perceive themselves to be a team.

Exhibit 7.1 briefly describes various types of teams in organizations. Some teams are permanent, whereas others are temporary; some are responsible for making products or providing services, whereas others exist to make decisions or share knowledge. Each type of team has been created deliberately to serve an organizational purpose. Some teams, such as skunkworks teams, are not initially sanctioned by management yet

▼**EXHIBIT 7.1** Types of Teams in Organizations

Team Type	Description
Departmental teams	Teams that consist of employees who have similar or complementary skills and are located in the same unit of a functional structure; usually have minimal task interdependence because each person works with employees in other departments.
Production/service/leadership teams	Typically multiskilled (employees have diverse competencies), team members collectively produce a common product/service or make ongoing decisions; production/service teams typically have an assembly-line type of interdependence, whereas leadership teams tend to have tight interactive (reciprocal) interdependence.
Self-directed teams	Similar to production/service teams except (1) they are organized around work processes that complete an entire piece of work requiring several interdependent tasks and (2) they have substantial autonomy over the execution of those tasks (i.e., they usually control inputs, flow, and outputs with little or no supervision).
Advisory teams	Teams that provide recommendations to decision makers; include committees, advisory councils, work councils, and review panels; may be temporary, but often permanent, some with frequent rotation of members.
Task force (project) teams	Usually multiskilled, temporary teams whose assignment is to solve a problem, realize an opportunity, or design a product or service.
Skunkworks	Multiskilled teams that are usually located away from the organization and are relatively free of its hierarchy; often initiated by an entrepreneurial team leader who borrows people and resources (*bootlegging*) to design a product or service.
Virtual teams	Teams whose members operate across space, time, and organizational boundaries and are linked through information technologies to achieve organizational tasks; may be a temporary task force or permanent service team.
Communities of practice	Teams (but often informal groups) bound together by shared expertise and passion for a particular activity or interest; main purpose is to share information; often rely on information technologies as the main source of interaction.

are called "teams" because members work toward an organizational objective.

Informal Groups

For the most part this chapter focuses on formal teams, but employees also belong to informal groups. All teams are groups, but many groups do not satisfy our definition of teams. Groups include people assembled together, whether or not they have any interdependence or organizationally focused objective. The friends you meet for lunch are an *informal group*, but they wouldn't be called a team because they have little or no interdependence (each person could just as easily eat lunch alone) and no organizationally mandated purpose. Instead they exist primarily for the benefit of their members. Although the terms are used interchangeably, *teams* has largely replaced *groups* in the language of business when referring to employees who work together to complete organizational tasks.[4]

Why do informal groups exist? One reason is that human beings are social animals. Our drive to bond is hardwired through evolutionary development, creating a need to belong to informal groups.[5] This is evidenced by the fact that people invest considerable time and effort forming and maintaining social

teams Groups of two or more people who interact and influence each other, are mutually accountable for achieving common goals associated with organizational objectives, and perceive themselves as a social entity within an organization.

Informal Groups and Organizational Outcomes Informal groups are not created to serve organizational objectives. Nevertheless, they have a profound influence on organizations and individual employees. Informal groups potentially minimize employee stress because, as just mentioned, group members provide emotional and informational social support. This stress-reducing capability of informal groups improves employee well-being, thereby improving organizational effectiveness. Informal groups are also the backbone of *social networks*, which are important sources of trust building, information sharing, power, influence, and employee well-being in the workplace.[8] Chapter 8 describes the growing significance of social networking sites similar to Facebook and MySpace to encourage the formation of informal groups and associated communication. Chapter 9 examines the importance of social networks as a source of influence in organizational settings. Employees with strong informal networks tend to have more power and influence because they receive better information and preferential treatment from others and their talent is more visible to key decision makers.

> [Informal groups are not created to serve organizational objectives, yet they have a profound influence on organizations and individual employees.]

relationships without any special circumstances or ulterior motives. A second explanation is provided by social identity theory, which states that individuals define themselves by their group affiliations (see Chapters 2 and 3). Thus we join groups—particularly those that are viewed favorably by others and that have values similar to our own—because they shape and reinforce our self-concepts.[6]

A third reason why people are motivated to form informal groups is that such groups accomplish tasks that cannot be achieved by individuals working alone. For example, employees will sometimes create a group to oppose organizational changes because the group collectively has more power than individuals who try to bring about change alone. A fourth explanation for informal groups is that we are comforted by the mere presence of other people and are therefore motivated to be near them in stressful situations. When in danger, people congregate near each other even though doing so serves no protective purpose. Similarly, employees tend to mingle more often after hearing rumors that the company might be acquired by a competitor. As Chapter 4 explained, this social support minimizes stress by providing emotional and informational support to buffer the stress experience.[7]

ADVANTAGES AND DISADVANTAGES OF TEAMS

Many corporate leaders are convinced that teams make a difference. Rackspace Hosting, Inc., organizes most of its 2,700 employees into teams of 12 to 20 people. The San Antonio, Texas, provider of enterprise-level Web infrastructure assigns every customer to one of these dedicated teams, which provides around-the-clock service. New Zealand Post's largest delivery branch was the poorest-performing branch in the country until employees were reorganized into teams. Now it is the company's model operation as measured by performance and morale. A cross-functional team of employees at the City of Indianapolis conducted a "chuckhole kaizen response" to identify more efficient ways to repair potholes. The team found ways to address pothole complaints in 48 hours rather than the previous average of 19 days.[9]

Why are teams so important in so many organizations around the world? The answer to this question has a long history.[11]

FACT. **Organizations That Value Teamwork**[10]

Company	What They Say about Teamwork
PricewaterhouseCoopers (New York)	The best solutions come from working together with colleagues and clients. Effective teamwork requires relationships, respect, and sharing.
Veolia Environnement (Paris)	Teamwork is a crucial element in the way Veolia Environnement works worldwide. Working together and pooling knowledge and experience ensure that every success is a shared victory.
Great Falls Clinic (Montana)	The combination of physicians and employees working together to improve patient care is our commitment and can be defined as "Team Care." . . . Our Great Falls Clinic team will continue to provide leadership in medicine through teamwork.
Whole Foods Market (Texas)	Working in our team environment means (a) communicating frequently, openly, and compassionately; (b) meeting regularly to discuss team operations and make consensus decisions; (c) appreciating each other's contributions; (d) working together to maximize rewards from team member incentive programs; (e) celebrating our successes together; and (f) having fun!
Colgate-Palmolive (New York)	All Colgate people are part of a global team, committed to working together across countries and throughout the world. Only by sharing ideas, technologies, and talents can the company achieve and sustain profitable growth.

Early research on British coal mining in the 1940s and the Japanese economic miracle of the 1970s, and a huge number of investigations since then, have revealed that *under the right conditions,* teams make better decisions, develop better products and services, and create a more engaged workforce than do employees working alone.[12] Similarly, team members can quickly share information and coordinate tasks, whereas these processes are slower and prone to more errors in traditional departments led by supervisors. Teams typically provide superior customer service because they provide more breadth of knowledge and expertise to customers than individual "stars" can offer.

In many situations, people are potentially more motivated when working in teams than when working alone.[13] One reason for this motivation is that, as we mentioned a few paragraphs ago, employees have a drive to bond and are motivated to fulfill the goals of groups to which they belong. This motivation is particularly strong when the team is part of the employee's social identity. "Our employees really value teamwork," says Lucie Bennett, a manager at Ergon Energy, which supplies electricity throughout most of Queensland, Australia. "It is a real key to our success and there's a real family culture, a sort of feeling that everyone is your mate."[14]

In addition, people are more motivated in teams because they are accountable to fellow team members, who monitor performance more closely than a traditional supervisor. This is particularly true where the team's performance depends on the

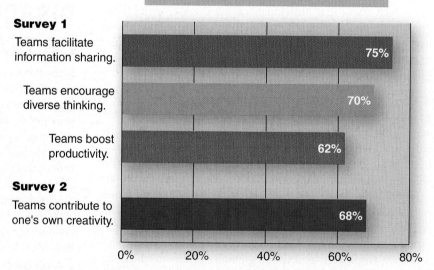

Companies/Employees See the Benefits of Teams[15]

Survey 1
Teams facilitate information sharing. 75%

Teams encourage diverse thinking. 70%

Teams boost productivity. 62%

Survey 2
Teams contribute to one's own creativity. 68%

Percentage of respondents who agree that each is a benefit of working in teams. Survey 1 consisted of 278 human resource professionals in the United States. Survey 2 consisted of a representative sample of 1,000 working Canadians.

worst performer, such as on an assembly line, where how fast the product is assembled depends on the speed of the slowest employee. In some circumstances, performance improves when employees work near others because coworkers become benchmarks of comparison. Employees are also motivated to work harder because of apprehension that their performance will be compared to others' performance.

The Challenges of Teams

Despite the many benefits of teams, they are not always as effective as individuals working alone.[16] Teams are usually better suited to complex work, such as designing a building or auditing a company's financial records. Under these circumstances, one person rarely has all the necessary knowledge and skills. Instead the work is performed better if its tasks are divided into more specialized roles, with people in those specialized jobs coordinating with each other. In contrast, work is typically performed more effectively by individuals alone when they have all the necessary

process losses
Resources (including time and energy) expended toward team development and maintenance rather than the task.

Brooks's law
Also called the "mythical man-month," this principle says that adding more people to a late software project only makes it later.

> ❝ If I could solve all the problems myself, I would.
> —Thomas Edison (when asked why he had a team of 21 people) ❞

knowledge and skills and the work cannot be divided into specialized tasks or is not complex enough to benefit from specialization. Even where the work can and should be specialized, a team structure might not be necessary if the tasks performed by several people require minimal coordination.

The main problem with teams is that they have additional costs called **process losses**—resources (including time and energy) expended toward team development and maintenance rather than the task.[17] It is much more efficient for an individual to work out an issue alone than to resolve differences of opinion with other people. For a team to perform well, team members need to agree and have mutual understanding of their goals, the strategy for accomplishing those goals, their specific roles, and informal rules of conduct.[18] Developing and maintaining these team requirements divert time and energy away from performing the work. The process loss problem is particularly apparent when more staff are added or replace others on the team. Team performance suffers when a team adds members because those employees need to learn how the team operates and how to coordinate efficiently with other team members. When people are added, process losses also occur in redistributing the workload, sometimes with the result that tasks are duplicated or accidentally forgotten.

The software industry even has a name for this phenomenon: **Brooks's law** (also called the "mythical man-month") says that adding more people to a late software project only makes it later! According to some sources, Apple Computer may have fallen into this trap in the recent development of its professional photography software program, called Aperture.

When the project started to fall behind schedule, the manager in charge of the Aperture project increased the size of the team—some sources say it ballooned from 20 to almost 150 engineers and quality assurance staff within a few weeks. Unfortunately adding so many people further bogged down the project. The result? When Aperture was finally released, it was nine months late and considered one of Apple's buggier software offerings.[19]

Social Loafing Perhaps the best-known limitation of teams is the risk of productivity loss due to **social loafing**. Social loafing occurs when people exert less effort (and usually perform at a lower level) when working in teams than when working alone.[20] Social loafing tends to be more serious when the individual's performance is less likely to be noticed, such as when people work together in large teams. The individual's output is also less noticeable where the team produces a single output (rather than each team member producing output), such as finding a single solution to a customer's problem. There is less social loafing when each team member's contribution is more noticeable; this can be achieved by reducing the size of the team, for example, or measuring each team member's performance.

Social loafing also depends on the employee's motivation to perform the work. Social loafing is less prevalent when the task is interesting because individuals are more motivated by the work itself to perform their duties. For example, one recent study revealed that student apathy explains some of the social loafing that occurs in university student teams. Social loafing is also less common when the team's objective is important, possibly because individuals experience more pressure from coworkers to perform well. Finally, social loafing occurs less frequently among members who value team membership and believe in working toward the team's objectives.[21]

In summary, teams can be powerful forces for competitive advantage, or they can be more trouble than they are worth—so much so that job performance and morale decline when employees are placed in teams. To understand when teams are better than individuals working alone, we need to more closely examine the conditions that make teams effective or ineffective. The next few sections of this chapter discuss the model of team effectiveness.

Minimizing Social Loafing

- Make each team member's contribution more visible/identifiable.
- Redesign the work so it is more interesting (more job enrichment).
- Assign team objectives that are important or valued by team members.
- Increase the extent to which team members value their membership in the team.

social loafing
Occurs when people exert less effort (and usually perform at a lower level) when working in groups than when working alone.

Learning Objectives

After reading the next two sections, you should be able to

LO2 Outline the team effectiveness model and discuss how task characteristics, team size, and team composition influence team effectiveness.

A MODEL OF TEAM EFFECTIVENESS

Why are some teams effective while others fail? Before answering this question, let's clarify the meaning of *team effectiveness*. A team is effective when it benefits the organization, its members, and its own survival.[22] First, most teams exist to serve some organizational purpose, so effectiveness is measured partly by the achievement of those objectives. Second, a team's effectiveness relies on the satisfaction and well-being of its members. People join groups to fulfill their personal needs, so effectiveness is measured partly by this need fulfillment. Finally, team effectiveness includes the team's viability—its ability to survive. It must be able to maintain the commitment of its members, particularly during the turbulence of the team's development. The team will fall apart without this commitment because members leave or provide minimal effort. The team must also secure sufficient resources and find a benevolent environment in which to operate.

Researchers have developed several models over the years to identify the features or conditions that make some teams more effective than others.[23] Exhibit 7.2 integrates the main components of these team effectiveness models. We will closely examine each component over the next several pages. This exhibit is really a meta-model that connects several theories because each component (team development, team cohesion, and so forth) includes its own set of theories and models to explain how that component operates.

Organizational and Team Environment

The organizational and team environment represents all conditions beyond the team's boundaries that influence its effectiveness. Team members tend to work together more effectively when they are at least partly rewarded for team performance.[24] Another environmental factor is the organizational structure; teams flourish when organized around work processes because this structure increases interaction and interdependence among team members and reduces interaction with people outside the team. High-performance teams also depend on organizational leaders who provide support and strategic direction while team members focus on operational efficiency and flexibility.[25] The physical layout of the team's workspace can

▼ **EXHIBIT 7.2** Team Effectiveness Model

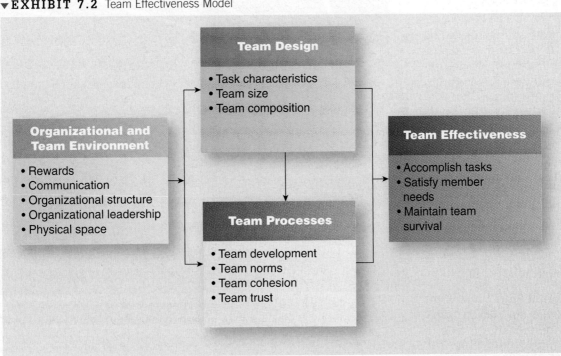

task interdependence
The extent that team members must share materials, information, or expertise in order to perform their jobs.

also make a difference. For instance, Toyota Motor Corporation occasionally congregates developers or department managers in a large open-space room (called an *obeya*) to resolve issues and improve collaboration across functions. Toyota claims the obeya arrangement has significantly cut product development time and costs.[26]

TEAM DESIGN ELEMENTS

Along with setting up a team-friendly environment, leaders need to carefully design the team itself, including task characteristics, team size, team composition, and team roles.

Task Characteristics

What type of work is best for teams? Recall that teams operate better than individuals working alone on work that is sufficiently complex, such as launching a business in a new market, developing a computer operating system, or constructing a bridge. Complex work requires skills and knowledge beyond the competencies of one person. Teams are particularly well suited when the complex work can be divided into more specialized roles and the people in the specialized roles require frequent coordination with each other. Some evidence also suggests that teams work best with well-structured tasks because it is easier to coordinate such work among several people.[27]

For example, La-Z-Boy, Inc., previously organized production staff around their respective trades. "You would have a group of upholsterers in one place, the sewing people in another section, the framing people in another area, and everyone would just work in the same place all day," recalls Jovie Dabu, general manager of La-Z-Boy's manufacturing facility in Redlands, California. Now the company organizes one or two people from each trade into teams of five to seven employees who work side by side to build an entire piece of furniture. La-Z-Boy executives say the new team structure has improved coordination, communication, and team bonding. "The idea is to help make workers accountable, but also to give them a sense of ownership of what they do," said Greg Bachman, La-Z-Boy's production manager.[28]

One task characteristic that is particularly important for teams is **task interdependence**—the extent to which team members must share materials, information, or expertise to perform their jobs.[29] Apart from complete independence, there are three levels of task interdependence, as illustrated in Exhibit 7.3. The lowest level of interdependence, called *pooled interdependence*, occurs when an employee or work unit shares a common resource, such as machinery, administrative support, or a budget, with other employees or work units. This would occur in a team setting where each member works alone but shares raw materials or machinery to perform her or his otherwise independent tasks. Interdependence is higher under *sequential interdependence*, in which the output of one person becomes the direct input for another person or unit. Sequential interdependence occurs where team members are organized in an assembly line.

Reciprocal interdependence, in which work output is exchanged back and forth among individuals, produces the highest degree of interdependence. People who design a new product or service would typically have reciprocal interdependence because their design decisions affect others involved in the design process. Any decision made by the design engineers would influence the work of the manufacturing engineer and purchasing specialist, and vice versa. Employees with reciprocal interdependence should be organized into teams to facilitate coordination in their interwoven relationship.

As a rule, the higher the level of task interdependence, the greater the need to organize people into teams rather than have them work alone. A team structure improves interpersonal communication and thus results in better coordination. High

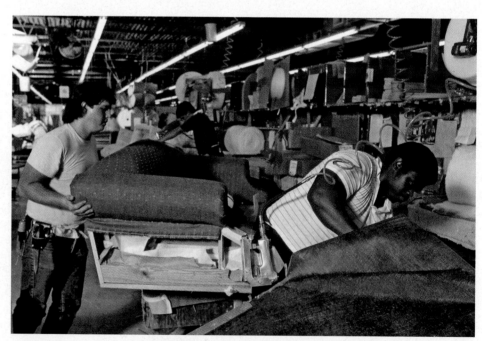

La-Z-Boy, Inc., organized production employees into teams because making entire piece of furniture requires coordination and working together increases their mutual accountability and sense of ownership for the entire piece of furniture they build.

> # TEAMS SHOULD BE LARGE ENOUGH TO PROVIDE THE NECESSARY COMPETENCIES AND PERSPECTIVES TO PERFORM THE WORK, YET SMALL ENOUGH TO MAINTAIN EFFICIENT COORDINATION AND MEANINGFUL INVOLVEMENT OF EACH MEMBER.

▼ **EXHIBIT 7.3** Levels of Task Interdependence

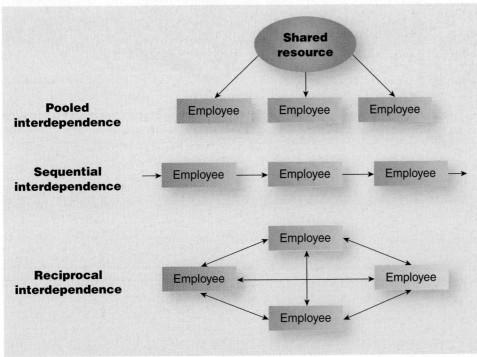

task interdependence also motivates most people to be part of the team. However, the rule that a team should be formed when employees have high interdependence applies when team members have the same task goals, such as serving the same clients or collectively assembling the same product. When team members have different goals (such as serving different clients) but must depend on other team members to achieve those unique goals, teamwork might create excessive conflict. Under these circumstances, the company should try to reduce the level of interdependence or rely on supervision as a buffer or mediator among employees.

Team Size

What is the ideal size for a team? One popular (but untested) rule is that the optimal team size is between five and seven people. Yet some observers have recently argued that tasks are getting so complex that many teams need to have more than 100 members.[30] Unfortunately the former piece of advice is excessively simplistic, and the latter seems to have lost sight of the meaning and dynamics of real teams. Generally teams should be large enough to provide the necessary competencies and perspectives to perform the work, yet small enough to maintain efficient coordination and meaningful involvement of each member.[31]

"You need to have a balance between having enough people to do all the things that need to be done, while keeping the team small enough so that it is cohesive and can make decisions effectively and speedily," says Jim Hassell, a senior executive at Broadcast Australia (which operates one of the most extensive terrestrial broadcast transmission networks in the world).[32] Small teams (say, less than a dozen members) operate effectively because they have less process loss. Members of smaller teams also tend to feel more engaged because they get to know the other team members (which improves trust), have more influence on the group's norms and goals, and feel more responsible for the team's success and failure.

Should companies have 100-person teams if the task is highly complex? The answer is that a group this large probably isn't a team, even if management calls it one. A team exists when its members interact and influence each other, are mutually accountable for achieving common goals associated with organizational objectives, and perceive themselves as a social entity within an organization. It is very difficult for everyone in a 100-person work unit to influence each other and experience enough cohesion to perceive themselves as team members. Executives at Whole Foods Market were aware that

real teams are much smaller than 100 people when the food retailer opened its huge store in New York City's Columbus Circle. The store had 140 cashiers—far too many people for one cashier team—so Whole Foods Market divided the group into teams with a dozen employees each. All cashiers meet as one massive group every month to discuss production issues, but the smaller teams work effectively on a day-to-day basis.[33]

Team Composition

To work effectively in a team, employees must have more than technical skills to perform their own work; they must also be able and willing to perform that work in a team environment. The most frequently mentioned characteristics or behaviors of effective team members are the "five C's" illustrated in Exhibit 7.4: cooperating, coordinating, communicating, comforting, and conflict resolving. The first three competencies are mainly (but not entirely) task-related, while the last two primarily assist team maintenance:[34]

- *Cooperating:* Effective team members are willing and able to work together rather than alone. This includes sharing resources and being sufficiently adaptive or flexible to accommodate the needs and preferences of other team members, such as rescheduling use of machinery so another team member with a tighter deadline can use it.

- *Coordinating:* Effective team members actively manage the team's work so it is performed efficiently and harmoniously. For example, effective team members keep the team on track and help integrate the work performed by different members. This typically requires that effective team members know the work of other team members, not just their own.

- *Communicating:* Effective team members transmit information freely (rather than hoarding), efficiently (using the best channel and language), and respectfully (minimizing arousal of negative emotions). They also listen actively to coworkers.

- *Comforting:* Effective team members help coworkers maintain positive and healthy psychological states. They show empathy, provide psychological comfort, and build coworker feelings of confidence and self-worth.

Sources: Based on information in V. Rousseau, C. Aubé, and A. Savoie, "Teamwork Behaviors: A Review and an Integration of Frameworks," *Small Group Research* 37, no. 5 (2006), pp. 540–70; M. L. Loughry, M. W. Ohland, and D. D. Moore, "Development of a Theory-Based Assessment of Team Member Effectiveness," *Educational and Psychological Measurement* 67, no. 3 (2007), pp. 505–24.

opposing effects of diversity on team effectiveness.[36] One effect is that diverse teams make better decisions under some circumstances, for three reasons. One reason is that people from different backgrounds tend to see a problem or opportunity from different angles. Team members have different mental models, so they are more likely to identify viable solutions to difficult problems.

A second reason why diverse teams tend to make better decisions is that they have a broader pool of technical competencies. For example, each team at Rackspace Hosting consists of more than a dozen people with diverse skills such as account management, systems engineering, technical support, billing expertise, and data center support. The enterprise-level Web infrastructure company requires these diverse technical competencies within each team to serve the needs of customers assigned to the team. A third reason favoring teams with diverse members is that they provide better representation of the team's constituents, such as other departments or clients from similarly diverse backgrounds. A team responsible for designing and launching a new service, for instance, should have representation from the organization's various specializations so people in those work units will support the team's decisions.

Team diversity offers many advantages, but it also presents a number of opposing challenges.[37] Specifically, diverse employees take longer to become a

> [Team diversity offers many advantages, but it also presents a number of opposing challenges.]

- *Conflict resolving:* Conflict is inevitable in social settings, so effective team members have the skills and motivation to resolve dysfunctional disagreements among team members. This requires effective use of various conflict-handling styles as well as diagnostic skills to identify and resolve the structural sources of conflict.

These characteristics of effective team members are associated with conscientiousness and extraversion personality traits, as well as with emotional intelligence. Furthermore, the old saying "One bad apple spoils the barrel" seems to apply to teams; one team member who lacks these teamwork competencies may undermine the dynamics of the entire team.[35]

Team Diversity Another important dimension of team composition is diversity. There are two distinct and sometimes

high-performing team. This occurs partly because team members take longer to bond with people who are different from them, particularly when others hold different perspectives and values (that is, when they have deep level diversity). Diverse teams are susceptible to "fault lines"—hypothetical dividing lines that may split a team into subgroups along gender, ethnic, professional, or other dimensions. These fault lines reduce team effectiveness by reducing the motivation to communicate and coordinate with teammates across the hypothetical divisions. In contrast, members of teams with minimal diversity experience higher satisfaction, less conflict, and better interpersonal relations. Consequently, homogeneous teams tend to be more effective on tasks requiring a high degree of cooperation and coordination, such as emergency response teams.

role A set of behaviors that people are expected to perform because of the positions they hold in a team and organization.

team building Formal activities intended to improve the development and functioning of a work team.

Learning Objectives

After reading this section, you should be able to

LO3 Discuss how the four team processes—team development, norms, cohesion, and trust—influence team effectiveness.

TEAM PROCESSES

The third set of elements in the team effectiveness model, collectively known as *team processes*, includes team development, norms, cohesion, and trust. These elements represent characteristics of the team that continuously evolve.

Team Development

Team members must resolve several issues and pass through several stages of development before emerging as an effective work unit. They need to get to know and trust each other, understand and agree on their respective roles, discover appropriate and inappropriate behaviors, and learn how to coordinate with each other. The longer team members work together, the better they develop common or complementary mental models, mutual understanding, and effective performance routines to complete the work.

A popular model that captures many team development activities is shown in Exhibit 7.5.[38] The model shows teams moving systematically from one stage to the next, while the dashed lines illustrate that teams might fall back to an earlier stage of development as new members join or other conditions disrupt the team's maturity. *Forming,* the first stage of team development, is a period of testing and orientation in which members learn about each other and evaluate the benefits and costs of continued membership. People tend to be polite, will defer to authority, and try to find out what is expected of them and how they will fit into the team. The *storming* stage is marked by interpersonal conflict as members become more proactive and compete for various team roles. Members try to establish norms of appropriate behavior and performance standards.

During the *norming* stage, the team develops its first real sense of cohesion as roles are established and a consensus forms around group objectives and a common or complementary team-based mental model. By the *performing* stage, team members have learned to efficiently coordinate and resolve conflicts. In high-performance teams, members are highly cooperative, have a high level of trust in each other, are committed to group objectives, and identify with the team. Finally, the *adjourning* stage occurs when the team is about to disband. Team members shift their attention away from task orientation to a relationship focus.

U.S. Air Force Security Forces Squadrons are deployed for special "outside-the-wire" operations, so they achieve high team development through ongoing training, including this simulated fire team assignment. "I have 13 guys under me, and every single day I work with the same 13 guys," explains squad leader Staff Sgt. Eric Hammons. "They're going to know that when I go into a room I'm going to the right. And they know that since I'm going right they go left."[41]

The five-stage model in Exhibit 7.5 masks two distinct processes during team development.[39] The first process—*developing team identity*—refers to the transition that individuals make from viewing the team as something "out there" to something that is part of themselves. In other words, team development occurs when employees shift their view of the team from "them" to "us." This relates to becoming familiar with the team, making it part of their social identity, and shaping the team to better fit their prototype of an ideal team. The other process—*developing team competence*—includes developing habitual routines with teammates and forming shared or complementary mental models.[40] Team mental models are visual or relational mental images that are shared by team members. For example, members of a

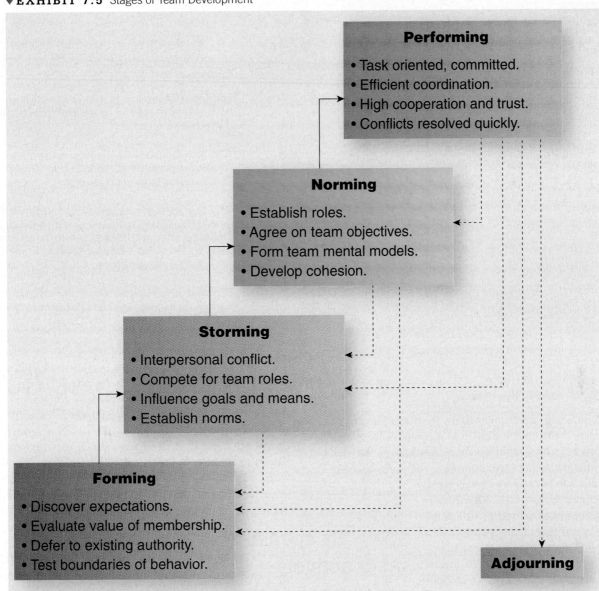

Performing
- Task oriented, committed.
- Efficient coordination.
- High cooperation and trust.
- Conflicts resolved quickly.

Norming
- Establish roles.
- Agree on team objectives.
- Form team mental models.
- Develop cohesion.

Storming
- Interpersonal conflict.
- Compete for team roles.
- Influence goals and means.
- Establish norms.

Forming
- Discover expectations.
- Evaluate value of membership.
- Defer to existing authority.
- Test boundaries of behavior.

Adjourning

newly formed team might have different views about customer service (quality of interaction, speed of service, technical expertise provided, and the like). As the team develops, these views converge into a shared mental model of customer service.

Team Roles An important part of the team development process is forming and reinforcing team roles. A **role** is a set of behaviors that people are expected to perform because they hold certain positions in a team and organization.[42] In a team setting, some roles help the team achieve its goals; other roles maintain relationships within the team. Some team roles are formally assigned to specific people. For example, team leaders are usually expected to initiate discussion, ensure that everyone has an opportunity to present his or her views, and help the team reach agreement on the issues discussed.

Team members are assigned specific roles within their formal job responsibilities. Yet team members also assume informal roles that suit their personalities and values as well as the wishes of other team members. These informal roles, which are negotiated throughout the team development process, range from supporting others to initiating new ideas. Informal team roles are shared, but many are eventually associated with one or two people on the team.[43]

Accelerating Team Development through Team Building **Team building** consists of formal activities intended to improve the development and functioning of a work team.[44] To a large extent, team building attempts to speed up the team development process. This process may be applied to new teams, but it is more commonly introduced for existing teams that

Team-Building Activity	Description	Example
Team volunteering events	Teams of employees spend a day providing a public service to the community.	Timberland Co. employees work in teams to clean up the environment, plant trees, and work on community revitalization projects.
Team scavenger/ treasure hunt competitions	Teams follow instructions to find clues or objects collected throughout the community.	With instructions and GPS devices, teams of Verizon Wireless employees track down 32 clues around Tampa within a three-hour time limit.
Team sports/ exercise competitions	Wide variety of sports or health activities, ranging from volleyball tournaments across departments to teams competing globally in health activities.	More than 200 teams (seven employees per team) at Nestlé UK compete each year in the Global Corporate Challenge. Each team has the challenge of taking a virtual walk around the world in 125 days, which is about 10,000 steps per person.
Team cooking competitions	Employees work in teams to prepare a meal under the guidance of a master chef.	Employees at the Singapore operations of German engineering firm Siemens attend lessons at a bakery and then test their baking skills in teams.

have regressed to earlier stages of team development due to membership turnover or loss of focus.

Some team-building interventions clarify the team's performance goals, increase the team's motivation to accomplish these goals, and establish a mechanism for systematic feedback on the team's goal performance. Others try to improve the team's problem-solving skills. A third category of team building clarifies and reconstructs each member's perceptions of her or his role as well as the role expectations that member has of other team members. Role definition team building also helps the team develop shared mental models—common internal representations of the external world, such as how to interact with clients, maintain machinery, and engage in meetings. Research indicates that team processes and performance depend on how well team members share common mental models about how they should work together.[45]

A popular form of team building is aimed at improving relations among team members. This includes activities that help team members learn more about each other, build trust in each other, and develop ways to manage conflict within the team. Popular interventions such as wilderness team activities, paintball wars, and obstacle course challenges are typically offered to build trust. "If two colleagues hold the rope for you while you're climbing 10 meters up, that is truly team-building," suggests a partner in a German communications consulting firm who participated in that team-building event.[46]

> " By speaking up or actively coaching the team, leaders can often subdue dysfunctional norms while developing useful norms. "

Although team-building activities are popular, their success is less certain than many claim.[48] One problem is that team-building activities are used as general solutions to general team problems. A better approach is to begin with a sound diagnosis of the team's health and then select team-building interventions that address weaknesses.[49] Another problem is that team building is applied as a one-shot medical inoculation that every team should receive when it is formed. In truth, team building is an ongoing process, not a three-day jump start.[50] Finally, we must remember that team building occurs on the job, not just on an obstacle course or in a national park. Organizations should encourage team members to reflect on their work experiences and to experiment with just-in-time learning for team development.

Team Norms

Norms are the informal rules and shared expectations that groups establish to regulate the behavior of their members. Norms apply only to behavior, not to private thoughts or feelings. Furthermore, norms exist only for behaviors that are important to the team.[51] Norms are enforced in various ways. Coworkers grimace if we are late for a meeting, or they make sarcastic comments if we don't have our part of the project completed on time. Norms are also directly reinforced through praise from high-status members, more access to valued resources, or other rewards available to the team. But team members often conform to prevailing norms without direct reinforcement or punishment because they identify with the group and want to align their behavior with the team's values. The more closely a person's social identity is connected to a group, the more the individual is motivated to avoid negative sanctions from that group.[52]

How Team Norms Develop Norms develop when teams form because people need to anticipate or predict how others will act. Even subtle events during the team's formation, such as how team members initially greet each other and where they sit in the first meetings, can initiate norms that are later difficult to change. Norms also form as team members discover behaviors that help them function more effectively (such as the need to respond quickly to e-mail). In particular, a critical event in the team's history can trigger formation of a norm or sharpen a previously vague one. A third influence on team norms are the experiences and values that members bring to the team. If members of a new team value work/life balance, norms are likely to develop that discourage long hours and work overload.[53]

Preventing and Changing Dysfunctional Team Norms Team norms often become deeply anchored, so the best way to avoid norms that undermine organizational success or employee well-being is to establish desirable norms when the team is first formed. One way to do this is to clearly state desirable norms when the team is created. Another approach is to select people with appropriate values. If organizational leaders want their teams to have strong safety norms, they should hire people who already value safety and who clearly identify the importance of safety when the team is formed.

The suggestions so far refer to new teams, but how can organizational leaders maintain desirable norms in older teams? First, as one recent study affirmed, leaders often have the capacity to alter existing norms.[54] By speaking up or actively coaching the team, they can often subdue dysfunctional norms while developing useful norms. Team-based reward systems can also weaken counterproductive norms; however, studies report that employees might continue to adhere to a dysfunctional team norm (such as limiting output) even though this behavior reduces their paycheck. Finally, if dysfunctional norms are deeply ingrained and the previous solutions don't work, it may be necessary to disband the group and replace it with people having more favorable norms.

Team Cohesion

Team cohesion refers to the degree of attraction people feel toward the team and their motivation to remain members. It is a characteristic of the team, including the extent to which its members are attracted to the team, are committed to the team's goals or tasks, and feel a collective sense of team pride.[55] Thus team cohesion is an emotional experience, not just a calculation of whether to stay in or leave the team. It exists when team members make the team part of their social identity. Team cohesion is associated with team development because members develop a team identity as part of the team development process.

Influences on Team Cohesion Several factors influence team cohesion: member similarity, team size, member interaction, difficult entry, team success, and external competition or challenges. For the most part, these factors reflect the individual's social identity with the group and beliefs about how team membership will fulfill personal needs.

norms The informal rules and shared expectations that groups establish to regulate the behavior of their members.

team cohesion The degree of attraction people feel toward the team and their motivation to remain members.

- *Member similarity:* Teams have higher cohesion or become cohesive more quickly when members are similar to each other. This influence on cohesion is due to the similarity–attraction effect, which states that people with similar backgrounds and values are more comfortable with and attracted to each other. It is usually more difficult or takes longer for teams with diverse members to become cohesive, but this depends on the form of diversity. For example, teams consisting of people from different job groups seem to gel together just as well as teams of people from the same job.[56]

- *Team size:* Smaller teams tend to have more cohesion than larger teams because it is easier for a few people to agree on goals and coordinate work activities. However, small teams have less cohesion when they lack enough members to perform the required tasks.

- *Member interaction:* Teams tend to have more cohesion when team members interact with each other fairly regularly. This occurs when team members perform highly interdependent tasks and work in the same physical area.

- *Somewhat difficult entry:* Teams tend to have more cohesion when entry to the team is restricted. The more elite the team, the more prestige it confers on its members, and the more they tend to value their membership in the unit. However, research suggests that severe initiations can weaken team cohesion because of the adverse effects of humiliation, even for those who successfully endure the initiation.[57]

- *Team success:* Cohesion is both emotional and instrumental, with the latter referring to the notion that people feel more cohesion to teams that fulfill their needs and goals. Consequently, cohesion increases with the team's level of success.[58] Furthermore, individuals are more likely to attach their social identities to successful teams than to those with a string of failures.[59]

- *External competition and challenges:* Team cohesion tends to increase when members face external competition or have a valued objective that is challenging. This might include a threat from an external competitor or friendly competition

> People who belong to high-cohesion teams are motivated to maintain their membership and to help the team perform effectively.

from other teams. Employees value their membership on the team because of its ability to overcome the threat or competition and as a form of social support. However, cohesion can dissipate when external threats are severe because these threats are stressful and cause teams to make less effective decisions.[60]

Consequences of Team Cohesion Every team must have some minimal level of cohesion to maintain its existence. People who belong to high-cohesion teams are motivated to maintain their membership and to help the team perform effectively. Compared to low-cohesion teams, high-cohesion team members spend more time together, share information more frequently, and are more satisfied with each other. They provide each other with better social support in stressful situations.[61]

Members of high-cohesion teams are generally more sensitive to each other's needs and develop better interpersonal relationships, thereby reducing dysfunctional conflict. When conflict does arise, members tend to resolve their differences

swiftly and effectively. With better cooperation and more conformity to norms, high-cohesion teams usually perform better than low-cohesion teams.[62] However, as Exhibit 7.6 illustrates, this relationship holds true only when team norms are compatible with organizational values and objectives. Cohesion motivates employees to perform at a level more consistent with team norms, so when those norms conflict with the organization's success (such as when norms support high absenteeism or acting unethically), high cohesion will reduce team performance.[63]

Team Trust

Any relationship—including the relationship among team members—depends on a certain degree of trust.[64] **Trust** refers to positive expectations one person has toward another person in situations involving risk (see Chapter 4).[65] A high level of trust occurs when others affect you in situations where you are at risk but you believe they will not harm you. Trust includes both your beliefs and conscious feelings about the relationship with other team members. In other words, a person both logically evaluates

▼ **EXHIBIT 7.6** Effect of Team Cohesion on Task Performance

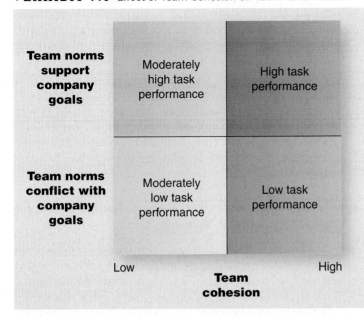

	Low	High
Team norms support company goals	Moderately high task performance	High task performance
Team norms conflict with company goals	Moderately low task performance	Low task performance

Team cohesion

the situation as trustworthy and feels that it is trustworthy.[66] Trust is built on three foundations: calculus, knowledge, and identification (see Exhibit 7.7).

Calculus-based trust represents a logical calculation that other team members will act appropriately because they face sanctions if their actions violate reasonable expectations.[67] It offers the lowest potential trust and is easily broken by a violation of expectations. Generally, calculus-based trust alone cannot sustain a team's relationship because it relies on deterrence.

Knowledge-based trust is based on the predictability of another team member's behavior. Even if we don't agree with a particular team member's actions, his or her consistency generates some level of trust. Knowledge-based trust also relates to confidence in the other person's ability or competence, such as the confidence that exists when we trust a physician.[68] Knowledge-based trust offers a higher potential level of trust and is more stable because it develops over time.

Identification-based trust is based on mutual understanding and an emotional bond among team members. It occurs when team members think, feel, and act like each other. High-performance teams exhibit this level of trust because they share the same values and mental models. Identification-based trust is potentially the strongest and most robust of all three types of trust. The individual's self-concept is based partly on membership in the team, and he or she believes the members' values highly overlap, so any transgressions by other team members are quickly forgiven. People are more reluctant to acknowledge a violation of this high-level trust because it strikes at the heart of their self-concept.

Dynamics of Team Trust Employees typically join a team with a moderate or high level—not a low level—of trust in their new coworkers. The main explanation for the initially high trust (called *swift trust*) in organizational settings is that people usually believe fellow team members are reasonably competent (knowledge-based trust) and they tend to develop some degree of social identity with the team (identification-based trust). Even when working with strangers, most of us display some level of trust, if only because it supports our self-concept of being a good person.[69] However, trust is fragile in new relationships because it is based on assumptions rather than well-established experience. Consequently, studies report that trust tends to decrease rather than increase over time. This is unfortunate because employees become less forgiving and less cooperative toward others as their level of trust decreases, and this undermines team and organizational effectiveness.[70]

The team effectiveness model is a useful template for understanding how teams work—and don't work—in organizations. With this knowledge in hand, let's briefly investigate two types of teams that have received considerable attention among OB experts and practitioners: self-directed teams and virtual teams.

▼ **EXHIBIT 7.7** Three Foundations of Trust in Teams

	Type of trust	Description
High ↑	**Identification-based trust**	• Based on common mental models and values. • Increases with person's social identity with team.
Potential level of trust	**Knowledge-based trust**	• Based on predictability and competence. • Fairly robust.
Low ↓	**Calculus-based trust**	• Based on deterrence. • Fragile and limited potential because dependent on punishment.

Every Whole Foods Market store is divided into about 10 self-directed teams (prepared-foods team, seafood team, and so on) who make decisions about inventory, product placement, scheduling, and other matters affecting their work unit.[72]

Learning Objectives

After reading the next three sections, you should be able to

LO4 Discuss the characteristics and factors required for success of self-directed teams and virtual teams.

LO5 Identify four constraints on team decision making and discuss the advantages and disadvantages of four structures aimed at improving team decision making.

SELF-DIRECTED TEAMS

Self-directed teams (SDTs) are cross-functional groups, organized around work processes, that complete an entire piece of work requiring several interdependent tasks and that have substantial autonomy over the execution of those tasks.[71] From this definition we see two distinct features of SDTs. First, these teams complete an entire piece of work requiring several interdependent tasks. This type of work arrangement clusters the team members together while minimizing interdependence and interaction with employees outside the team. The result is a close-knit group of employees who depend on each other to accomplish their individual tasks. For example, Whole Foods Market employees responsible for a store's fish department would naturally work more closely with each other than with members of other teams.

The second distinctive feature of SDTs is that they have substantial autonomy over the execution of their tasks. In particular, these teams plan, organize, and control work activities with little or no direct involvement of a higher-status supervisor. The teams at Whole Foods Market, for instance, are considered self-directed because they have considerable autonomy and responsibility for decisions in their work area, including managing inventory, profitability, scheduling, and hiring.

Self-directed teams are found in many industries, ranging from petrochemical plants to aircraft parts manufacturing. Some sources estimate that most of the top-rated manufacturing firms in North America rely on SDTs.[73] The popularity of SDTs is consistent with research indicating that they potentially increase both productivity and job satisfaction. For instance, one study found that car dealership service shops that organize employees into SDTs are significantly more profitable than shops where employees work without a team structure. Another study reported that both short- and long-term measures of customer satisfaction increased after street cleaners in a German city were organized into SDTs.[74]

Success Factors for Self-Directed Teams

Whether self-directed teams succeed or fail depends on several factors.[75] SDTs should be responsible for an entire work process, such as making an entire product or providing a service. This structure keeps each team sufficiently independent from other teams, yet it demands a relatively high degree of interdependence among employees within the team.[76] SDTs should also have sufficient autonomy to organize and coordinate their work. Autonomy allows them to respond quickly and effectively to client and stakeholder demands. It also motivates team members through feelings of empowerment. Finally, SDTs are more successful when the work site and technology support coordination and communication among team members and increase job enrichment.[77] Too often management

calls a group of employees a "team," yet the work layout, assembly-line structure, and other technologies isolate the employees from each other.

VIRTUAL TEAMS

Virtual teams are teams whose members operate across space, time, and organizational boundaries and are linked through information technologies to achieve organizational tasks.[78] Virtual teams differ from traditional teams in two ways: (1) They are not usually colocated (do not work in the same physical area), and (2) due to their lack of colocation, members of virtual teams depend primarily on information technologies rather than face-to-face interaction to communicate and coordinate their work effort.

Virtual teams have become more common across most organizations. One reason for this trend is that information technologies have made it easy to communicate and coordinate with people at a distance.[79] The shift from production-based to knowledge-based work is a second reason why virtual teamwork is feasible. It isn't yet possible to make a product when team members are located apart, but most of us are now in jobs that process mainly knowledge.

Information technologies and knowledge-based work make virtual teams *possible,* but organizational learning and globalization are two reasons why they are increasingly *necessary.* Virtual teams represent a natural part of the organizational learning process because they encourage employees to share and use knowledge where geography limits more direct forms of collaboration. Globalization makes virtual teams increasingly necessary because employees are spread around the planet rather than around one city. Thus global businesses depend on virtual teamwork to leverage their human capital.

self-directed teams (SDTs)
Cross-functional work groups organized around work processes, that complete an entire piece of work requiring several interdependent tasks, and that have substantial autonomy over the execution of those tasks.

virtual teams
Teams whose members operate across space, time, and organizational boundaries and are linked through information technologies to achieve organizational tasks.

Success Factors for Virtual Teams

Virtual teams have all the challenges of traditional teams, along with the complications of distance and time. Fortunately OB researchers have been keenly interested in virtual teams, and their studies are now yielding ways to improve virtual team effectiveness.[81] First, along with having the team competencies described earlier in this chapter, members of successful virtual teams must have good communication technology skills, strong self-leadership skills to motivate and guide their behavior without peers or bosses nearby, and higher emotional intelligence so they can decipher the feelings of other team members from e-mail and other limited communication media.

A second recommendation is that virtual teams should have a toolkit of communication channels (e-mail, virtual whiteboards, video conferencing, and so on) as well as the freedom to choose the channels that work best for them. This may sound obvious, but unfortunately senior management tends to impose technology on virtual teams, often based on advice from external consultants, and expects team members to use the same communication technology throughout their work. In contrast, research suggests that communication channels gain and lose importance over time, depending on the task and level of trust.

Third, virtual teams need plenty of structure. In one recent review of effective virtual teams, many of the principles for successful virtual teams related mostly to creating these structures, such as clear operational objectives, documented work processes, and agreed-upon roles and responsibilities.[82] The final recommendation is that virtual team members should meet face-to-face fairly early in the team development process. This idea may seem contradictory to the entire notion of virtual teams, but so far no technology has replaced face-to-face interaction for high-level bonding and mutual understanding.

More Virtual Teams
More Virtual Challenges[80]

80% of managers polled in large American companies who say that their firm's reliance on virtual teams will grow in importance over the next three years.

58% of American managers who say that it is somewhat or very important that all members of their department work from the same location.

70% of American chief information officers polled who indicate that managing virtual teams is a very important globalization challenge (highest-rated issue on the list).

production blocking A time constraint in team decision making due to the procedural requirement that only one person may speak at a time.

evaluation apprehension Occurs when individuals are reluctant to mention ideas that seem silly because they believe (often correctly) that other team members are silently evaluating them.

groupthink The tendency of highly cohesive groups to value consensus at the price of decision quality.

TEAM DECISION MAKING

Self-directed teams, virtual teams, and practically all other groups are expected to make decisions. Under certain conditions, teams are more effective than individuals at identifying problems, choosing alternatives, and evaluating their decisions. To leverage these benefits, however, we first need to understand the constraints on effective team decision making. Then we look at specific team structures that try to overcome these constraints.

Constraints on Team Decision Making

Anyone who has spent enough time in the workplace can reel off several ways in which teams stumble in decision making. The four most common problems are time constraints, evaluation apprehension, pressure to conform, and groupthink.

Time Constraints There's a saying that committees keep minutes and waste hours. This reflects the fact that teams take longer than individuals to make decisions.[83] Unlike individuals, teams require extra time to organize, coordinate, and maintain relationships. The larger the group, the more time is required to make a decision. Team members need time to learn about each other and build rapport. They need to manage an imperfect communication process so there is sufficient understanding of each other's ideas. They also need to coordinate roles and rules of order within the decision process.

Another time-related constraint found in most team structures is that only one person can speak at a time.[84] This problem, known as **production blocking**, undermines idea generation in several ways. First, team members need to listen in on the conversation to find an opportune time to speak up, and this monitoring makes it difficult for them to concentrate on their own ideas. Second, ideas are fleeting, so the longer they wait to speak up, the more likely these flickering ideas will die out. Third, team members might remember their fleeting thoughts by concentrating on them, but this causes them to pay less attention to the conversation. By ignoring what others are saying, team members miss other potentially good ideas as well as the opportunity to convey their ideas to others in the group.

> **Individuals are reluctant to mention ideas that seem silly because they believe (often correctly) that other team members are silently evaluating them.**

Evaluation Apprehension Individuals are reluctant to mention ideas that seem silly because they believe (often correctly) that other team members are silently evaluating them.[85] This **evaluation apprehension** is based on the individual's desire to create a favorable self-presentation and need to protect self-esteem. It is most common when meetings are attended by people with different levels of status or expertise or when members formally evaluate each other's performance throughout the year (as in 360-degree feedback). Creative ideas often sound bizarre or illogical when first presented, so evaluation apprehension tends to discourage employees from mentioning them in front of coworkers.

Pressure to Conform Team cohesion leads employees to conform to the team's norms. This control keeps the group organized around common goals, but it may also cause team members to suppress their dissenting opinions, particularly when a strong team norm is related to the issue. When someone does state a point of view that violates the majority opinion, other members might punish the violator or try to persuade him or her that the opinion is incorrect. Conformity can also be subtle. To some extent, we depend on the opinions that others hold to validate our own views. If coworkers don't agree with us, we begin to question our own opinions even without overt peer pressure.

Groupthink **Groupthink** is the tendency of highly cohesive groups to value consensus at the price of decision quality.[86] The concept includes the dysfunctional effects of conformity on team decision

Improving Team Decision Making

- Encourage critical thinking and vigorous debate.

- Provide opportunities for everyone to present their ideas (be sure the discussion is not dominated by one or two people).

- The meeting should have enough people to provide necessary knowledge, yet few enough people that everyone has opportunities to participate in the discussion.

- Get everyone's preferences out in the open quickly.

- Narrow discussion to a few plausible options.

- Recognize that the most senior person may have to make the final decision after everyone has debated the issue, particularly when the issue is messy or filled with conflict.

sense of invulnerability, which makes them less attentive in decision making than are moderately confident teams.[88]

Team Structures to Improve Decision Making

Team decision making is fraught with problems, but several solutions also emerge from these bad-news studies. Team members need to be confident in their decision making but not so confident that they collectively feel invulnerable. This calls for team norms that encourage critical thinking as well as team membership with sufficient diversity. Checks and balances need to be in place to prevent one or two people from dominating the discussion. The team should also be large enough to possess the collective knowledge to resolve the problem yet small enough that the team doesn't consume too much time or restrict

> "When two [people] in business always agree, one of them is unnecessary.[91]
>
> —William Wrigley, Jr.

making, which were already described. It also includes the dysfunctional consequences of trying to maintain harmony within the team. This desire for harmony exists as a group norm and is most apparent when team members have a strong social identity with the group. Groupthink supposedly occurs most often when the team is isolated from outsiders, the team leader is opinionated (rather than impartial), the team is under stress due to an external threat, the team has experienced recent failures or other decision-making problems, and the team lacks clear guidance from corporate policies or procedures.

The term *groupthink* is now part of everyday language, but experts have dismissed the concept. The elements of groupthink do not cluster together; some groupthink characteristics improve rather than undermine decision making in some situations; and flaws have been found in the case studies that previously supported the existence of groupthink.[87]

Despite the problems with the groupthink concept, some of its specific elements continue to be relevant because they explain specific problems with team decision making. One of these elements, conformity, was just described as a concern. Another important element is the team's overconfidence. Studies consistently report that highly confident teams have a false

individual input. One recent perspective is that executives typically face messy (ill-defined, incomplete information) problems and that members of the executive team represent their constituents (divisions, departments, regions, and the like). Therefore, the

To foster constructive conflict, NASA's mission management team at Johnson Space Center replaced its assigned-seating rectangular table with a C-shaped arrangement where people sit wherever they want (shown in photo). None of the 24 members stands out above the others in the new setup.[93]

constructive conflict (also known as *task* or *cognitive conflict*)
Occurs when people focus their discussion on the issue while maintaining respectfulness for people having other points of view.

brainstorming
A freewheeling, face-to-face meeting where team members aren't allowed to criticise, but are encouraged to speak freely, generate as many ideas as possible, and build on the ideas of others.

electronic brainstorming
A recent form of brainstorming that relies on networked computers to submit and share creative ideas.

nominal group technique
A variation of traditional brainstorming that tries to combine the benefits of team decision making without the problems mentioned earlier.

best strategy is to get everyone's preferences out in the open quickly, have them vigorously debated, create a few plausible options, and in most cases acknowledge that the CEO needs to make the final decision because consensus is rarely possible.[89]

Team structures also help to minimize the problems described over the previous few pages. Four structures potentially improve team decision making in team settings: constructive conflict, brainstorming, electronic brainstorming, and the nominal group technique.

Constructive Conflict

A popular way to improve team decision making at Corning Inc. is to assign promising ideas to two-person teams, who spend up to four months analyzing the feasibility of their assigned ideas. The unique feature about this process is that the team is deliberately designed so that one person is from marketing and the other has technical expertise. This oil-and-water combination sometimes ruffles feathers, but it seems to generate better ideas and evaluations. "We find great constructive conflict this way," says Deborah Mills, who leads Corning's early-stage marketing team.[90]

or their ideas; (3) provide as many ideas as possible—the quality of ideas increases with the quantity of ideas; and (4) build on the ideas that others have presented. These rules are supposed to encourage divergent thinking while minimizing evaluation apprehension and other team dynamics problems.

Lab studies using university students concluded many years ago that brainstorming isn't very effective, largely because production blocking and evaluation apprehension still interfere with team dynamics.[94] However, brainstorming may be more beneficial than the earlier studies indicated.[95] The earlier lab studies measured the number of ideas generated, whereas recent investigations within companies using brainstorming indicate that this team structure results in more *creative* ideas, which is the main reason why companies use brainstorming. Also, evaluation apprehension is less of a problem in high-performing teams that embrace a learning orientation culture than it is for students brainstorming in lab experiments.

Another overlooked advantage of brainstorming is that participants interact and participate directly, thereby increasing decision

> [Many years ago, lab studies concluded that brainstorming isn't very effective, but more recent field studies have found that brainstorming can be beneficial.]

Constructive conflict occurs when people focus on the issue and maintain respect for people having other points of view. This conflict is called "constructive" because different viewpoints are encouraged so ideas and recommendations can be clarified, redesigned, and tested for logical soundness. The main advantage of this debate is that it presents different points of view and thus encourages all participants to reexamine their assumptions and logic. The main challenge with constructive conflict is that healthy debate too often slides into personal attacks—a problem that may explain why the evidence of constructive conflict on team decision making is inconsistent.[92] We explore this issue further in Chapter 10, along with specific strategies for minimizing the emotional effects of conflict while maintaining constructive debate.

Brainstorming

Brainstorming tries to leverage the creative potential of teams by establishing four simple rules: (1) Speak freely—describe even the craziest ideas; (2) don't criticize others

acceptance and team cohesion. Finally, brainstorming sessions often spread enthusiasm, which tends to generate more creativity. Overall, while brainstorming might not always be the best team structure, it seems to be more valuable than some of the earlier research studies indicated.

Electronic Brainstorming

Electronic brainstorming is a more recent form of brainstorming that relies on networked computers for submitting and sharing creative ideas. After receiving the question or issue, participants enter their ideas using special computer software. The ideas are distributed anonymously to other participants, who are encouraged to piggyback on those ideas. Team members eventually vote electronically on the ideas presented. Face-to-face discussion usually follows. Electronic brainstorming can be quite effective at generating creative ideas with minimal production blocking, evaluation apprehension, or conformity problems.[96] Despite these numerous advantages, electronic brainstorming seems to be too structured and technology-bound for some executives. Some leaders may also feel threatened by the honesty of statements generated through this process and by their limited ability to control the discussion.

Nominal Group Technique

The **nominal group technique** is a variation of traditional brainstorming that tries to combine the benefits of team decision making without the problems mentioned earlier.[97] The method is called "nominal" because participants form a group only in name during two of its three stages. After the problem is described, team members silently and independently write down as many solutions as they can. In the second stage, participants describe their solutions to the other team members, usually in a round-robin format. As with brainstorming, there is no criticism or debate, although members are encouraged to ask for clarification of the ideas presented. In the third stage, participants silently and independently rank order or vote on each proposed solution. Nominal group technique tends to generate a higher number of ideas and better-quality ideas than do traditional interacting and possibly brainstorming groups.[98] Due to its high degree of structure, nominal group technique usually maintains a high task orientation and relatively low potential for conflict within the team. However, production blocking and evaluation apprehension still occur to some extent. ■

CHECK IT OUT!

mhhe.com/McShaneM

for study materials

including quizzes

and Internet resources

chapter eight

communicating in
teams and organizations

When times get tough, it's time to increase the volume and quality of internal communication. Career coach Mark Schnurman and others at the New York City–based firm where he works followed that advice during the recent economic downturn. The company, which has 60 locations across the country, holds monthly lunches or other gatherings where employees have an opportunity to mingle and receive updates on how well the company is doing. The company president regularly writes matter-of-fact, yet upbeat, e-mail messages to all employees, which help to quash distorted rumors. Senior executives at Schnurman's firm are encouraged to get a better sense of staff morale and concerns by leaving their offices regularly to chat with employees. Finally, the company is finding more opportunities for employees to be involved in company decisions, such as evaluating health plan options.[1]

Communication is the lifeblood of all organizations, and communicating effectively is particularly important when conditions are as unsettling as the recent recession and financial crisis. **Communication** refers to the process by which information is transmitted and *understood* between two or more people. We emphasize the word "understood" because transmitting the sender's intended meaning is the essence of good communication. This chapter begins by discussing the importance of effective communication and outlining a model of the communication process. Next we identify types of communication channels, including computer-mediated or Internet-based communication, followed by factors to consider when choosing a communication medium. This chapter then identifies barriers to effective communication. This is followed by an overview of ways to communicate in organizational hierarchies and the pervasive organizational grapevine. ■

LEARNING OBJECTIVES

After reading this chapter, you should be able to

LO1 Explain why communication is important in organizations and discuss four influences on effective communication encoding and decoding.

LO2 Compare and contrast the advantages of and problems with electronic mail, other verbal communication media, and nonverbal communication.

LO3 Discuss social acceptance and media richness as factors when selecting a communication channel.

LO4 Identify various barriers (noise) to effective communication, and describe strategies for getting your message across and engaging in active listening.

LO5 Summarize communication strategies in organizational hierarchies, including the role and relevance of the organizational grapevine.

Learning Objectives

After reading the next two sections, you should be able to

LO1 Explain why communication is important in organizations and discuss four influences on effective communication encoding and decoding.

THE IMPORTANCE OF COMMUNICATION

Effective communication is vital to all organizations—so much so that no company could exist without it. The reason is that organizations consist of groups of people who work interdependently toward some purpose (see Chapter 1). People can work interdependently only through communication. They need to share information to clarify their expectations and co-ordinate work, which allows them to achieve organizational objectives more efficiently and effectively. Chester Barnard, a telecommunications CEO and a respected pioneer in organizational behavior theory, stated this point back in 1938: "An organization is born when there are individuals who are able to communicate."[2]

isolation are much more susceptible to colds, cardiovascular disease, and other physical and mental illnesses.[5] This effect occurs because people have an inherent drive to bond, to validate their self-worth, and to maintain their social identity. Communication is the means through which these drives and needs are fulfilled.

A MODEL OF COMMUNICATION

The communication process model presented in Exhibit 8.1 provides a useful "conduit" metaphor for thinking about the communication process.[6] According to this model, communication flows through channels between the sender and receiver. The sender forms a message and encodes it into words, gestures, voice intonations, and other symbols or signs. Next the encoded message is transmitted to the intended receiver through one or more communication channels (media). The receiver senses the incoming message and decodes it into something meaningful. Ideally the decoded meaning is what the sender intended.

In most situations, the sender looks for evidence that the other person received and understood the transmitted message. This feedback may be a formal acknowledgment, such as "Yes, I know what you mean," or indirect evidence from the

> The greatest problem with communication is the illusion that it has been accomplished.
> —George Bernard Shaw

Effective communication is an important instrument for organizational learning and decision making. Employees are the organization's brain cells, and communication represents the nervous system that carries this information and shared meaning to vital parts of the organizational body. Effective communication brings knowledge into the organization and disseminates it quickly to employees who require that information. Effective communication minimizes the "silos of knowledge" problem that undermines an organization's potential. This, in turn, allows employees to make more informed choices about corporate actions.[3]

Communication also aids employee well-being, which is why Mark Schnurman and other leaders at his company are trying to communicate more often during the economic downturn.[4] Information communicated from coworkers helps employees to manage their work environment, such as how to complete work procedures correctly or handle difficult customers. Equally important, employee well-being benefits from the communication experience itself; people who experience social

receiver's subsequent actions. Notice that feedback repeats the communication process. Intended feedback is encoded, transmitted, received, and decoded from the receiver to the sender of the original message. This model recognizes that communication is not a free-flowing conduit. Rather, the transmission of meaning from one person to another is hampered by *noise*—the psychological, social, and structural barriers that distort and obscure the sender's intended message. If any part of the communication process is distorted or broken, the sender and receiver will not have a common understanding of the message.

Influences on Effective Encoding and Decoding

The communication process model suggests that communication effectiveness depends on the ability of sender and receiver to efficiently and accurately encode and decode information. Experts have identified four factors that influence the effectiveness of the encoding–decoding process.[7] One factor is the

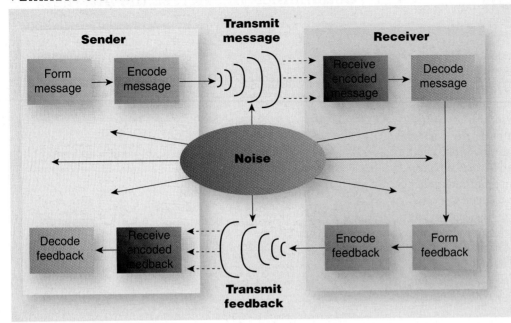

is less need for redundancy (such as saying the same thing in different ways) and less need for confirmation feedback ("So, you are saying that . . . ?").

A third factor influencing encoding–decoding process effectiveness is the extent to which both parties have shared mental models about the topic's context. Mental models are internal representations of the external world that allow us to visualize elements of a setting and relationships among those elements (see Chapter 3). When sender and receiver have shared mental models, they have a common understanding of the environment relating to the information, so less communication is necessary to clarify meaning about that context. Notice that sharing the same codebook differs from sharing the same mental models of the topic context. Codebooks are symbols used to convey message content, whereas mental models are knowledge structures of the communication topic setting. For example, a Russian cosmonaut and American astronaut might have shared mental models of the design and technology onboard the international space station (communication context), yet they experience poor communication because of language differences (different codebooks).

sender's and receiver's ability and motivation to communicate through the communication channel. Some people are better and more motivated to communicate through face-to-face conversations. Others are awkward in conversations, yet are quite good at communicating via BlackBerry or similar text message technologies. The encoding–decoding process is generally more effective when both parties are skilled in and enjoy using the selected communication channel.[8]

A second factor is the extent to which both parties have similar "codebooks"—dictionaries of symbols, language, gestures, idioms, and other tools used to convey information. With similar codebooks, the communication participants can encode and decode more accurately because they both have the same or similar meaning. Communication efficiency also improves because there

A fourth factor influencing encoding–decoding process effectiveness is the sender's experience at communicating the message. As people become more familiar with the subject matter, they become more proficient at using the codebook of symbols to convey the message. For example, after speaking to several groups of employees about the company's new product development, you learn which words and phrases help to communicate that particular message better to the audience. This is similar to the effect of job training or sports practice. The more experience and practice gained at communicating a subject, the more people learn how to effectively transmit that information to others.

Encoding and Decoding More Effectively

Communication encoding and decoding are more effective when

- Both sender and receiver are skilled and motivated to use that particular communication channel.
- Both sender and receiver possess similar codebooks of symbols, language, gestures, and the like.
- Both sender and receiver have shared mental models about the topic's context.
- The sender has experience encoding that particular message.

Learning Objectives

After reading the next two sections, you should be able to

L02 Compare and contrast the advantages of and problems with electronic mail, other verbal communication media, and nonverbal communication.

L03 Discuss social acceptance and media richness as factors when selecting a communication channel.

COMMUNICATION CHANNELS

A critical part of the communication model is the channel or medium through which information is transmitted. There are two main types of channels: verbal and nonverbal. Verbal communication uses words and occurs through either spoken or written channels. Nonverbal communication is any part of communication that does not use words. Spoken and written communication are both verbal (they both use words); but they are quite different from each other and have different strengths and weaknesses in communication effectiveness, which we discuss later in this section. Also, written communication has traditionally been much slower than spoken communication at transmitting messages, although electronic mail, Twitter "tweets," and other Internet-based communication channels have significantly improved written communication efficiency.

Communicating Across the Internet: Statistical Estimates[11]

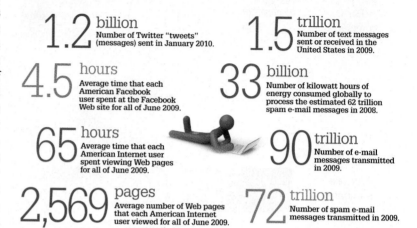

1.2 billion Number of Twitter "tweets" (messages) sent in January 2010.

1.5 trillion Number of text messages sent or received in the United States in 2009.

4.5 hours Average time that each American Facebook user spent at the Facebook Web site for all of June 2009.

33 billion Number of kilowatt hours of energy consumed globally to process the estimated 62 trillion spam e-mail messages in 2008.

65 hours Average time that each American Internet user spent viewing Web pages for all of June 2009.

90 trillion Number of e-mail messages transmitted in 2009.

2,569 pages Average number of Web pages that each American Internet user viewed for all of June 2009.

72 trillion Number of spam e-mail messages transmitted in 2009.

Computer-Mediated and Internet-Based Communication

In the early 1960s university researchers with funding from the U.S. Department of Defense began discussing how to collaborate better by connecting their computers through a network. Their rough vision of connected computers became a reality in 1969 as the Advanced Research Projects Agency Network (ARPANET). ARPANET initially had only a dozen or so connections and was very slow and expensive by today's standards, but it marked the birth of the Internet.

Two years later a computer engineer at the Cambridge, Massachusetts, company contracted to develop ARPANET sent the first electronic mail (e-mail) message between different computers on a network. (Computer experts had previously been able to send messages between terminals connected to the same computer.) By 1973 most communication on ARPANET was through e-mail. ARPANET was mostly restricted to U.S. Defense–funded research centers, so in 1979 two graduate students at Duke University developed a public network system called Usenet. Usenet allowed people to post information that could be retrieved by anyone else on the network, making it the first public computer-mediated social network.[9]

We have come a long way since the early days of ARPANET and Usenet. The most popular form of computer-mediated and Internet-based communication in organizational settings today is e-mail. E-mail has become the medium of choice in most workplaces because messages are quickly written, edited, and transmitted. Information can be appended and conveyed to many people with a simple click of a mouse. It is asynchronous (messages are sent and received at different times), so there is no need to coordinate a communication session. E-mail software has also become an efficient filing cabinet.[10]

E-mail tends to be the preferred medium for coordinating work (such as confirming deadlines with a coworker's schedule) and for sending well-defined information for decision making. It often increases the volume of communication and significantly alters the flow of information within groups and throughout the organization.[12] Specifically, it reduces some face-to-face and telephone communication but increases communication with people further up the hierarchy. Some social and organizational status differences still exist with e-mail,[13] but they are somewhat less apparent than in face-to-face communication. By hiding age, race, and other features, e-mail reduces stereotype biases. However, it also tends to increase reliance on stereotypes when we are already aware of the other person's characteristics.[14]

Problems with E-mail Despite the wonders of e-mail, anyone who has used this communication medium knows that it has limitations. Here are the top four complaints:

1. *Poor medium for communicating emotions:* People rely on facial expressions and other nonverbal cues to interpret the emotional meaning of words; e-mail lacks this parallel communication channel. Senders try to clarify the emotional tone of their messages by using expressive language ("Wonderful to hear from you!"), highlighting phrases in boldface or quotation marks, and inserting graphic faces (called emoticons or "smileys") representing the desired emotion. These actions help, but they do not replace the full complexity of real facial expressions, voice intonation, and hand movements.[15]

2. *Less politeness and respect:* E-mail messages are often less diplomatic than written letters—so much so that the term "flaming" refers mainly to e-mail and other electronic messages. There are at least three reasons why people are more likely to send disparaging messages by e-mail than other forms of verbal communication. First, individuals can post e-mail messages before their emotions subside, whereas the sender of a traditional memo or letter would have time for sober second thoughts. Second, e-mail has low social presence (it's more impersonal), so people are more likely to write things they would never say in face-to-face conversation. Third, for the same reasons that e-mail is a poor medium for communicating emotions, it is also easier for the receiver to misinterpret the emotional tone of the e-mail message. Fortunately research has found that flaming decreases as teams move to later stages of development and when explicit norms and rules of communication are established.[16]

3. *Poor medium for ambiguous, complex, and novel situations:* E-mail is usually fine for well-defined situations, such as giving basic instructions or presenting a meeting agenda, but it can be cumbersome in ambiguous, complex, and novel situations. As we will describe later in this section, these circumstances require communication channels that transmit a larger volume of information with more rapid feedback. In other words, when the issue gets messy, stop e-mailing and start talking, preferably face-to-face.

4. *More information overload:* E-mail contributes to information overload.[17] Approximately 20 trillion e-mail messages (excluding spam) are now transmitted annually around the world, up from just 1.1 trillion in 1998. The e-mail glut occurs

partly because messages are created and copied to many people without much effort. The number of e-mail messages will probably decrease as people become more familiar with it; until then, e-mail volume will continue to rise.

Workplace Communication through Social Media

Although e-mail continues to dominate computer-mediated or Internet-based communication in organizations, emerging Internet technologies have sparked development of various social media, such as Facebook, MySpace, LinkedIn, and Twitter.[18] These communication channels allow people to form communities around friendships, common interests, expertise, and other themes, resulting in closer interaction in the communication experience. Indeed, many of these social network media gain value as more people participate in the technology.[19]

Yet just as corporate leaders stumbled their way through Web 1.0 (the Internet's first stage) over the past two decades, many are fighting rather than leveraging the potential of this more socially interactive second stage (called Web 2.0). A large number of companies have banned employee access to social network sites after discovering that staff spend too much

> "Despite the wonders of e-mail, anyone who has used this communication medium knows that it has limitations."

wikis Collaborative Web spaces at which anyone in a group can write, edit, or remove material from the Web site.

emotional contagion The nonconscious process of "catching" or sharing another person's emotions by mimicking that person's facial expressions and other nonverbal behavior.

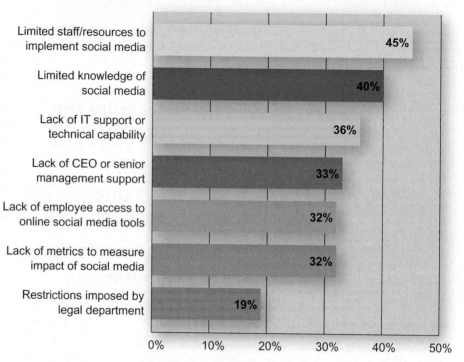

Top Reasons Why Companies Don't Use Social Media for Workplace Communication[20]

Percentage of 328 large organizations giving each reason why they have not implemented or expanded the use of social media in their organization. Firms in this sample originate from the United States (43 percent), Europe (20 percent), and other parts of the world.

work time looking at these sites. Recognizing the popularity of social media, a few organizational leaders are experimenting with ways to use it as a conduit for employees to communicate productively with each other, as well as with customers and other external stakeholders. One such vanguard is Serena Software, which has made Facebook its new corporate intranet. The Redwood City, California, company introduced "Facebook Fridays" sessions in which teenagers are hired to teach older staff how to use Facebook. Most Serena employees now have Facebook pages, and the company's Facebook site links employees to confidential documents behind the company's firewall.[21]

IBM has been at the forefront of another form of social networking communication called **wikis**. Wikis are collaborative Web spaces in which anyone in a group can write, edit, or remove material from the Web site. Wikipedia, the popular online encyclopedia, is a massive public example of a wiki. Wikis hold considerable promise for communicating in organizational settings because they are democratic, collaborative social networking spaces that rapidly document new knowledge. For example, IBM's WikiCentral now hosts more than 20,000 wiki projects involving 100,000 employees. The accuracy of wikis depends on the quality of participants, but IBM experts say that errors are quickly identified by IBM's online community. Also, some wikis have failed to gain employee support, likely because wiki involvement takes time and the company does not reward or recognize those who provide this time for wiki development.[22]

Nonverbal Communication

Nonverbal communication includes facial gestures, voice intonation, physical distance, and even silence. This communication channel is necessary where noise or physical distance prevent effective verbal exchanges and the need for immediate feedback

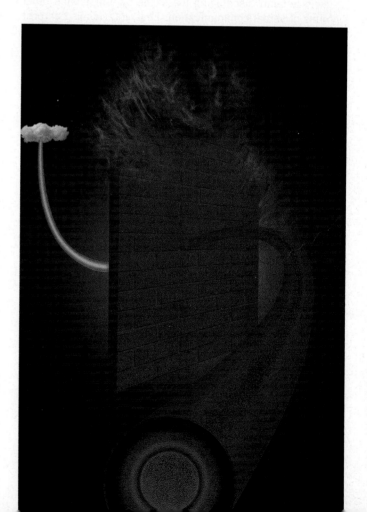

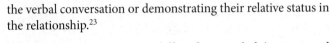

> # The most important thing in communication is hearing what isn't said.
>
> —Peter Drucker

precludes written communication. But even in quiet face-to-face meetings, most information is communicated nonverbally. Rather like a parallel conversation, nonverbal cues signal subtle information to both parties, such as reinforcing their interest in

the verbal conversation or demonstrating their relative status in the relationship.[23]

Nonverbal communication differs from verbal (written and spoken) communication in a couple of ways. First, it is less rule-bound than verbal communication. We receive considerable formal training in how to understand spoken words, but very little for understanding the nonverbal signals that accompany those words. Consequently, nonverbal cues are generally more ambiguous and susceptible to misinterpretation. At the same time, many facial expressions (such as smiling) are hardwired and universal, thereby providing the only reliable means of communicating across cultures.

The other difference between verbal and nonverbal communication is that the former is typically conscious, whereas most nonverbal communication is automatic and nonconscious. We normally plan the words we say or write, but we rarely plan every blink, smile, or other gesture during a conversation. Indeed, as we just mentioned, many of these facial expressions communicate the same meaning across cultures because they are hardwired nonconscious responses to human emotions.[24] For example, pleasant emotions cause the brain center to widen the mouth, whereas negative emotions produce constricted facial expressions (squinting eyes, pursed lips, and so forth).

Emotional Contagion One of the most fascinating effects of emotions on nonverbal communication is the phenomenon called **emotional contagion**, which is the automatic process of "catching" or sharing another person's emotions by mimicking that person's facial expressions and other nonverbal behavior. Consider what happens when you see a coworker accidentally bang his or her head against a filing cabinet. Chances are that you wince and put your hand on your own head as if you had hit the cabinet. Similarly, while listening to someone describe a positive event, you tend to smile and exhibit other emotional displays of happiness. Although some of our nonverbal communication is planned, emotional contagion represents nonconscious behavior—we automatically mimic and synchronize our nonverbal behaviors with those of other people.[25]

Emotional contagion serves three purposes. First, mimicry provides continuous feedback, communicating that we understand and empathize with the sender. To consider the significance of this, imagine employees remaining expressionless after watching

media richness
A medium's data-carrying capacity, that is, the volume and variety of information that can be transmitted during a specific time.

a coworker bang his or her head: the lack of parallel behavior would convey a lack of understanding or caring. Second, mimicking the nonverbal behaviors of other people seems to be a way of receiving emotional meaning from those people. If a coworker is angry with a client, your tendency to frown and show anger while listening helps you share that emotion more fully. In other words, we receive meaning by expressing the sender's emotions as well as by listening to the sender's words.

The third function of emotional contagion is to fulfill the drive to bond that was described in Chapter 5. Social solidarity is built out of each member's awareness of a collective sentiment. Through nonverbal expressions of emotional contagion, people see others share the same emotions that they feel. This strengthens relations among team members as well as between leaders and followers by providing evidence of their similarity.[26]

CHOOSING THE BEST COMMUNICATION CHANNEL

Which communication channel is most appropriate in a particular situation? Two important sets of factors to consider are (a) social acceptance and (b) media richness.

Social Acceptance

Social acceptance refers to how well a communication medium is approved and supported by the organization, teams, and individuals.[27] One factor in social acceptance is organizational and team norms regarding the use of specific communication channels. Norms partly explain why telephone conversations are more common among staff in some firms, whereas e-mail or text messaging is the medium of choice in other organizations. Some companies expect employees to meet face-to-face, whereas meetings and similar conversations are rare events elsewhere. Norms also shape the use of communication media for people in specific positions. For instance, frontline employees are more

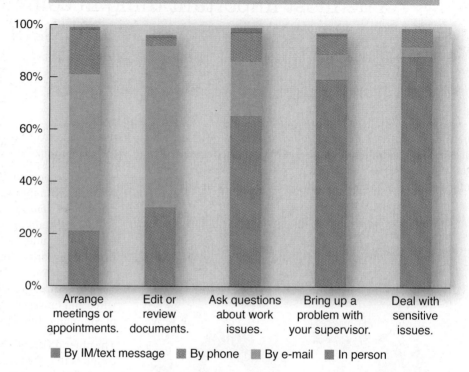

Some Things Are Better Communicated in Person[29]

Percentage of employed Americans who indicate each communication medium is the most effective for that workplace situation. N = 655. The sample included only people who use e-mail at work. The numbers do not add up to 100 percent because some people did not give an answer.

likely to write an e-mail message and less likely to telephone or personally visit the company's CEO. A second social acceptance factor is individual preferences for specific communication channels.[28] You may have noticed that some coworkers ignore (or rarely check) voice mail, yet they quickly respond to text messages or Twitter "tweets." These preferences are due to personality traits as well as previous experience and reinforcement with particular channels.

A third social acceptance factor is the symbolic meaning of a channel. Some communication channels are viewed as impersonal whereas others are more personal; some are considered professional whereas others are casual; some are "cool" whereas others are old-fashioned. To illustrate the importance of a channel's symbolic meaning, consider stories about managers who use e-mail or text messages to inform employees that they are fired or laid off. These communication events make headlines because e-mail and text messages are considered inappropriate (too impersonal) for transmission of such important information.[30]

Media Richness

Along with social acceptance, people select communication media based on their **media richness**. Media richness refers to the medium's data-carrying capacity—the volume and

variety of information that can be transmitted during a specific time.[31] Exhibit 8.2 illustrates various communication channels arranged in a hierarchy of richness, with face-to-face interaction at the top and lean data-only reports at the bottom. A communication channel has high richness when it is able to convey multiple cues (such as both verbal and non-verbal information), allows timely feedback from receiver to sender, allows the sender to customize the message to the receiver, and makes use of complex symbols (such as words and phrases with multiple meanings). Face-to-face communication is at the top of media richness because it allows us to communicate both verbally and nonverbally at the same time, to receive feedback almost immediately from the receiver, to quickly adjust our message and style, and to use complex language such as metaphors and idioms (such as "spilling the beans").

According to media richness theory, rich media are better than lean media when the communication situation is nonroutine and ambiguous. In nonroutine situations (such as an unexpected and unusual emergency), the sender and receiver have little common experience, so they need to transmit a

▼**EXHIBIT 8.2** Media Richness Hierarchy

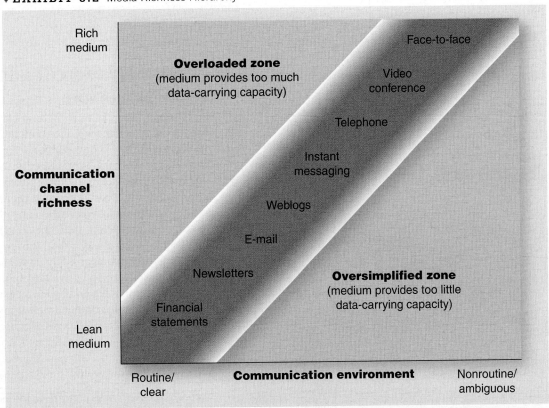

Sources: Based on R. Lengel and R. Daft, "The Selection of Communication Media as an Executive Skill," *Academy of Management Executive* 2, no. 3 (August, 1988), p. 226; R. L. Daft and R. H. Lengel, "Information Richness: A New Approach to Managerial Behavior and Organization Design," *Research in Organizational Behavior*, 1984, p. 199.

persuasion The use of facts, logical arguments, and emotional appeals to change another person's beliefs and attitudes, usually for the purpose of changing the person's behavior.

large volume of information with immediate feedback. Lean media work well in routine situations because the sender and receiver have common expectations through shared mental models. Ambiguous situations require rich media because the parties must share large amounts of information with immediate feedback to resolve multiple and conflicting interpretations of their observations and experiences.[32] Choosing the wrong medium reduces communication effectiveness. When the situation is routine or clear, using a rich medium—such as holding a special meeting—would seem like a waste of time. On the other hand, if a unique and ambiguous issue is handled through e-mail or another lean medium, issues take longer to resolve and misunderstandings are more likely to occur.

Evaluating Media Richness Theory Research generally supports the relevance of media richness for traditional channels (face-to-face, written memos, and the like). However, the model doesn't fit reality nearly as well when computer-mediated communication channels are studied. Three factors seem to override or blur the medium's richness:

1. *The ability to multicommunicate:* It is usually difficult (as well as rude) to communicate face-to-face with someone while simultaneously transmitting messages to someone else using another medium. Most computer-mediated technologies, on the other hand, require less sensory attention, so employees can easily engage in two or more communication events at the same time. In other words, they can multicom-

municate.[34] For example, people routinely scan Web pages while carrying on telephone conversations. Some write text messages to a client while simultaneously listening to a discussion at a large meeting. People don't multitask as efficiently as they believe, but some are good enough that they likely exchange as much information through two or more lean media as through one high media richness channel.

2. *More varied proficiency levels:* Earlier in this chapter we explained that communication effectiveness is determined partially by the sender's competence with the communication channel. Those with higher proficiency can "push" more information through the channel, thereby increasing the channel's information flow. Experienced BlackBerry users, for instance, can whip through messages in a flash, whereas new users struggle to type notes and organize incoming messages. In contrast, there is less variation in the ability to communicate through casual conversation and other natural channels because most of us develop good proficiency throughout life and possibly through hardwired evolutionary development.[35]

3. *Social distractions of rich channels:* Channels with high media richness tend to involve more direct social interaction. However, this social presence sensitizes both parties to their relative status and self-presentation, which diverts their attention from the message.[36] In other words, the benefits of media richness channels such as face-to-face communication may be offset by social distractions from the message content, whereas lean media have much less social presence.

Communication Channels and Persuasion

Media richness as well as social issues lay the foundation for understanding which communication channels are more effective for **persuasion**—that is, changing another person's beliefs and attitudes. Recent studies support the long-held view that spoken communication, particularly face-to-face interaction, is more persuasive than e-mail, Web sites, and other forms of written communication. There are three main reasons for this persuasive effect.[37] First, spoken communication is typically accompanied by nonverbal communication. People are often persuaded more when they receive both emotional and logical messages, and the combination of spoken with nonverbal communication provides this dual punch. A lengthy pause, raised voice tone, and (in face-to-face interaction) animated hand gestures can amplify the emotional tone of the message, thereby signaling the vitality of the issue.

Second, spoken communication offers the sender high-quality immediate feedback showing whether the receiver understands and accepts the message (is being persuaded). This feedback allows the sender to adjust the content and emotional tone of the message

Every day at 11:15 a.m., employees at I Love Rewards Inc. meet face-to-face for 10 minutes to communicate priorities and share news. The Toronto-based firm has these quick meetings because their high media richness provides a personal connection and highly interactive feedback on timely issues.[33]

more quickly than with written communication. Third, people are persuaded more under conditions of high social presence than low social presence. In face-to-face conversations (high social presence), people are more sensitive to how they are perceived by others in that social setting, so they pay attention to the sender's message and are more willing to actively consider that viewpoint. This is particularly true when the sender is a member of the receiver's social identity group. In contrast, when people receive persuasion attempts through a Web site, e-mail, or other source of written communication, they experience a higher degree of anonymity and psychological distance from the persuader. These conditions reduce the motivation to think about and accept the persuasive message.

Although spoken communication tends to be more persuasive, written communication can also persuade others to some extent. Written messages have the advantage of presenting more technical detail than can occur through conversation. This factual information is valuable when the issue is important to the receiver. Also, people experience a moderate degree of social presence in written communication when they are exchanging messages with close associates, so messages from friends and coworkers can be persuasive.

Learning Objectives

After reading the next three sections, you should be able to

LO4 Identify various barriers (noise) to effective communication, and describe strategies for getting your message across and engaging in active listening.

COMMUNICATION BARRIERS (NOISE)

Despite the best intentions of sender and receiver to communicate, several barriers (called "noise" earlier in Exhibit 8.1) inhibit the effective exchange of information. One barrier is the imperfect perceptual processes of both sender and receiver. As receivers, we don't listen as well as senders assume, and our needs and expectations influence what signals get noticed and ignored. We aren't any better as senders, either. Some studies suggest that we have difficulty stepping out of our own perspectives and stepping into the perspectives of others, so we

overestimate how well other people understand the messages we are communicating.[38]

Language differences also produce communication noise. Yet even when people speak the same language, translation errors occur because of cultural differences in the meaning of particular words and phrases. For example, a French executive might call an event a "catastrophe" as a casual exaggeration, whereas

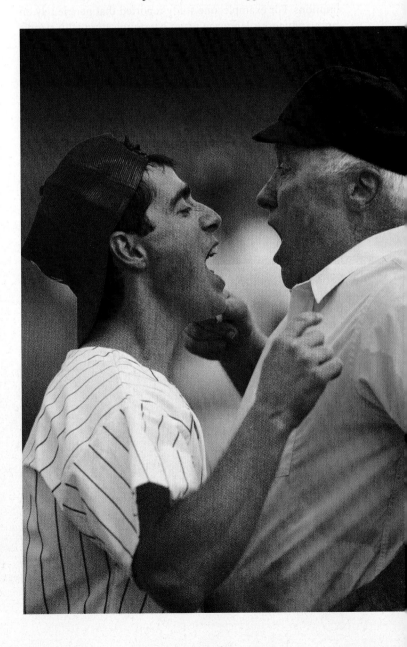

information overload A condition in which the volume of information received exceeds the person's capacity to process it.

someone in Germany usually interprets this word literally as an earth-shaking event.[39] The English language (among others) also has built-in ambiguities that cause misunderstandings. Consider the question "Can you close the door?" You might assume the sender is asking whether shutting the door is permitted. However, the question might be asking whether you are physically able to shut the door or whether the door is designed so that it can be shut. Or this question might not be a question at all; the person could be politely *telling* you to shut the door.[40]

The ambiguity of language isn't always dysfunctional noise.[41] Corporate leaders sometimes rely on metaphors and other vague language to describe ill-defined or complex ideas. Ambiguity is also used to avoid conveying or creating undesirable emotions. For example, one study reported that people rely on more ambiguous language when communicating with people who have different values and beliefs. In these situations, ambiguity minimizes the risk of conflict.

Jargon—specialized words and phrases for specific occupations or groups—is usually designed to improve communication efficiency. However, it is a source of communication noise when transmitted to people who do not possess the jargon codebook. Furthermore, people who use jargon excessively put themselves in an unflattering light. For example, Chrysler's former CEO Robert Nardelli announced, "I'm blessed to have individuals with me who can take areas of responsibility and do vertical dives to really get the granularity and make sure that we're coupling horizontally across those functions so that we have a pure line of sight toward the customer." Business journalists weren't impressed, even if they did figure out what Nardelli meant.[42]

Another source of noise in the communication process is the tendency to filter messages. Filtering may involve deleting or delaying negative information or using less harsh words so a message sounds more favorable.[43] Filtering is less likely to occur when corporate leaders create a "culture of candor." This culture develops when leaders themselves communicate truthfully, seek out diverse sources for information, and protect and reward those who speak openly and truthfully.[44]

How Leaders Can Create a Culture of Candor[45]

- Tell the truth; tell everyone the same unvarnished story.
- Give employees the courage to tell higher-ups unpalatable truths.
- Reward contrarians—those who challenge others' assumptions.
- Learn how to deliver bad news in a way that doesn't unnecessarily hurt others.
- Diversify your sources of information.
- Admit your mistakes, which provides a model for others to do the same.
- Build organizational support for transparency, such as protecting whistleblowers and supporting those who speak honestly.
- Set information free; start with the assumption that employees can be trusted, rather than that they can't be trusted.

Information Overload

Start with a daily avalanche of e-mail, then add in cell phone calls, text messages, PDF file downloads, Web pages, hard copy documents, some Twitter tweets, blogs, wikis, and other sources of incoming information. This creates a perfect recipe for **information overload**.[46] As Exhibit 8.3 illustrates, information overload occurs whenever a job's information load exceeds

▼**EXHIBIT 8.3** Dynamics of Information Overload

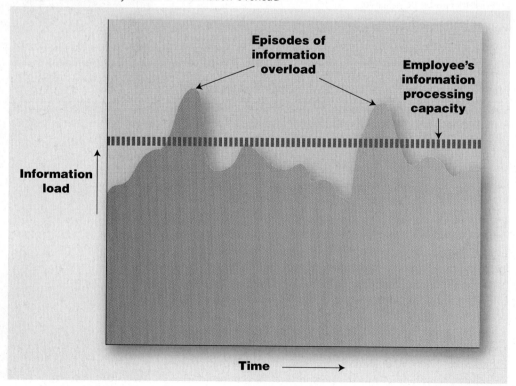

an individual's capacity to get through it. Employees have a certain *information processing capacity*—the amount of information they can process in a fixed unit of time. At the same time, jobs have a varying *information load*—the amount of information to be processed per unit of time. Information overload creates noise in the communication system because information gets overlooked or misinterpreted when people can't process it fast enough. The result is poorer-quality decisions as well as higher stress.[47]

Information overload problems can be minimized by increasing our information processing capacity, reducing the job's information load, or through a combination of both. Studies suggest that employees often increase their information processing capacity by temporarily reading faster, scanning through documents more efficiently, and removing distractions that slow information processing speed. Time management also increases information processing capacity. When information overload is temporary, we can increase information processing capacity by working longer hours. Information load can be reduced by buffering, omitting, and summarizing. Buffering involves having incoming communication filtered, usually by an assistant. Omitting occurs when we decide to overlook messages, such as using software rules to redirect e-mail from distribution lists to folders we never look at. An example of summarizing would be where we read executive summaries rather than the full report.

CROSS-CULTURAL AND GENDER COMMUNICATION

As globalization and cultural diversity increase, we can be sure cross-cultural communication problems will also increase.[48] As we noted earlier, language is an obvious cross-cultural communication challenge. Words are easily misunderstood in verbal communication, either because the receiver has a limited vocabulary or because the sender's accent distorts the usual sound of some words. Voice intonation is another cross-cultural communication barrier. How loudly, deeply, and quickly people speak vary across cultures, and these voice intonations send secondary messages that have different meaning in different cultures.

> Communication includes silence, but its use and meaning varies from one culture to another.

Communication includes silence, but its use and meaning vary from one culture to another.[49] One study estimated that silence and pauses represented 30 percent of conversation time between Japanese doctors and patients, compared to only 8 percent of the time between American doctors and patients. Why is there more silence in Japanese conversations? In Japan, silence symbolizes respect and indicates that the listener is thoughtfully contemplating what has just been said.[50] Empathy is important in Japan, and this shared understanding is demonstrated without using words. In contrast, most people in the United States and many other cultures view silence as a *lack* of communication and often interpret long breaks as a sign of disagreement.

Conversational overlaps also send different messages in different cultures. Japanese people usually stop talking when they are interrupted, whereas talking over another person's speech is more common in Brazil, France, and some other countries. The difference in communication behavior is again due to interpretations. Talking while someone is speaking to you is considered quite rude in Japan, whereas Brazilians and French are more likely to interpret this as the person's interest and involvement in the conversation.

Nonverbal Differences across Cultures

Nonverbal communication represents another potential area for misunderstanding across cultures. Many nonconscious or involuntary nonverbal cues (such as smiling) have the same meaning around the world, but deliberate gestures often have different interpretations. For example, most of us shake our heads from side to side to say "No," but a variation of head shaking means "I understand" to many people in India. Filipinos raise their eyebrows to give an affirmative answer, yet Arabs interpret this expression (along with clicking one's tongue) as a negative response. Most Americans are taught to maintain eye contact with a speaker to show interest and respect, whereas some North American native groups learn at an early age to show respect by looking down when an older or more senior person is talking to them.[51]

Gender Differences in Communication

Men and women have similar communication practices, but there are subtle distinctions that can occasionally lead to misunderstanding and conflict (see Exhibit 8.4).[52] One distinction is that men are more likely than women to view conversations as negotiations of relative status and power. They assert their power by directly giving advice to others ("You should do the following") and using combative language. There is also evidence that men dominate the talk time in conversations with women, as well as interrupt more and adjust their speaking styles less than do women.

Men engage in more "report talk," in which the primary function of the conversation is impersonal and efficient information exchange. Women also use report talk, particularly when conversing with men, but conversations among women have a higher incidence of relationship building through "rapport talk." Women make more use of indirect requests ("Do you think you should . . . "), apologize more often, and seek advice from others more quickly than do men. Finally, research fairly consistently indicates that women are more sensitive than men to nonverbal cues in face-to-face meetings.[53] Together these conditions can create communication conflicts. Women who describe problems get frustrated that men offer advice rather than rapport, whereas men become frustrated because they can't understand why women don't appreciate their advice.

IMPROVING INTERPERSONAL COMMUNICATION

Effective interpersonal communication depends on the sender's ability to get the message across and the receiver's performance as an active listener. In this section we outline these two essential features of effective interpersonal communication.

Getting Your Message Across

This chapter began with the statement that effective communication occurs when the other person receives and understands the message. This is more difficult to accomplish than most people believe. To get your message across to the other person, you first need to empathize with the receiver, such as being sensitive to words that may be ambiguous or trigger the wrong emotional response. Second, be sure that you repeat the message,

> ## Men engage in more "report talk," whereas conversations among women have a higher incidence of relationship building through "rapport talk."

▼**EXHIBIT 8.4** Gender Differences in Communication

When Men Communicate	When Women Communicate
Report talk: functional, asserts power.	Rapport talk: relationship building.
Give advice directly.	Give advice indirectly.
Dominant conversation style.	Flexible conversation style.
Apologize less often.	Apologize more often.
Less sensitive to nonverbal cues.	More sensitive to nonverbal cues.

such as by rephrasing the key points a couple of times. Third, your message competes with other messages and noise, so find a time when the receiver is less likely to be distracted by these other matters. Finally, if you are communicating bad news or criticism, focus on the problem, not the person.

Active Listening

Active listening is a process of actively sensing the sender's signals, evaluating them accurately, and responding appropriately. These three components of listening—sensing, evaluating, and responding—reflect the listener's side of the communication model described at the beginning of this chapter. Listeners receive the sender's signals, decode them as

Getting Your Message Across

Communication encoding and decoding are more effective when you

- Empathize with the person receiving the message.
- Repeat the key points of your message a couple of times.
- Actively determine the best time to speak to the other person.
- Be descriptive by directing any negative comments toward the issue, not the person.

sensing in three ways. First, they postpone evaluation by not forming an opinion until the speaker has finished. Second, they avoid interrupting the speaker's conversation. Third, they remain motivated to listen to the speaker.

Evaluating This component of listening includes understanding the message meaning, evaluating the message, and remembering the message. To improve their evaluation of the conversation, active listeners empathize with the speaker—they try to understand and be sensitive to the speaker's feelings, thoughts, and situation. Evaluation also improves by organizing the speaker's ideas during the communication episode.

> "Nature gave us one tongue, but two ears, so we may listen twice as much as we speak.[55]
>
> —Epictetus

intended, and provide appropriate and timely feedback to the sender (see Exhibit 8.5). Active listeners constantly cycle through sensing, evaluating, and responding during the conversation and engage in various activities to improve these processes.[54]

Sensing Sensing is the process of receiving signals from the sender and paying attention to them. Active listeners improve

Responding Responding, the third component of listening, is feedback to the sender, which motivates and directs the speaker's communication. Active listeners accomplish this by maintaining sufficient eye contact and sending back channel signals (such as "I see"), both of which showing interest. They also respond by clarifying the message—rephrasing the speaker's ideas at appropriate breaks ("So you're saying that . . . ?").

▼ **EXHIBIT 8.5** Active Listening Process and Strategies

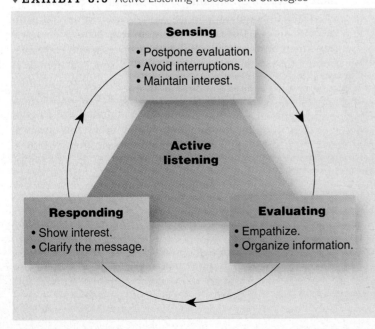

Learning Objectives

After reading the next two sections, you should be able to

LO5 Summarize communication strategies in organizational hierarchies, including the role and relevance of the organizational grapevine.

IMPROVING COMMUNICATION THROUGHOUT THE HIERARCHY

So far we have focused on micro-level issues in the communication process—namely, the dynamics of sending and receiving information between two employees or the informal exchanges of information across several people. But in this era where knowledge is competitive advantage,

management by walking around (MBWA) A communication practice in which executives get out of their offices and learn from others in the organization through face-to-face dialogue.

grapevine An unstructured and informal network founded on social relationships rather than organizational charts or job descriptions.

corporate leaders also need to maintain an open flow of communication up, down, and across the organization. In this section we discuss three communication strategies: workspace design, Web-based communication, and direct communication with top management.

Workspace Design

Some organizations are improving communication among staff by tearing down walls.[56] The location and design of hallways, offices, cubicles, and communal areas (cafeterias, elevators) all shape whom we speak to as well as the frequency of that communication. Some firms are replacing traditional offices with an open space where all employees (including management) work together. "We do not have doors," explains an executive at Continuum, the Boston-based design and innovation firm. "It's structured that way to stimulate conversation and to allow people to work collaboratively."[57] Although these open space arrangements increase communication, they also potentially increase noise, distractions, and loss of privacy.[58] The challenge is to increase social interaction without these stressors.

FACT. **Open Communication at Zappos**

Zappos encourages employees to communicate with each other and with customers. One-third of the online retailer's 1,500 employees have Twitter accounts, and tweeting (sending messages through Twitter) is part of the employee training program. Zappos CEO Tony Hsieh is equally serious about encouraging face-to-face communication. For example, he has the ultimate open-door policy by locating in an open cubicle where anyone can speak with him. Hsieh was also concerned about opportunities for informal communication when Zappos moved to its current Las Vegas offices. The previous tenant installed several exits, so people would come and go without crossing paths with anyone from other departments. Hsieh's solution was to lock most of the side exit doors so employees had to leave the building through the front entrance reception area. "The reason for that is to create this kind of central hub that everyone has to pass through to help build community and culture," Hsieh explains.[60]

Another workspace strategy is to cloister employees into team spaces, but also encourage sufficient interaction with people from other teams. Pixar Animation Studios constructed its campus in Emeryville, California, with these principles in mind. The building encourages communication among team members. At the same time, the campus encourages happenstance interactions with people on other teams. Pixar executives call this the "bathroom effect" because team members must leave their isolated pods to fetch their mail, have lunch, or visit the restroom.[59]

Internet-Based Organizational Communication

For decades, employees received official company news through hard copy newsletters and magazines. Many firms still use these communication devices, but most have supplemented or replaced them completely with Web-based sources of information. The traditional company magazine is now typically published on Web pages or distributed in PDF format. The advantage of these *e-zines* is that company news can be prepared and distributed quickly. However, employees are increasingly skeptical of information that has been screened and packaged by management. In response, a few companies such as IBM are encouraging employees to post their own news on internal blogs and wikis. A very small number of companies, such as Zappos, post news publicly on Facebook and Twitter and encourages employees to use these sites to post personal news and photos.

Direct Communication with Top Management

"The best fertilizer in any field is that of the farmer's footsteps!" This old Chinese saying suggests that farmers will be more successful by spending more time in the fields directly observing the crop's development. Translated into an organizational context, this means that senior executives will understand their business better if they meet directly with employees and other stakeholders. Nearly 40 years ago people at Hewlett-Packard coined a phrase for this communication strategy: **management by walking around (MBWA)**.

Brian Scudamore, founder and CEO of 1-800-Got-Junk?, takes this practice further. "I don't have my own office, and I very often move around to different departments for a day at a time," says Scudamore.[61]

Along with MBWA, executives communicate more directly with employees through "town hall meetings." Some executives also conduct employee roundtable forums to hear opinions from a

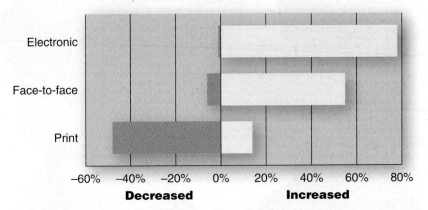

Decline of Print Media in Corporate Internal Communications[62]

Electronic

Face-to-face

Print

−60% −40% −20% 0% 20% 40% 60% 80%

Decreased   **Increased**

Percentage of 328 large organizations that are increasing or decreasing use of each medium to communicate with employees. This chart indicates that most firms plan to increase their use of electronic and face-to-face communication, and decrease their use of print media. Firms in this sample originate from the United States (43 percent), Europe (20 percent), and other parts of the world.

COMMUNICATING THROUGH THE GRAPEVINE

No matter how much organizations try to get messages to employees quickly through e-zines, blogs, wikis, MBWA, and other means, employees still use the oldest communication channel: the corporate **grapevine**. The grapevine is an unstructured and informal network founded on social relationships rather than organizational charts or job descriptions. What do employees think about the grapevine? Surveys of employees in two firms—one in Florida, the other in California—found that almost all employees use the grapevine, but few of them prefer this source of information. The California survey also reported that only one-third of employees

[A rumor without a leg to stand on will get around some other way.]

—John Tudor

small representation of staff about various issues. At the departmental level, some companies hold daily or weekly "huddles"— brief stand-up meetings in which staff and their manager discuss goals and hear good news stories. These direct communication strategies potentially minimize filtering because executives listen directly to employees. They also help executives acquire a deeper meaning and quicker understanding of internal organizational problems. A third benefit of direct communication is that employees might have more empathy for decisions made further up the corporate hierarchy.

believe grapevine information is credible. In other words, employees turn to the grapevine when they have few other options.[64]

Grapevine Characteristics

Research conducted several decades ago reported that the grapevine transmits information rapidly in all directions throughout the organization. The typical pattern is a cluster chain, whereby a few people actively transmit rumors to many others. The grapevine works through informal social networks, so it is more active where employees have similar backgrounds and can communicate easily. Many rumors seem to have at least a kernel of truth, possibly because they are transmitted through media-rich communication channels (face-to-face) and employees are motivated to communicate effectively. Nevertheless, the grapevine distorts information by deleting fine details and exaggerating key points of stories.[65]

Some of these characteristics might still be true, but the grapevine almost certainly has changed as e-mail, social networking sites, and Twitter tweets have replaced the traditional water cooler as sources of gossip. For example, several Facebook sites are themed around specific companies, allowing employees and customers to vent their complaints about the organization. Along with altering the speed and network of corporate

FACT. **Google's TGIF Communication**

Google has become a large organization, but that hasn't stopped its founders and executives from answering employee questions. Google employees submit their questions online and vote on the questions submitted. Questions that receive the most votes are answered by Google's founders and executives most Fridays in a forum called "Thank Goodness It's Friday" (TGIF).[63]

> "E-mail, social networking sites, and Twitter tweets have replaced the traditional water cooler as sources of gossip for the corporate grapevine.

grapevines, the Internet has expanded these networks around the globe, not just around the next cubicle.

Grapevine Benefits and Limitations

Should the grapevine be encouraged, tolerated, or quashed? The difficulty in answering this question is that the grapevine has both benefits and limitations.[66] One benefit, as was mentioned earlier, is that employees rely on the grapevine when information is not available through formal channels. It is also the main conduit through which organizational stories and other symbols of the organization's culture are communicated. A third benefit of the grapevine is that this social interaction relieves anxiety. This explains why rumor mills are most active during times of uncertainty.[67] Finally, the grapevine is associated with the drive to bond. Being a recipient of gossip is a sign of inclusion, according to evolutionary psychologists. Trying to quash the grapevine is, in some respects, an attempt to undermine the natural human drive for social interaction.[68]

While the grapevine offers these benefits, it is not a preferred communication medium. Grapevine information is sometimes so distorted that it escalates rather than reduces employee anxiety. Furthermore, employees develop more negative attitudes toward the organization when management is slower than the grapevine in communicating information. What should corporate leaders do with the grapevine? The best advice seems to be to listen to the grapevine as a signal of employee anxiety, then correct the cause of this anxiety. Some companies also listen to the grapevine and step in to correct blatant errors and fabrications. Most important, corporate leaders need to view the grapevine as a competitor, and meet this challenge by directly informing employees of news before it spreads throughout the grapevine. ■

CHECK IT OUT!

mhhe.com/McShaneM

for study materials

including quizzes

and Internet resources

power and influence in the workplace

Engineering and environmental consulting firm MWH Global reorganized its information technology (IT) operations into a single global division and located its main service center in New Zealand. Ken Loughridge was transferred from England to manage the new service center, but he didn't know who the key players were in his New Zealand team. "By and large, the staff I'd adopted were strangers," he says. Fortunately Loughridge was able to consult a report displaying the informal social network of relationships among his staff. MWH Global had surveyed its IT employees a few months earlier about whom they communicated with most often for information. These data produced a web-like diagram of nodes (people) connected by a maze of lines (relationships). From this picture Loughridge could identify the employees on whom others depend for information. "It's as if you took the top off an ant hill and could see where there's a hive of activity," he says of the map. "It really helped me understand who the players were."[1]

MWH Global and many other organizations recognize that an organizational chart does not tell the whole story about who has power in an organization. Much of a person's or team's power lies under the surface. Social network analysis can reveal that power to some extent, although some forms of power are more complex and subtle than any systematic study can fully detect. This chapter looks at the meaning and dynamics of power and influence in organizational settings. First we define *power* and present a model depicting the dynamics of power in organizational settings. The chapter then discusses the five sources of power, as well as information as a power

continued on p. 180

LEARNING OBJECTIVES

After reading this chapter, you should be able to

LO1 Define power and describe the five sources of power in organizations as well as the two types of information-based power.

LO2 Discuss the four contingencies of power and explain how social networking increases a person's power.

LO3 Describe eight types of influence tactics, three consequences of influencing others, and three contingencies to consider when choosing an influence tactic.

LO4 Identify the organizational conditions and personal characteristics that support organizational politics, as well as ways to minimize organizational politics.

continued from p. 179

base. Next we look at the contingencies necessary to translate those sources into meaningful power. The latter part of this chapter examines the various types of influence in organizational settings as well as the contingencies of effective influence strategies. The final section of this chapter looks at situations in which influence becomes organizational politics, as well as ways of minimizing dysfunctional politics. ■

Learning Objectives

After reading the next three sections, you should be able to

LO1 Define power and describe the five sources of power in organizations as well as the two types of information-based power.

LO2 Discuss the four contingencies of power and explain how social networking increases a person's power.

THE MEANING OF POWER

Power is the capacity of a person, team, or organization to influence others.[2] Power is not the act of changing someone's attitudes or behavior; it is only the potential to do so. People frequently have power they do not use; they might not even know they have power. Also power is not a personal feeling of power. You might feel powerful or think you have power over someone else, but this is not power unless you truly have the capacity to influence that person. The most basic prerequisite of power is that one person or group believes it is dependent on another person or group for a resource of value.[3] This relationship, shown in Exhibit 9.1, occurs where Person A has power over Person B by controlling something that Person B wants. You might have power over others by controlling a desired job assignment, useful information, important resources, or even the privilege of being associated with you! However, power requires the *perception* of dependence, so people might gain power by convincing others that they have something of value, whether or not they actually control that resource. Thus power exists when others believe you control resources they want.

Although dependence is a key element of power relationships, it is really more accurate to say that the parties are *interdependent*.[4]

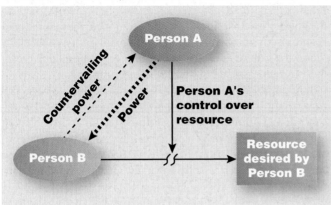

In Exhibit 9.1, Person A dominates in the power relationship, but Person B also has some **countervailing power**—enough power to keep Person A in the exchange relationship and ensure that he or she uses the dominant power judiciously. For example, executives have power over subordinates by controlling their job security and promotional opportunities. At the same time, employees have countervailing power by possessing skills and knowledge to keep production humming and customers happy, something that executives can't accomplish alone. Finally, the power relationship depends on some minimum level of trust. Trust indicates a level of expectation that the more powerful party will deliver the resource. For example, you trust your employer to give you a paycheck at the end of each pay period. Even those in extremely dependent situations will usually walk away from a relationship if they lack a minimum level of trust in the more powerful party.

A Model of Power in Organizations

Power involves more than just dependence or interdependence. As Exhibit 9.2 illustrates, power is derived from five sources: legitimate, reward, coercive, expert, and referent. The model also indicates that these sources yield power only under certain conditions. The four contingencies of power include the employee's or department's substitutability, centrality, discretion, and visibility. Finally, as you will read later in this chapter, the type of power applied affects the type of influence the power holder has over the other person or work unit.

SOURCES OF POWER IN ORGANIZATIONS

Power derives from several sources and a few contingencies that determine the potential of those power sources.[5] Three sources of power—legitimate, reward, and coercive—originate mostly from the power holder's formal position or informal role. In other words, the person is granted these sources of power formally by the organization or informally by coworkers. Two other sources of power—expert and referent—originate from the power holder's own characteristics; that is, he or she brings these power bases to the organization. Sources of power are resources that help the dependent person directly or indirectly achieve his or her goals. For example, your expertise is a source of power when others need that expertise to accomplish their objectives.

Legitimate Power

Legitimate power is an agreement among organizational members that people in certain roles can request certain behaviors of others. This perceived right originates from formal job descriptions as well as informal rules of

power The capacity of a person, team, or organization to influence others.

countervailing power The capacity of a person, team, or organization to keep a more powerful person or group in the exchange relationship.

legitimate power An agreement among organizational members that people in certain roles can request certain behaviors of others.

▼ **EXHIBIT 9.2** A Model of Power within Organizations

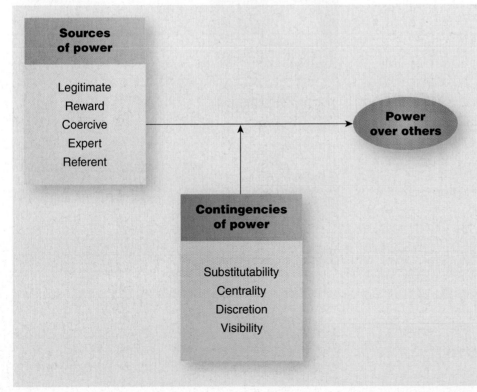

The size of this zone of indifference (and consequently the magnitude of legitimate power) increases with the extent to which the power holder is trusted and makes fair decisions. Some people are also more obedient than others to authority, particularly those who value conformity and tradition. People in high power distance cultures (that is, those who accept an unequal distribution of power) also tend to have higher obedience to authority compared with people in low power distance cultures. The organization's culture represents a third factor. A 3M scientist might continue to work on a project after being told by superiors to stop working on it because the 3M culture supports an entrepreneurial spirit, which includes ignoring your boss's authority from time to time.[7]

Reward Power

Reward power is derived from the person's ability to control the allocation of rewards valued by others and to remove negative sanctions (i.e., negative reinforcement). Managers have formal authority that gives them power over the distribution of organizational rewards such as pay, promotions, time off, vacation schedules, and work assignments. Employees also have reward power over their bosses through their feedback and ratings in 360-degree feedback systems. These ratings affect supervisors' promotions and other rewards, so supervisors tend to behave differently toward employees after 360-degree feedback is introduced.

conduct. This legitimate power extends to employees, not just managers. For example, an organization might give employees the right to request customer files if this information is required for their jobs. Legitimate power depends on more than job descriptions. It also depends on mutual agreement from those expected to abide by this authority. Your boss's power to make you work overtime partly depends on your agreement to this authority. Legitimate power operates within a "zone of indifference"—the range within which people are willing to accept someone else's authority.[6]

FACT. Legitimate Power Takes People to the Extreme[8]

French reality television recently revealed how far people are willing to submit to authority. As a variation of the 1960s experiments conducted by Stanley Milgram, 80 contestants administered electric shocks whenever a volunteer (an actor who didn't receive the shocks at all) answered a question incorrectly. Shocks increased in 20-volt increments, from 20 volts for the first mistake to 460 volts, which is more than enough to kill a human being. Most contestants who hesitated to administer strong shocks (after hearing loud screams from the volunteer) continued the treatment after the host told them to continue. Audience support also encouraged contestants to continue giving shocks. Only 16 of the 80 contestants refused to administer the strongest shocks. Eighty percent followed orders . . . to the end.

referent power
The capacity to influence others on the basis of an identification with and respect for the power-holder.

who own the company. And without this control over production, owners are more dependent on employees to achieve their corporate objectives.

Referent Power

People have **referent power** when others identify with them, like them, or otherwise respect them. Like expert power, referent power comes from within the person. It is largely a function of the person's interpersonal skills and tends to develop slowly. Referent power is usually associated with charismatic leadership. Experts have difficulty agreeing on the meaning of *charisma*, but it is most often described as a form of interpersonal attraction whereby followers ascribe almost magical powers to the charismatic individual.[12] Some experts describe charisma as a special "gift" or trait within the charismatic person, whereas others say it exists mainly in the eyes of beholders. However, all agree that charisma produces a high degree of trust, respect, and devotion toward the charismatic individual.

Information and Power

Information is power.[13] In one form, people gain information power when they control (through legitimate power) the flow of information to others. Employees are ultimately dependent on these information gatekeepers to release the information required to perform their jobs. Furthermore, by deciding what information is distributed to whom, those who control information flow also control perceptions of the situation by releasing information favoring one perspective more than another.[14] This right to control information flow is a form of legitimate power and is most common in highly bureaucratic firms. The wheel formation in Exhibit 9.3 depicts this highly centralized control over information flow. The all-channels structure, on

Coercive Power Coercive power is the ability to apply punishment. For many of us, the first thought is managers threatening employees with dismissal. Yet employees also have coercive power, such as being sarcastic toward coworkers or threatening to ostracize them if they fail to conform to team norms. Many firms rely on this coercive power to control coworker behavior in team settings. Nucor is one such example: "If you're not contributing with the team, they certainly will let you know about it," says Dan Krug, manager of HR and organizational development at the Charlotte, North Carolina, steelmaker. "The few poor players get weeded out by their peers." Similarly, when asked how AirAsia maintained attendance and productivity after the Malaysian discount airline removed the time clocks, chief executive Tony Fernandes replied, "Simple. Peer pressure sees to that. The fellow employees, who are putting their shoulders to the wheel, will see to that."[9]

Expert Power

For the most part, legitimate, reward, and coercive power originate from the position.[10] In contrast, expert power originates within the person. It is an individual's or work unit's capacity to influence others by possessing knowledge or skills that they value. Employees are gaining expert power as our society moves from an industrial to a knowledge-based economy.[11] The reason is that employee knowledge becomes the means of production and is ultimately outside the control of those

▼**EXHIBIT 9.3** Power through the Control of Information

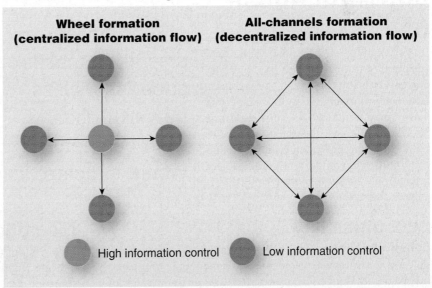

**Wheel formation
(centralized information flow)**

**All-channels formation
(decentralized information flow)**

High information control   Low information control

substitutability
A contingency of power referring to the availability of alternatives.

centrality A contingency of power referring to the degree and nature of interdependence between the powerholder and others.

the other hand, depicts a situation where no one has control over the flow of information. The former would occur when information must flow through your boss to you, whereas the latter occurs when information is distributed to many people, such as coworkers in a self-directed team.

The other form of information power occurs when a person or work unit has the ability—or is believed to have the ability—to manage environmental uncertainties. This capability, which is a derivative of expert power, is valued because organizations are more effective when they can operate in predictable environments. A groundbreaking study of breweries and container companies identified three general strategies to help organizations cope with uncertainty. These coping strategies are arranged in a hierarchy of importance, with prevention being the most powerful:[15]

- *Prevention:* The most effective strategy is to prevent environmental changes from occurring. For example, financial experts acquire power by preventing the organization from experiencing a cash shortage or defaulting on loans.

- *Forecasting:* The next best strategy is to predict environmental changes or variations. In this respect, trend spotters and other marketing specialists gain power by predicting changes in consumer preferences.

- *Absorption:* People and work units also gain power by absorbing or neutralizing the impact of environmental shifts as they occur. An example is the ability of maintenance crews to come to the rescue when machines break down and the production process stops.

CONTINGENCIES OF POWER

Let's say you have expert power because of your ability to forecast and possibly even prevent dramatic changes in the organization's environment. Does this expertise mean you are influential? Not necessarily. As Exhibit 9.2 has illustrated, sources of power generate power only under certain conditions. Four important contingencies of power are substitutability, centrality, discretion, and visibility.[16]

Substitutability

Substitutability refers to the availability of alternatives. Power is strongest when someone has a monopoly over a valued resource. Conversely, power decreases as the number of

alternative sources of the critical resource increases. If you—and no one else—have expertise across the organization on an important issue, you would be more powerful than if several people in your company possessed this valued knowledge. Substitutability refers not only to other sources that offer the resource, but also to substitutions for the resource itself. For instance, labor unions are weakened when companies introduce technologies that replace the need for their union members. Technology is a substitute for employees and consequently reduces union power.

Nonsubstitutability is strengthened by controlling access to the resource. Professions and labor unions gain power by controlling knowledge, tasks, or labor to perform important activities. For instance, the medical profession is powerful because it controls who can perform specific medical procedures. Labor unions that dominate an industry effectively control access to labor needed to perform key jobs. Employees become nonsubstitutable when they possess knowledge (such as operating equipment or serving clients) that is not documented or readily available to others. Nonsubstitutability also occurs when people differentiate their resource from the alternatives. Some people claim that consultants use this tactic. They take skills and knowledge that many other consulting firms can provide and wrap them into a package (with the latest buzzwords, of course) that looks like a service no one else can offer.

Centrality

Centrality refers to the degree and nature of interdependence between the power holder and others.[17] Think about your own centrality for a moment. If you decided not to show up for work or school tomorrow, how many people would be affected, and how much time would pass before they were affected? If you have high centrality, most people in the organization would be adversely affected by your absence, and they would be affected quickly.

The extent to which centrality leverages power is apparent in well-timed labor union strikes, such as the New York City transit strike during the busy Christmas shopping season a few years ago. The illegal three-day work stoppage clogged roads and caused half the city's workers to miss or arrive very late for work. "[The Metropolitan Transit Authority] told us we got no power, but we got power," said one striking transit worker. "We got the power to stop the city."[18]

> " The lack of discretion makes supervisors less powerful than their positions would indicate. "

Discretion

The freedom to exercise judgment—to make decisions without referring to a specific rule or receiving permission from someone else—is another important contingency of power in

Airlines are almost completely shut down when their pilots go on strike. This occurs because pilots have expert power that is amplified by their high centrality in the organization.

organizations. Consider the plight of first-line supervisors. It may seem that they have legitimate, reward, and coercive power over employees, but this power is often curtailed by specific rules. The lack of discretion makes supervisors less powerful than their positions would indicate. "Middle managers are very much 'piggy-in-the-middle,'" complains a middle manager at Britain's National Health System. "They have little power, only what senior managers are allowed to give them."[19] More generally, research indicates that managerial discretion varies considerably across industries, and that managers with an internal locus of control are viewed as more powerful because they don't act as though they lack discretion in their jobs.[20]

Visibility

Power does not flow to unknown people in the organization. Those who control valued resources or knowledge will wield power only when others are aware of these sources of power—in

other words, when the power is visible. One way to increase visibility is to take people-oriented jobs and work on projects that require frequent interaction with senior executives. "You can take visibility in steps," advises an executive at a pharmaceutical firm. "You can start by making yourself visible in a small group, such as a staff meeting. Then when you're comfortable with that, seek out larger arenas."[21]

Employees also gain visibility by being, quite literally, visible. Some people strategically locate themselves in more visible offices, such as those closest to the elevator or staff coffee room. People often use public symbols as subtle (and not-so-subtle) cues to make their power sources known to others. Many professionals display their educational diplomas and awards on office walls to remind visitors of their expertise. Medical professionals wear white coats with stethoscopes around their necks to symbolize their legitimate and expert power in hospital settings. Other people play the game of "face time"—spending more time at work and showing that they are working productively.

Recession-Proofing Your Career through Power and Its Contingencies[22]

- *Take on vital tasks that your boss doesn't like doing.* These responsibilities make you more valuable (nonsubstitutable), visible, and appreciated.

- *Becoming a spokesperson for the work unit or organization.* Increase your visibility and possibly centrality by seeking out opportunities where you publicly represent the company to stakeholders, such as attending industry events.

- *Continually develop your social capital.* Develop and maintain strong and diverse networks with people inside and outside your organization long before you need their assistance. Be sure to help and support them whenever you can without expecting anything in return.

- *Be a great team member.* People are perceived as more valuable when they get along with and support coworkers rather than being an irritant to the team.

- *Continually develop your intellectual capital.* Expert power is perishable. Keep up to date with knowledge, technology, and the latest trends in your field.

- *Maintain a positive can-do attitude.* When the economy tanks, those with fighting spirit who seek out new revenue or cost-saving ideas are appreciated more than ever. You also personally need positive self-talk and a can-do attitude to remain motivated when job security becomes less certain.

- *Be reliable.* Companies need reliable performers more than sporadic top performers. Be sure you can be counted on to get the job done.

- *Make your job substitutable.* Within some caution, earn income outside your job, such as a small online business that doesn't compete with your employer.

- *Document and carefully publicize your accomplishments.* Keep track of your achievements and, without boasting, make them known in subtle ways, such as mentioning them in a personal blog.

to a durable network that connects them to others. Networks consist of people who trust each other, which increases the flow of knowledge among those within the network. The more you network, the more likely you will receive valuable information that increases your expert power in the organization.[23] Second, people tend to identify more with partners within their own networks, which increases referent power among people within each network. This network-based referent power may lead to more favorable decisions by others in the network.

Third, effective networkers are better known by others in the organization, so their talents are more readily recognized. This power increases when networkers place themselves in strategic positions in the network, thereby gaining centrality.[24] For example, an individual might be regarded as the main person who distributes information in the network or who keeps the network connected through informal

Social Networking and Power

"It's not what you know, but whom you know that counts!" This often-heard statement reflects the idea that employees get ahead not just by developing their competencies, but by *social networking*—cultivating social relationships with others to accomplish one's goals. Networking increases a person's power in three ways. First, networks represent a critical component of **social capital**—the knowledge and other resources available to people or social units (teams, organizations) due

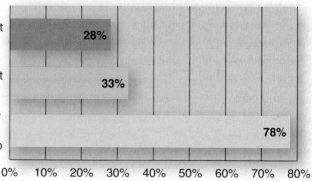

The Power of Personal Networks for Job Hunting[25]

- Employees who found current job through networking: **28%**
- Managers who found current job through networking: **33%**
- College graduates who say personal networks are the most useful for finding a job: **78%**

Percentage of 2,024 American employees and managers surveyed who say they found their current jobs through personal networks, and percentage of 1,250 recent college students and graduates who say personal networks are the most useful means of finding jobs.

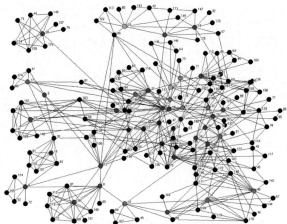

What does this diagram tell you about social networks at Raytheon's engineering center in Colorado? To Raytheon engineering director Karl Arunski, it reveals that some communication and power dynamics are functioning well, whereas others are not achieving the work unit's potential for innovation and performance.[29]

gatherings. Social networks are important foundations of power for individuals, and companies are applying social network analysis tools to discover who has this power. By identifying who is the most connected, leaders know whom to approach for information, who might be the most influential over other employees, and who would be most costly if they leave the company.

Social networks are natural elements of all organizations, yet they can create a formidable barrier to those who are not actively connected to them.[26] Women are often excluded from informal management networks because they do not participate in golf games and other male-dominated social events. Nina Smith, who leads Sage Software's Business Management Division, has had several conversations with female executives about these power dynamics. "I'm still trying to knock down the Boys' Club, and I still have women at Sage coming to me and saying, 'Nina, that's the boys' network and I can't get in.'"[27] Several years ago executives at Deloitte Touche Tohmatsu discovered that inaccessibility to powerful social networks partly explained why many junior female employees left the accounting and consulting firm before reaching partnership level. The Swiss-based accounting firm now relies on mentoring, formal women's network groups, and measurement of career progress to ensure that female staff members have the same career development opportunities as their male colleagues.[28]

Consequences of Power

How does power affect the power holder? We partly answered this question earlier in this book when describing empowerment—an individual's feelings of self-determination, meaning, competence, and impact in the organization. Under the right conditions, employees who receive more power feel more empowered, which tends to increase their motivation, job satisfaction, organizational commitment, and job performance. In addition, research suggests that as people become more powerful, they are more goal directed and tend to act on their environment rather than hide from it.

At the same time, increasing power over others can potentially undermine an individual's effectiveness and interpersonal relations. Some studies have found that people who have (or believe they have) power over others are more likely to cling to stereotypes, have difficulty empathizing, and generally have less accurate perceptions compared with people with less power. They also engage in more automatic rather than mindful thinking, possibly because powerful people are less concerned about the consequences of their actions.[30]

social capital
The knowledge and other resources available to people or social units (teams, organizations) due to a durable network that connects them to others.

influence Any behavior that attempts to alter someone's attitudes or behavior.

Learning Objectives

After reading this section, you should be able to

LO3 Describe eight types of influence tactics, three consequences of influencing others, and three contingencies to consider when choosing an influence tactic.

INFLUENCING OTHERS

We have focused on the sources and contingencies of power. But power is only the *capacity* to influence others. It represents the potential to change someone's attitudes and behavior. **Influence**, on the other hand, refers to any behavior that attempts to alter someone's attitudes or behavior.[31] Influence is power in motion. It applies one or more sources of power to get people to alter their beliefs, feelings, and activities. Consequently our interest in the remainder of this chapter is on how people use power to influence others.

> ## NOTHING MORE ENHANCES AUTHORITY THAN SILENCE. IT IS THE CROWNING VIRTUE OF THE STRONG, THE REFUGE OF THE WEAK, THE MODESTY OF THE PROUD, THE PRIDE OF THE HUMBLE, THE PRUDENCE OF THE WISE, AND THE SENSE OF FOOLS.[35]
>
> —CHARLES DE GAULLE

Influence tactics are woven throughout the social fabric of all organizations. This is because influence is an essential process through which people coordinate their effort and act in concert to achieve organizational objectives. Indeed, influence is central to the definition of leadership. Influence operates down, across, and up the corporate hierarchy. Executives ensure that subordinates complete required tasks. Employees influence coworkers to help them with their job assignments. Subordinates engage in upward influence tactics so corporate leaders make decisions compatible with subordinates' needs and expectations.

Types of Influence Tactics

Organizational behavior researchers have devoted considerable attention to the various types of influence tactics found in organizational settings. They do not agree on a definitive list of influence tactics, but the most commonly identified are listed in Exhibit 9.4 and described over the next few pages.[32] The first five are known as "hard" influence tactics because they force behavior change through position power (legitimate, reward, and coercion). The latter three—persuasion, ingratiation and impression management, and exchange—are called "soft" tactics because they rely more on personal sources of power (referent, expert) and appeal to the target person's attitudes and needs.

Silent Authority The silent application of authority occurs when someone complies with a request because of the requester's legitimate power as well as the target person's role expectations. This condition is known as *deference to authority*.[33] This deference occurs when you comply with your boss's request to complete a particular task. If the task is within your job scope and your boss has the right to make this request, then this influence strategy operates without negotiation, threats, persuasion, or other tactics. Silent authority is the most common form of influence in high power distance cultures.[34]

Assertiveness In contrast to silent authority, assertiveness might be called "vocal authority" because it involves actively applying legitimate and coercive power to influence others. Assertiveness includes persistently reminding the target of his or her obligations, frequently checking the target's work, confronting the target, and using threats of sanctions to force compliance. Assertiveness typically applies or threatens to apply

▼**EXHIBIT 9.4** Types of Influence Tactics in Organizations

Influence Tactic	Description
Silent authority	Influencing behavior through legitimate power without explicitly referring to that power base.
Assertiveness	Actively applying legitimate and coercive power by applying pressure or threats.
Information control	Explicitly manipulating someone else's access to information for the purpose of changing their attitudes and/or behavior.
Coalition formation	Forming a group that attempts to influence others by pooling the resources and power of its members.
Upward appeal	Gaining support from one or more people with higher authority or expertise.
Persuasion	Using logical arguments, factual evidence, and emotional appeals to convince people of the value of a request.
Ingratiation/impression management	Attempting to increase liking by, or perceived similarity to, some targeted person.
Exchange	Promising benefits or resources in exchange for the target person's compliance.

punishment if the target does not comply. Explicit or implicit threats range from job loss to losing face by letting down the team. Extreme forms of assertiveness include blackmailing colleagues, such as by threatening to reveal the other person's previously unknown failures unless he or she complies with your request.

coalition A group that attempts to influence people outside the group by pooling the resources and power of its members.

upward appeal A type of influence in which someone with higher authority or expertise is called upon in reality or symbolically to support the influencer's position.

persuasion Presenting facts, logical arguments, and emotional appeals to change another person's attitudes and behavior.

Information Control

Information control involves explicitly manipulating others' access to information for the purpose of changing their attitudes and/or behavior. With limited access to potentially valuable information, others are at a disadvantage. According to one major survey, almost half of employees believe coworkers keep others in the dark about work issues if it helps their own cause. Employees also influence executive decisions by screening out (filtering) information flowing up the hierarchy. One study found that CEOs influence their boards of directors by selectively feeding and withholding information.[36]

Coalition Formation

When people lack sufficient power alone to influence others in the organization, they might form a **coalition** of people who support the proposed change. A coalition is influential in three ways.[37] First, it pools the power and resources of many people, so the coalition potentially has more influence than any number of people operating alone. Second, the coalition's mere existence can be a source of power by symbolizing the legitimacy of the issue. In other words, a coalition creates a sense that the issue deserves attention because it has broad support. Third, coalitions tap into the power of the social identity process introduced in Chapter 2. A coalition is essentially an informal group that advocates a new set of norms and behaviors. If the coalition has a broad-based membership (that is, if its members come from various parts of the organization), other employees are more likely to identify with that group and consequently accept the ideas the coalition is proposing.

Upward Appeal

Upward appeal involves calling upon higher authority or expertise, or symbolically relying on these sources to support the influencer's position. It occurs when someone says, "The boss likely agrees with me on this matter; let's find out!" Upward appeal also occurs when people rely on the authority of the firm's policies or values. By reminding others that your request is consistent with the organization's overarching goals, you are implying support from senior executives without formally involving them.

> ❝ Persuasion is one of the most effective influence strategies for career success. ❞

Persuasion

Persuasion is one of the most effective influence strategies for career success. The ability to present facts, logical arguments, and emotional appeals to change another person's attitudes and behavior is not just an acceptable way to influence others; in many societies, it is a noble art and a quality of effective leaders. The effectiveness of persuasion as an influence tactic depends on characteristics of the persuader, message content, communication medium, and the audience being persuaded (see Exhibit 9.5).[38] People are more persuasive when listeners believe they have expertise and credibility, as well as demonstrate impartiality, such as when persuaders acknowledge information that favors an opposing position.

The message is more important than the messenger when the issue is important to the audience. Persuasive message content acknowledges several points of view so the audience does

▼**EXHIBIT 9.5** Elements of Persuasion

Persuasion Element	Characteristics of Effective Persuasion
Persuader characteristics	Expertise.
	Credibility.
	No apparent personal gain.
	Appears somewhat neutral (acknowledges benefits of the opposing view).
Message content	Multiple viewpoints (not exclusively supporting the supported option).
	Limited to a few strong arguments (not many arguments).
	Repeat arguments, but not excessively.
	Use emotional appeals in combination with logical arguments.
	Offers specific solutions to overcome the stated problems.
	Inoculation effect—warn audience about counterarguments that opposition will present.
Communication medium	Media-rich channels are usually more persuasive.
Audience characteristics (that resist persuasion)	Self-esteem.
	Intelligence.
	Self-concept tied to the opposing view.

inoculation effect A persuasive communication strategy of warning listeners that others will try to influence them in the future and that they should be wary about the opponent's arguments.

ingratiation Any attempt to increase liking by, or perceived similarity to, some targeted person.

impression management The practice of actively shaping our public images.

not feel cornered by the speaker. The message should also be limited to a few strong arguments that are repeated a few times, but not too frequently. The message should use emotional appeals (such as graphically showing the unfortunate consequences of a bad decision), but only in combination with logical arguments and specific recommendations to overcome the threat. Finally, message content is more persuasive when the audience is warned about opposing arguments. This **inoculation effect** causes listeners to generate counterarguments to the anticipated persuasion attempts, which makes the opponent's subsequent persuasion attempts less effective.[39]

Two other considerations when persuading people are the medium of communication and characteristics of the audience. Persuasion usually works best in face-to-face conversations and through other media-rich communication channels. The personal nature of face-to-face communication increases the persuader's credibility, and the richness of this channel provides faster feedback to show whether the influence strategy is working. With respect to audience characteristics, it is more difficult to persuade people who have high self-esteem and intelligence, as well as a self-concept that is strongly tied to the opposing viewpoint.[40]

Ingratiation and Impression Management
Silent authority, assertiveness, information control, coalitions, and upward appeals are somewhat (or very) forceful ways to influence other people. In contrast, a "soft" influence tactic is **ingratiation**—any attempt to increase liking by, or perceived similarity to, some targeted person.[41] Ingratiation comes in several flavors. Employees might flatter their boss in front of others, demonstrate that they have similar attitudes as their boss (such as by agreeing with the boss's proposal), and ask their boss for advice. Ingratiation is one of the more effective influence tactics at boosting a person's career success (in terms of performance appraisal feedback, salaries, and promotions).[42] However, people who engage in high levels of ingratiation are less (not more) influential and less likely to get promoted.[43] The

explanation for the contrasting evidence is that those who engage in too much ingratiation are viewed as insincere and self-serving. The terms "apple polishing" and "brown-nosing" are applied to those who ingratiate to excess or in ways that suggest selfish motives for the ingratiation.

Ingratiation is part of a larger influence tactic known as impression management. **Impression management** is the practice of actively shaping our public images.[44] These public images might be crafted as being important, vulnerable, threatening, or pleasant. For the most part, employees routinely engage in pleasant impression management behaviors to satisfy the basic norms of social behavior, such as the way they dress and how they behave toward colleagues and customers. Impression management is a common strategy for people trying to get ahead in the workplace. In fact, career professionals encourage people to develop a personal "brand"—that is, to demonstrate and symbolize a distinctive competitive advantage.[45] Just as running shoes and soft drinks have brand images that represent an expectation, successful individuals build a personal brand in which they deliver valued knowledge or skills. Furthermore, people who are adept at personal branding rely on impression management through distinctive personal characteristics. You can more easily recall people who wear distinctive clothing or accoutrements.

Unfortunately a few individuals carry impression management beyond ethical boundaries by exaggerating their credentials and accomplishments on their résumés. For instance, a Lucent Technologies executive lied about having a PhD from Stanford University and hid his criminal past involving forgery and embezzlement. Ironically the executive was Lucent's director of recruiting![47] One of the most elaborate misrepresentations occurred several years ago when a Singaporean entrepreneur sent out news releases claiming to be a renowned artificial intelligence researcher, the author of several books, and the recipient of numerous awards from MIT and Stanford University (one of the awards was illustrated on his Web site). These falsehoods were so convincing that the entrepreneur almost received a real award, the "Internet Visionary of the Year" at the Internet World Asia Industry Awards.[48]

Exchange
Exchange activities involve the promise of benefits or resources in exchange for the target person's compliance with

> "People who engage in high levels of ingratiation (such as 'apple polishing') are less influential because their actions are viewed as insincere and self-serving."

Impression Management in Job Interviews[46]

Interviewer Question	Impression Management Principle	Do Say ...	Don't Say ...
What interests you about this job?	Demonstrate your interest in and respect for this company by seeking a specific job or career here.	"There are exciting things happening at this company, and this position would be a great way for me to grow my skills."	"Well, I just need a job, and this place looks as good as any to find one."
What are your greatest weaknesses?	Demonstrate honesty, self-awareness, and ability to develop yourself.	"Sometimes I take on more tasks than I should. I need to learn how to delegate more for better workload balance and to give others opportunities to develop their skills."	"Gee, I really don't have any weaknesses. I'm a model employee."
Why did you leave your last job?	Demonstrate that you are a positive forward thinker who values this company's career opportunities. Avoid dwelling on negative past events.	"I have a goal to become head of marketing someday. The experience and new skills I would gain here look like an excellent fit with that aspiration."	"Working in my last job was like being on the *Titanic*. Also, I didn't like my boss. He always wanted me to work late, and it caused me to miss my favorite TV show a few times."
Describe a situation in which you had to deal with a professional disagreement or conflict.	Demonstrate that you are a good team player, such as diplomatic conflict handling and problem solving.	"My coworker and I once disagreed on (describe situation). We discussed our different methods and came up with a better way that combined the best of each of our methods."	"I've never had a disagreement. Everyone tends to know I'm right."
How many times do a clock's hands overlap in a day?	These unusual problem-solving questions test more than your technical skills; they also test your motivation and "can-do" attitude to solve problems.	"Let's see, there are 24 hours in a day and every time on the clock happens twice, so ..."	"Gosh, I have no idea. I'm not that good at math."

your request. This tactic also includes reminding the target of past benefits or favors with the expectation that the target will now make up for that debt. The *norm of reciprocity* is a central and explicit theme in exchange strategies. According to the norm of reciprocity, individuals are expected to help those who have helped them.[49] Negotiation is also an integral part of exchange influence activities. For instance, you might negotiate with your boss for a day off in return for working a less desirable shift at a future date.

Networking is another form of exchange as an influence strategy. Active networkers build up "exchange credits" by helping colleagues in the short term for reciprocal benefits in the long term. *Guanxi,* a Chinese term referring to special relationships and active interpersonal connectedness, is well-established in Confucian culture. Guanxi develops the norm of reciprocity, but some Asian governments are concerned that guanxi might lead to favoritism in decisions.[50]

Consequences and Contingencies of Influence Tactics

Now that the main influence strategies have been described, you are probably wondering which ones are best. The best way to answer this question is to identify the three ways that people react when others try to influence them: resistance, compliance, or commitment.[51] *Resistance* occurs when people or work units oppose the behavior desired by the influencer and consequently refuse, argue, or delay engaging in the behavior. *Compliance* occurs when people are motivated to implement the influencer's request at a minimal level of effort and for purely instrumental reasons. Compliance-based behavior occurs only when external sources motivate it. *Commitment* is the strongest form of influence, whereby people identify with the influencer's request and are highly motivated to implement it even when extrinsic sources of motivation are no longer present.

organizational politics Behaviors that others perceive as self-serving tactics for personal gain at the expense of other people and possibly the organization.

▼**EXHIBIT 9.6** Consequences of Hard and Soft Influence Tactics

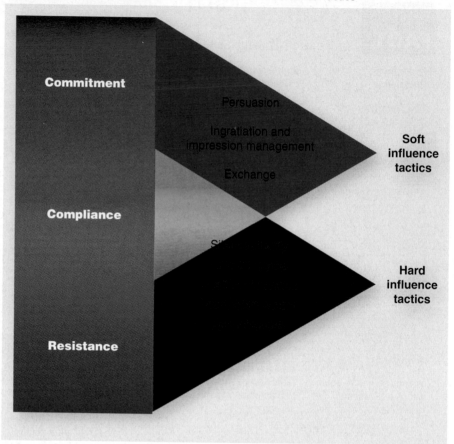

Generally people react more favorably to "soft" tactics than to "hard" tactics (see Exhibit 9.6). Soft influence tactics rely on personal sources of power (expert and referent power), which tend to build commitment to the influencer's request. In contrast, hard tactics rely on position power (legitimate, reward, and coercion), so they tend to produce compliance or, worse, resistance. Hard tactics also tend to undermine trust, which can hurt future relationships.

Apart from the general preference for soft rather than hard tactics, the most appropriate influence strategy depends on a few contingencies. One obvious contingency is which sources of power are strongest. Those with expertise tend to have more influence using persuasion, whereas those with a strong legitimate power base are usually more successful applying silent authority.[52] A second contingency is whether the person being influenced is higher, lower, or at the same level in the organization. As an example, employees may face adverse career consequences by being too assertive with their boss. Meanwhile, supervisors who engage in ingratiation and impression management tend to lose the respect of their staff.

Finally, the most appropriate influence tactic depends on personal, organizational, and cultural values.[53] People with a strong power orientation might feel more comfortable using assertiveness, whereas those who value conformity might feel more comfortable with upward appeals. At an organizational level, firms with a competitive culture might sanction the use of information control and coalition formation, whereas companies with a learning orientation would likely encourage more influence through persuasion. The preferred influence tactics also vary across societal cultures. Research indicates that ingratiation is much more common among managers in the United States than in Hong Kong, possibly because this tactic disrupts the more distant roles that managers and employees expect in high power distance cultures.

Learning Objectives

After reading this section, you should be able to

LO4 Identify the organizational conditions and personal characteristics that support organizational politics, as well as ways to minimize organizational politics.

INFLUENCE TACTICS AND ORGANIZATIONAL POLITICS

You might have noticed that organizational politics has not been mentioned yet, even though some of the practices and examples described over the past few pages are usually considered political tactics. The phrase was carefully avoided because, for the most part, organizational politics is in the eye of the beholder. You might perceive a coworker's attempt to influence the boss as acceptable behavior for the good of the organization,

[Soft influence tactics tend to build commitment to the influencer's request, whereas hard tactics tend to produce compliance or, worse, resistance.]

SWALLOWED!

whereas someone else might perceive the coworker's tactic as brazen organizational politics.

This perceptual issue explains why OB experts increasingly discuss influence tactics as behaviors and organizational politics as

perceptions.[55] The influence tactics described earlier are perceived as **organizational politics** when they seem to be self-serving behaviors at the expense of others and possibly contrary to the interests of the entire organization. Of course some tactics are so blatantly selfish and counterproductive that almost everyone correctly sees them as political. In other situations, however, a person's behavior might be viewed either as political or in the organization's best interest.

When employees perceive many incidents of organizational politics, the result is lower job satisfaction, organizational commitment, organizational citizenship, and task performance, as well as higher levels of work-related stress and motivation to leave the organization.[56] And because political tactics serve individuals rather than organizations, they potentially divert resources away from the organization's effective functioning and can threaten its survival.

Office Politics
by the Numbers[54]

53% of British managers polled who feel that organizational politics is a major cause of stress at work (top-ranked cause of stress.)

47% of American employees polled who say that office politics cuts into productive time (second highest cause, after fixing someone else's work).

36% of Canadian employees polled who say that office politics is one of the biggest roadblocks to productivity.

19% of Canadian employees polled 10 years ago who said that office politics is one of the biggest roadblocks to productivity.

29% of American employees polled who say a coworker has taken credit for one of their ideas.

58% of Canadian employees polled who say a coworker has taken credit for one of their ideas.

Conditions Supporting Organizational Politics

Employees are more likely to engage in organizational politics (that is, use influence tactics for personal gain) under certain conditions.[57] One of those conditions is scarce resources. When budgets are slashed, people rely on political tactics to safeguard their resources and maintain the status quo. Office politics also flourishes when resource allocation decisions are ambiguous, complex, or lack formal rules. This occurs because decision makers are given more

Machiavellian values The beliefs that deceit is a natural and acceptable way to influence others.

discretion over resource allocation, so potential recipients of those resources use political tactics to influence the factors that should be considered in the decision. Organizational change encourages political behaviors for this reason. Change creates uncertainty and ambiguity as the company moves from an old set of rules and practices to a new set. During these times, employees apply political strategies to protect their valued resources, positions, and self-concepts.[58]

Personal Characteristics of Organizational Politicians

Several personal characteristics affect a person's motivation to engage in self-serving behavior.[59] This includes a strong need for personal as opposed to socialized power. Those with a need for personal power seek power for its own sake and try to acquire more power. Some individuals have strong **Machiavellian values**. Machiavellianism is named after Niccolò Machiavelli, the 16th-century Italian philosopher who wrote *The Prince*, a famous treatise about political behavior. People with high Machiavellian values are comfortable with getting more than they deserve, and they believe that deceit is a natural and acceptable way to achieve this goal. They seldom trust coworkers and tend to use cruder influence tactics, such as bypassing one's boss or being assertive, to get their own way.[60]

Minimizing Organizational Politics and Its Consequences

The conditions that fuel organizational politics also give us some clues about how to control dysfunctional political activities.[62] One strategy to keep organizational politics in check is to introduce clear rules and regulations to specify the use of scarce resources. Organizational politics can become a problem during times of organizational change, so politics can be minimized through effective organizational change practices. Leaders also need to actively manage group norms to

> ## "Keep your friends close and your enemies closer.[63]
> ### —Attributed to Sun Tzu"

curtail self-serving influence activities. In particular, they can support organizational values that oppose political tactics, such as altruism and customer focus. One of the most important strategies is for leaders to become role models of organizational citizenship rather than symbols of successful organizational politicians.

FACT. **Coming up Next, Philadelphia's Top Political Story . . .[61]**

Over a two-year period, Philadelphia news coanchor Alycia Lane was subject to malicious news stories from anonymous sources about her off-air behavior. Lane's coanchor, Larry Mendte, showed concern when these stories emerged; but, Lane claims, he suggested that the best solution would be for her to move to another city. Soon after she lost her job (partly due to the rumors), Lane discovered why Mendte offered this advice: he was likely the person who fed private information about Lane to the media. The FBI found that Mendte used keystroke software to gain access to Lane's e-mail, and that he looked at her e-mail at least 500 times. Lane's attorney claims that Mendte sent Lane's e-mail messages to newspapers because "[Alycia Lane's] star was climbing, while his was not climbing. . . . His conduct was designed to undermine her." Mendte's e-mail tampering surprised most people, but not everyone who knew him. One former colleague claims that "[Mendte] was great to my face and manipulative and destructive behind my back." Another TV insider suggests that "Larry worked hard to take Alycia down."

Along with minimizing organizational politics, companies can limit the adverse effects of political perceptions by giving employees more control over their work and keeping them informed about organizational events. Research has found that employees who are kept informed about what is going on in the organization and who are involved in organizational decisions are less likely to experience organizational politics, which reduces stress, job dissatisfaction, and absenteeism. ■

CHECK IT OUT!

mhhe.com/McShaneM

for study materials
including quizzes
and Internet resources

understanding and managing
workplace conflict

To reward themselves for a job well done, a team of young employees at Western Technical College create funny mock videos or throw a pizza party during office hours. Those events bother some older staff at the La Crosse, Wisconsin, college. This conflict comes as no surprise to Linda Gravett. "We had a sense that there was tension," says Gravett, a human resources consultant at Xavier University in Cincinnati. Gravett and colleague Robin Throckmorton identified many forms of intergenerational conflict in their recent book about this subject. "This was confirmed in our research. We found there was a lot of generational tension around the use of technology and work ethics."[1]

One of the facts of life is that people hold different points of view. They have unique values hierarchies, develop unique perceptions of reality, and establish different norms about acceptable behavior in social settings. At the same time, organizations are living systems that demand dynamic rather than static relationships among employees. In other words, employees at Western Technical College and other organizations need to frequently agree on new work arrangements, revise the company's strategic direction, and renegotiate the allocation of scarce resources required to perform their jobs. ■

LEARNING OBJECTIVES

After reading this chapter, you should be able to

LO1 Debate the positive and negative consequences of conflict in the workplace.

LO2 Distinguish constructive from relationship conflict and describe three strategies to minimize relationship conflict during constructive conflict episodes.

LO3 Diagram the conflict process model and describe six structural sources of conflict in organizations.

LO4 Outline the five conflict handling styles and discuss the circumstances in which each would be most appropriate.

LO5 Compare and contrast six structural approaches to managing conflict and three types of third-party dispute resolution.

conflict Is a process in which one party perceives that its interests are being opposed or negatively affected by another party.

Given that people do not have identical viewpoints, this dynamic relationship necessarily leads to conflict. **Conflict** is a process in which one party perceives that its interests are being opposed or negatively affected by another party.[3] It may occur when one party obstructs or plans to obstruct another's goals in some way. For example, baby boomer managers experience conflict with younger employees who spend time on Facebook, believing that this interferes with the manager's goal of completing departmental deadlines on time. Facebook-loving employees experience conflict with their bosses because they view this form of communication as a valuable way to network, keep informed, and (contrary to the boss's opinion) achieve departmental objectives. Conflict is ultimately based on perceptions; it exists whenever one party *believes* that another might obstruct its efforts, whether the other party actually intends to do so.

This chapter investigates the dynamics of conflict in organizational settings. We begin by considering this age-old question: Is conflict good or bad? Next we describe the conflict process and examine in detail the main factors that cause or amplify conflict. The five styles of handling conflict are then described, followed by a discussion of the structural approaches to conflict management. The last section of this chapter reviews the role of managers and others in third-party conflict resolution.

Learning Objectives

After reading this section, you should be able to

LO1 Debate the positive and negative consequences of conflict in the workplace.

LO2 Distinguish constructive from relationship conflict and describe three strategies to minimize relationship conflict during constructive conflict episodes.

IS CONFLICT GOOD OR BAD?

For the past century, and likely much longer, experts have been debating whether conflict is good or bad for organizations. The "conflict-is-bad" perspective has prevailed for most of that time.[4] According to this perspective, even moderately low levels of disagreement tatter the fabric of workplace relations and sap energy away from productive activities. Although the "conflict-is-bad" perspective is now considered too simplistic, numerous studies report that conflict can have negative consequences (Exhibit 10.1).[5] Conflict can be stressful and distracting, which undermines productivity and job satisfaction. In some cases valuable employees quit because they can no longer endure the conflict episodes. When people experience conflict, they are less motivated to share resources with the other party. Conflict fuels organizational politics, such as motivating employees to find ways to undermine the credibility of their opponents. Decision making suffers because people are less motivated to communicate valuable information. Ironically, with less communication, the feuding parties are more likely to escalate their disagreement because each side relies increasingly on distorted perceptions and stereotypes of the other party. Finally, conflict among team members may undermine team cohesion.

Despite these well-documented problems with conflict, Mary Parker Follett suggested more than 80 years ago that moderate levels of conflict can produce desirable outcomes.[6] Follett was a popular political scientist, social worker, and management theorist, but her ideas about conflict were slow to gain support. It wasn't until the 1970s that conflict management experts began to embrace the "optimal conflict" perspective, which states that organizations are most effective when there is neither too little nor too much conflict among employees.[7] The optimal conflict view was based on growing evidence that a moderate level of conflict sparks debate, which energizes people to evaluate alternatives more thoroughly by testing the logic of arguments and reexamining basic assumptions about the decision

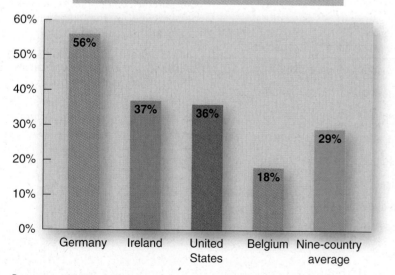

Frequently or Always Dealing with Workplace Conflict[2]

Percentage of 5,000 employees surveyed in nine countries (Belgium, Brazil, Denmark, France, Germany, Ireland, the Netherlands, the United Kingdom, and the United States) who say they always or frequently have to deal with workplace conflict. Selected countries and average results are shown in this chart.

> " Conflict is the gadfly of thought. It stirs us to observation and memory. It instigates to invention. It shocks us out of sheeplike passivity, and sets us at noting and contriving.[10]
>
> —John Dewey "

▼**EXHIBIT 10.1** Outcomes of Workplace Conflict

Negative Outcomes	Positive Outcomes
Less information sharing.	Better decision making; tests logic of arguments; questions assumptions.
Higher stress and job dissatisfaction.	
Valued employees quit.	More responsive to changing environment.
Increases organizational politics.	
Wastes resources.	Stronger team cohesion (when conflict occurs between the team and an outside source).
Weakens team cohesion (when conflict occurs among team members).	

maker's preferences. By generating active thinking, conflict potentially also improves creativity.[8]

A second apparent benefit of moderate conflict is that it prevents organizations from stagnating and becoming nonresponsive to their external environment. Through conflict, employees continuously question current practices and become more sensitive to dissatisfaction from stakeholders. In other words, conflict generates more vigilance.[9] A third benefit is that some degree of conflict with people outside the team potentially increases cohesion

within the team (see Chapter 7). People are more motivated to work together when faced with an external threat, such as conflict with people outside the team.

The Emerging View: Constructive and Relationship Conflict

Although the "optimal conflict" perspective still dominates conflict management writing, an emerging school of thought formed in the 1990s. This emerging perspective proposes that there are two types of conflict with opposing consequences: constructive conflict and relationship conflict.[11] **Constructive conflict** occurs when people focus their discussion around the issue while showing respect for people with other points of view. This conflict is called "constructive" because different positions are encouraged so ideas and recommendations can be clarified, redesigned, and tested for logical soundness. Keeping the debate focused on the issue helps participants to reexamine their assumptions and beliefs without triggering the drive to defend and its associated negative emotions and ego defense mechanism behaviors. Teams and organizations with very low levels of constructive conflict are less effective, but there is also likely an upper limit to the level of intensity of constructive conflict.[12]

In contrast to constructive conflict, **relationship conflict** focuses on the other party as the source of conflict. This type of conflict is apparent when the conflict is explained in terms of interpersonal incompatibilities or "personality clashes" rather than legitimate differences of opinion regarding tasks or decisions. When relationship conflict dominates, the parties attack each other's credibility, intelligence, and competence. These actions are more likely to trigger defense mechanisms and a competitive orientation. The verbal attacks reduce the motivation to communicate or share information, making it more difficult for the parties to discover common ground and ultimately resolve the conflict. Instead they increasingly rely on distorted perceptions and stereotypes, which further escalate the conflict. Relationship conflict is sometimes called "socioemotional" or "affective" conflict because people experience and react to strong emotional responses during these conflict episodes.

> " Most of us experience some degree of relationship conflict during and after any constructive debate. "

Separating Constructive from Relationship Conflict The current perspective that there are two types of conflict leads to the logical conclusion that we should encourage constructive conflict and minimize relationship conflict. This recommendation sounds good in theory, but recent evidence suggests that separating these two types of conflict isn't easy. Most of us experience some degree of relationship conflict during and after any constructive debate.[14] In other words, any attempt to engage in constructive conflict, no matter how calmly and rationally, may still sow the seeds of relationship conflict. The stronger the level of debate and the more the issue is tied to the individual's self-concept, the higher the chance that the constructive conflict will evolve into (or mix with) relationship conflict.

Constructive Confrontation inside Intel[13]

Until a few years ago, Intel engineers were obsessed with designing computer processors that were faster, smaller, and ultimately hotter and more power-hungry. But key people at Intel's Israeli operations saw trouble brewing. Almost weekly, they would fly from Haifa to Intel's headquarters in California, "pestering" top executives with data and arguments that the company would soon hit the limits of chip speed. The Israeli crew also warned that Intel would lose out to competitors for cooler and more power-efficient "mobility" chips for laptops and other mobility devices. The conflict may have rankled some Intel bosses, but the Israeli staff convinced Intel to change direction. Their persistent arguing also demonstrated the value of "constructive confrontation"—the art of argument and respectful debate that Intel cofounder Andy Grove encouraged long ago. The practice is so important that new Intel employees are taught the fine art of confrontation through supervised debates and role plays. "The goal of a leader should be to maximize resistance—in the sense of encouraging disagreement and dissent," says Dov Frohman, founder of Intel Israel.

constructive conflict Occurs when people focus their discussion on the issue while maintaining respectfulness for people having other points of view.

relationship conflict Occurs when people focus on characteristics of other individuals rather than the issues as the source of conflict.

- *Supportive team norms:* Various team norms can hold relationship conflict at bay during constructive debate. When team norms encourage openness, for instance, team members learn to appreciate honest dialogue without personally reacting to any emotional display during the disagreements.[16] Other norms might discourage team members from displaying negative emotions toward coworkers. Team norms can also encourage tactics that diffuse relationship conflict when it first appears. For instance, research has found that teams with low relationship conflict use humor to maintain positive group emotions, which offsets negative feelings team members might develop toward some coworkers during debate.

Fortunately conflict management experts have identified three strategies that potentially minimize the level of relationship conflict during constructive conflict episodes:[15]

- *Emotional intelligence:* Relationship conflict is less likely to occur, or is less likely to escalate, when team members have high levels of emotional intelligence. Emotionally intelligent employees are better able to regulate their emotions during debate, which reduces the risk of escalating perceptions of interpersonal hostility. People with high emotional intelligence are also more likely to view a coworker's emotional reaction as valuable information about that person's needs and expectations, rather than as a personal attack.

- *Cohesive team:* Relationship conflict is suppressed when the conflict occurs within a highly cohesive team. The longer people work together, get to know each other, and develop mutual trust, the more latitude they give to each other to show emotions without being personally offended. Strong cohesion also allows team members to know about and anticipate the behaviors and emotions of their teammates. Another benefit is that cohesion produces a stronger social identity with the group, so team members are motivated to avoid escalating relationship conflict during otherwise emotionally turbulent discussions.

Learning Objectives

After reading the next two sections, you should be able to

L03 Diagram the conflict process model and describe six structural sources of conflict in organizations.

CONFLICT PROCESS MODEL

Now that we have outlined the history and current knowledge about conflict and its outcomes, let's look at the model of the conflict process, shown in Exhibit 10.2.[17] This model begins with the sources of conflict, which we will describe in more detail in the next section. At some point, the sources of conflict lead one or both parties to perceive that conflict exists. They

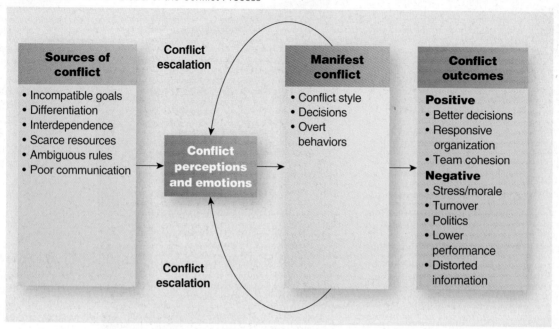

become aware that one party's statements and actions are incompatible with their own goals. These perceptions usually interact with emotions experienced about the conflict.[18] Conflict perceptions and emotions manifest themselves in the decisions and behaviors of one party toward the other. These *conflict episodes* may range from subtle nonverbal behaviors to warlike aggression. Particularly when people experience high levels of conflict emotions, they have difficulty finding words and expressions that communicate effectively without further irritating the relationship.[19] Conflict is also manifested by the style each side uses to resolve the conflict. Some people tend to avoid the conflict, whereas others try to defeat those with opposing views.

Exhibit 10.2 shows arrows looping back from manifest conflict to conflict perceptions and emotions. These arrows illustrate that the conflict process is really a series of episodes that potentially cycle into conflict escalation.[20] It doesn't take much to start this conflict cycle—just an inappropriate comment, a misunderstanding, or an action that lacks diplomacy. These behaviors cause the other party to perceive that conflict exists. Even if the first party did not intend to demonstrate conflict, the second party's response may create that perception.

STRUCTURAL SOURCES OF CONFLICT IN ORGANIZATIONS

The conflict model starts with the sources of conflict, so we need to understand these sources to effectively diagnose conflict episodes and subsequently resolve a conflict or occasionally

to generate conflict where it is lacking. The six main conditions that cause conflict in organizational settings are incompatible goals, differentiation, interdependence, scarce resources, ambiguous rules, and communication problems.

Incompatible Goals

Goal incompatibility occurs when the goals of one person or department seem to interfere with another person's or department's goals.[21] For example, the production department strives for cost efficiency by scheduling long production runs, whereas the sales team emphasizes customer service by delivering the client's product as quickly as possible. If the company runs out of a particular product, the production team would prefer to have clients wait until the next production run. This infuriates sales representatives, who would rather change production quickly to satisfy consumer demand.

Goal incompatibility partly explains some of the conflicts reported at Microsoft in recent years. For example, Microsoft's MSN group fought against the Microsoft Office Group over MSN's desire to connect their online calendar with the calendar in Office. The Office group balked because "then MSN could cannibalize Office," says an employee who left Microsoft. "Windows and Office would never let MSN have more budget or more control."[22] MSN's goal of providing users with better calendar integration threatened the Microsoft Office group's product territory, which might have undermined its profitability or control over the calendar feature.

Differentiation

Another source of conflict is differentiation—differences among people, departments, and other entities regarding their training, values, beliefs, and experiences. Differentiation can be distinguished from goal incompatibility because two people or departments may agree on a common goal but have profound differences in how to achieve that goal. Consider the classic tension between employees from two companies brought together through a merger. Staff in each organization fight over the "right way" to do things because of their unique experiences in the separate companies.

Intergenerational conflicts, which were described at the beginning of this chapter, are also mainly caused by differentiation. Younger and older employees have different needs, different expectations, and different workplace practices, which sometimes produce conflicting preferences and actions. Recent studies suggest that intergenerational differences occur because people develop social identities around technological developments and other pivotal social events.[24]

Interdependence

Conflict tends to increase with the level of interdependence. Interdependence exists when team members must share common inputs to their individual tasks, need to interact in the process of executing their work, or receive outcomes (such as rewards) that are partly determined by the performance of others.[26] Higher interdependence increases the risk of conflict because there is a greater chance that each side will disrupt or interfere with the other side's goals.[27]

Other than complete independence, employees tend to have the lowest risk of conflict when working with others in a pooled interdependence relationship. Pooled interdependence occurs where individuals operate independently except for reliance on a common resource or authority (see Chapter 7). The potential for conflict is higher in sequential interdependence work relationships, such as an assembly line. The highest risk of conflict tends to occur in reciprocal interdependence situations. With reciprocal interdependence, employees are highly dependent on each other and, consequently, have a higher probability of interfering with each other's work and personal goals.

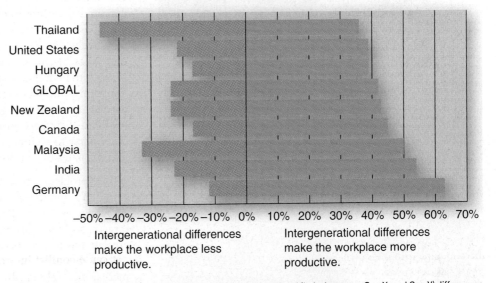

Percentage of employees by country who believe that intergenerational (baby boomers, Gen X, and Gen Y) differences have a positive or negative effect on workplace productivity. The chart does not show the percentage of people who say generational differences have no effect on productivity. Based on a survey of 100,000 employees in 33 countries.

Scarce Resources

Resource scarcity generates conflict because each person or unit requiring the same resource necessarily undermines others who also need that resource to fulfill their goals. Consider the famed lively debates among employees at Intel. These conflict episodes occur partly because there aren't enough financial, human capital, and other resources for everyone to accomplish their goals, so employees need to justify why they should receive the resources. If one camp of Intel employees believes the future is in

and resources.[28] When clear rules exist, on the other hand, employees know what to expect from each other and have agreed to abide by those rules.

Communication Problems

Conflict often occurs due to the lack of opportunity, ability, or motivation to communicate effectively. Let's look at each of these causes. First, when two parties lack the opportunity to communicate, they tend to rely more on stereotypes to understand the other party in the conflict. Unfortunately, stereotypes are sufficiently subjective that emotions can negatively distort the meaning of an opponent's actions, thereby escalating perceptions of conflict. Second, some people lack the necessary skills to communicate in a diplomatic, nonconfrontational manner. When one party communicates its disagreement arrogantly, opponents are more likely to heighten their perception of the conflict. This may lead the other party to reciprocate with a similar response, which further escalates the conflict.[29]

A third problem is that the perception of conflict reduces motivation to communicate. Relationship conflict is uncomfortable, so people are less motivated to communicate with others in a disagreement. Unfortunately, less communication can further escalate the conflict because each side has less accurate information about the other side's intentions. To fill in the missing pieces, they rely on distorted images and stereotypes of the other party. Perceptions are further distorted because people in conflict situations tend to engage in more differentiation with those who are different from them (see Chapter 3). This differentiation creates a more positive self-concept and a more negative image of the opponent. We begin to see competitors less favorably so our self-concept remains positive during these uncertain times.[30]

faster (and more power-hungry) chips and another camp believes the future is in low-power mobility chips, conflict will occur if there are not enough financial and human resources to invest in both directions. In other words, the more resources one project receives, the fewer resources another project will have available to accomplish its goals.

Ambiguous Rules

Ambiguous rules—or the complete lack of rules—breed conflict. This occurs because uncertainty increases the risk that one party intends to interfere with the other party's goals. Ambiguity also encourages political tactics, and in some cases, employees enter a free-for-all battle to win decisions in their favor. This explains why conflict is more common during mergers and acquisitions. Employees from both companies have conflicting practices and values, and few rules have developed to minimize the maneuvering for power

Learning Objectives

After reading this section, you should be able to

LO4 Outline the five conflict handling styles and discuss the circumstances in which each would be most appropriate.

INTERPERSONAL CONFLICT HANDLING STYLES

The six structural conditions just described set the stage for conflict, and these sources lead to conflict perceptions and emotions that, in turn, motivate people to take some sort of action to address the conflict. Mary Parker Follett, who first proposed that some

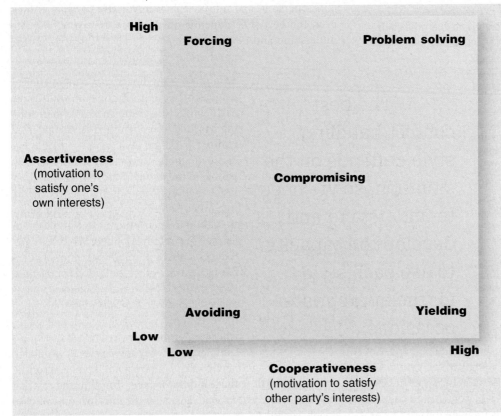

Sources: C. K. W. de Dreu, A. Evers, B. Beersma, E. S. Kluwer, and A. Nauta, "A Theory-Based Measure of Conflict Management Strategies in the Workplace," *Journal of Organizational Behavior*, 22 (2001), pp. 645–68. For other variations of this model, see T. L. Ruble and K. Thomas, "Support For a Two-Dimensional Model of Conflict Behavior," *Organizational Behavior and Human Performance*, 16 (1976), p. 145; R. R. Blake, H. A. Shepard, and J. S. Mouton. *Managing Intergroup Conflict in Industry* (Houston: Gulf Publishing, 1964); and M. A. Rahim, "Toward a Theory of Managing Organizational Conflict," *International Journal of Conflict Management* 13, no. 3 (2002), pp. 206–35.

win–win orientation
The belief that the parties will find a mutually beneficial solution to their disagreement.

win–lose orientation
The belief that conflicting parties are drawing from a fixed pie, so the more one party receives, the less the other party will receive.

conflict is beneficial, also identified several conflict handling styles. Conflict management experts have developed and refined our understanding of these styles, with the most common variations depicted in the five-category model shown in Exhibit 10.3 and described here:[31]

- *Problem solving:* Problem solving tries to find a solution that is beneficial for both parties. This is known as the **win–win orientation** because people using this style believe the resources at stake are expandable rather than fixed if the parties work together to find a creative solution. Information sharing is an important feature of this

> [The more arguments you win, the fewer friends you will have.[32]
> —Mid-20th-century American proverb]

style because both parties collaborate to identify common ground and potential solutions that satisfy everyone involved.

- *Forcing:* Forcing tries to win the conflict at the other's expense. People who use this style typically have a **win–lose orientation**—they believe the parties are drawing from a fixed pie, so the more one party receives, the less the other party will receive. Consequently this style relies on some of the "hard" influence tactics described in Chapter 9, particularly assertiveness, to get one's own way.

- *Avoiding:* Avoiding tries to smooth over or avoid conflict situations altogether. It represents a low concern for both self and the other party; in other words, avoiders try to suppress thinking about the conflict. For example, some employees will rearrange their work area or tasks to minimize interaction with certain coworkers.[33]

- *Yielding:* Yielding is giving in completely to the other side's wishes, or at least cooperating with little or no attention to your own interests. This style involves making unilateral concessions and unconditional promises, as well as offering help with no expectation of reciprocal help.

- *Compromising:* Compromising is looking for a position in which your losses are offset by equally valued gains. It involves matching the other party's concessions, making conditional promises or threats, and actively searching for a middle ground between the interests of the two parties.

Choosing the Best Conflict Handling Style

Chances are that you have a preferred conflict handling style. You might have a tendency toward avoiding or yielding because disagreement makes you feel uncomfortable and is inconsistent with your self-concept as someone who likes to get along with everyone. Or perhaps you prefer the compromising and forcing strategies because they reflect your strong need for achievement and control over your environment. People usually gravitate toward one or

> The best conflict-handling style depends on the situation, so we need to understand and develop the capacity to use each style for the appropriate occasions.

two preferred conflict handling styles that match their personalities, personal and cultural values, and past experiences. However, the best style depends on the situation, so we need to understand and develop the capacity to use each style for the appropriate occasions.[34]

Exhibit 10. 4 summarizes the main contingencies of, as well as problems with using, each conflict handling style. Problem solving has long been identified as the preferred conflict handling style where possible because dialogue and clever thinking help people to break out of the limited boundaries of their opposing alternatives to find an integrated solution where both gain value. In addition, recent studies report that problem solving improves long-term relationships, reduces stress, and minimizes emotional defensiveness and other indications of relationship conflict.[35] However, problem solving is the best choice of conflict handling only when there is some potential for mutual gains, which is more likely to occur when the issue is complex, and when the parties have enough trust, openness, and time to share information. If problem solving is used under the wrong conditions, there is an increased risk that the other party will take advantage of the information you have openly shared.

▼**EXHIBIT 10.4** Conflict Handling Style Contingencies and Problems

Conflict Handling Style	Preferred Style When . . .	Problems with this Style
Problem solving	• Interests are not perfectly opposing (i.e., not pure win–lose). • The parties have trust, openness, and time to share information. • The issues are complex.	• Sharing information that the other party might use to their advantage.
Forcing	• You have a deep conviction about your position (e.g., you believe the other person's behavior is unethical). • The dispute requires a quick solution. • The other party would take advantage of more cooperative strategies.	• Highest risk of relationship conflict. • May damage long-term relations, reducing future problem solving.
Avoiding	• The conflict has become too emotionally charged. • The cost of trying to resolve the conflict outweighs the benefits.	• Doesn't usually resolve the conflict. • May increase the other party's frustration.
Yielding	• The other party has substantially more power. • The issue is much less important to you than to the other party. • The value and logic of your position are not as clear.	• Increases the other party's expectations in future conflict episodes.
Compromising	• The parties have equal power. • There is time pressure to resolve the conflict. • The parties lack trust/openness for problem solving.	• Suboptimal solution where mutual gains are possible.

You might think that avoiding is an ineffective conflict management strategy, but it is actually the best approach if a conflict has become emotionally charged or if negotiating has a higher cost than the benefits of conflict resolution.[36] At the same time, conflict avoidance is often ineffective because it doesn't resolve the conflict and may increase the other party's frustration. The forcing style of conflict resolution is usually inappropriate because research indicates that it generates relationship conflict more quickly or intensely than other conflict handling styles. However, forcing may be necessary when you know you are correct (for example, if the other party's position is unethical or is based on obviously flawed logic), the dispute requires a quick solution, or the other party would take advantage of a more cooperative conflict handling style.

The yielding style may be appropriate when the other party has substantially more power, the issue is not as important to you as to the other party, and you aren't confident that your position has the best value or logical consistency. On the other hand, yielding behaviors may give the other side unrealistically high expectations, thereby motivating them to seek more from you in the future. In the long run, yielding may produce more conflict rather than resolving it. The compromising style may be best when there is little hope for mutual gain through problem solving, both parties have equal power, and both are under time pressure to settle their differences. However, we rarely know for certain that mutual gains are not available, so entering a conflict with the compromising style may cause the parties to overlook better solutions.

Steering Clear of Workplace Conflict[37]

67% of employees polled* who have gone out of their way to avoid a colleague because of a disagreement at work.

24% of employees polled* who have stayed away from a work-related social event to avoid a workplace conflict.

10% of employees polled* who have failed to attend meetings to avoid a workplace conflict.

14% of employees polled* who have missed a day of work to avoid a workplace conflict.

*5,000 employees from nine countries in Europe and the Americas.

Cultural and Gender Differences in Conflict Handling Styles

Cultural differences are more than just a source of conflict. Cultural background also affects the preferred conflict handling style.[38] Some research suggests that people from collectivist cultures— where group goals are valued more than individual goals—are motivated to maintain harmonious relations and, consequently, are more likely than those from low collectivist cultures to manage disagreements through avoidance or problem solving. However, this view may be somewhat simplistic because people in some collectivist cultures are also more likely to publicly shame those whose actions conflict with expectations.[39]

Some writers suggest that men and women also tend to rely on different conflict handling styles.[40] They suggest that, compared to men, women pay more attention to the relationship between the parties. Consequently, women tend to adopt a compromising or occasionally problem-solving style in business settings and are more willing to compromise to protect the relationship. Men tend to be more competitive and take a short-term orientation to the relationship. In low collectivist cultures, men are more likely than women to use the forcing approach to conflict handling. However, we must be cautious about these observations because gender usually has a weak influence on conflict management style.

Learning Objectives

After reading the next two sections, you should be able to

LO5 Compare and contrast six structural approaches to managing conflict and three types of third-party dispute resolution.

STRUCTURAL APPROACHES TO CONFLICT MANAGEMENT

Conflict handling styles describe how we approach the other party in a conflict situation. But conflict management also involves altering the underlying structural causes of potential conflict. The main structural

AS PEOPLE DEVELOP A SHARED REPOSITORY OF EXPERIENCES AND BELIEFS, THEY BECOME MORE MOTIVATED TO COORDINATE ACTIVITIES AND RESOLVE THEIR DISPUTES THROUGH CONSTRUCTIVE DISCUSSION.

approaches are emphasizing superordinate goals, reducing differentiation, improving communication and understanding, reducing task interdependence, increasing resources, and clarifying rules and procedures.

Emphasizing Superordinate Goals

One of the oldest recommendations for resolving conflict is to seek out common goals.[41] In organizational settings, this typically takes the form of a superordinate goal, which is any goal that both conflicting parties value and whose attainment is beyond the resources and effort of either party alone.[42] By increasing commitment to corporate-wide goals, employees pay less attention to competing individual or departmental-level goals, which reduces their perceived conflict with coworkers. They also potentially reduce the problem of differentiation by establishing a common frame of reference. For example, research indicates that the most effective executive teams frame their decisions as superordinate goals that rise above each executive's departmental or divisional goals.[43]

Reducing Differentiation

Another way to minimize dysfunctional conflict is to reduce the differences that generate conflict. As people develop a shared repository of experiences and beliefs, they become more motivated to coordinate activities and resolve their disputes through constructive discussion.[44]

One way to reduce differentiation is by creating common experiences. SAP, the German enterprise software company, applied this strategy when it recently acquired Business Objects, a French company with a strong U.S. presence. Conflict is common following many acquisitions because employees at each company have different cultures, experiences, and loyalties. SAP minimized this differentiation by immediately intermingling people from the two organizations. "In the first six months after the acquisition, more than 35 percent of senior managers transferred from SAP while all the original Business Objects corporate services people are now a part of a global shared services team," says Business Objects CEO John Schwarz. "We also encourage cross-border, cross-functional teamwork on projects such as major product releases. In this way team members come to depend on each other."[45]

Improving Communication and Understanding

A third way to resolve dysfunctional conflict is to give the conflicting parties more opportunities to communicate and understand each other. This recommendation applies the contact hypothesis (see Chapter 3)—namely that we rely less on stereotypes to understand someone as we have more meaningful interaction with that person.[46] There are two warnings, however. First, communication and understanding interventions should be applied only *after* differentiation between the two sides has been reduced or where differentiation is already sufficiently low. If perceived differentiation remains high, attempts to manage conflict through dialogue might escalate rather than reduce relationship conflict. The reason is that when forced to interact with people who we believe are quite different and in conflict with us, we tend to select information that reinforces that view.[47] Thus communication and understanding interventions are effective only when differentiation is sufficiently low.

The second warning is that people in collectivist and high power distance cultures are less comfortable with the practice of resolving differences through direct and open communication.[48] As noted earlier, people in Confucian cultures prefer an avoidance conflict management style because it is the most consistent with harmony and face saving. Direct communication is a high-risk strategy because it easily threatens the need to save face and maintain harmony.

Reducing Interdependence

Conflict occurs where people are dependent on each other, so another way to reduce dysfunctional conflict is to minimize the level of interdependence between the parties. Here are three strategies to reduce interdependence among employees and work units.

Create Buffers A buffer is any mechanism that loosens the coupling between two or more people or work units. By decoupling the relationship, buffers help to reduce the potential for

conflict. Building up inventories between people in an assembly line would be a buffer, for example, because each employee is less dependent in the short term on the previous person along that line. In contrast, a just-in-time inventory system (where supplies are provided just before they are needed) has tight coupling, which increases the potential for conflict.

Use Integrators *Integrators* are employees who coordinate the activities of differentiated work units toward the completion of a common task. For example, an individual might be responsible for coordinating the efforts of the research, production, advertising, and marketing departments in launching a new product line. In some respects, integrators are human buffers; they reduce the frequency of direct interaction among work units with diverse goals and perspectives. Integrators rarely have direct authority over the departments they integrate, so they must rely on referent power and persuasion to manage conflict and accomplish the work. Integrators need to work effectively with each unit, so they must possess sufficient knowledge of each area.

Combine Jobs Combining jobs is both a form of job enrichment and a way to reduce task interdependence. Consider a toaster assembly system where one person inserts the heating element, another adds the sides, and so on. By combining these tasks so that each person assembles an entire toaster, the employees now have a pooled rather than sequential form of task interdependence, and the likelihood of dysfunctional conflict is reduced.

Increasing Resources

An obvious way to reduce conflict caused by resource scarcity is to increase the amount of resources available. Corporate decision makers might quickly dismiss this solution because of the costs involved. However, they need to carefully compare these costs with the costs of dysfunctional conflict due to resource scarcity.

Action PLAN

Resolving Conflict through Dialogue[49]

- Begin with an open, curious, and emotionally stable frame of mind.
- Ask the other people in the conflict to describe their perspectives of the situation.
- Listen actively to the stories told by the others, focusing on their perceptions, not on who is right or wrong.
- Acknowledge and demonstrate that you understand the others' viewpoints as well as their feelings about the situation.
- Present your perspective of the situation, describing it as your perception (not facts).
- Refer to the others' viewpoints while you are describing your viewpoint.
- Ask other people in the conflict for their ideas about how to overcome these differences.
- Create solutions that incorporate ideas from everyone involved in the discussion.

third-party conflict resolution Any attempt by a relatively neutral person to help the parties resolve their differences.

alternative dispute resolution (ADR) An orderly process of third-party dispute resolution, typically including mediation followed by arbitration.

Clarifying Rules and Procedures

Conflicts that arise from ambiguous rules can be minimized by establishing rules and procedures. If two departments are fighting over the use of a new laboratory, a schedule might be established that allocates the lab exclusively to each team at certain times of the day or week. Armstrong World Industries, Inc., applied the clarifying rules and procedures strategy when consultants and information systems employees clashed while working together on development of a client–server network. Information systems employees at the flooring and building materials company thought they should be in charge, whereas consultants believed they had the senior role. Also, the consultants wanted to work long hours and take Fridays off to fly home, whereas Armstrong employees wanted to work regular hours. The company reduced these conflicts by having both parties agree on specific responsibilities and roles. The agreement also assigned two senior executives at the companies to establish rules if future disagreements arose.[50]

THIRD-PARTY CONFLICT RESOLUTION

Most of this chapter has focused on people directly involved in a conflict, yet many disputes in organizational settings are resolved with the assistance of the manager of the feuding employees, or some other third party. **Third-party conflict resolution** is any attempt by a relatively neutral person to help the parties resolve their differences. There are generally three types of third-party dispute resolution activities: arbitration, inquisition, and mediation. These activities can be classified by their level of control over the process and control over the decision (see Exhibit 10.5).[51]

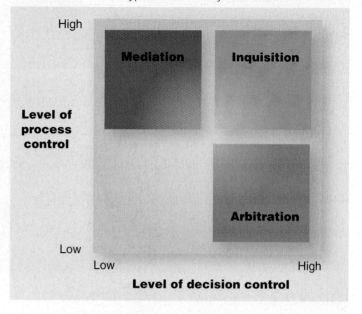

▼ **EXHIBIT 10.5** Types of Third-Party Intervention

- *Arbitration:* Arbitrators have high control over the final decision but low control over the process. Executives engage in this strategy by following previously agreed rules of due process, listening to arguments from the disputing employees, and making a binding decision. Arbitration is applied as the final stage of grievances by unionized employees in many countries, but it is also becoming more common in non-union conflicts.

- *Inquisition:* Inquisitors control all discussion about the conflict. Like arbitrators, they have high decision control because they choose the form of conflict resolution. However, they also have high process control because they choose which information to examine and how to examine it, and they generally decide how the conflict resolution process will be handled.

- *Mediation:* Mediators have high control over the intervention process. In fact, their main purpose is to manage the process and context of interaction between the disputing parties. However, the parties make the final decision about how to resolve their differences. Thus mediators have little or no control over the conflict resolution decision.

Choosing the Best Third-Party Intervention Strategy

Team leaders, executives, and coworkers regularly intervene in disputes between employees and departments. Sometimes they adopt a mediator role; other times they serve as arbitrators. Occasionally they begin with one approach and then switch to another. However, research suggests that people in positions of authority (such as managers) usually adopt an inquisitional approach whereby they dominate the intervention process as well as make a binding decision.[52]

Managers tend to rely on the inquisition approach because it is consistent with the decision-oriented nature of managerial jobs, gives them control over the conflict process and outcome, and tends to resolve disputes efficiently. However, inquisition is usually the least effective third-party conflict resolution method in organizational settings.[53] One problem is that leaders who take an inquisitional role tend to collect limited information about the problem, so their imposed decision may produce an ineffective solution to the conflict. Another problem is that employees often view inquisitional procedures and outcomes as unfair because they have little control over this approach. In particular, the inquisitional approach potentially violates several practices required to support procedural justice (see Chapter 5).

Which third-party intervention is most appropriate in organizations? The answer partly depends on the situation, such as the type of dispute, the relationship between the manager and employees, and cultural values such as power distance.[54] But generally speaking, for everyday disagreements between two employees, the mediation approach is usually best because this gives employees more responsibility for resolving their own disputes. The third-party representative merely establishes an appropriate context for conflict resolution. Although not as efficient as other strategies, mediation potentially offers the highest level of employee satisfaction with the conflict process and outcomes.[55] When employees cannot resolve their differences through mediation, arbitration seems to work best because the predetermined rules of evidence and other processes create a higher sense of procedural fairness.[56] Moreover, arbitration is preferred where the organization's goals should take priority over individual goals.

Alternative Dispute Resolution Rather than battle each other in court or external arbitration, the U.S. Air Force and its civilian staff have resolved most workplace conflicts quickly and with improved mutual understanding through alternative dispute resolution (ADR). "The parties, in essence, maintain control over the [ADR] process and its outcome," explains Air Mobility Command civilian programs branch chief Diana Hendrix. Some Air Force bases retain a mediator to identify issues and explore options with the parties without imposing a solution. Other bases use peer review panels, consisting of four or six union and nonunion employees who examine facts, listen to the parties, and make a final binding decision. But even with these formal third-party systems in place, Hendrix explains that supervisors are the first line of defense in resolving workplace conflict. "Ultimately, it's about Air Force employees and supervisors resolving conflicts in an efficient and effective manner so they can continue performing the Air Force mission of supporting and defending the United States of America," she says.[57]

The U.S. Air Force has joined a growing list of organizations that have taken third-party resolution one step further through an **alternative dispute resolution (ADR)** process (for employees only, also called *internal dispute resolution* or *employee dispute resolution*). ADR combines third-party dispute resolution in an orderly sequence. ADR typically begins with a meeting between the employee and employer to clarify and negotiate their differences. If this fails, a mediator is brought in to help the parties reach a mutually agreeable solution. If mediation fails, the parties submit their case to an arbitrator whose decision may be either binding or voluntarily accepted by the employer. Although most ADR systems rely on professional arbitrators, some firms, such as Eastman Kodak and some U.S. Air Force bases, prefer peer arbitration, which includes a panel of coworkers and managers who are not involved in the dispute.[58]

Whether resolving conflict through third-party dispute resolution or direct dialogue, we need to recognize that many solutions come from the sources of conflict that were identified earlier in this chapter. This may seem obvious, but in the heat of conflict, people often focus on each other rather than the underlying causes. Recognizing these conflict sources is the role of effective leadership, which is discussed in the next chapter. ■

CHECK IT OUT!

mhhe.com/McShaneM

for study materials
including quizzes
and Internet resources

leadership in
organizational settings

Leadership is one of the most researched and discussed topics in the field of organizational behavior. Google returns a whopping 324 million Web pages where either "leader" or "leadership" is mentioned. Google Scholar lists 173,000 journal articles and books with one or both words in the title. Proquest identifies more than 1.8 million scholarly and practitioner articles where one or both of these words appear in the title or abstract. Amazon lists more than 20,000 printed books in the English language with "leader" or "leadership" in the title. From 2000 to 2009 the U.S. Library of Congress catalog added 7,336 books or documents with the word "leader" or "leadership" in the citation, compared with 3,054 items added in the 1990s and only 146 items with these words (many of which were newspaper names) added during the first decade of the 1900s. ■

LEARNING OBJECTIVES

After reading this chapter, you should be able to

LO1 Define *leadership* and *shared leadership*.

LO2 Describe the competency and behavioral perspectives of leadership.

LO3 Discuss the key elements of path–goal theory, Fiedler's contingency model, and leadership substitutes.

LO4 Describe the four elements of transformational leadership and distinguish this theory from transactional and charismatic leadership.

LO5 Describe the implicit leadership perspective.

LO6 Discuss the similarities and differences in leadership across cultures and between genders.

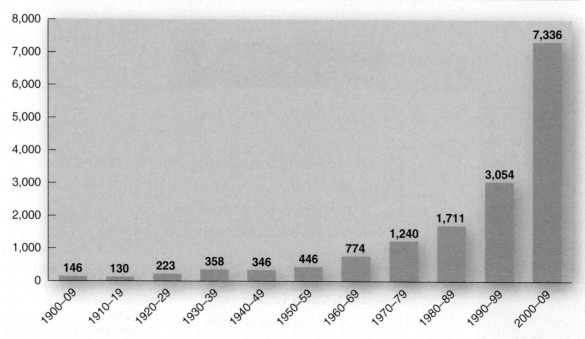

Filling the U.S. Library of Congress with Leadership Books and Materials

Number of books and other materials with "leader" or "leadership" in the title or citation catalogued by the U.S. Library of Congress and currently listed in its catalog, by decade that the item was published or produced. The U.S. Library of Congress is the world's largest library.

The topic of leadership captivates us because we are awed by individuals who influence and motivate others beyond expectations and who build commitment to a better future. Leadership also makes a difference in an organization's effectiveness. Consider Anne Sweeney, cochair of Disney Media Networks and president of Disney-ABC Television Group. Sweeney successfully built the Disney, Nickelodeon, and FX cable networks and led the turnaround of the ABC television network. Although Sweeney credits ABC's managers and creative talent, these people point to Sweeney's leadership as the key factor that unleashed their potential.

organization and the future of the entire industry," says ABC News President David Westin. "In short, none of us could wish for a better leader, through whatever may come our way."[1]

Learning Objectives

After reading this section, you should be able to

LO1 Define *leadership* and *shared leadership*.

[Leadership is one of the most researched and discussed topics in the field of organizational behavior.]

Television producer and executive Fred Silverman points out that Sweeney has "great resolve and strength." Albert Cheng, a Disney media executive, notes that "Anne makes it a point to engage with everyone." Still others say that Sweeney's leadership strength is her ability to engage staff in a vision of the future. "Anne draws upon her optimism and her grace in keeping her focus firmly on the future—the future of our own

WHAT IS LEADERSHIP?

A few years ago, 54 leadership experts from 38 countries reached a consensus that **leadership** is influencing, motivating, and enabling others to contribute toward the effectiveness and success of the organizations of which they are members.[2] Leaders apply various forms of influence—from subtle persuasion to direct

The Leadership Report Card[3]

82% of U.K. board of directors polled who rate senior leadership in their organization as either good or excellent.

52% of U.K. middle managers polled who rate senior leadership in their organization as either good or excellent.

51% of U.K. public sector employees polled who rate their leadership as poor or very poor.

55% of senior executives polled in the United States and eight other countries who say their organizations are able to develop leaders with the aptitude and skills to adapt to rapid change and new learning.

53% of American employees polled who rate management in their companies as "so-so" or worse.

15% of American employees polled who rate management in their companies as either "barely deserving the name 'management'" or "hopeless."

application of power—to ensure that followers have the motivation and role clarity to achieve specified goals. Leaders also arrange the work environment—such as allocating resources and altering communication patterns—so employees can achieve organizational objectives more easily.

Anyone can be a leader if he or she has an idea or vision that other employees are eager to follow.

Shared leadership flourishes in organizations where the formal leaders are willing to delegate power and encourage employees to take initiative and risks without fear of failure (that is, in a learning orientation culture). Shared leadership also calls for a collaborative rather than internally competitive culture because employees take on shared leadership roles when coworkers support them for their initiative. Furthermore, shared leadership lacks formal authority, so it operates best when employees learn to influence others through their enthusiasm, logical analysis, and involvement of coworkers in their ideas or visions.

Consider, for example, the emergence of shared leadership at Rolls-Royce Engine Services in Oakland, California. As part of its employee engagement initiative, the aircraft engine repair facility involved employees directly with clients, encouraged weekly huddles for information sharing, and accepted employee requests for less micromanagement. Employees not only experienced higher levels of engagement and empowerment; they also accepted more leadership responsibilities. "I saw people around me, all frontline employees, who were leaders," says a machine programmer at the Rolls-Royce Oakland plant. "They weren't

> **leadership** Influencing, motivating, and enabling others to contribute toward the effectiveness and success of the organizations of which they are members.

> **shared leadership** The view that leadership is broadly distributed rather than assigned to one person, such that people within the team and organization lead each other.

> "We've abandoned the Great Man model of leadership that long characterized Fiat and have created a culture where everyone is expected to lead.[6]
>
> —Sergio Marchionne

Shared Leadership

Leadership isn't restricted to the executive suite. Anyone in the organization may be a leader in various ways and at various times.[4] This view is known as **shared leadership** or the *leaderful organization*. From this emerging view, *leadership* is plural, not singular. It doesn't operate out of one formally assigned position or role. Instead a team or work unit may have several leaders at the same time. One team member might champion the introduction of new technology, while a coworker keeps the work unit focused on key performance indicators. Some organizations, such as Semco SA and W. L. Gore & Associates, depend on shared leadership because there are no formal leaders.[5]

actually leading the company, but they were people you would listen to and follow. We didn't have titles, but people had respect for what we did."[7]

Most of the enormous volume of leadership literature can be distilled and organized into five perspectives: competency, behavioral, contingency, transformational, and implicit.[9] Although some of these perspectives are currently more popular than others, each helps us to more fully understand the complex issue of leadership. This chapter explores each of these five perspectives of leadership. In the final section we also consider cross-cultural and gender issues in organizational leadership.

a

FACT. **Shared Leadership at W. L. Gore & Associates**

W. L. Gore & Associates has no formal (called vertical) leaders. Instead the company's 7,000 associates work with champions of projects and other initiatives because they are willing to follow them. "There is no positional power," explains a Gore team leader. "You are only a leader if teams decide to respect and follow you." Diane Davidson discovered this extreme version of shared leadership when the newly hired apparel industry sales executive asked her "starting sponsor" to identify her boss. The sponsor replied that she had no boss and eventually advised her to "stop using the B-word." Davidson initially thought the company must have formal managers who downplayed their position, but she soon realized that Gore really is a shared leadership organization. "Your team is your boss because you don't want to let them down," says Davidson. "Everyone's your boss, and no one's your boss." In fact, when Gore employees are asked in annual surveys, "Are you a leader?" more than 50 percent of them answer "Yes."[8]

of effective leaders. However, a major review in the late 1940s concluded that no consistent list of traits could be distilled from this research. This conclusion was revised a decade later, suggesting that a few traits are associated with effective leaders.[11] These nonsignificant findings caused many scholars to give up their search for personal characteristics that distinguish effective leaders.

Over the past two decades, leadership experts have returned to the notion that effective leaders possess specific personal characteristics.[12] The earlier research was apparently plagued by methodological problems, lack of theoretical foundation, and inconsistent definitions of leadership. The emerging work has identified several leadership *competencies*—that is, skills, knowledge, aptitudes, and other personal characteristics that lead to superior performance (see Chapter 2). The main categories of leadership competencies are listed in Exhibit 11.1 and described here:[13]

- *Personality:* Most of the Big Five personality dimensions (see Chapter 2) are associated with effective leadership to some extent, but the strongest predictors are high levels of extraversion (outgoing, talkative, sociable, and assertive) and conscientiousness (careful, dependable, and self-disciplined). With high extraversion, effective leaders are comfortable having an influential role in social settings. With high conscientiousness,

Learning Objectives

After reading the next two sections, you should be able to

LO2 Describe the competency and behavioral perspectives of leadership.

COMPETENCY PERSPECTIVE OF LEADERSHIP

Since the beginning of recorded civilization, people have been interested in the personal characteristics that distinguish great leaders from the rest of us.[10] In the 6th century BC, the Chinese philosopher Lao Tzu described effective leaders as selfless, honest, fair, and hardworking. The Greek philosopher Plato claimed that great leaders have wisdom and a superior capacity for logical thinking. For the past century, hundreds of leadership studies have tried to empirically identify the traits

effective leaders set ambitious goals for themselves (and others) and are motivated to pursue those goals.

- *Self-concept:* Successful leaders have a positive self-evaluation, including high self-esteem, self-efficacy, and internal locus of control (see Chapter 2).[14] They are confident in their leadership skills and ability to achieve objectives. These lead-

ers also have a complex, internally consistent, and clear self-concept.

- *Drive:* Related to their high conscientiousness and positive self-concept, successful leaders have a high need for achievement (see Chapter 5). This drive represents the inner motivation that leaders possess to pursue their goals and encourage

▼ **EXHIBIT 11.1** Competencies of Effective Leaders

Leadership Competency	Description
Personality	The leader's higher levels of extraversion (outgoing, talkative, sociable, and assertive) and conscientiousness (careful, dependable, and self-disciplined).
Self-concept	The leader's self-beliefs and positive self-evaluation about his or her own leadership skills and ability to achieve objectives.
Drive	The leader's inner motivation to pursue goals.
Integrity	The leader's truthfulness and tendency to translate words into deeds.
Leadership motivation	The leader's need for socialized power to accomplish team or organizational goals.
Knowledge of the business	The leader's tacit and explicit knowledge about the company's environment, enabling the leader to make more intuitive decisions.
Cognitive and practical intelligence	The leader's above-average cognitive ability to process information (cognitive intelligence) and ability to solve real-world problems by adapting to, shaping, or selecting appropriate environments (practical intelligence).
Emotional intelligence	The leader's ability to monitor his or her own and others' emotions, discriminate among them, and use the information to guide his or her thoughts and actions.

How Much Do Employees Trust Their Senior Leaders?[16]

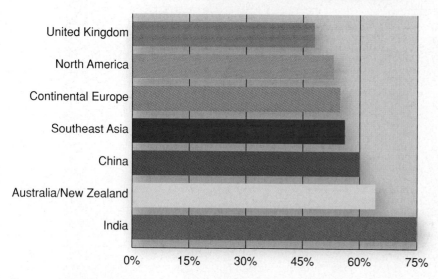

United Kingdom
North America
Continental Europe
Southeast Asia
China
Australia/New Zealand
India

0% 15% 30% 45% 60% 75%

Percentage of employees polled, by country/region, who agree or strongly agree that they trust senior leaders in their organization.

others to do the same. Drive inspires inquisitiveness, an action orientation, and boldness to take the organization or team into uncharted waters.

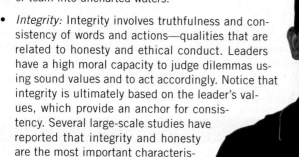

- *Integrity:* Integrity involves truthfulness and consistency of words and actions—qualities that are related to honesty and ethical conduct. Leaders have a high moral capacity to judge dilemmas using sound values and to act accordingly. Notice that integrity is ultimately based on the leader's values, which provide an anchor for consistency. Several large-scale studies have reported that integrity and honesty are the most important characteristics of effective leaders.[15]

- *Leadership motivation:* Effective leaders are motivated to lead others. They have a strong need for *socialized power,* meaning that they want power as a means to accomplish organizational objectives and similar good deeds. This contrasts with a need for *personalized power,* which is the desire to have power for personal gain or for the thrill one might experience from wielding power over others (see Chapter 5).[17] Leadership motivation is also necessary because, even in collegial firms, leaders are in contests for positions further up the hierarchy. Effective leaders thrive rather than wither in the face of this competition.[18]

- *Knowledge of the business:* Effective leaders possess tacit and explicit knowledge of the business environment in which they operate.

- *Cognitive and practical intelligence:* Leaders have above-average cognitive ability to process enormous amounts of information. Leaders aren't necessarily geniuses; rather, they have a superior ability to analyze a variety of complex alternatives and opportunities. Furthermore, leaders have practical intelligence. Unlike cognitive intelligence, which is assessed by performance on clearly defined problems with sufficient information and usually one best answer, practical intelligence is assessed by performance in real-world settings, where problems are poorly defined, information is missing, and more than one solution may be plausible.[19]

- *Emotional intelligence:* Effective leaders have a high level of emotional intelligence.[20] They can perceive and express emotion, assimilate emotion in thought, understand and reason with emotion, and regulate emotion in themselves and others (see Chapter 4).

Authentic Leadership

Several competencies associated with effective leaders relate to another important characteristic, called **authentic leadership** (Exhibit 11.2).[21] Authentic leadership refers to how well leaders are aware of, feel comfortable with, and act consistently with their self-concepts. In other words, authenticity is knowing yourself and being yourself. Leaders learn more about their personality, values, thoughts, and habits by reflecting on various situations and personal experiences. They also improve this self-awareness by receiving feedback from trusted people inside and outside the organization. Both self-reflection and receptivity to feedback require high levels of emotional intelligence. As people learn more about themselves, they gain a greater understanding of their inner

▼**EXHIBIT 11.2** Authentic Leadership

Know yourself:
- Engage in self-reflection.
- Receive feedback from trusted sources.
- Understand your life story.

Be yourself:
- Develop your own style.
- Apply your values.
- Maintain a positive core self-evaluation.

purpose, which in turn generates a long-term passion for achieving something worthwhile for the organization or society. Some leadership experts suggest that this inner purpose emerges from a life story—typically a critical event or experience earlier in life that clarifies the leader's core values and is a source of inner strength throughout his or her career.

Authentic leadership is more than self-awareness; it also involves behaving consistently with that self-concept rather than pretending to be someone else. To be themselves, great leaders regulate their decisions and behavior in several ways. First, they develop their own style and, where appropriate, seek positions where that style is most effective. Although effective leaders adapt their behavior to situations to some extent, they invariably understand and rely on decision methods and interpersonal styles that feel most comfortable to them.

Second, effective leaders continually think about and consistently apply their stable hierarchy of personal values to those decisions and behaviors. Leaders face many pressures and temptations, such as achieving short-term stock price targets at the cost of long-term profitability. Experts note that authentic leaders demonstrate self-discipline by remaining anchored to their values. Third, leaders maintain consistency around their self-concepts by having strong, positive core self-evaluations. They have high self-esteem and self-efficacy as well as an internal locus of control (Chapter 2).

> " Competencies indicate only leadership potential, not leadership performance. "

Competency Perspective Limitations and Practical Implications

Although the competency perspective is gaining popularity (again), it has a few limitations.[22] First, it assumes that all effective leaders have the same personal characteristics that are equally important in all situations. This is probably a false assumption; leadership is far too complex to have a universal list of traits that apply to every condition. Some competencies might not be important all the time. Second, alternative combinations of competencies may be equally successful; two people with different sets of competencies might be equally good leaders. Third, the competency perspective views leadership as something within a person, yet experts emphasize that leadership is relational. People are effective leaders because of their favorable relationships with followers, so effective leaders cannot be identified without considering the quality of these relationships.[23]

As we will learn later in this chapter, several leadership researchers have also warned that some personal characteristics might influence only our perception that someone is a leader, not whether the individual really makes a difference to the organization's success. People who exhibit self-confidence, extraversion, and other traits are called leaders because they fit our stereotype of an effective leader. Or we might see a successful person, call that person a leader, and then attribute unobservable traits that we consider essential for great leaders.

The competency perspective of leadership does not necessarily imply that leadership is a talent acquired at birth rather than developed throughout life. On the contrary, competencies indicate only leadership *potential,* not leadership performance. People with these characteristics become effective leaders only after they have developed and mastered the necessary leadership behaviors. People with somewhat lower leadership competencies may become very effective leaders because they have leveraged their potential more fully.

BEHAVIORAL PERSPECTIVE OF LEADERSHIP

In the 1940s and 1950s leadership experts at several universities launched an intensive research investigation to answer the question "What behaviors make leaders effective?" Questionnaires were administered to subordinates, asking them to rate their supervisors on a large number of behaviors. These studies revealed two distinct leadership styles (see Exhibit 11.3) from literally thousands of leadership behavior items.[24]

▼ **EXHIBIT 11.3** People and Task-Oriented Leadership Styles

Leaders are people-oriented when they...	Leaders are task-oriented when they...
• Listen to employees. • Make the workplace more pleasant. • Show interest in others as people. • Compliment employees for their work. • Are considerate of employee needs.	• Assign work and clarify responsibilities. • Set deadlines. • Evaluate and provide feedback on work quality. • Establish well-defined best work procedures. • Plan future work activities.

path–goal leadership theory
A contingency theory of leadership based on the expectancy theory of motivation that relates several leadership styles to specific employee and situational contingencies.

servant leadership
The view that leaders serve followers, rather than vice versa; they help employees fulfil their needs and are coaches, stewards, and facilitators of employee performance.

One cluster represents people-oriented behaviors. This cluster includes behaviors such as showing mutual trust and respect for subordinates, demonstrating a genuine concern for their needs, and having a desire to look out for their welfare. Leaders with a strong people-oriented style listen to employee suggestions, do personal favors for employees, support their interests when required, and treat employees as equals. The other cluster represents a task-oriented leadership style and includes behaviors that define and structure work roles. Task-oriented leaders assign employees to specific tasks, clarify their work duties and procedures, ensure that they follow company rules, and push them to reach their performance capacity. They establish challenging goals and motivate employees to excel beyond those high standards.

Choosing Task- versus People-Oriented Leadership

Should leaders be task-oriented or people-oriented? This is a difficult question to answer because each style has advantages and disadvantages. Recent evidence suggests that both styles are positively associated with leader effectiveness, but differences are often apparent only in very high or very low levels of each style. Absenteeism, grievances, turnover, and job dissatisfaction tend to be higher among employees who work with supervisors with very low levels of people-oriented leadership. Job performance is lower among employees who work for supervisors with low levels of task-oriented leadership.[25] Research suggests that university students value task-oriented instructors because they want clear objectives and well-prepared lectures that abide by the unit's objectives.[26]

One problem with the behavioral leadership perspective is that the two categories are broad generalizations that mask specific behaviors within each category. For instance, task-oriented leadership includes planning work activities, clarifying roles, and monitoring operations and performance. Each of these clusters of activities is fairly distinct and likely has different effects on employee well-being and performance. A second concern is that the behavioral approach assumes that high levels of both styles are best in all situations. In reality, the best leadership style depends on the situation.[27] In spite of these limitations, the behavioral perspective lays the foundation for two of the main leadership styles—people-oriented and task-oriented—found in many contemporary leadership theories. These contemporary theories adopt a contingency perspective, which is described next.

Learning Objectives

After reading this section, you should be able to

LO3 Discuss the key elements of path–goal theory, Fiedler's contingency model, and leadership substitutes.

CONTINGENCY PERSPECTIVE OF LEADERSHIP

The contingency perspective of leadership is based on the idea that the most appropriate leadership style depends on the situation. Most (although not all) contingency leadership theories assume that effective leaders must be both insightful and flexible.[28] They must be able to adapt their behaviors and styles to the immediate situation. This isn't easy to do, however. Leaders typically have a preferred style. It takes considerable effort for leaders to choose and enact different styles to match their situations. As we noted earlier, leaders must have high emotional intelligence so they can diagnose their circumstances and match their behaviors accordingly.

Path–Goal Theory of Leadership

Several contingency theories have been proposed over the years, but **path–goal leadership theory** has withstood scientific critique better than the others. Indeed, one recent study found that the path–goal theory explained more about effective leadership than did another popular perspective of leadership (transformational, which we describe later in this chapter).[29] Path–goal leadership theory has its roots in the expectancy theory of motivation (see Chapter 5) because leaders create paths (expectancies) to effective performance (goals) for their employees.[30]

Path–goal theory states that effective leaders ensure that good performers receive more valued rewards than poor performers. Effective leaders also provide the information, support, and other resources necessary to help employees complete their tasks.[31] In other words, path–goal theory advocates **servant leadership**.[32] Servant leaders do not view leadership as a position of power; rather, they are coaches, stewards, and facilitators. Leadership is an obligation to understand employee needs and to facilitate their work performance. Servant leaders ask, "How can I help you?" rather than expecting employees to serve them.

Path–Goal Leadership Styles
Exhibit 11.4 presents the path–goal theory of leadership. This model specifically highlights four leadership styles and several contingency factors leading to three indicators of leader effectiveness. Here are the four leadership styles:[33]

- *Directive:* This leadership style consists of clarifying behaviors that provide a psychological structure for subordinates. The leader clarifies performance goals, the means to reach

those goals, and the standards against which performance will be judged. It also includes judicious use of rewards and disciplinary actions. Directive leadership is the same as task-oriented leadership, described earlier, and echoes our discussion in Chapter 2 of the importance of clear role perceptions in employee performance.

- *Supportive:* In this style, the leader's behaviors provide psychological support for subordinates. The leader is friendly and approachable; makes the work more pleasant; treats employees with equal respect; and shows concern for the status, needs, and well-being of employees. Supportive leadership is the same as people-oriented leadership, described earlier, and reflects the benefits of social support to help employees cope with stressful situations.

- *Participative:* Participative leadership behaviors encourage and facilitate subordinate involvement in decisions beyond their normal work activities. The leader consults with employees, asks for their suggestions, and seriously considers these ideas before making a decision. Participative leadership applies the employee involvement model described in Chapter 6.

- *Achievement-oriented:* This leadership style emphasizes behaviors that encourage employees to reach their peak performance. The leader sets challenging goals, expects employees to perform at their

▼**EXHIBIT 11.4** Path–Goal Leadership Theory

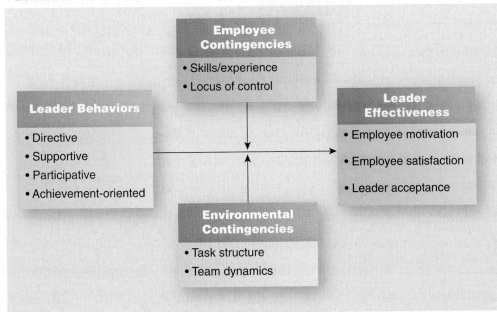

highest level, continuously seeks improvement in employee performance, and shows a high degree of confidence that employees will assume responsibility and accomplish challenging goals. Achievement-oriented leadership applies goal-setting theory as well as positive expectations in self-fulfilling prophecy.

The path–goal model contends that effective leaders are capable of selecting the most appropriate behavioral style (or styles) for each situation. Leaders might simultaneously use two or more styles.

Contingencies of Path–Goal Theory

As a contingency theory, path–goal theory states that each of the four leadership styles will be effective in some situations but not in others. The path–goal leadership model specifies two sets of situational variables that moderate the relationship between a leader's style and effectiveness: (1) employee characteristics and (2) characteristics of the employee's work environment. Several contingencies have already been studied within the path–goal framework, and the model is open for more variables in the future.[34] However, only four contingencies are reviewed here:

- *Skill and experience:* A combination of directive and supportive leadership is best for employees who are (or perceive themselves to be) inexperienced and unskilled.[35] Directive leadership gives subordinates information about how to accomplish the task, whereas supportive leadership helps them cope with the uncertainties of unfamiliar work situations. Directive leadership is detrimental when employees are skilled and experienced because it introduces too much supervisory control.

- *Locus of control:* Recall from Chapter 2 that people with an internal locus of control believe they have control over their

work environment. Consequently, these employees prefer participative and achievement-oriented leadership styles and may become frustrated with a directive style. In contrast, people with an external locus of control believe their performance is due more to luck and fate, so they tend to be more satisfied with directive and supportive leadership.

Choosing the Best Leadership Style for the Situation

- Employee lacks skill or experience: use directive and supportive styles.

- Employee is highly skilled and has plenty of experience: use participative and achievement-oriented styles.

- Employee has an internal locus of control: use participative and achievement-oriented styles.

- Employee has an external locus of control: use directive and supportive styles.

- Employee performs highly routine (repetitive) tasks: use supportive style.

- Employee performs nonroutine tasks: use directive style if employee also lacks experience; otherwise use participative style.

- Employee works in a low cohesion team: use supportive style.

- Employee works in a team with counterproductive norms: use directive style.

- *Task structure:* Leaders should adopt a directive style when a task is nonroutine because this style minimizes the role ambiguity that tends to occur in complex work situations (particularly for inexperienced employees).[36] The directive style is ineffective when employees have routine and simple tasks because the manager's guidance serves no purpose and may be viewed as unnecessarily close control. Employees in highly routine and simple jobs may require supportive leadership to help them cope with the tedious nature of the work and lack of control over the pace of work. Participative leadership is preferred for employees performing nonroutine tasks because the lack of rules and procedures gives them more discretion to achieve challenging goals. The participative style is ineffective for employees in routine tasks because they lack discretion over their work.

- *Team dynamics:* Cohesive teams with performance-oriented norms act as a substitute for most leader interventions. High team cohesion substitutes for supportive leadership, whereas performance-oriented team norms substitute for directive and possibly achievement-oriented leadership. Thus when team cohesion is low, leaders should use the supportive style. Leaders should apply a directive style to counteract team norms that oppose the team's formal objectives. For example, the team leader may need to use legitimate power if team members have developed a norm to "take it easy" rather than get a project completed on time.

Path–goal theory has received more research support than other contingency leadership models, but the evidence is far from complete. A few contingencies (such as task structure) have limited research support. Other contingencies and leadership styles in the path–goal leadership model haven't been investigated at all.[37] Another concern is that as path–goal theory expands, the model may become too complex for practical use. Few people would be able to remember all the contingencies and the appropriate leadership styles for those contingencies. Despite these limitations, path–goal theory remains a relatively robust contingency leadership theory.

Other Contingency Theories

Many leadership theories have developed over the years, most of which are found in the contingency perspective of leadership. Some overlap with the path–goal model's leadership styles, but most use simpler and more abstract contingencies. We will briefly mention only two here because of their popularity and historical significance to the field.

Situational Leadership Theory
One of the most popular contingency theories among practitioners is the **situational leadership theory (SLT)**, developed by Paul Hersey and Ken Blanchard.[38] SLT suggests that effective leaders vary their style with the ability and motivation (or commitment) of followers. The earliest versions of the model compressed the employee's ability and motivation into a single situational condition called maturity or readiness. The most recent version uses four labels, such as "enthusiastic beginner" (low ability, high motivation) and "disillusioned learner" (moderate ability and low motivation).

The situational leadership model also identifies four leadership styles—telling, selling, participating, and delegating—that Hersey and Blanchard distinguish by the amount of directive and supportive behavior provided. For example, "telling" has high task behavior and low supportive behavior. The situational leadership model has four quadrants, with each quadrant showing the leadership style that is most appropriate under different circumstances.

Despite its popularity, several studies and at least three reviews have concluded that the situational leadership model lacks empirical support.[39] Only one part of the model apparently works—namely that leaders should use "telling" (directive style) when employees lack motivation and ability. (Recall that this is also documented in path–goal theory.) The model's elegant simplicity is attractive and entertaining, but most parts don't represent reality well.

Fiedler's Contingency Model
Fiedler's contingency model, developed by Fred Fiedler and his associates, is the earliest contingency theory of leadership.[41] According to this model, leader effectiveness depends on whether the person's natural leadership style is appropriately matched to the situation. The theory examines two leadership styles that essentially correspond to the previously described people-oriented and task-oriented styles. Unfortunately Fiedler's model relies on a questionnaire that does not measure either leadership style well.

situational leadership theory (SLT) A commercially popular but poorly supported leadership model, stating that effective leaders vary their style (telling, selling, participating, delegating) with followers' motivation and ability.

Fiedler's contingency model Developed by Fred Fiedler, this early contingency leadership model suggests that leader effectiveness depends on whether the person's natural leadership style is appropriately matched to the situation.

Situational Leadership Theory:
Widely Adopted Despite the Evidence[40]

1972	**70%**	**14 million**	**3 million**
Year that Hersey and Blanchard introduced situational leadership theory (then known as "life-cycle leadership").	of Fortune 500 companies that currently use one or more situational leadership training products.	Estimated number of people who have received situational leadership training (as of 2010).	Estimated number of people who have received situational leadership training (as of 1997).

leadership substitutes A theory identifying contingencies that either limit the leader's ability to influence subordinates or make that particular leadership style unnecessary.

transformational leadership A leadership perspective that explains how leaders change teams or organizations by creating, communicating and modeling a vision for the organization or work unit, and inspiring employees to strive for that vision.

transactional leadership Leadership that helps organizations achieve their current objectives more efficiently, such as linking job performance to valued rewards and ensuring that employees have the resources needed to get the job done.

Fiedler's model suggests that the best leadership style depends on the level of *situational control*—that is, the degree of power and influence the leader possesses in a particular situation. Situational control is affected by three factors in the following order of importance: leader–member relations, task structure, and position power.[42] *Leader–member relations* refers to how much employees trust and respect the leader and are willing to follow

recent scholars have also proposed that leadership styles are "hardwired" more than most contingency leadership theories assume.[44]

If leadership style is influenced by a leader's personality, organizations should engineer the situation to fit the leader's dominant style, rather than expecting leaders to change their styles to fit situations. A directive leader might be assigned inexperienced employees who need direction rather than seasoned people who work less effectively under a directive style. Alternatively, companies might transfer supervisors to workplaces where their dominant style fits best. For instance, directive leaders might be parachuted into work teams with counterproductive norms, whereas leaders who prefer a supportive style should be sent to departments in which employees face work pressures and other stressors.

> [Fiedler's contingency model suggests that leadership style is related to the individual's personality and, consequently, is relatively stable over time.]

his or her guidance. *Task structure* refers to the clarity or ambiguity of operating procedures. *Position power* is the extent to which the leader possesses legitimate, reward, and coercive power over subordinates. These three contingencies form the eight possible combinations of *situation favorableness* from the leader's viewpoint. Good leader–member relations, high task structure, and strong position power create the most favorable situation for the leader because he or she has the most power and influence under these conditions.

Fiedler has gained considerable respect for pioneering the first contingency theory of leadership. However, his theory has fared less well. As mentioned, the leadership style scale used by Fiedler has been widely criticized. There is also no scientific justification for placing the three situational control factors in a hierarchy. Furthermore, the concept of leader–member relations is really an indicator of leader effectiveness (as in path–goal theory) rather than a situational factor. Finally, the theory considers only two leadership styles, whereas other models present a more complex and realistic array of behavior options. These concerns explain why the theory has limited empirical support.[43]

Changing the Situation to Match the Leader's Natural Style

Fiedler's contingency model may have become a historical footnote, but it does make an important and lasting contribution by suggesting that leadership style is related to the individual's personality and, consequently, is relatively stable over time. Leaders might be able to alter their style temporarily, but they tend to use a preferred style in the long term. More

Leadership Substitutes

So far we have looked at theories that recommend using different leadership styles in various situations. But one theory, called **leadership substitutes**, identifies conditions that either limit the leader's ability to influence subordinates or make a particular leadership style unnecessary. The literature identifies several conditions that possibly substitute for task-oriented or people-oriented leadership. For example, performance-based reward systems keep employees directed toward organizational goals, so they might replace or reduce the need for task-oriented leadership. Task-oriented leadership is also less important when employees are skilled and experienced. These propositions are similar to path–goal leadership theory, which states that directive leadership is unnecessary—and may be detrimental—when employees are skilled or experienced.[45]

Some research suggests that effective leaders help team members learn to lead themselves through leadership substitutes; in other words, coworkers substitute for leadership in high-involvement team structures.[46] Coworkers instruct new employees, thereby providing directive leadership. They also provide social support, which reduces stress among fellow employees. Teams with norms that support organizational goals may substitute for achievement-oriented leadership because employees encourage (or pressure) coworkers to stretch their performance levels.[47]

The leadership substitutes model has intuitive appeal, but the evidence so far is mixed. Some studies show that a few substitutes do reduce the need for task- or people-oriented leadership, but others do not. The difficulties of statistically testing for leadership substitutes may account for some problems, but a few writers contend that the limited support is evidence that leadership plays a critical role regardless of the situation.[48] At this point, we can conclude that leadership substitutes might reduce the need for leaders, but they certainly do not completely replace leaders in these situations.

Learning Objectives

After reading this section, you should be able to

L04 Describe the four elements of transformational leadership and distinguish this theory from transactional and charismatic leadership.

TRANSFORMATIONAL PERSPECTIVE OF LEADERSHIP

Transformational leadership is by far the most popular perspective of leadership today. Unlike the contingency and behavioral perspectives, which examine how leaders improve employee performance and well-being, transformational leadership views effective leaders as agents of change in the work unit or organization. They create, communicate, and model a shared vision for the team or organization, and they inspire followers to strive for that vision.[49]

Transformational versus Transactional Leadership

Leadership experts often contrast transformational leadership with **transactional leadership**.[50] Transactional leaders influence others mainly by using rewards and penalties as well as by negotiating services from employees. James McGregor

Burns, who coined the term four decades ago, describes transactional leadership with reference to political leaders who engage in vote buying or make transactional promises ("I'll have a new hospital built if you vote for me").[51] Managers in organizations are rarely elected, yet transactional leadership has become the focus of study in organizational behavior. The problem is compounded by a confusing and sometimes conflicting array of definitions and measures for transactional leadership. For example, Burns (and others) argue that transformational leadership is distinct from transactional leadership because the former leaders motivate employees through their values and aspirations. Yet Burns acknowledges that transactional leaders also appeal to follower wants and convictions about morality and justice, and that they engage in reciprocity, trustworthiness, and promise keeping.[52]

We will avoid the "transactional leadership" phrase, focusing instead on the elements of transformational leadership. A better distinction is "leading" versus "managing." Transformational leadership is about "leading"—changing the organization's strategies and culture so they better fit the surrounding environment. Transformational leaders are change agents who energize and direct employees to a new vision and corresponding behaviors. "Managing," on the other hand, refers to helping employees become more proficient and satisfied in the current

> ## Managers are people who do things right, and leaders are people who do the right thing.[54]
>
> —Warren Bennis (also often attributed to Peter Drucker)

situation.[53] To a large degree, the contingency and behavioral theories of leadership described earlier refer to managing employees because they focus on leader behaviors that improve employee performance and well-being rather than on behaviors that move the organization and work unit in a new direction.

Organizations require leaders who both manage employees and transform the work unit or organization.[55] Managing improves organizational efficiency, whereas transformational leadership steers companies to a better course of action. Transformational leadership is particularly important in organizations that require significant alignment with the external environment. Unfortunately too many leaders get trapped in the daily activities that represent managerial leadership.[56] They lose touch with the transformational aspect of effective leadership. Without transformational leaders, organizations stagnate and eventually become seriously misaligned with their environments.

Transformational versus Charismatic Leadership

Another topic that has generated some confusion and controversy is the distinction between *transformational* and *charismatic* leadership.[57] Many researchers either use the words interchangeably, as if they have the same meaning, or view charismatic leadership as an essential ingredient of transformational leadership. Others take this view further by suggesting that charismatic leadership is the highest degree of transformational leadership.

However, the emerging view, which this book adopts, comes from a third group of experts who contend that charisma is distinct from transformational leadership. These scholars point out that charisma is a personal trait or relational quality that provides referent power over followers, whereas transformational leadership is a set of behaviors that people use to lead the change process.[58] Charismatic leaders might be transformational leaders; indeed, their personal power through charisma is a tool to change the behavior of followers. However, some research points out that charismatic leaders easily build allegiance in followers but do not necessarily change the organization. Other research suggests that charismatic leaders produce dependent followers, whereas transformational leaders have the opposite effect—they build follower empowerment, which tends to reduce dependence on the leader. For example, one study reported a negative relationship between charismatic leadership and the self-efficacy of followers.[59]

The main point here is that transformational leaders are not necessarily charismatic, and charismatic leaders are not necessarily transformational. Alan G. Lafley, the CEO of Procter & Gamble, is not known for being charismatic, but he has transformed the household goods company like no leader in recent memory. Similarly, IBM CEO Sam Palmisano speaks with humility yet continues to drive IBM's success. "I don't have much curb appeal," Palmisano says of his minimal charisma, adding that IBM has more than 300,000 brilliant people to drive the organization. "I just try to lead them and get them to come together around a common point of view," he explains.[61] In other words, Palmisano and Lafley lead by applying transformational leadership behaviors.

Elements of Transformational Leadership

There are several descriptions of transformational leadership, but most include the following four elements: create a strategic vision, communicate the vision, model the vision, and build commitment toward the vision (see Exhibit 11.5).

▼ **EXHIBIT 11.5** Elements of Transformational Leadership

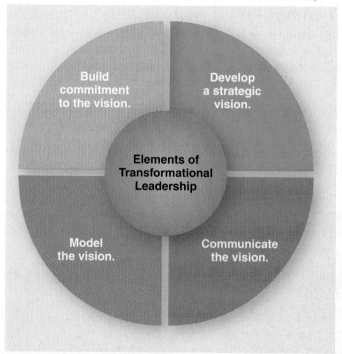

> # THE WORLD IS MADE UP OF:
> # THOSE WHO MAKE THINGS HAPPEN;
> # THOSE WHO WATCH THINGS HAPPEN;
> # AND THOSE WHO ASK WHAT HAPPENED.[60]
> ## —NORMAN AUGUSTINE

Create a Strategic Vision Transformational leaders establish a vision of the company's future state that engages employees to objectives they didn't think possible. These leaders shape a strategic vision of a realistic and attractive future that bonds employees together and focuses their energy toward a superordinate organizational goal.[62] A shared strategic vision represents the substance of transformational leadership. It reflects a future for the company or work unit that is ultimately accepted and valued by organizational members.

A strategic vision creates a "higher purpose" or superordinate goal that energizes and unifies employees.[63] This vision might originate with the leader, but it is just as likely to emerge from employees, clients, suppliers, or other stakeholders. A shared strategic vision plays an important role in organizational effectiveness.[64] Visions offer the motivational benefits of goal setting, but they are compelling future states that bond employees and motivate them to strive for those objectives. Visions are typically described in a way that distinguishes them from the current situation yet makes the goal both appealing and achievable.

Communicate the Vision If vision is the substance of transformational leadership, communicating that vision is the process. CEOs say that the most important leadership quality is being able to build and share their vision for the organization. "Part of a leader's role is to set the vision for the company and to communicate that vision to staff to get their buy-in," explains Dave Anderson, president of WorkSafeBC (the Workers' Compensation Board of British Columbia, Canada).[65]

Transformational leaders communicate meaning and elevate the importance of the visionary goal to employees. They frame messages around a grand purpose with emotional appeal that captivates employees and other corporate stakeholders. Framing helps transformational leaders establish a common mental model so the group or organization will act collectively toward the desirable goal.[66] Transformational leaders bring their visions to life through symbols, metaphors, stories, and other vehicles that transcend plain language. Metaphors borrow images of other experiences, thereby creating richer meaning of the vision that has not yet been experienced.

Model the Vision Transformational leaders not only talk about a vision; they enact it. They "walk the talk" by stepping outside the executive suite and doing things that symbolize the vision.[68] For example, when Anne Sweeney became president of Disney-ABC Television Group, she put much effort into communicating her vision of the future and ensuring that

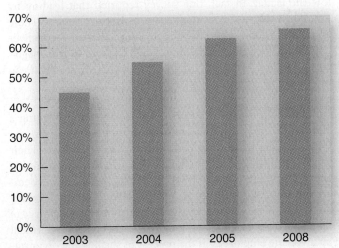

Does the Company's Senior Leadership Communicate a Clear Vision?[67]

Percentage of American employees, by year, who agree that senior management in their organization communicates a clear vision of the future.

implicit leadership
theory A theory stating
that people evaluate a
leader's effectiveness in
terms of how well that
person fits preconceived
beliefs about the features
and behaviors of effective
leaders (leadership
prototypes), and that
they tend to inflate the
influence of leaders on
organizational events.

her actions were consistent with her words. "There was a lot of uncertainty about who this new team was, what they were going to be about, and how the company would be managed," she recalls. "My job was to let people know what my management philosophy was and to not just talk the talk, but walk the [talk]."[69]

Leaders walk the talk through significant events such as visiting customers, moving their offices closer to employees, and holding ceremonies to destroy outdated policy manuals. However, they also alter mundane activities—meeting agendas, dress codes, executive schedules—so the activities are more consistent with the vision and its underlying values. Modeling the vision is important because doing so legitimizes and demonstrates what the vision looks like in practice. Modeling the vision is also important because it builds employee trust in the leader.

Evaluating the Transformational Leadership Perspective

Transformational leaders make a difference. Subordinates are more satisfied and have higher affective organizational commitment under transformational leaders. They also perform their jobs better, engage in more organizational citizenship behaviors, and make better or more creative decisions. One study of bank branches reported that organizational commitment and financial performance seemed to increase where the branch manager completed a transformational leadership training program.[72]

Transformational leadership is currently the most popular leadership perspective, but it faces a number of challenges. One problem is that some writers engage in circular logic.[73] These scholars define and measure transformational leadership by the leader's success rather than by whether they engage in behaviors we call transformational (such as communicating a vision). This approach makes it impossible to evaluate transformational leadership because, by definition and measurement, all transformational leaders are effective!

> "As an executive, you're always being watched by employees, and everything you say gets magnified. So you teach a lot by how you conduct yourself.[71]
>
> —Carl Bass

The greater the consistency between the leader's words and actions, the more employees will believe in and be willing to follow the leader. In fact, one survey reported that leading by example is the most important characteristic of a leader. "There are lots of people who talk a good story, but very few deliver one," warns Peter Farrell, founder and chairman of San Diego–based ResMed. "You've got to mean what you say, say what you mean, and be consistent."[70]

Build Commitment toward the Vision Transforming a vision into reality requires employee commitment. Transformational leaders build this commitment in several ways. Their words, symbols, and stories build a contagious enthusiasm that energizes people to adopt the vision as their own. Leaders demonstrate a "can do" attitude by enacting their vision and staying on course. Their persistence and consistency reflect an image of honesty, trust, and integrity. Finally, leaders build commitment by involving employees in the process of shaping the organization's vision.

Another concern is that transformational leadership is usually described as a universal rather than contingency-oriented model. Only recently have writers begun to explore the idea that transformational leadership is more valuable in some situations than others.[74] For instance, transformational leadership is probably more appropriate when organizations need to adapt than when environmental conditions are stable. Preliminary evidence suggests that the transformational leadership perspective is relevant across cultures. However, specific elements of transformational leadership, such as the way visions are formed and communicated, may be more appropriate in North America than in other cultures.

Learning Objectives

After reading the next two sections, you should be able to

LO5 Describe the implicit leadership perspective.

LO6 Discuss the similarities and differences in leadership across cultures and between genders.

IMPLICIT LEADERSHIP PERSPECTIVE

The competency, behavior, contingency, and transformational leadership perspectives include the basic assumption that leaders "make a difference." Certainly there is evidence that senior executives influence organizational performance. However, leadership also involves followers' perceptions of the characteristics and influence of people they call leaders. This perceptual perspective of leadership, called **implicit leadership theory**, has two components: leader prototypes and the romance or attribution of leadership.[75]

Prototypes of Effective Leaders

One aspect of implicit leadership theory states that everyone has *leadership prototypes*—preconceived beliefs about the features and behaviors of effective leaders. These prototypes, which develop through socialization within the family and society,[76] shape our expectations and acceptance of others as leaders, and this in turn affects our willingness to serve as followers. In other words, we are more willing to allow someone to influence us as a leader if that person looks and acts like our prototype of a leader. For example, one recent study established that inherited personality characteristics significantly influence the perception that someone is a leader in a leaderless situation.[77] Such leadership prototypes not only support a person's role as leader; they also form or influence our perception of the leader's effectiveness. If a leader looks like and acts consistently with our prototype, we are more likely to believe that the leader is effective.[78] This prototype comparison process occurs because people have an inherent need to quickly evaluate individuals as leaders, yet leadership effectiveness is often ambiguous and might not be apparent for a long time.

The Romance of Leadership

Along with relying on implicit prototypes of effective leaders, followers tend to distort their perceptions of the influence that leaders have on the environment. This "romance of leadership" effect exists because in most cultures people want to believe leaders make a difference. Consider the experience of Ricardo Semler, the charismatic CEO of Brazilian conglomerate Semco SA:

> At the company, no matter what you do, people will naturally create and nurture a charismatic figure. The charismatic figure, on the other hand, feeds this; it doesn't just happen, and it is very difficult to check your ego at the door. The people at Semco don't look and act like me. They are not yes-men by any means. What is left, however, is a certain feeling that has to do with the cult of personality. They credit me with successes that are not my own, and they don't debit me my mistakes. They give undue importance to what I say, and I think that doesn't go away.[80]

There are two basic reasons why people inflate their perceptions of the leader's influence over the environment.[81] First, leadership is a useful way for us to simplify life events. It is easier to explain organizational successes and failures in terms of the leader's ability than by analyzing a complex array of other forces. Second, there is a strong tendency in the United States and other Western cultures to believe that life events are generated more from people than from uncontrollable natural forces.[82] This illusion of control is satisfied by believing that events result from the rational actions of leaders. In other words, employees feel better believing that leaders make a difference, so they actively look for evidence that this is so.

One way that followers support their perceptions that leaders make a difference is through fundamental attribution error (see Chapter 3). Research has found that (at least in Western cultures) leaders are given credit or blame for the company's success or failure because employees do not readily see the external forces that also influence these events. Leaders reinforce this belief by taking credit for organizational successes.[83]

The implicit leadership perspective provides valuable advice to improve leadership acceptance. It highlights the fact that leadership is a perception of followers as much as the actual behaviors and formal roles of people calling themselves leaders. Potential leaders must be sensitive to this fact, understand what followers expect, and act accordingly. Individuals who do not make an effort to fit leadership prototypes will have more difficulty bringing about necessary organizational change.

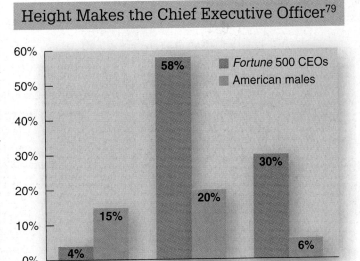

Height Makes the Chief Executive Officer[79]

Fortune 500 CEOs / American males

- Under 66": 4% / 15%
- 72" (6ft)+: 58% / 20%
- 74"+: 30% / 6%

The average male *Fortune* 500 chief executive officer is currently about 6 feet tall (72 inches), whereas the average adult American male is almost three inches shorter. A 1980 survey also reported that the average male *Fortune* 500 CEO at that time was about 6 feet tall.

expectations is more likely to be perceived as an ineffective leader. Furthermore, leaders who deviate from those values may experience various forms of influence to get them to conform to the leadership norms and expectations of the society. In other words, implicit leadership theory, described in the previous section of this chapter, explains differences in leadership practices across cultures.

Over the past few years, 150 researchers from dozens of countries have worked together on Project GLOBE (Global Leadership and Organizational Behavior Effectiveness) to identify the effects of cultural values on leadership.[84] The project organized countries into 10 regional clusters, of which the United States, Great Britain, and similar countries were grouped into the "Anglo" cluster. The results of this massive investigation suggest that some features of leadership are universal and some differ across cultures. Specifically, the GLOBE project reported that "charismatic visionary" is a universally recognized concept and that middle managers around the world

FACT. Microsoft Germany's Gender Leadership Boom

Europe's population is shrinking and aging, two trends that worried Achim Berg when he was recently hired as CEO of Microsoft Germany. Fortunately, in a country where men still overwhelmingly dominate the executive suite, the former Deutsche Telekom executive has a straightforward solution: hire more female managers and create a work environment that motivates them to stay. Berg now has 5 women on the 12-person management board and a growing pool of junior female staff members working their way into leadership positions. Berg also welcomes the gender balance because it brings more diverse leadership styles. "Women have a different management style," Berg claims. Dorothee Belz, Microsoft Germany's director of legal and corporate affairs, agrees. Women, she suggests, look at issues differently and are more willing than men to discuss problems. Berg says that working with more female colleagues has also altered his own leadership style; it has become more consultative, with less focus on "speed and quick results." He has also noticed less politics in executive meetings. "It seems that there is a noticeable decline in territorial behavior. But perhaps we'd be better off consulting a zoologist," says Berg, laughing.[88]

CROSS-CULTURAL AND GENDER ISSUES IN LEADERSHIP

Along with the five perspectives of leadership presented throughout this chapter, cultural values and practices affect what leaders do. Culture shapes the leader's values and norms, which influence his or her decisions and actions. Cultural values also shape the expectations that followers have of their leaders. An executive who acts inconsistently with cultural

believe that it is characteristic of effective leaders. *Charismatic visionary* represents a cluster of concepts including visionary, inspirational, performance orientation, integrity, and decisiveness.[85] In contrast, participative leadership is perceived as characteristic of effective leadership in low power distance cultures but less so in high power distance cultures. For instance, one study reported that Mexican employees expect managers to make decisions affecting their work. Mexico is a high power distance culture, so followers expect leaders to apply their authority rather than delegate their power most of the time.[86] In summary, there are similarities and differences in the concept and preferred practice of leadership across cultures.

With respect to gender, studies in field settings have generally found that male and female leaders do not differ in their levels of task-oriented or people-oriented leadership. The main explanation is that real-world jobs require similar behavior from male and female leaders.[87] However, women adopt a participative leadership style more readily than their male counterparts do. One possible reason is that, compared to boys, girls are often raised to be more egalitarian and less status-oriented, which is consistent with being participative. There is also some evidence that women have somewhat better interpersonal skills than men, and this translates into their relatively greater use of the participative leadership style. A third explanation is that subordinates, on the basis of their own gender stereotypes, expect female leaders to be more participative, so female leaders comply with follower expectations to some extent.

Several surveys report that women are rated higher than men on the emerging leadership qualities of coaching, teamwork, and empowering employees.[89] Yet research also suggests that women are evaluated negatively when they try to apply the full range of leadership styles, particularly more directive and autocratic approaches. Thus, ironically, women may be well suited to contemporary leadership roles, yet they often continue to face limitations of leadership through the gender stereotypes and prototypes of leaders that are held by followers.[90] Overall, both male and female leaders must be sensitive to the fact that followers have expectations about how leaders should act, and negative evaluations may go to leaders who deviate from those expectations. ■

CHECK IT OUT!

mhhe.com/McShaneM

for study materials
including quizzes
and Internet resources

chapter twelve

designing
organizational structures

In the early 1990s Nokia Corporation was a diversified organization with operations in consumer electronics (televisions, audio equipment), cable for construction and power transmission, and industrial rubber (tires, footwear), as well as its recently acquired businesses in telecommunications networks and cell (mobile) phones.[1] The Finnish company became the market leader in cell phones by 1998 (overtaking Motorola), so it sold most other divisions and designed a new organizational structure around its cell phone and consumer electronics businesses as well as several functional groups (finance, human resources, and so on). The consumer

electronics business was not sufficiently profitable, so it was sold and Nokia drew a new organizational chart in 1999 around cell phones, the emerging business of mobile networks, ventures (emerging Internet mobile technology), and communication products (digital terminals). By 2003 the cell phone market was converging with photography, games, music, and other multimedia content, so Nokia added a new "multimedia" division to keep the company at the forefront of those developments. In 2006 the company's burgeoning network business merged with Siemens through an ongoing joint venture.

continued on p. 234

organizational structure The division of labor as well as the patterns of coordination, communication, workflow, and formal power that direct organizational activities.

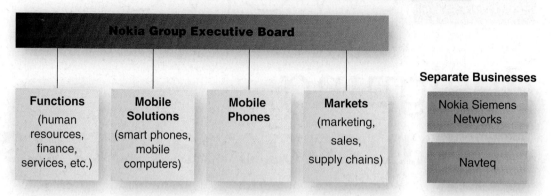

Nokia Corporation's New Organizational Structure[2]

continued from p. 233

Nokia's earlier organizational structures gave some priority to Internet and multimedia technologies, enough to put the company at the forefront of the quickly emerging "smart phone" market. But with increasing competition from Research in Motion (which makes the Blackberry) and Apple (which makes the iPhone), Nokia recently announced a new organizational structure that will focus more power and resources around this segment. The new chart includes a mobile solutions division (mobile computers and smart phones), mobile phones division, a markets division (responsible for global sales and supply chain operations), and a few functional groups (such as finance and human resources). "Nokia's new organizational structure is designed to speed up execution and accelerate innovation, both short-term and longer term," explains a senior Nokia executive. "We believe that this will allow us to build stronger mobile solutions." ■

organizational activities. It formally dictates what activities receive the most attention as well as financial, power, and information resources. For example, Nokia created new divisions to capture the potential of mobile networks, Internet telephony, mobile-based multimedia content, and more recently smart phone technology. The formation of these business units allowed the company to give priority to emerging business opportunities.

Nokia's changing organizational chart is only part of its organizational structure. In fact, throughout this chapter, we hope to show that an organization's structure is much more than an organizational chart diagramming which employees report to which managers. Organizational structure includes reporting relationships, but it also relates to job design, information flow, work standards and rules, team dynamics, and power relationships. As such, the organization's structure is an important instrument in an executive's toolkit for organizational change because it establishes new communication patterns and aligns employee behavior with the corporate vision.[3]

This chapter begins by introducing the two fundamental processes in organizational structure: division of labor and

> ## [The organization's structure is an important instrument in an executive's toolkit for organizational change.]

This brief summary of Nokia's evolution over the past two decades reveals that organizational structure is an important instrument for guiding and providing resources around the organization's strategy. **Organizational structure** refers to the division of labor as well as the patterns of coordination, communication, workflow, and formal power that direct

coordination. This is followed by a detailed investigation of the four main elements of organizational structure: span of control, centralization, formalization, and departmentalization. The latter part of this chapter examines the contingencies of organizational design, including external environment, organizational size, technology, and strategy.

> ## ALL THINGS WILL BE PRODUCED IN SUPERIOR QUANTITY AND QUALITY, AND WITH GREATER EASE, WHEN EACH PERSON WORKS AT A SINGLE OCCUPATION, IN ACCORDANCE WITH HIS OR HER NATURAL GIFTS, AND AT THE RIGHT MOMENT, WITHOUT MEDDLING WITH ANYTHING ELSE.[6]
>
> —PLATO

Learning Objectives

After reading the next two sections, you should be able to

LO1 Describe three types of coordination in organizational structures.

LO2 Discuss the advantages and disadvantages of span of control, centralization and formalization and relate these elements to organic and mechanistic organizational structures.

DIVISION OF LABOR AND COORDINATION

All organizational structures include two fundamental requirements: the division of labor into distinct tasks and the coordination of that labor so employees can accomplish common goals.[4] Organizations are groups of people who work interdependently toward some purpose. To efficiently accomplish their goals, these groups typically divide the work into manageable chunks, particularly when there are many different tasks to perform. They also introduce various coordinating mechanisms to ensure that everyone is working effectively toward the same objectives.

Division of Labor

Division of labor refers to the subdivision of work into separate jobs assigned to different people. Subdivided work leads to job specialization because each job includes a narrow subset of the tasks necessary to complete the product or service. Nokia organizes employees into thousands of specific jobs to more effectively design and market cell phones. It further divides people into work units and divisions. As companies get larger, this horizontal division of labor is usually accompanied by vertical division of labor: some people are assigned the task of supervising employees, others are responsible for managing those supervisors, and so on.

Why do companies divide the work required to design and market cell phones into several jobs? As you learned earlier in this book, job specialization increases work efficiency.[5] Job incumbents can master their tasks quickly because work cycles are short. Less time is wasted changing from one task to another. Training costs are reduced because employees require fewer physical and mental skills to accomplish the assigned work. Finally, job specialization makes it easier to match people with specific aptitudes or skills to the jobs for which they are best suited. Although one person working alone might be able to design a cell phone, doing so would take much longer than having the phone designed by a team of specialists, manufactured by others, and marketed by a third group of employees. Some employees are gifted at innovating cell phone features, whereas others are more talented at efficiently manufacturing those devices.

Coordinating Work Activities

When people divide work among themselves, they require coordinating mechanisms to ensure that everyone works in concert. Coordination is so closely connected to division of labor that the optimal level of specialization is limited by the feasibility of coordinating the work. In other words, an organization should divide work among many people only to the extent that those people can coordinate with each other. Otherwise individual effort is wasted due to misalignment, duplication, and mistiming of tasks. Coordination also tends to become more expensive and difficult as the division of labor increases, so companies specialize jobs only to the point where it isn't too costly or challenging to coordinate the people in those jobs.[7]

Every organization—from the two-person corner convenience store to the largest corporate entity—uses one or more of the following coordinating mechanisms:[8] informal communication, formal hierarchy, and standardization (see Exhibit 12.1). These forms of coordination align the work of staff within the same department as well as across work units. These coordinating mechanisms are also critical when several organizations work together, such as in joint ventures and humanitarian aid programs.[9]

Form of Coordination	Description	Subtypes/Strategies
Informal communication	Sharing information about mutual tasks; forming common mental models to synchronize work activities.	• Direct communication. • Liaison roles. • Integrator roles. • Temporary teams.
Formal hierarchy	Assigning legitimate power to individuals, who use this power to direct work processes and allocate resources.	• Direct supervision. • Formal communication channels.
Standardization	Creating routine patterns of behavior or output.	• Standardized skills. • Standardized processes. • Standardized output.

Sources: Based on information in J. Galbraith, *Designing Complex Organizations* (Reading, MA: Addison-Wesley, 1973), pp. 8–19; H. Mintzberg, *The Structuring of Organizations* (Englewood Cliffs, NJ: Prentice Hall, 1979), Chap. 1; D. A. Nadler and M. L. Tushman, *Competing by Design: The Power of Organizational Architecture* (New York: Oxford University Press, 1997), Chap. 6.

Coordination through Informal Communication

Informal communication is a coordinating mechanism in all organizations. It includes sharing information about mutual tasks as well as forming common mental models so employees synchronize work activities using the same mental road map.[10] Informal communication is vital in nonroutine and ambiguous situations because employees can exchange a large volume of information through face-to-face communication and other media-rich channels.

Coordination through informal communication is easiest in small firms, although information technologies have further leveraged this coordinating mechanism in large organizations.[11] Companies employing thousands of people also support informal communication by keeping each production site small. Magna International, the global auto parts manufacturer, keeps its plants to a maximum size of around 200 employees. Magna's leaders believe employees have difficulty remembering each other's names in plants that are any larger, a situation that makes informal communication more difficult as a coordinating mechanism.[12]

Larger organizations also encourage coordination through informal communication by assigning *liaison roles* to employees, who are expected to communicate and share information with coworkers in other work units. Where coordination is required among several work units, companies create *integrator roles*. These people are responsible for coordinating a work process by encouraging employees in each work unit to share information and informally coordinate work activities. Brand managers at Procter & Gamble have integrator roles because they coordinate work among marketing, production, and design groups.[13] Integrators do not have authority over the people involved in that process, so they must rely on persuasion and commitment.

Another way that larger organizations encourage coordination through informal communication is by organizing employees from several departments into temporary teams. **Concurrent engineering** applies this coordinating strategy for development of products or services. Concurrent engineering typically consists of a cross-functional project team of people from various functional departments, such as design engineering, manufacturing, marketing, and purchasing. By being assigned to a team, rather than working within their usual specialized departments, these employees have more authority and opportunity to coordinate with each other using informal communication. When the design engineer begins to form the product specifications, representatives from manufacturing, engineering, marketing, purchasing, and other departments can offer feedback as well as begin their contribution to the process. By coordinating through information-rich informal communication, concurrent engineering teams tend to produce higher-quality products with dramatically less development time compared to situations where employees work in their own departments and coordinate through other means.[14]

Coordination through Formal Hierarchy

Informal communication is the most flexible form of coordination, but it can become chaotic as the number of employees increases. Consequently, as organizations grow, they rely increasingly on a second coordinating mechanism: formal hierarchy.[15] Hierarchy assigns legitimate power to individuals, who use this power to direct work processes and allocate resources. In other words, work is coordinated through direct supervision—the chain of command.

The formal hierarchy has traditionally been applauded as the optimal coordinating mechanism for large organizations. Management scholars argued a century ago that organizations are most effective when managers exercise their authority and employees receive orders from only one supervisor. Coordination should occur through the chain of command—that is, up the hierarchy and across to the other work unit. Any organization with a formal structure coordinates work to some extent through this arrangement. For instance, managers at Nokia are responsible for ensuring that employees in their department remain on schedule and that their respective tasks are compatible with tasks completed by other employees. The formal hierarchy also coordinates work among executives through the division of organizational activities. If the organization is divided into geographic areas, the structure gives the regional group leaders legitimate power over executives responsible for production, customer service, and other activities in those areas. If the organization is divided into product groups, the heads of those groups have the right to coordinate work across regions.

The formal hierarchy can be efficient for simple and routine situations, but it is not as agile for coordination in complex and novel situations. Communicating through the chain of command is rarely as fast or accurate as direct communication between employees. For instance, we noted earlier that product development—typically a complex and novel activity—tends to occur more quickly and produce higher-quality results when people coordinate mainly through informal communication rather than formal hierarchy. Another concern with formal hierarchy is that managers can closely supervise only a limited number of employees. As

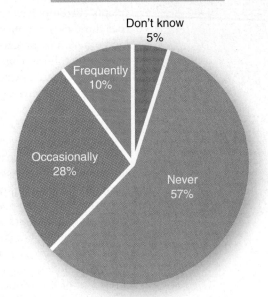

Coordination through Micromanagement[16]

Don't know
5%

Frequently
10%

Occasionally
28%

Never
57%

Percentage of 524 American employees polled who said they never, occasionally, or frequently feel micromanaged by their bosses.

concurrent engineering The organization of employees from several departments into a temporary team for the purpose of developing a product or service.

the business grows, the number of supervisors and layers of management must increase, resulting in a costly bureaucracy. Finally, today's workforce is less tolerant of rigid structures. For instance, Wegmans Food Market is one of the best places to work, partly because the Rochester, New York–based grocery chain minimizes formal hierarchy as a coordinating mechanism.

Coordination through Standardization

Standardization, the third means of coordination, involves creating routine patterns of behavior or output. This coordinating mechanism takes three distinct forms:

- *Standardized processes:* Quality and consistency of a product or service can often be improved by standardizing work activities through job descriptions and procedures.[17] This coordinating mechanism is feasible when the work is routine (such as mass production) or simple (such as making pizzas), but it is less effective in nonroutine and complex work such as product design.

- *Standardized outputs:* This form of standardization involves ensuring that individuals and work units have clearly defined goals and output measures (such as customer satisfaction or production efficiency). For instance, to coordinate the work of salespeople, companies assign sales targets rather than specific behaviors.

- *Standardized skills:* When work activities are too complex to standardize through processes or goals, companies often coordinate work effort by extensively training employees or hiring people who have learned precise role behaviors from educational programs. This form of coordination is used in hospital operating rooms. Surgeons, nurses, and other operating room professionals coordinate their work more through training than through goals or company rules.

Division of labor and coordination of work represent the two fundamental ingredients of all organizations. But how work is divided, which coordinating mechanisms are emphasized, who makes decisions, and other issues are related to the four elements of organizational structure.

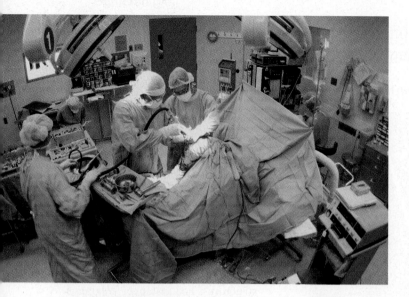

ELEMENTS OF ORGANIZATIONAL STRUCTURE

Organizational structure has four elements that apply to every organization. This section introduces three of them: span of control, centralization, and formalization. The fourth element—departmentalization—is presented in the next section.

Span of Control

Span of control (also called *span of management*) refers to the number of people directly reporting to the next level in the hierarchy. A narrow span of control exists when very few people report directly to a manager, whereas a wide span exists when a manager has many direct reports.[18] A century ago French engineer and management scholar Henri Fayol strongly recommended a relatively narrow span of control, typically no more than 20 employees per supervisor and 6 supervisors per manager. Fayol championed formal hierarchy as the primary coordinating mechanism, so he believed supervisors should closely monitor and coach employees. His views were similar to those of Napoleon and other military leaders, who declared that somewhere between 3 and 10 subordinates is the optimal span of control. These prescriptions were based on the belief

that managers simply could not monitor and control any more subordinates closely enough.[19]

Today we know better. The best-performing manufacturing plants currently have an average of 38 production employees per supervisor.[20] What's the secret here? Did Fayol, Napoleon, and others miscalculate the optimal span of control? The answer is that those sympathetic to hierarchical control believed employees should perform the physical tasks, whereas supervisors and other management personnel should make the decisions and monitor employees to make sure they performed their tasks. In contrast, the best-performing manufacturing operations today rely on self-directed teams, so direct supervision (formal hierarchy) is supplemented with other coordinating mechanisms. Self-directed teams coordinate mainly through informal communication and specialized knowledge, so formal hierarchy plays a minor role. Many firms that employ doctors, lawyers, and other professionals have a larger span of control because these staff members coordinate their work mainly through standardized skills. For example, more than two dozen people report directly to Cindy Zollinger, president of Boston-based litigation consulting firm Cornerstone Research. Zollinger explains that this large number of direct reports is possible because she leads professional staff who don't require close supervision. "They largely run themselves," Zollinger explains. "I help them in dealing with obstacles they face, or in making the most of opportunities that they find."[21]

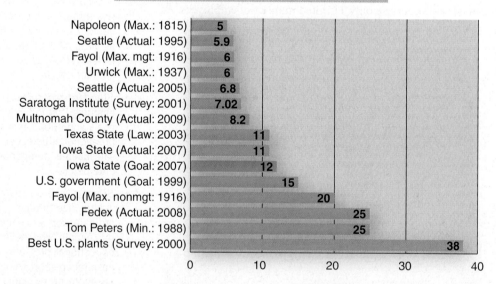

Ideal and Actual Spans of Control[22]

Napoleon (Max.: 1815)	5
Seattle (Actual: 1995)	5.9
Fayol (Max. mgt: 1916)	6
Urwick (Max.: 1937)	6
Seattle (Actual: 2005)	6.8
Saratoga Institute (Survey: 2001)	7.02
Multnomah County (Actual: 2009)	8.2
Texas State (Law: 2003)	11
Iowa State (Actual: 2007)	11
Iowa State (Goal: 2007)	12
U.S. government (Goal: 1999)	15
Fayol (Max. nonmgt: 1916)	20
Fedex (Actual: 2008)	25
Tom Peters (Min.: 1988)	25
Best U.S. plants (Survey: 2000)	38

Figures represent the average number of direct reports per manager. "Max." figures represent the maximum spans of control recommended by Napoleon Bonaparte, Henri Fayol, and Lindall Urwick. "Min." figure represents the minimum span of control recommended by Tom Peters. "Goal" figures represent span of control targets that the U.S. government and the state of Iowa have tried to achieve. The state of Texas figure represents the span of control mandated by law. The Saratoga Institute figure is the average span of control among U.S. companies surveyed. The best U.S. plants figure is the average span of control in American manufacturing facilities identified by *Industry Week* magazine as the most effective. "Actual" figures are spans of control at the city of Seattle, Multnomah County (including Portland, Oregon), the state of Iowa, and FedEx Corporation in the years indicated.

A second factor influencing the best span of control is whether employees perform routine tasks. A wider span of control is possible when employees perform routine jobs because there is less frequent need for direction or advice from supervisors. A narrow span of control is necessary when employees perform novel or complex tasks because these employees tend to require more supervisory decisions and coaching. This principle is illustrated in a survey of American property and casualty insurers. The average span of control in commercial policy processing departments is around 15 employees per supervisor, whereas the span of control is 6.1 in claims service and 5.5 in commercial underwriting. Staff members in the latter two departments perform more technical work, so they have more novel and complex tasks. Commercial policy processing, on the other hand, is like production work, where tasks are routine and have few exceptions.[23]

A third influence on span of control is the degree of interdependence among employees within the department or team.[24] Generally a narrow span of control is necessary where employees perform highly interdependent work with others. More supervision is required for highly interdependent jobs because employees tend to experience more conflict with each other, which requires more of a manager's time to resolve. Also, employees are less clear on their personal work performance in highly interdependent tasks, so supervisors spend more time providing coaching and feedback.

Tall versus Flat Structures Span of control is interconnected with organizational size (number of employees) and the number of layers in the organizational hierarchy. Consider two companies with the same number of employees. If Company A has a wider span of control (more direct reports per manager) than Company B, then Company A must have fewer layers of management (a flatter structure) than does Company B. The reason for this relationship is that a company with a wider span of control necessarily has more employees per supervisor, more supervisors for each middle manager, and so on. This larger number of direct reports, compared to a company with a narrower span of control, is possible only by removing layers of management. The interconnection of span of control, organizational size (number of employees), and number of management layers also means that as companies employ more people, they must widen the span of control, build a taller hierarchy, or both. Most companies end up building taller structures because they rely on direct supervision to some extent as a coordinating mechanism, and there are limits to how many people each manager can coordinate.

Unfortunately building a taller hierarchy (more layers of management) creates problems. First, tall structures have higher overhead costs because most layers of hierarchy consist of managers rather than employees who actually make the product or supply the service. Second, senior managers in tall structures often receive lower-quality and less timely information from the external environment because information from frontline employees is transmitted slowly or not at all up the hierarchy. Also, the more layers of management through which information must pass, the higher the probability that managers will filter out information that does not put them in a positive light. Finally, tall hierarchies tend to undermine employee empowerment and engagement because they focus power around managers rather than employees.[26]

These problems have prompted leaders to "delayer"—remove one or more levels in the organizational hierarchy.[27] Soon after Mark Hurd was hired as CEO of HP (Hewlett-Packard), he stripped the high-technology company's 11 layers of hierarchy down to 8 layers. He argued that this action reduced costs and would make HP more nimble. BASF's European Seal Sands plant went even further when it was dramatically restructured around self-directed teams. "Seven levels of management have been cut basically to two," says a BASF executive.[28]

FACT. The Struggle to Stay Flat[25]

For more than four decades, Nucor Corporation maintained a flat structure with only four layers of management. Crew supervisors reported to their functional managers (production, shipping, maintenance), who reported to the plant manager, who reported to Nucor's CEO. By allowing each plant to operate as an independent business, this flat structure was manageable even as Nucor grew to more than two dozen plants. But Nucor has become America's largest steelmaker in terms of shipments, employing 20,000 people at more than four dozen facilities worldwide. Managing 50 or more direct reports would itself be a full-time job, so Nucor's current chairman and CEO, Dan DiMicco, reluctantly added another layer of management (five executive vice presidents). "I needed to be free to make decisions on trade battles," says DiMicco, shown in this photo. Even with this additional layer, Nucor's structure has half the hierarchy of most similar-sized companies. DiMicco also emphasizes that he continues to stay involved by checking his own e-mail and meeting with staff at every opportunity.

centralization The degree to which formal decision authority is held by a small group of people, typically those at the top of the organizational hierarchy.

formalization The degree to which organizations standardize behavior through rules, procedures, formal training, and related mechanisms.

mechanistic structure An organizational structure with a narrow span of control and a high degree of formalization and centralization.

organic structure An organizational structure with a wide span of control, little formalization and decentralized decision making.

[Organizational experts warn that there are also negative long-term consequences of cutting out too much middle management.]

Although many companies enjoy reduced costs and more empowered employees when they delayer the organizational hierarchy, organizational experts warn that there are also negative long-term consequences of cutting out too much middle management.[29] These include undermining necessary managerial functions, increasing workload and stress among management, and restricting managerial career development:

- *Undermines managerial functions:* Critics of delayering point out that all companies need managers to guide work activities, coach subordinates, and manage company growth. Furthermore, managers are needed to make quick decisions and represent a source of appeal over conflicts. These valuable functions are underserved when the span of control becomes too wide.

- *Increases workload and stress:* Delayering increases the number of direct reports per manager and thus significantly increases management workload and corresponding levels of stress. Managers partly reduce the workload by learning to give subordinates more autonomy rather than micromanaging them. However, this role adjustment itself is stressful (same responsibility, but less authority or control), and many companies increase the span of control beyond the point at which many managers are capable of coaching or leading their direct reports.

- *Restricts managerial career development:* Delayering results in fewer managerial jobs, so companies have less maneuverability to develop managerial skills. Promotions are also riskier because they involve a larger jump in responsibility in flatter, compared to taller, hierarchies. Furthermore, having fewer promotion opportunities means that managers experience more career plateauing, which reduces their motivation and loyalty. Chopping back managerial career structures also sends a signal that managers are no longer valued. "Delayering has had an adverse effect on morale, productivity, and performance," argues a senior executive in the Australian federal government. "Disenfranchising middle management creates negative perceptions and lower commitment to the organization with consequent reluctance to accept responsibility."[30]

Centralization and Decentralization

Centralization/decentralization is a second element to consider when designing an organizational structure. **Centralization** means formal decision-making authority is held by a small group of people, typically those at the top of the organizational hierarchy. Most organizations begin with centralized structures: the founder makes most of the decisions and tries to direct the business toward his or her vision. As organizations grow, however, they diversify and their environments become more complex. Senior executives aren't able to process all the decisions that significantly influence the business. Consequently, larger organizations typically *decentralize*—that is, they disperse decision authority and power throughout the organization.

The optimal level of centralization or decentralization depends on several contingencies that we will examine later in this chapter. However, we also need to keep in mind that different degrees of decentralization can occur simultaneously in different parts of an organization. Nestlé, the Swiss-based food company, has decentralized marketing decisions to remain responsive to local markets, but it has centralized production, logistics, and supply chain management activities to improve cost efficiencies and avoid having too much complexity across the organization. "If you are too decentralized, you can become too complicated—you get too much complexity in your production system," explains a Nestlé executive.[31]

Likewise, 7-Eleven relies on both centralization and decentralization in different parts of the organization. The convenience store chain leverages buying power and efficiencies by centralizing decisions about information technology and supplier purchasing. At the same time, it decentralizes local inventory decisions to store managers so they can adapt quickly to changing circumstances at the local level. Along with receiving ongoing product training and guidance from regional consultants, store managers have the best information about their customers and can respond quickly to local market needs. "We could never predict a busload of football players on a Friday night, but the store manager can," explains a 7-Eleven executive.[32]

THE CHALLENGE THAT COMPANIES FACE AS THEY GET LARGER AND OLDER IS TO AVOID TOO MUCH FORMALIZATION.

Formalization

Formalization is the degree to which organizations standardize behavior through rules, procedures, formal training, and related mechanisms.[33] In other words, companies become more formalized as they increasingly rely on various forms of standardization to coordinate work. McDonald's restaurants and most other efficient fast-food chains typically have a high degree of formalization because they rely on standardization of work processes as a coordinating mechanism. Employees have precisely defined roles, right down to how much mustard should be dispensed, how many pickles should be applied, and how long each hamburger should be cooked.

Older companies tend to become more formalized because work activities become routinized, making them easier to document into standardized practices. Larger companies also tend to have more formalization because direct supervision and informal communication among employees do not operate as easily when large numbers of people are involved. External influences, such as government safety legislation and strict accounting rules, also encourage formalization.

Formalization may increase efficiency and compliance, but it can also create problems.[34] Rules and procedures reduce organizational flexibility, so employees follow prescribed behaviors even when the situation clearly calls for a customized response. High levels of formalization tend to undermine organizational learning and creativity. Some work rules become so convoluted that organizational efficiency would decline if they were actually followed as prescribed. Formalization is also a source of job dissatisfaction and work stress. Finally, rules and procedures have been known to take on a life of their own in some organizations. They become the focus of attention rather than the organization's ultimate objectives of producing a product or service and serving its dominant stakeholders.

The challenge that companies face as they get larger and older is to avoid too much formalization. Yahoo! seems to be a case in point. A decade ago the world's most popular Web portal site was a creative hotspot among Web-based companies. Through strategic acquisitions (Flickr, del.icio.us, Yahoo! 360, and so forth), the company continues to launch new services, but observers and former staff say internal innovations have been hampered by creeping bureaucracy. "In a small company [the attitude] is, 'Hey, let's launch it and let's see if the users like it,'" says a senior Yahoo! staffer who has since moved to a smaller firm. "There was a time a few years ago where Yahoo! had more of that mentality. But as companies get bigger and bigger, many of them reach a point where they can't do that as quickly." Another former Yahoo! employee is more blunt: "If you are on the Internet, you have to be fast and you have to take risks. The organizational structure that Yahoo! has is completely antithetical to the industry they are in."[36]

Mechanistic versus Organic Structures

We discussed span of control, centralization, and formalization together because they cluster around two broader organizational forms: mechanistic and organic structures (see Exhibit 12.2).[37] A **mechanistic structure** is characterized by a narrow span of control and a high degree of formalization and centralization. Mechanistic structures have many rules and procedures, limited decision making at lower levels, tall hierarchies of people in specialized roles, and vertical rather than horizontal communication flows. Tasks are rigidly defined and are altered only when sanctioned by higher authorities. Companies with an **organic structure** have the opposite characteristics. They operate with a wide span of control, decentralized decision making, and little formalization. Tasks are fluid, adjusting to new situations and organizational needs.

As a general rule, mechanistic structures operate better in stable environments because they rely on efficiency and routine behaviors, whereas organic structures work better in rapidly changing (dynamic) environments because they are more flexible and responsive to the changes. Organic structures are also more compatible with organizational learning, high-performance

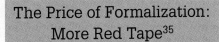
The Price of Formalization: More Red Tape[35]

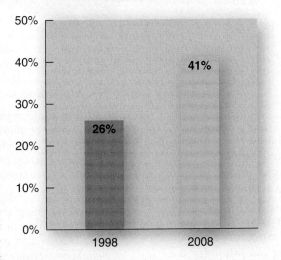

Percentage of 1,200 Canadian employees polled in 1998 and of 2,052 Canadian employees polled in 2008 who identified "red tape and bureaucracy" as one of the biggest barriers to their work productivity.

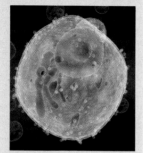

Mechanistic Structure	Organic Structure
• Narrow span of control.	• Wide span of control.
• High centralization.	• High decentralization.
• High formalization.	• Low formalization.

workplaces, and quality management because they emphasize information sharing and an empowered workforce rather than hierarchy and status.[38] However, the advantages of organic structures, rather than mechanistic structures, in dynamic environments occur only when employees have developed well-established roles and expertise.[39] Without these conditions, employees are unable to coordinate effectively with each other, resulting in errors and gross inefficiencies.

Start-up companies often face this problem, known as the *liability of newness*. Newness makes start-up firms more organic—they tend to be smaller organizations with few rules and considerable delegation of authority. However, employees in new organizations often lack industry experience, and their teams have not developed sufficiently for peak performance. As a result, the organic structures of new companies cannot compensate for the poorer coordination and significantly lower efficiencies caused by the lack of structure from past experience and team mental models. Fortunately, companies can minimize the liability of newness by launching businesses with existing teams of people or with industry veterans guiding the novices.

Learning Objectives

After reading this section, you should be able to

LO3 Identify and evaluate six types of departmentalization.

FORMS OF DEPARTMENTALIZATION

Span of control, centralization, and formalization are important elements of organizational structure, but most people think about organizational charts when the discussion of organizational structure arises. The organizational chart represents the fourth element in the structuring of organizations, called *departmentalization*. Departmentalization specifies how employees and their activities are grouped together. It is a fundamental strategy for coordinating organizational activities because it influences organizational behavior in the following ways:[40]

- Departmentalization establishes the chain of command—the system of common supervision among positions and units within the organization. It frames the membership of formal work teams and typically determines which positions and units must share resources. Thus departmentalization establishes interdependencies among employees and subunits.

- Departmentalization focuses people around common mental models or ways of thinking, such as serving clients, developing products, or supporting a particular skill set. This focus is typically anchored around the common budgets and measures of performance assigned to employees within each departmental unit.

- Departmentalization encourages specific people and work units to coordinate through informal communication. With common supervision and resources, members within each configuration typically work near each other, so they can use frequent and informal interaction to get the work done.

[Departmentalization establishes the chain of command, focuses people around common mental models, and encourages specific people to coordinate through informal communication.]

There are almost as many organizational charts as there are businesses, but the six most common pure types of departmentalization are simple, functional, divisional, team-based, matrix, and network.

Simple Structure

Most companies begin with a *simple structure*.[42] They employ only a few people and typically offer only one distinct product or service. There is minimal hierarchy—usually just employees reporting to the owners. Employees perform broadly defined roles because there are insufficient economies of scale to assign them to specialized jobs. The simple structure is highly flexible and minimizes the walls that form between employees in other structures. However, the simple structure usually depends on the owner's direct supervision to coordinate work activities, so it is difficult to operate as the company grows and becomes more complex.

see people with common issues and expertise.[43]

The functional structure also has limitations.[44] Grouping employees around their skills tends to focus attention on those skills and related professional needs rather than on the company's product, service, or client needs. Unless people are transferred from one function to the next, they might not develop a broader understanding of the business. Compared with other structures, the functional structure usually produces higher dysfunctional conflict and poorer coordination in serving clients or developing products. These problems occur because employees need to work with coworkers in other departments to

functional structure
An organizational structure in which employees are organized around specific knowledge or other resources.

divisional structure
An organizational structure in which employees are organized around geographic areas, outputs (products/services), or clients.

> " Every company has two organizational structures: The formal one is written on the charts; the other is the everyday relationship of the men and women in the organization.[41]
> —Harold S. Geneen "

Functional Structure

Growing organizations usually introduce a functional structure at some level of the hierarchy or at some time in their history. A **functional structure** organizes employees around specific knowledge or other resources (see Exhibit 12.3). Employees with marketing expertise are grouped into a marketing unit, those with production skills are located in manufacturing, engineers are found in product development, and so on. Organizations with functional structures are typically centralized to coordinate their activities effectively.

Evaluating the Functional Structure

The functional structure creates specialized pools of talent that typically serve everyone in the organization. This provides more economies of scale than are possible if functional specialists are spread over different parts of the organization. It increases employee identity with the specialization or profession. Direct supervision is easier in functional structures because managers over-

complete organizational tasks, yet they have different subgoals and mental models of ideal work. Together these problems require substantial formal controls and coordination when people are organized around functions.

Divisional Structure

The **divisional structure** (sometimes called the *multidivisional* or *M-form* structure) groups employees around geographic areas,

▼ **EXHIBIT 12.3** A Functional Organizational Structure

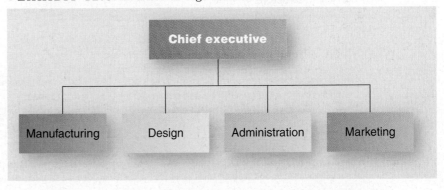

globally integrated enterprise
An organizational structure in which work processes and executive functions are distributed around the world through global centers, rather than developed in a home country and replicated in satellite countries or regions.

outputs (products or services), or clients. Exhibit 12.4 illustrates these three variations of divisional structure. The *geographic divisional structure* organizes employees around distinct regions of the country or world. Exhibit 12.4(a) illustrates a geographic divisional structure recently adopted by Barrick Gold Corporation, the world's largest gold mining company. The *product/ service divisional structure* organizes employees around distinct outputs. Exhibit 12.4(b) illustrates a simplified version of this type of structure at Philips. The Dutch electronics company divides its workforce mainly into three divisions: health care products, lighting products, and consumer products. The *client divisional structure* organizes employees around specific customer groups. Exhibit 12.4(c) illustrates a customer-focused divisional structure similar to one adopted by the U.S. Internal Revenue Service.[45]

Which form of divisional structure should large organizations adopt? The answer depends mainly on the primary source of environmental diversity or uncertainty.[46] Suppose an organization has one type of product sold to people across the country. If customers have different needs across regions, or if state governments impose different regulations on the product, then a geographic structure would be best to be more vigilant of this diversity. On the other hand, if the company sells several types of products across the country and customer preferences and government regulations are similar everywhere, then a product structure would likely work best.

Coca-Cola, Nestlé, and many other food and beverage companies are organized mainly around geographic regions because consumer tastes and preferred marketing strategies vary considerably around the world. Even though McDonald's makes the same Big Mac throughout the world, the company has more fish products in Hong Kong and more vegetarian products in India, in line with traditional diets in those countries. Philips, on the other hand, is organized around products because

▼ **EXHIBIT 12.4** Three Types of Divisional Structure

(a) Geographic structure

- Chief executive officer
  - North America
  - South America
  - Australia Pacific
  - Africa

(b) Product structure

- Chief executive officer
  - Health care
  - Lighting products
  - Consumer lifestyle

(c) Client structure

- Commissioner (chief executive)
  - Wage and investment (individual taxpayers)
  - Small business and self-employed
  - Large and midsize business
  - Tax-exempt and government entities

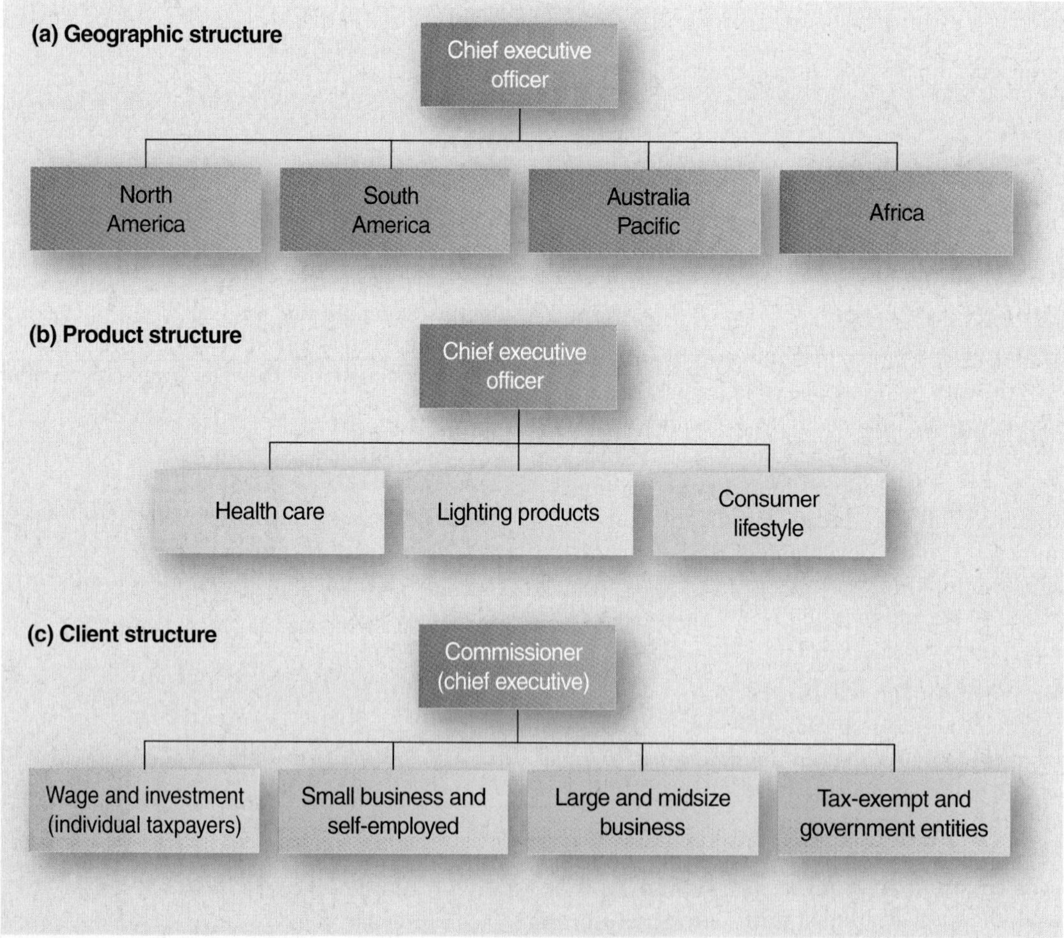

Note: Diagram (a) shows a global geographic divisional structure similar to that of Barrick Gold Corp.; diagram (b) is similar to the product divisions at Philips; diagram (c) is similar to the customer-focused structure at the U.S. Internal Revenue Service.

> ## WE ARE MOVING AGGRESSIVELY FROM [A] MULTINATIONAL MODEL TO A FUNDAMENTALLY NEW ARCHITECTURE OF THE CORPORATION—WHAT WE CALL THE GLOBALLY INTEGRATED ENTERPRISE.[50]
>
> —SAM PALMISANO

consumer preferences around the world are similar within each product group. Hospitals from Geneva, Switzerland, to Santiago, Chile, buy similar medical equipment from Philips, whereas the manufacturing and marketing of these products are quite different from Philips' consumer electronics business.

The Globally Integrated Enterprise Many companies are moving away from structures that organize people around geographic clusters.[47] One reason is that clients can purchase products online and communicate with businesses from almost anywhere in the world, so local representation is less critical. Reduced geographic variation is another reason for the shift away from geographic structures; freer trade has reduced government intervention, and consumer preferences for many products and services are becoming more similar (converging) around the world. The third reason is that large companies increasingly have global business customers who demand one global point of purchase, not one in every country or region.

This shift away from geographic and toward product or client-based divisional structures reflects the trend toward the **globally integrated enterprise**.[49] As the label implies, a globally integrated enterprise connects work processes around the world rather than replicating them within each country or region. This type of organization typically organizes people around product or client divisions. Even functional units—production, marketing, design, human resources, and so on—serve the company worldwide rather than within specific geographic clusters. These functions are sensitive to cultural and market differences and have local representation to support that sensitivity, but local representatives are associates of a global function rather than a local subsidiary copied across several regions. Indeed, a globally integrated enterprise is marked by a dramatic increase in virtual teamwork because employees are assigned global projects and ongoing responsibilities for work units that transcend geographic boundaries.

FACT. Organizations Going Global: Consistent Reputations across Regions[48]

Rank	Asia	Central Europe	Central and South America	North America	Northern Europe
1	The Walt Disney Company	Sony	Nestlé	Johnson & Johnson	Google
2	Daimler/Mercedes Benz	BMW	Sony	Google	IKEA
3	BMW	Google	Google	Nestlé	Sony
4	Sony	Volkswagen	BMW	The Walt Disney Company	The Walt Disney Company
5	Singapore Airlines	Daimler/Mercedes Benz	Johnson & Johnson	Sony	Singapore Airlines

Companies with highest reputations, by region. Data are based on 181,000 ratings by several thousand consumers in 24 countries of the reputations of the world's 600 largest companies. These results suggest that people around the world identify similar companies as highest ranked for reputations, a sign that these are globalized organizations.

team-based organizational structure
An organizational structure built around self-directed teams that complete an entire piece of work.

matrix structure
An organizational structure that overlays two structures (such as a geographic divisional and a functional structure) in order to leverage the benefits of both.

The globally integrated enterprise no longer orchestrates its business from a single headquarters in one "home" country. Instead its divisional and functional operations are led from where the work is concentrated, and this concentration depends on economics (cost of labor, infrastructure, and the like), expertise, and openness (trade, capital flow, knowledge sharing, and so forth). For example, IBM has moved toward a globally integrated enterprise structure by locating its global data centers in Colorado, Web site management in Ireland, back-office finance in Brazil,

revise their structures back and forth or create complex structures that attempt to give all three dimensions equal status. This waffling and complexity generate further complications because organizational structure decisions shift power and status among executives. If the company switches from a geographic to product structure, people who lead the geographic fiefdoms suddenly get demoted under the product chiefs. In short, leaders of global organizations struggle to find the best divisional structure, often resulting in the departure of some executives and frustration among those who remain.

Team-Based Structure

A **team-based organizational structure** is built around self-directed teams that complete an entire piece of work, such as manufacturing a product or developing an electronic game. This

[Leaders of global organizations struggle to find the best divisional structure, often resulting in the departure of some executives and frustration among those who remain.]

software in India, and procurement in China. IBM's vice president of worldwide engineering, responsible for procurement, moved from Armonk, New York, to China, where the procurement center is located. "These people are not leading teams focused on China or India or Brazil or Ireland—or Colorado or Vermont," says IBM CEO Sam Palmisano. "They are leading integrated global operations."[51]

Evaluating the Divisional Structure The divisional organizational structure is a building-block structure; it accommodates growth relatively easily and focuses employee attention on products or customers rather than tasks. Different products, services, or clients can be accommodated by sprouting new divisions. These advantages are offset by a number of limitations. First, the divisional structure tends to duplicate resources, such as production equipment and engineering or information technology expertise. Also, unless the division is quite large, resources are not used as efficiently as they are in functional structures where resources are pooled across the entire organization. The divisional structure also creates silos of knowledge. Expertise is spread across several autonomous business units, and this reduces the ability and perhaps motivation of the people in one division to share their knowledge with counterparts in other divisions. In contrast, a functional structure groups experts together, thereby supporting knowledge sharing.

Finally, the preferred divisional structure depends on the company's primary source of environmental diversity or uncertainty. This principle seems to be applied easily enough at Coca-Cola, McDonald's, and Philips, but many global organizations experience diversity and uncertainty in terms of geography, product, *and* clients. Consequently some organizations

type of structure is usually organic. There is a wide span of control because teams operate with minimal supervision. In extreme situations, there is no formal leader—just someone selected by other team members to help coordinate the work and liaise with top management. Team structures are highly decentralized because almost all day-to-day decisions are made by team members rather than someone further up the organizational hierarchy. Finally, many team-based structures have low formalization because teams are given relatively few rules about how to organize their work. Instead executives assign quality and quantity output targets and often productivity improvement goals to each team. Teams are then encouraged to use available resources and their own initiative to achieve those objectives.

Team-based structures are usually found within the manufacturing or service operations of larger divisional structures. For example, several GE Aircraft Engines plants are organized as team-based structures, but these plants operate within GE's larger divisional structure. However, a small number of firms apply the team-based structure from top to bottom, including W. L. Gore & Associates and Semco SA, where almost all associates work in teams.

Evaluating the Team-Based Structure

The team-based structure has gained popularity because it tends to be flexible and responsive in turbulent environments.[52] It tends to reduce costs because teams have less reliance on formal hierarchy (direct supervision). A cross-functional team structure improves communication and cooperation across traditional boundaries. With greater autonomy, this structure also allows quicker and more informed decision making.[53] For this reason, some hospitals have shifted from functional departments to cross-functional teams. Teams composed of nurses, radiologists, anesthetists, a pharmacology representative, possibly social workers, a rehabilitation therapist, and other specialists communicate and coordinate more efficiently, thereby reducing delays and errors.[54]

> The team-based structure has gained popularity because it tends to be flexible and responsive in turbulent environments.

Against these benefits, the team-based structure can be costly to maintain due to the need for ongoing interpersonal skill training. Teamwork potentially takes more time to coordinate than formal hierarchy during the early stages of team development. Employees may experience more stress due to increased ambiguity in their roles. Team leaders also experience more stress due to increased conflict, loss of functional power, and unclear career progression ladders. In addition, team structures suffer from duplication of resources and potential competition (and lack of resource sharing) across teams.[55]

Matrix Structure

When physicians Ray Muzyka and Greg Zeschuk and a third partner (who later returned to medical practice) founded Bio-Ware Corp., they initially organized employees at the electronic games company into a simple structure in which everyone worked together on the first game, *Shattered Steel*. Soon after, Muzyka and Zeschuk decided to create a second game (*Baldur's Gate*), but they weren't sure what organizational structure would be best. Simply creating a second team might duplicate resources, undermine information sharing across teams, and weaken employee loyalty to the overall company. Alternatively, the game developer could adopt a functional structure by assigning employees to specialized departments such as art, programming, audio, quality assurance, and design. A functional structure would encourage employees within each specialization to share information, but it might undermine team dynamics on game projects and reduce employee commitment to the game they were developing.[56]

After carefully weighing the various organizational structure options, Muzyka and Zeschuk adopted a **matrix structure** to gain the benefits of both a functional structure and a project-based (team) structure. BioWare's matrix structure, which is similar to the diagram in Exhibit 12.5, is organized around both functions (art, audio, programming, and so on) and team-based game development projects. Employees are assigned to a cross-functional team responsible for a specific game project, yet they also belong to a permanent functional unit from which they are reassigned when their work is completed on a particular project.[57]

Muzyka and Zeschuk say the matrix structure focuses employees on the final product yet keeps them organized around their expertise to encourage knowledge sharing. "The matrix structure also supports our overall company culture where BioWare is the team, and everyone is always willing to help each other whether they are on the same project or not," they add. BioWare's matrix structure was a good choice, particularly as the company (which recently became an independent division of Electronic Arts) has grown to almost 400 employees working on more than a half-dozen game projects in Austin, Texas, and Edmonton, Canada.

BioWare's structure, in which project teams overlap with functional departments, is just one form of matrix structure. Another variation, found mainly in large global firms, is to have geography on one axis and products/services or client groups on the other. A few years ago Procter & Gamble moved toward this type of global matrix structure with geographic divisions (called "market development organizations") on one axis and "global business units," representing global brands, on the other axis. P&G previously had a geographic divisional structure, which gave too much power to country managers and not enough power or priority to globalizing its major brands (such as Pantene, Tide, and Pringles). P&G's leaders believe the new matrix structure will balance this power, thereby supporting its

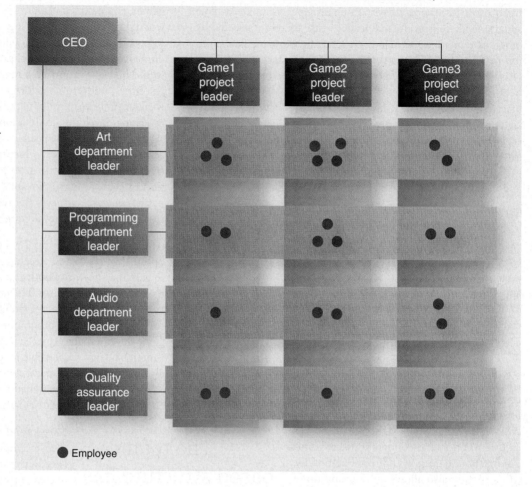

● Employee

philosophy of thinking globally and acting locally.[58]

Evaluating the Matrix Structure

The matrix structure usually makes good use of resources and expertise, making it ideal for project-based organizations with fluctuating workloads. When properly managed, it improves communication efficiency, project flexibility, and innovation, compared to purely functional or divisional designs. It focuses employees on serving clients or creating products yet keeps people organized around their specialization, so knowledge sharing improves and resources are used more efficiently. The matrix structure is also a logical choice when, as in the case of Procter & Gamble, two different dimensions (regions and products) are equally important. Structures determine executive power and what is important; the matrix structure works when two different dimensions deserve equal attention.

Despite these advantages, the matrix structure has several well-known problems.[59] One concern is that it increases conflict among managers who equally share power. Employees working at the matrix level have two bosses and, consequently, two sets of priorities that aren't always aligned with each other. Project leaders might squabble with functional leaders regarding the assignment of specific employees to projects as well as regarding the employee's technical competence. For example, Citigroup, Inc., recently adopted a geographic–product matrix structure and apparently is already experiencing dysfunctional conflict between the regional and product group executives.[60] Aware of these potential conflicts, BioWare holds several "synchronization meetings" each year involving all department directors (art, design, audio, and so forth), producers (that is, game project leaders), and the human resource manager. These meetings sort out differences and ensure that staff members are properly assigned to each game project.

Another challenge is that the existence of two bosses can dilute accountability. In a functional or divisional structure, one manager is responsible for everything, even the most unexpected issues. But in a matrix structure, the unusual problems don't get resolved because neither manager takes ownership of them.[61]

Mark Hurd was so concerned about accountability that he replaced Hewlett-Packard's matrix structure soon after becoming CEO. "The more accountable I can make you, the easier it is for you to show you're a great performer," Hurd declared. "The more I use a matrix, the easier I make it to blame someone else."[62] The combination of dysfunctional conflict and ambiguous accountability in matrix structures also explains why some employees experience more stress and some managers are less satisfied with their work arrangements.

Network Structure

BMW and Daimler Benz aren't eager to let you know this, but some of their vehicles designed and constructed with German precision are designed and constructed neither by them nor in Germany. Much of BMW's X3, for example, was designed by Magna Steyr in Austria. Magna also manufactured the vehicle in Austria until BMW transferred this work to its manufacturing plant in the United States. The contract manufacturer also builds Daimler's off-road G-class Mercedes. Both BMW and Daimler Benz are hub organizations that own and market their respective brands, whereas Magna and other suppliers are spokes around the hub that provide production, engineering, and other services that get the auto firms' luxury products to customers.[64]

FACT. Losing Data in the Matrix[63]

Soon after Britain's Inland Revenue and Customs/Excise departments merged to become HM Revenue & Customs (HMRC), the combined department experienced a series of errors that violated individual privacy rights. The most serious of these incidents occurred when HMRC staff somehow lost two computer disks containing confidential details of 25 million child welfare claimants. The U.K. government's investigation into the security lapse concluded that along with resulting from poor security procedures, the error was partly due to "muddled accountabilities" created by the matrix organizational structure under which the new department operated. The investigator's initial briefing stated that the matrix structure and numerous departments made it "difficult to relate roles and responsibilities amongst senior management to accountability." In fact, responsibility for data security was assigned to no fewer than five departments, each of which reported to different director generals. The final report concluded that "[HMRC] is not suited to the so-called 'constructive friction' matrix type organization [that was] in place at the time of the data loss." HMRC has since changed to a more traditional, single-command organizational structure.

BMW, Daimler Benz, and many other organizations are moving toward a **network structure** as they design and build a product or serve a client through an alliance of several organizations.[65] As Exhibit 12.6 illustrates, this collaborative structure typically consists of several satellite organizations beehived around a hub or core firm. The core firm orchestrates the network process and provides one or two other core competencies, such as marketing or product development. In our example, BMW or Mercedes is the hub that provides marketing and management, whereas other firms perform many other functions. The core firm might be the main contact with customers, but most of the product or service delivery and

support activities are farmed out to satellite organizations located anywhere in the world. Extranets (Web-based networks with partners) and other technologies ensure that information flows easily and openly between the core firm and its array of satellites.[66]

One of the main forces pushing toward a network structure is the recognition that an organization has only a few *core competencies*. A core competency is a knowledge base that resides throughout the organization and provides a strategic advantage. As companies discover their core competencies, they "unbundle" noncritical tasks to other organizations that have a core competency at performing those tasks. For instance, BMW decided long ago that its core competency is not facilities management, so it outsourced this function at its British engine plant to Dalkia, which specializes in facility maintenance and energy management.[67]

Companies are also more likely to form network structures when technology is changing quickly and production processes are complex or varied.[68] Many firms cannot keep up with the hyperfast changes in information technology, so they have outsourced their entire information system departments to IBM, EDS, and other firms that specialize in information system services. Similarly, many high-technology firms form networks with Flextronics, Celestica, and other electronic equipment manufacturers that have expertise in diverse production processes.

Evaluating the Network Structure
For several years, organizational behavior theorists have argued that organizational leaders must develop a metaphor of organizations as plasmalike organisms rather than rigid machines.[69] Network structures come close to the organism metaphor because they offer the flexibility to realign their structure with changing environmental requirements. If customers demand a new product or service, the core firm forms new alliances with other firms offering the appropriate resources. For example, by working with Magna International, BMW was probably able to develop and launch the X3 vehicle much sooner than would have been the case if it had performed these tasks on its own. When BMW

> ## Network structures come close to the organism metaphor because they offer the flexibility to realign their structure with changing environmental requirements.

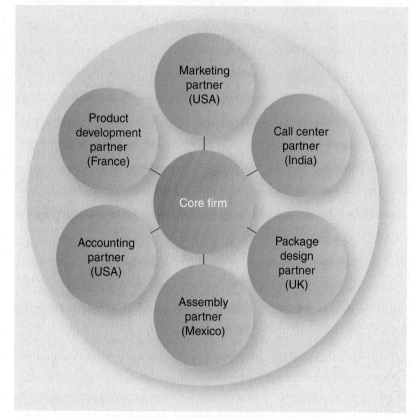

compared to maintaining the quality of work performed by in-house employees.

Learning Objectives

After reading this section, you should be able to

LO4 Explain how the external environment, organizational size, technology, and strategy are relevant when designing an organizational structure.

CONTINGENCIES OF ORGANIZATIONAL DESIGN

Most organizational behavior theories and concepts have contingencies; ideas that work well in one situation might not work as well in another situation. This contingency approach is certainly relevant when choosing the most appropriate organizational structure.[71] In this section we introduce four contingencies of organizational design: external environment, size, technology, and strategy.

needs a different type of manufacturing, it isn't saddled with nonessential facilities and resources. Network structures also offer efficiencies because the core firm becomes globally competitive as it shops worldwide for subcontractors with the best people and the best technology at the best price. Indeed, the pressures of global competition have made network structures more vital, and computer-based information technology has made them possible.[70]

A potential disadvantage of network structures is that they expose the core firm to market forces. Other companies may bid up the price for subcontractors, whereas the short-term cost would be lower if the company hired its own employees to perform the same function. Another problem is that although information technology makes worldwide communication much easier, it will never replace the degree of control organizations have when manufacturing, marketing, and other functions are in-house. The core firm can use arm's-length incentives and contract provisions to maintain the subcontractor's quality, but these actions are relatively crude

External Environment

The best structure for an organization depends on its external environment. The external environment includes anything outside the organization, including most stakeholders (such as clients, suppliers, government), resources (raw materials, human resources, information, finances, and so forth), and competitors. Four characteristics of external environments influence the type of organizational structure best suited to a particular situation: dynamism, complexity, diversity, and hostility.[72]

Dynamic versus Stable Environments Dynamic environments have a high rate of change, leading to novel situations and a lack of identifiable patterns. Organic structures are better suited to this type of environment so the organization can adapt more quickly to changes, but only if employees are experienced and coordinate well in teamwork.[73] In contrast, stable environments are characterized by regular cycles of activity and steady changes in supply and demand for inputs and outputs. Events are more predictable, enabling the

> ## " DECENTRALIZATION IS A LOGICAL CHOICE IN COMPLEX ENVIRONMENTS BECAUSE DECISIONS ARE PUSHED DOWN TO PEOPLE AND SUBUNITS WITH THE NECESSARY INFORMATION TO MAKE INFORMED CHOICES. "

Choosing the Best Organizational Structure for the Environment

- Organic structures are better suited for dynamic environments; mechanistic structures are usually more effective for stable environments.

- Organizations should be more decentralized as environments become more complex.

- Diverse environments call for a divisional structure aligned with the highest form of diversity.

- Organic structures are better suited for hostile environments; mechanistic structures are usually more effective in munificent environments.

firm to apply rules and procedures. Mechanistic structures are more efficient than organic structures when the environment is predictable.

Complex versus Simple Environments
Complex environments have many elements, whereas simple environments have few things to monitor. As an example, a major university library operates in a more complex environment than a small-town public library. The university library's clients require several types of services—book borrowing, online full-text databases, research centers, course reserve collections, and so on. A small-town public library has fewer of these demands placed on it. The more complex the environment, the more decentralized the organization should become. Decentralization is a logical choice in complex environments because decisions are pushed down to people and subunits with the necessary information to make informed choices.

Diverse versus Integrated Environments
Organizations located in diverse environments have a greater variety of products or services, clients, and regions. In contrast, an integrated environment has only one client, product, and geographic area. The more diversified the environment, the more the firm needs to use a divisional structure aligned with that diversity. If it sells a single product around the world, a geographic divisional structure would align best with the firm's geographic diversity, for example.

Hostile versus Munificent Environments
Firms located in a hostile environment face resource scarcity and more competition in the marketplace. Hostile environments are typically dynamic ones because they reduce the predictability of access to resources and demand for outputs. Organic structures tend to be best in hostile environments. However, when the environment is extremely hostile—such as a severe shortage of supplies or sudden intense competition—organizations tend to temporarily centralize so decisions can be made more quickly and executives feel more comfortably in control.[74] Ironically, centralization may result in lower-quality decisions during organizational crises because top management has less information, particularly when the environment is complex.

Organizational Size
Larger organizations should have different structures than smaller organizations.[75] As the number of employees increases, job specialization increases due to a greater division of labor. The greater division of labor requires more elaborate coordinating mechanisms. Thus larger firms make greater use of standardization (particularly work processes and outcomes) to coordinate work activities. These coordinating mechanisms create an administrative hierarchy and greater formalization. Historically, larger organizations have made less use of informal communication as a coordinating mechanism. However, emerging information technologies and increased emphasis on empowerment have caused informal communication to regain importance in large firms.[76]

Larger organizations also tend to be more decentralized. Executives have neither sufficient time nor expertise to process all the decisions that significantly influence the business as it grows. Therefore, decision-making authority is pushed down to lower levels, where incumbents can cope with the narrower range of issues under their control.

> Organizational structures don't evolve as a natural response to environmental conditions; they result from conscious human decisions.

Technology

Technology is another factor to consider when designing the best organizational structure.[77] *Technology* refers to the mechanisms or processes by which an organization turns out its product or service. One technological contingency is *variability*—the number of exceptions to standard procedure that tend to occur. In work processes with low variability, jobs are routine and follow standard operating procedures. Another contingency is *analyzability*—the predictability or difficulty of the required work. The less analyzable the work, the more it requires experts with sufficient discretion to address the work challenges. An organic, rather than a mechanistic, structure should be introduced where employees perform tasks with high variety and low analyzability, such as in a research setting. The reason is that employees face unique situations with little opportunity for repetition. In contrast, a mechanistic structure is preferred where the technology has low variability and high analyzability, such as an assembly line. Here the work is routine and highly predictable—an ideal situation for a mechanistic structure to operate efficiently.

Organizational Strategy

Organizational strategy refers to the way the organization positions itself in its setting in relation to its stakeholders, given the organization's resources, capabilities, and mission.[78] In other words, strategy represents the decisions and actions applied to achieve the organization's goals. Although size, technology, and environment influence the optimal organizational structure, these contingencies do not necessarily determine structure. Instead corporate leaders formulate and implement strategies that shape both the characteristics of these contingencies as well as the organization's resulting structure.

This concept is summed up with the simple phrase "Structure follows strategy."[79] Organizational leaders decide how large to grow and which technologies to use. They take steps to define and manipulate their environments rather than letting the organization's fate be entirely determined by external influences. Furthermore, organizational structures don't evolve as a natural response to environmental conditions; they result from conscious human decisions. Thus organizational strategy influences both the contingencies of structure and the structure itself. If a company's strategy is to compete through innovation, a more organic structure would be preferred because it is easier for employees to share knowledge and be creative. If a company chooses a low-cost strategy, a mechanistic structure is preferred because it maximizes production and service efficiency.[80] Overall, it is now apparent that organizational structure is influenced by size, technology, and environment; but the organization's strategy may reshape these elements and loosen their connection to organizational structure. ■

organizational strategy The way the organization positions itself in its setting in relation to its stakeholders, given the organization's resources, capabilities, and mission.

CHECK IT OUT!

mhhe.com/McShaneM

for study materials
including quizzes
and Internet resources

chapter thirteen

organizational **culture**

"Secretive Culture Led Toyota Astray" (*The Wall Street Journal*)[1]

"BP Culture Needs Closer Examination" (*Altoona Mirror*)[2]

"Cultures Clash as Merrill Herd Meets 'Wal-Mart of Banking'" (*The Wall Street Journal*)[3]

"Damning Insight into Corporate Culture Sheds Light on Fall of a Wall Street Giant" (*Financial Times*)[4]

It seems that whenever a company is very successful or in deep trouble, its organizational culture is part of the explanation. These recent newspaper and magazine headlines illustrate this point. The *Wall Street Journal* article argues that Toyota's slow response to vehicle defects was due to its "secretive culture." The *Altoona Mirror* piece suggests that BP's culture was a factor in the disastrous Gulf of Mexico oil spill as well as other environmental and safety incidents in which BP has been responsible. The article about

continued on p. 256

LEARNING OBJECTIVES

After reading this chapter, you should be able to

LO1 Describe the elements of organizational culture and discuss the importance of organizational subcultures.

LO2 List four categories of artifacts through which corporate culture is deciphered.

LO3 Discuss the importance of organizational culture and the conditions under which organizational culture strength improves organizational performance.

LO4 Compare and contrast four strategies for merging organizational cultures.

LO5 Identify four strategies for changing or strengthening an organization's culture, including the application of attraction-selection-attrition theory.

LO6 Describe the organizational socialization process and identify strategies to improve that process.

organizational culture The values and assumptions shared within an organization.

continued from p. 255

clashing cultures refers to frictions between Merrill Lynch and Bank of America after the latter hastily acquired the investment firm. And London's *Financial Times* states that a U.S. court report identified a dysfunctional corporate culture as a major cause of the financial collapse of investment giant Lehman Brothers. ■

Organizational culture consists of the values and assumptions shared within an organization.[5] It defines what is important and unimportant in the company and, consequently, directs everyone in the organization toward the "right way" of doing things. You might think of organizational culture as the company's DNA—invisible to the naked eye, yet a powerful template that shapes what happens in the workplace.

This chapter begins by identifying the elements of organizational culture and then describing how culture is deciphered through artifacts. This is followed by a discussion of the relationship between organizational culture and performance, including the effects of cultural strength, fit, and adaptability. Then we examine the challenges of and solutions to merging organizational cultures. The final sections of this chapter turn our attention to ways to change or strengthen organizational culture, including a closer look at the related topic of organizational socialization.

Learning Objectives

After reading the next two sections, you should be able to

L01 Describe the elements of organizational culture and discuss the importance of organizational subcultures.

ELEMENTS OF ORGANIZATIONAL CULTURE

As its definition states, organizational culture consists of shared values and assumptions. Exhibit 13.1 illustrates how these shared values and assumptions relate to each other and are

▼**EXHIBIT 13.1** Organizational Culture Assumptions, Values, and Artifacts

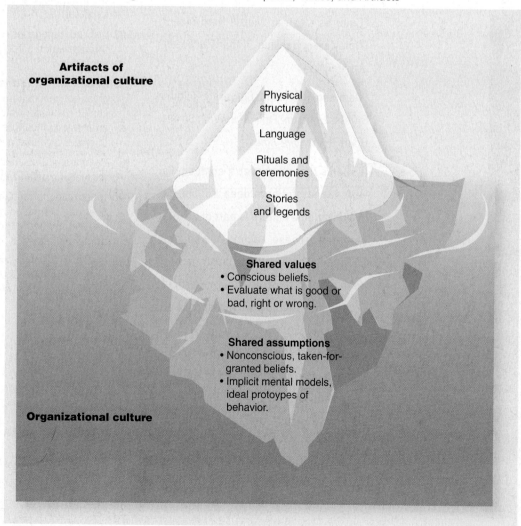

Artifacts of organizational culture

Physical structures

Language

Rituals and ceremonies

Stories and legends

Shared values
• Conscious beliefs.
• Evaluate what is good or bad, right or wrong.

Shared assumptions
• Nonconscious, taken-for-granted beliefs.
• Implicit mental models, ideal protoypes of behavior.

Organizational culture

associated with artifacts, which are discussed later in this chapter. *Values* are stable, evaluative beliefs that guide our preferences for outcomes or courses of action in a variety of situations (see Chapters 1 and 2).[6] They are conscious perceptions about what is good or bad, right or wrong. In the context of organizational culture, values are discussed as *shared values,* which are values that people within the organization or work unit have in common and place near the top of their hierarchy of values.[7] For example, various reports suggest that BP's culture prized cost efficiency and placed safety and environmentalism much further down the values hierarchy.

values—progressive, responsible, innovative, and performance-driven—that "guide us in the conduct of our business." Korean steelmaker POSCO identifies five core values: customer focus, execution (achieving goals), integrity, recognizing the value of people, and challenge (an indomitable spirit of transforming the impossible into reality). POSCO is one of Asia's most admired companies and is rated by senior university students as the most desired company to work for in Korea.

Do these values really represent the cultural content of BP and POSCO? Possibly, to some extent. However, corporate leaders typically describe *espoused values*—the values they want others

The thing I have learned at IBM is that culture is everything.[8]

—Louis V. Gerstner, Jr.

Organizational culture also consists of *shared assumptions*—a deeper element that some experts believe is the essence of corporate culture. Shared assumptions are nonconscious, taken-for-granted perceptions or ideal prototypes of behavior that are considered the correct way to think and act toward problems and opportunities. Shared assumptions are so deeply ingrained that you probably wouldn't discover them by surveying employees. Only by observing employees, analyzing their decisions, and debriefing them on their actions would these assumptions rise to the surface.

It has become a popular practice for leaders to identify and publicly state their organization's culture or, more precisely, their shared values. BP, the British energy giant, lists four core

to believe guide their decisions and actions.[9] Espoused values are usually socially desirable, so they present a positive public image. Even if top management actually enacts the espoused values, lower-level employees might not do so. Organizational culture is not represented by these espoused values. Instead it consists of shared *enacted values*—the values that most leaders and employees truly rely on to guide their decisions and actions. These "values-in-use" are apparent by watching people in action.

To illustrate the distinction between espoused and enacted values, consider BP's values, particularly its "responsible" value. The energy giant describes this value as being "committed to the safety and development of our people and the communities and societies

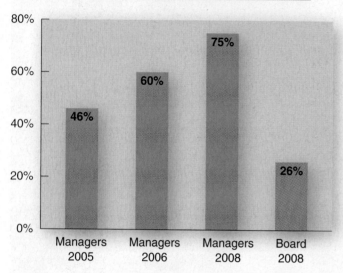

Company's Actions are Inconsistent with their Espoused Values[11]

Percentage of junior managers and (for 2008) boards of directors polled in the United Kingdom who believe there is a mismatch between their company's "espoused values" and what actually goes on in the company.

in which we operate. We aim for no accidents, no harm to people, and no damage to the environment." Even though BP's leaders claim this value guides their decisions and actions, BP's track record on safety and environmentalism suggests otherwise. In 2010 the company was at the center of the Gulf of Mexico oil spill, one of America's worst environmental disasters. A few months before the spill occurred, the U.S. government's Occupational Safety and Health Administration (OSHA) penalized BP with the largest fine in OSHA's history for failing to sufficiently improve safety at its Texas City refinery. Four years earlier, 15 employees died in an explosion at that refinery. A U.S. government report on that explosion concluded that BP "did not provide effective safety culture leadership." A few years before the Texas refinery explosion, the Norwegian government concluded that "a poor HES (Health, Environment, and Safety) culture" contributed to a fatality on a BP oil platform. And a prominent newspaper concluded that a series of spills, accidents, and alleged hush-ups at the Alaskan operations managed by BP "raises serious questions about BP's safety culture."[10] In short, being safety conscious and environmentally "responsible" is an espoused value at BP but is not likely part of the company's current or recent culture.

CONTENT OF ORGANIZATIONAL CULTURE

Organizations differ in their cultural content—that is, the relative ordering of values. Consider the following companies and their apparent dominant cultures:

- SAS Institute: Burning the midnight oil is a way of life at many high-technology companies, but SAS Institute has a completely

different culture. The American software company shoos out its employees by 6 p.m. and locks the doors to be sure they practice work/life balance. Located on a 200-acre campus, SAS supports employee well-being with free on-site medical care, unlimited sick days, heavily subsidized child care, ski trips, personal trainers, inexpensive gourmet cafeterias, and tai chi classes. CEO Jim Goodnight has fended off dozens of potential acquiring companies because he wants to keep the employee-friendly culture intact. "We spent many years building a culture here that's honed out of respect for our employees, and is one of innovation and creativity, one of exceeding customer expectations," Goodnight explains. "I don't want to see that end by SAS being merged into another company."[12]

- Argo Investments: In an era when investment firms are better known for their corporate excesses than financial performance, Australian-based Argo Investments is decisively frugal. CEO Robert Patterson explains that this culture dates back to the company's founder Alf Adamson. "He was old school, very conservative, and paid himself a pittance, and me, too!" Patterson recalls. "There was no company car in his time, no expense allowances or things like that." Argo Investments now has two company cars among its 15 staff, but the frugal culture is still apparent. The company has bare-boned offices without expensive artwork, and Patterson receives a salary that "many fund managers wouldn't get out of bed for."[13]

- ICICI Bank: India's second-largest bank exudes a performance-oriented culture focused on growth. Its organizational practices place a premium on training, career development, goal setting, and pay for performance, all with the intent of maximizing employee achievement and customer service. A small percentage of staff receives generous rewards while the bottom 5 percent are cut from the payroll. "Growth happens only when there are differential rewards for differential performers," explains ICICI's head of human resources.[14]

Employee-friendly and creative. Frugal. Performance-oriented. How many corporate cultures are there? Several models and measures classify organizational culture into a handful of easy-to-remember categories. One of these, shown in Exhibit 13.2, identifies seven corporate cultures. Another popular model identifies four organizational cultures organized in a two-by-two table representing internal versus external focus and flexibility versus control. Other models organize cultures around a circle with 8 or 12 categories. These circumplex models suggest that some cultures are opposite to others, such as an avoidance culture versus a self-actualization culture, or a power culture versus a collegial culture.[15]

These organizational culture models and surveys are popular with corporate leaders faced with the messy business of diagnosing their company's culture and identifying what kind of culture they want to develop. Unfortunately they also present a distorted view of organizational culture. One problem is that these models oversimplify the diversity of cultural values in organizations. There are dozens of individual values and many more combinations of values, so the number of organizational cultures these models describe likely falls considerably short of

Organizational Culture Dimension	Characteristics of the Dimension
Innovation	Experimenting, opportunity seeking, risk taking, few rules, low cautiousness.
Stability	Predictability, security, rule-oriented.
Respect for people	Fairness, tolerance.
Outcome orientation	Action-oriented, high expectations, results-oriented.
Attention to detail	Precise, analytic.
Team orientation	Collaboration, people-oriented.
Aggressiveness	Competitive, low emphasis on social responsibility.

Source: Based on information in C. A. O'Reilly III, J. Chatman, and D. F. Caldwell, "People and Organizational Culture: A Profile Comparison Approach to Assessing Person–Organization Fit," *Academy of Management Journal* 34, no. 3 (1991), pp. 487–518.

the full set. A second concern is that organizational culture includes shared assumptions about the right way to do things, not just shared values. Few models and measures take this more subterranean aspect of culture into account.

A third concern is that many organizational culture models and measures incorrectly assume that organizations have a fairly clear, unified culture that is easily decipherable.[16] This "integration" perspective, as it is called, further assumes that when an organization's culture changes, it shifts from one unified condition to a new unified condition with only temporary ambiguity or weakness during the transition. These assumptions are probably incorrect or, at best, oversimplified. An organization's culture is usually blurry; it varies across work units and is somewhat indistinct even within work units. For example, after BP's Texas refinery explosion a few years ago, an independent panel investigated the energy company's safety culture across the United States. The panel concluded that most of BP's U.S. operations required a much stronger safety culture, but a couple of sites already had a strong safety culture.[17]

Organizations do not have a single homogeneous culture because values and assumptions are ultimately unique to every individual. As long as employees differ, an organization's culture will have noticeable variability. Furthermore, as we discuss next, organizations consist of diverse subcultures because employees

> " Many organizational culture models and measures incorrectly assume that organizations have a fairly clear, unified culture that is easily decipherable. "

across the organization have different clusters of experiences and backgrounds that have shaped their values and priorities. Thus many of the popular organizational culture models and measures oversimplify the variety of organizational cultures and falsely presume that organizations can easily be identified within these categories.

Organizational Subcultures

When discussing organizational culture, we are really referring to the *dominant culture*—that is, the values and assumptions shared most consistently and widely by the organization's members. The dominant culture is usually supported by senior management, but cultures persist despite senior management's desire for another culture. Furthermore, as mentioned in the previous section, an organization's dominant culture is not as unified or clear as many consultants and business leaders assume. Instead organizations are composed of *subcultures* located throughout their various divisions, geographic regions, and occupational groups.[18] Some subcultures enhance the dominant culture by espousing parallel assumptions and values; others differ from but do not oppose the dominant culture; still others are called *countercultures* because they embrace values or assumptions that directly oppose the organization's dominant culture. It is also possible that some organizations (including some universities, according to one study) operate with subcultures and no decipherable dominant culture at all.[19]

Subcultures, particularly countercultures, potentially create conflict and dissension among employees, but they also serve two important functions.[20] First, they maintain the organization's standards of performance and ethical behavior. Employees who hold countercultural values are an important source of surveillance and critical review of the dominant order. They encourage constructive conflict and more creative thinking about how the organization should interact with its environment. Subcultures potentially support ethical conduct by preventing employees from blindly following one set of values. Subculture members continually question the "obvious" decisions and actions of the majority, thereby making everyone more mindful of the consequences of their actions.

The second function of subcultures is that they are the spawning grounds for emerging values that keep the firm aligned with the needs of customers, suppliers, society, and other stakeholders. Companies eventually need to replace their dominant values with ones that are more appropriate for the changing environment. If subcultures are suppressed, the organization may take longer to discover and adopt values aligned with the emerging environment.

artifacts The observable symbols and signs of an organization's culture.

rituals The programmed routines of daily organizational life that dramatize the organization's culture.

ceremonies Planned displays of organizational culture, conducted specifically for the benefit of an audience.

and its collective assumptions too deeply ingrained to be measured through surveys. Instead we need to observe workplace behavior, listen to everyday conversations among staff and with customers, study written documents and e-mail, note physical structures and settings, and interview staff about corporate stories. In other words, to truly understand an organization's culture, we need to sample information from a variety of organizational artifacts.

The Mayo Clinic conducted such an assessment a few years ago. An anthropologist was hired to decipher the medical organization's culture at its headquarters in Minnesota and to identify ways of transferring that culture to its two newer sites in Florida and Arizona. For six weeks the anthropologist shadowed employees, posed as a patient in waiting rooms, did countless interviews, and accompanied physicians on patient visits. The final report outlined Mayo's dominant culture and how its satellite operations varied from that culture.[23]

In this section we review the four broad categories of artifacts: organizational stories and legends, rituals and ceremonies, language, and physical structures and symbols.

Organizational Stories and Legends

David Ogilvy is a legend in the advertising industry, but equally significant are the stories about him that have continued to reinforce the values he instilled. For example, Ogilvy's board of directors arrived at one meeting to discover a Russian matryoshka doll at each of their seats. The directors opened each doll, one nested inside the other, until they discovered this message inside the tiniest doll: "If you hire people who are smaller than you are, we shall become a company of dwarfs. If you hire people who are bigger than you are, we shall become a company of giants." The Russian dolls became part of Ogilvy's culture, which demands hiring the very best talent.[24]

Stories such as Ogilvy's Russian dolls permeate strong organizational cultures. Some tales recount heroic deeds, whereas others ridicule past events that deviate from the firm's core values. Organizational stories and legends serve as powerful social prescriptions of the way things should (or should not) be done. They add human realism to corporate expectations, individual performance standards, and the criteria for getting fired. Stories also produce emotions in listeners, and this tends to improve listeners' memory of the lesson within the story.[25] Stories have the greatest effect on communicating corporate culture when they describe real people, are assumed to be true, and are known by employees throughout the organization. Stories are also prescriptive—they advise people what to do or not to do.[26]

Learning Objective

After reading the next section, you should be able to

LO2 List four categories of artifacts through which corporate culture is deciphered.

DECIPHERING ORGANIZATIONAL CULTURE THROUGH ARTIFACTS

We can't directly see an organization's shared values and assumptions. Instead, as Exhibit 13.1 illustrated earlier, we decipher organizational culture indirectly through artifacts. **Artifacts** are the observable symbols and signs of an organization's culture, such as the way visitors are greeted, the organization's physical layout, and how employees are rewarded.[21] A few experts suggest that artifacts are the essence of organizational culture, whereas most others (including the authors of this book) view artifacts as symbols or indicators of culture. Either way, artifacts are important because they reinforce and potentially support changes to an organization's culture.

Artifacts provide valuable evidence about a company's culture.[22] An organization's culture is usually too ambiguous and complex

Rituals and Ceremonies

Rituals are the programmed routines of daily organizational life that dramatize an organization's culture. They include how visitors are greeted, how often senior executives visit subordinates, how people communicate with each other, how much time employees take for lunch, and so on. For instance, BMW's fast-paced culture is quite literally apparent in the way employees walk around the German carmaker's offices. "When you move through the corridors and hallways of other companies' buildings, people kind of crawl, they walk slowly," observes a BMW executive. "But BMW people tend to move faster."[27] **Ceremonies** are more formal artifacts than rituals. Ceremonies are planned activities conducted specifically for the benefit of an audience. This would include publicly rewarding (or punishing) employees or celebrating the launch of a new product or newly won contract.

Organizational Language

The language of the workplace speaks volumes about the company's culture. How employees talk to each other, describe customers, express anger, and greet stakeholders are all verbal symbols of cultural values. For example, employees at The Container Store compliment each other about "being Gumby," meaning that they are being as flexible as the once-popular green toy to help a customer or another employee.[28] Language also highlights values held by organizational subcultures. Consultants working at Whirlpool kept hearing employees talk about the appliance company's "PowerPoint culture." This phrase, which names Microsoft's presentation software, implied that Whirlpool has a hierarchical culture in which communication is one-way (from executives to employees).[29]

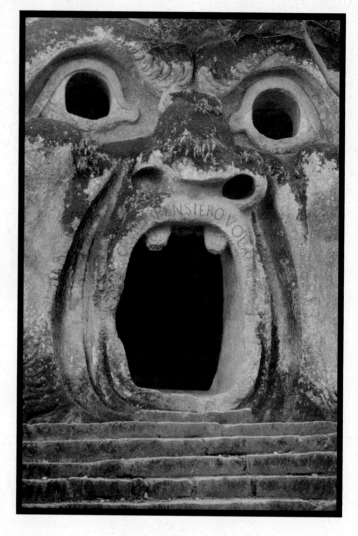

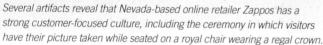

Several artifacts reveal that Nevada-based online retailer Zappos has a strong customer-focused culture, including the ceremony in which visitors have their picture taken while seated on a royal chair wearing a regal crown.

Physical Structures and Symbols

Buildings both reflect and influence an organization's culture. The size, shape, location, and age of buildings might suggest a company's emphasis on teamwork, environmental friendliness, flexibility, or any other set of values.[30] Even if the building doesn't make much of a statement, there is a treasure trove of physical artifacts inside. Desks, chairs, office space, and wall hangings (or lack of them) are just a few of the items that might convey cultural meaning.[31]

Consider the physical artifacts that you might notice when visiting the headquarters of Mother. Housed in a converted warehouse in an artsy district of London, the creative agency has a large reception hall with an adjoining casual lounge on one side and a large cafeteria on the other, where staff can get free fruit, cereals, toast, and similar snacks any time they want. A wide staircase leads from reception to the next floor, which has meeting rooms separated only by dividers made of hanging strips of opaque plastic. The top floor of Mother's offices is one room dominated by a large rectangular concrete table around which dozens of staff work. Each of these physical artifacts alone might not say much, but put enough of them together and you

[We shape our buildings; thereafter, they shape us.[33]
—Winston Churchill]

> "Culture is one of the most precious things a company has, so you must work harder on it than anything else.[36]"
>
> —Herb Kelleher

can see how they symbolize Mother's edgy creative culture with a strong team orientation.[32]

Learning Objective

After reading the next two sections, you should be able to

LO3 Discuss the importance of organizational culture and the conditions under which organizational culture strength improves organizational performance.

IS ORGANIZATIONAL CULTURE IMPORTANT?

Does organizational culture improve organizational effectiveness? Leaders at The Container Store, Mayo Clinic, Cirque du Soleil, and other companies think so. "If you get the people right, and the culture right, you will get the success," says a former CEO of National Australia Bank. Many writers of popular press management books also assert that the most successful companies have strong cultures. In fact one popular management book, *Built to Last*, suggests that successful companies are "cultlike" (although not actually cults, the authors are careful to point out).[34]

So does organizational culture make a difference? The research evidence suggests that companies with strong cultures tend to be more successful, but only under a particular set of conditions.[35] Before discussing these contingencies, let's examine the meaning of a "strong" organizational culture and its potential benefits. The strength of an organization's culture refers to how widely and deeply employees hold the company's dominant values and assumptions. In a strong organizational culture, most employees across all subunits understand and embrace the dominant values. These values and assumptions are also institutionalized through well-established artifacts, thereby making it difficult to change the culture. Furthermore, strong cultures tend to be long-lasting; some can be traced back to the values and assumptions established by the company's founder. In contrast, companies have weak cultures when the dominant values are held mainly by a few people at the top of the organization, are barely discernible, and are in flux.

As mentioned, companies with stronger cultures are potentially more effective, and this occurs through the three important functions listed in Exhibit 13.3 and described here:

1. *Control system:* Organizational culture is a deeply embedded form of social control that influences employee decisions and behavior.[37] Culture is pervasive and operates nonconsciously. You might think of it as an automatic pilot, directing employees in ways that are consistent with organizational expectations.

2. *Social glue:* Organizational culture is the "social glue" that bonds people together and makes them feel part of the organizational experience.[38] Employees are motivated to internalize the organization's dominant culture because it fulfills their need for social identity. This social glue is increasingly important as a way to attract new staff and retain top performers. It also becomes the common thread that holds together employees in global organizations.

▼**EXHIBIT 13.3** Potential Benefits and Contingencies of Culture Strength

Benefits of culture strength depend on . . .
- Whether culture content fits the environment.
- Moderate strength (not a cult).
- An adaptive culture.

Functions of strong cultures
- Control system.
- Social glue.
- Sense making.

Organizational outcomes
- Organizational performance.
- Employee well-being.

> IF YOU'RE MANAGING A COMPANY WHICH HAS A GLOBAL FOOTPRINT, DIVERSE NATIONALITIES, DIVERSE CLIENTS, DIVERSE ALL OVER THE PLACE, THE VALUES OF THE COMPANY ARE REALLY THE BEDROCK—THE GLUE WHICH HOLDS THE FIRM TOGETHER.[41]
>
> —NANDAN NILEKANI

3. *Sense making:* Organizational culture assists the sense-making process.[39] It helps employees understand what goes on and why things happen in the company. Corporate culture also makes it easier for them to understand what is expected of them and to interact with other employees who know the culture and believe in it. For instance, one recent study reported that organizational culture strength increases role clarity, which reduces stress among sales staff.[40]

CONTINGENCIES OF ORGANIZATIONAL CULTURE AND EFFECTIVENESS

Studies have found only a modestly positive relationship between culture strength and organizational effectiveness because three contingencies need to be considered: (1) whether the culture content is aligned with the environment, (2) whether the culture is moderately strong, not a cult, and (3) whether the culture incorporates an adaptive culture (see Exhibit 13.3).

Culture Content Alignment with Environment

One contingency between cultural strength and organizational effectiveness is whether the organization's culture content—its dominant values and assumptions—is aligned with the external environment. Consider the situation that Dell recently faced. Dell's culture gave the highest priority to cost efficiency and competitiveness, yet these values and assumptions are no longer sufficient for the marketplace. Low-cost computers are still popular, but consumers increasingly demand computers that are innovative with elegant styling. Dell had a strong culture, but it was no longer the best culture for the external environment. "Dell's culture is not inspirational or aspirational," suggests one industry expert. "[Its] culture only wants to talk about execution."[42]

Avoiding a Corporate Cult

A second contingency is the degree of culture strength. Various experts suggest that companies with very strong cultures (corporate "cults") may be less effective than companies with moderately strong cultures.[43] One reason why corporate cults may undermine organizational effectiveness is that they lock people into mental models, which can blind them to new opportunities and unique problems. They overlook or incorrectly define subtle misalignments between the organization's activities and the changing environment.

The other reason why very strong cultures may be dysfunctional is that they suppress dissenting subcultural values. At Dell, for instance, anyone who questioned the company's almost sacred values and assumptions was quickly silenced, even though the dissenting values could have helped Dell to realign its culture more quickly. The challenge for organizational leaders is to maintain not only a strong culture but one that allows subcultural diversity. Subcultures encourage constructive conflict, which improves creative thinking and offers some level of ethical vigilance over the dominant culture. In the long run, a subculture's nascent values could become important dominant values as the environment changes. Corporate cults suppress subcultures, thereby undermining these benefits.

Culture Is Adaptive

A third contingency between cultural strength and organizational effectiveness is whether the culture content includes an **adaptive culture**.[44] An adaptive culture exists when employees are receptive to change—they assume that the organization needs to continuously adapt to its external environment and that they need to be flexible in their roles within the organization. Employees in an adaptive culture embrace an open-systems perspective, in which the organization's survival and success require ongoing adaptation to the external environment, which itself is continuously changing. They assume that their future depends on monitoring the external environment and serving stakeholders with the resources available. Thus employees in adaptive cultures have a strong sense of ownership. They take responsibility for the organization's performance and alignment with the external environment.

In an adaptive culture, receptivity to change extends to internal processes and roles. Employees recognize that satisfying stakeholder needs requires continuous improvement of internal work processes. They also support changing internal work processes as well as flexibility in their own work roles. The phrase "That's not my job" is not found in adaptive cultures. Finally, an adaptive culture has a strong *learning orientation* because being receptive to change necessarily means that the company also supports action-oriented discovery. With a learning orientation, employees welcome new learning opportunities, actively experiment with new ideas and practices, view reasonable mistakes as a natural part of the learning process, and continuously question past practices.[45]

Organizational Culture and Business Ethics

An organization's culture influences the ethical conduct of its employees. This makes sense because good behavior is driven by ethical values, and ethical values can become embedded into an organization's dominant culture. Michael Dell and his executive team saw this connection between culture and ethics when they launched the "Soul of Dell" a few years ago. One of the computer maker's revised values was defined as "behaving ethically in every interaction and in every aspect of how we conduct business." Unfortunately the Soul of Dell initiative probably didn't change the company's culture. Two years after the Soul of Dell cultural change program was launched, the company reported that some executives had manipulated the company books to reach performance targets that would give them a larger bonus.[46]

diligence audits of their respective corporate cultures.[47] Some forms of integration (which we discuss later in this section) may allow successful mergers between companies with different cultures. However, research concludes that mergers typically suffer when organizations with significantly divergent corporate cultures merge into a single entity with a high degree of integration.[48]

adaptive culture
An organizational culture in which employees are receptive to change, including the ongoing alignment of the organization to its environment and continuous improvement of internal processes.

One of the more recent culture clashes has been the side effect of Bank of America's (BofA) hasty acquisition of Merrill Lynch. BofA's "Main Street" culture is about serving middle America with broad-based accessible services, whereas Merrill Lynch had a much more exclusive culture catering to wealthy clients. Consistent with these divergent client orientations, BofA's culture embraces cost efficiencies and penny pinching, whereas Merrill Lynch had more of an entitlement culture that encouraged big spending and bigger bonuses. To illustrate, despite the company's staggering losses during the previous year, Merrill Lynch's CEO spent more than $1 million renovating his office, hired an executive with a $25 million signing bonus, and handed out billions in bonuses. BofA's culture is also more cautious and bureaucratic, requiring more signatures and higher-level authority, whereas Merrill Lynch's "thundering herd" culture was more aggressive, entrepreneurial, and, some say, more likely to venture into ethically questionable territory.[50]

Learning Objective

After reading the next section, you should be able to

LO4 Compare and contrast four strategies for merging organizational cultures.

MERGING ORGANIZATIONAL CULTURES

4C Corporate Culture Clash and Chemistry is a company with an unusual name and mandate. The Dutch consulting firm helps clients determine whether their culture is aligned ("chemistry") or incompatible ("clash") with a potential acquisition or merger partner. The firm also analyzes the company's culture with its strategy. There should be plenty of demand for 4C's expertise. According to various studies, most corporate mergers and acquisitions fail in terms of subsequent performance of the merged organization. Evidence suggests that such failures occur partly because corporate leaders are so focused on the financial or marketing logistics of a merger that they fail to conduct due

Losing Value and Talent with Mergers and Acquisitions[49]

85% of executives of failed mergers who identify organizational culture differences as the major cause of the failure.

71% Average percentage of acquisitions in three major studies that destroyed rather than enhanced shareholder value.

75% of executives interviewed who believed their acquisition was successful.

40% of executives in acquired firms who left within two years after the acquisition (twice the usual executive turnover rate).

> "So many mergers fail to deliver what they promise that there should be a presumption of failure. The burden of proof should be on showing that anything really good is likely to come out of one.[53]
> —Warren Hellman

Bicultural Audit

Organizational leaders can minimize these cultural collisions and fulfill their duty of due diligence by conducting a bicultural audit.[51] A **bicultural audit** diagnoses cultural relations between the companies and determines the extent to which cultural clashes will likely occur. The bicultural audit process begins by identifying cultural differences between the merging companies. The bicultural audit data are then analyzed to determine which differences between the two firms will result in conflict and which cultural values provide common ground on which to build a cultural foundation in the merged organization. The final stage involves identifying strategies and preparing action plans to bridge the two organizations' cultures.

A classic example of a bicultural audit occurred several years ago when pulp-and-paper conglomerate Abitibi-Price proposed a merger with rival Stone Consolidated. Abitibi developed the Merging Cultures Evaluation Index (MCEI), an evaluation system that helped Abitibi executives compare its culture with other companies in the industry. The MCEI examined several dimensions of corporate culture, such as concentration of power versus diffusion of power, innovation versus tradition, wide versus narrow flow of information, and consensus versus authoritative decision making. Abitibi and Stone executives completed the questionnaire to assess their own culture, and then they compared the results. The MCEI results, along with financial and infrastructural information, served as the basis for

Abitibi-Price to merge with Stone Consolidated to become Abitibi-Consolidated (now Abitibi Bowater).[52]

Strategies for Merging Different Organizational Cultures

In some cases the bicultural audit results in a decision to end merger talks because the two cultures are too different to merge effectively. However, even with substantially different cultures, two companies may form a workable union if they apply the appropriate merger strategy. The four main strategies for merging different corporate cultures are assimilation, deculturation, integration, and separation (see Exhibit 13.4).[54]

Assimilation Assimilation occurs when employees at the acquired company willingly embrace the cultural values of the acquiring organization. This strategy typically works best when the acquired company has a weak, dysfunctional culture and the acquiring company's culture is strong and aligned with the external environment. Culture clash is rare with assimilation because the acquired firm's culture is weak and employees are looking for better cultural alternatives. Research in Motion (RIM), the Blackberry wireless device maker, applies the assimilation strategy by deliberately acquiring only small start-up firms. "Small companies . . . don't have cultural issues," says RIM co-CEO Jim Balsillie, adding that they are typically absorbed into RIM's culture with little fuss or attention.[55]

▼ **EXHIBIT 13.4** Strategies for Merging Different Organizational Cultures

Merger Strategy	Description	Works best when . . .
Assimilation	Acquired company embraces acquiring firm's culture.	Acquired firm has a weak culture.
Deculturation	Acquiring firm imposes its culture on unwilling acquired firm.	Rarely works—may be necessary only when acquired firm's culture doesn't work but employees don't realize it.
Integration	Merging companies combine two or more cultures into a new composite culture.	Existing cultures can be improved.
Separation	Merging companies remain distinct entities with minimal exchange of culture or organizational practices.	Firms operate successfully in different businesses requiring different cultures.

Sources: Based on ideas in A. R. Malekazedeh and A. Nahavandi, "Making Mergers Work by Managing Cultures," *Journal of Business Strategy,* May–June 1990, pp. 55–57; and K. W. Smith, "A Brand-New Culture for the Merged Firm," *Mergers and Acquisitions,* 35 (June 2000), pp. 45–50.

Deculturation Assimilation is rare. Employees usually resist organizational change, particularly when they are asked to throw away personal and cultural values. Under these conditions, some acquiring companies apply a *deculturation* strategy by imposing their culture and business practices on the acquired organization. The acquiring firm strips away artifacts and reward systems that support the old culture. People who cannot adopt the acquiring company's culture often lose their jobs. Deculturation may be necessary when the acquired firm's culture doesn't work, even when employees in the acquired company aren't convinced of this. However, this strategy is difficult to apply effectively because the acquired firm's employees resist the cultural intrusions from the buying firm, thereby delaying or undermining the merger process.

Integration A third strategy is to combine the two or more cultures into a new composite culture that preserves the best features of the previous cultures. Integration is slow and potentially risky because many forces preserve the existing cultures. Still, this strategy should be considered when the companies have relatively weak cultures or when their cultures include several overlapping values. Integration also works best when people realize that their existing cultures are ineffective and therefore are motivated to adopt a new set of dominant values.

Separation A separation strategy occurs when the merging companies agree to remain distinct entities with minimal exchange of culture or organizational practices. This strategy is most appropriate when the two merging companies are in unrelated industries or operate in different countries because the most appropriate cultural values tend to differ by industry and national culture. This strategy is also relevant advice for the corporate cultures of diversified conglomerates.

For example, Australian conglomerate Wesfarmers has a strong performance and employee ownership culture across all of its businesses, but each business also has a distinct culture in many respects. "We do have a couple of common principles across all our business," says Wesfarmers CEO Richard Goyders. "However, each individual business has been encouraged to develop its own culture, as long as, of course, it is a healthy culture. . . . We don't necessarily want exactly the same culture in all our individual businesses, as retail is different from industrial distribution, which is different again from mining, and so on."[56] Wesfarmers' cultural separation approach is rare, however. Executives in acquiring firms usually have difficulty keeping their hands off the acquired firm. It's not surprising, therefore, that only 15 percent of mergers leave the acquired company as a stand-alone unit.[57]

Learning Objectives

After reading the next section, you should be able to

LO5 Identify four strategies for changing or strengthening an organization's culture, including the application of attraction-selection-attrition theory.

CHANGING AND STRENGTHENING ORGANIZATIONAL CULTURE

Is it possible to change an organization's culture? Yes—but doing so isn't easy, the change rarely occurs quickly, and often the culture ends up changing (or replacing) corporate leaders. A few experts argue that an organization's culture "cannot be managed," so attempting to change the company's values and assumptions is a waste of time.[58] This view is more extreme than most, but organizational culture experts generally agree that changing an organization's culture is a considerable challenge. However, it is sometimes necessary to change a company's culture because the alignment of that culture with the external environment can influence the organization's survival and success. Over the next few pages we will highlight four strategies that have had some success at altering corporate cultures. These strategies, illustrated in Exhibit 13.5, are not exhaustive; but each seems to work well under the right circumstances.

Aligning Artifacts

Artifacts represent more than just the visible indicators of a company's culture. They are also mechanisms that keep the culture in place. By altering artifacts—or creating new ones—leaders can potentially adjust shared values and assumptions. Corporate cultures are also altered and strengthened through the artifacts of stories and behaviors. According to Max De Pree, former CEO of furniture manufacturer Herman Miller Inc., every organization needs "tribal storytellers" to keep the

> [Unconsciously or consciously, senior people leave their marks on an organization's culture and legacy.[61]
> —Max de Pree]

Actions of Founders and Leaders

An organization's culture begins with its founders.[59] Founders are often visionaries who provide a powerful role model for others to follow. The company's culture sometimes reflects the founder's personality, and this cultural imprint can remain with the organization for decades. Despite the founder's cultural imprint, subsequent leaders are sometimes able to reshape that culture by applying transformational leadership and organizational change practices.[60]

▼**EXHIBIT 13.5** Strategies for Changing and Strengthening Organizational Culture

organization's history and culture alive.[62] Leaders play a role by creating memorable events that symbolize the cultural values they want to develop or maintain. Companies also strengthen culture in new operations by transferring current employees who abide by the culture.

Introducing Culturally Consistent Rewards

Reward systems are artifacts that often have a powerful effect on strengthening or reshaping an organization's culture.[63] Robert Nardelli used rewards to change Home Depot's freewheeling culture. Nardelli introduced precise measures of corporate performance and drilled managers with weekly performance objectives related to those metrics. A two-hour weekly conference call became a ritual in which Home Depot's top executives were held accountable for the previous week's goals. These actions reinforced a more disciplined (and centralized) performance-oriented culture.[64]

Attracting, Selecting, and Socializing Employees

Organizational culture is strengthened by attracting and hiring people who already embrace the cultural values. This process, along with weeding out people who don't fit the culture, is explained by **attraction–selection–attrition (ASA) theory**.[65] ASA theory states that organizations have a natural tendency to attract, select, and retain people with values and personality characteristics that are consistent with the organization's character, resulting in a more homogeneous organization and a stronger culture.

- *Attraction:* Job applicants engage in self-selection by avoiding employment in companies whose values seem incompatible with their own values.[67] Companies often encourage this self-selection by actively describing their cultures, but applicants will look for evidence of the company's culture even when it is not advertised. Applicants also inspect organizational artifacts when visiting the company.

- *Selection:* How well the person fits in with the company's culture is often a factor in deciding which job applicants to hire. Companies with strong cultures often put applicants through several interviews and other selection tests, in part to better gauge applicants' values and their congruence with the company's values.[68] Consider Park Place Dealerships. As one of America's top-rated luxury car dealerships, the Dallas–Fort Worth company relies on interviews and selection tests to carefully screen applicants for their culture fit. "Testing is one piece of our hiring process that enables us to find people who will not only be successful in our culture, but thrive and enjoy our culture," says Park Place chairman Ken Schnitzer. When Park Place recently acquired a Lexus dealership in California, several people left when they realized they did not fit Park Place's culture. "We've had some turnover," Schnitzer acknowledges in reference to the Lexus dealership. "We're looking for people to fit into our culture. It's not easy to get hired by Park Place."[69]

- *Attrition:* People are motivated to seek environments that are sufficiently congruent with their personal values and to leave environments that are a poor fit. This occurs because person–organization value congruence supports their social identity and minimizes internal role conflict. Even if employees aren't forced out, many quit when values incongruence is sufficiently high. This likely occurred when Park Place Dealerships acquired the Lexus dealership in California—some staff members left voluntarily or otherwise because they did not fit Park Place's unique culture.[70]

Organizational Culture
During the Hiring Process[66]

58%
of 1,500 American job seekers polled who, during the hiring process, wanted to know about the **company's culture.**

61%
of 500 Canadian executives polled who say **cultural fit** is more important than skills for selecting (promoting) internal candidates.

75%
of 500 Canadian executives polled who say **cultural fit** is more important than skills for selecting external candidates.

44%
of Fortune 500 companies that take steps to describe their **corporate culture** to job seekers.

attraction–selection–attrition (ASA) theory States that organizations have a natural tendency to attract, select, and retain people with values and personality characteristics that are consistent with the organization's character, resulting in a more homogeneous organization and a stronger culture.

organizational socialization The process by which individuals learn the values, expected behaviors, and social knowledge necessary to assume their roles in the organization.

Learning Objectives

After reading the next section, you should be able to

LO6 Describe the organizational socialization process and identify strategies to improve that process.

ORGANIZATIONAL SOCIALIZATION

Along with their use of attraction, selection, and attrition, organizations rely on organizational socialization to maintain a strong corporate culture. **Organizational socialization** is the process by which individuals learn the values, expected behaviors, and social knowledge necessary to assume their roles in the organization.[71] When a company clearly communicates its culture, job candidates and new hires are more likely to internalize its values quickly and deeply. Socialization is an important process for absorbing corporate culture as well as helping newcomers adjust to coworkers, work procedures, and other corporate realities. Research indicates that when employees are effectively socialized into the organization, they tend to perform better, have higher job satisfaction, and remain longer with the organization.[72]

Socialization as a Learning and Adjustment Process

Organizational socialization is a process of both learning and adjustment. It is a learning process because newcomers try to make sense of the company's physical workplace, social dynamics, and strategic and cultural environment. They learn about the organization's performance expectations, power dynamics, corporate culture, company history, and jargon. They also need to form successful and satisfying relationships with other people from whom they can learn the ropes.[73] Thus effective socialization enables new employees to form a cognitive map of the physical, social, and

reality shock
The stress that results when employees perceive discrepancies between their pre-employment expectations and on-the-job reality.

strategic and cultural dynamics of the organization without information overload.

Organizational socialization is also a process of adjustment because individuals need to adapt to their new work environment. They develop new work roles that reconfigure their social identity, adopt new team norms, and practice new behaviors.[74] Research reports that the adjustment process is fairly rapid for many people, usually occurring within a few months. However, newcomers with diverse work experience seem to adjust better than those with limited previous experience, possibly because they have a larger toolkit of knowledge and skills to make the adjustment possible.[75]

Stages of Organizational Socialization

Socialization is a continuous process, beginning long before the first day of employment and continuing throughout one's career within the company. However, it is most intense when people move across organizational boundaries, such as when they first join a company or get transferred to an international assignment. Each of these transitions is a process that can be divided into three stages. Our focus here is on the socialization of new employees, so the three stages are called preemployment socialization, encounter, and role management (see Exhibit 13.6). These stages parallel the individual's transition from outsider to newcomer and then to insider.[77]

Stage 1: Preemployment Socialization

Think back to the months and weeks before you began working in a new job (or attending a new school). You actively searched for information about the company, formed expectations about working there, and felt some anticipation about fitting into that environment. The preemployment socialization stage encompasses all the learning and adjustment that occurs before the first day of

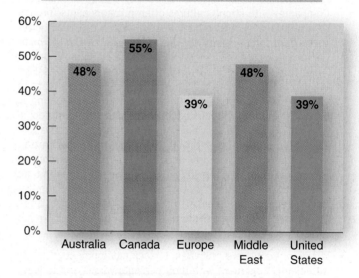

Company Perceptions of How Effectively Their Internal Communication Processes Integrate Newcomers into the Organization[76]

Percentage of 328 organizations (collectively employing 5 million people) who report that their internal communication function is effective at integrating new employees into the organization, by country/region.

work. In fact, a large part of the socialization adjustment process occurs during this stage.[78]

The main problem with preemployment socialization is that outsiders rely on indirect information about what it is like to work in the organization. This information is often distorted by inherent conflicts during the mating dance between employer and applicant.[79] One conflict occurs between the employer's need to attract qualified applicants and the applicant's need for complete information to make accurate employment

▼**EXHIBIT 13.6** Stages of Organizational Socialization

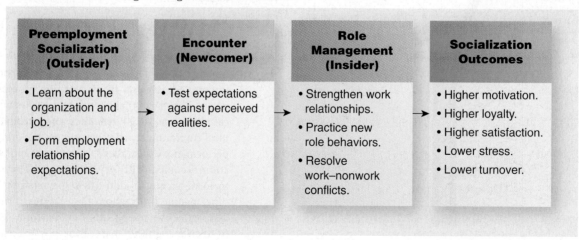

Preemployment Socialization (Outsider)	Encounter (Newcomer)	Role Management (Insider)	Socialization Outcomes
• Learn about the organization and job. • Form employment relationship expectations.	• Test expectations against perceived realities.	• Strengthen work relationships. • Practice new role behaviors. • Resolve work–nonwork conflicts.	• Higher motivation. • Higher loyalty. • Higher satisfaction. • Lower stress. • Lower turnover.

decisions. Many firms use a "flypaper" approach by describing only positive aspects of the job and company, causing applicants to accept job offers from incomplete or false expectations. Another conflict that prevents accurate exchange of information occurs when applicants avoid asking important questions about the company because they don't want to convey an unfavorable image to their prospective employer. For instance, applicants usually don't like to ask about starting salaries and promotion opportunities because it makes them sound greedy or overaggressive. Yet unless the employer provides this information, applicants might fill in the missing information with false assumptions that produce an inaccurate psychological contract.

Two other types of conflict tend to distort preemployment information for employers. Applicants engage in impression management when seeking employment, and this tends to motivate them to hide negative information, act out of character, and occasionally embellish information about their past accomplishments. At the same time, employers are sometimes reluctant to ask certain questions or use potentially valuable selection devices because they might scare off applicants. Unfortunately exaggerated résumés from applicants and reluctance to ask for some information causes employers to form a less accurate opinion of the job candidate's potential as an employee.

> From the first day on the job, newcomers test how well their preemployment expectations fit reality. Many companies fail the test.

Stage 2: Encounter The first day on the job typically marks the beginning of the encounter stage of organizational socialization. This is the stage in which newcomers test how well their preemployment expectations fit reality. Many companies fail the test, resulting in **reality shock**—the stress that results when employees perceive discrepancies between their preemployment expectations and on-the-job reality.[80] Reality shock doesn't necessarily occur on the first day; it might develop over several weeks or even months as newcomers form a better understanding of their new work environment.

Reality shock is common in many organizations.[81] Unmet expectations sometimes occur because the employer is unable to live up to its promises, such as failing to provide challenging projects or the resources to get the work done. Reality shock also occurs because new hires develop distorted work expectations through the information exchange conflicts just described. Whatever the cause, reality shock impedes the socialization process because the newcomer's energy is directed toward managing the stress rather than learning and accepting organizational knowledge and roles.[82]

realistic job preview (RJP) Giving job applicants a balance of positive and negative information about the job and work context.

Greatest Challenge When Starting a New Marketing/Advertising Job[83]

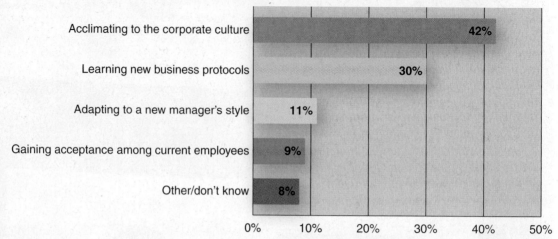

Acclimating to the corporate culture	42%
Learning new business protocols	30%
Adapting to a new manager's style	11%
Gaining acceptance among current employees	9%
Other/don't know	8%

0% 10% 20% 30% 40% 50%

Percentage of 125 randomly selected advertising executives and 125 senior marketing executives in the United States who identify each factor as the greatest challenge when a person is starting a new staff-level marketing/advertising job.

Stage 3: Role Management

Role management, the third stage of organizational socialization, really begins during preemployment socialization, but it is most active as employees make the transition from newcomers to insiders. They strengthen relationships with co-workers and supervisors, practice new role behaviors, and adopt attitudes and values consistent with their new positions and the organization. Role management also involves resolving the conflicts between work and nonwork activities, including resolving discrepancies between their existing values and those emphasized by the organizational culture.

Improving the Socialization Process

One potentially effective way to improve the socialization process is through a **realistic job preview (RJP)**—a balance of positive and negative information about the job and work context.[84] Unfortunately, as mentioned earlier, many companies overpromise. They often exaggerate positive features of the job and neglect to mention the undesirable elements in the hope that the best applicants will get "stuck" on the organization.

In contrast, an RJP helps job applicants decide for themselves whether their skills, needs, and values are compatible with the job and organization. RJPs scare away some applicants, but they also tend to reduce turnover and increase job performance.[86] This occurs because RJPs help applicants develop more accurate preemployment expectations, which, in turn, minimize reality shock. RJPs represent a type of vaccination by preparing employees for the more challenging and troublesome aspects of work life. There is also some evidence that RJPs increase organizational loyalty. A possible explanation for this is that companies providing candid information are easier to trust. They also

FACT. **Lindblad's Reality Check for Job Applicants**

Lindblad Expeditions can't afford to have crew members jump ship soon after starting the job. To minimize reality shock, the 500-employee adventure cruise company gives applicants a DVD showing a realistic picture of what it's like to work on board. The program shows not one but two scenes in which staff members are cleaning toilets. One scene reveals the cramped quarters for crew members. In another scene, a dishwasher talks about washing 5,000 dishes in one day. The video is meant to scare off applicants who cannot adjust easily to the challenges of working on a ship. The realistic job preview video does have this effect, says Lindblad human resources manager Kris Thompson, but the attrition is well worth it if it reduces turnover soon after staff are hired. "If [new hires] get on board and say, 'This is not what I expected,' then shame on us," says Thompson.[85]

show respect for the psychological contract and concern for employee welfare.[87]

Socialization Agents

Ask new employees what most helped them to adjust to their jobs and chances are they will mention helpful coworkers, bosses, or maybe even friends who work for the company. The fact is, organizational socialization occurs mainly through these socialization agents.[88] Supervisors tend to provide technical information, performance feedback, and information about job duties. They also improve the socialization process by giving newcomers reasonably challenging first assignments, buffering them from excessive demands, and helping them form social ties with coworkers.

Coworkers are important socialization agents because they are easily accessible, can answer questions when problems arise, and serve as role models for appropriate behavior. New employees tend to receive this information and support when coworkers integrate them into the work team. Coworkers also aid the socialization process by being flexible and tolerant in their interactions with new hires. The challenge for some companies is helping newcomers to learn from coworkers about the company's culture when opening new stores where most employees are new to the company.

At Whole Foods Market, yogurt is the solution to socialization of a large group of new employees to the company's culture. "One of our secrets is what I refer to as our 'yogurt culture,'" explains John McKey, cofounder of the health-focused food retailer. This strategy involves transferring employees who carry Whole Foods Market's unique culture to new stores so that recently hired employees learn and embrace that culture more quickly. "For example, in our Columbus Circle store in New York, about 25 percent of the team members transferred from existing stores," McKey recalls. "They were the starting culture for the fermentation that turned Columbus Circle into a true Whole Foods store."[89]

Several organizations rely on a "buddy system," whereby newcomers are assigned to coworkers for sources of information and social support. Meridian Technology Centre relies on a buddy system in the socialization of new staff members. Buddies introduce new hires to other employees, give them campus tours, and generally familiarize them with the physical layout of the workplace. They have lunch with employees on their first day and meet weekly with them for their first two months. Cxtec, the networking and voice technology company in Syracuse, New York, helps new staff meet other employees through food. On the first Friday of each month, new staff members take charge of the doughnut cart, introducing themselves as they distribute the morning snack to the company's 350 employees.[90] Collectively, these practices help newcomers to form social networks, which are powerful means of gaining information and influence in the organization. ■

CHECK IT OUT!

mhhe.com/McShaneM

for study materials

including quizzes

and Internet resources

organizational
change

With blue-chip clients such as McDonald's and Walmart, Lopez Foods Inc. has built an impressive business over the past two decades. And with annual sales of $500 million, the Oklahoma City–based beef patty and sausage manufacturer has become the 10th-largest Hispanic-owned company in America. To ensure that the next two decades will be equally successful, CEO Eduardo Sanchez recently introduced a major organizational change initiative aimed at making "a quantum leap" in the company's efficiency and performance. The company held several "brown paper" sessions in which the current production process was mapped out on a large wall of brown paper. Employees were asked to verify that these maps accurately represented the production process. Then they were asked to figure out how to improve the process. "Things we thought would be a hard sell on the employees, they themselves have come up to us and said, 'We can do this better,' or 'We don't need five people here, we only need three,'" says Sanchez.[1]

LEARNING OBJECTIVES

After reading this chapter, you should be able to

LO1 Describe the elements of Lewin's force field analysis model.

LO2 Discuss the reasons why people resist organizational change and outline six strategies for minimizing this resistance.

LO3 Debate the importance of leadership in organizational change and outline the conditions for effectively diffusing change from a pilot project.

LO4 Describe and compare action research, appreciative inquiry, large group interventions, and parallel learning structures as formal approaches to organizational change.

LO5 Discuss two cross-cultural and three ethical issues in organizational change.

force field analysis Kurt Lewin's model of system-wide change that helps change agents diagnose the forces that drive and restrain proposed organizational change.

unfreezing The first part of the change process whereby the change agent produces disequilibrium between the driving and restraining forces.

refreezing The latter part of the change process in which systems and structures are introduced that reinforce and maintain the desired behaviors.

The productivity improvement initiative that Eduardo Sanchez orchestrated at Lopez Foods went more smoothly than most change activities across the corporate landscape. It is challenging enough to envision a new strategic direction for an organization, department, or team. However, a greater challenge is in the execution of this strategy. The first hurdle is for leaders to recognize early enough that changes are needed. When leaders discover the need for change and identify some ideas about the preferred route to a better future, the change process requires considerable leadership capabilities to navigate around the numerous obstacles and gain organizationwide support for that change.

The challenges of leading change are continuous because, to repeat a well-worn statement, change has become the only constant in organizations. Organizations are, after all, open systems that need to remain compatible with their external environments (see Chapter 1). These environments—such as consumer needs, global competition, technology, community expectations, government (de)regulation, and environmental standards—are constantly changing, so organizations must recognize these shifts and respond accordingly to survive and remain effective. Successful organizations monitor their environments and take appropriate

> ## "The velocity of change is so rapid, so quick, that if you don't accept the change and move with the change, you're going to be left behind.
>
> —Jacques Nasser[3]

How Successful Are Organizational Change Initiatives?[2]

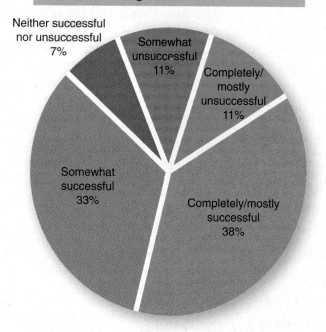

- Neither successful nor unsuccessful 7%
- Somewhat unsuccessful 11%
- Completely/mostly unsuccessful 11%
- Somewhat successful 33%
- Completely/mostly successful 38%

Evaluation by 1,536 executives globally of the degree of success of an organizational transformation they have been involved in over the previous five years.

steps to maintain a compatible fit with new external conditions. Rather than resisting change, employees in successful companies embrace change as an integral part of organizational life.

This chapter unfolds as follows. We begin by introducing Lewin's model of change and its component parts. This discussion includes sources of resistance to change, ways to minimize this resistance, and ways to stabilize desired behaviors. Next the chapter examines four approaches to organizational change—action research, appreciative inquiry, large group interventions, and parallel learning structures. The last section of this chapter considers both cross-cultural and ethical issues in organizational change.

Learning Objectives

After reading the next two sections, you should be able to

LO1 Describe the elements of Lewin's force field analysis model.

LO2 Discuss the reasons why people resist organizational change and outline six strategies for minimizing this resistance.

> IT SHOULD BE BORNE IN MIND THAT THERE IS NOTHING MORE DIFFICULT TO MANAGE, OR MORE DOUBTFUL OF SUCCESS, OR MORE DANGEROUS TO HANDLE THAN TO TAKE THE LEAD IN INTRODUCING A NEW ORDER OF THINGS.[7]
>
> —NICCOLÒ MACHIAVELLI

LEWIN'S FORCE FIELD ANALYSIS MODEL

It is easy to see that environmental forces push companies to change the way they operate. What is more difficult to see is the complex interplay of these forces on the internal dynamics of organizations. Social psychologist Kurt Lewin developed the force field analysis model to describe this process using the metaphor of a force field (see Exhibit 14.1).[4] Although it was developed more than 50 years ago, recent reviews affirm that Lewin's **force field analysis** model remains one of the most widely respected ways of viewing the change process.[5]

One side of the force field model represents the *driving forces* that push organizations toward a new state of affairs. These might include new competitors or technologies, evolving workforce expectations, or a host of other environmental changes. Corporate leaders also produce driving forces even when external forces for change aren't apparent. For instance, some experts call for "divine discontent" as a key feature of successful organizations, meaning that leaders continually urge employees to strive for higher standards or better practices even when the company outshines the competition.

The other side of Lewin's model represents the *restraining forces* that maintain the status quo. These restraining forces are commonly called "resistance to change" because they appear to block the change process. Stability occurs when the driving and restraining forces are roughly in equilibrium—that is, they are of approximately equal strength in opposite directions.

Lewin's force field model emphasizes that effective change occurs by **unfreezing** the current situation, moving to a desired condition, and then **refreezing** the system so it remains in the desired state. Unfreezing involves producing disequilibrium between the driving and restraining forces. As we will describe later, this may occur by increasing the driving forces, reducing the restraining forces, or having a combination of both. Refreezing occurs when the organization's systems and structures are aligned with the desired behaviors. They must support and reinforce the new role patterns and prevent the organization from slipping back into the old way of doing things. Over the next few pages, we use Lewin's model to understand why change is blocked and how the process can evolve more smoothly.

Restraining Forces

Robert Nardelli pushed hard to transform Home Depot from a loose configuration of fiefdoms to a more performance-oriented operation that delivered a consistent customer experience. Change did occur at the world's largest home improvement retailer, but at a price. A large number of talented managers and employees left the company, and some of those remaining continued to resent Nardelli's transformation. Disenchanted staff referred to the company as "Home Despot" because the changes took away their autonomy. Others named it "Home GEpot," a disparaging reference to the many former GE executives that Nardelli hired into top positions. After five years, the Home Depot board decided to replace Nardelli, partly because he made some unsuccessful strategic decisions and partly because of the aftereffects of Nardelli's changes.[6]

Robert Nardelli experienced plenty of *resistance to change* at Home Depot. Resistance to change takes many forms, ranging from overt work stoppages to subtle attempts to continue the old ways.

▼ **EXHIBIT 14.1** Lewin's Force Field Analysis Model

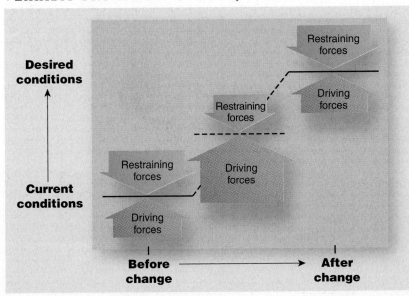

One study of bank employees reported that subtle resistance is much more common than overt resistance. Some employees in that study avoided the desired changes by moving into different jobs. Others continued to perform tasks the old way as long as management didn't notice. Even when employees complied with the planned changes, they engaged in resistance by performing their work without corresponding cognitive or emotional support for the change.[8] In other words, they resisted by letting customers know that they disapproved of the changes forced on them.

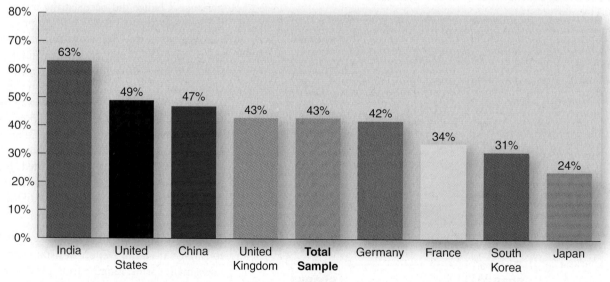

How Effectively Do Organizations around the World Handle Change?[9]

India	63%	
United States	49%	
China	47%	
United Kingdom	43%	
Total Sample	43%	
Germany	42%	
France	34%	
South Korea	31%	
Japan	24%	

Percentage of employees, by selected countries, who agree or strongly agree that "change is handled effectively in my organization." Not all 28,810 employees across the 15 countries surveyed are shown here, but all are included in the "total sample" figure.

FACT.

Hoppy Change

Hoppy, a carbonated low-alcohol malt-and-hops beverage, was popular around Tokyo after World War II as a cheap alternative to expensive beer, but it fell out of favor as beer became affordable. Mina Ishiwatari (center in photo), granddaughter of Hoppy Beverage Co.'s founder, was determined to improve Hoppy's image when she joined the company a decade ago. Unfortunately the company's 30 employees—mostly men in their fifties who were family relatives—didn't want to disturb their cozy jobs. "It was a turbulent decade of eliminating evils from the company and rebuilding a new organization from scratch," recalls Ishiwatari, who began as a rank-and-file employee and is now the company's executive vice president. "I tried to take a new marketing approach to change the image of Hoppy . . . but no one would listen to me." With limited support and budget, Ishiwatari developed a Web site that informed the public about the product, sold it online, and documented Ishiwatari's views in an early Weblog. As the contemporary marketing caught the attention of health-conscious young people, Hoppy sales have doubled to about $25 million (US) annually, even though it is sold only around Tokyo. Most employees who opposed Ishiwatari's radical changes have since left the company; almost all of the 43 current staff members were hired by Ishiwatari and support her vision of Hoppy's future.[12]

Employee Resistance as a Resource for Change

Although Symantec's CEO was probably frustrated by the executive's passive resistance to change, change agents need to realize that resistance is a common and natural human response. Even when people support change, they typically assume that it is others—not themselves—who need to change. The problem, however, isn't so much that resistance to change exists. The main problem is that change agents typically view resistance as an unreasonable, dysfunctional, and irrational response to a desirable initiative. They often form an "us versus them" perspective without considering that the causes of resistance may, in fact, be traced back to their own actions or inaction.[13]

The emerging view among change management experts is that resistance to change needs to be seen as a resource, rather than as an impediment to change. Resistance to change is a resource in three ways. First, resistance is a signal—a warning system—that the change agent has not sufficiently addressed the underlying conditions that block effective organizational change.[14]

Some experts point out that these subtle forms of resistance create the greatest obstacles to change because they are not as visible. In the words of one manager, "[Change efforts] never die because of direct confrontation. Direct confrontation you can work with because it is known. Rather, they die a death of a thousand cuts. People and issues you never confront drain the life out of important [initiatives] and result in solutions that simply do not have the performance impact that they should have."[10]

John Thompson experienced this subtle resistance to change soon after he became CEO of Symantec Corporation. To reduce costs, Thompson suggested that the computer cable included in all Symantec software packages was an unnecessary expense because most customers already owned these cables. Everyone at the cost-cutting meeting agreed that the cables should no longer be shipped with the software but would be provided free to customers who requested them. Yet several weeks later Thompson discovered that computer cables were still being shipped with the software, so he reminded the executive responsible that the team makes these decisions only once. "If you've got a disagreement or a point of view, bring it up when we're going through the discussion," Thompson advised the executive. "Don't hold back and give me this smiley kind of benign agreement. Go back and get it fixed. We're not shipping cables any more."[11]

In some situations, employees may be worried about the *consequences* of change, such as how the new conditions will take away their power and status. In other situations, employees show resistance because of concerns about the *process* of change itself, such as the effort required to break old habits and learn new skills.

Second, resistance should be recognized as a form of constructive conflict. Recall from earlier chapters that constructive conflict can potentially improve decision making, including identifying better ways to improve the organization's success. However, constructive conflict is typically accompanied by dysfunctional relationship conflict. This appears to be the case when change agents see resistance to change as an impediment rather than a resource. They describe the people who resist as the problem, whereas their focus should be on understanding the reasons why these people resist. Thus, by viewing resistance as a form of constructive conflict, change agents may be able to improve the change strategy or change process.

clarity occurs when people misunderstand or magnify what is expected of them in the future. These three factors—motivation, ability, and role (mis)perceptions—are the foundations of the six most commonly cited reasons why people resist change, which are summarized here:[18]

- *Direct costs:* People tend to oppose changes that they believe will put them in a worse situation. For example, the Malaysian government has introduced sweeping changes in which managers are expected to delegate more power and responsibility to staff. However, many government managers believe these reforms will give them less power and prestige, so they have hindered the change by delegating responsibility slowly.

- *Saving face:* Some people resist change as a political strategy to "prove" that the decision is wrong or that the person encouraging change is incompetent. For example, senior executives in a manufacturing firm bought a computer other than the system recommended by the information systems department. Soon after the system was in place, several information systems

> "Faced with the choice between changing one's mind and proving that there is no need to do so, almost everyone gets busy on the proof.[15]
>
> —John Kenneth Galbraith

Finally, resistance should be viewed in the context of justice and motivation. Resistance is a form of voice, so it potentially improves procedural justice (see Chapter 5). By redirecting initial forms of resistance into constructive conversations, change agents can increase employee perceptions and feelings of fairness. Furthermore, resistance is motivational; it potentially engages people to think about the change strategy and process. Change agents can harness that motivational force to ultimately strengthen commitment to the change initiative.

Why Employees Resist Change Change management experts have developed a long list of reasons why people do not embrace change.[17] Many of these reasons relate to a lack of motivation, which typically occurs when employees believe the change will be costly to them personally. This cost might be in the form of lost rewards and status, or might represent negative consequences if they attempt to support the change. Another reason for resistance is the person's inability (or perceived inability) to change due to inadequate skills and knowledge. A third reason is that employees lack role clarity about the change. This lack of role

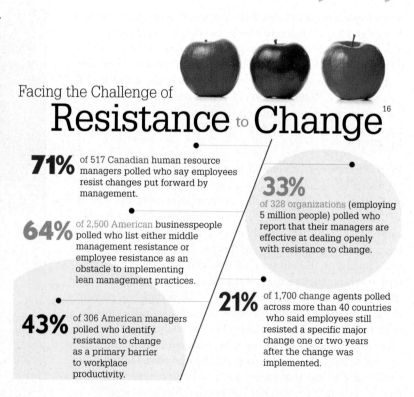

Facing the Challenge of

Resistance to Change [16]

71% of 517 Canadian human resource managers polled who say employees resist changes put forward by management.

64% of 2,500 American businesspeople polled who list either middle management resistance or employee resistance as an obstacle to implementing lean management practices.

43% of 306 American managers polled who identify resistance to change as a primary barrier to workplace productivity.

33% of 328 organizations (employing 5 million people) polled who report that their managers are effective at dealing openly with resistance to change.

21% of 1,700 change agents polled across more than 40 countries who said employees still resisted a specific major change one or two years after the change was implemented.

employees let minor implementation problems escalate to demonstrate that senior management had made a poor decision. This not-invented-here syndrome is widespread, according to change experts. Says one consultant, "Unless employees are scared enough to listen, they'll never forgive you for being right and for knowing something they don't."[19]

- *Fear of the unknown:* People resist change out of worry that they cannot adjust to the new work requirements. This fear of the unknown increases the *risk* of personal loss, and this uncertainty is usually considered less desirable than the relative certainty of the status quo.

- *Breaking routines:* People typically resist initiatives that force them out of their comfort zones and require them to invest time and energy in learning new role patterns. For instance, employees in one survey admitted they don't follow through with organizational changes because they "like to keep things the way they are" or the changes seem too complicated or time wasting.[20]

desired state. Unfreezing occurs when the driving forces are stronger than the restraining forces. This happens by making the driving forces stronger, weakening or removing the restraining forces, or combining both.

The first option is to increase the driving forces, motivating employees to change through fear or threats (real or contrived). This strategy rarely works, however, because the action of increasing the driving forces alone is usually met with an equal and opposing increase in the restraining forces. A useful metaphor is pushing against the coils of a mattress. The harder corporate leaders push for change, the stronger the restraining forces push back. This antagonism threatens the change effort by producing tension and conflict within the organization.

The second option is to weaken or remove the restraining forces. The problem with this change strategy is that it provides no motivation for change. To some extent, weakening the

> [Even when we want to change, and *do* change, we tend to relax and the rubber band snaps us back into our comfort zones.[21]]
>
> —Ray Davis

- *Incongruent team dynamics:* Teams develop and enforce conformity to a set of norms that guide behavior. However, conformity to existing team norms may discourage employees from accepting organizational change. This form of resistance occurred at electronics retailer Best Buy when it introduced the results-only work environment (ROWE). ROWE evaluates employees by their results, not their face time, so employees can come to work and leave when they want. Yet coworkers often responded to deviations from the standard work schedule with half-humorous barbs such as "Forgot to set your alarm clock again?" These jibes supported the old employment model but undermined the ROWE program. Best Buy's consultants eventually set up sessions that warned employees about these taunts, which they called "sludge."[22]

- *Incongruent organizational systems:* Rewards, information systems, patterns of authority, career paths, selection criteria, and other systems and structures are both friends and foes of organizational change. When properly aligned, they reinforce desired behaviors. When misaligned, they pull people back into their old attitudes and behavior. Even enthusiastic employees lose momentum after failing to overcome the structural confines of the past.

UNFREEZING, CHANGING, AND REFREEZING

According to Lewin's force field analysis model, effective change occurs by unfreezing the current situation, moving to a desired condition, and then refreezing the system so it remains in this

restraining forces is like clearing a pathway for change. An unobstructed road makes it easier to travel to the destination but does not motivate anyone to go there. The preferred option, therefore, is to both increase the driving forces and reduce or remove the restraining forces. Increasing the driving forces

"IN MANY ORGANIZATIONS, LEADERS BUFFER EMPLOYEES FROM THE EXTERNAL ENVIRONMENT TO SUCH AN EXTENT THAT EXTERNAL DRIVING FORCES ARE HARDLY FELT BY ANYONE BELOW THE TOP EXECUTIVE LEVEL."

creates an urgency for change, while reducing the restraining forces lessens motivation to oppose the change and removes obstacles such as lack of ability and situational constraints.

Creating an Urgency for Change

It is almost a cliché to say that organizations today operate in more dynamic, fast-paced environments than they did a few decades ago. The environmental pressures represent the driving forces that push employees out of their comfort zones. They energize people to face the risks that change creates. In many organizations, however, leaders buffer employees from the external environment to such an extent that these driving forces are hardly felt by anyone below the top executive level. The result is that employees don't understand why they need to change and leaders are surprised when their change initiatives do not have much effect. The change process therefore necessarily begins by ensuring that employees develop an urgency for change. This typically occurs by informing employees about competitors, changing consumer trends, impending government regulations, and other driving forces in the external environment.[23]

Customer-Driven Change
Some companies fuel the urgency to change by putting employees in direct contact with customers. Dissatisfied customers represent a compelling driving force for change because the organization's survival typically depends on having customers who are satisfied with the product or service. Customers also provide a human element that further energizes employees to change current behavior patterns.[24]

Executives at Shell Europe applied customer-driven change a few years ago. Many middle managers at the energy company seemed blissfully unaware that Shell wasn't achieving either its financial goals or its customer needs; so to create an urgency for change, the European managers were loaded onto buses and taken out to talk with customers and employees who work with customers every day. "We called these 'bus rides.' The idea was to encourage people to think back from the customer's perspective rather than from the head office," explains Shell Europe's vice president of retailing. "The bus rides were difficult for a lot of people who, in their work history, had hardly ever had to talk to a customer and find out what was good and not so good about Shell from the customer's standpoint."[25]

Creating an Urgency for Change without External Forces
Exposing employees to external forces can strengthen the urgency for change, but leaders often need to begin the change process before problems come knocking at the company's door. "You want to create a burning platform for change even when there isn't a need for one," says Steve Bennett, CEO of financial software company Intuit.[26] Creating an urgency for change when the organization is riding high requires rare persuasive capability that helps employees visualize future competitive threats and environmental shifts.

For instance, Apple Computer's iPod dominates the digital music market, but Steve Jobs wants the company to be its own toughest competitor. Just when sales of the iPod Mini were soaring, Jobs challenged a gathering of 100 top executives and engineers to develop a better product to replace it. "Playing it safe is the most dangerous thing we can do," Jobs warned. Nine months later the company launched the iPod Nano, which replaced the still-popular iPod Mini before competitors could offer a better alternative.[27]

Experts warn, however, that employees may see the burning-platform strategy as manipulative—a view that produces cynicism about change and undermines trust in the change agent.[28] Also, the urgency for change doesn't need to originate from problems or threats to the company; this motivation can also develop through a change champion's vision of a more appealing future. By creating a future vision of a better organization, leaders effectively make the current situation less appealing. When the vision connects to employee values and needs, it can be a motivating force for change even when external problems are not strong.

Reducing the Restraining Forces

Employee resistance should be viewed as a resource, but its underlying causes—the restraining forces—need to be addressed. As we explained earlier using the mattress coil metaphor, it is not enough to increase the driving forces because employees often push back harder to offset the opposing force. Exhibit 14.2 summarizes six strategies for addressing the sources of employee resistance. If feasible, communication, learning, employee involvement, and stress management should be attempted first.[29] However, negotiation and coercion are necessary for people who will clearly lose something from the change and in cases where the speed of change is critical.

Communication
Communication is the highest priority and first strategy required for any organizational change. According to one recent survey, communication (together with involvement) is considered the top strategy for engaging employees in the change process.[30] Communication improves the change process in at least two ways. First, communication illuminates the future and thereby reduces fear of the unknown. The more corporate leaders communicate their vision of the future, particularly details about that future and milestones already achieved, the more easily employees can understand their own roles in that future. Similarly, as the leader

Strategy	Example	When Applied	Problems
Communication	Customer complaint letters are shown to employees.	When employees don't feel an urgency for change, don't know how the change will affect them, or resist change due to a fear of the unknown.	Time-consuming and potentially costly.
Learning	Employees learn how to work in teams as company adopts a team-based structure.	When employees need to break old routines and adopt new role patterns.	Time-consuming and potentially costly.
Employee involvement	Company forms task force to recommend new customer service practices.	When the change effort needs more employee commitment, some employees need to save face, and/or employee ideas would improve decisions about the change strategy.	Very time-consuming. Might lead to conflict and poor decisions if employees' interests are incompatible with organizational needs.
Stress management	Employees attend sessions to discuss their worries about the change.	When communication, training, and involvement do not sufficiently ease employee worries.	Time-consuming and potentially expensive. Some methods may not reduce stress for all employees.
Negotiation	Employees agree to replace strict job categories with multiskilling in return for increased job security.	When employees will clearly lose something of value from the change and would not otherwise support the new conditions. Also necessary when the company must change quickly.	May be expensive, particularly if other employees want to negotiate their support. Also tends to produce compliance but not commitment to the change.
Coercion	Company president tells managers to "get on board" the change or leave.	When other strategies are ineffective and the company needs to change quickly.	Can lead to more subtle forms of resistance, as well as long-term antagonism with the change agent.

Sources: Adapted from J. P. Kotter and L. A. Schlesinger, "Choosing Strategies for Change," *Harvard Business Review* 57 (1979), pp. 106–114; P. R. Lawrence, "How to Deal with Resistance to Change," *Harvard Business Review,* May–June 1954, pp. 49–57.

communicates the future state more clearly, employees better understand how the change relates to their jobs and responsibilities.

The second way that communication minimizes resistance to change is by generating an urgency to change. In particular, leaders motivate employees to support the change by candidly telling them about the external threats and opportunities that make change so important. Whether through town hall meetings with senior management or by directly meeting with disgruntled customers, employees become energized to change when they understand and visualize those external forces. For this reason, communication has been an important approach to managing change at the Federal Bureau of Investigation (FBI) as it shifts its mandate from law enforcement to intelligence gathering. "The word is out. Terrorism is the No. 1 priority, and intelligence is what the bureau is about," says former assistant attorney

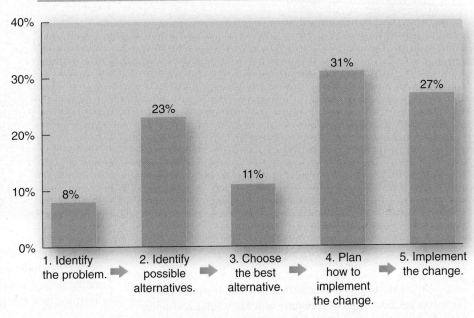

At What Stage in the Change Process Do Companies Activate the Internal Communication Function?[32]

Figures indicate percentage of 328 organizations (employing 5 million people) who activate the internal communication function at each stage of the change process. More than half (58 percent) of companies do not involve the internal communication function until after the change strategy has been selected.

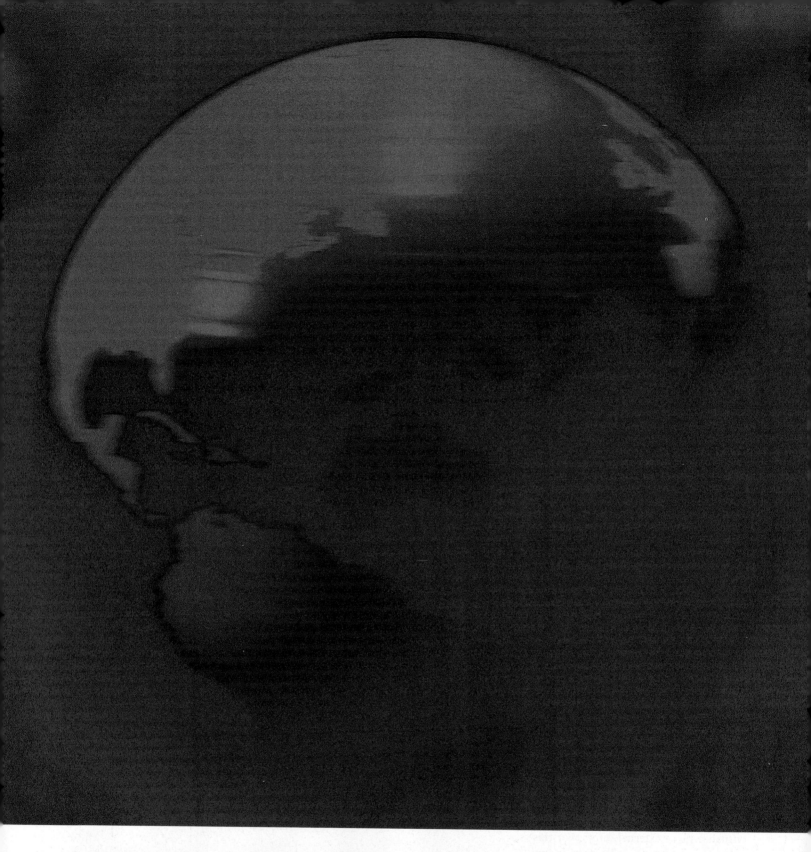

general Paul R. Corts, who has worked closely with the FBI during the change process. "You've got to say it, say it, and say it again."[31]

Learning Learning is an important process in most change initiatives because employees require new knowledge and skills to fit the organization's evolving requirements. When a company introduces a new sales database, for instance, representatives need to learn how to use the system as well as learn to adapt their previous behavior patterns to benefit from the new system. Training is time-consuming, but it helps people break routines by learning new role patterns.

Employee Involvement Unless the change must occur quickly or employee interests are highly incompatible with the organization's needs, employee involvement is almost an essential part of the change process. Earlier in this book (Chapter 6) we described several potential benefits of employee involvement, all of which are relevant to organizational change. Employees who participate in decisions about a change tend to feel more personal responsibility for its successful implementation, rather than being disinterested agents of someone else's decisions.[33] This sense of ownership also minimizes the problems of saving face and fear of the unknown. Furthermore, the complexity of today's work environment demands that more people provide ideas regarding the best direction of the change effort. Employee involvement is such an important component of organizational change that special initiatives have been developed to allow participation in large groups. These change interventions are described later in the chapter.

Stress Management Organizational change is a stressful experience for many people because it threatens self-esteem and creates uncertainty about the future.[34] Communication, learning, and employee involvement can reduce some of the stressors. However, research indicates that companies also need to introduce stress management practices to help employees cope with changes.[35] In particular, stress management minimizes resistance by removing some of the direct costs and fear of the unknown of the change process. Stress also saps energy, so minimizing stress potentially increases employee motivation to support the change process.

Firing people is the least desirable way to change organizations. However, dismissals and other forms of coercion are sometimes necessary when speed is essential and other tactics are ineffective. For example, it may be necessary to remove several members of an executive team who are unwilling or unable to change their existing mental models of the ideal organization. This is also a radical form of organizational "unlearning" (see Chapter 1) because when executives leave, they take knowledge of the organization's past routines, which potentially opens up opportunities for new practices to take hold.[37] At the same time, coercion is a risky strategy because survivors (employees who do not leave) may have less trust in corporate leaders and engage in more political tactics to protect their own job security.

Refreezing the Desired Conditions

Unfreezing and changing behavior won't produce lasting change. People are creatures of habit, so they easily slip back into past patterns. Therefore, leaders need to refreeze the new behaviors by realigning organizational systems and team dynamics with the desired changes.[38] The desired patterns of behavior can be "nailed down" by changing the physical structure and situational conditions. Organizational rewards are also powerful systems that refreeze behaviors.[39] If the change process is supposed to encourage efficiency, then rewards should be realigned to

> People are creatures of habit, so leaders need to refreeze the new behaviors by realigning organizational systems and team dynamics with the desired changes.

Negotiation As long as people resist change, organizational change strategies will require some influence tactics. Negotiation is a form of influence that involves the promise of benefits or resources in exchange for the target person's compliance with the influencer's request. This strategy potentially gains support from those who would otherwise lose out from the change. However, this support is mostly compliance with, rather than commitment to, the change effort, so it might not be effective in the long term.

Coercion If all else fails, leaders rely on coercion to change organizations. Coercion can include persistently reminding people of their obligations, frequently monitoring behavior to ensure compliance, confronting people who do not change, and using threats of sanctions to force compliance. Replacing people who will not support the change is an extreme step, but it is fairly common. One year after Robert Nardelli was hired as CEO of Home Depot, most of the retailer's top management team had voluntarily or involuntarily left the company. Several years earlier, when Gordon Bethune and Greg Brenneman orchestrated the turnaround of Continental Airlines, 50 of the company's 61 executive officers left the organization.[36]

motivate and reinforce efficient behavior. Information systems play a complementary role in the change process, particularly as conduits for feedback.[40] Feedback mechanisms help employees learn how well they are moving toward the desired objectives, and they provide a permanent architecture to support the new behavior patterns in the long term. The adage "What gets measured, gets done" applies here. Employees concentrate on the new priorities when they receive a continuous flow of feedback about how well they are achieving those goals.

CHANGE AGENTS, STRATEGIC VISIONS, AND DIFFUSING CHANGE

Kurt Lewin's force field analysis model is a useful template to explain the dynamics of organizational change. But it overlooks three ingredients in effective change processes: change agents, strategic visions, and diffusing change.

Change Agents and Strategic Visions

The beginning of this chapter described how Lopez Foods CEO Eduardo Sanchez engaged employees in the change process by challenging them to identify better ways to organize the production process. Leadership plays a critical role in organizational change. As we learned in the chapter about leadership (Chapter 11), transformational leaders are agents of change because they develop an appealing vision of the desired future state, communicate that vision in ways that are meaningful to others, make decisions and act in ways that are consistent with that vision, and build commitment to that vision.[41] Change agents come in different forms,

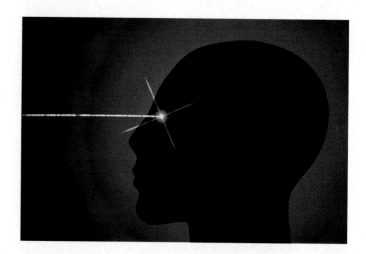

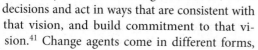

Insights about Leading Change[43]

Insights about Leading Change	Explanation
Creating a Compelling Story	
1. What motivates you doesn't motivate most of your employees.	Employees are motivated by their personal needs and values, so the vision for change must be more compatible with those motivations, such as benefit to themselves, society, etc.
2. You're better off letting them write their own story.	Employees have their own views of the company's problems and opportunities, so leaders need to listen to those views and incorporate them into the vision and rationale for change.
3. It takes a story with both positive and negative elements to create real energy.	The problem-oriented ("what's wrong") and appreciative ("what might be") approaches to organizational change have advantages and disadvantages, so use both approaches together in organizational change.
Role Modeling	
4. Leaders believe mistakenly that they already "are the change."	Leaders believe they embrace the change and are acting consistently with it. In reality, they also need to change. This change is assisted through concrete sources of feedback (e.g., 360-degree feedback) to help them align their behavior with the change.
5. "Influence leaders" aren't a panacea for making change happen.	Employee support for the change is strengthened through persuasive and respected leaders and change champions. Yet these change agents alone are not enough. Change still requires application of all the insights listed here.
Reinforcing Mechanisms	
6. Money is the most expensive way to motivate people.	Trying to align the organization's compensation system to the organizational change objectives is difficult, expensive, and rarely successful. Instead use symbolic recognition and rewards to support the change process.
7. The process and the outcome need to be fair.	Employees will oppose a seemingly logical change if they perceive unfairness in the process or secondary consequences of that change. Therefore, pay attention to employee perceptions of fairness in how various stakeholders are affected by the change.
Capability Building	
8. Employees are what they think, feel, and believe in.	Effective change pays attention to employee attitudes, not just behavior. Therefore, pay attention to employee attitudes toward the new versus previous roles (e.g., sales versus administration) as well as alignment of their personalities and beliefs to those new roles.
9. Good intentions aren't enough.	Change programs that train employees in new skills often fail because the training is not transferred back to the job. New skills are more likely to be applied on the job when the training includes field assignments (performing trained skills on the job) and when the work environment is also changed to support the new skills and behaviors.

and more than one person is often required to fulfill these different roles.[42] In most situations, however, transformational leaders are the primary agents of change.

A key element of leading change is a strategic vision. A leader's vision provides a sense of direction and establishes the critical success factors against which the real changes are evaluated. Furthermore, a vision provides an emotional foundation to the change because it links the individual's values and self-concept to the desired change.[44] A strategic vision also minimizes employee fear of the unknown and provides a better understanding of what behaviors employees must learn for the desired future.

Diffusion of Change

Earlier in this chapter (as well as earlier in this book) we described Best Buy's results-only work environment (ROWE) initiative, which was introduced to support work/life balance and emerging employment expectations. ROWE evaluates employees by their results, not their face time. This new arrangement gives employees at the Minneapolis-based retailer the freedom to come to work when it suits them. ROWE is a significant departure from the traditional employment relationship, so Best Buy wisely introduced an early version of it as a pilot project. Specifically, the program was first tested with a retail division of 320 employees that suffered from low morale and high turnover. Only after employee engagement scores increased and turnover fell over several months was the ROWE program expanded to other parts of the organization.[45]

As at Best Buy, change agents often test the transformation process with a pilot project and then diffuse what has been learned from this experience to other parts of the organization. Unlike centralized, systemwide changes, pilot projects are more flexible and less risky.[46] The pilot project approach also makes it easier to select organizational groups that are most ready for change, thus increasing the pilot project's success.

But how do we ensure that the change process started in the pilot project is adopted by other segments of the organization? The MARS model introduced in Chapter 2 offers a useful template to structure the answer to this question. First, employees are more likely to adopt the practices of a pilot project when they are motivated to do so.[47] This occurs when they see that the pilot project is successful and people in the pilot project receive recognition and rewards for changing their previous work practices. Diffusion also occurs more successfully when managers support and reinforce the desired behaviors. More generally, change agents need to minimize the sources of resistance to change that we discussed earlier in this chapter.

Second, employees must have the ability—the required skills and knowledge—to adopt the practices introduced in the pilot project. According to innovation diffusion studies, people adopt ideas more readily when they have an opportunity to interact

Action PLAN

Strategies for Diffusing Change from a Pilot Project

Motivation

- The pilot project is successful, and that success is widely communicated.
- Employees who participated in the pilot project receive recognition and rewards for their achievement.
- Managers support and reinforce the desired behaviors related to the pilot project's success.
- Managers apply strategies to minimize resistance to change.

Ability

- Employees have the opportunity to interact with and learn from those in the pilot project.
- Some employees from the pilot project are reassigned or temporarily seconded to other work units to coach others and serve as role models.
- Employees receive technical training required to implement practices identified in the pilot project.

Role Perceptions

- Employees discover how the pilot project practices are relevant for their own functional areas.
- The company describes the pilot project intervention to employees in other work units in a way that is neither too specific nor too general.

Situational Factors

- The organization provides sufficient time and resources for employees to learn and implement the pilot project practices in their work units.

with and learn from others who have already applied the new practices.[48] In other words, pilot projects get diffused when employees in the original pilot are dispersed to other work units as role models and knowledge sources.

Third, pilot projects get diffused when employees have clear role perceptions—that is, when they understand how the practices in a pilot project apply to them even though they are in a completely different functional area. For instance, accounting department employees won't easily recognize how they can adopt quality improvement practices developed by employees in the production department. The challenge here is for change agents to provide guidance that is not too specific (not too narrowly defined around the pilot project environment) because it might not seem relevant to other areas of the organization. At the same time, the pilot project intervention should not be described too broadly or abstractly to other employees because this makes the information and role model too vague. Finally, employees require supportive situational factors, including the resources and time necessary to adopt the practices demonstrated in the pilot project.

Action research maintains that meaningful change is a combination of action orientation (changing attitudes and behavior) and research orientation (testing theory).

Learning Objectives

After reading the next two sections, you should be able to

LO4 Describe and compare action research, appreciative inquiry, large group interventions, and parallel learning structures as formal approaches to organizational change.

LO5 Discuss two cross-cultural and three ethical issues in organizational change.

FOUR APPROACHES TO ORGANIZATIONAL CHANGE

So far, this chapter has examined the dynamics of change that occur every day in organizations. However, organizational change agents and consultants also apply various structured approaches to organizational change. This section introduces four of the leading approaches: action research, appreciative inquiry, large group interventions, and parallel learning structures.

Action Research Approach

Along with introducing the force field model, Kurt Lewin recommended an **action research** approach to the change process. Action research maintains that meaningful change is a combination of action orientation (changing attitudes and behavior) and research orientation (testing theory).[49] On one hand, the change process needs to be action-oriented because the ultimate goal is to change the workplace. An action orientation involves diagnosing current problems and applying interventions that resolve those problems. On the other hand, the change process is a research study because change agents apply a conceptual framework (such as team dynamics or

organizational culture) to a real situation. As with any good research, the change process involves collecting data to diagnose problems more effectively and to systematically evaluate how well the theory works in practice.[50]

Within this dual framework of action and research, the action research approach adopts an open-systems view. It recognizes that organizations have many interdependent parts, so change agents need to anticipate both the intended and the unintended consequences of their interventions. Action research is also a highly participative process because open-systems change requires both the knowledge and the commitment of members within that system. Indeed, employees are essentially co-researchers as well as participants in the intervention. Overall, action research is a data-based, problem-oriented process that diagnoses the need for change, introduces the intervention, and then evaluates and stabilizes the desired changes. The main phases of action research are illustrated in Exhibit 14.3 and described here:[51]

1. *Form client–consultant relationship.* Action research usually assumes that the change agent originates outside the system (such as a consultant), so the process begins by forming the client–consultant relationship. Consultants need to determine the client's readiness for change, including whether people are motivated to participate in the process, are open to meaningful change, and possess the abilities to complete the process.

2. *Diagnose the need for change.* Action research is a problem-oriented activity that carefully diagnoses the problem through systematic analysis of the situation. Organizational diagnosis identifies the appropriate direction for the change effort by gathering and analyzing data about an ongoing system, such as through interviews and surveys of employees and other stakeholders. Organizational diagnosis also includes employee involvement in agreeing on the appropriate change method, the schedule for the actions involved, and the expected standards of successful change.

▼**EXHIBIT 14.3** The Action Research Process

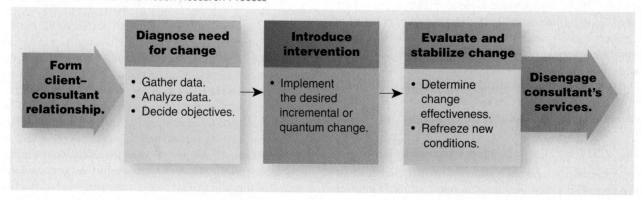

3. *Introduce intervention.* This stage in the action research model applies one or more actions to correct the problem. It may include any of the prescriptions mentioned in this book, such as building more effective teams, managing conflict, building a better organizational structure, or changing the corporate culture. An important issue is how quickly the changes should occur.[52] Some experts recommend *incremental change,* in which the organization fine-tunes the system and takes small steps toward a desired state. Others claim that *quantum change* is often required, in which the system is overhauled decisively and quickly. Quantum change is usually traumatic to employees and offers little opportunity for correction. But incremental change is also risky when the organization is seriously misaligned with its environment, thereby facing a threat to its survival.

4. *Evaluate and stabilize change.* Action research recommends evaluating the effectiveness of the intervention against the standards established in the diagnostic stage. Unfortunately, even when these standards are clearly stated, the effectiveness of an intervention might not be apparent for several years or might be difficult to separate from other factors. If the activity has the desired effect, the change agent and participants need to stabilize the new conditions. This refers to the refreezing process that was described earlier. Rewards, information systems, team norms, and other conditions are redesigned so they support the new values and behaviors.

The action research approach has dominated organizational change thinking since it was introduced in the 1940s. However, some experts are concerned that the problem-oriented nature of action research—in which something is wrong that must be fixed—focuses on the negative dynamics of the group or system rather than its positive opportunities and potential. This concern with action research has led to the development of a more positive approach to organizational change, called *appreciative inquiry.*[53]

Appreciative Inquiry Approach

Appreciative inquiry tries to break out of the problem-solving mentality of traditional change management practices by reframing relationships around the positive and the possible. It searches for organizational (or team) strengths and capabilities and then adapts or applies that knowledge for further success and well-being. Appreciative inquiry is therefore deeply grounded in the emerging philosophy of *positive organizational behavior,* which suggests that focusing on the positive rather than the negative aspects of life will improve organizational success and individual well-being. In other words, this approach emphasizes building on strengths rather than trying to directly correct problems.[54]

Appreciative inquiry typically examines successful events, organizations, and work units. This focus becomes a form of behavioral modeling, but it also increases open dialogue by redirecting the group's attention away from its own problems. Appreciative inquiry is especially useful when participants are aware of their problems or already suffer from negativity in their relationships. The positive orientation of appreciative inquiry enables groups to overcome these negative tensions and build a more hopeful perspective of their future by focusing on what is possible.[55]

action research
A problem-focused change process that combines action orientation (changing attitudes and behavior) and research orientation (testing theory through data collection and analysis).

appreciative inquiry
An organizational change strategy that directs the group's attention away from its own problems and focuses participants on the group's potential and positive elements.

Appreciative inquiry's positive focus is illustrated by the intervention conducted a few years ago by the British Broadcasting Corporation.[56] Almost 40 percent of BBC's workforce attended one of 200 appreciative inquiry meetings held over six months. Participants at each session were organized into pairs, where they asked each other three questions: (1) What has been the most creative/valued experience in your time at the BBC? (2) What were the conditions that made that experience possible? (3) If those experiences were to become the norm, how would the BBC have to change? These questions focused participants on the positive and the possible rather than on problems. They also produced 98,000 ideas, which were distilled into 15,000 unique suggestions and ultimately 35 concrete initiatives.

Appreciative Inquiry Principles The positive focus is one of five principles embraced by appreciative inquiry (see Exhibit 14.4).[57] A second principle, called the *constructionist principle,* takes the position that conversations don't describe reality; they shape that reality. In other words, how we come to understand something depends on the questions we ask and the language we use. Thus appreciative inquiry requires sensitivity to and proactive

The British Broadcasting Corporation (BBC) launched an appreciative inquiry intervention to help the media organization discover ways of becoming more innovative. The process involved more than 10,000 employees (about 40 percent of BBC's workforce) in 200 meetings held over six months.

Appreciative Inquiry Principle	Description
Positive principle	Focusing on positive events and potential produces more positive, effective, and enduring change.
Constructionist principle	How we perceive and understand the change process depends on the questions we ask and language we use throughout that process.
Simultaneity principle	Inquiry and change are simultaneous, not sequential.
Poetic principle	Organizations are open books, so we have choices in how they may be perceived, framed, and described.
Anticipatory principle	People are motivated and guided by the vision they see and believe in for the future.

management of the words and language used as well as the thoughts and feelings behind that communication. This relates to a third principle, called the *simultaneity principle,* which states that inquiry and change are simultaneous, not sequential. The moment we ask questions of others, we are changing those people. Furthermore, the questions we ask determine the information we receive, which in turn affects which change intervention we choose. The key learning point from this principle is to be mindful of effects that the inquiry has on the direction of the change process.

A fourth principle, called the *poetic principle,* states that organizations are open books, so we have choices in how they may be perceived, framed, and described. The poetic principle is reflected in the notion that a glass of water can be viewed as half full or half empty. Thus appreciative inquiry actively frames reality in a way that provides constructive value for future development. *The anticipatory principle,* the fifth principle of appreciative inquiry, emphasizes the importance of a positive collective vision of the future state. People are motivated and guided by the vision they see and believe in for the future. Images that are mundane or disempowering will affect current effort and behavior differently than will images that are inspiring and engaging. We noted the importance of visions earlier in this chapter (change agents) and in our discussion of transformational leadership (Chapter 11).

The Four-D Model of Appreciative Inquiry Building on these five principles, appreciative inquiry generally follows the "Four-D" process (named after its four stages) shown in Exhibit 14.5. Appreciative inquiry begins with *discovery*—identifying the positive elements of the observed events or organization.[58] This might involve documenting positive customer experiences elsewhere in the organization. Or it might include interviewing members of another organization to discover its fundamental strengths. As participants discuss their findings, they shift into the *dreaming* stage by envisioning what might be possible in an ideal organization. By pointing out a hypothetical ideal organization or situation, participants feel safer revealing their hopes and aspirations than they would if they were discussing their own organization or predicament.

As participants make their private thoughts public to the group, the process shifts into the third stage, called *designing.* Designing involves dialogue in which participants listen with selfless receptivity to each other's models and assumptions and eventually form a collective model for thinking within the team. In effect, they create a common image of what should be. As this model takes shape, group members shift the focus back to their own situation. In the final stage of appreciative inquiry, called *delivering* (also known as *destiny*), participants establish specific

▼EXHIBIT 14.5 The Four-D Model of Appreciative Inquiry

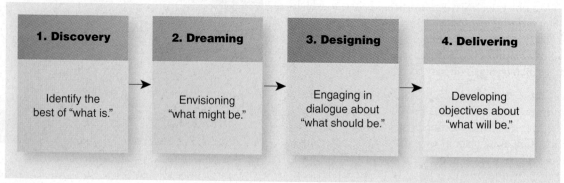

1. Discovery	2. Dreaming	3. Designing	4. Delivering
Identify the best of "what is."	Envisioning "what might be."	Engaging in dialogue about "what should be."	Developing objectives about "what will be."

Sources: Based on F. J. Barrett and D. L. Cooperrider, "Generative Metaphor Intervention: A New Approach for Working with Systems Divided by Conflict and Caught in Defensive Perception," *Journal of Applied Behavioral Science* 26 (1990), p. 229; D. Whitney and C. Schau, "Appreciative Inquiry: An Innovative Process for Organization Change," *Employment Relations Today* 25 (Spring 1998), pp. 11–21; and J. M. Watkins and B. J. Mohr, *Appreciative Inquiry: Change at the Speed of Imagination* (San Francisco: Jossey-Bass, 2001), pp. 25, 42–45.

objectives and direction for their own organization on the basis of their model of what will be.

Appreciative inquiry was developed 20 years ago, but it really gained popularity only within the past few years. Several success stories of organizational change from appreciative inquiry have emerged in a variety of organizational settings, including the British Broadcasting Corporation, Castrol Marine, Canadian Tire, AVON Mexico, American Express, Green Mountain Coffee Roasters, and Hunter Douglas.[59] However, experts warn that appreciative inquiry is not always the best approach to changing teams or organizations, and, indeed, it has not always been successful. For appreciative inquiry to work, participants need to let go of the problem-oriented approach, including the "blame game" of determining who may have been responsible for past problems. It also requires leaders who are willing to accept appreciative inquiry's less structured process.[60] Another concern is that research has not yet examined the contingencies of this approach.[61] In other words, we don't yet know under what conditions appreciative inquiry is a useful approach to organizational change and under what conditions it is less effective. Overall, appreciative inquiry has much to offer the organizational change process, but we are just beginning to understand its potential and limitations.

Large Group Interventions

Appreciative inquiry can occur in small teams, but it is often designed to involve a large number of people, such as the 10,000 employees who participated in the process at the British Broadcasting Corporation. As such, appreciative inquiry is often identified as one of several large group organizational change interventions. Another large group intervention, known as **future search** (and its variations—*search conferences* and *open-space technology*), "puts the entire system in the room," meaning that the process tries to involve as many employees and other stakeholders as possible who are associated with the organizational system.[62] Future search conferences are typically held over a few days and involve participants in the search for trends or issues that are emerging. These events also ask participants to develop strategic solutions for those future conditions.

For example, Emerson & Cuming's chemical manufacturing facility in Canton, Massachusetts, relied on a future search conference in which managers, supervisors, and production employees were organized into five stakeholder teams to identify initiatives that would improve the plant's safety, efficiency, and cooperation. Lawrence Public Schools in Kansas conducted a future search conference involving parents, teachers, students, community partners, and other stakeholders to help the board allocate resources more effectively. "The goals that were developed at the future search conference reflect what the community envisioned for its school district," says superintendent Randy Weseman. Those goals have since become the foundation of the board's strategic decision making.[63]

Future search meetings and similar large group change events potentially minimize resistance to change and assist the quality of the change process, but they also have limitations.[64] One problem is that involving so many people invariably limits the opportunity to contribute and increases the risk that a few people will dominate the process. Another concern is that these events focus on finding common ground, and this may prevent the participants from discovering substantive differences that interfere with future progress. A third issue is that these events generate high expectations about an ideal future state that are difficult to satisfy in practice. Employees become even more cynical and resistant to change if they do not see meaningful decisions and actions resulting from these meetings. The Washington State Department of Corrections held a future search event that tried to minimize these problems. The event involved a representation of 75 employees and managers, who reached a consensus on the department's future direction. Department executives were then assigned specific recommendations to ensure that the conference results were put into place.[65]

Parallel Learning Structure Approach

Parallel learning structures are highly participative arrangements composed of people from most levels of the organization who follow the action research model to produce meaningful organizational change. They are social structures developed alongside the formal hierarchy with the purpose of increasing the organization's learning.[66] Ideally participants in parallel learning structures are sufficiently free from the constraints of the larger organization that they can effectively solve organizational issues.

Royal Dutch/Shell relied on a parallel learning structure to introduce a more customer-focused organization.[67] Rather than try to change the entire organization at once, executives held weeklong "retail boot camps" with six country teams of frontline people (such as gas station managers, truck drivers, and marketing professionals). Participants learned about competitive trends in their regions and were taught powerful marketing tools to identify new opportunities. The teams then returned home to study their markets and develop proposals for improvement. Four months later, boot camp teams returned for a second workshop, at which time each proposal was critiqued by Royal/Dutch Shell executives. Each team had 60 days to put its ideas into action; then the teams returned for a third workshop to analyze what worked and what didn't. This parallel learning process did much more than introduce new marketing ideas. It created enthusiasm in participants that spread contagiously to their coworkers, including managers above them, when they returned to their home countries.

future search System-wide group sessions, usually lasting a few days, in which participants identify trends and identify ways to adapt to those changes.

parallel learning structure Highly participative arrangements, composed of people from most levels of the organization who follow the action research model to produce meaningful organizational change.

CROSS-CULTURAL AND ETHICAL ISSUES IN ORGANIZATIONAL CHANGE

One concern is that many organizational change models are built around American and other Western cultural assumptions and values, which may differ from and sometimes conflict with assumptions and values in other cultures.[68] One possible cross-cultural limitation is that many Western organizational change models, such as Lewin's force field analysis, assume that change has a beginning and an ending in a logical linear sequence (that is, a straight line from point A to point B). Yet in some cultures change is viewed more as a cyclical phenomenon, such as the earth's revolution around the sun or a pendulum swinging back and forth. Other cultures have more of an interconnected view of change, whereby one change leads to another (often unplanned) change, which leads to another change, and so on until the change objective is ultimately achieved in a more circuitous way.

Another cross-cultural problem with some organizational change interventions is that they assume effective organizational change is necessarily punctuated by tension and overt conflict. Indeed, some change interventions encourage such conflict. But this direct confrontation view is incompatible with cultures that emphasize harmony and equilibrium. These cross-cultural differences suggest that a more contingency-oriented perspective is required for organizational change to work effectively in a globalized world.

Some organizational change practices also face ethical issues.[69] One ethical concern is the risk of violating individual privacy rights. The action research model is built on the idea of collecting information from organizational members, yet this requires that employees provide personal information and emotions that they may not want to divulge.[70] A second ethical concern is that some change activities potentially increase management's power by inducing compliance and conformity in organizational members. For instance, action research is a systemwide activity that requires employee participation rather than allowing individuals to get involved voluntarily. A third concern is that some organizational change interventions undermine the individual's self-esteem. The unfreezing process requires that participants disconfirm their existing beliefs, sometimes including their own competence at certain tasks or interpersonal relations.

> "Take away my people, but leave my factories, and soon grass will grow on the factory floors. Take away my factories, but leave my people, and soon we will have a new and better factory.[71]
>
> —Attributed to Andrew Carnegie

Organizational change is usually more difficult than it initially seems. Yet the dilemma is that most organizations operate in hyperfast environments that demand continuous and rapid adaptation. Organizations survive and gain competitive advantage by mastering the complex dynamics of moving people through the continuous process of change as quickly as the external environment is changing.

ORGANIZATIONAL BEHAVIOR: THE JOURNEY CONTINUES

Nearly 100 years ago American industrialist Andrew Carnegie said, "Take away my people, but leave my factories, and soon grass will grow on the factory floors. Take away my factories, but leave my people, and soon we will have a new and better factory." Carnegie's statement reflects the message woven throughout this book: Organizations are not buildings or machinery or financial assets; rather, they are the people in them. Organizations are human entities—full of life, sometimes fragile, and always exciting. ■

CHECK IT OUT!

mhhe.com/McShaneM

for study materials

including quizzes

and Internet resources

endnotes

CHAPTER 1

1. E. A. Robinson, "America's Most Admired Companies," *Fortune,* March 3, 1997, pp. 68–76; J. Kahn, "The World's Most Admired Companies," *Fortune,* October 26, 1998, pp. 206–16; A. Bernasek, "The World's Most Admired Companies," *Fortune,* March 22, 2010, pp. 121–26.

2. Bernasek, "The World's Most Admired Companies."

3. B. Schlender, "The Three Faces of Steve," *Fortune,* November 9, 1998, pp. 96–101.

4. M. Warner, "Organizational Behavior Revisited," *Human Relations* 47 (October 1994), pp. 1151–66; R. Westwood and S. Clegg, "The Discourse of Organization Studies: Dissensus, Politics, and Peradigms," in *Debating Organization: Point–Counterpoint in Organization Studies,* ed. R. Westwood and S. Clegg (Malden, MA: Blackwood, 2003), pp. 1–42.

5. D. Katz and R. L. Kahn, *The Social Psychology of Organizations* (New York: Wiley, 1966), Chap. 2; R. N. Stern and S. R. Barley, "Organizations as Social Systems: Organization Theory's Neglected Mandate," *Administrative Science Quarterly* 41 (1996), pp. 146–62.

6. L. E. Greiner, "A Recent History of Organizational Behavior," in *Organizational Behaviour,* ed. S. Kerr (Columbus, Ohio: Grid, 1979), pp. 3–14; J. Micklethwait and A. Wooldridge, *The Company: A Short History of a Revolutionary Idea* (New York: Random House, 2003).

7. "World's 8 Biggest Employers" (Rediff.com Business, 2009), http://business.rediff.com (accessed March 27, 2010). Other data are from *Fortune* magazine's Global 500, 2009 (accessed March 27, 2010) and Wikipedia entries for the specific companies listed.

8. N. Hooper, "Call Me Irresistable," *Australian Financial Review,* December 5, 2003, p. 38.

9. S. L. Rynes et al., "Behavioral Coursework in Business Education: Growing Evidence of a Legitimacy Crisis," *Academy of Management Learning & Education* 2, no. 3 (2003), pp. 269–83; R. P. Singh and A. G. Schick, "Organizational Behavior: Where Does It Fit in Today's Management Curriculum?" *Journal of Education for Business* 82, no. 6 (July 2007), p. 349.

10. P. R. Lawrence and N. Nohria, *Driven: How Human Nature Shapes Our Choices* (San Francisco: Jossey-Bass, 2002), Chap. 6.

11. P. R. Lawrence "Historical Development of Organizational Behavior," in *Handbook of Organizational Behavior,* ed. L. W. Lorsch (Englewood Cliffs, NJ: Prentice Hall, 1987), pp. 1–9; S. A. Mohrman, C. B. Gibson, and A. M. Mohrman Jr., "Doing Research That Is Useful to Practice: A Model and Empirical Exploration," *Academy of Management Journal* 44 (April 2001), pp. 357–75. For a contrary view, see A. P. Brief and J. M. Dukerich, "Theory in Organizational Behavior: Can It Be Useful?" *Research in Organizational Behavior* 13 (1991), pp. 327–52.

12. M. S. Myers, *Every Employee a Manager* (New York: McGraw-Hill, 1970).

13. B. N. Pfau and I. T. Kay, *The Human Capital Edge* (New York: McGraw-Hill, 2002); I. S. Fulmer, B. Gerhart, and K. S. Scott, "Are the 100 Best Better? An Empirical Investigation of the Relationship between Being a 'Great Place to Work' and Firm Performance," *Personnel Psychology* 56, no. 4 (Winter 2003), pp. 965–93; Y.H. Ling and B.S. Jaw, "The Influence of International Human Capital on Global Initiatives and Financial Performance," *The International Journal of Human Resource Management* 17, no. 3 (2006), pp. 379–98; M. A. West et al., "Reducing Patient Mortality in Hospitals: The Role of Human Resource Management," *Journal of Organizational Behavior* 27, no. 7 (2006), pp. 983–1002. However, one study warns about the direction of causation. Although OB practices seem to predict subsequent firm performance, firm performance also seems to predict the presence of OB practices (such as employee involvement, training, and pay for performance). See P. M. Wright et al., "The Relationship between HR Practices and Firm Performance: Examining Causal Order," *Personnel Psychology* 58, no. 2 (2005), pp. 409–46.

14. For a sample of specific studies of OB practices and share performance, see Deloitte & Touche, *Human Capital ROI Study: Creating Shareholder Value through People* (Toronto: Deloitte & Touche, 2002); D. Wheeler and J. Thomson, *Human Capital Based Investment Criteria for Total Shareholder Returns: A Canadian and International Perspective* (Toronto: Schulich School of Business, York University, June 2004).

15. Mohrman, Gibson, and Mohrman Jr., "Doing Research That Is Useful to Practice: A Model and Empirical Exploration"; J. P. Walsh et al., "On the Relationship between Research and Practice: Debate and Reflections," *Journal of Management Inquiry* 16, no. 2 (June 2007), pp. 128–54. Similarly, in 1961 Harvard business professor Fritz Roethlisberger proposed that the field of OB is concerned with human behavior "from the points of view of both (a) its determination . . . and (b) its improvement." See P. B. Vaill, "F. J. Roethlisberger and the Elusive Phenomena of Organizational Behavior," *Journal of Management Education* 31, no. 3 (June 2007), pp. 321–38.

16. R. H. Hall, "Effectiveness Theory and Organizational Effectiveness," *Journal of Applied Behavioral Science* 16, no. 4 (Oct. 1980), pp. 536–45; K. Cameron, "Organizational Effectiveness: Its Demise and Re-Emergence through Positive Organizational Scholarship," in *Great Minds in Management,* ed. K. G. Smith and M. A. Hitt (New York: Oxford University Press, 2005), pp. 304–30.

17. J. L. Price, "The Study of Organizational Effectiveness," *The Sociological Quarterly* 13 (1972), pp. 3–15.

18. P. Aldhous and P. McKenna, "Hey, Green Spender, Spend a Buck on Me," *New Scientist,* February 20, 2010, pp. 6–9.

19. S. C. Selden and J. E. Sowa, "Testing a Multi-Dimensional Model of Organizational Performance: Prospects and Problems," *Journal of Public Administration Research and Theory* 14, no. 3 (July 2004), pp. 395–416.

20. F. E. Kast and J. E. Rosenweig, "General Systems Theory: Applications for Organization and Management," *Academy of Management Journal* (1972), pp. 447–65; P. M. Senge, *The Fifth Discipline: The Art and Practice of the Learning Organization* (New York: Doubleday Currency, 1990); A. De Geus, *The Living Company* (Boston: Harvard Business School Press, 1997); R. T. Pascale, M. Millemann, and L. Gioja, *Surfing on the Edge of Chaos* (London: Texere, 2000).

21. V. P. Rindova and S. Kotha, "Continuous 'Morphing': Competing through Dynamic Capabilities, Form, and Function," *Academy of Management Journal* 44 (2001), pp. 1263–80; J. McCann, "Organizational Effectiveness: Changing Concepts for Changing

Environments," *Human Resource Planning* 27, no. 1 (2004), pp. 42–50.

22. J. Arlidge, "McJobs That All the Family Can Share," *Daily Telegraph (London),* January 26, 2006, p. 1.

23. C. Ostroff and N. Schmitt, "Configurations of Organizational Effectiveness and Efficiency," *Academy of Management Journal* 36, no. 6 (1993), p. 1345.

24. P. S. Adler et al., "Performance Improvement Capability: Keys to Accelerating Performance Improvement in Hospitals," *California Management Review* 45, no. 2 (2003), pp. 12–33; J. Jamrog, M. Vickers, and D. Bear, "Building and Sustaining a Culture That Supports Innovation," *Human Resource Planning* 29, no. 3 (2006), pp. 9–19.

25. J. O. Bray and P. Watkins, "Technical Change in Corn Production in the United States, 1870–1960," *Journal of Farm Economics* 46, no. 4 (1964), 751–65; U.S. Department of Agriculture, "A History of American Agriculture," (USDA and Utah State University, 2010), http://www.agclassroom.org/gan/timeline/farm_tech.htm (accessed 6 April 2010).

26. G. Huber, "Organizational Learning: The Contributing Processes and Literature," *Organizational Science* 2 (1991), pp. 88–115; D. A. Garvin, *Learning in Action: A Guide to Putting the Learning Organization to Work* (Boston: Harvard Business School Press, 2000); H. Shipton, "Cohesion or Confusion? Towards a Typology for Organizational Learning Research," *International Journal of Management Reviews* 8, no. 4 (2006), pp. 233–52.

27. W. C. Bogner and P. Bansal, "Knowledge Management as the Basis of Sustained High Performance," *Journal of Management Studies* 44, no. 1 (2007), pp. 165–88; D. Jiménez-Jiménez and J. G. Cegarra-Navarro, "The Performance Effect of Organizational Learning and Market Orientation," *Industrial Marketing Management* 36, no. 6 (2007), pp. 694–708.

28. R. Garud and A. Kumaraswamy, "Vicious and Virtuous Circles in the Management of Knowledge: The Case of Infosys Technologies," *MIS Quarterly* 29, no. 1 (March 2005), pp. 9–33.

29. M. Liedtke, "Google vs. Yahoo: Heavyweights Attack from Different Angles," *Associated Press Newswires,* December 18, 2004; R. Basch, "Doing Well by Doing Good," *Searcher Magazine,* January 2005, pp. 18–28; A. Ignatius and L. A. Locke, "In Search of the Real Google," *Time,* February 20, 2006, p. 36.

30. W. Cohen and D. Levinthal, "Absorptive Capacity: A New Perspective on Learning and Innovation," *Administrative Science Quarterly* 35 (1990), pp. 128–52; G. Todorova and B. Durisin, "Absorptive Capacity: Valuing a Reconceptualization," *Academy of Management Review* 32, no. 3 (2007), pp. 774–86.

31. M. Rogers, "Absorptive Capacity and Economic Growth: How Do Countries Catch Up?" *Cambridge Journal of Economics* 28, no. 4 (July 2004), pp. 577–96.

32. T. A. Stewart, *Intellectual Capital: The New Wealth of Organizations* (New York: Currency/Doubleday, 1997); H. Saint-Onge and D. Wallace, *Leveraging Communities of Practice for Strategic Advantage* (Boston: Butterworth-Heinemann, 2003), pp. 9–10; J.-A. Johannessen, B. Olsen, and J. Olaisen, "Intellectual Capital as a Holistic Management Philosophy: A Theoretical Perspective," *International Journal of Information Management* 25, no. 2 (2005), pp. 151–71.

33. M. N. Wexler, "Organizational Memory and Intellectual Capital," *Journal of Intellectual Capital* 3, no. 4 (2002), pp. 393–414.

34. "A Cornerstone for Learning," *T&D,* October 2008, pp. 66–89.

35. M. E. McGill and J. W. Slocum Jr., "Unlearn the Organization," *Organizational Dynamics* 22, no. 2 (1993), pp. 67–79; A. E.

Akgün, G. S. Lynn, and J. C. Byrne, "Antecedents and Consequences of Unlearning in New Product Development Teams," *Journal of Product Innovation Management* 23 (2006), pp. 73–88.

36. P. Lyman et al., *How Much Information? 2003* (Berkeley: Regents of the University of California, October 27, 2003); L. o. Congress, "About the Library" (Washington: Library of Congress, 2010), http://www.loc.gov/about/generalinfo.html (accessed April 2, 2010). For the meaning of data, information, knowledge, and wisdom, see I. Nonaka and H. Takeuchi, *The Knowledge-Creating Company* (New York: Oxford University Press, 1995); T. Davenport et al., "Data to Knowledge to Results: Building an Analytic Capability," *California Management Review* 43, no. 2 (2001), pp. 117–38.

37. J. Pfeffer, *The Human Equation: Building Profits by Putting People First* (Boston: Harvard University Press, 1998); E. Appelbaum et al., *Manufacturing Advantage: Why High-Performance Work Systems Pay Off* (Ithaca, NY: Cornell University Press, 2000); G. S. Benson, S. M. Young, and E. E. Lawler III, "High-Involvement Work Practices and Analysts' Forecasts of Corporate Earnings," *Human Resource Management* 45, no. 4 (2006), pp. 519–37; L. Sels et al., "Unravelling the HRM–Performance Link: Value-Creating and Cost-Increasing Effects of Small Business HRM," *Journal of Management Studies* 43, no. 2 (2006), pp. 319–42.

38. M. A. Huselid, "The Impact of Human Resource Management Practices on Turnover, Productivity, and Corporate," *Academy of Management Journal* 38, no. 3 (1995), p. 635; B. E. Becker and M. A. Huselid, "Strategic Human Resources Management: Where Do We Go from Here?" *Journal of Management* 32, no. 6 (December 2006), pp. 898–925; J. Combs et al., "How Much Do High-Performance Work Practices Matter? A Meta-Analysis of Their Effects on Organizational Performance," *Personnel Psychology* 59, no. 3 (2006), pp. 501–28.

39. J. Barney, "Firm Resources and Sustained Competitive Advantage," *Journal of Management* 17, no. 1 (1991), pp. 99–120.

40. E. E. Lawler III, S. A. Mohrman, and G. E. Ledford Jr., *Strategies for High Performance Organizations* (San Francisco: Jossey-Bass, 1998); S. H. Wagner, C. P. Parker, and D. Neil, "Employees That Think and Act Like Owners: Effects of Ownership Beliefs and Behaviors on Organizational Effectiveness," *Personnel Psychology* 56, no. 4 (Winter 2003), pp. 847–71; P. J. Gollan, "High Involvement Management and Human Resource Sustainability: The Challenges and Opportunities," *Asia Pacific Journal of Human Resources* 43, no. 1 (April 2005), pp. 18–33; Y. Liu et al., "The Value of Human Resource Management for Organizational Performance," *Business Horizons* 50 (2007), pp. 503–11; P. Tharenou, A. M. Saks, and C. Moore, "A Review and Critique of Research on Training and Organizational-Level Outcomes," *Human Resource Management Review* 17, no. 3 (2007), pp. 251–73.

41. S. Fleetwood and A. Hesketh, "HRM-Performance Research: Under-Theorized and Lacking Explanatory Power," *International Journal of Human Resource Management* 17, no. 12 (December 2006), pp. 1977–93.

42. J. Godard, "High Performance and the Transformation of Work? The Implications of Alternative Work Practices for the Experience and Outcomes of Work," *Industrial and Labor Relations Review* 54, no. 4 (July 2001), pp. 776–805; G. Murray et al., eds., *Work and Employment Relations in the High-Performance Workplace* (London: Continuum, 2002); B. Harley, "Hope or Hype? High Performance Work Systems," in *Participation and Democracy at Work: Essays in Honour of*

Harvie Ramsay, ed. B. Harley, J. Hyman, and P. Thompson (Houndsmills, UK: Palgrave Macmillan, 2005), pp. 38–54.

43. A. L. Friedman and S. Miles, *Stakeholders: Theory and Practice* (New York: Oxford University Press, 2006); M. L. Barnett, "Stakeholder Influence Capacity and the Variability of Financial Returns to Corporate Social Responsibility," *Academy of Management Review* 32, no. 3 (2007), pp. 794–816; R. E. Freeman, J. S. Harrison, and A. C. Wicks, *Managing for Stakeholders: Survival, Reputation, and Success* (New Haven, CT: Yale University Press, 2007).

44. C. Eden and F. Ackerman, *Making Strategy: The Journey of Strategic Management* (London: Sage, 1998).

45. T. A. Hemphill, "Rejuvenating Wal-Mart's Reputation," *Business Horizons* 48, no. 1 (2005), pp. 11–21; A. Bianco, *The Bully of Bentonville: How the High Cost of Wal-Mart's Everyday Low Prices Is Hurting America* (New York: Random House, 2006); C. Fishman, *The Wal-Mart Effect* (New York: Penguin, 2006). For a description of Walmart's recent corrective actions on environmentalism, see E. L. Plambeck and L. Denend, "Wal-Mart," *Stanford Social Innovation Review* 6, no. 2 (Spring 2008), pp. 53–59.

46. G. R. Salancik and J. Pfeffer, *The External Control of Organizations: A Resource Dependence Perspective* (New York: Harper & Row, 1978); T. Casciaro and M. J. Piskorski, "Power Imbalance, Mutual Dependence, and Constraint Absorption: A Closer Look at Dependence Theory," *Administrative Science Quarterly* 50 (2005), pp. 167–99; N. Roome and F. Wijen, "Stakeholder Power and Organizational Learning in Corporate Environmental Management," *Organization Studies* 27, no. 2 (2005), pp. 235–63.

47. R. E. Freeman, A. C. Wicks, and B. Parmar, "Stakeholder Theory and 'the Corporate Objective Revisited'," *Organization Science* 15, no. 3 (May–June 2004), pp. 364–69; D. Balser and J. McClusky, "Managing Stakeholder Relationships and Nonprofit Organization Effectiveness," *Nonprofit Management & Leadership* 15, no. 3 (Spring 2005), pp. 295–315; Friedman and Miles, *Stakeholders: Theory and Practice,* Chap. 3.

48. B. M. Meglino and E. C. Ravlin, "Individual Values in Organizations: Concepts, Controversies, and Research," *Journal of Management* 24, no. 3 (1998), pp. 351–89; B. R. Agle and C. B. Caldwell, "Understanding Research on Values in Business," *Business and Society* 38, no. 3 (September 1999), pp. 326–87; A. Bardi and S. H. Schwartz, "Values and Behavior: Strength and Structure of Relations," *Personality and Social Psychology Bulletin* 29, no. 10 (October 2003), pp. 1207–20; S. Hitlin and J. A. Pilavin, "Values: Reviving a Dormant Concept," *Annual Review of Sociology* 30 (2004), pp. 359–93.

49. K. Kernaghan, "Integrating Values into Public Service: The Values Statement as Centrepiece," *Public Administration Review* 63, no. 6 (November/December 2003), pp. 711–19. Some popular books that emphasize the importance of values include J. C. Collins and J. I. Porras, *Built to Last: Successful Habits of Visionary Companies* (London: Century, 1995); C. A. O'Reilly III and J. Pfeffer, *Hidden Value* (Cambridge, MA: Harvard Business School Press, 2000); R. Barrett, *Building a Values-Driven Organization: A Whole System Approach to Cultural Transformation* (Burlington, MA: Butterworth-Heinemann, 2006); J. M. Kouzes and B. Z. Posner, *The Leadership Challenge,* 4th ed. (San Francisco: Jossey-Bass, 2007).

50. Aspen Institute, *Where Will They Lead? MBA Student Attitudes about Business & Society* (Washington, DC: Aspen Institute, April 2008).

51. M. van Marrewijk, "Concepts and Definitions of CSR and Corporate Sustainability: Between Agency and Communion," *Journal of Business Ethics* 44 (May 2003), pp. 95–105; Barnett, "Stakeholder Influence Capacity and the Variability of Financial Returns to Corporate Social Responsibility."

52. L. S. Paine, *Value Shift* (New York: McGraw-Hill, 2003); A. Mackey, T. B. Mackey, and J. B. Barney, "Corporate Social Responsibility and Firm Performance: Investor Preferences and Corporate Strategies," *Academy of Management Review* 32, no. 3 (2007), pp. 817–35.

53. S. Zadek, *The Civil Corporation: The New Economy of Corporate Citizenship* (London: Earthscan, 2001); S. Hart and M. Milstein, "Creating Sustainable Value," *Academy of Management Executive* 17, no. 2 (2003), pp. 56–69.

54. D. McGinn, "The Greenest Big Companies in America," *Newsweek,* September 28, 2009, pp. 34–54.

55. "Canadians Inclined to Punish Companies Deemed Socially Irresponsible, Study Suggests," *Canadian Press,* April 23, 2005; M. Johne, "Show Us the Green, Workers Say," *Globe & Mail,* October 10, 2007, p. C1; Aspen Institute, *Where Will They Lead? MBA Student Attitudes about Business & Society;* "1/3 of American Workers More Inclined to Work for a "Green" Company," Adecco news release (New York: September 29, 2009).

56. A. Fox, "Corporate Social Responsibility Pays Off," *HRMagazine* 52, no. 8 (August 2007), pp. 42–47.

57. J. P. Campbell, "The Definition and Measurement of Performance in the New Age," in *The Changing Nature of Performance: Implications for Staffing, Motivation, and Development,* ed. D. R. Ilgen and E. D. Pulakos (San Francisco: Jossey-Bass, 1999), pp. 399–429; R. D. Hackett, "Understanding and Predicting Work Performance in the Canadian Military," *Canadian Journal of Behavioural Science* 34, no. 2 (2002), pp. 131–40.

58. D. W. Organ, "Organizational Citizenship Behavior: It's Construct Clean-up Time," *Human Performance* 10 (1997), pp. 85–97; S. J. Motowidlo, "Some Basic Issues Related to Contextual Performance and Organizational Citizenship Behavior in Human Resource Management," *Human Resource Management Review* 10, no. 1 (2000), pp. 115–26; J. A. LePine, A. Erez, and D. E. Johnson, "The Nature and Dimensionality of Organizational Citizenship Behavior: A Critical Review and Meta-Analysis," *Journal of Applied Psychology* 87 (February 2002), pp. 52–65.

59. K. Lee and N. J. Allen, "Organizational Citizenship Behavior and Workplace Deviance: The Role of Affect and Cognitions," *Journal of Applied Psychology* 87, no. 1 (2002), pp. 131–42.

60. M. Rotundo and P. Sackett, "The Relative Importance of Task, Citizenship, and Counterproductive Performance to Global Ratings of Job Performance: A Policy-Capturing Approach," *Journal of Applied Psychology* 87 (February 2002), pp. 66–80; and P. D. Dunlop and K. Lee, "Workplace Deviance, Organizational Citizenship Behaviour, and Business Unit Performance: The Bad Apples Do Spoil the Whole Barrel," *Journal of Organizational Behavior* 25 (2004), pp. 67–80.

61. Watson Wyatt, "U.S. Workers City Hypocrisy and Favoritism— Rather Than Financial Misdeeds—as Biggest Ethical Lapses at Work," Watson Wyatt News release (Washington, DC: January 12, 2005); Watson Wyatt, *WorkCanada 2004/2005—Pursuing Productive Engagement* (Toronto: Watson Wyatt, January 2005).

62. P. W. Singer, "Meet the Sims . . . and Shoot Them," *Foreign Policy* (March/April 2010).

63. "One in Four Working Malaysians Say Work Has Negative Impact on Health," *Bernama Daily Malaysian News,* December 10, 2008; M. Fahmy, "Survey Says Work Really Is Hazardous to Your Health," *Reuters (London),* December 5, 2008.

64. D. A. Harrison and J. J. Martocchio, "Time for Absenteeism: A 20-Year Review of Origins, Offshoots, and Outcomes," *Journal of Management* 24 (Spring 1998), pp. 305–50; C. M. Mason and M. A. Griffin, "Group Absenteeism and Positive Affective Tone: A Longitudinal Study," *Journal of Organizational Behavior* 24 (2003), pp. 667–87; A. Vaananen et al., "Job Characteristics, Physical and Psychological Symptoms, and Social Support as Antecedents of Sickness Absence among Men and Women in the Private Industrial Sector," *Social Science & Medicine* 57, no. 5 (2003), pp. 807–24.

65. N. Chaudhury et al., "Missing in Action: Teacher and Health Worker Absence in Developing Countries," *The Journal of Economic Perspectives* 20, no. 1 (2006), pp. 91–116.

66. S. Fischer, "Globalization and Its Challenges," *American Economic Review* (May 2003), pp. 1–29. For discussion of the diverse meanings of *globalization,* see M. F. Guillén, "Is Globalization Civilizing, Destructive or Feeble? A Critique of Five Key Debates in the Social Science Literature," *Annual Review of Sociology* 27 (2001), pp. 235–60.

67. The ongoing debate regarding the advantages and disadvantages of globalization is discussed in Guillén, "Is Globalization Civilizing, Destructive or Feeble?"; D. Doane, "Can Globalization Be Fixed?" *Business Strategy Review* 13, no. 2 (2002), pp. 51–58; J. Bhagwati, *In Defense of Globalization* (New York: Oxford University Press, 2004); and M. Wolf, *Why Globalization Works* (New Haven, CT: Yale University Press, 2004).

68. K. Ohmae, *The Next Global Stage* (Philadelphia: Wharton School Publishing, 2005).

69. R. House, M. Javidan, and P. Dorfman, "Project GLOBE: An Introduction," *Applied Psychology: An International Journal* 50 (2001), pp. 489–505; M. A. Von Glinow, E. A. Drost, and M. B. Teagarden, "Converging on IHRM Best Practices: Lessons Learned from a Globally Distributed Consortium on Theory and Practice," *Human Resource Management* 41, no. 1 (April 2002), pp. 123–40; M. M. Javidan et al., "In the Eye of the Beholder: Cross Cultural Lessons in Leadership from Project GLOBE," *Academy of Management Perspectives* 20, no. 1 (February 2006), pp. 67–90.

70. "For the Second Time in Three Years Verizon Ranked No. 1 on Diversityinc Magazine's List of Top 50 Companies for Diversity," PR Newswire News release (New York: April 2, 2008); Verizon, *Doing the Work: 2007 Verizon Corporate Responsibility Report* (New York: Verizon, 2008).

71. M. F. Riche, "America's Diversity and Growth: Signposts for the 21st Century," *Population Bulletin* (June 2000), pp. 3–43; U.S. Census Bureau, *Statistical Abstract of the United States: 2004–2005* (Washington: U.S. Census Bureau, May 2005).

72. D. A. Harrison et al., "Time, Teams, and Task Performance: Changing Effects of Surface- and Deep-Level Diversity on Group Functioning," *Academy of Management Journal* 45, no. 5 (2002), pp. 1029–46.

73. R. Zemke, C. Raines, and B. Filipczak, *Generations at Work: Managing the Clash of Veterans, Boomers, Xers, and Nexters in Your Workplace* (New York: Amacom, 2000); M. R. Muetzel, *They're Not Aloof, Just Generation X* (Shreveport, LA: Steel Bay, 2003); S. H. Applebaum, M. Serena, and B. T. Shapiro, "Generation X and the Boomers: Organizational Myths and Literary Realities," *Management Research News* 27, no. 11/12

(2004), pp. 1–28; N. Howe and W. Strauss, "The Next 20 Years: How Customer and Workforce Attitudes Will Evolve," *Harvard Business Review* (July–August 2007), pp. 41–52.

74. U.S. Bureau of Labor Statistics, *Household Data, Annual Averages: Employment Status of the Civilian Noninstitutional Population by Age, Sex, and Race* (Washington, DC: U.S. Bureau of Labor Statistics, 2010).

75. O. C. Richard, "Racial Diversity, Business Strategy, and Firm Performance: A Resource-Based View," *Academy of Management Journal* 43 (2000), pp. 164–77; D. D. Frink et al., "Gender Demography and Organization Performance: A Two-Study Investigation with Convergence," *Group & Organization Management* 28 (March 2003), pp. 127–47; T. Kochan et al., "The Effects of Diversity on Business Performance: Report of the Diversity Research Network," *Human Resource Management* 42 (2003), pp. 3–21; R. J. Burke and E. Ng, "The Changing Nature of Work and Organizations: Implications for Human Resource Management," *Human Resource Management Review* 16 (2006), pp. 86–94.

76. D. Porras, D. Psihountas, and M. Griswold, "The Long-Term Performance of Diverse Firms," *International Journal of of Diversity* 6, no. 1 (2006), pp. 25–34; R. A. Weigand, "Organizational Diversity, Profits and Returns in U.S. Firms," *Problems & Perspectives in Management,* no. 3 (2007), pp. 69–83.

77. C. Hymowitz, "The New Diversity," *The Wall Street Journal,* November 14, 2005, p. R1.

78. R. J. Ely and D. A. Thomas, "Cultural Diversity at Work: The Effects of Diversity Perspectives on Work Group Processes and Outcomes," *Administrative Science Quarterly* 46 (June 2001), pp. 229–73; Kochan et al., "The Effects of Diversity on Business Performance: Report of the Diversity Research Network"; D. van Knippenberg and S. A. Haslam, "Realizing the Diversity Dividend: Exploring the Subtle Interplay between Identity, Ideology and Reality," in *Social Identity at Work: Developing Theory for Organizational Practice,* ed. S. A. Haslam et al. (New York: Taylor and Francis, 2003), pp. 61–80; D. van Knippenberg, C. K. W. De Dreu, and A. C. Homan, "Work Group Diversity and Group Performance: An Integrative Model and Research Agenda," *Journal of Applied Psychology* 89, no. 6 (2004), pp. 1008–22; E. Molleman, "Diversity in Demographic Characteristics, Abilities and Personality Traits: Do Faultlines Affect Team Functioning?" *Group Decision and Negotiation* 14, no. 3 (2005), pp. 173–93.

79. A. Birritteri, "Workplace Diversity: Realizing the Benefits of an All-Inclusive Employee Base," *New Jersey Business,* November 2005, p. 36.

80. W. G. Bennis and R. J. Thomas, *Geeks and Geezers* (Boston: Harvard Business School Press, 2002), pp. 74–79; E. D. Y. Greenblatt, "Work/Life Balance: Wisdom or Whining," *Organizational Dynamics* 31, no. 2 (2002), pp. 177–93.

81. M. Conlin, "The Easiest Commute of All," *BusinessWeek,* December 12, 2005, p. 78.

82. WorldatWork, *Telework Trendlines 2006* (Scottsdale, AZ: WorldatWork, August 2006); WorldatWork, *Telework Trendlines 2009* (Scottsdale, AZ: WorldatWork, February 2009).

83. "AT&T Telecommute Survey Indicates Productivity Is Up," AT&T news release (New York: August 6, 2002); L. Duxbury and C. Higgins, "Telecommute: A Primer for the Millennium Introduction," in *The New World of Work: Challenges and Opportunities,* ed. C. L. Cooper and R. J. Burke (Oxford: Blackwell, 2002), pp. 157–99; V. Illegems and A. Verbeke, "Telework: What Does It Mean for Management?" *Long Range*

Planning 37 (2004), pp. 319–34; S. Raghuram and B. Wiesenfeld, "Work–Nonwork Conflict and Job Stress among Virtual Workers," *Human Resource Management* 43, no. 2/3 (Summer/Fall 2004), pp. 259–77.

84. D. E. Bailey and N. B. Kurland, "A Review of Telework Research: Findings, New Directions, and Lessons for the Study of Modern Work," *Journal of Organizational Behavior* 23 (2002), pp. 383–400; D. W. McCloskey and M. Igbaria, "Does 'Out of Sight' Mean 'Out of Mind'? An Empirical Investigation of the Career Advancement Prospects of Telecommuters," *Information Resources Management Journal* 16 (April–June 2003), pp. 19–34; Sensis, *Sensis® Insights Report: Teleworking* (Melbourne: Sensis, June 2005).

85. M. N. Zald, "More Fragmentation? Unfinished Business in Linking the Social Sciences and the Humanities," *Administrative Science Quarterly* 41 (1996), pp. 251–61. Concerns about the "trade deficit" in OB are raised in C. Heath and S. B. Sitkin, "Big-B versus Big-O: What Is Organizational about Organizational Behavior?" *Journal of Organizational Behavior* 22 (2001), pp. 43–58.

86. J. Pfeffer and R. I. Sutton, *Hard Facts, Dangerous Half-Truths, and Total Nonsense* (Boston: Harvard Business School Press, 2006); D. M. Rousseau and S. McCarthy, "Educating Managers from an Evidence-Based Perspective," *Academy of Management Learning & Education* 6, no. 1 (2007), pp. 84–101.

87. Pfeffer and Sutton, *Hard Facts, Dangerous Half-Truths, and Total Nonsense*.

88. C. M. Christensen and M. E. Raynor, "Why Hard-Nosed Executives Should Care about Management Theory," *Harvard Business Review* (September 2003), pp. 66–74. For an excellent critique of the "one best way" approach in early management scholarship, see P. F. Drucker, "Management's New Paradigms," *Forbes* (October 5 1998), pp. 152–77.

89. H. L. Tosi and J. W. Slocum Jr., "Contingency Theory: Some Suggested Directions," *Journal of Management* 10 (1984), pp. 9–26.

90. D. M. Rousseau and R. J. House, "Meso Organizational Behavior: Avoiding Three Fundamental Biases," in *Trends in Organizational Behavior,* ed. C. L. Cooper and D. M. Rousseau (Chichester, UK: John Wiley & Sons, 1994), pp. 13–30.

CHAPTER 2

1. J. Becker and L. Layton, "Safety Warnings Often Ignored at Metro," *Washington Post,* June 6, 2005, p. A01; M. Ahlers, "NTSB Says Train Detection System Failed in Days before D.C. Crash," *CNN,* July 1, 2009; D. Stroup, "The Price of Safety: Parts I and II," *District Daily (Washington, D.C.),* October 11 and 17, 2009.

2. L. L. Thurstone, "Ability, Motivation, and Speed," *Psychometrika* 2, no. 4 (1937), pp. 249–54; N. R. F. Maier, *Psychology in Industry,* 2nd ed. (Boston: Houghton Mifflin Company, 1955); V. H. Vroom, *Work and Motivation* (New York: John Wiley & Sons, 1964); J. P. Campbell et al., *Managerial Behavior, Performance, and Effectiveness* (New York: McGraw-Hill, 1970).

3. E. E. I. Lawler and L. W. Porter, "Antecedent Attitudes of Effective Managerial Performance," *Organizational Behavior and Human Performance* 2 (1967), pp. 122–42; M. A. Griffin, A. Neal, and S. K. Parker, "A New Model of Work Role Performance: Positive Behavior in Uncertain and Interdependent Contexts," *Academy of Management Journal* 50, no. 2 (April 2007), pp. 327–47.

4. Only a few literature reviews have included all four factors. These include J. P. Campbell and R. D. Pritchard, "Motivation Theory in Industrial and Organizational Psychology," in *Handbook of Industrial and Organizational Psychology,* ed. M. D. Dunnette (Chicago: Rand McNally, 1976), pp. 62–130; T. R. Mitchell, "Motivation: New Directions for Theory, Research, and Practice," *Academy of Management review* 7, no. 1 (January 1982), pp. 80–88; G. A. J. Churchill et al., "The Determinants of Salesperson Performance: A Meta-Analysis," *Journal of Marketing Research (JMR)* 22, no. 2 (1985), pp. 103–18; R. E. Plank and D. A. Reid, "The Mediating Role of Sales Behaviors: An Alternative Perspective of Sales Performance and Effectiveness," *Journal of Personal Selling & Sales Management* 14, no. 3 (Summer 1994), pp. 43–56. The MARS acronym was coined by senior officers in the Singapore armed forces. Chris Perryer at the University of Western Australia suggests the full model should be called the "MARS BAR" because the outcomes might be labeled "behavior and results"!

5. Technically, the model proposes that situation factors moderate the effects of the three within-person factors. For instance, the effect of employee motivation on behavior and performance depends on (is moderated by) the situation.

6. C. C. Pinder, *Work Motivation in Organizational Behavior* (Upper Saddle River, NJ: Prentice-Hall, 1998); G. P. Latham and C. C. Pinder, "Work Motivation Theory and Research at the Dawn of the Twenty-First Century," *Annual Review of Psychology* 56 (2005), pp. 485–516.

7. T. J. Watson Jr., *A Business and Its Beliefs* (New York: McGraw-Hill, 2003, 1963), p. 4.

8. L. M. Spencer and S. M. Spencer, *Competence at Work: Models for Superior Performance* (New York: Wiley, 1993); R. Kurz and D. Bartram, "Competency and Individual Performance: Modelling the World of Work," in *Organizational Effectiveness: The Role of Psychology,* ed. I. T. Robertson, M. Callinan, and D. Bartram (Chichester, UK: John Wiley & Sons, 2002), pp. 227–58; D. Bartram, "The Great Eight Competencies: A Criterion-Centric Approach to Validation," *Journal of Applied Psychology* 90, no. 6 (2005), pp. 1185–1203; H. Heinsman et al., "Competencies through the Eyes of Psychologists: A Closer Look at Assessing Competencies," *International Journal of Selection and Assessment* 15, no. 4 (December 2007), pp. 412–27.

9. U.S. Department of Health and Human Services, *HHS Competency Framework* (Washington, DC: U.S. Department of Health and Human Services, 2007).

10. P. Tharenou, A. M. Saks, and C. Moore, "A Review and Critique of Research on Training and Organizational-Level Outcomes," *Human Resource Management Review* 17, no. 3 (2007), pp. 251–73; T. W. H. Ng and D. C. Feldman, "How Broadly Does Education Contribute to Job Performance?" *Personnel Psychology* 62, no. 1 (Spring 2009), pp. 89–134.

11. M. Johnson and C. Roebuck, "Nurturing a New Kind of Capital," *Financial Executive,* July 2008, p. 32.

12. Canada Newswire, "Canadian Organizations Must Work Harder to Productively Engage Employees," news release, January 25, 2005.

13. K. F. Kane, "Special Issue: Situational Constraints and Work Performance," *Human Resource Management Review* 3 (Summer 1993), pp. 83–175; S. B. Bacharach and P. Bamberger, "Beyond Situational Constraints: Job Resources Inadequacy and Individual Performance at Work," *Human Resource Management Review* 5, no. 2 (1995), pp. 79–102; G. Johns, "Commentary: In Praise of Context," *Journal of Organizational Behavior* 22 (2001), pp. 31–42.

14. Personality researchers agree on one point about the definition of personality: it is difficult to pin down. A definition necessarily captures one perspective of the topic more than others, and the concept of personality is itself broad. The definition presented here is based on C. S. Carver and M. F. Scheier, *Perspectives on Personality,* 6th ed. (Boston: Allyn & Bacon, 2007); and D. C. Funder, *The Personality Puzzle,* 4th ed. (New York: W. W. Norton & Company, 2007).

15. C. M. Schwab, *Ten Commandments of Success: An Interview,* by B. C. Forbes with Charles M. Schwab (Chicago: La Salle Extension University, 1920).

16. D. P. McAdams and J. L. Pals, "A New Big Five: Fundamental Principles for an Integrative Science of Personality," *American Psychologist* 61, no. 3 (2006), pp. 204–17.

17. B. Reynolds and K. Karraker, "A Big Five Model of Disposition and Situation Interaction: Why a 'Helpful' Person May Not Always Behave Helpfully," *New Ideas in Psychology* 21 (April 2003), pp. 1–13; W. Mischel, "Toward an Integrative Science of the Person," *Annual Review of Psychology* 55 (2004), pp. 1–22.

18. B. W. Roberts and A. Caspi, "Personality Development and the Person–Situation Debate: It's Déjà Vu All Over Again," *Psychological Inquiry* 12, no. 2 (2001), pp. 104–9.

19. K. L. Jang, W. J. Livesley, and P. A. Vernon, "Heritability of the Big Five Personality Dimensions and Their Facets: A Twin Study," *Journal of Personality* 64, no. 3 (1996), pp. 577–91; N. L. Segal, *Entwined Lives: Twins and What They Tell Us about Human Behavior* (New York: Plume, 2000); T. Bouchard and J. Loehlin, "Genes, Evolution, and Personality," *Behavior Genetics* 31, no. 3 (May 2001), pp. 243–73; G. Lensvelt-Mulders and J. Hettema, "Analysis of Genetic Influences on the Consistency and Variability of the Big Five across Different Stressful Situations," *European Journal of Personality* 15, no. 5 (2001), pp. 355–71; P. Borkenau et al., "Genetic and Environmental Influences on Person X Situation Profiles," *Journal of Personality* 74, no. 5 (2006), pp. 1451–80.

20. Segal, *Entwined Lives,* 116–18. For critiques of the genetics perspective of personality, see J. Joseph, "Separated Twins and the Genetics of Personality Differences: A Critique," *American Journal of Psychology* 114, no. 1 (Spring 2001), pp. 1–30; and P. Ehrlich and M. W. Feldman, "Genes, Environments & Behaviors," *Daedalus* 136, no. 2 (Spring 2007), pp. 5–12.

21. B. W. Roberts and W. F. DelVecchio, "The Rank-Order Consistency of Personality Traits from Childhood to Old Age: A Quantitative Review of Longitudinal Studies," *Psychological Bulletin* 126, no. 1 (2000), pp. 3–25; A. Terracciano, P. T. Costa, and R. R. McCrae, "Personality Plasticity after Age 30," *Personality and Social Psychology Bulletin* 32, no. 8 (August 2006), pp. 999–1009.

22. M. Jurado and M. Rosselli, "The Elusive Nature of Executive Functions: A Review of Our Current Understanding," *Neuropsychology Review* 17, no. 3 (2007), pp. 213–33.

23. B. W. Roberts and E. M. Pomerantz, "On Traits, Situations, and Their Integration: A Developmental Perspective," *Personality & Social Psychology Review* 8, no. 4 (2004), pp. 402–16; W. Fleeson, "Situation-Based Contingencies Underlying Trait-Content Manifestation in Behavior," *Journal of Personality* 75, no. 4 (2007), pp. 825–62.

24. J. M. Digman, "Personality Structure: Emergence of the Five-Factor Model," *Annual Review of Psychology* 41 (1990), pp. 417–40; O. P. John and S. Srivastava, "The Big Five Trait Taxonomy: History, Measurement, and Theoretical Perspectives," in *Handbook of Personality: Theory and Research,* ed. L. A. Pervin and O. P. John (New York: Guildford Press, 1999), pp. 102–38; A. Caspi, B. W. Roberts, and R. L. Shiner, "Personality Development: Stability and Change," *Annual Review of Psychology* 56, no. 1 (2005), pp. 453–84; McAdams and Pals, "A New Big Five: Fundamental Principles for an Integrative Science of Personality,"

25. S. J. Rubenzer, T. R. Faschingbauer, and D. S. Ones, "Assessing the U.S. Presidents Using the Revised Neo Personality Inventory," *Assessment* 7, no. 4 (December 2000), pp. 403–19.

26. J. Hogan and B. Holland, "Using Theory to Evaluate Personality and Job-Performance Relations: A Socioanalytic Perspective," *Journal of Applied Psychology* 88, no. 1 (2003), pp. 100–12; D. S. Ones, C. Viswesvaran, and S. Dilchert, "Personality at Work: Raising Awareness and Correcting Misconceptions," *Human Performance* 18, no. 4 (2005), pp. 389–404.

27. G. D. Steel et al., "People in High Latitudes: The "Big Five" Personality Characteristics of the Circumpolar Sojourner," *Environment and Behavior* 29, no. 3 (May 1, 1997), pp. 324–47; D. M. Musson et al., "Personality Testing in Antarctic Expeditioners; Cross Cultural Comparisons and Evidence for Generalizability," paper presented at 53rd International Astronautical Congress, The World Space Congress, Houston, October 10–19, 2002; A. Sarris, "Personality, Culture Fit, and Job Outcomes on Australian Antarctic Stations," *Environment and Behavior* 38, no. 3 (May 2006), pp. 356–72; L. A. Palinkas and P. Suedfeld, "Psychological Effects of Polar Expeditions," *The Lancet* 371, no. 9607 (January 18, 2008), pp. 153–63.

28. M. R. Barrick and M. K. Mount, "Yes, Personality Matters: Moving on to More Important Matters," *Human Performance* 18, no. 4 (2005), pp. 359–72.

29. M. R. Barrick, M. K. Mount, and T. A. Judge, "Personality and Performance at the Beginning of the New Millennium: What Do We Know and Where Do We Go Next?" *International Journal of Selection and Assessment* 9, no. 1&2 (2001), pp. 9–30; T. A. Judge and R. Ilies, "Relationship of Personality to Performance Motivation: A Meta-Analytic Review," *Journal of Applied Psychology* 87, no. 4 (2002), pp. 797–807; A. Witt, L. A. Burke, and M. R. Barrick, "The Interactive Effects of Conscientiousness and Agreeableness on Job Performance," *Journal of Applied Psychology* 87 (February 2002), pp. 164–69; J. Moutafi, A. Furnham, and J. Crump, "Is Managerial Level Related to Personality?" *British Journal of Management* 18, no. 3 (2007), pp. 272–80.

30. K. M. DeNeve and H. Cooper, "The Happy Personality: A Meta-Analysis of 137 Personality Traits and Subjective Well-Being," *Psychological Bulletin* 124 (September 1998), pp. 197–229; R. Ilies, M. W. Gerhardt, and H. Le, "Individual Differences in Leadership Emergence: Integrating Meta-Analytic Findings and Behavioral Genetics Estimates," *International Journal of Selection and Assessment* 12, no. 3 (September 2004), pp. 207–19; B. Kozak, J. Strelau, and J. N. V. Miles, "Genetic Determinants of Individual Differences in Coping Styles," *Anxiety, Stress & Coping* 18, no. 1 (March 2005), pp. 1–15.

31. C. G. Jung, *Psychological Types,* trans. H. G. Baynes (Princeton, NJ: Princeton University Press, 1971); I. B. Myers, *The Myers-Briggs Type Indicator* (Palo Alto, CA: Consulting Psychologists Press, 1987).

32. Adapted from an exhibit found at http://www.16-personality-types.com.

33. M. Gladwell, "Personality Plus," *New Yorker,* September 20, 2004, pp. 42–48; R. B. Kennedy and D. A. Kennedy, "Using the Myers-Briggs Type Indicator in Career Counseling," *Journal of Employment Counseling* 41, no. 1 (March 2004), pp. 38–44.

34. K. M. Butler, "Using Positive Four-Letter Words," *Employee Benefit News,* April 2007; M. Weinstein, "Personality Assessment Soars at Southwest," *Training,* January 3 2008.

35. W. L. Johnson et al., "A Higher Order Analysis of the Factor Structure of the Myers-Briggs Type Indicator," *Measurement and Evaluation in Counseling and Development* 34 (July 2001), pp. 96–108; R. M. Capraro and M. M. Capraro, "Myers-Briggs Type Indicator Score Reliability across Studies: A Meta-Analytic Reliability Generalization Study," *Educational and Psychological Measurement* 62 (August 2002), pp. 590–602; J. Michael, "Using the Myers-Briggs Type Indicator as a Tool for Leadership Development? Apply with Caution," *Journal of Leadership & Organizational Studies* 10 (Summer 2003), pp. 68–81.

36. R. R. McCrae and P. T. Costa, "Reinterpreting the Myers-Briggs Type Indicators Form the Perspective of the Five-Factor Model of Personality," *Journal of Personality* 57 (1989), pp. 17–40; A. Furnham, "The Big Five Versus the Big Four: The Relationship between the Myers-Briggs Type Indicator (MBTI) and NEO-PI Five Factor Model of Personality," *Personality and Individual Differences* 21, no. 2 (1996), pp. 303–7.

37. R. Hogan, "In Defense of Personality Measurement: New Wine for Old Whiners," *Human Performance* 18, no. 4 (2005), pp. 331–41; K. Murphy and J. L. Dzieweczynski, "Why Don't Measures of Broad Dimensions of Personality Perform Better as Predictors of Job Performance?" *Human Performance* 18, no. 4 (2005), pp. 343–57; F. P. Morgeson et al., "Reconsidering the Use of Personality Tests in Personnel Selection Contexts," *Personnel Psychology* 60, no. 3 (2007), pp. 683–729; R. P. Tett and C. N. D., "Personality Tests at the Crossroads: A Response to Morgeson, Campion, Dipboye, Hollenbeck, Murphy, and Schmitt (2007)," *Personnel Psychology* 60, no. 4 (2007), pp. 967–93.

38. H. Tatham, "Conforming or Conscientious?" *New Zealand Management,* May 2008, pp. 60–65.

39. V. Baker, "Why Men Can't Manage Women," *The Guardian,* April 14, 2007, p. 1.

40. J. D. Campbell, S. Assanand, and A. Di Paula, "The Structure of the Self-Concept and Its Relation to Psychological Adjustment," *Journal of Personality* 71, no. 1 (2003), pp. 115–40; M. J. Constantino et al., "The Direct and Stress-Buffering Effects of Self-Organization on Psychological Adjustment," *Journal of Social & Clinical Psychology* 25, no. 3 (2006), pp. 333–60.

41. C. Sedikides and A. P. Gregg, "Portraits of the Self," in *The Sage Handbook of Social Psychology,* ed. M. A. Hogg and J. Cooper (London: Sage Publications, 2003), pp. 110–38; M. R. Leary, "Motivational and Emotional Aspects of the Self," *Annual Review of Psychology* 58, no. 1 (2007), pp. 317–44.

42. D. A. Moore, "Not So Above Average after All: When People Believe They Are Worse Than Average and Its Implications for Theories of Bias in Social Comparison," *Organizational Behavior and Human Decision Processes* 102, no. 1 (2007), pp. 42–58.

43. D. A. Moore and P. J. Healy, "The Trouble with Overconfidence," *Psychological Review* 115, no. 2 (2008), pp. 502–17.

44. N. J. Hiller and D. C. Hambrick, "Conceptualizing Executive Hubris: The Role of (Hyper-)Core Self-Evaluations in Strategic Decision-Making," *Strategic Management Journal* 26, no. 4 (2005), pp. 297–319; U. Malmendier and G. Tate, "CEO Overconfidence and Corporate Investment," *The Journal of Finance* 60, no. 6 (2005), pp. 2661–700; J. A. Doukas and D. Petmezas, "Acquisitions, Overconfident Managers and Self-Attribution Bias," *European Financial Management* 13, no. 3 (2007), pp. 531–77.

45. "New Worldatwork Survey: Trends in Employee Recognition 2008," WorldatWork news release (Scottsdale, AZ: April 23, 2008); A. Gostick and C. Elton, *The Carrot Principle,* reissued ed. (New York: Free Press, 2009). The WorldatWork survey provided the percentage of companies with recognition programs. Other statistics are from the Gostick and Elton book.

46. W. B. Swann Jr., "To Be Adored or to Be Known? The Interplay of Self-Enhancement and Self-Verification," in *Foundations of Social Behavior,* ed. R. M. Sorrentino and E. T. Higgins (New York: Guildford, 1990), pp. 408–48; W. B. Swann Jr., P. J. Rentfrow, and J. S. Guinn, "Self-Verification: The Search for Coherence," in *Handbook of Self and Identity,* ed. M. R. Leary and J. Tagney (New York: Guildford, 2002), pp. 367–83.

47. Leary, "Motivational and Emotional Aspects of the Self."

48. T. A. Judge and J. E. Bono, "Relationship of Core Self-Evaluations Traits—Self-Esteem, Generalized Self-Efficacy, Locus of Control, and Emotional Stability—with Job Satisfaction and Job Performance: A Meta-Analysis," *Journal of Applied Psychology* 86, no. 1 (2001), pp. 80–92; T. A. Judge and C. Hurst, "Capitalizing on One's Advantages: Role of Core Self-Evaluations," *Journal of Applied Psychology* 92, no. 5 (2007), pp. 1212–27. We have described the three most commonly noted components of self-evaluation. The full model also includes emotional stability (low neuroticism). However, the core self-evaluation model has received limited research, and its dimensions are being debated. For example, see R. E. Johnson, C. C. Rosen, and P. E. Levy, "Getting to the Core of Core Self-Evaluation: A Review and Recommendations," *Journal of Organizational Behavior* 29 (2008), pp. 391–413.

49. W. B. Swann Jr, C. Chang-Schneider, and K. L. McClarty, "Do People's Self-Views Matter? Self-Concept and Self-Esteem in Everyday Life," *American Psychologist* 62, no. 2 (2007), pp. 84–94.

50. A. Bandura, *Self-Efficacy: The Exercise of Control* (New York: W. H. Freeman, 1997).

51. G. Chen, S. M. Gully, and D. Eden, "Validation of a New General Self-Efficacy Scale," *Organizational Research Methods* 4, no. 1 (January 2001), pp. 62–83.

52. P. E. Spector, "Behavior in Organizations as a Function of Employee's Locus of Control," *Psychological Bulletin* 91 (1982), pp. 482–97; K. Hattrup, M. S. O'Connell, and J. R. Labrador, "Incremental Validity of Locus of Control after Controlling for Cognitive Ability and Conscientiousness," *Journal of Business and Psychology* 19, no. 4 (2005), pp. 461–81; T. W. H. Ng, K. L. Sorensen, and L. T. Eby, "Locus of Control at Work: A Meta-Analysis," *Journal of Organizational Behavior* 27 (2006), pp. 1057–87.

53. H. Tajfel, *Social Identity and Intergroup Relations* (Cambridge: Cambridge University Press, 1982); B. E. Ashforth and F. Mael, "Social Identity Theory and the Organization," *Academy of Management Review* 14 (1989), pp. 20–39; M. A. Hogg and D. J. Terry, "Social Identity and Self-Categorization Processes in Organizational Contexts," *Academy of Management Review* 25 (January 2000), pp. 121–40; S. A. Haslam, R. A. Eggins, and K. J. Reynolds, "The Aspire Model: Actualizing Social and Personal Identity Resources to Enhance Organizational Outcomes," *Journal of Occupational and Organizational Psychology* 76 (2003), pp. 83–113.

54. Sedikides and Gregg, "Portraits of the Self." The history of the social self in human beings is described in M. R. Leary and N. R. Buttermore, "The Evolution of the Human Self: Tracing the Natural History of Self-Awareness," *Journal for the Theory of Social Behaviour* 33, no. 4 (2003), pp. 365–404.

55. M. R. Edwards, "Organizational Identification: A Conceptual and Operational Review," *International Journal of Management Reviews* 7, no. 4 (2005), pp. 207–30; D. A. Whetten, "Albert and Whetten Revisited: Strengthening the Concept of Organizational Identity," *Journal of Management Inquiry* 15, no. 3 (September 2006), pp. 219–34.

56. B. M. Meglino and E. C. Ravlin, "Individual Values in Organizations: Concepts, Controversies, and Research," *Journal of Management* 24, no. 3 (1998), pp. 351–89; B. R. Agle and C. B. Caldwell, "Understanding Research on Values in Business," *Business and Society* 38, no. 3 (September 1999), pp. 326–87; S. Hitlin and J. A. Pilavin, "Values: Reviving a Dormant Concept," *Annual Review of Sociology* 30 (2004), pp. 359–93.

57. D. Lubinski, D. B. Schmidt, and C. P. Benbow, "A 20-Year Stability Analysis of the Study of Values for Intellectually Gifted Individuals from Adolescence to Adulthood," *Journal of Applied Psychology* 81 (1996), pp. 443–51.

58. Hitlin and Pilavin, "Values: Reviving a Dormant Concept"; A. Pakizeh, J. E. Gebauer, and G. R. Maio, "Basic Human Values: Inter-Value Structure in Memory," *Journal of Experimental Social Psychology* 43, no. 3 (2007), pp. 458–65.

59. S. H. Schwartz, "Universals in the Content and Structure of Values: Theoretical Advances and Empirical Tests in 20 Countries," *Advances in Experimental Social Psychology* 25 (1992), pp. 1–65; S. H. Schwartz, "Are There Universal Aspects in the Structure and Contents of Human Values?" *Journal of Social Issues* 50 (1994), pp. 19–45; D. Spini, "Measurement Equivalence of 10 Value Types from the Schwartz Value Survey across 21 Countries," *Journal of Cross-Cultural Psychology* 34, no. 1 (January 2003), pp. 3–23; S. H. Schwartz and K. Boehnke, "Evaluating the Structure of Human Values with Confirmatory Factor Analysis," *Journal of Research in Personality* 38, no. 3 (2004), pp. 230–55.

60. Schwartz, "Universals in the Content and Structure of Values: Theoretical Advances and Empirical Tests in 20 Countries"; Schwartz and Boehnke, "Evaluating the Structure of Human Values with Confirmatory Factor Analysis."

61. G. R. Maio and J. M. Olson, "Values as Truisms: Evidence and Implications," *Journal of Personality and Social Psychology* 74, no. 2 (1998), pp. 294–311; G. R. Maio et al., "Addressing Discrepancies between Values and Behavior: The Motivating Effect of Reasons," *Journal of Experimental Social Psychology* 37, no. 2 (2001), pp. 104–17; B. Verplanken and R. W. Holland, "Motivated Decision Making: Effects of Activation and Self-Centrality of Values on Choices and Behavior," *Journal of Personality and Social Psychology* 82, no. 3 (2002), pp. 434–47; A. Bardi and S. H. Schwartz, "Values and Behavior: Strength and Structure of Relations," *Personality and Social Psychology Bulletin* 29, no. 10 (October 2003), pp. 1207–20; M. M. Bernard and G. R. Maio, "Effects of Introspection about Reasons for Values: Extending Research on Values-as-Truisms," *Social Cognition* 21, no. 1 (2003), pp. 1–25.

62. N. Mazar, O. Amir, and D. Ariely, "The Dishonesty of Honest People: A Theory of Self-Concept Maintenance," *Journal of Marketing Research* 45 (December 2008), pp. 633–44.

63. K. Hornyak, "Upward Move: Cynthia Schwalm," *Medical Marketing & Media,* June 2008, p. 69. For research on the consequences on value congruence, see A. L. Kristof, "Person–Organization Fit: An Integrative Review of Its Conceptualizations, Measurement, and Implications," *Personnel Psychology* 49, no. 1 (Spring 1996), pp. 1–49; M. L. Verquer, T. A. Beehr, and

S. H. Wagner, "A Meta-Analysis of Relations between Person–Organization Fit and Work Attitudes," Journal of Vocational Behavior 63 (2003), pp. 473–89; J. W. Westerman and L. A. Cyr, "An Integrative Analysis of Person–Organization Fit Theories," *International Journal of Selection and Assessment* 12, no. 3 (September 2004), pp. 252–61; D. Bouckenooghe et al., "The Prediction of Stress by Values and Value Conflict," *Journal of Psychology* 139, no. 4 (2005), pp. 369–82.

64. Aspen Institute, *Where Will They Lead?* (New York: Aspen Institute, April 17, 2008).

65. T. Simons, "Behavioral Integrity: The Perceived Alignment between Managers' Words and Deeds as a Research Focus," *Organization Science* 13, no. 1 (January–February 2002), pp. 18–35; Watson Wyatt, "Employee Ratings of Senior Management Dip, Watson Wyatt Survey Finds," Watson Wyatt news release (New York: January 4, 2007).

66. T. A. Joiner, "The Influence of National Culture and Organizational Culture Alignment on Job Stress and Performance: Evidence from Greece," *Journal of Managerial Psychology* 16 (2001), pp. 229–42; Z. Aycan, R. N. Kanungo, and J. B. P. Sinha, "Organizational Culture and Human Resource Management Practices: The Model of Culture Fit," *Journal of Cross-Cultural Psychology* 30 (July 1999), pp. 501–26.

67. V. Galt, "A World of Opportunity for Those in Mid-Career," *Globe & Mail,* June 7, 2006, p. C1.

68. A. Fisher, "How to Be a Better Global Manager," *Fortune,* July 9, 2009.

69. D. Oyserman, H. M. Coon, and M. Kemmelmeier, "Rethinking Individualism and Collectivism: Evaluation of Theoretical Assumptions and Meta-Analyses," *Psychological Bulletin* 128 (2002), pp. 3–72; C. P. Earley and C. B. Gibson, "Taking Stock in Our Progress on Individualism–Collectivism: 100 Years of Solidarity and Community," *Journal of Management* 24 (May 1998), pp. 265–304; F. S. Niles, "Individualism–Collectivism Revisited," *Cross-Cultural Research* 32 (November 1998), pp. 315–41.

70. Oyserman, Coon, and Kemmelmeier, "Rethinking Individualism and Collectivism: Evaluation of Theoretical Assumptions and Meta-Analyses." Also see F. Li and L. Aksoy, "Dimensionality of Individualism–Collectivism and Measurement Equivalence of Triandis and Gelfand's Scale," *Journal of Business and Psychology* 21, no. 3 (2007), pp. 313–29. The relationship between individualism and collectivism is still being debated, but most experts now agree that individualism and collectivism have serious problems with conceptualization and measurement.

71. G. Hofstede, *Culture's Consequences: Comparing Values, Behaviors, Institutions, and Organizations across Nations,* 2nd ed. (Thousand Oaks, CA: Sage, 2001).

72. Hofstede, *Culture's Consequences: Comparing Values, Behaviors, Institutions, and Organizations across Nations.* Hofstede used the terms *masculinity* and *femininity* for *achievement* and *nurturing orientation,* respectively. We (along with other writers) have adopted the latter two terms to minimize the sexist perspective of these concepts.

73. M. Voronov and J. A. Singer, "The Myth of Individualism–Collectivism: A Critical Review," *Journal of Social Psychology* 142 (August 2002), pp. 461–80; N. Jacob, "Cross-Cultural Investigations: Emerging Concepts," *Journal of Organizational Change Management* 18, no. 5 (2005), pp. 514–28.

74. W. K. W. Choy, A. B. E. Lee, and P. Ramburuth, "Multinationalism in the Workplace: A Myriad of Values in a Singaporean Firm," *Singapore Management Review* 31, no. 1 (January 2009).

75. J. S. Osland et al., "Beyond Sophisticated Stereotyping: Cultural Sensemaking in Context," *Academy of Management Executive* 14 (February 2000), pp. 65–79; S. S. Sarwono and R. W. Armstrong, "Microcultural Differences and Perceived Ethical Problems: An International Business Perspective," *Journal of Business Ethics* 30 (March 2001), pp. 41–56.

76. C. Savoye, "Workers Say Honesty Is Best Company Policy," *Christian Science Monitor,* June 15, 2000; J. M. Kouzes and B. Z. Posner, *The Leadership Challenge,* 3rd ed. (San Francisco: Jossey-Bass, 2002); J. Schettler, "Leadership in Corporate America," *Training & Development,* September 2002, pp. 66–73; "Healthcare Workers Sick of Stress," SEEK Ltd news release (Melbourne: February 18, 2009).

77. Ethics Resource Center, *The 2009 National Business Ethics Survey: Ethics in the Recession* (Arlington, VA: Ethics Resource Center, 2009).

78. P. L. Schumann, "A Moral Principles Framework for Human Resource Management Ethics," *Human Resource Management Review* 11 (Spring–Summer 2001), pp. 93–111; J. Boss, *Analyzing Moral Issues,* 3rd ed. (New York: McGraw-Hill, 2005), Chap. 1; M. G. Velasquez, *Business Ethics: Concepts and Cases,* 6th ed. (Upper Saddle River, NJ: Prentice-Hall, 2006), Chap. 2.

79. Transparency International, *Transparency International Corruption Perceptions Index 2009* (Berlin, Germany: Transparency International, November 2009).

80. T. J. Jones, "Ethical Decision Making by Individuals in Organizations: An Issue Contingent Model," *Academy of Management Review* 16 (1991), pp. 366–95; B. H. Frey, "The Impact of Moral Intensity on Decision Making in a Business Context," *Journal of Business Ethics* 26 (August 2000), pp. 181–95; D. R. May and K. P. Pauli, "The Role of Moral Intensity in Ethical Decision Making," *Business and Society* 41 (March 2002), pp. 84–117.

81. J. R. Sparks and S. D. Hunt, "Marketing Researcher Ethical Sensitivity: Conceptualization, Measurement, and Exploratory Investigation," *Journal of Marketing* 62 (April 1998), pp. 92–109.

82. K. F. Alam, "Business Ethics in New Zealand Organizations: Views from the Middle and Lower Level Managers," *Journal of Business Ethics* 22 (November 1999), pp. 145–53; Human Resource Institute, *The Ethical Enterprise: State-of-the-Art* (St. Petersburg, FL: Human Resource Institute, January 2006).

83. "Gradfacts 2008," *The Guardian (London),* 2008; Aspen Institute, *Where Will They Lead?*; Sinead English & Associates, *What Graduates Want from Their Employers: Attracting and Retaining Graduates in the Irish Market—Report of Survey Findings* (Limerick: Sinead English & Associates, April 2009).

84. B. Farrell, D. M. Cobbin, and H. M. Farrell, "Codes of Ethics: Their Evolution, Development, and Other Controversies," *Journal of Management Development* 21, no. 2 (2002), pp. 152–63; G. Wood and M. Rimmer, "Codes of Ethics: What Are They Really and What Should They Be?" *International Journal of Value-Based Management* 16, no. 2 (2003), p. 181.

85. S. Greengard, "Golden Values," *Workforce Management,* March 2005, pp. 52–53; K. Tyler, "Do the Right Thing," *HRMagazine,* February 2005, pp. 99–102.

86. T. F. Lindeman, "A Matter of Choice," *Pittsburgh Post-Gazette,* March 30, 2004; J. Fortier, "Trust in the Workplace," *Ottawa Business Journal,* January 4, 2007.

87. Ethics Resource Center, *The 2009 National Business Ethics Survey: Ethics in the Recession.*

88. E. Aronson, "Integrating Leadership Styles and Ethical Perspectives," *Canadian Journal of Administrative Sciences* 18 (December 2001), pp. 266–76; D. R. May et al., "Developing the Moral Component of Authentic Leadership," *Organizational Dynamics* 32 (2003), pp. 247–60. The Vodafone director quotation is from R. Van Lee, L. Fabish, and N. McGaw, "The Value of Corporate Values," *strategy+business,* no. 39 (Summer 2005), pp. 1–13.

CHAPTER 3

1. K. A. Findley and M. Scott, "The Multiple Dimensions of Tunnel Vision in Criminal Cases," *Wisconsin Law Review* 2 (2006), pp. 291–397; V. Geberth, "10 Most Common Errors in Death Investigations: Part 1," *Law & Order* 55, no. 11 (November 2007), pp. 84–89; M. Allen, "Unsolved Killings," *Roanoke Times (Virginia),* August 10, 2008; C. Lo, A. Lamand, and J. But, "Police Step Up Hunt after Fourth Prostitute Found Dead in City," *South China Morning Post (Hong Kong),* March 18, 2008.

2. S. A. C. Doyle, "A Study in Scarlet," in *The Complete Sherlock Holmes* (New York: Fine Creative Media, 2003), pp. 3–96. Sherlock Holmes offers similar advice in "A Scandal in Bohemia," p. 189.

3. Plato, *The Republic,* trans. D. Lee (Harmondsworth, England: Penguin, 1955).

4. The effect of the target in selective attention is known as "bottom-up selection"; the effect of the perceiver's psychodynamics on this process is known as "top-down selection." See C. E. Connor, H. E. Egeth, and S. Yantis, "Visual Attention: Bottom-Up versus Top-Down," *Current Biology* 14, no. 19 (2004), pp. R850–52; E. I. Knudsen, "Fundamental Components of Attention," *Annual Review of Neuroscience* 30, no. 1 (2007), pp. 57–78.

5. A. Mack et al., "Perceptual Organization and Attention," *Cognitive Psychology* 24, no. 4 (1992), pp. 475–501; A. R. Damasio, *Descartes' Error: Emotion, Reason, and the Human Brain* (New York: Putnam Sons, 1994); C. Frith, "A Framework for Studying the Neural Basis of Attention," *Neuropsychologia* 39, no. 12 (2001), pp. 1367–71; N. Lavie, "Distracted and Confused? Selective Attention under Load," *Trends in Cognitive Sciences* 9, no. 2 (2005), pp. 75–82; M. Shermer, "The Political Brain," *Scientific American* 295, no. 1 (July 2006), p. 36; D. Westen, *The Political Brain: The Role of Emotion in Deciding the Fate of the Nation* (Cambridge, MA: PublicAffairs, 2007).

6. Confirmation bias is defined as "unwitting selectivity in the acquisition and use of evidence." See R. S. Nickerson, "Confirmation Bias: A Ubiquitous Phenomenon in Many Guises," *Review of General Psychology* 2, no. 2 (1998), pp. 175–220. This occurs in a variety of ways, including overweighting positive information, perceiving only positive information, and restricting cognitive attention to a favored hypothesis. Research has found that confirmation bias is typically nonconscious and driven by emotions.

7. S. Lewandowsky et al., "Memory for Fact, Fiction, and Misinformation. The Iraq War 2003," *Psychological Science* 16, no. 3 (2005), pp. 190–95.

8. D. J. Simons and C. F. Chabris, "Gorillas in Our Midst: Sustained Inattentional Blindness for Dynamic Events," *Perception* 28 (1999), pp. 1059–74.

9. D. Woods, "Managers Make Decisions about People Based on Gut Instinct Rather Than Objective Data," *HR Magazine (UK),* February 16, 2010, http://www.hrmagazine.co.uk.

10. K. A. Lane, J. Kang, and M. R. Banaji, "Implicit Social Cognition and Law," *Annual Review of Law and Social Science* 3, no. 1 (2007).

11. C. N. Macrae and G. V. Bodenhausen, "Social Cognition: Thinking Categorically about Others," *Annual Review of Psychology* 51 (2000), pp. 93–120. For literature about the automaticity of the perceptual organization and interpretation process, see J. A. Bargh, "The Cognitive Monster: The Case against the Controllability of Automatic Stereotype Effects," in *Dual Process Theories in Social Psychology,* ed. S. Chaiken and Y. Trope (New York: Guilford, 1999), pp. 361–82; J. A. Bargh and M. J. Ferguson, "Beyond Behaviorism: On the Automaticity of Higher Mental Processes," *Psychological Bulletin* 126, no. 6 (2000), pp. 925–45; and M. Gladwell, *Blink: The Power of Thinking without Thinking* (New York: Little, Brown, 2005).

12. E. M. Altmann and B. D. Burns, "Streak Biases in Decision Making: Data and a Memory Model," *Cognitive Systems Research* 6, no. 1 (2005), pp. 5–16. For a discussion of cognitive closure and perception, see A. W. Kruglanski, *The Psychology of Closed Mindedness* (New York: Psychology Press, 2004).

13. N. Ambady and R. Rosenthal, "Half a Minute: Predicting Teacher Evaluations from Thin Slices of Nonverbal Behavior and Physical Attractiveness," *Journal of Personality and Social Psychology* 64, no. 3 (March 1993), pp. 431–41. For other research on thin slices, see N. Ambady and R. Rosenthal, "Thin Slices of Expressive Behavior as Predictors of Interpersonal Consequences: A Meta-Analysis," *Psychological Bulletin* 111, no. 2 (1992), pp. 256–74; N. Ambady et al., "Surgeons' Tone of Voice: A Clue to Malpractice History," *Surgery* 132, no. 1 (July 2002), pp. 5–9.

14. P. M. Senge, *The Fifth Discipline: The Art and Practice of the Learning Organization* (New York: Doubleday Currency, 1990), Chap. 10; P. N. Johnson-Laird, "Mental Models and Deduction," *Trends in Cognitive Sciences* 5, no. 10 (2001), pp. 434–42; A. B. Markman and D. Gentner, "Thinking," *Annual Review of Psychology* 52 (2001), pp. 223–47; T. J. Chermack, "Mental Models in Decision Making and Implications for Human Resource Development," *Advances in Developing Human Resources* 5, no. 4 (2003), pp. 408–22.

15. M. A. Hogg et al., "The Social Identity Perspective: Intergroup Relations, Self-Conception, and Small Groups," *Small Group Research* 35, no. 3 (June 2004), pp. 246–76; J. Jetten, R. Spears, and T. Postmes, "Intergroup Distinctiveness and Differentiation: A Meta-Analytic Integration," *Journal of Personality and Social Psychology* 86, no. 6 (2004), pp. 862–79.

16. J. W. Jackson and E. R. Smith, "Conceptualizing Social Identity: A New Framework and Evidence for the Impact of Different Dimensions," *Personality & Social Psychology Bulletin* 25 (January 1999), pp. 120–35.

17. L. Falkenberg, "Improving the Accuracy of Stereotypes within the Workplace," *Journal of Management* 16 (1990), pp. 107–18; S. T. Fiske, "Stereotyping, Prejudice, and Discrimination," in *Handbook of Social Psychology,* ed. D. T. Gilbert, S. T. Fiske, and G. Lindzey, 4th ed. (New York: McGraw-Hill, 1998), pp. 357–411; Macrae and Bodenhausen, "Social Cognition: Thinking Categorically about Others."

18. C. N. Macrae, A. B. Milne, and G. V. Bodenhausen, "Stereotypes as Energy-Saving Devices: A Peek inside the Cognitive Toolbox," *Journal of Personality and Social Psychology* 66 (1994), pp. 37–47; J. W. Sherman et al., "Stereotype Efficiency Reconsidered: Encoding Flexibility under Cognitive Load," *Journal of Personality and Social Psychology* 75 (1998), pp. 589–606; Macrae and Bodenhausen, "Social Cognition: Thinking Categorically about Others."

19. L. Sinclair and Z. Kunda, "Motivated Stereotyping of Women: She's Fine If She Praised Me but Incompetent If She Criticized Me," *Personality and Social Psychology Bulletin* 26 (November 2000), pp. 1329–42; J. C. Turner and S. A. Haslam, "Social Identity, Organizations, and Leadership," in *Groups at Work: Theory and Research,* ed. M. E. Turner (Mahwah, NJ: Lawrence Erlbaum Associates, 2001), pp. 25–65.

20. S. N. Cory, "Quality and Quantity of Accounting Students and the Stereotypical Accountant: Is There a Relationship? " *Journal of Accounting Education* 10, no. 1 (1992), pp. 1–24; P. D. Bougen, "Joking Apart: The Serious Side to the Accountant Stereotype," *Accounting, Organizations and Society* 19, no. 3 (1994), pp. 319–35; A. L. Friedman and S. R. Lyne, "The Beancounter Stereotype: Towards a General Model of Stereotype Generation," *Critical Perspectives on Accounting* 12, no. 4 (2001), pp. 423–51; A. Hoffjan, "The Image of the Accountant in a German Context," *Accounting and the Public Interest* 4 (2004), pp. 62–89; T. Dimnik and S. Felton, "Accountant Stereotypes in Movies Distributed in North America in the Twentieth Century," *Accounting, Organizations and Society* 31, no. 2 (2006), pp. 129–55.

21. Friedman and Lyne, "The Beancounter Stereotype: Towards a General Model of Stereotype Generation."

22. "Employers Face New Danger: Accidental Age Bias," *Omaha World-Herald,* October 10, 2005, p. D1; "Tiptoeing through the Employment Minefield of Race, Sex, and Religion? Here's Another One," *North West Business Insider (Manchester, UK),* February 2006.

23. E. Cediey and F. Foroni, *Discrimination in Access to Employment on Grounds of Foreign Origin in France* (Geneva: International Labour Organization, 2008).

24. S. O. Gaines and E. S. Reed, "Prejudice: From Allport to Dubois," *American Psychologist* 50 (February 1995), pp. 96–103; Fiske, "Stereotyping, Prejudice, and Discrimination"; M. Hewstone, M. Rubin, and H. Willis, "Intergroup Bias," *Annual Review of Psychology* 53 (2002), pp. 575–604.

25. M. Weinstein, "Racism, Sexism, Ageism: Workplace Not Getting Any Friendlier," *Training,* May 2006, p. 11.

26. M. Patriquin, "Quebec Farm Segregated Black Workers," *Globe & Mail,* April 30, 2005, p. A1; S. Foley, "The Women Who Took on a Banking Giant and Won a $33m Sexism Case," *The Independent (London),* April 5, 2008.

27. Equal Employment Opportunity Commission, *Charge Statistics, FY 1997 through FY 2009* (Washington, DC: Equal Employment Opportunity Commission, 2010).

28. J. A. Bargh and T. L. Chartrand, "The Unbearable Automaticity of Being," *American Psychologist* 54, no. 7 (July 1999), pp. 462–79; S. T. Fiske, "What We Know Now about Bias and Intergroup Conflict, the Problem of the Century," *Current Directions in Psychological Science* 11, no. 4 (August 2002), pp. 123–28. For recent evidence that shows that intensive training can minimize stereotype activation, see K. Kawakami et al., "Just Say No (to Stereotyping): Effects of Training in the Negation of Stereotypic Associations on Stereotype Activation," *Journal of Personality and Social Psychology* 78, no. 5 (2000), pp. 871–88; E. A. Plant, B. M. Peruche, and D. A. Butz, "Eliminating Automatic Racial Bias: Making Race Non-Diagnostic for Responses to Criminal

Suspects," *Journal of Experimental Social Psychology* 41, no. 2 (2005), p. 141.

29. H. H. Kelley, *Attribution in Social Interaction* (Morristown, NJ: General Learning Press, 1971).

30. J. M. Feldman, "Beyond Attribution Theory: Cognitive Processes in Performance Appraisal," *Journal of Applied Psychology* 66 (1981), pp. 127–48.

31. J. M. Crant and T. S. Bateman, "Assignment of Credit and Blame for Performance Outcomes," *Academy of Management Journal* 36 (1993), pp. 7–27; B. Weiner, "Intrapersonal and Interpersonal Theories of Motivation from an Attributional Perspective," *Educational Psychology Review* 12 (2000), pp. 1–14; N. Bacon and P. Blyton, "Worker Responses to Teamworking: Exploring Employee Attributions of Managerial Motives," *International Journal of Human Resource Management* 16, no. 2 (February 2005), pp. 238–55.

32. Fundamental attribution error is part of a larger phenomenon known as correspondence bias. See D. T. Gilbert and P. S. Malone, "The Correspondence Bias," *Psychological Bulletin* 117, no. 1 (1995), pp. 21–38.

33. I. Choi, R. E. Nisbett, and A. Norenzayan, "Causal Attribution across Cultures: Variation and Universality," *Psychological Bulletin* 125, no. 1 (1999), pp. 47–63; D. S. Krull et al., "The Fundamental Fundamental Attribution Error: Correspondence Bias in Individualist and Collectivist Cultures," *Personality and Social Psychology Bulletin* 25, no. 10 (October 1999), pp. 1208–19; R. E. Nisbett, *The Geography of Thought: How Asians and Westerners Think Differently—and Why* (New York: Free Press, 2003), Chap. 5.

34. E. W. K. Tsang, "Self-Serving Attributions in Corporate Annual Reports: A Replicated Study," *Journal of Management Studies* 39, no. 1 (January 2002), pp. 51–65; F. Lee, C. Peterson, and L. Z. Tiedens, "Mea Culpa: Predicting Stock Prices from Organizational Attributions," *Pers Soc Psychol Bull* 30, no. 12 (December 1, 2004), pp. 1636–49; N. J. Roese and J. M. Olson, "Better, Stronger, Faster: Self-Serving Judgment, Affect Regulation, and the Optimal Vigilance Hypothesis," *Perspectives on Psychological Science* 2, no. 2 (2007), pp. 124–41; R. Hooghiemstra, "East–West Differences in Attributions for Company Performance: A Content Analysis of Japanese and U.S. Corporate Annual Reports," *Journal of Cross-Cultural Psychology* 39, no. 5 (September 1, 2008), pp. 618–29.

35. Similar models are presented in D. Eden, "Self-Fulfilling Prophecy as a Management Tool: Harnessing Pygmalion," *Academy of Management Review* 9 (1984), pp. 64–73; R. H. G. Field and D. A. Van Seters, "Management by Expectations (MBE): The Power of Positive Prophecy," *Journal of General Management* 14 (Winter 1988), pp. 19–33; D. O. Trouilloud et al., "The Influence of Teacher Expectations on Student Achievement in Physical Education Classes: Pygmalion Revisited," *European Journal of Social Psychology* 32 (2002), pp. 591–607.

36. D. Eden, "Interpersonal Expectations in Organizations," in *Interpersonal Expectations: Theory, Research, and Applications* (Cambridge, UK: Cambridge University Press, 1993), pp. 154–78.

37. D. Eden, "Pygmalion Goes to Boot Camp: Expectancy, Leadership, and Trainee Performance," *Journal of Applied Psychology* 67 (1982), pp. 194–99; R. P. Brown and E. C. Pinel, "Stigma on My Mind: Individual Differences in the Experience of Stereotype Threat," *Journal of Experimental Social Psychology* 39, no. 6 (2003), pp. 626–33.

38. S. Madon, L. Jussim, and J. Eccles, "In Search of the Powerful Self-Fulfilling Prophecy," *Journal of Personality and Social Psychology* 72, no. 4 (April 1997), pp. 791–809; A. E. Smith, L. Jussim, and J. Eccles, "Do Self-Fulfilling Prophecies Accumulate, Dissipate, or Remain Stable over Time?" *Journal of Personality and Social Psychology* 77, no. 3 (1999), pp. 548–65; S. Madon et al., "Self-Fulfilling Prophecies: The Synergistic Accumulative Effect of Parents' Beliefs on Children's Drinking Behavior," *Psychological Science* 15, no. 12 (2005), pp. 837–45.

39. W. H. Cooper, "Ubiquitous Halo," *Psychological Bulletin* 90 (1981), pp. 218–44; K. R. Murphy, R. A. Jako, and R. L. Anhalt, "Nature and Consequences of Halo Error: A Critical Analysis," *Journal of Applied Psychology* 78 (1993), pp. 218–25; T. H. Feeley, "Comment on Halo Effects in Rating and Evaluation Research," *Human Communication Research* 28, no. 4 (October 2002), pp. 578–86. For a variation of the classic halo effect in business settings, see P. Rosenzweig, *The Halo Effect . . . and the Eight Other Business Delusions That Deceive Managers* (New York: Free Press, 2007).

40. C. L. Kleinke, *First Impressions: The Psychology of Encountering Others* (Englewood Cliffs, NJ: Prentice Hall, 1975); E. A. Lind, L. Kray, and L. Thompson, "Primacy Effects in Justice Judgments: Testing Predictions from Fairness Heuristic Theory," *Organizational Behavior and Human Decision Processes* 85 (July 2001), pp. 189–210; O. Ybarra, "When First Impressions Don't Last: The Role of Isolation and Adaptation Processes in the Revision of Evaluative Impressions," *Social Cognition* 19 (October 2001), pp. 491–520; S. D. Bond et al., "Information Distortion in the Evaluation of a Single Option," *Organizational Behavior and Human Decision Processes* 102, no. 2 (2007), pp. 240–54.

41. "Survey: Candidates with Strong Résumés Often Fail to Meet Expectations in Interview," PR news release, (Menlo Park, CA: July 23, 2009); L. Smith, "How Typos on Résumé Can Ruin Your Career Prospects," *ABC15 (Phoenix, AZ),* July 15, 2009.

42. D. D. Steiner and J. S. Rain, "Immediate and Delayed Primacy and Recency Effects in Performance Evaluation," *Journal of Applied Psychology* 74 (1989), pp. 136–42; K. T. Trotman, "Order Effects and Recency: Where Do We Go from Here?" *Accounting & Finance* 40 (2000), pp. 169–82; W. Green, "Impact of the Timing of an Inherited Explanation on Auditors' Analytical Procedures Judgements," *Accounting and Finance* 44 (2004), pp. 369–92.

43. R. W. Clement and J. Krueger, "The Primacy of Self-Referent Information in Perceptions of Social Consensus," *British Journal of Social Psychology* 39 (2000), pp. 279–99; R. L. Gross and S. E. Brodt, "How Assumptions of Consensus Undermine Decision Making," *Sloan Management Review* (January 2001), pp. 86–94; J. Oliver et al., "Projection of Own on Others' Job Characteristics: Evidence for the False Consensus Effect in Job Characteristics Information," *International Journal of Selection and Assessment* 13, no. 1 (2005), pp. 63–74.

44. D. Eden et al., "Implanting Pygmalion Leadership Style through Workshop Training: Seven Field Experiments," *Leadership Quarterly* 11 (2000), pp. 171–210; S. S. White and E. A. Locke, "Problems with the Pygmalion Effect and Some Proposed Solutions," *Leadership Quarterly* 11 (Autumn 2000), pp. 389–415; M. Bendick, M. L. Egan, and S. M. Lofhjelm, "Workforce Diversity Training: From Anti-Discrimination Compliance to Organizational Development HR," *Human Resource Planning* 24 (2001), pp. 10–25; L. Roberson, C. T. Kulik, and M. B. Pepper, "Using Needs Assessment to Resolve

Controversies in Diversity Training Design," *Group & Organization Management* 28, no. 1 (March 2003), pp. 148–74; D. E. Hogan and M. Mallott, "Changing Racial Prejudice through Diversity Education," *Journal of College Student Development* 46, no. 2 (March/April 2005), pp. 115–25.

45. T. W. Costello and S. S. Zalkind, *Psychology in Administration: A Research Orientation* (Englewood Cliffs, NJ: Prentice Hall, 1963), pp. 45–46; J. M. Kouzes and B. Z. Posner, The Leadership Challenge, 4th ed. (San Francisco: Jossey-Bass, 2007), Chap. 3.

46. B. George, *Authentic Leadership* (San Francisco: Jossey-Bass, 2004); W. L. Gardner et al., "'Can You See the Real Me?' A Self-Based Model of Authentic Leader and Follower Development," *Leadership Quarterly* 16 (2005), pp. 343–72; B. George, *True North* (San Francisco: Jossey-Bass, 2007).

47. For a discussion of the Implicit Association Test, including critique, see H. Blanton et al., "Decoding the Implicit Association Test: Implications for Criterion Prediction," *Journal of Experimental Social Psychology* 42, no. 2 (2006), pp. 192–212; A. G. Greenwald, B. A. Nosek, and N. Sriram, "Consequential Validity of the Implicit Association Test: Comment on Blanton and Jaccard (2006)," *American Psychologist* 61, no. 1 (2006), pp. 56–61; W. Hofmann et al., "Implicit and Explicit Attitudes and Interracial Interaction: The Moderating Role of Situationally Available Control Resources," *Group Processes Intergroup Relations* 11, no. 1 (January 2008), pp. 69–87.

48. Hofmann et al., "Implicit and Explicit Attitudes and Interracial Interaction: The Moderating Role of Situationally Available Control Resources"; J. T. Jost et al., "The Existence of Implicit Bias Is beyond Reasonable Doubt: A Refutation of Ideological and Methodological Objections and Executive Summary of Ten Studies That No Manager Should Ignore," *Research in Organizational Behavior* 29 (2009), pp. 39–69.

49. J. Luft, *Group Processes* (Palo Alto, CA: Mayfield Publishing, 1984). For a variation of this model, see J. Hall, "Communication Revisited," *California Management Review* 15 (Spring 1973), pp. 56–67.

50. L. C. Miller and D. A. Kenny, "Reciprocity of Self-Disclosure at the Individual and Dyadic Levels: A Social Relations Analysis," *Journal of Personality and Social Psychology* 50 (1986), pp. 713–19.

51. J. Dixon and K. Durrheim, "Contact and the Ecology of Racial Division: Some Varieties of Informal Segregation," *British Journal of Social Psychology* 42 (March 2003), pp. 1–23; P. J. Henry and C. D. Hardin, "The Contact Hypothesis Revisited: Status Bias in the Reduction of Implicit Prejudice in the United States and Lebanon," *Psychological Science* 17, no. 10 (2006), pp. 862–68; T. F. Pettigrew and L. R. Tropp, "A Meta-Analytic Test of Intergroup Contact Theory," *Journal of Personality and Social Psychology* 90, no. 5 (2006), pp. 751–83; C. Tredoux and G. Finchilescu, "The Contact Hypothesis and Intergroup Relations 50 Years On: Introduction to the Special Issue," *South African Journal of Psychology* 37, no. 4 (2007), pp. 667–78; T. F. Pettigrew, "Future Directions for Intergroup Contact Theory and Research," *International Journal of Intercultural Relations* 32, no. 3 (2008), pp. 187–99.

52. C. Hymowitz, "IBM Combines Volunteer Service, Teamwork to Cultivate Emerging Markets," *The Wall Street Journal,* August 4, 2008, p. B6.

53. W. Frey, "Rubbish Boy Doing Well as Junk Man," *Metro-Vancouver,* April 25, 2005, p. 11; "Domino's Pizza Named One of Michigan's 'Cool Places to Work,'" PR Newswire news release

(Ann Arbor: September 10, 2007); G. Thomas, "Fye Rewrites the Tune at ANZ," *Air Transport World,* September 2007, p. 61.

54. W. G. Stephen and K. A. Finlay, "The Role of Empathy in Improving Intergroup Relations," *Journal of Social Issues* 55 (Winter 1999), pp. 729–43; S. K. Parker and C. M. Axtell, "Seeing Another Viewpoint: Antecedents and Outcomes of Employee Perspective Taking," *Academy of Management Journal* 44 (December 2001), pp. 1085–100; G. J. Vreeke and I. L. van der Mark, "Empathy, an Integrative Model," *New Ideas in Psychology* 21, no. 3 (2003), pp. 177–207.

55. I. Nonaka and H. Takeuchi, *The Knowledge-Creating Company* (New York: Oxford University Press, 1995); P. Duguid, "'The Art of Knowing': Social and Tacit Dimensions of Knowledge and the Limits of the Community of Practice," *The Information Society* 21 (2005), pp. 109–18.

56. B. F. Skinner, *About Behaviorism* (New York: Alfred A. Knopf, 1974); J. Komaki, T. Coombs, and S. Schepman, "Motivational Implications of Reinforcement Theory," in *Motivation and Leadership at Work,* ed. R. M. Steers, L. W. Porter, and G. A. Bigley (New York: McGraw-Hill, 1996), pp. 34–52; R. G. Miltenberger, *Behavior Modification: Principles and Procedures* (Pacific Grove, CA: Brooks/Cole, 1997).

57. T. K. Connellan, *How to Improve Human Performance* (New York: Harper & Row, 1978), pp. 48–57; F. Luthans and R. Kreitner, *Organizational Behavior Modification and Beyond* (Glenview, IL: Scott, Foresman, 1985), pp. 85–88.

58. Miltenberger, *Behavior Modification: Principles and Procedures,* Chap. 4–6.

59. Punishment can also include removing a pleasant consequence, such as when employees must switch from business-class to economy-class flying when their sales fall below the threshold for top-tier sales "stars."

60. T. R. Hinkin and C. A. Schriesheim, "If You Don't Hear from Me You Know You Are Doing Fine," *Cornell Hotel & Restaurant Administration Quarterly* 45, no. 4 (November 2004), pp. 362–72.

61. L. K. Trevino, "The Social Effects of Punishment in Organizations: A Justice Perspective," *Academy of Management Review* 17 (1992), pp. 647–76; L. E. Atwater et al., "Recipient and Observer Reactions to Discipline: Are Managers Experiencing Wishful Thinking?" *Journal of Organizational Behavior* 22, no. 3 (May 2001), pp. 249–70.

62. G. P. Latham and V. L. Huber, "Schedules of Reinforcement: Lessons from the Past and Issues for the Future," *Journal of Organizational Behavior Management* 13 (1992), pp. 125–49; B. A. Williams, "Challenges to Timing-Based Theories of Operant Behavior," *Behavioural Processes* 62 (April 2003), pp. 115–23.

63. ExxonMobil, *UK and Ireland Corporate Citizenship* (ExxonMobil, August 2004); H. Wecsler, "Sick Day Incentive Plan Favored by NLR Board," *Arkansas Democrat Gazette,* February 17, 2006, p. 14.

64. D. Gibson, "Investing in Employees' Health," *Lane Report (Kentucky),* December 2007, p. 28.

65. Bargh and Ferguson, "Beyond Behaviorism." Some writers argue that behaviorists long ago accepted the relevance of cognitive processes in behavior modification. See I. Kirsch et al., "The Role of Cognition in Classical and Operant Conditioning," *Journal of Clinical Psychology* 60, no. 4 (April 2004), pp. 369–92.

66. A. Bandura, *Social Foundations of Thought and Action: A Social Cognitive Theory* (Englewood Cliffs, NJ: Prentice Hall, 1986).

67. A. Pescuric and W. C. Byham, "The New Look of Behavior Modeling," *Training & Development* 50 (July 1996), pp. 24–30.

68. M. E. Schnake, "Vicarious Punishment in a Work Setting," *Journal of Applied Psychology* 71 (1986), pp. 343–45; Trevino, "The Social Effects of Punishment in Organizations: A Justice Perspective"; J. B. DeConinck, "The Effect of Punishment on Sales Managers' Outcome Expectancies and Responses to Unethical Sales Force Behavior," *American Business Review* 21, no. 2 (June 2003), pp. 135–40.

69. A. Bandura, "Self-Reinforcement: Theoretical and Methodological Considerations," *Behaviorism* 4 (1976), pp. 135–55; C. A. Frayne and J. M. Geringer, "Self-Management Training for Improving Job Performance: A Field Experiment Involving Salespeople," *Journal of Applied Psychology* 85, no. 3 (June 2000), pp. 361–72; J. B. Vancouver and D. V. Day, "Industrial and Organisation Research on Self-Regulation: From Constructs to Applications," *Applied Psychology: An International Journal* 54, no. 2 (April 2005), pp. 155–85.

70. D. A. Kolb, *Experiential Learning* (Englewood Cliffs, NJ: Prentice-Hall, 1984); S. Gherardi, D. Nicolini, and F. Odella, "Toward a Social Understanding of How People Learn in Organizations," *Management Learning* 29 (September 1998), pp. 273–97; D. A. Kolb, R. E. Boyatzis, and C. Mainemelis, "Experiential Learning Theory: Previous Research and New Directions," in *Perspectives on Thinking, Learning, and Cognitive Styles,* ed. R. J. Sternberg and L. F. Zhang (Mahwah, NJ: Lawrence Erlbaum, 2001), pp. 227–48.

71. P.-E. Ellström, "Integrating Learning and Work: Problems and Prospects," *Human Resource Development Quarterly* 12, no. 4 (2001), pp. 421–35.

72. W. E. Baker and J. M. Sinkula, "The Synergistic Effect of Market Orientation and Learning Orientation on Organizational Performance," *Academy of Marketing Science Journal* 27, no. 4 (Fall 1999), pp. 411–27; Z. Emden, A. Yaprak, and S. T. Cavusgil, "Learning from Experience in International Alliances: Antecedents and Firm Performance Implications," *Journal of Business Research* 58, no. 7 (2005), pp. 883–92.

73. R. Farson and R. Keyes, "The Failure-Tolerant Leader," *Harvard Business Review* 80 (August 2002), pp. 64–71; T. C. Li, "Loyalty Pays Off for Chief of Malaysia's CIMB," *the Wall Street Journal Asia*, June 23, 2008, p. 36.

74. W. H. Agor, *Intuitive Management: Integrating Left and Right Brain Management Skills* (Englewood Cliffs, NJ: Prentice-Hall, 1984), p. 67.

CHAPTER 4

1. "CCW-Update," Customer Contact Management Association News release (Australia: December 7, 2007); E. G. Brown and J. Lubahn, "We Need 'to Talk,'" *Bank Marketing* 39, no. 7 (2007), pp. 32–36; J. Penman, "Clydesdale Rings the Changes," *Sunday Times (London),* February 4, 2007, p. 13; T. Russell, "Centres of Excellence," *Personnel Today,* January 23, 2007, pp. 24–25.

2. The centrality of emotions in marketing, economics, and sociology is discussed in G. Loewenstein, "Emotions in Economic Theory and Economic Behavior," *American Economic Review* 90, no. 2 (May 2000), pp. 426–32; D. S. Massey, "A Brief History of Human Society: The Origin and Role of Emotion in Social Life," *American Sociological Review* 67 (February 2002), pp. 1–29; J. O'Shaughnessy and N. J. O'Shaughnessy, *The Marketing Power of Emotion* (New York: Oxford University Press, 2003).

3. The definition presented here is constructed from the following sources: N. M. Ashkanasy, W. J. Zerbe, and C. E. J. Hartel, "Introduction: Managing Emotions in a Changing Workplace," in *Managing Emotions in the Workplace,* ed. N. M. Ashkanasy, W. J. Zerbe, and C. E. J. Hartel (Armonk, NY: M. E. Sharpe, 2002), pp. 3–18; H. M. Weiss, "Conceptual and Empirical Foundations for the Study of Affect at Work," in *Emotions in the Workplace,* ed. R. G. Lord, R. J. Klimoski, and R. Kanfer (San Francisco: Jossey-Bass, 2002), pp. 20–63. However, the meaning of emotions is still being debated. See, for example, M. Cabanac, "What Is Emotion?" *Behavioral Processes* 60 (2002), pp. 69–83.

4. R. Kanfer and R. J. Klimoski, "Affect and Work: Looking Back to the Future," in *Emotions in the Workplace,* ed. R. G. Lord, R. J. Klimoski, and R. Kanfer (San Francisco: Jossey-Bass, 2002), pp. 473–90; J. A. Russell, "Core Affect and the Psychological Construction of Emotion," *Psychological Review* 110, no. 1 (2003), pp. 145–72.

5. R. B. Zajonc, "Emotions," in *Handbook of Social Psychology,* ed. D. T. Gilbert, S. T. Fiske, and L. Gardner (New York: Oxford University press, 1998), pp. 591–634.

6. N. A. Remington, L. R. Fabrigar, and P. S. Visser, "Reexamining the Circumplex Model of Affect," *Journal of Personality and Social Psychology* 79, no. 2 (2000), pp. 286–300; R. J. Larson, E. Diener, and R. E. Lucas, "Emotion: Models, Measures, and Differences," in *Emotions in the Workplace,* ed. R. G. Lord, R. J. Klimoski, and R. Kanfer (San Francisco: Jossey-Bass, 2002), pp. 64–113; L. F. Barrett et al., "The Experience of Emotion," *Annual Review of Psychology* 58, no. 1 (2007), pp. 373–403.

7. A. H. Eagly and S. Chaiken, *The Psychology of Attitudes* (Orlando, FL: Harcourt Brace Jovanovich, 1993); A. P. Brief, *Attitudes in and around Organizations* (Thousand Oaks, CA: Sage, 1998). There is an amazing lack of consensus on the definition of attitudes. This book adopts the three-component model, whereas some experts define attitude as only the "feelings" component, with "beliefs" as a predictor and "intentions" as an outcome. Some writers specifically define attitudes as an "evaluation" of an attitude object, whereas others distinguish attitudes from evaluations of an attitude object. For some of these definitional variations, see I. Ajzen, "Nature and Operation of Attitudes," *Annual Review of Psychology* 52 (2001), pp. 27–58; D. Albarracín et al., "Attitudes: Introduction and Scope," in *The Handbook of Attitudes,* ed. D. Albarracín, B. T. Johnson, and M. P. Zanna (Mahwah, NJ: Lawrence Erlbaum Associates, 2005), pp. 3–20; W. A. Cunningham and P. D. Zelazo, "Attitudes and Evaluations: A Social Cognitive Neuroscience Perspective," *TRENDS in Cognitive Sciences* 11, no. 3 (2007), pp. 97–104.

8. C. D. Fisher, "Mood and Emotions While Working: Missing Pieces of Job Satisfaction?" *Journal of Organizational Behavior* 21 (2000), pp. 185–202; Cunningham and Zelazo, "Attitudes and Evaluations"; M. D. Lieberman, "Social Cognitive Neuroscience: A Review of Core Processes," *Annual Review of Psychology* 58, no. 1 (2007), pp. 259–89.

9. S. Orbell, "Intention–Behavior Relations: A Self-Regulation Perspective," in *Contemporary Perspectives on the Psychology of Attitudes,* ed. G. Haddock and G. R. Maio (East Sussex, UK: Psychology Press, 2004), pp. 145–68.

10. H. M. Weiss and R. Cropanzano, "Affective Events Theory: A Theoretical Discussion of the Structure, Causes, and Consequences of Affective Experiences at Work," *Research in Organizational Behavior* 18 (1996), pp. 1–74; J. Wegge et al., "A Test of Basic Assumptions of Affective Events Theory (AET)

in Call Centre Work," *British Journal of Management* 17 (2006), pp. 237–54.

11. J. A. Bargh and M. J. Ferguson, "Beyond Behaviorism: On the Automaticity of Higher Mental Processes," *Psychological Bulletin* 126, no. 6 (2000), pp. 925–45; R. H. Fazio, "On the Automatic Activation of Associated Evaluations: An Overview," *Cognition and Emotion* 15, no. 2 (2001), pp. 115–41; M. Gladwell, *Blink: The Power of Thinking without Thinking* (New York: Little, Brown, 2005).

12. A. R. Damasio, *Descartes' Error: Emotion, Reason, and the Human Brain* (New York: Putnam Sons, 1994); A. Damasio, *The Feeling of What Happens* (New York: Harcourt Brace and Co., 1999); P. Ekman, "Basic Emotions," in *Handbook of Cognition and Emotion*, ed. T. Dalgleish and M. Power (San Francisco: Jossey-Bass, 1999), pp. 45–60; J. E. LeDoux, "Emotion Circuits in the Brain," *Annual Review of Neuroscience* 23 (2000), pp. 155–84; R. J. Dolan, "Emotion, Cognition, and Behavior," *Science* 298, no. 5596 (November 8, 2002), pp. 1191–94.

13. N. Schwarz, "Emotion, Cognition, and Decision Making," *Cognition and Emotion* 14, no. 4 (2000), pp. 433–40; M. T. Pham, "The Logic of Feeling," *Journal of Consumer Psychology* 14, no. 4 (2004), pp. 360–69.

14. These lists are found at www.greatplacetowork.com. Hewitt Associates produces a related list for Asia and the Middle East. See http://was2.hewitt.com/bestemployers/asia/english/results_2009.htm.

15. S. Davies, "Razer Employees Wear Shorts, T-Shirts and Flip-Flops to Work," *Straits Times (Singapore)*, May 10, 2008; C. Eggleston, "Dixon Schwabl #1 to Work for in America," *R-News (Rochester, NY)*, June 23, 2008; E. Maltby, "Boring Meetings? Get Out the Water Guns," *The Wall Street Journal*, January 7, 2010, p. B5.

16. B. Ott, N. Blacksmith, and K. Royal, "What Generation Gap?" *Gallup Management Journal* (March 13, 2008); E. Lamm and M. D. Meeks, "Workplace Fun: The Moderating Effects of Generational Differences," *Employee Relations* 31, no. 6 (2009), pp. 613–31.

17. G. R. Maio, V. M. Esses, and D. W. Bell, "Examining Conflict between Components of Attitudes: Ambivalence and Inconsistency Are Distinct Constructs," *Canadian Journal of Behavioural Science* 32, no. 2 (2000), pp. 71–83.

18. P. C. Nutt, *Why Decisions Fail* (San Francisco, CA: Berrett-Koehler, 2002); S. Finkelstein, *Why Smart Executives Fail* (New York: Viking, 2003); P. C. Nutt, "Search during Decision Making," *European Journal of Operational Research* 160 (2005), pp. 851–76.

19. Weiss and Cropanzano, "Affective Events Theory."

20. L. Festinger, *A Theory of Cognitive Dissonance* (Evanston, IL: Row, Peterson, 1957); G. R. Salancik, "Commitment and the Control of Organizational Behavior and Belief," in *New Directions in Organizational Behavior*, ed. B. M. Staw and G. R. Salancik (Chicago: St. Clair, 1977), pp. 1–54; A. D. Galinsky, J. Stone, and J. Cooper, "The Reinstatement of Dissonance and Psychological Discomfort Following Failed Affirmation," *European Journal of Social Psychology* 30, no. 1 (2000), pp. 123–47.

21. T. A. Judge, E. A. Locke, and C. C. Durham, "The Dispositional Causes of Job Satisfaction: A Core Evaluations Approach," *Research in Organizational Behavior* 19 (1997), pp. 151–88; Massey, "A Brief History of Human Society: The Origin and Role of Emotion in Social Life."

22. C. M. Brotheridge and A. A. Grandey, "Emotional Labor and Burnout: Comparing Two Perspectives of 'People Work," *Journal of Vocational Behavior* 60 (2002), pp. 17–39; P. G. Irving, D. F. Coleman, and D. R. Bobocel, "The Moderating Effect of Negative Affectivity in the Procedural Justice–Job Satisfaction Relation," *Canadian Journal of Behavioural Science* 37, no. 1 (January 2005), pp. 20–32.

23. J. Schaubroeck, D. C. Ganster, and B. Kemmerer, "Does Trait Affect Promote Job Attitude Stability?" *Journal of Organizational Behavior* 17 (1996), pp. 191–96; C. Dormann and D. Zapf, "Job Satisfaction: A Meta-Analysis of Stabilities," *Journal of Organizational Behavior* 22 (2001), pp. 483–504.

24. B. E. Ashforth and R. H. Humphrey, "Emotional Labor in Service Roles: The Influence of Identity," *Academy of Management Review* 18 (1993), pp. 88–115. For a recent review of the emotional labor concept, see T. M. Glomb and M. J. Tews, "Emotional Labor: A Conceptualization and Scale Development," *Journal of Vocational Behavior* 64, no. 1 (2004), pp. 1–23.

25. J. A. Morris and D. C. Feldman, "The Dimensions, Antecedents, and Consequences of Emotional Labor," *Academy of Management Review* 21 (1996), pp. 986–1010; D. Zapf, "Emotion Work and Psychological Well-Being: A Review of the Literature and Some Conceptual Considerations," *Human Resource Management Review* 12 (2002), pp. 237–68.

26. "Reach for the Sky," *New Sunday Times (Kuala Lumpur)*, November 16, 2008, p. 4; C. Platt, "Inside Flight Attendant School," *WA Today (Perth)*, February 24, 2009.

27. F. Trompenaars and C. Hampden-Turner, *Riding the Waves of Culture*, 2nd ed. (New York: McGraw-Hill, 1998), p. 71. Cultural differences in emotional expression are also discussed in A. E. Raz and A. Rafaeli, "Emotion Management in Cross-Cultural Perspective: 'Smile Training' in Japanese and North American Service Organizations," *Research on Emotion in Organizations* 3 (2007), pp. 199–220; S. Ravid, A. Rafaeli, and A. Grandey, "Expressions of Anger in Israeli Workplaces: The Special Place of Customer Interactions," *Human Resource Management Review* in press, corrected proof (2010).

28. "We're Bottom of Fun Table," *Blackpool Gazette (UK)*, February 3, 2008.

29. This relates to the automaticity of emotion, which is summarized in P. Winkielman and K. C. Berridge, "Unconscious Emotion," *Current Directions in Psychological Science* 13, no. 3 (2004), pp. 120–23; K. N. Ochsner and J. J. Gross, "The Cognitive Control of Emotions," *TRENDS in Cognitive Sciences* 9, no. 5 (May 2005), pp. 242–49.

30. W. J. Zerbe, "Emotional Dissonance and Employee Well-Being," in *Managing Emotions in the Workplace,* ed. N. M. Ashkanasy, W. J. Zerbe, and C. E. J. Hartel (Armonk, NY: M. E. Sharpe, 2002), pp. 189–214; R. Cropanzano, H. M. Weiss, and S. M. Elias, "The Impact of Display Rules and Emotional Labor on Psychological Well-Being at Work," *Research in Occupational Stress and Well Being* 3 (2003), pp. 45–89.

31. Brotheridge and Grandey, "Emotional Labor and Burnout: Comparing Two Perspectives of 'People Work"; Zapf, "Emotion Work and Psychological Well-Being"; J. M. Diefendorff, M. H. Croyle, and R. H. Gosserand, "The Dimensionality and Antecedents of Emotional Labor Strategies," *Journal of Vocational Behavior* 66, no. 2 (2005), pp. 339–57.

32. J. D. Mayer, P. Salovey, and D. R. Caruso, "Models of Emotional Intelligence," in *Handbook of Human Intelligence,* ed. R. J. Sternberg, 2nd ed. (New York: Cambridge University

Press, 2000), pp. 396–420. This definition is also recognized in C. Cherniss, "Emotional Intelligence and Organizational Effectiveness," in *The Emotionally Intelligent Workplace,* ed. C. Cherniss and D. Goleman (San Francisco: Jossey-Bass, 2001), pp. 3–12; M. Zeidner, G. Matthews, and R. D. Roberts, "Emotional Intelligence in the Workplace: A Critical Review," *Applied Psychology: An International Review* 53, no. 3 (2004), pp. 371–99.

33. These four dimensions of emotional intelligence are discussed in detail in D. Goleman, R. Boyatzis, and A. McKee, *Primal Leadership* (Boston: Harvard Business School Press, 2002), Chap. 3. Slight variations of this model are presented in R. Boyatzis, D. Goleman, and K. S. Rhee, "Clustering Competence in Emotional Intelligence," in *The Handbook of Emotional Intelligence,* ed. R. Bar-On and J. D. A. Parker (San Francisco: Jossey-Bass, 2000), pp. 343–62; and D. Goleman, "An EI-Based Theory of Performance," in *The Emotionally Intelligent Workplace,* ed. C. Cherniss and D. Goleman (San Francisco: Jossey-Bass, 2001), pp. 27–44. Which model best represents EI and its abilities is debated in several sources, including several chapters in K. R. Murphy, ed., *A Critique of Emotional Intelligence: What Are the Problems and How Can They Be Fixed?* (Mahwah, NJ: Lawrence Erlbaum Associates, 2006).

34. H. A. Elfenbein and N. Ambady, "Predicting Workplace Outcomes from the Ability to Eavesdrop on Feelings," *Journal of Applied Psychology* 87, no. 5 (2002), pp. 963–71.

35. The hierarchical nature of the four EI dimensions is discussed by Goleman, but it is more explicit in the Salovey and Mayer model. See D. R. Caruso and P. Salovey, *The Emotionally Intelligent Manager* (San Francisco: Jossey-Bass, 2004).

36. P. N. Lopes et al., "Emotional Intelligence and Social Interaction," *Personality and Social Psychology Bulletin* 30, no. 8 (August 2004), pp. 1018–34; C. S. Daus and N. M. Ashkanasy, "The Case for the Ability-Based Model of Emotional Intelligence in Organizational Behavior," *Journal of Organizational Behavior* 26 (2005), pp. 453–66; J. E. Barbuto Jr and M. E. Burbach, "The Emotional Intelligence of Transformational Leaders: A Field Study of Elected Officials," *Journal of Social Psychology* 146, no. 1 (2006), pp. 51–64; M. A. Brackett et al., "Relating Emotional Abilities to Social Functioning: A Comparison of Self-Report and Performance Measures of Emotional Intelligence," *Journal of Personality and Social Psychology* 91, no. 4 (2006), pp. 780–95; D. L. Reis et al., "Emotional Intelligence Predicts Individual Differences in Social Exchange Reasoning," *NeuroImage* 35, no. 3 (2007), pp. 1385–91; S. K. Singh, "Role of Emotional Intelligence in Organisational Learning: An Empirical Study," *Singapore Management Review* 29, no. 2 (2007), pp. 55–74.

37. W. Lau, "Staff with High EQ Help Motivate Team Members Events Watch," *South China Morning Post (Hong Kong),* August 23, 2008, p. 22.

38. Some studies have reported situations where EI has a limited effect on individual performance. For example, see A. L. Day and S. A. Carroll, "Using an Ability-Based Measure of Emotional Intelligence to Predict Individual Performance, Group Performance, and Group Citizenship Behaviors," *Personality and Individual Differences* 36 (2004), pp. 1443–58; Z. Ivcevic, M. A. Brackett, and J. D. Mayer, "Emotional Intelligence and Emotional Creativity," *Journal of Personality* 75, no. 2 (2007), pp. 199–236; and J. C. Rode et al., "Emotional Intelligence and Individual Performance: Evidence of Direct and Moderated Effects," *Journal of Organizational Behavior* 28, no. 4 (2007), pp. 399–421.

39. D. McGinn, "The Emotional Workplace," *National Post,* August 18, 2007, p. FW3.

40. Goleman, Boyatzis, and McKee, *Primal Leadership;* S. C. Clark, R. Callister, and R. Wallace, "Undergraduate Management Skills Courses and Students' Emotional Intelligence," *Journal of Management Education* 27, no. 1 (February 2003), pp. 3–23; Lopes et al., "Emotional Intelligence and Social Interaction"; H. A. Elfenbein, "Learning in Emotion Judgments: Training and the Cross-Cultural Understanding of Facial Expressions," *Journal of Nonverbal Behavior* 30, no. 1 (2006), pp. 21–36; C.-S. Wong et al., "The Feasibility of Training and Development of EI: An Exploratory Study in Singapore, Hong Kong and Taiwan," *Intelligence* 35, no. 2 (2007), pp. 141–50.

41. C. Fox, "Shifting Gears," *Australian Financial Review,* August 13, 2004, p. 28; J. Thomson, "True Team Spirit," *Business Review Weekly,* March 18, 2004, p. 92; R. Johnson, "Can You Feel It?" *People Management,* August 23, 2007, pp. 34–37.

42. D. A. Harrison, D. A. Newman, and P. L. Roth, "How Important Are Job Attitudes? Meta-Analytic Comparisons of Integrative Behavioral Outcomes and Time Sequences," *Academy of Management Journal* 49, no. 2 (2006), pp. 305–25.

43. E. A. Locke, "The Nature and Causes of Job Satisfaction," in *Handbook of Industrial and Organizational Psychology,* ed. M. Dunnette (Chicago: Rand McNally, 1976), pp. 1297–1350; H. M. Weiss, "Deconstructing Job Satisfaction: Separating Evaluations, Beliefs and Affective Experiences," *Human Resource Management Review,* no. 12 (2002), pp. 173–94. Some definitions still include emotion as an element of job satisfaction, whereas the definition presented in this book views emotion as a cause of job satisfaction. Also, this definition views job satisfaction as a "collection of attitudes," not several "facets" of job satisfaction.

44. The problems with measuring attitudes and values across cultures are discussed in G. Law, "If You're Happy & You Know It, Tick the Box," *Management-Auckland* 45 (March 1998), pp. 34–37; P. E. Spector et al., "Do National Levels of Individualism and Internal Locus of Control Relate to Well-Being: An Ecological Level International Study," *Journal of Organizational Behavior* 22 (2001), pp. 815–32; L. Saari and T. A. Judge, "Employee Attitudes and Job Satisfaction," *Human Resource Management* 43, no. 4 (Winter 2004), pp. 395–407.

45. T. W. Smith, *Job Satisfaction in America: Trends and Socio-Demographic Correlates* (Chicago: National Opinion Research Center/University of Chicago, August 2007); G. Langer, "Happy at Work? Depends Who's Asking," *ABC News,* January 5, 2010, http://blogs.abcnews.com/thenumbers/2010/01/happy-at-work-depends-whos-asking.html.

46. H. Rao and R. I. Sutton, "Innovation Lessons from Pixar: An Interview with Oscar-Winning Director Brad Bird," *McKinsey Quarterly* (April 2008), pp. 1–9.

47. M. J. Withey and W. H. Cooper, "Predicting Exit, Voice, Loyalty, and Neglect," *Administrative Science Quarterly,* no. 34 (1989), pp, 521–39; W. H. Turnley and D. C. Feldman, "The Impact of Psychological Contract Violations on Exit, Voice, Loyalty, and Neglect," *Human Relations,* no. 52 (July 1999), pp. 895–922. Subdimensions of silence and voice also exist. See L. van Dyne, S. Ang, and I. C. Botero, "Conceptualizing Employee Silence and Employee Voice as Multidimensional Constructs," *Journal of Management Studies* 40, no. 6 (September 2003), pp. 1359–92.

48. T. R. Mitchell, B. C. Holtom, and T. W. Lee, "How to Keep Your Best Employees: Developing an Effective Retention Policy," *Academy of Management Executive* 15 (November 2001), pp. 96–108; C. P. Maertz and M. A. Campion, "Profiles of Quitting: Integrating Process and Content Turnover Theory," *Academy of Management Journal* 47, no. 4 (2004), pp. 566–82; K. Morrell, J. Loan-Clarke, and A. Wilkinson, "The Role of Shocks in Employee Turnover," *British Journal of Management* 15 (2004), pp. 335–49; B. C. Holtom, T. R. Mitchell, and T. W. Lee, "Increasing Human and Social Capital by Applying Job Embeddedness Theory," *Organizational Dynamics* 35, no. 4 (2006), pp. 316–31.

49. A. A. Luchak, "What Kind of Voice Do Loyal Employees Use?" *British Journal of Industrial Relations* 41 (March 2003), pp. 115–34.

50. A. O. Hirschman, *Exit, Voice, and Loyalty: Responses to Decline in Firms, Organizations, and States* (Cambridge, MA: Harvard University Press, 1970); E. A. Hoffmann, "Exit and Voice: Organizational Loyalty and Dispute Resolution Strategies," *Social Forces* 84, no. 4 (June 2006), pp. 2313–30.

51. J. D. Hibbard, N. Kumar, and L. W. Stern, "Examining the Impact of Destructive Acts in Marketing Channel Relationships," *Journal of Marketing Research* 38 (February 2001), pp. 45–61; J. Zhou and J. M. George, "When Job Dissatisfaction Leads to Creativity: Encouraging the Expression of Voice," *Academy of Management Journal* 44 (August 2001), pp. 682–96.

52. M. J. Withey and I. R. Gellatly, "Situational and Dispositional Determinants of Exit, Voice, Loyalty and Neglect," *Proceedings of the Administrative Sciences Association of Canada, Organizational Behaviour Division* (June 1998); D. C. Thomas and K. Au, "The Effect of Cultural Differences on Behavioral Responses to Low Job Satisfaction," *Journal of International Business Studies* 33, no. 2 (2002), pp. 309–26; S. F. Premeaux and A. G. Bedeian, "Breaking the Silence: The Moderating Effects of Self-Monitoring in Predicting Speaking Up in the Workplace," *Journal of Management Studies* 40, no. 6 (2003), pp. 1537–62.

53. T. A. Judge et al., "The Job Satisfaction–Job Performance Relationship: A Qualitative and Quantitative Review," *Psychological Bulletin* 127 (2001), pp. 376–407; Saari and Judge, "Employee Attitudes and Job Satisfaction." Other studies report stronger correlations with job performance when both the belief and feeling components of job satisfaction are consistent with each other and when overall job attitude (satisfaction and commitment combined) is being measured. See D. J. Schleicher, J. D. Watt, and G. J. Greguras, "Reexamining the Job Satisfaction–Performance Relationship: The Complexity of Attitudes," *Journal of Applied Psychology* 89, no. 1 (2004), pp. 165–77; and Harrison, Newman, and Roth, "How Important Are Job Attitudes?" The positive relationship between job satisfaction and employee performance is also consistent with emerging research on the outcomes of positive organizational behavior. For example, see J. R. Sunil, "Enhancing Employee Performance through Positive Organizational Behavior," *Journal of Applied Social Psychology* 38, no. 6 (2008), pp. 1580–600.

54. J. I. Heskett, W. E. Sasser, and L. A. Schlesinger, *The Service Profit Chain* (New York: Free Press, 1997); D. J. Koys, "The Effects of Employee Satisfaction, Organizational Citizenship Behavior, and Turnover on Organizational Effectiveness: A Unit-Level, Longitudinal Study," *Personnel Psychology* 54 (April 2001), pp. 101–14; W.-C. Tsai and Y.-M. Huang, "Mechanisms Linking Employee Affective Delivery and Customer Behavioral Intentions," *Journal of Applied Psychology* 87, no. 5 (2002), pp. 1001–8; T. DeCotiis et al., "How Outback Steakhouse Created a Great Place to Work, Have Fun, and Make Money," *Journal of Organizational Excellence* 23, no. 4 (Autumn 2004), pp. 23–33; G. A. Gelade and S. Young, "Test of a Service Profit Chain Model in the Retail Banking Sector," *Journal of Occupational & Organizational Psychology* 78 (2005), pp. 1–22.

55. This model is based on similar models presented or described in Heskett, Sasser, and Schlesinger, *The Service Profit Chain*; A. J. Rucci, S. P. Kirn, and R. T. Quinn, "The Employee–Customer–Profit Chain at Sears," *Harvard Business Review* 76 (January–February 1998), pp. 83–97.

56. P. Guenzi and O. Pelloni, "The Impact of Interpersonal Relationships on Customer Satisfaction and Loyalty to the Service Provider," *International Journal Of Service Industry Management* 15, no. 3–4 (2004), pp. 365–84; S. J. Bell, S. Auh, and K. Smalley, "Customer Relationship Dynamics: Service Quality and Customer Loyalty in the Context of Varying Levels of Customer Expertise and Switching Costs," *Journal of the Academy of Marketing Science* 33, no. 2 (Spring 2005), pp. 169–83; P. B. Barger and A. A. Grandey, "Service with a Smile and Encounter Satisfaction: Emotional Contagion and Appraisal Mechanisms," *Academy of Management Journal* 49, no. 6 (2006), pp. 1229–38.

57. "The Greatest Briton in Management and Leadership," *Personnel Today,* February 18, 2003, p. 20.

58. R. T. Mowday, L. W. Porter, and R. M. Steers, *Employee Organization Linkages: The Psychology of Commitment, Absenteeism, and Turnover* (New York: Academic Press, 1982).

59. J. P. Meyer, "Organizational Commitment," *International Review of Industrial and Organizational Psychology* 12 (1997), pp. 175–228. Along with affective and continuance commitment, Meyer identifies "normative commitment," which refers to employee feelings of obligation to remain with the organization. This commitment has been excluded so that students focus on the two most common perspectives of commitment.

60. R. D. Hackett, P. Bycio, and P. A. Hausdorf, "Further Assessments of Meyer and Allen's (1991) Three-Component Model of Organizational Commitment," *Journal of Applied Psychology* 79 (1994), pp. 15–23.

61. J. P. Meyer et al., "Affective, Continuance, and Normative Commitment to the Organization: A Meta-Analysis of Antecedents, Correlates, and Consequences," *Journal of Vocational Behavior* 61 (2002), pp. 20–52; M. Riketta, "Attitudinal Organizational Commitment and Job Performance: A Meta-Analysis," *Journal of Organizational Behavior* 23 (2002), pp. 257–66.

62. J. P. Meyer et al., "Organizational Commitment and Job Performance: It's the Nature of the Commitment That Counts," *Journal of Applied Psychology* 74 (1989), pp. 152–56; A. A. Luchak and I. R. Gellatly, "What Kind of Commitment Does a Final-Earnings Pension Plan Elicit?" *Relations Industrielles* 56 (Spring 2001), pp. 394–417; Z. X. Chen and A. M. Francesco, "The Relationship between the Three Components of Commitment and Employee Performance in China," *Journal of Vocational Behavior* 62, no. 3 (2003), pp. 490–510; D. M. Powell and J. P. Meyer, "Side-Bet Theory and the Three-Component Model of Organizational Commitment," *Journal of Vocational Behavior* 65, no. 1 (2004), pp. 157–77.

63. Data provided in several country-specific news releases from Kelly Services. For a white paper summary of the survey, see Kelly Services, *Employee Loyalty Rises during Global*

Economic Recession, Kelly International Workforce Survey Finds (Troy, MI: Kelly Services, March 8, 2010).

64. J. E. Finegan, "The Impact of Person and Organizational Values on Organizational Commitment," *Journal of Occupational and Organizational Psychology* 73 (June 2000), pp. 149–69; A. Panaccio and C. Vandenberghe, "Perceived Organizational Support, Organizational Commitment and Psychological Well-Being: A Longitudinal Study," *Journal of Vocational Behavior* 75, no. 2 (2009), pp. 224–36; R. J. Riggle, D. R. Edmondson, and J. D. Hansen, "A Meta-Analysis of the Relationship between Perceived Organizational Support and Job Outcomes: 20 Years of Research," *Journal of Business Research* 62, no. 10 (2009), pp. 1027–30.

65. D. M. Cable and T. A. Judge, "Person–Organization Fit, Job Choice Decisions, and Organizational Entry," *Organizational Behavior and Human Decision Processes* 67, no. 3 (1996), pp. 294–311; J. W. Westerman and L. A. Cyr, "An Integrative Analysis of Person-Organization Fit Theories," *International Journal of Selection and Assessment* 12, no. 3 (September 2004), pp. 252–61; J. R. Edwards and D. M. Cable, "The Value of Value Congruence," *Journal of Applied Psychology* 94, no. 3 (2009), pp. 654–77.

66. D. M. Rousseau et al., "Not So Different after All: A Cross-Discipline View of Trust," *Academy of Management Review* 23 (1998), pp. 393–404.

67. S. Ashford, C. Lee, and P. Bobko, "Content, Causes, and Consequences of Job Insecurity: A Theory-Based Measure and Substantive Test," *Academy of Management Journal* 32 (1989), pp. 803–29; C. Hendry and R. Jenkins, "Psychological Contracts and New Deals," *Human Resource Management Journal* 7 (1997), pp. 38–44.

68. T. S. Heffner and J. R. Rentsch, "Organizational Commitment and Social Interaction: A Multiple Constituencies Approach," *Journal of Vocational Behavior* 59 (2001), pp. 471–90.

69. H. Samuel, "Why Have 24 France Telecom Workers Killed Themselves in the Past 19 Months?" *The Telegraph (London, UK)*, October 4, 2009; "Doctor or Decorator?" *Economist*, April 8, 2010; F. Aizicovici, "France TéLéCom : La Lutte Contre le Stress au Travail Se Met en Place Lentement," *Le Monde (Paris)*, January 26, 2010; R. Tomlinson and G. Viscusi, "Suicides inside France Telecom Prompting Sarkozy Stress Testing," *BusinessWeek*, January 25, 2010.

70. J. C. Quick et al., *Preventive Stress Management in Organizations* (Washington, DC: American Psychological Association, 1997), pp. 3–4; R. S. DeFrank and J. M. Ivancevich, "Stress on the Job: An Executive Update," *Academy of Management Executive* 12 (August 1998), pp. 55–66; A. L. Dougall and A. Baum, "Stress, Coping, and Immune Function," in *Handbook of Psychology*, ed. M. Gallagher and R. J. Nelson (Hoboken, NJ: John Wiley & Sons, 2003), pp. 441–55. There are at least three schools of thought regarding the meaning of stress, and some reviews of the stress literature describe these schools without pointing to any one as the preferred definition. One reviewer concluded that the stress concept is so broad that it should be considered an umbrella concept, capturing a broad array of phenomena and providing a simple term for the public to use. See T. A. Day, "Defining Stress as a Prelude to Mapping Its Neurocircuitry: No Help from Allostasis," *Progress in Neuro-Psychopharmacology and Biological Psychiatry* 29, no. 8 (2005), pp. 1195–200; R. Cropanzano and A. Li, "Organizational Politics and Workplace Stress," in *Handbook of Organizational Politics*, ed. E. Vigoda-Gadot and A. Drory (Cheltenham, UK: Edward Elgar, 2006), pp. 139–60; R. L.

Woolfolk, P. M. Lehrer, and L. A. Allen, "Conceptual Issues Underlying Stress Management," in *Principles and Practice of Stress Management*, ed. P. M. Lehrer, R. L. Woolfolk, and W. E. Sime (New York: Guilford Press, 2007), pp. 3–15.

71. Finegan, "The Impact of Person and Organizational Values on Organizational Commitment"; Dougall and Baum, "Stress, Coping, and Immune Function"; R. S. Lazarus, *Stress and Emotion: A New Synthesis* (New York: Springer Publishing, 2006); L. W. Hunter and S. M. B. Thatcher, "Feeling the Heat: Effects of Stress, Commitment, and Job Experience on Job Performance," *Academy of Management Journal* 50, no. 4 (2007), pp. 953–68.

72. Quick et al., *Preventive Stress Management in Organizations*, pp. 5–6; B. L. Simmons and D. L. Nelson, "Eustress at Work: The Relationship between Hope and Health in Hospital Nurses," *Health Care Management Review* 26, no. 4 (October 2001), p. 7ff.

73. "The Anxious American Worker: Jobs, the Economy, and a Call for Help," Rutgers University news release (New Brunswick, NJ: August 28, 2008); M. Fahmy, "Survey Says Work Really Is Hazardous to Your Health," *Reuters (Singapore)*, December 5, 2008; Towers Watson, "Debunking Workforce Myths," Towers Watson news release (March 2008); L. Saad, *Job Security Slips in U.S. Worker Satisfaction Rankings* (Princeton, NJ: Gallup, August 27, 2009).

74. H. Selye, "A Syndrome Produced by Diverse Nocuous Agents," *Nature* 138, no. 1 (July 4, 1936), p. 32; H. Selye, *Stress without Distress* (Philadelphia: J. B. Lippincott, 1974). The earliest use of the word *stress* is reported in R. M. K. Keil, "Coping and Stress: A Conceptual Analysis," *Journal of Advanced Nursing* 45, no. 6 (2004), pp. 659–65.

75. S. E. Taylor, R. L. Repetti, and T. Seeman, "Health Psychology: What Is an Unhealthy Environment and How Does It Get under the Skin?" *Annual Review of Psychology* 48 (1997), pp. 411–47.

76. D. Ganster, M. Fox, and D. Dwyer, "Explaining Employees' Health Care Costs: A Prospective Examination of Stressful Job Demands, Personal Control, and Physiological Reactivity," *Journal of Applied Psychology* 86 (May 2001), pp. 954–64; M. Kivimaki et al., "Work Stress and Risk of Cardiovascular Mortality: Prospective Cohort Study of Industrial Employees," *British Medical Journal* 325 (October 19, 2002), pp. 857–60; S. Andrew and S. Ayers, "Stress, Health, and Illness," in *The Sage Handbook of Health Psychology*, ed. S. Sutton, A. Baum, and M. Johnston (London: Sage, 2004), pp. 169–96; A. Rosengren et al., "Association of Psychosocial Risk Factors with Risk of Acute Myocardial Infarction in 11 119 Cases and 13 648 Controls from 52 Countries (the Interheart Study): Case–Control Study," *The Lancet* 364, no. 9438 (September 11, 2004), pp. 953–62.

77. R. C. Kessler, "The Effects of Stressful Life Events on Depression," *Annual Review of Psychology* 48 (1997), pp. 191–214; L. Greenburg and J. Barling, "Predicting Employee Aggression against Coworkers, Subordinates and Supervisors: The Roles of Person Behaviors and Perceived Workplace Factors," *Journal of Organizational Behavior* 20 (1999), pp. 897–913; M. Jamal and V. V. Baba, "Job Stress and Burnout among Canadian Managers and Nurses: An Empirical Examination," *Canadian Journal of Public Health* 91, no. 6 (November–December 2000), pp. 454–58; L. Tourigny, V. V. Baba, and T. R. Lituchy, "Job Burnout among Airline Employees in Japan: A Study of the Buffering Effects of Absence and Supervisory Support," *International Journal of Cross Cultural Management* 5, no. 1 (April 2005), pp. 67–85;

M. S. Hershcovis et al., "Predicting Workplace Aggression: A Meta-Analysis," *Journal of Applied Psychology* 92, no. 1 (2007), pp. 228–38.

78. C. Maslach, W. B. Schaufeli, and M. P. Leiter, "Job Burnout," *Annual Review of Psychology* 52 (2001), pp. 397–422; J. R. B. Halbesleben and M. R. Buckley, "Burnout in Organizational Life," *Journal of Management* 30, no. 6 (2004), pp. 859–79.

79. K. Danna and R. W. Griffin, "Health and Well-Being in the Workplace: A Review and Synthesis of the Literature," *Journal of Management,* Spring 1999, pp. 357–84.

80. This is a slight variation of the definition in the Quebec anti-harassment legislation. See www.cnt.gouv.qc.ca. For related definitions and discussion of workplace incivility, see H. Cowiea et al., "Measuring Workplace Bullying," *Aggression and Violent Behavior* 7 (2002), pp. 33–51; C. M. Pearson and C. L. Porath, "On the Nature, Consequences and Remedies of Workplace Incivility: No Time for 'Nice'? Think Again," *Academy of Management Executive* 19, no. 1 (February 2005), pp. 7–18.

81. Pearson and Porath, "On the Nature, Consequences and Remedies of Workplace Incivility"; A. Yeung and B. Griffin, "Workplace Incivilty: Does It Matter in Asia?" *People & Strategy* 31, no. 1 (December 2008), pp. 14–19.

82. For a legal discussion of types of sexual harassment, see B. Lindemann and D. D. Kadue, *Sexual Harassment in Employment Law* (Washington: BNA Books, 1999), pp. 7–9.

83. Past predictions of future work hours are described in B. K. Hunnicutt, *Kellogg's Six-Hour Day* (Philadelphia: Temple University Press, 1996). For a history of working hours, including review of recent increases, see L. Golden, "A Brief History of Long Work Time and the Contemporary Sources of Overwork," *Journal of Business Ethics* 84, no. 0 (2009), pp. 217–27.

84. R. Konrad, "For Some Techies, an Interminable Workday," *Associated Press (Santa Clara, CA),* May 10, 2005.

85. R. Drago, D. Black, and M. Wooden, *The Persistence of Long Work Hours,* Melbourne Institute Working Paper Series (Melbourne: Melbourne Institute of Applied Economic and Social Research, University of Melbourne, August 2005).

86. C. B. Meek, "The Dark Side of Japanese Management in the 1990s: Karoshi and Ijime in the Japanese Workplace," *Journal of Managerial Psychology* 19, no. 3 (2004), pp. 312–31; A. Kanai, "Karoshi (Work to Death) in Japan," *Journal of Business Ethics* 84, no. 0 (2009), pp. 209–16; P. Novotny, "Overwork a Silent Killer in Japan," *Agence France Presse,* January 11, 2009.

87. "Nagoya Court Rules Toyota Employee Died from Overwork," *Japan Times,* December 1, 2007; Y. Kageyama, "Questions Rise about Temps, Overwork at Toyota," *Associated Press Newswires,* September 10, 2008; National Labor Committee, *The Toyota You Don't Know: The Race to the Bottom in the Auto Industry* (Pittsburgh, PA: National Labor Committee, June 2008).

88. A. Bakker, E. Demerouti, and W. Verbeke, "Using the Job Demands–Resources Model to Predict Burnout and Performance," *Human Resources Management* 43, no. 1 (2004), pp. 83–104; W. B. Schaufeli, "Job Demands, Job Resources, and Their Relationship with Burnout and Engagement: A Multisample Study," *Journal of Organizational Behavior* 25 (2004), pp. 293–315; A. Bakker and E. Demerouti, "The Job Demands–Resources Model: State of the Art," *Journal of Managerial Psychology* 22, no. 3 (2007), p. 309.

89. R. Karasek and T. Theorell, *Healthy Work: Stress, Productivity, and the Reconstruction of Working Life* (New York: Basic Books, 1990); N. Turner, N. Chmiel, and M. Walls, "Railing for Safety: Job Demands, Job Control, and Safety Citizenship Role Definition," *Journal of Occupational Health Psychology* 10, no. 4 (2005), pp. 504–12.

90. S. Johnson et al., "The Experience of Work-Related Stress across Occupations," in *Stress and the Quality of Working Life,* ed. A. M. Rossi, J. C. Quick, and P. L. Perrewé (Charlotte, NC: Information Age Publishing, 2009), pp. 67–77.

91. S. J. Havlovic and J. P. Keenen, "Coping with Work Stress: The Influence of Individual Differences; Handbook on Job Stress [Special Issue]," *Journal of Social Behavior and Personality* 6 (1991), pp. 199–212.

92. S. S. Luthar, D. Cicchetti, and B. Becker, "The Construct of Resilience: A Critical Evaluation and Guidelines for Future Work," *Child Development* 71, no. 3 (May–June 2000), pp. 543–62; F. Luthans, "The Need for and Meaning of Positive Organizational Behavior," *Journal of Organizational Behavior* 23 (2002), pp. 695–706; G. A. Bonanno, "Loss, Trauma, and Human Resilience: Have We Underestimated the Human Capacity to Thrive after Extremely Aversive Events?" *American Psychologist* 59, no. 1 (2004), pp. 20–28.

93. M. Beasley, T. Thompson, and J. Davidson, "Resilience in Response to Life Stress: The Effects of Coping Style and Cognitive Hardiness," *Personality and Individual Differences* 34, no. 1 (2003), pp. 77–95; M. M. Tugade, B. L. Fredrickson, and L. Feldman Barrett, "Psychological Resilience and Positive Emotional Granularity: Examining the Benefits of Positive Emotions on Coping and Health," *Journal of Personality* 72, no. 6 (2004), pp. 1161–90; I. Tsaousis and I. Nikolaou, "Exploring the Relationship of Emotional Intelligence with Physical and Psychological Health Functioning," *Stress and Health* 21, no. 2 (2005), pp. 77–86; L. Campbell-Sills, S. L. Cohan, and M. B. Stein, "Relationship of Resilience to Personality, Coping, and Psychiatric Symptoms in Young Adults," *Behaviour Research and Therapy* 44, no. 4 (April 2006), pp. 585–99.

94. J. T. Spence and A. S. Robbins, "Workaholism: Definition, Measurement and Preliminary Results," *Journal of Personality Assessment* 58 (1992), pp. 160–78; R. J. Burke, "Workaholism in Organizations: Psychological and Physical Well-Being Consequences," *Stress Medicine* 16, no. 1 (2000), pp. 11–16; I. Harpaz and R. Snir, "Workaholism: Its Definition and Nature," *Human Relations* 56 (2003), pp. 291–319; R. J. Burke, A. M. Richardson, and M. Martinussen, "Workaholism among Norwegian Senior Managers: New Research Directions," *International Journal of Management* 21, no. 4 (December 2004), pp. 415–26.

95. R. J. Burke and G. MacDermid, "Are Workaholics Job Satisfied and Successful in Their Careers?" *Career Development International* 4 (1999), pp. 277–82; R. J. Burke and S. Matthiesen, "Short Communication: Workaholism among Norwegian Journalists: Antecedents and Consequences," *Stress and Health* 20, no. 5 (2004), pp. 301–8.

96. "Workaholics Anonymous," *Human Capital Magazine,* November 26, 2008; "What Is HR's Greatest Downfall?" Human Resources Leader, November 25, 2008.

97. L. T. Eby et al., "Work and Family Research in IO/OB: Content Analysis and Review of the Literature (1980–2002)," *Journal of Vocational Behavior* 66, no. 1 (2005), pp. 124–97; B. Harrington and J. J. Ladge, "Work–Life Integration: Present Dynamics and Future Directions for Organizations,"

Organizational Dynamics 38, no. 2 (2009), pp. 148–57. The ongoing debate about the effects of work/life balance on organizational performance is reviewed in T. A. Beauregard and L. C. Henry, "Making the Link between Work–Life Balance Practices and Organizational Performance," *Human Resource Management Review* 19, no. 1 (2009), pp. 9–22.

98. M. Conlin, "Smashing the Clock," *BusinessWeek,* December 11, 2006, pp. 60–68; L. Gresham, "A New Dawn," *Employee Benefits News,* March 2007; B. Ward, "Power to the People," *Star-Tribune (Minneapolis-St. Paul),* June 1, 2008, p. 1E.

99. S. R. Madsen, "The Effects of Home-Based Teleworking on Work–Family Conflict," *Human Resource Development Quarterly* 14, no. 1 (2003), pp. 35–58.

100. Organization for Economic Cooperation and Development, *Babies and Bosses: Reconciling Work and Family Life,* vol. 4 (Canada, Finland, Sweden and the United Kingdom) (Paris: OECD Publishing, 2005); B. Pettit and J. Hook, "The Structure of Women's Employment in Comparative Perspective," *Social Forces* 84, no. 2 (December 2005), pp. 779–801; J. Heymann et al., *The Work, Family, and Equity Index: How Does the United States Measure Up?* Project on Global Working Families (Montreal: Institute for Health and Social Policy, June 2007).

101. M. Secret, "Parenting in the Workplace: Child Care Options for Consideration," *The Journal of Applied Behavioral Science* 41, no. 3 (September 2005), pp. 326–47.

102. A. E. Carr and T. L.-P. Tang, "Sabbaticals and Employee Motivation: Benefits, Concerns, and Implications," *Journal of Education for Business* 80, no. 3 (January/February 2005), pp. 160–64; S. Overman, "Sabbaticals Benefit Companies as Well as Employees," *Employee Benefit News,* April 15, 2006.

103. M. Waung, "The Effects of Self-Regulatory Coping Orientation on Newcomer Adjustment and Job Survival," *Personnel Psychology* 48 (1995), pp. 633–50; M. H. Abel, "Humor, Stress, and Coping Strategies," *Humor: International Journal of Humor Research* 15, no. 4 (2002), pp. 365–81; N. A. Kuiper et al., "Humor Is Not Always the Best Medicine: Specific Components of Sense of Humor and Psychological Well-Being," Humor: International Journal of Humor Research 17, no. 1/2 (2004), pp. 135–68; E. J. Romero and K. W. Cruthirds, "The Use of Humor in the Workplace," *Academy of Management Perspectives* 20, no. 2 (2006), pp. 58–69; M. McCreaddie and S. Wiggins, "The Purpose and Function of Humor in Health, Health Care and Nursing: A Narrative Review," *Journal of Advanced Nursing* 61, no. 6 (2008), pp. 584–95.

104. W. M. Ensel and N. Lin, "Physical Fitness and the Stress Process," *Journal of Community Psychology* 32, no. 1 (January 2004), pp. 81–101.

105. S. Armour, "Rising Job Stress Could Affect Bottom Line," *USA Today,* July 29, 2003; V. A. Barnes, F. A. Treiber, and M. H. Johnson, "Impact of Transcendental Meditation on Ambulatory Blood Pressure in African-American Adolescents," *American Journal of Hypertension* 17, no. 4 (2004), pp. 366–69; P. Manikonda et al., "Influence of Non-Pharmacological Treatment (Contemplative Meditation and Breathing Technique) on Stress Induced Hypertension—a Randomized Controlled Study," *American Journal of Hypertension* 18, no. 5, Supplement 1 (2005), pp. A89–A90.

106. S. E. Taylor et al., "Biobehavioral Responses to Stress in Females: Tend-and-Befriend, Not Fight-or-Flight," *Psychological Review* 107, no. 3 (July 2000), pp. 411–29; R. Eisler and D. S. Levine, "Nurture, Nature, and Caring: We Are Not Prisoners of Our Genes," *Brain and Mind* 3 (2002), pp. 9–52.

107. Ipsos Public Affairs, "Nearly Half of Working Adults Socialize with Colleagues," Ipsos Public Affairs news release (New York: February 24, 2010).

CHAPTER 5

1. E. Pofeldt, "What Makes a Great Boss?" *Fortune,* October 16, 2006, p. 192B; "Employee Engagement-Design for Working," *Human Resources,* February 2008, p. 54; A. McCall, "24 Rackspace," *Sunday Times: 100 Best Companies to Work For 2008,* March 9, 2008, p. 38; Rackspace Hosting, *2008 Racker Letter to Investors* (San Antonio, TX: Rackspace Hosting, August 7, 2008).

2. C. C. Pinder, *Work Motivation in Organizational Behavior* (Upper Saddle River, NJ: Prentice-Hall, 1998); R. M. Steers, R. T. Mowday, and D. L. Shapiro, "The Future of Work Motivation Theory," *Academy of Management Review* 29 (2004), pp. 379–87.

3. A. B. Bakker and W. B. Schaufeli, "Positive Organizational Behavior: Engaged Employees in Flourishing Organizations," *Journal of Organizational Behavior* 29, no. 2 (2008), pp. 147–54; W. H. Macey and B. Schneider, "The Meaning of Employee Engagement," *Industrial and Organizational Psychology* 1 (2008), pp. 3–30.

4. "Gallup Study: Feeling Good Matters in the Workplace," *Gallup Management Journal,* January 12, 2006; "Few Workers Are 'Engaged' at Work and Most Want More from Execs," *Dow Jones Business News* (San Francisco), October 22, 2007; Blessing-White, *The State of Employee Engagement 2008: Asia Pacific Overview* (Princeton, NJ: Blessing White, March 3, 2009); Gallup Consulting, *The Gallup Q12-Employee Engagement-Poll 2008 Results* (Gallup Consulting, February 2009).

5. M. Millar, "Getting the Measure of Its People," *Personnel Today,* December 14, 2004, p. 6; K. Ockenden, "Inside Story," *Utility Week,* January 28, 2005, p. 26; J. Engen, "Are Your Employees Truly Engaged?" *Chief Executive,* March 2008, p. 42; P. Flade, "Employee Engagement Drives Shareholder Value," *Director of Finance Online,* February 13, 2008; S. Flander, "Terms of Engagement," *Human Resource Executive Online,* January 2008.

6. G. Ginsberg, ed., *Essential Techniques for Employee Engagement, The Practitioner's Guide To . . .* (London: Melcrum Publishing, 2007).

7. Several sources attempt to identify and organize the drivers of employee engagement. See, for example, D. Robinson, S. Perryman, and S. Hayday, *The Drivers of Employee Engagement* (Brighton, UK: Institute for Employment Studies, 2004); W. H. Macey et al., *Employee Engagement: Tools for Analysis, Practice, and Competitive Advantage* (Malden, MA: Wiley-Blackwell, 2009); M. Stairs and M. Galpin, "Positive Engagement: From Employee Engagement to Workplace Happiness," in *Oxford Handbook of Positive Psychology of Work,* ed. P. A. Linley, S. Harrington, and N. Garcea (New York: Oxford University Press, 2010), pp. 155–72.

8. "Event Brief of Q2 2006 JCPenney Earnings Conference Call," *Voxant Fair Disclosure Wire,* August 10, 2006; S. Edelson, "The Penney Program," *Women's Wear Daily,* February 12, 2007, p. 1; Engen, "Are Your Employees Truly Engaged?"

9. The confusing array of definitions about drives and needs has been the subject of criticism for a half century. See, for example, R. S. Peters, "Motives and Motivation," *Philosophy* 31 (1956), pp. 117–30; H. Cantril, "Sentio, Ergo Sum: 'Motivation' Reconsidered," *Journal of Psychology* 65, no. 1 (January 1967), pp. 91–107; G. R. Salancik and J. Pfeffer, "An Examination of Need-Satisfaction Models of Job Attitudes,"

Administrative Science Quarterly 22, no. 3 (September 1977), pp. 427–56.

10. A. Blasi, "Emotions and Moral Motivation," *Journal for the Theory of Social Behaviour* 29, no. 1 (1999), pp. 1–19; D. W. Pfaff, *Drive: Neurobiological and Molecular Mechanisms of Sexual Motivation* (Cambridge, MA: MIT Press, 1999); T. V. Sewards and M. A. Sewards, "Fear and Power-Dominance Drive Motivation: Neural Representations and Pathways Mediating Sensory and Mnemonic Inputs, and Outputs to Premotor Structures," *Neuroscience and Biobehavioral Reviews* 26 (2002), pp. 553–79; K. C. Berridge, "Motivation Concepts in Behavioral Neuroscience," *Physiology & Behavior* 81, no. 2 (2004), pp. 179–209. We distinguish drives from emotions, but future research may find that the two concepts are not so different as is stated here.

11. G. Loewenstein, "The Psychology of Curiosity: A Review and Reinterpretation," *Psychological Bulletin* 116, no. 1 (1994), pp. 75–98; R. E. Baumeister and M. R. Leary, "The Need to Belong: Desire for Interpersonal Attachments as a Fundamental Human Motivation," *Psychological Bulletin* 117 (1995), pp. 497–529; A. E. Kelley, "Neurochemical Networks Encoding Emotion and Motivation: An Evolutionary Perspective," in *Who Needs Emotions? The Brain Meets the Robot,* ed. J.-M. Fellous and M. A. Arbib (New York: Oxford University Press, 2005), pp. 29–78.

12. K. Passyn and M. Sujan, "Self-Accountability Emotions and Fear Appeals: Motivating Behavior," *Journal of Consumer Research* 32, no. 4 (2006), pp. 583–89; S. G. Barsade and D. E. Gibson, "Why Does Affect Matter in Organizations?" *Academy of Management Perspectives* 21, no. 2 (February 2007), pp. 36–59.

13. S. Hitlin, "Values as the Core of Personal Identity: Drawing Links between Two Theories of Self," *Social Psychology Quarterly* 66, no. 2 (2003), pp. 118–37; D. D. Knoch and E. E. Fehr, "Resisting the Power of Temptations. The Right Prefrontal Cortex and Self-Control," *Annals of the New York Academy of Sciences* 1104, no. 1 (2007), p. 123; B. Monin, D. A. Pizarro, and J. S. Beer, "Deciding Versus Reacting: Conceptions of Moral Judgment and the Reason-Affect Debate," *Review of General Psychology* 11, no. 2 (2007), pp. 99–111.

14. V. Lombardi Jr., *What It Takes to Be #1: Vince Lombardi on Leadership* (New York: McGraw-Hill, 2001), p. 39.

15. A. H. Maslow, "A Theory of Human Motivation," *Psychological Review* 50 (1943), pp. 370–96; A. H. Maslow, *Motivation and Personality* (New York Harper & Row, 1954).

16. Australian Institute of Management, *There Are No Limits: What Keeps Employees Engaged with Their Workplace?* (St. Kilda, VIC: Australian Institute of Management, November 29, 2006); Society of Petroleum Engineers, "SPE Survey Rates Employee Satisfaction," *Talent & Technology,* 2007.

17. D. T. Hall and K. E. Nougaim, "An Examination of Maslow's Need Hierarchy in an Organizational Setting," *Organizational Behavior and Human Performance* 3, no. 1 (1968), p. 12; M. A. Wahba and L. G. Bridwell, "Maslow Reconsidered: A Review of Research on the Need Hierarchy Theory," *Organizational Behavior and Human Performance* 15 (1976), pp. 212–40; E. L. Betz, "Two Tests of Maslow's Theory of Need Fulfillment," *Journal of Vocational Behavior* 24, no. 2 (1984), pp. 204–20; P. A. Corning, "Biological Adaptation in Human Societies: A 'Basic Needs' Approach," *Journal of Bioeconomics* 2, no. 1 (2000), pp. 41–86.

18. K. Dye, A. J. Mills, and T. G. Weatherbee, "Maslow: Man Interrupted-Reading Management Theory in Context," *Management Decision* 43, no. 10 (2005), pp. 1375–95.

19. A. H. Maslow, "A Preface to Motivation Theory," *Psychsomatic Medicine* 5 (1943), pp. 85–92.

20. A. H. Maslow, *Maslow on Management* (New York: John Wiley & Sons, 1998).

21. F. F. Luthans, "Positive Organizational Behavior: Developing and Managing Psychological Strengths," *The Academy of Management Executive* 16, no. 1 (2002), pp. 57–72; S. L. Gable and J. Haidt, "What (and Why) Is Positive Psychology?" *Review of General Psychology* 9, no. 2 (2005), pp. 103–10; M. E. P. Seligman et al., "Positive Psychology Progress: Empirical Validation of Interventions," *American Psychologist* 60, no. 5 (2005), pp. 410–21.

22. B. A. Agle and C. B. Caldwell, "Understanding Research on Values in Business," *Business and Society* 38 (September 1999), pp. 326–87; B. Verplanken and R. W. Holland, "Motivated Decision Making: Effects of Activation and Self-Centrality of Values on Choices and Behavior," *Journal of Personality and Social Psychology* 82, no. 3 (2002), pp. 434–47; S. Hitlin and J. A. Pilavin, "Values: Reviving a Dormant Concept," *Annual Review of Sociology* 30 (2004), pp. 359–93.

23. D. C. McClelland, *The Achieving Society* (New York: Van Nostrand Reinhold, 1961); D. C. McClelland and D. H. Burnham, "Power Is the Great Motivator," *Harvard Business Review* 73 (January–February 1995), pp. 126–39; D. Vredenburgh and Y. Brender, "The Hierarchical Abuse of Power in Work Organizations," *Journal of Business Ethics* 17 (September 1998), pp. 1337–47; S. Shane, E. A. Locke, and C. J. Collins, "Entrepreneurial Motivation," *Human Resource Management Review* 13, no. 2 (2003), pp. 257–79.

24. McClelland, *The Achieving Society.*

25. Shane, Locke, and Collins, "Entrepreneurial Motivation."

26. McClelland and Burnham, "Power Is the Great Motivator"; J. L. Thomas, M. W. Dickson, and P. D. Bliese, "Values Predicting Leader Performance in the U.S. Army Reserve Officer Training Corps Assessment Center: Evidence for a Personality-Mediated Model," *The Leadership Quarterly* 12, no. 2 (2001), pp. 181–96.

27. R. J. Moretti and E. D. Rossini, "The Thematic Apperception Test (Tat)," in *Comprehensive Handbook of Psychological Assessment,* ed. M. J. Hilsenroth and D. L. Segal (Hoboken, NJ: John Wiley & Sons, 2004), pp. 356–71.

28. Vredenburgh and Brender, "The Hierarchical Abuse of Power in Work Organizations."

29. D. Miron and D. C. McClelland, "The Impact of Achievement Motivation Training on Small Business," *California Management Review* 21 (1979), pp. 13–28.

30. P. R. Lawrence and N. Nohria, *Driven: How Human Nature Shapes Our Choices* (San Francisco: Jossey-Bass, 2002).

31. L. Gaertner et al., "The 'I,' the 'We,' and the 'When': A Meta-Analysis of Motivational Primacy in Self-Definition," *Journal of Personality and Social Psychology* 83, no. 3 (2002), pp. 574–91; M. R. Leary, "Motivational and Emotional Aspects of the Self," *Annual Review of Psychology* 58, no. 1 (2007), pp. 317–44.

32. Baumeister and Leary, "The Need to Belong."

33. J. Litman, "Curiosity and the Pleasures of Learning: Wanting and Liking New Information," *Cognition and Emotion* 19, no. 6 (2005), pp. 793–814; T. G. Reio Jr. et al., "The Measurement and Conceptualization of Curiosity," *Journal of Genetic Psychology* 167, no. 2 (2006), pp. 117–35.

34. W. H. Bexton, W. Heron, and T. H. Scott, "Effects of Decreased Variation in the Sensory Environment," *Canadian Journal of*

Psychology 8 (1954), pp. 70–76; Loewenstein, "The Psychology of Curiosity."

35. A. R. Damasio, *Descartes' Error: Emotion, Reason, and the Human Brain* (New York: Putnam sons, 1994); J. E. LeDoux, "Emotion Circuits in the Brain," *Annual Review of Neuroscience* 23 (2000), pp. 155–84; P. Winkielman and K. C. Berridge, "Unconscious Emotion," *Current Directions in Psychological Science* 13, no. 3 (2004), pp. 120–23.

36. Lawrence and Nohria, *Driven,* pp. 145–47.

37. Lawrence and Nohria, *Driven,* Chap. 11.

38. Expectancy theory of motivation in work settings originated in V. H. Vroom, *Work and Motivation* (New York: Wiley, 1964). The version of expectancy theory presented here was developed by Edward Lawler. Lawler's model provides a clearer presentation of the model's three components. P-to-O expectancy is similar to "instrumentality" in Vroom's original expectancy theory model. The difference is that instrumentality is a correlation whereas P-to-O expectancy is a probability. See J. P. Campbell et al., *Managerial Behavior, Performance, and Effectiveness* (New York: McGraw-Hill, 1970); E. E. Lawler III, *Motivation in Work Organizations* (Monterey, CA: Brooks-Cole, 1973); and D. A. Nadler and E. E. Lawler, "Motivation: A Diagnostic Approach," in *Perspectives on Behavior in Organizations,* ed. J. R. Hackman, E. E. Lawler III, and L. W. Porter, 2nd ed. (New York: McGraw-Hill, 1983), pp. 67–78.

39. M. Zeelenberg et al., "Emotional Reactions to the Outcomes of Decisions: The Role of Counterfactual Thought in the Experience of Regret and Disappointment," *Organizational Behavior and Human Decision Processes* 75, no. 2 (1998), pp. 117–41; B. A. Mellers, "Choice and the Relative Pleasure of Consequences," *Psychological Bulletin* 126, no. 6 (November 2000), pp. 910–24; R. P. Bagozzi, U. M. Dholakia, and S. Basuroy, "How Effortful Decisions Get Enacted: The Motivating Role of Decision Processes, Desires, and Anticipated Emotions," *Journal of Behavioral Decision Making* 16, no. 4 (October 2003), pp. 273–95.

40. Nadler and Lawler, "Motivation: A Diagnostic Approach."

41. Watson Wyatt, *WorkCanada 2004/2005—Pursuing Productive Engagement* (Toronto: Watson Wyatt, January 2005); Hudson, *Rising above the Average: 2007 Compensation & Benefits Report* (New York: June 2007).

42. T. Matsui and T. Terai, "A Cross-Cultural Study of the Validity of the Expectancy Theory of Motivation," *Journal of Applied Psychology* 60 (1975), pp. 263–65; D. H. B. Welsh, F. Luthans, and S. M. Sommer, "Managing Russion Factory Workers: The Impact of U.S.-Based Behavioral and Participative Techniques," *Academy of Management Journal* 36 (1993), pp. 58–79.

43. This limitation was recently acknowledged by Victor Vroom, who had introduced expectancy theory in his 1964 book. See G. P. Latham, *Work Motivation: History, Theory, Research, and Practice* (Thousand Oaks, CA: Sage, 2007), pp. 47–48.

44. J. Greenberg and E. A. Lind, "The Pursuit of Organizational Justice: From Conceptualization to Implication to Application," in *Industrial and Organizational Psychology: Linking Theory with Practice,* ed. C. L. Cooper and E. A. Locke (London: Blackwell, 2000), pp. 72–108; R. Cropanzano and M. Schminke, "Using Social Justice to Build Effective Work Groups," in *Groups at Work: Theory and Research,* ed. M. E. Turner (Mahwah, NJ: Lawrence Erlbaum Associates, 2001), pp. 143–71; D. T. Miller, "Disrespect and the Experience of Injustice," *Annual Review of Psychology* 52 (2001), pp. 527–53.

45. J. S. Adams, "Toward an Understanding of Inequity," *Journal of Abnormal and Social Psychology* 67 (1963), pp. 422–36; R. T. Mowday, "Equity Theory Predictions of Behavior in Organizations," in *Motivation and Work Behavior,* ed. L. W. Porter and R. M. Steers, 5th ed. (New York: McGraw-Hill, 1991), pp. 111–31; R. G. Cropanzano, J., "Progress in Organizational Justice: Tunneling through the Maze," in *International Review of Industrial and Organizational Psychology,* ed. C. L. Cooper and I. T. Robertson (New York: Wiley, 1997), pp. 317–72; L. A. Powell, "Justice Judgments as Complex Psychocultural Constructions: An Equity-Based Heuristic for Mapping Two- and Three-Dimensional Fairness Representations in Perceptual Space," *Journal of Cross-Cultural Psychology* 36, no. 1 (January 2005), pp. 48–73.

46. K. Jenkins et al., *The Anxious American Worker* (New Brunswick, NJ: John J. Heldrich Center for Workforce Development, Summer 2008).

47. C. T. Kulik and M. L. Ambrose, "Personal and Situational Determinants of Referent Choice," *Academy of Management Review* 17 (1992), pp. 212–37; G. Blau, "Testing the Effect of Level and Importance of Pay Referents on Pay Level Satisfaction," *Human Relations* 47 (1994), pp. 1251–68.

48. T. P. Summers and A. S. DeNisi, "In Search of Adams' Other: Reexamination of Referents Used in the Evaluation of Pay," *Human Relations* 43 (1990), pp. 497–511.

49. Y. Cohen-Charash and P. E. Spector, "The Role of Justice in Organizations: A Meta-Analysis," *Organizational Behavior and Human Decision Processes* 86 (November 2001), pp. 278–321.

50. Canadian Press, "Pierre Berton, Canadian Cultural Icon, Enjoyed Long and Colourful Career," *Times Colonist* (Victoria, BC), November 30, 2004.

51. M. Ezzamel and R. Watson, "Pay Comparability across and within UK Boards: An Empirical Analysis of the Cash Pay Awards to CEOs and Other Board Members," *Journal of Management Studies* 39, no. 2 (March 2002), pp. 207–32; J. Fizel, A. C. Krautman, and L. Hadley, "Equity and Arbitration in Major League Baseball," *Managerial and Decision Economics* 23, no. 7 (October–November 2002), pp. 427–35.

52. S. Friedman, "The Compelling Case for Setting Executive Compensation," *Management Review,* March 1988, p. 61; J. Reingold, "Executive Pay," *BusinessWeek Online,* April 21, 1997; J. Gill, "We're Back to Serfs and Royalty," *BusinessWeek Online,* April 9, 2001; L. Mishel, J. Bernstein, and H. Shierholz, *The State of Working America,* 2008/2009 (New York: Economic Policy Institute, 2008), p. 221; R. Wartzman, "Put a Cap on CEO Pay," *BusinessWeek,* September 15, 2008.

53. Greenberg and Lind, "The Pursuit of Organizational Justice: From Conceptualization to Implication to Application"; K. Roberts and K. S. Markel, "Claiming in the Name of Fairness: Organizational Justice and the Decision to File for Workplace Injury Compensation," *Journal of Occupational Health Psychology* 6 (October 2001), pp. 332–47; J. B. Olson-Buchanan and W. R. Boswell, "The Role of Employee Loyalty and Formality in Voicing Discontent," *Journal of Applied Psychology* 87, no. 6 (2002), pp. 1167–74.

54. R. Hagey et al., "Immigrant Nurses' Experience of Racism," *Journal of Nursing Scholarship* 33 (Fourth Quarter 2001), pp. 389–95; Roberts and Markel, "Claiming in the Name of Fairness: Organizational Justice and the Decision to File for Workplace Injury Compensation"; D. A. Jones and D. P. Skarlicki, "The Effects of Overhearing Peers Discuss an Authority's Fairness Reputation on Reactions to Subsequent Treatment," *Journal of Applied Psychology* 90, no. 2 (2005), pp. 363–72.

55. Miller, "Disrespect and the Experience of Injustice."

56. M. L. Ambrose, M. A. Seabright, and M. Schminke, "Sabotage in the Workplace: The Role of Organizational Injustice," *Organizational Behavior and Human Decision Processes* 89, no. 1 (2002), pp. 947–65.

57. S. Zeller, "Good Calls," *Government Executive,* May 15, 2005; C. Bailor, "Checking the Pulse of the Contact Center," *Customer Relationship Management,* November 2007, pp. 24–29.

58. A. Shin, "What Customers Say and How They Say It," *Washington Post,* October 18, 2006, p. D01; D. Ververidis and C. Kotropoulos, "Emotional Speech Recognition: Resources, Features, and Methods," *Speech Communication* 48, no. 9 (2006), pp. 1162–81.

59. G. P. Latham, "Goal Setting: A Five-Step Approach to Behavior Change," *Organizational Dynamics* 32, no. 3 (2003), pp. 309–18; E. A. Locke and G. P. Latham, *A Theory of Goal Setting and Task Performance* (Englewood Cliffs, NJ: Prentice Hall, 1990). The acronym *SMART* refers to goals that are specific, measurable, acceptable, relevant, and timely. However, notice that this list duplicates some characteristics (such as specific goals that are measurable *and* timely) and overlooks the characteristics of challenging (not just acceptable) and feedback-related.

60. A. Li and A. B. Butler, "The Effects of Participation in Goal Setting and Goal Rationales on Goal Commitment: An Exploration of Justice Mediators," *Journal of Business and Psychology* 19, no. 1 (Fall 2004), pp. 37–51.

61. Locke and Latham, *A Theory of Goal Setting and Task Performance,* Chap. 6 and 7; J. Wegge, "Participation in Group Goal Setting: Some Novel Findings and a Comprehensive Model as a New Ending to an Old Story," *Applied Psychology: An International Review* 49 (2000), pp. 498–516.

62. M. London, E. M. Mone, and J. C. Scott, "Performance Management and Assessment: Methods for Improved Rater Accuracy and Employee Goal Setting," *Human Resource Management* 43, no. 4 (Winter 2004), pp. 319–36; G. P. Latham and C. C. Pinder, "Work Motivation Theory and Research at the Dawn of the Twenty-First Century," *Annual Review of Psychology* 56 (2005), pp. 485–516.

63. S. P. Brown, S. Ganesan, and G. Challagalla, "Self-Efficacy as a Moderator of Information-Seeking Effectiveness," *Journal of Applied Psychology* 86, no. 5 (2001), pp. 1043–51; P. A. Heslin and G. P. Latham, "The Effect of Upward Feedback on Managerial Behaviour," *Applied Psychology: An International Review* 53, no. 1 (2004), pp. 23–37; D. Van-Dijk and A. N. Kluger, "Feedback Sign Effect on Motivation: Is It Moderated by Regulatory Focus?" *Applied Psychology: An International Review* 53, no. 1 (2004), pp. 113–35; J. E. Bono and A. E. Colbert, "Understanding Responses to Multi-Source Feedback: The Role of Core Self-Evaluations," *Personnel Psychology* 58, no. 1 (Spring 2005), pp. 171–203.

64. P. Drucker, *The Effective Executive* (Oxford, UK: Butterworth-Heinemann, 2007), p. 22.

65. M. Buckingham, *Go Put Your Strengths to Work* (New York: Free Press, 2007); S. L. Orem, J. Binkert, and A. L. Clancy, *Appreciative Coaching: A Positive Process for Change* (San Francisco: Jossey-Bass, 2007); S. Gordon, "Appreciative Inquiry Coaching," *International Coaching Psychlogy Review* 3, no. 2 (March 2008), pp. 19–31.

66. A. Terracciano, P. T. Costa, and R. R. McCrae, "Personality Plasticity after Age 30," *Personality and Social Psychology Bulletin* 32, no. 8 (August 2006), pp. 999–1009; Leary, "Motivational and Emotional Aspects of the Self."

67. M. Buckingham and D. O. Clifton, *Now, Discover Your Strengths* (New York: Free Press, 2001).

68. S. J. Ashford and G. B. Northcraft, "Conveying More (or Less) Than We Realize: The Role of Impression Management in Feedback Seeking," *Organizational Behavior and Human Decision Processes* 53 (1992), pp. 310–34; J. R. Williams et al., "Increasing Feedback Seeking in Public Contexts: It Takes Two (or More) to Tango," *Journal of Applied Psychology* 84 (December 1999), pp. 969–76.

69. D. Hendry, "Game-Playing: The Latest Business Tool," *Globe & Mail,* November 17, 2006, p. C11.

70. J. B. Miner, "The Rated Importance, Scientific Validity, and Practical Usefulness of Organizational Behavior Theories: A Quantitative Review," *Academy of Management Learning and Education* 2, no. 3 (2003), pp. 250–68. Also see C. C. Pinder, *Work Motivation in Organizational Behavior* (Upper Saddle River, NJ: Prentice-Hall, 1997), p. 384.

71. P. M. Wright, "Goal Setting and Monetary Incentives: Motivational Tools That Can Work Too Well," *Compensation and Benefits Review* 26 (May–June 1994), pp. 41–49; E. A. Locke and G. P. Latham, "Building a Practically Useful Theory of Goal Setting and Task Motivation: A 35–Year Odyssey," *American Psychologist* 57, no. 9 (2002), pp. 705–17.

72. Latham, *Work Motivation,* p. 188.

73. J. R. Edwards, J. A. Scully, and M. D. Brtek, "The Nature and Outcomes of Work: A Replication and Extension of Interdisciplinary Work-Design Research," *Journal of Applied Psychology* 85, no. 6 (2000), pp. 860–68; F. P. Morgeson and M. A. Campion, "Minimizing Tradeoffs When Redesigning Work: Evidence from a Longitudinal Quasi-Experiment," *Personnel Psychology* 55, no. 3 (Autumn 2002), pp. 589–612.

74. H. Fayol, *General and Industrial Management,* trans. C. Storrs (London: Pitman, 1949); Lawler III, *Motivation in Work Organizations,* Chap. 7; M. A. Campion, "Ability Requirement Implications of Job Design: An Interdisciplinary Perspective," *Personnel Psychology* 42 (1989), pp. 1–24.

75. F. W. Taylor, *The Principles of Scientific Management* (New York: Harper & Row, 1911); R. Kanigel, *The One Best Way: Frederick Winslow Taylor and the Enigma of Efficiency* (New York: Viking, 1997).

76. C. R. Walker and R. H. Guest, *The Man on the Assembly Line* (Cambridge, MA: Harvard University Press, 1952); W. F. Dowling, "Job Redesign on the Assembly Line: Farewell to Blue-Collar Blues?" *Organizational Dynamics* (Autumn 1973), pp. 51–67; E. E. Lawler III, *High-Involvement Management* (San Francisco: Jossey-Bass, 1986).

77. M. Keller, *Rude Awakening* (New York: Harper Perennial, 1989), p. 128.

78. F. Herzberg, B. Mausner, and B. B. Snyderman, *The Motivation to Work* (New York: Wiley, 1959).

79. S. K. Parker, T. D. Wall, and J. L. Cordery, "Future Work Design Research and Practice: Towards an Elaborated Model of Work Design," *Journal of Occupational and Organizational Psychology* 74 (November 2001), pp. 413–40. For a decisive critique of motivator–hygiene theory, see N. King, "Clarification and Evaluation of the Two Factor Theory of Job Satisfaction," *Psychological Bulletin* 74 (1970), pp. 18–31.

80. J. R. Hackman and G. Oldham, *Work Redesign* (Reading, MA: Addison-Wesley, 1980).

81. D. Whitford, "A Human Place to Work," *Fortune,* January 8, 2001, pp. 108–19.

82. Data provided in several country-specific news releases from Kelly Services. For a white paper summary of the survey, see Kelly Services, *Employee Loyalty Rises during Global Economic*

Recession, Kelly International Workforce Survey Finds (Troy, MI: Kelly Services, March 8, 2010). The percentages of employees in India choosing higher salary/benefits and employees in China choosing meaningful responsibility are inferred (they were not stated in available sources, but received a lower percentage than the other two identified categories).

83. J. E. Champoux, "A Multivariate Test of the Job Characteristics Theory of Work Motivation," *Journal of Organizational Behavior* 12, no. 5 (September 1991), pp. 431–46; R. B. Tiegs, L. E. Tetrick, and Y. Fried, "Growth Need Strength and Context Satisfactions as Moderators of the Relations of the Job Characteristics Model," *Journal of Management* 18, no. 3 (September 1992), pp. 575–93.

84. M. A. Campion and C. L. McClelland, "Follow-up and Extension of the Interdisciplinary Costs and Benefits of Enlarged Jobs," *Journal of Applied Psychology* 78 (1993), pp. 339–51; N. G. Dodd and D. C. Ganster, "The Interactive Effects of Variety, Autonomy, and Feedback on Attitudes and Performance," *Journal of Organizational Behavior* 17 (1996), pp. 329–47.

85. J. R. Hackman et al., "A New Strategy for Job Enrichment," *California Management Review* 17, no. 4 (1975), pp. 57–71; R. W. Griffin, *Task Design: An Integrative Approach* (Glenview, IL: Scott Foresman, 1982).

86. P. E. Spector and S. M. Jex, "Relations of Job Characteristics from Multiple Data Sources with Employee Affect, Absence, Turnover Intentions, and Health," *Journal of Applied Psychology* 76 (1991), pp. 46–53; P. Osterman, "How Common Is Workplace Transformation and Who Adopts It?" *Industrial and Labor Relations Review* 47 (1994), pp. 173–88; R. Saavedra and S. K. Kwun, "Affective States in Job Characteristics Theory," *Journal of Organizational Behavior* 21 (2000), pp. 131–46.

87. Hackman and Oldham, *Work Redesign,* pp. 137–38.

88. A. Hertting et al., "Personnel Reductions and Structural Changes in Health Care: Work-Life Experiences of Medical Secretaries," *Journal of Psychosomatic Research* 54 (February 2003), pp. 161–70.

89. This definition is based mostly on G. M. Spreitzer and R. E. Quinn, *A Company of Leaders: Five Disiplines for Unleashing the Power in Your Workforce* (San Francisco: Jossey-Bass, 2001). However, most elements of this definition appear in other discussions of empowerment. See, for example, R. Forrester, "Empowerment: Rejuvenating a Potent Idea," *Academy of Management Executive* 14 (August 2000), pp. 67–80; W. A. Randolph, "Re-Thinking Empowerment: Why Is It So Hard to Achieve?" *Organizational Dynamics* 29 (November 2000), pp. 94–107; S. T. Menon, "Employee Empowerment: An Integrative Psychological Approach," *Applied Psychology: An International Review* 50 (2001), pp. 153–80.

90. The positive relationship between these structural empowerment conditions and psychological empowerment is reported in H. K. S. Laschinger et al., "A Longitudinal Analysis of the Impact of Workplace Empowerment on Work Satisfaction," *Journal of Organizational Behavior* 25, no. 4 (June 2004), pp. 527–45.

91. C. S. Koberg et al., "Antecedents and Outcomes of Empowerment," *Group and Organization Management* 24 (1999), pp. 71–91; Y. Melhem, "The Antecedents of Customer-Contact Employees' Empowerment," *Employee Relations* 26, no. 1/2 (2004), pp. 72–93.

92. B. J. Niehoff et al., "The Influence of Empowerment and Job Enrichment on Employee Loyalty in a Downsizing Environment," *Group and Organization Management* 26 (March 2001), pp. 93–113; J. Yoon, "The Role of Structure and Motivation for Workplace Empowerment: The Case of Korean Employees," *Social Psychology Quarterly* 64 (June 2001), pp. 195–206; T. D. Wall, J. L. Cordery, and C. W. Clegg, "Empowerment, Performance, and Operational Uncertainty: A Theoretical Integration," *Applied Psychology: An International Review* 51 (2002), pp. 146–69.

93. G. M. Spreitzer, "Social Structural Characteristics of Psychological Empowerment," *Academy of Management Journal* 39 (April 1996), pp. 483–504; J. Godard, "High Performance and the Transformation of Work? The Implications of Alternative Work Practices for the Experience and Outcomes of Work," *Industrial & Labor Relations Review* 54 (July 2001), pp. 776–805; P. A. Miller, P. Goddard, and H. K. Spence Laschinger, "Evaluating Physical Therapists' Perception of Empowerment Using Kanter's Theory of Structural Power in Organizations," *Physical Therapy* 81 (December 2001), pp. 1880–88.

94. J.-C. Chebat and P. Kollias, "The Impact of Empowerment on Customer Contact Employees' Role in Service Organizations," *Journal of Service Research* 3 (August 2000), pp. 66–81; H. K. S. Laschinger, J. Finegan, and J. Shamian, "The Impact of Workplace Empowerment, Organizational Trust on Staff Nurses' Work Satisfaction and Organizational Commitment," *Health Care Management Review* 26 (Summer 2001), pp. 7–23.

CHAPTER 6

1. S. Marchionne, "Fiat's Extreme Makeover," *Harvard Business Review,* December 2008, pp. 45–48; "Marchionne's Weekend Warriors," *Automotive News,* June 22, 2009; D. Welch, D. Kiley, and C. Matlack, "Tough Love at Chrysler," *BusinessWeek,* August 24, 2009; B. Wernie and L. Ciferri, "Life under Marchionne: New Stars, Hasty Exits," *Automotive News,* October 12, 2009, 1, 42; J. Reed, "High Stakes for Fiat's Sergio Marchionne," *Financial Times (London),* February 19, 2010.

2. F. A. Shull Jr., A. L. Delbecq, and L. L. Cummings, *Organizational Decision Making* (New York: McGraw-Hill, 1970), p. 31.

3. R. E. Nisbett, *The Geography of Thought: How Asians and Westerners Think Differently—and Why* (New York: Free Press, 2003); R. Hanna, "Kant's Theory of Judgment," (Stanford Encyclopedia of Philosophy, 2004), http://plato.stanford.edu/entries/kant-judgment/ (accessed March 31, 2008); D. Baltzly, "Stoicism," (Stanford Encyclopedia of Philosophy, 2008), http://plato.stanford.edu/entries/stoicism/ (accessed March 30, 2008).

4. J. G. March and H. A. Simon, *Organizations* (New York: John Wiley & Sons, 1958).

5. *U.K. Bosses Labeled Bad Decision Makers* (London: Investors in People, August 6, 2007).

6. This model is adapted from several sources, including H. A. Simon, *The New Science of Management Decision* (New York: Harper & Row, 1960); H. Mintzberg, D. Raisinghani, and A. Théorét, "The Structure of 'Unstructured' Decision Processes," *Administrative Science Quarterly* 21 (1976), pp. 246–75; and W. C. Wedley and R. H. G. Field, "A Predecision Support System," *Academy of Management Review* 9 (1984), pp. 696–703.

7. P. F. Drucker, *The Practice of Management* (New York: Harper & Brothers, 1954), pp. 353–57; B. M. Bass, *Organizational Decision Making* (Homewood, IL: Irwin, 1983), Chap. 3.

8. L. R. Beach and T. R. Mitchell, "A Contingency Model for the Selection of Decision Strategies," *Academy of Management Review* 3 (1978), pp. 439–49; I. L. Janis, *Crucial Decisions* (New York: The Free Press, 1989), pp. 35–37; W. Zhongtuo, "Meta-Decision Making: Concepts and Paradigm," *Systematic Practice and Action Research* 13, no. 1 (February 2000), pp. 111–15.

9. N. Schwarz, "Social Judgment and Attitudes: Warmer, More Social, and Less Conscious," *European Journal of Social Psychology* 30 (2000), pp. 149–76; N. M. Ashkanasy and C. E. J. Hartel, "Managing Emotions in Decision Making," in *Managing Emotions in the Workplace,* ed. N. M. Ashkanasy, W. J. Zerbe, and C. E. J. Hartel (Armonk, NY: M. E. Sharpe, 2002); S. Maitlis and H. Ozcelik, "Toxic Decision Processes: A Study of Emotion and Organizational Decision Making," *Organization Science* 15, no. 4 (July–August 2004), pp. 375–93.

10. A. Howard, "Opinion," *Computing* (July 8, 1999), p. 18.

11. A. R. Damasio, *Descartes' Error: Emotion, Reason, and the Human Brain* (New York: Putnam Sons, 1994); P. Winkielman and K. C. Berridge, "Unconscious Emotion," *Current Directions in Psychological Science* 13, no. 3 (2004), pp. 120–23; A. Bechara and A. R. Damasio, "The Somatic Marker Hypothesis: A Neural Theory of Economic Decision," *Games and Economic Behavior* 52, no. 2 (2005), pp. 336–72.

12. T. K. Das and B. S. Teng, "Cognitive Biases and Strategic Decision Processes: An Integrative Perspective," *Journal of Management Studies* 36, no. 6 (November 1999), pp. 757–78; P. Bijttebier, H. Vertommen, and G. V. Steene, "Assessment of Cognitive Coping Styles: A Closer Look at Situation-Response Inventories," *Clinical Psychology Review* 21, no. 1 (2001), pp. 85–104; P. C. Nutt, "Expanding the Search for Alternatives during Strategic Decision Making," *Academy of Management Executive* 18, no. 4 (November 2004), pp. 13–28.

13. W. Ocasio, "Toward an Attention-Based View of the Firm," *Strategic Management Journal* 18, no. S1 (1997), pp. 187–206; S. Kaplan, "Framing Contests: Strategy Making under Uncertainty," *Organization Science* 19, no. 5 (September 2008), pp. 729–52; J. S. McMullen, D. A. Shepherd, and H. Patzelt, "Managerial (in)Attention to Competitive Threats," *Journal of Management Studies* 46, no. 2 (2009), pp. 157–81.

14. P. C. Nutt, *Why Decisions Fail* (San Francisco, CA: Berrett-Koehler, 2002); S. Finkelstein, *Why Smart Executives Fail* (New York: Viking, 2003).

15. E. Witte, "Field Research on Complex Decision-Making Processes—the Phase Theorum," *International Studies of Management and Organization,* no. 56 (1972), pp. 156–82; J. A. Bargh and T. L. Chartrand, "The Unbearable Automaticity of Being," *American Psychologist* 54, no. 7 (July 1999), pp. 462–79.

16. A. H. Maslow, *The Psychology of Science: A Reconnaissance* (Chapel Hill, NC: Maurice Bassett Publishing, 2002)

17. J. Brandtstadter, A. Voss, and K. Rothermund, "Perception of Danger Signals: The Role of Control," *Experimental Psychology* 51, no. 1 (2004), pp. 24–32; M. Hock and H. W. Krohne, "Coping with Threat and Memory for Ambiguous Information: Testing the Repressive Discontinuity Hypothesis," *Emotion* 4, no. 1 (2004), pp. 65–86.

18. "NASA Managers Differed over Shuttle Strike," *Reuters* (July 22, 2003); Columbia Accident Investigation Board, *Report, Volume 1* (Washington, DC: Government Printing Office, August 2003); C. Gibson, "Columbia: The Final Mission," *NineMSN* (July 13, 2003); S. Jefferson, "NASA Let Arrogance on Board," *Palm Beach Post,* August 30, 2003; R. J. Smith, "NASA Culture, Columbia Probers Still Miles Apart," *Washington Post* (August 22, 2003), p. A3.

19. R. Rothenberg, "Ram Charan: The Thought Leader Interview," *strategy + business,* Fall 2004.

20. H. A. Simon, *Administrative Behavior,* 2nd ed. (New York: The Free Press, 1957); H. A. Simon, "Rational Decision Making in Business Organizations," *American Economic Review* 69, no. 4 (September 1979), pp. 493–513.

21. Simon, *Administrative Behavior,* pp. xxv, 80–84.

22. P. O. Soelberg, "Unprogrammed Decision Making," *Industrial Management Review* 8 (1967), pp. 19–29; J. E. Russo, V. H. Medvec, and M. G. Meloy, "The Distortion of Information during Decisions," *Organizational Behavior & Human Decision Processes* 66 (1996), pp. 102–10. This is consistent with the observations by Milton Rokeach, who famously stated, "Life is ipsative, because decisions in everyday life are inherently and phenomenologically ipsative decisions." M. Rokeach, "Inducing Changes and Stability in Belief Systems and Personality Structures," *Journal of Social Issues* 41, no. 1 (1985), pp. 153–71.

23. A. L. Brownstein, "Biased Predecision Processing," *Psychological Bulletin* 129, no. 4 (2003), pp. 545–68.

24. H. A. Simon, "Rational Choice and the Structure of Environments," *Psychological Review* 63 (1956), pp. 129–38.

25. S. Botti and S. S. Iyengar, "The Dark Side of Choice: When Choice Impairs Social Welfare," *Journal of Public Policy and Marketing* 25, no. 1 (2006), pp. 24–38; K. D. Vohs et al., "Making Choices Impairs Subsequent Self-Control: A Limited-Resource Account of Decision Making, Self-Regulation, and Active Initiative," *Journal of Personality and Social Psychology* 94, no. 5 (2008), pp. 883–98.

26. S. S. Iyengar and M. R. Lepper, "When Choice Is Demotivating: Can One Desire Too Much of a Good Thing?" *Journal of Personality and Social Psychology* 79, no. 6 (2000), pp. 995–1006.

27. P. C. Nutt, "Search during Decision Making," *European Journal of Operational Research* 160 (2005), pp. 851–76.

28. P. Winkielman et al., "Affective Influence on Judgments and Decisions: Moving Towards Core Mechanisms," *Review of General Psychology* 11, no. 2 (2007), pp. 179–92.

29. J. P. Forgas, "Affective Intelligence: Towards Understanding the Role of Affect in Social Thinking and Behavior," in *Emotional Intelligence in Everyday Life,* ed. J. V. Ciarrochi, J. P. Forgas, and J. D. Mayer (New York: Psychology Press, 2001), pp. 46–65; J. P. Forgas and J. M. George, "Affective Influences on Judgments and Behavior in Organizations: An Information Processing Perspective," *Organizational Behavior and Human Decision Processes* 86 (September 2001), pp. 3–34; G. Loewenstein and J. S. Lerner, "The Role of Affect in Decision Making," in *Handbook of Affective Sciences,* ed. R. J. Davidson, K. R. Scherer, and H. H. Goldsmith (New York: Oxford University Press, 2003), pp. 619–42; J. S. Lerner, D. A. Small, and G. Loewenstein, "Heart Strings and Purse Strings: Carryover Effects of Emotions on Economic Decisions," *Psychological Science* 15, no. 5 (2004), pp. 337–41; M. T. Pham, "Emotion and Rationality: A Critical Review and Interpretation of Empirical Evidence," *Review of General Psychology* 11, no. 2 (2007), pp. 155–78.

30. D. Miller, *The Icarus Paradox* (New York: HarperBusiness, 1990); D. Miller, "What Happens after Success: The Perils of Excellence," *Journal of Management Studies* 31, no. 3 (1994), pp. 325–68; A. C. Amason and A. C. Mooney, "The Icarus Paradox Revisited: How Strong Performance Sows the Seeds of Dysfunction in Future Strategic Decision Making," *Strategic Organization* 6, no. 4 (November 2008), pp. 407–34.

31. M. T. Pham, "The Logic of Feeling," *Journal of Consumer Psychology* 14 (September 2004), pp. 360–69; N. Schwarz, "Metacognitive Experiences in Consumer Judgment and Decision Making," *Journal of Consumer Psychology* 14 (September 2004), pp. 332–49.

32. L. Sjöberg, "Intuitive vs. Analytical Decision Making: Which Is Preferred?" *Scandinavian Journal of Management* 19 (2003), pp. 17–29.

33. W. H. Agor, "The Logic of Intuition," *Organizational Dynamics* (Winter 1986), pp. 5–18; H. A. Simon, "Making Management Decisions: The Role of Intuition and Emotion," *Academy of Management Executive* (February 1987), pp. 57–64; O. Behling and N. L. Eckel, "Making Sense out of Intuition," *Academy of Management Executive* 5 (February 1991), pp. 46–54. This process is also known as naturalistic decision making. For a discussion of research on naturalistic decision making, see the special issue in *Organization Studies:* R. Lipshitz, G. Klein, and J. S. Carroll, "Introduction to the Special Issue: Naturalistic Decision Making and Organizational Decision Making: Exploring the Intersections," *Organization Studies* 27, no. 7 (2006), pp. 917–23.

34. D. Woods, "Managers Make Decisions about People Based on Gut Instinct Rather Than Objective Data," *HR Magazine,* February 16, 2010.

35. M. D. Lieberman, "Intuition: A Social Cognitive Neuroscience Approach," *Psychological Bulletin* 126 (2000), pp. 109–37; G. Klein, *Intuition at Work* (New York: Currency/Doubleday, 2003); E. Dane and M. G. Pratt, "Exploring Intuition and Its Role in Managerial Decision Making," *Academy of Management Review* 32, no. 1 (2007), pp. 33–54.

36. Klein, *Intuition at Work,* pp. 12–13, 16–17.

37. Y. Ganzach, A. H. Kluger, and N. Klayman, "Making Decisions from an Interview: Expert Measurement and Mechanical Combination," *Personnel Psychology* 53 (Spring 2000), pp. 1–20; A. M. Hayashi, "When to Trust Your Gut," *Harvard Business Review* 79 (February 2001), pp. 59–65. Evidence of high failure rates from quick decisions is reported in Nutt, *Why Decisions Fail;* Nutt, "Search during Decision Making"; P. C. Nutt, "Investigating the Success of Decision Making Processes," *Journal of Management Studies* 45, no. 2 (March 2008), pp. 425–55.

38. P. Goodwin and G. Wright, "Enhancing Strategy Evaluation in Scenario Planning: A Role for Decision Analysis," *Journal of Management Studies* 38 (January 2001), pp. 1–16; R. Bradfield et al., "The Origins and Evolution of Scenario Techniques in Long Range Business Planning," *Futures* 37, no. 8 (2005), pp. 795–812; G. Wright, G. Cairns, and P. Goodwin, "Teaching Scenario Planning: Lessons from Practice in Academe and Business," *European Journal of Operational Research* 194, no. 1 (April 2009), pp. 323–35.

39. *Whatif... Edition: Shipping* (Harstad, Norway: Dreyer Kompetense, July 16, 2009); Z. A. Wahab, "Norwegian Firm Offers Board Game as Training Tool," *Bernama Daily Malaysian News (Kuala Lumpur),* March 25, 2010.

40. J. Pfeffer and R. I. Sutton, "Knowing 'What' to Do Is Not Enough: Turning Knowledge into Action," *California Management Review* 42, no. 1 (Fall 1999), pp. 83–108; R. Charan, C. Burke, and L. Bossidy, *Execution: The Discipline of Getting Things Done* (New York: Crown Business, 2002).

41. R. N. Taylor, *Behavioral Decision Making* (Glenview, IL: Scott, Foresman, 1984), pp. 163–66; R. S. Nickerson, "Confirmation Bias: A Ubiquitous Phenomenon in Many Guises," *Review of General Psychology* 2, no. 2 (1998), pp. 175–220.

42. G. Whyte, "Escalating Commitment to a Course of Action: A Reinterpretation," *Academy of Management Review* 11 (1986), pp. 311–21; J. Brockner, "The Escalation of Commitment to a Failing Course of Action: Toward Theoretical Progress," *Academy of Management Review* 17, no. 1 (January 1992), pp. 39–61.

43. F. D. Schoorman and P. J. Holahan, "Psychological Antecedents of Escalation Behavior: Effects of Choice, Responsibility, and Decision Consequences," *Journal of Applied Psychology* 81 (1996), pp. 786–93.

44. G. Whyte, "Escalating Commitment in Individual and Group Decision Making: A Prospect Theory Approach," *Organizational Behavior and Human Decision Processes* 54 (1993), pp. 430–55; D. J. Sharp and S. B. Salter, "Project Escalation and Sunk Costs: A Test of the International Generalizability of Agency and Prospect Theories," *Journal of International Business Studies* 28, no. 1 (1997), pp. 101–21.

45. M. Keil, G. Depledge, and A. Rai, "Escalation: The Role of Problem Recognition and Cognitive Bias," *Decision Sciences* 38, no. 3 (August 2007), pp. 391–421.

46. P. Hall, *Great Planning Disasters* (New York: Penguin Books, 1980), Chap. 5; H. Drummond, *Escalation in Decision Making: The Tragedy of Taurus* (Oxford: Oxford University Press, 1996); R. Matas, "Spiralling Costs Torpedoed Fast Ferries," *Globe & Mail,* June 13, 2000, A2; C. McInnes, "Victoria Sinks Fast Ferries," *Vancouver Sun,* March 14, 2000; R. Montealagre and M. Keil, "De-Escalating Information Technology Projects: Lessons from the Denver International Airport," *MIS Quarterly* 24, no. 3 (September 2000), pp. 417–47; I. Swanson, "Holyrood Firms Face Grilling over Costs," *Evening News (Edinburgh),* June 6, 2003, 2; Lord Fraser of Carmyllie QC, *The Holyrood Inquiry* (Edinborough: Scottish Parliamentary Corporate Body, 2004); P. Murray, *The Saga of Sydney Opera House* (London: Taylor & Francis, 2004); M. Sheehan, "Throwing Good Money after Bad," *Sunday Independent (Dublin),* October 9, 2005; D. Ferry, "Computer System Was Budgeted at Eur9m...It's Cost Eur170m...Now Health Chiefs Want a New One," *The Mirror (London),* July 7, 2007, p. 16.

47. J. D. Bragger et al., "When Success Breeds Failure: History, Hysteresis, and Delayed Exit Decisions," *Journal of Applied Psychology* 88, no. 1 (2003), pp. 6–14. A second logical reason for escalation, called the Martingale strategy, is described in J. A. Aloysius, "Rational Escalation of Costs by Playing a Sequence of Unfavorable Gambles: The Martingale," *Journal of Economic Behavior & Organization* 51 (2003), pp. 111–29.

48. I. Simonson and B. M. Staw, "De-Escalation Strategies: A Comparison of Techniques for Reducing Commitment to Losing Courses of Action," *Journal of Applied Psychology* 77 (1992), pp. 419–26; W. Boulding, R. Morgan, and R. Staelin, "Pulling the Plug to Stop the New Product Drain," *Journal of Marketing Research,* no. 34 (1997), pp. 164–76; B. M. Staw, K. W. Koput, and S. G. Barsade, "Escalation at the Credit Window: A Longitudinal Study of Bank Executives' Recognition and Write-Off of Problem Loans," *Journal of Applied Psychology,* no. 82 (1997), pp. 130–42; M. Keil and D. Robey, "Turning around Troubled Software Projects: An Exploratory Study of the Deescalation of Commitment to Failing Courses of Action," *Journal of Management Information Systems* 15 (Spring 1999), pp. 63–87.

49. D. Ghosh, "De-Escalation Strategies: Some Experimental Evidence," *Behavioral Research in Accounting* 9 (1997), pp. 88–112.

50. M. Gardner, "Democratic Principles Making Businesses More Transparent," *Christian Science Monitor,* March 19, 2007, p. 13.

51. M. Fenton-O'Creevy, "Employee Involvement and the Middle Manager: Saboteur or Scapegoat?" *Human Resource Management Journal,* no. 11 (2001), pp. 24–40. Also see V. H. Vroom and A. G. Jago, *The New Leadership: Managing Participation in Organizations* (Englewood Cliffs, NJ: Prentice Hill, 1988).

52. "Survey Finds Most Workers in Big Companies (65%) Rely on One Another," *Enhanced News Online (New York),* July 31, 2007.

53. Some of the early OB writing on employee involvement includes C. Argyris, *Personality and Organization* (New York: Harper &

Row, 1957); D. McGregor, *The Human Side of Enterprise* (New York: McGraw-Hill, 1960); and R. Likert, *New Patterns of Management* (New York: McGraw-Hill, 1961).

54. A. G. Robinson and D. M. Schroeder, *Ideas Are Free* (San Francisco: Berrett-Koehler, 2004).

55. R. J. Ely and D. A. Thomas, "Cultural Diversity at Work: The Effects of Diversity Perspectives on Work Group Processes and Outcomes," *Administrative Science Quarterly* 46 (June 2001), pp. 229–73; E. Mannix and M. A. Neale, "What Differences Make a Difference? The Promise and Reality of Diverse Teams in Organizations," *Psychological Science in the Public Interest* 6, no. 2 (2005), pp. 31–55.

56. D. Berend and J. Paroush, "When Is Condorcet's Jury Theorem Valid?" *Social Choice and Welfare* 15, no. 4 (1998), pp. 481–88.

57. K. T. Dirks, L. L. Cummings, and J. L. Pierce, "Psychological Ownership in Organizations: Conditions under Which Individuals Promote and Resist Change," *Research in Organizational Change and Development,* no. 9 (1996), pp. 1–23; J. P. Walsh and S.-F. Tseng, "The Effects of Job Characteristics on Active Effort at Work," *Work & Occupations,* no. 25 (February 1998), pp. 74–96; B. Scott-Ladd and V. Marshall, "Participation in Decision Making: A Matter of Context?" *Leadership & Organization Development Journal* 25, no. 8 (2004), pp. 646–62.

58. J. Zhou and C. E. Shalley, "Research on Employee Creativity: A Critical Review and Directions for Future Research," *Research in Personnel and Human Resources Management* 22 (2003), pp. 165–217; M. A. Runco, "Creativity," *Annual Review of Psychology* 55 (2004), pp. 657–87.

59. G. Wallas, *The Art of Thought* (New York: Harcourt Brace Jovanovich, 1926). For recent applications of Wallas's classic model, see T. Kristensen, "The Physical Context of Creativity," *Creativity and Innovation Management* 13, no. 2 (June 2004), pp. 89–96; U.-E. Haner, "Spaces for Creativity and Innovation in Two Established Organizations," *Creativity and Innovation Management* 14, no. 3 (2005), pp. 288–98.

60. R. S. Nickerson, "Enhancing Creativity," in *Handbook of Creativity,* ed. R. J. Sternberg (New York: Cambridge University Press, 1999), pp. 392–430.

61. R. I. Sutton, *Weird Ideas That Work* (New York: Free Press, 2002), p. 26.

62. For a thorough discussion of insight, see R. J. Sternberg and J. E. Davidson, *The Nature of Insight* (Cambridge, MA: MIT Press, 1995).

63. R. J. Sternberg and L. A. O' Hara, "Creativity and Intelligence," in *Handbook of Creativity,* ed. R. J. Sternberg (New York: Cambridge University Press, 1999), pp. 251–72; S. Taggar, "Individual Creativity and Group Ability to Utilize Individual Creative Resources: A Multilevel Model," *Academy of Management Journal* 45 (April 2002), pp. 315–30.

64. G. J. Feist, "The Influence of Personality on Artistic and Scientific Creativity," in *Handbook of Creativity,* ed. R. J. Sternberg (New York: Cambridge University Press, 1999), pp. 273–96; Sutton, *Weird Ideas That Work,* pp. 8–9, Chap. 10; T. Åsterbro, S. A. Jeffrey, and G. K. Adomdza, "Inventor Perseverance after Being Told to Quit: The Role of Cognitive Biases," *Journal of Behavioral Decision Making* 20 (2007), pp. 253–72.

65. R. W. Weisberg, "Creativity and Knowledge: A Challenge to Theories," in *Handbook of Creativity,* ed. R. J. Sternberg (New York: Cambridge University Press, 1999), pp. 226–50.

66. Sutton, *Weird Ideas That Work,* pp. 121, 153–54; C. Andriopoulos, "Six Paradoxes in Managing Creativity: An Embracing Act," *Long Range Planning* 36 (2003), pp. 375–88.

67. R. J. Sternberg and T. I. Lubart, *Defying the Crowd: Cultivating Creativity in a Culture of Conformity* (New York: Free Press, 1995); Feist, "The Influence of Personality on Artistic and Scientific Creativity"; S. J. Dollinger, K. K. Urban, and T. A. James, "Creativity and Openness to Experience: Validation of Two Creative Product Measures," *Creativity Research Journal* 16, no. 1 (2004), pp. 35–47; C. E. Shalley, J. Zhou, and G. R. Oldham, "The Effects of Personal and Contextual Characteristics on Creativity: Where Should We Go from Here?" *Journal of Management* 30, no. 6 (2004), pp. 933–58; T. S. Schweizer, "The Psychology of Novelty-Seeking, Creativity and Innovation: Neurocognitive Aspects within a Work-Psychological Perspective," *Creativity and Innovation Management* 15, no. 2 (2006), pp. 164–72.

68. T. M. Amabile et al., "Leader Behaviors and the Work Environment for Creativity: Perceived Leader Support," *The Leadership Quarterly* 15, no. 1 (2004), pp. 5–32; Shalley, Zhou, and Oldham, "The Effects of Personal and Contextual Characteristics on Creativity"; S. T. Hunter, K. E. Bedell, and M. D. Mumford, "Climate for Creativity: A Quantitative Review," *Creativity Research Journal* 19, no. 1 (2007), pp. 69–90; T. C. DiLiello and J. D. Houghton, "Creative Potential and Practised Creativity: Identifying Untapped Creativity in Organizations," *Creativity and Innovation Management* 17, no. 1 (2008), pp. 37–46.

69. R. Westwood and D. R. Low, "The Multicultural Muse: Culture, Creativity and Innovation," *International Journal of Cross Cultural Management* 3, no. 2 (2003), pp. 235–59.

70. V. Khanna, "The Voice of Google," *Business Times Singapore,* January 12, 2008.

71. "Samsung CEO Yun Picks Google as New Role Model," *Korea Times,* October 1, 2007.

72. T. M. Amabile, "Motivating Creativity in Organizations: On Doing What You Love and Loving What You Do," *California Management Review* 40 (Fall 1997), pp. 39–58; A. Cummings and G. R. Oldham, "Enhancing Creativity: Managing Work Contexts for the High Potential Employee," *California Management Review,* no. 40 (Fall 1997), pp. 22–38.

73. T. M. Amabile, "Changes in the Work Environment for Creativity during Downsizing," *Academy of Management Journal* 42 (December 1999), pp. 630–40.

74. J. Moultrie et al., "Innovation Spaces: Towards a Framework for Understanding the Role of the Physical Environment in Innovation," *Creativity & Innovation Management* 16, no. 1 (2007), pp. 53–65.

75. J. M. Howell and K. Boies, "Champions of Technological Innovation: The Influence of Contextual Knowledge, Role Orientation, Idea Generation, and Idea Promotion on Champion Emergence," *The Leadership Quarterly* 15, no. 1 (2004), pp. 123–43; Shalley, Zhou, and Oldham, "The Effects of Personal and Contextual Characteristics on Creativity"; S. Powell, "The Management and Consumption of Organisational Creativity," *Journal of Consumer Marketing* 25, no. 3 (2008), pp. 158–66.

76. A. Hiam, "Obstacles to Creativity—and How You Can Remove Them," *Futurist* 32 (October 1998), pp. 30–34.

77. M. A. West, *Developing Creativity in Organizations* (Leicester, UK: BPS Books, 1997), pp. 33–35.

78. S. Hemsley, "Seeking the Source of Innovation," *Media Week,* August 16, 2005, p. 22.

79. A. Hargadon and R. I. Sutton, "Building an Innovation Factory," *Harvard Business Review* 78 (May-June 2000), pp. 157–66; T. Kelley, *The Art of Innovation* (New York: Currency Doubleday, 2001), pp. 158–62.

80. M. Burton, "Open Plan, Open Mind," *Director* (March 2005), pp. 68–72; A. Benady, "Mothers of Invention," *The Independent (London),* November 27, 2006; B. Murray, "Agency Profile: Mother London," *Ihaveanidea,* January 28, 2007, www.ihaveanidea.org.

81. "John Collee-Biography" (IMDB (Internet Movie Database), 2009), http://www.imdb.com/name/nm0171722/bio (accessed April 27, 2009).

CHAPTER 7

1. "Trends: Are Many Meetings a Waste of Time? Study Says So," MeetingsNet news release (November 1, 1998); "Go Teams! Firms Can't Do without Them" (American Management Association, 2008), http://amalearning.com (accessed April 21, 2010).

2. S. Wuchty, B. F. Jones, and B. Uzzi, "The Increasing Dominance of Teams in Production of Knowledge," *Science* 316 (May 18, 2007), pp. 1036–39.

3. M. E. Shaw, *Group Dynamics,* 3rd ed. (New York: McGraw-Hill, 1981), p. 8; S. A. Mohrman, S. G. Cohen, and A. M. Mohrman Jr., *Designing Team-Based Organizations: New Forms for Knowledge Work* (San Francisco: Jossey-Bass, 1995), pp. 39–40; E. Sundstrom, "The Challenges of Supporting Work Team Effectiveness," in *Supporting Work Team Effectiveness,* ed. E. Sundstrom and Associates (San Francisco, CA: Jossey-Bass, 1999), pp. 6–9.

4. R. A. Guzzo and M. W. Dickson, "Teams in Organizations: Recent Research on Performance and Effectiveness," *Annual Review of Psychology* 47 (1996), pp. 307–38; D. A. Nadler, "From Ritual to Real Work: The Board as a Team," *Directors and Boards* 22 (Summer 1998), pp. 28–31; L. R. Offerman and R. K. Spiros, "The Science and Practice of Team Development: Improving the Link," *Academy of Management Journal* 44 (April 2001), pp. 376–92.

5. B. D. Pierce and R. White, "The Evolution of Social Structure: Why Biology Matters," *Academy of Management Review* 24 (October 1999), pp. 843–53; P. R. Lawrence and N. Nohria, *Driven: How Human Nature Shapes Our Choices* (San Francisco: Jossey-Bass, 2002); J. R. Spoor and J. R. Kelly, "The Evolutionary Significance of Affect in Groups: Communication and Group Bonding," *Group Processes & Intergroup Relations* 7, no. 4 (2004), pp. 398–412. For a critique of this view, see G. Sewell, "What Goes Around, Comes Around," *Journal of Applied Behavioural Science* 37, no. 1 (March 2001), pp. 70–91.

6. M. A. Hogg et al., "The Social Identity Perspective: Intergroup Relations, Self-Conception, and Small Groups," *Small Group Research* 35, no. 3 (June 2004), pp. 246–76; N. Michinov, E. Michinov, and M.-C. Toczek-Capelle, "Social Identity, Group Processes, and Performance in Synchronous Computer-Mediated Communication," *Group Dynamics: Theory, Research, and Practice* 8, no. 1 (2004), pp. 27–39; M. Van Vugt and C. M. Hart, "Social Identity as Social Glue: The Origins of Group Loyalty," *Journal of Personality and Social Psychology* 86, no. 4 (2004), pp. 585–98.

7. S. Schacter, *The Psychology of Affiliation* (Stanford, CA: Stanford University Press, 1959), pp. 12–19; R. Eisler and D. S. Levine, "Nurture, Nature, and Caring: We Are Not Prisoners of Our Genes," *Brain and Mind* 3 (2002), pp. 9–52; A. C. DeVries, E. R. Glasper, and C. E. Detillion, "Social Modulation of Stress Responses," *Physiology & Behavior* 79, no. 3 (August 2003), pp. 399–407; S. Cohen, "The Pittsburgh Common Cold Studies: Psychosocial Predictors of Susceptibility to Respiratory Infectious Illness," *International Journal of Behavioral Medicine* 12, no. 3 (2005), pp. 123–31.

8. Cohen, "The Pittsburgh Common Cold Studies: Psychosocial Predictors of Susceptibility to Respiratory Infectious Illness"; M. T. Hansen, M. L. Mors, and B. Løvås, "Knowledge Sharing in Organizations: Multiple Networks, Multiple Phases," *Academy of Management Journal* 48, no. 5 (2005), pp. 776–93; R. Cross et al., "Using Social Network Analysis to Improve Communities of Practice," *California Management Review* 49, no. 1 (2006), pp. 32–60; P. Balkundi et al., "Demographic Antecedents and Performance Consequences of Structural Holes in Work Teams," *Journal of Organizational Behavior* 28, no. 2 (2007), pp. 241–60; W. Verbeke and S. Wuyts, "Moving in Social Circles: Social Circle Membership and Performance Implications," *Journal of Organizational Behavior* 28, no. 4 (2007), pp. 357–79.

9. "Mayor Announces Plan to Reduce Pot-Hole Wait Times to Two Days," *US Fed News,* August 7, 2008; "Transformational Business Project and Top Professionals among HR Awards Winners," Mediacom news release (Auckland: March 3, 2009); Rackspace Hosting, *Rackspace Hosting, Inc. - Form 10-K,* (San Antonio, TX: February 26, 2010).

10. This information is from the Web sites of these companies.

11. M. Moldaschl and W. Weber, "The 'Three Waves' of Industrial Group Work: Historical Reflections on Current Research on Group Work," *Human Relations* 51 (March 1998), pp. 347–88. Several popular books in the 1980s encouraged teamwork, based on the Japanese economic miracle. These books include W. Ouchi, *Theory Z: How American Management Can Meet the Japanese Challenge* (Reading, MA: Addison-Wesley, 1981); and R. T. Pascale and A. G. Athos, *Art of Japanese Management* (New York: Simon and Schuster, 1982).

12. C. R. Emery and L. D. Fredenhall, "The Effect of Teams on Firm Profitability and Customer Satisfaction," *Journal of Service Research* 4 (February 2002), pp. 217–29; G. S. Van der Vegt and O. Janssen, "Joint Impact of Interdependence and Group Diversity on Innovation," *Journal of Management* 29 (2003), pp. 729–51.

13. R. E. Baumeister and M. R. Leary, "The Need to Belong: Desire for Interpersonal Attachments as a Fundamental Human Motivation," *Psychological Bulletin* 117 (1995), pp. 497–529; S. Chen, H. C. Boucher, and M. P. Tapias, "The Relational Self Revealed: Integrative Conceptualization and Implications for Interpersonal Life," *Psychological Bulletin* 132, no. 2 (2006), pp. 151–79; J. M. Feinberg and J. R. Aiello, "Social Facilitation: A Test of Competing Theories," *Journal of Applied Social Psychology* 36, no. 5 (2006), pp. 1087–109; A. M. Grant, "Relational Job Design and the Motivation to Make a Prosocial Didifference," *Academy of Management Review* 32, no. 2 (2007), pp. 393–417; N. L. Kerr et al., "Psychological Mechanisms Underlying the Kohler Motivation Gain," *Personality & Social Psychology Bulletin* 33, no. 6 (2007), pp. 828–41.

14. "Powerhouse Team Switched on by Pride," *The Australian,* August 23, 2008, p. 4.

15. "Canadians Name Diversity as Key Ingredient in Formula for Innovation Success," Canada News Wire news release for X. R. C. o. Canada (Toronto: September 25, 2007); Institute for Corporate Productivity, "Two out of Three Companies Say They Will Rely More on Virtual Teams in the Future," Institute for Corporate Productivity news release (Seattle: September 4, 2008).

16. E. A. Locke et al, "The Importance of the Individual in an Age of Groupism," in *Groups at Work: Theory and Research,* ed. M. E. Turner (Mahwah, NJ: Lawrence Erbaum Associates, 2001),

pp. 501–28; N. J. Allen and T. D. Hecht, "The 'Romance of Teams': Toward an Understanding of Its Psychological Underpinnings and Implications," *Journal of Occupational and Organizational Psychology* 77 (2004), pp. 439–61.

17. I. D. Steiner, *Group Process and Productivity* (New York: Academic Press, 1972); N. L. Kerr and S. R. Tindale, "Group Performance and Decision Making," *Annual Review of Psychology* 55 (2004), pp. 623–55.

18. D. Dunphy and B. Bryant, "Teams: Panaceas or Prescriptions for Improved Performance?" *Human Relations* 49 (1996), pp. 677–99. For a discussion of Brooks's Law, see F. P. Brooks, ed., *The Mythical Man-Month: Essays on Software Engineering,* 2nd ed. (Reading, MA: Addison-Wesley, 1995).

19. J. Gruber, "More Aperture Dirt" (Daring Fireball, May 4, 2006), http://daringfireball.net/2006/05/more_aperture_dirt (accessed June 7, 2006); J. Gruber, "Aperture Dirt" (Daring Fireball, April 28, 2006), http://daringfireball.net/2006/04/aperture_dirt (accessed April 30, 2006).

20. S. J. Karau and K. D. Williams, "Social Loafing: A Meta-Analytic Review and Theoretical Integration," *Journal of Personality and Social Psychology* 65 (1993), pp. 681–706; R. C. Liden et al., "Social Loafing: A Field Investigation," *Journal of Management* 30 (2004), pp. 285–304; L. L. Chidambaram, "Is out of Sight, out of Mind? An Empirical Study of Social Loafing in Technology-Supported Groups," *Information Systems Research* 16, no. 2 (2005), pp. 149–68; U.-C. Klehe and N. Anderson, "The Moderating Influence of Personality and Culture on Social Loafing in Typical Versus Maximum Performance Situations," *International Journal of Selection and Assessment* 15, no. 2 (2007), pp. 250–62.

21. M. Erez and A. Somech, "Is Group Productivity Loss the Rule or the Exception? Effects of Culture and Group-Based Motivation," *Academy of Management Journal* 39 (1996), pp. 1513–37; Kerr and Tindale, "Group Performance and Decision Making"; A. Jassawalla, H. Sashittal, and A. Malshe, "Students' Perceptions of Social Loafing: Its Antecedents and Consequences in Undergraduate Business Classroom Teams," *Academy of Management Learning and Education* 8, no. 1 (March 2009), pp. 42–54.

22. G. P. Shea and R. A. Guzzo, "Group Effectiveness: What Really Matters?" *Sloan Management Review* 27 (1987), pp. 33–46; J. R. Hackman et al., "Team Effectiveness in Theory and in Practice," in *Industrial and Organizational Psychology: Linking Theory with Practice,* ed. C. L. Cooper and E. A. Locke (Oxford, UK: Blackwell, 2000), pp. 109–29.

23. M. A. West, C. S. Borrill, and K. L. Unsworth, "Team Effectiveness in Organizations," *International Review of Industrial and Organizational Psychology* 13 (1998), pp. 1–48; R. Forrester and A. B. Drexler, "A Model for Team-Based Organization Performance," *Academy of Management Executive* 13 (August 1999), pp. 36–49; J. E. McGrath, H. Arrow, and J. L. Berdahl, "The Study of Groups: Past, Present, and Future," *Personality & Social Psychology Review* 4, no. 1 (2000), pp. 95–105; M. A. Marks, J. E. Mathieu, and S. J. Zaccaro, "A Temporally Based Framework and Taxonomy of Team Processes," *Academy of Management Review* 26, no. 3 (July 2001), pp. 356–76.

24. J. S. DeMatteo, L. T. Eby, and E. Sundstrom, "Team-Based Rewards: Current Empirical Evidence and Directions for Future Research," *Research in Organizational Behavior* 20 (1998), pp. 141–83; E. E. Lawler III, *Rewarding Excellence: Pay Strategies for the New Economy* (San Francisco: Jossey-Bass, 2000), pp. 207–14; G. Hertel, S. Geister, and U. Konradt, "Managing Virtual Teams: A Review of Current Empirical Research," *Human Resource Management Review* 15 (2005), pp. 69–95.

25. These and other environmental conditions for effective teams are discussed in R. Wageman, "Case Study: Critical Success Factors for Creating Superb Self-Managing Teams at Xerox," *Compensation and Benefits Review* 29 (September-October 1997), pp. 31–41; Sundstrom, "The Challenges of Supporting Work Team Effectiveness"; J. N. Choi, "External Activities and Team Effectiveness: Review and Theoretical Development," *Small Group Research* 33 (April 2002), pp. 181–208; T. L. Doolen, M. E. Hacker, and E. M. Van Aken, "The Impact of Organizational Context on Work Team Effectiveness: A Study of Production Team," *IEEE Transactions on Engineering Management* 50, no. 3 (August 2003), pp. 285–96; S. D. Dionne et al., "Transformational Leadership and Team Performance," *Journal Of Organizational Change Management* 17, no. 2 (2004), pp. 177–93.

26. A. Niimi, "The Slow and Steady Climb toward True North," Toyota Motor Manufacturing North America news release, August 7, 2003; L. Adams, "Medrad Works and Wins as a Team," *Quality Magazine,* October 2004, p. 42; J. Teresko, "Toyota's Real Secret," *Industry Week,* February 1, 2007.

27. M. A. Campion, E. M. Papper, and G. J. Medsker, "Relations between Work Team Characteristics and Effectiveness: A Replication and Extension," *Personnel Psychology* 49 (1996), pp. 429–52; D. C. Man and S. S. K. Lam, "The Effects of Job Complexity and Autonomy on Cohesiveness in Collectivistic and Individualistic Work Groups: A Cross-Cultural Analysis," *Journal of Organizational Behavior* 24 (2003), pp. 979–1001.

28. L. Hirsh, "Manufacturing in Action," *Press-Enterprise* (*Riverside, CA*), June 21, 2008, p. E01.

29. G. S. Van der Vegt, J. M. Emans, and E. Van de Vliert, "Patterns of Interdependence in Work Teams: A Two-Level Investigation of the Relations with Job and Team Satisfaction," *Personnel Psychology* 54 (Spring 2001), pp. 51–69; R. Wageman, "The Meaning of Interdependence," in *Groups at Work: Theory and Research*, ed. M. E. Turner (Mahwah, NJ: Lawrence Erlbaum Associates, 2001), pp. 197–217; S. M. Gully et al., "A Meta-Analysis of Team-Efficacy, Potency, and Performance: Interdependence and Level of Analysis as Moderators of Observed Relationships," *Journal of Applied Psychology* 87, no. 5 (October 2002), pp. 819–32; M. R. Barrick et al., "The Moderating Role of Top Management Team Interdependence: Implications for Real Teams and Working Groups," *Academy of Management Journal* 50, no. 3 (2007), pp. 544–57.

30. L. Gratton and T. J. Erickson, "Ways to Build Collaborative Teams," *Harvard Business Review,* November 2007, pp. 100–109.

31. G. Stasser, "Pooling of Unshared Information during Group Discussion," in *Group Process and Productivity,* ed. S. Worchel, W. Wood, and J. A. Simpson (Newbury Park, CA: Sage, 1992); J. R. Katzenbach and D. K. Smith, *The Wisdom of Teams: Creating the High-Performance Organization* (Boston: Harvard University Press, 1993), pp. 45–47.

32. J. O'Toole, "The Power of Many: Building a High-Performance Management Team," *ceoforum.com.au,* March 2003.

33. C. Fishman, "The Anarchist's Cookbook," *Fast Company,* July 2004, p. 70.

34. F. P. Morgeson, M. H. Reider, and M. A. Campion, "Selecting Individuals in Team Setting: The Importance of Social Skills, Personality Characteristics, and Teamwork Knowledge," *Personnel Psychology* 58, no. 3 (2005), pp. 583–611; V. Rousseau, C. Aubé, and A. Savoie, "Teamwork Behaviors: A Review and an Integration of Frameworks," *Small Group Research* 37, no. 5 (2006), pp. 540–70. For a detailed

examination of the characteristics of effective team members, see M. L. Loughry, M. W. Ohland, and D. D. Moore, "Development of a Theory-Based Assessment of Team Member Effectiveness," *Educational and Psychological Measurement* 67, no. 3 (June 2007), pp. 505–24.

35. C. O. L. H. Porter et al., "Backing up Behaviors in Teams: The Role of Personality and Legitimacy of Need," *Journal of Applied Psychology* 88, no. 3 (2003), pp. 391–403; C. E. Hårtel and D. Panipucci, "How 'Bad Apples' Spoil the Bunch: Faultlines, Emotional Levers, and Exclusion in the Workplace," *Research on Emotion in Organizations* 3 (2007), pp. 287–310. The bad apple phenomenon is also identified in executive team "derailers." See R. Wageman et al., *Senior Leadership Teams* (Boston: Harvard Business School Press, 2008), pp. 97–102.

36. D. van Knippenberg, C. K. W. De Dreu, and A. C. Homan, "Work Group Diversity and Group Performance: An Integrative Model and Research Agenda," *Journal of Applied Psychology* 89, no. 6 (2004), pp. 1008–22; E. Mannix and M. A. Neale, "What Differences Make a Difference? The Promise and Reality of Diverse Teams in Organizations," *Psychological Science in the Public Interest* 6, no. 2 (2005), pp. 31–55.

37. D. C. Lau and J. K. Murnighan, "Interactions within Groups and Subgroups: The Effects of Demographic Faultlines," *Academy of Management Journal* 48, no. 4 (August 2005), pp. 645–59; R. Rico et al., "The Effects of Diversity Faultlines and Team Task Autonomy on Decision Quality and Social Integration," *Journal of Management* 33, no. 1 (February 2007), pp. 111–32.

38. B. W. Tuckman and M. A. C. Jensen, "Stages of Small-Group Development Revisited," *Group and Organization Studies* 2 (1977), pp. 419–42; B. W. Tuckman, "Developmental Sequence in Small Groups," *Group Facilitation* (Spring 2001), pp. 66–81.

39. G. R. Bushe and G. H. Coetzer, "Group Development and Team Effectiveness: Using Cognitive Representations to Measure Group Development and Predict Task Performance and Group Viability," *Journal of Applied Behavioral Science* 43, no. 2 (June 2007), pp. 184–212.

40. J. E. Mathieu and G. F. Goodwin, "The Influence of Shared Mental Models on Team Process and Performance," *Journal of Applied Psychology* 85 (April 2000), pp. 273–84; J. Langan-Fox and J. Anglim, "Mental Models, Team Mental Models, and Performance: Process, Development, and Future Directions," *Human Factors and Ergonomics in Manufacturing* 14, no. 4 (2004), pp. 331–52; B.-C. Lim and K. J. Klein, "Team Mental Models and Team Performance: A Field Study of the Effects of Team Mental Model Similarity and Accuracy," *Journal of Organizational Behavior* 27 (2006), pp. 403–18; R. Rico, M. Sánchez-Manzanares, and C. Gibson, "Team Implicit Coordination Processes: A Team Knowledge-Based Approach," *Academy of Management Review* 33, no. 1 (2008), pp. 163–84.

41. J. P. Croxon, "Footsteps of the Ghostwalkers," *Airman Magazine,* March/April 2010, pp. 25–29.

42. A. P. Hare, "Types of Roles in Small Groups: A Bit of History and a Current Perspective," *Small Group Research* 25 (1994), pp. 443–48; A. Aritzeta, S. Swailes, and B. Senior, "Belbin's Team Role Model: Development, Validity and Applications for Team Building," *Journal of Management Studies* 44, no. 1 (January 2007), pp. 96–118.

43. S. H. N. Leung, J. W. K. Chan, and W. B. Lee, "The Dynamic Team Role Behavior: The Approaches of Investigation," *Team Performance Management* 9 (2003), pp. 84–90; G. L. Stewart, I. S. Fulmer, and M. R. Barrick, "An Exploration of Member Roles as a Multilevel Linking Mechanism for Individual Traits and Team Outcomes," *Personnel Psychology* 58, no. 2 (2005), pp. 343–65.

44. W. G. Dyer, *Team Building: Current Issues and New Alternatives,* 3rd ed. (Reading, MA: Addison-Wesley, 1995); C. A. Beatty and B. A. Barker, *Building Smart Teams: Roadmap to High Performance* (Thousand Oaks, CA: Sage Publications, 2004).

45. Langan-Fox and Anglim, "Mental Models, Team Mental Models, and Performance: Process, Development, and Future Directions"; J. E. Mathieu et al., "Scaling the Quality of Teammates' Mental Models: Equifinality and Normative Comparisons," *Journal of Organizational Behavior* 26 (2005), pp. 37–56.

46. "German Businesswoman Demands End to Fun at Work," *Reuters,* July 9, 2003.

47. A. Zayas, "A Search for Teamwork," *St. Petersburg Times (Florida),* June 29, 2008, p. 1F; "Team Nestlé Stride out in GCC Walking Challenge" (Croydon, UK: Nestlé UK, 2009), www.nestle.co.uk (accessed April 23, 2010); S. W. Leow, "Firms Whip up a Dash of Team Spirit," *Straits Times (Singapore),* December 4, 2009; D. Moss, "The Value of Giving," *HRMagainze,* December 2009, p. 22.

48. R. W. Woodman and J. J. Sherwood, "The Role of Team Development in Organizational Effectiveness: A Critical Review," *Psychological Bulletin* 88 (1980), pp. 166–86.

49. L. Mealiea and R. Baltazar, "A Strategic Guide for Building Effective Teams," *Personnel Management* 34, no. 2 (Summer 2005), pp. 141–60.

50. G. E. Huszczo, "Training for Team Building," *Training and Development Journal* 44 (February 1990), pp. 37–43; P. McGraw, "Back from the Mountain: Outdoor Management Development Programs and How to Ensure the Transfer of Skills to the Workplace," *Asia Pacific Journal of Human Resources* 31 (Spring 1993), pp. 52–61.

51. D. C. Feldman, "The Development and Enforcement of Group Norms," *Academy of Management Review* 9 (1984), pp. 47–53; E. Fehr and U. Fischbacher, "Social Norms and Human Cooperation," *Trends in Cognitive Sciences* 8, no. 4 (2004), pp. 185–90.

52. N. Ellemers and F. Rink, "Identity in Work Groups: The Beneficial and Detrimental Consequences of Multiple Identities and Group Norms for Collaboration and Group Performance," *Advances in Group Processes* 22 (2005), pp. 1–41.

53. J. J. Dose and R. J. Klimoski, "The Diversity of Diversity: Work Values Effects on Formative Team Processes," *Human Resource Management Review* 9, no. 1 (Spring 1999), pp. 83–108.

54. S. Taggar and R. Ellis, "The Role of Leaders in Shaping Formal Team Norms," *Leadership Quarterly* 18, no. 2 (2007), pp. 105–20.

55. D. J. Beal et al., "Cohesion and Performance in Groups: A Meta-Analytic Clarification of Construct Relations," *Journal of Applied Psychology* 88, no. 6 (2003), pp. 989–1004; S. W. J. Kozlowski and D. R. Ilgen, "Enhancing the Effectiveness of Work Groups and Teams," *Psychological Science in the Public Interest* 7, no. 3 (2006), pp. 77–124.

56. K. A. Jehn, G. B. Northcraft, and M. A. Neale, "Why Differences Make a Difference: A Field Study of Diversity, Conflict, and Performance in Workgroups," *Administrative Science Quarterly* 44, no. 4 (1999), pp. 741–63; van Knippenberg, De Dreu, and Homan, "Work Group Diversity and Group Performance: An Integrative Model and Research Agenda." For evidence that diversity/similarity does not always influence cohesion, see S. S. Webber and L. M. Donahue, "Impact of Highly and Less

Job-Related Diversity on Work Group Cohesion and Performance: A Meta-Analysis," *Journal of Management* 27, no. 2 (2001), pp. 141–62.

57. E. Aronson and J. Mills, "The Effects of Severity of Initiation on Liking for a Group," *Journal of Abnormal and Social Psychology* 59 (1959), pp. 177–81; J. E. Hautaluoma and R. S. Enge, "Early Socialization into a Work Group: Severity of Initiations Revisited," *Journal of Social Behavior & Personality* 6 (1991), pp. 725–48.

58. B. Mullen and C. Copper, "The Relation between Group Cohesiveness and Performance: An Integration," *Psychological Bulletin* 115 (1994), pp. 210–27.

59. Wageman et al., *Senior Leadership Teams,* pp. 69–70.

60. M. Rempel and R. J. Fisher, "Perceived Threat, Cohesion, and Group Problem Solving in Intergroup Conflict," *International Journal of Conflict Management* 8 (1997), pp. 216–34; M. E. Turner and T. Horvitz, "The Dilemma of Threat: Group Effectiveness and Ineffectiveness under Adversity," in *Groups at Work: Theory and Research,* ed. M. E. Turner (Mahwah, NJ: Lawrence Erlbaum Associates, 2001), pp. 445–70.

61. W. Piper et al., "Cohesion as a Basic Bond in Groups," *Human Relations* 36 (1983), pp. 93–108; C. A. O'Reilly, D. E. Caldwell, and W. P. Barnett, "Work Group Demography, Social Integration, and Turnover," *Administrative Science Quarterly* 34 (1989), pp. 21–37.

62. Mullen and Copper, "The Relation between Group Cohesiveness and Performance"; A. V. Carron et al., "Cohesion and Performance in Sport: A Meta-Analysis," *Journal of Sport and Exercise Psychology* 24 (2002), pp. 168–88; Beal et al., "Cohesion and Performance in Groups."

63. C. Langfred, "Is Group Cohesiveness a Double-Edged Sword? An Investigation of the Effects of Cohesiveness on Performance," *Small Group Research* 29 (1998), pp. 124–43; K. L. Gammage, A. V. Carron, and P. A. Estabrooks, "Team Cohesion and Individual Productivity: The Influence of the Norm for Productivity and the Identifiablity of Individual Effort," *Small Group Research* 32 (February 2001), pp. 3–18.

64. S. L. Robinson, "Trust and Breach of the Psychological Contract," *Administrative Science Quarterly* 41 (1996), pp. 574–99; D. M. Rousseau et al., "Not So Different after All: A Cross-Discipline View of Trust," *Academy of Management Review* 23 (1998), pp. 393–404; D. L. Duarte and N. T. Snyder, *Mastering Virtual Teams: Strategies, Tools, and Techniques That Succeed,* 2nd ed. (San Francisco, CA: Jossey-Bass, 2000), pp. 139–55. For the importance of trust in virtual teams, see L. M. Peters and C. C. Manz, "Getting Virtual Teams Right the First Time," in *The Handbook of High-Performance Virtual Teams: A Toolkit for Collaborating across Boundaries,* ed. J. Nemiro and M. M. Beyerlein (San Francisco: Jossey Bass, 2008), pp. 105–30.

65. Rousseau et al., "Not So Different after All: A Cross-Discipline View of Trust."

66. D. J. McAllister, "Affect- and Cognition-Based Trust as Foundations for Interpersonal Cooperation in Organizations," *Academy of Management Journal* 38, no. 1 (February 1995), pp. 24–59; M. Williams, "In Whom We Trust: Group Membership as an Affective Context for Trust Development," *Academy of Management Review* 26, no. 3 (July 2001), pp. 377–96.

67. O. E. Williamson, "Calculativeness, Trust, and Economic Organization," *Journal of Law and Economics* 36, no. 1 (1993), pp. 453–86.

68. E. M. Whitener et al., "Managers as Initiators of Trust: An Exchange Relationship Framework for Understanding Managerial Trustworthy Behavior," *Academy of Management Review* 23 (July 1998), pp. 513–30; J. M. Kouzes and B. Z. Posner, *The Leadership Challenge,* 3rd ed. (San Francisco: Jossey-Bass, 2002), Chap. 2; T. Simons, "Behavioral Integrity: The Perceived Alignment between Managers' Words and Deeds as a Research Focus," *Organization Science* 13, no. 1 (January–February 2002), pp. 18–35.

69. S. L. Jarvenpaa and D. E. Leidner, "Communication and Trust in Global Virtual Teams," *Organization Science* 10 (1999), pp. 791–815; M. M. Pillutla, D. Malhotra, and J. Keith Murnighan, "Attributions of Trust and the Calculus of Reciprocity," *Journal of Experimental Social Psychology* 39, no. 5 (2003), pp. 448–55.

70. K. T. Dirks and D. L. Ferrin, "The Role of Trust in Organizations," *Organization Science* 12, no. 4 (July–August 2004), pp. 450–67.

71. Mohrman, Cohen, and Mohrman Jr., *Designing Team-Based Organizations: New Forms for Knowledge Work;* D. E. Yeatts and C. Hyten, *High-Performing Self-Managed Work Teams: A Comparison of Theory and Practice* (Thousand Oaks, CA: Sage, 1998); E. E. Lawler, *Organizing for High Performance* (San Francisco: Jossey-Bass, 2001); R. J. Torraco, "Work Design Theory: A Review and Critique with Implications for Human Resource Development," *Human Resource Development Quarterly* 16, no. 1 (Spring 2005), pp. 85–109.

72. Fishman, "The Anarchist's Cookbook"; J. Mackey, "Open Book Company," *Newsweek,* November 28, 2005, 42; K. Zimbalist, "Green Giant," *Time,* April 24, 2006, p. 24.

73. P. Panchak, "Production Workers Can Be Your Competitive Edge," *Industry Week,* October 2004, p. 11; S. K. Muthusamy, J. V. Wheeler, and B. L. Simmons, "Self-Managing Work Teams: Enhancing Organizational Innovativeness," *Organization Development Journal* 23, no. 3 (Fall 2005), pp. 53–66.

74. Emery and Fredenhall, "The Effect of Teams on Firm Profitability and Customer Satisfaction"; A. Krause and H. Dunckel, "Work Design and Customer Satisfaction: Effects of the Implementation of Semi-Autonomous Group Work on Customer Satisfaction Considering Employee Satisfaction and Group Performance (Translated Abstract)," *ZEITSCHRIFT FUR ARBEITS-UND ORGANISATIONSPSYCHOLOGIE* 47, no. 4 (2003), pp. 182–93; H. van Mierlo et al., "Self-Managing Teamwork and Psychological Well-Being: Review of a Multilevel Research Domain," *Group & Organization Management* 30, no. 2 (April 2005), pp. 211–35.

75. Moldaschl and Weber, "The 'Three Waves' of Industrial Group Work: Historical Reflections on Current Research on Group Work"; W. Niepce and E. Molleman, "Work Design Issues in Lean Production from Sociotechnical System Perspective: Neo-Taylorism or the Next Step in Sociotechnical Design?" *Human Relations* 51, no. 3 (March 1998), pp. 259–87.

76. E. Ulich and W. G. Weber, "Dimensions, Criteria, and Evaluation of Work Group Autonomy," in *Handbook of Work Group Psychology,* ed. M. A. West (Chichester, UK: John Wiley and Sons, 1996), pp. 247–82.

77. K. P. Carson and G. L. Stewart, "Job Analysis and the Sociotechnical Approach to Quality: A Critical Examination," *Journal of Quality Management* 1 (1996), pp. 49–65; C. C. Manz and G. L. Stewart, "Attaining Flexible Stability by Integrating Total Quality Management and Socio-Technical Systems Theory," *Organization Science* 8 (1997), pp. 59–70.

78. J. Lipnack and J. Stamps, *Virtual Teams: People Working across Boundaries with Technology* (New York: John Wiley and Sons, 2001); B. S. Bell and W. J. Kozlowski, "A Typology of Virtual

Teams: Implications for Effective Leadership," *Group & Organization Management* 27 (March 2002), pp. 14–49; Hertel, Geister, and Konradt, "Managing Virtual Teams."

79. G. Gilder, *Telecosm: How Infinite Bandwidth Will Revolutionize Our World* (New York: Free Press, 2001); L. L. Martins, L. L. Gilson, and M. T. Maynard, "Virtual Teams: What Do We Know and Where Do We Go from Here?" *Journal of Management* 30, no. 6 (2004), pp. 805–35.

80. "Absence Makes the Team Uneasy," OfficeTeam news release (Menlo Park, NJ: March 6, 2008); "Go Teams! Firms Can't Do without Them"; N. Weil, "Global Team Management: Continental Divides," *CIO,* January 23, 2008.

81. Martins, Gilson, and Maynard, "Virtual Teams"; G. Hertel, U. Konradt, and K. Voss, "Competencies for Virtual Teamwork: Development and Validation of a Web-Based Selection Tool for Members of Distributed Teams," *European Journal of Work and Organizational Psychology* 15, no. 4 (2006), pp. 477–504.

82. G. G. Harwood, "Design Principles for Successful Virtual Teams," in *The Handbook of High-Performance Virtual Teams: A Toolkit for Collaborating across Boundaries,* ed. J. Nemiro and M. M. Beyerlein (San Francisco: Jossey-Bass, 2008), pp. 59–84.

83. V. H. Vroom and A. G. Jago, *The New Leadership* (Englewood Cliffs, NJ: Prentice-Hall, 1988), pp. 28–29.

84. M. Diehl and W. Stroebe, "Productivity Loss in Idea-Generating Groups: Tracking Down the Blocking Effects," *Journal of Personality and Social Psychology* 61 (1991), pp. 392–403; R. B. Gallupe et al., "Blocking Electronic Brainstorms," *Journal of Applied Psychology* 79 (1994), pp. 77–86; B. A. Nijstad, W. Stroebe, and H. F. M. Lodewijkx, "Production Blocking and Idea Generation: Does Blocking Interfere with Cognitive Processes?" *Journal of Experimental Social Psychology* 39, no. 6 (November 2003), pp. 531–48; B. A. Nijstad and W. Stroebe, "How the Group Affects the Mind: A Cognitive Model of Idea Generation in Groups," *Personality & Social Psychology Review* 10, no. 3 (2006), pp. 186–213.

85. B. E. Irmer, P. Bordia, and D. Abusah, "Evaluation Apprehension and Perceived Benefits in Interpersonal and Database Knowledge Sharing," *Academy of Management Proceedings* (2002), pp. B1–B6.

86. I. L. Janis, *Groupthink: Psychological Studies of Policy Decisions and Fiascoes,* 2nd ed. (Boston: Houghton Mifflin, 1982); J. K. Esser, "Alive and Well after 25 Years: A Review of Groupthink Research," *Organizational Behavior and Human Decision Processes* 73, no. 2–3 (1998), pp. 116–41.

87. J. N. Choi and M. U. Kim, "The Organizational Application of Groupthink and Its Limitations in Organizations," *Journal of Applied Psychology* 84, no. 2 (April 1999), pp. 297–306; W.-W. Park, "A Comprehensive Empirical Investigation of the Relationships among Variables of the Groupthink Model," *Journal of Organizational Behavior* 21, no. 8 (December 2000), pp. 873–87; D. D. Henningsen et al., "Examining the Symptoms of Groupthink and Retrospective Sensemaking," *Small Group Research* 37, no. 1 (February 2006), pp. 36–64.

88. D. Miller, *The Icarus Paradox: How Exceptional Companies Bring About Their Own Downfall* (New York: HarperBusiness, 1990); S. Finkelstein, *Why Smart Executives Fail* (New York: Viking, 2003); K. Tasa and G. Whyte, "Collective Efficacy and Vigilant Problem Solving in Group Decision Making: A Non-Linear Model," *Organizational Behavior and Human Decision Processes* 96, no. 2 (March 2005), pp. 119–29.

89. B. Frisch, "When Teams Can't Decide," *Harvard Business Review* 86, no. 11 (2008), pp. 121–26.

90. H. Collingwood, "Best-Kept Secrets of the World's Best Companies: Outside-in R&D," *Business 2.0,* April 2006, p. 82.

91. Cited in F. Dearmond, *Executive Thinking and Action* (New York: McGraw-Hill, 1946). Also credited to Wrigley in a 1931 issue of *American Magazine.*

92. K. M. Eisenhardt, J. L. Kahwajy, and L. J. Bourgeois III, "Conflict and Strategic Choice: How Top Management Teams Disagree," *California Management Review* 39 (1997), pp. 42–62; R. Sutton, *Weird Ideas That Work* (New York: Free Press, 2002); C. J. Nemeth et al., "The Liberating Role of Conflict in Group Creativity: A Study in Two Countries," *European Journal of Social Psychology* 34, no. 4 (2004), pp. 365–74. For a discussion of how all conflict is potentially detrimental to teams, see C. K. W. De Dreu and L. R. Weingart, "Task Versus Relationship Conflict, Team Performance, and Team Member Satisfaction: A Meta-Analysis," *Journal of Applied Psychology* 88 (August 2003), pp. 587–604; and P. Hinds and D. E. Bailey, "Out of Sight, out of Sync: Understanding Conflict in Distributed Teams," *Organization Science* 14, no. 6 (2003), pp. 615–32.

93. K. Darce, "Ground Control: NASA Attempts a Cultural Shift," *Seattle Times,* April 24, 2005, p. A3; R. Shelton, "NASA Attempts to Change Mindset in Wake of Columbia Tragedy," *Macon Telegraph* (Macon, GA), July 7, 2005.

94. B. Mullen, C. Johnson, and E. Salas, "Productivity Loss in Brainstorming Groups: A Meta-Analytic Integration," *Basic and Applied Psychology* 12 (1991), pp. 2–23. The original description of brainstorming appeared in A. F. Osborn, *Applied Imagination* (New York: Scribner, 1957).

95. R. I. Sutton and A. Hargadon, "Brainstorming Groups in Context: Effectiveness in a Product Design Firm," *Administrative Science Quarterly* 41 (1996), pp. 685–718; T. Kelley, *The Art of Innovation* (New York: Currency Doubleday, 2001); V. R. Brown and P. B. Paulus, "Making Group Brainstorming More Effective: Recommendations from an Associative Memory Perspective," *Current Directions in Psychological Science* 11, no. 6 (2002), pp. 208–12; K. Leggett Dugosh and P. B. Paulus, "Cognitive and Social Comparison Processes in Brainstorming," *Journal of Experimental Social Psychology* 41, no. 3 (2005), pp. 313–20.

96. R. B. Gallupe, L. M. Bastianutti, and W. H. Cooper, "Unblocking Brainstorms," *Journal of Applied Psychology* 76 (1991), pp. 137–42; W. H. Cooper et al., "Some Liberating Effects of Anonymous Electronic Brainstorming," *Small Group Research* 29, no. 2 (April 1998), pp. 147–78; A. R. Dennis, B. H. Wixom, and R. J. Vandenberg, "Understanding Fit and Appropriation Effects in Group Support Systems Via Meta-Analysis," *MIS Quarterly* 25, no. 2 (June 2001), pp. 167–93; D. M. DeRosa, C. L. Smith, and D. A. Hantula, "The Medium Matters: Mining the Long-Promised Merit of Group Interaction in Creative Idea Generation Tasks in a Meta-Analysis of the Electronic Group Brainstorming Literature," *Computers in Human Behavior* 23, no. 3 (2007), pp. 1549–81.

97. A. L. Delbecq, A. H. Van de Ven, and D. H. Gustafson, *Group Techniques for Program Planning: A Guide to Nominal Group and Delphi Processes* (Middleton, WI: Green Briar Press, 1986).

98. S. Frankel, "NGT + MDS: An Adaptation of the Nominal Group Technique for Ill-Structured Problems," *Journal of Applied Behavioral Science* 23 (1987), pp. 543–51; H. Barki and A. Pinsonneault, "Small Group Brainstorming and Idea Quality: Is Electronic Brainstorming the Most Effective Approach?" *Small Group Research* 32, no. 2 (April 2001), pp. 158–205.

CHAPTER 8

1. M. Schnurman, "Employers Must Work Hard to Improve Morale, Productivity," *Star-Ledger (Newark, NJ),* April 25, 2010.

2. C. Barnard, *The Functions of the Executive* (Cambridge, MA: Harvard University Press, 1938).

3. M. T. Hansen, M. L. Mors, and B. Løvås, "Knowledge Sharing in Organizations: Multiple Networks, Multiple Phases," *Academy of Management Journal* 48, no. 5 (2005), pp. 776–93; R. Du, S. Ai, and Y. Ren, "Relationship between Knowledge Sharing and Performance: A Survey in Xu'an, China," *Expert Systems with Applications* 32 (2007), pp. 38–46; S. R. Murray and J. Peyrefitte, "Knowledge Type and Communication Media Choice in the Knowledge Transfer Process," *Journal of Managerial Issues* 19, no. 1 (Spring 2007), pp. 111–33.

4. N. Ellemers, R. Spears, and B. Doosje, "Self and Social Identity," *Annual Review of Psychology* 53 (2002), pp. 161–86; S. A. Haslam and S. Reicher, "Stressing the Group: Social Identity and the Unfolding Dynamics of Responses to Stress," *Journal of Applied Psychology* 91, no. 5 (2006), pp. 1037–52; M. T. Gailliot and R. F. Baumeister, "Self-Esteem, Belongingness, and Worldview Validation: Does Belongingness Exert a Unique Influence upon Self-Esteem?" *Journal of Research in Personality* 41, no. 2 (2007), pp. 327–45.

5. S. Cohen, "The Pittsburgh Common Cold Studies: Psychosocial Predictors of Susceptibility to Respiratory Infectious Illness," *International Journal of Behavioral Medicine* 12, no. 3 (2005), pp. 123–31; B. N. Uchino, "Social Support and Health: A Review of Physiological Processes Potentially Underlying Links to Disease Outcomes," *Journal of Behavioral Medicine* 29, no. 4 (2006), pp. 377–87.

6. C. E. Shannon and W. Weaver, *The Mathematical Theory of Communication* (Urbana, IL: University of Illinois Press, 1949); R. M. Krauss and S. R. Fussell, "Social Psychological Models of Interpersonal Communication," in *Social Psychology: Handbook of Basic Principles,* ed. E. T. Higgins and A. Kruglanski (New York: Guilford Press, 1996), pp. 655–701.

7. J. R. Carlson and R. W. Zmud, "Channel Expansion Theory and the Experiential Nature of Media Richness Perceptions," *Academy of Management Journal* 42 (April 1999), pp. 153–70.

8. P. Shachaf and N. Hara, "Behavioral Complexity Theory of Media Selection: A Proposed Theory for Global Virtual Teams," *Journal of Information Science* 33 (2007), pp. 63–75.

9. M. Hauben and R. Hauben, "Netizens: On the History and Impact of Usenet and the Internet," *First Monday* 3, no. 8 (August 1998); J. Abbate, *Inventing the Internet* (Cambridge, MA: MIT Press, 1999).

10. N. B. Ducheneaut and L. A. Watts, "In Search of Coherence: A Review of E-Mail Research," *Human–Computer Interaction* 20, no. 1–2 (2005), pp. 11–48.

11. "The Radicati Group Releases 'Email Statistics Report, 2009–2013,'" Radicati Group news release (Palo Alto, CA: May 6, 2009); *The Carbon Footprint of Email Spam Report* (Santa Clara, CA: McAfee, Inc., and ICF International, April 2009); "Nielson Provides Topline U.S. Data for June 2009," The Nielson Company news release (New York: July 13, 2009); "CTIA—the Wireless Association® Announces Semi-Annual Wireless Industry Survey Results," CTIA—The Wireless Association news release (Las Vegas: March 23, 2010); "Blogpulse Stats" (BlogPulse, 2010), www.blogpulse.com (accessed April 27, 2010); "Twitter: Now More Than 1 Billion Tweets Per Month" (pingdom, 2010), http://royal.pingdom.com.

12. W. Lucas, "Effects of E-Mail on the Organization," *European Management Journal* 16, no. 1 (February 1998), pp. 18–30; D. A. Owens, M. A. Neale, and R. I. Sutton, "Technologies of Status Management Status Dynamics in E-Mail Communications," *Research on Managing Groups and Teams* 3 (2000), pp. 205–30; N. B. Ducheneaut, "Ceci N'est Pas un Objet? Talking about Objects in E-Mail," *Human–Computer Interaction* 18, no. 1–2 (2003), pp. 85–110.

13. N. B. Ducheneaut, "The Social Impacts of Electronic Mail in Organizations: A Case Study of Electronic Power Games Using Communication Genres," *Information, Communication, & Society* 5, no. 2 (2002), pp. 153–88; N. Panteli, "Richness, Power Cues and Email Text," *Information & Management* 40, no. 2 (2002), pp. 75–86.

14. N. Epley and J. Kruger, "When What You Type Isn't What They Read: The Perseverance of Stereotypes and Expectancies over E-Mail," *Journal of Experimental Social Psychology* 41, no. 4 (2005), pp. 414–22.

15. J. B. Walther, "Language and Communication Technology: Introduction to the Special Issue," *Journal of Language and Social Psychology* 23, no. 4 (December 2004), pp. 384–96; J. B. Walther, T. Loh, and L. Granka, "Let Me Count the Ways: The Interchange of Verbal and Nonverbal Cues in Computer–Mediated and Face-to-Face Affinity," *Journal of Language and Social Psychology* 24, no. 1 (March 2005), pp. 36–65; K. Byron, "Carrying Too Heavy a Load? The Communication and Miscommunication of Emotion by Email," *Academy of Management Review* 33, no. 2 (2008), pp. 309–27.

16. G. Hertel, S. Geister, and U. Konradt, "Managing Virtual Teams: A Review of Current Empirical Research," *Human Resource Management Review* 15 (2005), pp. 69–95; H. Lee, "Behavioral Strategies for Dealing with Flaming in an Online Forum," *The Sociological Quarterly* 46, no. 2 (2005), pp. 385–403.

17. D. D. Dawley and W. P. Anthony, "User Perceptions of E-Mail at Work," *Journal of Business and Technical Communication* 17, no. 2 (April 2003), pp. 170–200; G. F. Thomas and C. L. King, "Reconceptualizing E-Mail Overload," *Journal of Business and Technical Communication* 20, no. 3 (July 2006), pp. 252–87; S. Carr, "Email Overload Menace Growing," *Silicon.com,* July 12, 2007.

18. R. D. Waters et al., "Engaging Stakeholders through Social Networking: How Nonprofit Organizations Are Using Facebook," *Public Relations Review* 35, no. 2 (2009), pp. 102–6; J. Cunningham, "New Workers, New Workplace? Getting the Balance Right," *Strategic Direction* 26, no. 1 (2010), p. 5; A. M. Kaplan and M. Haenlein, "Users of the World, Unite! The Challenges and Opportunities of Social Media," *Business Horizons* 53, no. 1 (February 2010), pp. 59–68.

19. A. F. Cameron and J. Webster, "Unintended Consequences of Emerging Communication Technologies: Instant Messaging in the Workplace," *Computers in Human Behavior* 21, no. 1 (2005), pp. 85–103.

20. Towers Watson, *Capitalizing on Effective Communication* (New York: Towers Watson, February 4, 2010).

21. S. Humphries, "Companies Warm up to Social Networks," *Christian Science Monitor,* September 8, 2008, 13; R. Weston, "Facebook: Your Company's Intranet?" *Forbes,* March 20, 2009.

22. C. Wagner and A. Majchrzak, "Enabling Customer-Centricity Using Wikis and the Wiki Way," *Journal of Management Information Systems* 23, no. 3 (2006), pp. 17–43; R. B. Ferguson, "Build a Web 2.0 Platform and Employees Will Use

It," *eWeek,* June 20, 2007; C. Karena, "Working the Wiki Way," *Sydney Morning Herald,* March 6, 2007.

23. L. Z. Tiedens and A. R. Fragale, "Power Moves: Complementarity in Dominant and Submissive Nonverbal Behavior," *Journal of Personality and Social Psychology* 84, no. 3 (2003), pp. 558–68.

24. P. Ekman and E. Rosenberg, *What the Face Reveals: Basic and Applied Studies of Spontaneous Expression Using the Facial Action Coding System* (Oxford, England: Oxford University Press, 1997); P. Winkielman and K. C. Berridge, "Unconscious Emotion," *Current Directions in Psychological Science* 13, no. 3 (2004), pp. 120–23.

25. E. Hatfield, J. T. Cacioppo, and R. L. Rapson, *Emotional Contagion* (Cambridge, UK: Cambridge University Press, 1993); S. G. Barsade, "The Ripple Effect: Emotional Contagion and Its Influence on Group Behavior," *Administrative Science Quarterly* 47 (December 2002), pp. 644–75; M. Sonnby-Borgstrom, P. Jonsson, and O. Svensson, "Emotional Empathy as Related to Mimicry Reactions at Different Levels of Information Processing," *Journal of Nonverbal Behavior* 27 (Spring 2003), pp. 3–23; S. G. Barsade and D. E. Gibson, "Why Does Affect Matter in Organizations?" *Academy of Management Perspectives* (February 2007), pp. 36–59; S. K. Johnson, "I Second That Emotion: Effects of Emotional Contagion and Affect at Work on Leader and Follower Outcomes," *Leadership Quarterly* 19, no. 1 (2008), pp. 1–19.

26. J. R. Kelly and S. G. Barsade, "Mood and Emotions in Small Groups and Work Teams," *Organizational Behavior and Human Decision Processes* 86 (September 2001), pp. 99–130.

27. L. K. Treviño, J. Webster, and E. W. Stein, "Making Connections: Complementary Influences on Communication Media Choices, Attitudes, and Use," *Organization Science* 11, no. 2 (2000), pp. 163–82; B. Barry and I. S. Fulmer, "The Medium Is the Message: The Adaptive Use of Communication Media in Dyadic Influence," *Academy of Management Review* 29, no. 2 (2004), pp. 272–92; J. W. Turner et al., "Exploring the Dominant Media: How Does Media Use Reflect Organizational Norms and Affect Performance?" *Journal of Business Communication* 43, no. 3 (July 2006), pp. 220–50; M. B. Watson-Manheim and F. Bélanger, "Communication Media Repertoires: Dealing with the Multiplicity of Media Choices," *MIS Quarterly* 31, no. 2 (2007), pp. 267–93.

28. R. C. King, "Media Appropriateness: Effects of Experience on Communication Media Choice," *Decision sciences* 28, no. 4 (1997), pp. 877–910.

29. M. Madden and S. Jones, *Networked Workers,* Pew Internet & American Life Project (Washington, DC: Pew Research Center, September 24, 2008).

30. K. Griffiths, "KPMG Sacks 670 Employees by E-Mail," *The Independent (London),* November 5, 2002, p. 19; "Shop Worker Sacked by Text Message," *The Post (Claremont/Nedlands, Western Australia),* July 28, 2007, pp. 1, 78.

31. R. L. Daft and R. H. Lengel, "Information Richness: A New Approach to Managerial Behavior and Organization Design," *Research in Organizational Behavior* 6 (1984), pp. 191–233; R. H. Lengel and R. L. Daft, "The Selection of Communication Media as an Executive Skill," *Academy of Management Executive* 2 (1988), pp. 225–32.

32. R. E. Rice, "Task Analyzability, Use of New Media, and Effectiveness: A Multi-Site Exploration of Media Richness," *Organization Science* 3 (1992), pp. 475–500.

33. "Employer Snapshots: 2008," *Toronto Star,* October 13, 2007; H. Schachter, "Strange but True: Some Staff Meetings Are Actually Efficient," *Globe & Mail,* July 23, 2007.

34. J. W. Turner and N. L. Reinsch Jr., "The Business Communicator as Presence Allocator," *Journal of Business Communication* 44, no. 1 (2007), pp. 36–58.

35. Carlson and Zmud, "Channel Expansion Theory and the Experiential Nature of Media Richness Perceptions"; N. Kock, "Media Richness or Media Naturalness? The Evolution of Our Biological Communication Apparatus and Its Influence on Our Behavior toward E-Communication Tools," *IEEE Transactions on Professional Communication* 48, no. 2 (June 2005), pp. 117–30.

36. D. Muller, T. Atzeni, and F. Butera, "Coaction and Upward Social Comparison Reduce the Illusory Conjunction Effect: Support for Distraction-Conflict Theory," *Journal of Experimental Social Psychology* 40, no. 5 (2004), pp. 659–65; L. P. Robert and A. R. Dennis, "Paradox of Richness: A Cognitive Model of Media Choice," *IEEE Transactions on Professional Communication* 48, no. 1 (2005), pp. 10–21.

37. E. V. Wilson, "Perceived Effectiveness of Interpersonal Persuasion Strategies in Computer-Mediated Communication," *Computers in Human Behavior* 19, no. 5 (2003), pp. 537–52; K. Sassenberg, M. Boos, and S. Rabung, "Attitude Change in Face-to-Face and Computer-Mediated Communication: Private Self-Awareness Ad Mediator and Moderator," *European Journal of Social Psychology* 35 (2005), pp. 361–74; P. Di Blasio and L. Milani, "Computer-Mediated Communication and Persuasion: Peripheral vs. Central Route to Opinion Shift," *Computers in Human Behavior* 24, no. 3 (2008), pp. 798–815.

38. J. Kruger et al., "Egocentrism over E-Mail: Can We Communicate as Well as We Think?" *Journal of Personality and Social Psychology* 89, no. 6 (2005), pp. 925–36.

39. D. Woodruff, "Crossing Culture Divide Early Clears Merger Paths," *Asian Wall Street Journal,* May 28, 2001, p. 9.

40. R. M. Krauss, "The Psychology of Verbal Communication," in *International Encyclopedia of the Social and Behavioral Sciences,* ed. N. Smelser and P. Baltes (London: Elsevier, 2002), pp. 161–65.

41. L. L. Putnam, N. Phillips, and P. Chapman, "Metaphors of Communication and Organization," in *Handbook of Organization Studies,* ed. S. R. Clegg, C. Hardy, and W. R. Nord (London: Sage, 1996), pp. 373–408; G. Morgan, *Images of Organization,* 2nd ed. (Thousand Oaks, CA: Sage, 1997); M. Rubini and H. Sigall, "Taking the Edge Off of Disagreement: Linguistic Abstractness and Self-Presentation to a Heterogeneous Audience," *European Journal of Social Psychology* 32 (2002), pp. 343–51.

42. T. Walsh, "Nardelli Brags on VIP Recruits, Game Plan," *Detroit Free Press,* September 8, 2007.

43. D. Goleman, R. Boyatzis, and A. McKee, *Primal Leaders* (Boston: Harvard Business School Press, 2002), pp. 92–95.

44. J. O'Toole and W. Bennis, "What's Needed Next: A Culture of Candor," *Harvard Business Review* 87, no. 6 (2009), pp. 54–61.

45. O'Toole and Bennis, "What's Needed Next: A Culture of Candor."

46. T. Koski, "Reflections on Information Glut and Other Issues in Knowledge Productivity," *Futures* 33 (August 2001), pp. 483–95.

47. A. G. Schick, L. A. Gordon, and S. Haka, "Information Overload: A Temporal Approach," *Accounting, Organizations & Society* 15

(1990), pp. 199–220; A. Edmunds and A. Morris, "The Problem of Information Overload in Business Organisations: A Review of the Literature," *International Journal of Information Management* 20 (2000), pp. 17–28; R. Pennington, "The Effects of Information Overload on Software Project Risk Assessment," *Decision Sciences* 38, no. 3 (August 2007), pp. 489–526.

48. D. C. Thomas and K. Inkson, *Cultural Intelligence: People Skills for Global Business* (San Francisco: Berrett-Koehler, 2004), Chap. 6; D. Welch, L. Welch, and R. Piekkari, "Speaking in Tongues," *International Studies of Management & Organization* 35, no. 1 (Spring 2005), pp. 10–27.

49. S. Ohtaki, T. Ohtaki, and M. D. Fetters, "Doctor-Patient Communication: A Comparison of the USA and Japan," *Family Practice* 20 (June 2003), pp. 276–82; M. Fujio, "Silence during Intercultural Communication: A Case Study," *Corporate Communications* 9, no. 4 (2004), pp. 331–39.

50. D. C. Barnlund, *Communication Styles of Japanese and Americans: Images and Realities* (Belmont, CA: Wadsworth, 1988); H. Yamada, *American and Japanese Business Discourse: A Comparison of Interaction Styles* (Norwood, NJ: Ablex, 1992), Chap. 2; H. Yamada, *Different Games, Different Rules* (New York: Oxford University Press, 1997), pp. 76–79.

51. P. Harris and R. Moran, *Managing Cultural Differences* (Houston: Gulf, 1987); H. Blagg, "A Just Measure of Shame?" *British Journal of Criminology* 37 (Autumn 1997), pp. 481–501; R. E. Axtell, *Gestures: The Do's and Taboos of Body Language around the World,* rev. ed. (New York: Wiley, 1998).

52. D. Tannen, *You Just Don't Understand: Men and Women in Conversation* (New York: Ballentine Books, 1990); D. Tannen, *Talking from 9 to 5* (New York: Avon, 1994); M. Crawford, *Talking Difference: On Gender and Language* (Thousand Oaks, CA: Sage, 1995), pp. 41–44; L. L. Namy, L. C. Nygaard, and D. Sauerteig, "Gender Differences in Vocal Accommodation: The Role of Perception," *Journal of Language and Social Psychology* 21, no. 4 (December 2002), pp. 422–32; H. Itakura and A. B. M. Tsui, "Gender and Conversational Dominance in Japanese Conversation," *Language in Society* 33, no. 2 (2004), pp. 223–48.

53. A. Mulac et al., "'Uh-Huh. What's That All About?' Differing Interpretations of Conversational Backchannels and Questions as Sources of Miscommunication across Gender Boundaries," *Communication Research* 25 (December 1998), pp. 641–68; N. M. Sussman and D. H. Tyson, "Sex and Power: Gender Differences in Computer-Mediated Interactions," *Computers in Human Behavior* 16 (2000), pp. 381–94; D. R. Caruso and P. Salovey, *The Emotionally Intelligent Manager* (San Francisco: Jossey-Bass, 2004), p. 23; D. Fallows, *How Women and Men Use the Internet* (Washington, DC: Pew Internet and American Life Project, December 28, 2005).

54. The three components of listening discussed here are based on several studies in the field of marketing, including S. B. Castleberry, C. D. Shepherd, and R. Ridnour, "Effective Interpersonal Listening in the Personal Selling Environment: Conceptualization, Measurement, and Nomological Validity," *Journal of Marketing Theory and Practice* 7 (Winter 1999), pp. 30–38; L. B. Comer and T. Drollinger, "Active Empathetic Listening and Selling Success: A Conceptual Framework," *Journal of Personal Selling & Sales Management* 19 (Winter 1999), pp. 15–29; and K. de Ruyter and M. G. M. Wetzels, "The Impact of Perceived Listening Behavior in Voice-to-Voice Service Encounters," *Journal of Service Research* 2 (February 2000), pp. 276–84.

55. This quotation is varied slightly from the original translations by E. Carter, *All the Works of Epictetus, Which Are Now Extant,* 3rd ed., vol. 2 (London: J. and F. Rivington, 1768), p. 333; T. W. Higginson, *The Works of Epictetus* (Boston: Little, Brown, and Company, 1866), p. 428.

56. A. Leaman and B. Bordass, "Productivity in Buildings: The Killer Variables," *Building Research & Information* 27, no. 1 (1999), pp. 4–19; T. J. Allen, "Architecture and Communication among Product Development Engineers," *California Management Review* 49, no. 2 (Winter 2007), pp. 23–41; F. Becker, "Organizational Ecology and Knowledge Networks," *California Management Review* 49, no. 2 (Winter 2007), pp. 42–61.

57. M. Gardner, "Democratic Principles Make Businesses More Transparent," *Christian Science Monitor,* March 19, 2007, p. 13.

58. G. Evans and D. Johnson, "Stress and Open-Office Noise," *Journal of Applied Psychology* 85 (2000), pp. 779–83; F. Russo, "My Kingdom for a Door," *Time Magazine,* October 23, 2000, p. B1.

59. S. P. Means, "Playing at Pixar," *Salt Lake Tribune* (Utah), May 30, 2003, p. D1; G. Whipp, "Swimming against the Tide," *Daily News of Los Angeles,* May 30, 2003, p. U6.

60. J. Vijayan, "Staying on Message," *Computerworld,* October 19, 2009; "Social Media Training Programs: Different Approaches, Common Goals," *PR News,* January 4, 2010; A. Bryant, "On a Scale of 1 to 10, How Weird Are You?" *The New York Times,* January 10, 2010.

61. T. Fenton, "Inside the Worldblu List: 1–800–Got-Junk?'s CEO on Why 'Being Democratic Is Extremely Important to Maintaining Our Competitive Advantage,'" (Atlanta: WorldBlu, January 3, 2008). The original term was "management by *wandering* around," but this has been replaced with "walking around" over the years. See W. Ouchi, *Theory Z* (New York: Avon Books, 1981), pp. 176–77; and T. Peters and R. Waterman, *In Search of Excellence* (New York: Harper and Row, 1982), p. 122.

62. Towers Watson, *Capitalizing on Effective Communication,* Figure 18.

63. "'Involve Your Employees,' Says Google, Ceb," *BusinessWeek,* December 11, 2009.

64. R. Rousos, "Trust in Leaders Lacking at Utility," *The Ledger* (Lakeland, FL), July 29, 2003, p. B1; B. Whitworth and B. Riccomini, "Management Communication: Unlocking Higher Employee Performance," *Communication World,* March–April 2005, pp. 18–21.

65. K. Davis, "Management Communication and the Grapevine," *Harvard Business Review* 31 (September–October 1953), pp. 43–49; W. L. Davis and J. R. O'Connor, "Serial Transmission of Information: A Study of the Grapevine," *Journal of Applied Communication Research* 5 (1977), pp. 61–72.

66. H. Mintzberg, *The Structuring of Organizations* (Englewood Cliffs, NJ: Prentice Hall, 1979), pp. 46–53; D. Krackhardt and J. R. Hanson, "Informal Networks: The Company behind the Chart," *Harvard Business Review* 71 (July–August 1993), pp. 104–11.

67. C. J. Walker and C. A. Beckerle, "The Effect of State Anxiety on Rumor Transmission," *Journal of Social Behaviour & Personality* 2 (August 1987), pp. 353–60; R. L. Rosnow, "Inside Rumor: A Personal Journey," *American Psychologist* 46 (May 1991), pp. 484–96; M. Noon and R. Delbridge, "News from Behind My Hand: Gossip in Organizations," *Organization Studies* 14 (1993), pp. 23–36.

68. N. Nicholson, "Evolutionary Psychology: Toward a New View of Human Nature and Organizational Society," *Human Relations*

50 (September 1997), pp. 1053–78; R. F. Baumeister, L. Zhang, and K. D. Vohs, "Gossip as Cultural Learning," *Review of General Psychology* 8, no. 2 (2004), pp. 111–21; E. K. Foster, "Research on Gossip: Taxonomy, Methods, and Future Directions," *Review of General Psychology* 8, no. 2 (2004), pp. 78–99.

CHAPTER 9

1. J. McGregor, "The Office Chart That Really Counts," *BusinessWeek,* February 27, 2006, p. 48.

2. J. R. P. French and B. Raven, "The Bases of Social Power," in *Studies in Social Power,* ed. D. Cartwright (Ann Arbor, MI: University of Michigan Press, 1959), pp. 150–67; A. D. Galinsky et al., "Power and Perspectives Not Taken," *Psychological Science* 17, no. 12 (2006), pp. 1068–74. Also see H. Mintzberg, *Power in and around Organizations* (Englewood Cliffs, NJ: Prentice Hall, 1983), Chap. 1; and J. Pfeffer, *Managing with Power* (Boston: Harvard Business University Press, 1992), pp. 17, 30.

3. R. A. Dahl, "The Concept of Power," *Behavioral Science* 2 (1957), pp. 201–18; R. M. Emerson, "Power-Dependence Relations," *American Sociological Review* 27 (1962), pp. 31–41; A. M. Pettigrew, *The Politics of Organizational Decision-Making* (London: Tavistock, 1973).

4. R. Gulati and M. Sytch, "Dependence Asymmetry and Joint Dependence in Interorganizational Relationships: Effects of Embeddedness on a Manufacturer's Performance in Procurement Relationships," *Administrative Science Quarterly* 52, no. 1 (2007), pp. 32–69.

5. French and Raven, "The Bases of Social Power"; P. Podsakoff and C. Schreisheim, "Field Studies of French and Raven's Bases of Power: Critique, Analysis, and Suggestions for Future Research," *Psychological Bulletin* 97 (1985), pp. 387–411; P. P. Carson and K. D. Carson, "Social Power Bases: A Meta-Analytic Examination of Interrelationships and Outcomes," *Journal of Applied Social Psychology* 23 (1993), pp. 1150–69.

6. C. Barnard, *The Function of the Executive* (Cambridge, MA: Harvard University Press, 1938); C. Hardy and S. R. Clegg, "Some Dare Call It Power," in *Handbook of Organization Studies,* ed. S. R. Clegg, C. Hardy, and W. R. Nord (London: Sage, 1996), pp. 622–41.

7. A. I. Shahin and P. L. Wright, "Leadership in the Context of Culture: An Egyptian Perspective," *Leadership & Organization Development Journal* 25, no. 5/6 (2004), pp. 499–511; Y. J. Huo et al., "Leadership and the Management of Conflicts in Diverse Groups: Why Acknowledging versus Neglecting Subgroup Identity Matters," *European Journal of Social Psychology* 35, no. 2 (2005), pp. 237–54.

8. B. Crumley, "Game of Death: France's Shocking TV Experiment," *Time,* March 17, 2010; R. L. Parry, "Contestants Turn Torturers in French TV Experiment," *Yahoo! News,* March 16, 2010.

9. L. S. Sya, "Flying to Greater Heights," *New Sunday Times (Kuala Lumpur),* July 31, 2005, p. 14; M. Bolch, "Rewarding the Team," *HRMagazine,* February 2007, pp. 91–93.

10. J. M. Peiro and J. L. Melia, "Formal and Informal Interpersonal Power in Organisations: Testing a Bifactorial Model of Power in Role-Sets," *Applied Psychology* 52, no. 1 (2003), pp. 14–35.

11. P. F. Drucker, "The New Workforce," *The Economist* (November 3, 2001), pp. 8–12.

12. K. Miyahara, "Charisma: From Weber to Contemporary Sociology," *Sociological Inquiry* 53, no. 4 (Fall 1983), pp. 368–88; J. D. Kudisch and M. L. Poteet, "Expert Power, Referent Power, and Charisma: Toward the Resolution of a Theoretical Debate," *Journal of Business & Psychology* 10 (Winter 1995), pp. 177–95; D. Ladkin, "The Enchantment of the Charismatic Leader: Charisma Reconsidered as Aesthetic Encounter," *Leadership* 2, no. 2 (May 2006), pp. 165–79.

13. G. Yukl and C. M. Falbe, "Importance of Different Power Sources in Downward and Lateral Relations," *Journal of Applied Psychology* 76 (1991), pp. 416–23; B. H. Raven, "Kurt Lewin Address: Influence, Power, Religion, and the Mechanisms of Social Control," *Journal of Social Issues* 55 (Spring 1999), pp. 161–86.

14. P. L. Dawes, D. Y. Lee, and G. R. Dowling, "Information Control and Influence in Emergent Buying Centers," *Journal of Marketing* 62, no. 3 (July 1998), pp. 55–68; D. Willer, "Power-at-a-Distance," *Social Forces* 81, no. 4 (2003), pp. 1295–1334; D. J. Brass et al., "Taking Stock of Networks and Organizations: A Multilevel Perspective," *Academy of Management Journal* 47, no. 6 (December 2004), pp. 795–817.

15. C. R. Hinings et al., "Structural Conditions of Intraorganizational Power," *Administrative Science Quarterly* 19 (1974), pp. 22–44. Also see C. S. Saunders, "The Strategic Contingency Theory of Power: Multiple Perspectives," *The Journal of Management Studies* 27 (1990), pp. 1–21.

16. D. J. Hickson et al., "A Strategic Contingencies' Theory of Intra-organizational Power," *Administrative Science Quarterly* 16 (1971), pp. 216–27; Hinings et al., "Structural Conditions of Intraorganizational Power"; R. M. Kanter, "Power Failure in Management Circuits," *Harvard Business Review* (July–August 1979), pp. 65–75.

17. Hickson et al., "A Strategic Contingencies' Theory of Intraorganizational Power"; J. D. Hackman, "Power and Centrality in the Allocation of Resources in Colleges and Universities," *Administrative Science Quarterly* 30 (1985), pp. 61–77; D. J. Brass and M. E. Burkhardt, "Potential Power and Power Use: An Investigation of Structure and Behavior," *Academy of Management Journal* 36 (1993), pp. 441–70.

18. S. D. Harrington and B. Ivry, "For Commuters, a Day to Adapt," *The Record (Bergen, N.J.),* December 21, 2005, p. A1; S. McCarthy, "Transit Strike Cripples New York," *Globe & Mail (Toronto),* December 21, 2005, p. A17.

19. Kanter, "Power Failure in Management Circuits"; B. E. Ashforth, "The Experience of Powerlessness in Organizations," *Organizational Behavior and Human Decision Processes* 43 (1989), pp. 207–42; L. Holden, "European Managers: HRM and an Evolving Role," *European Business Review* 12 (2000).

20. D. C. Hambrick and E. Abrahamson, "Assessing Managerial Discretion across Industries: A Multimethod Approach," *Academy of Management Journal* 38, no. 5 (1995), pp. 1427–41; M. A. Carpenter and B. R. Golden, "Perceived Managerial Discretion: A Study of Cause and Effect," *Strategic Management Journal* 18, no. 3 (1997), pp. 187–206.

21. R. Madell, "Ground Floor," *Pharmaceutical Executive (Women in Pharma Supplement),* June 2000, pp. 24–31.

22. This list is derived from several sources, including I. Randall, "10 Ways to Make Yourself Indispensable at Work," *Black Enterprise,* January 1993, pp. 79–81; V. Elmer, "Recession-Proof Your Career," *Washington Post,* February 24, 2008; A. Zelenka, "5 Ways to Recession-Proof Your Career" (GigaOM Network, January 21, 2008), accessed May 4, 2010.

23. D. Krackhardt and J. R. Hanson, "Informal Networks: The Company behind the Chart," *Harvard Business Review* 71 (July–August 1993), pp. 104–11; P. S. Adler and S.-W. Kwon,

"Social Capital: Prospects for a New Concept," *Academy of Management Review* 27, no. 1 (2002), pp. 17–40.

24. A. Mehra, M. Kilduff, and D. J. Brass, "The Social Networks of High and Low Self-Monitors: Implications for Workplace Performance," *Administrative Science Quarterly* 46 (March 2001), pp. 121–46.

25. "It Still Comes Down to Who You Know," Hudson news release (New York: February 21, 2007); "Monstercollege Survey Shows Grads Are Optimistic, but Expect a Long Haul," *Marketing Weekly News,* May 8, 2010.

26. B. R. Ragins and E. Sundstrom, "Gender and Power in Organizations: A Longitudinal Perspective," *Psychological Bulletin* 105 (1989), pp. 51–88; M. Linehan, "Barriers to Women's Participation in International Management," *European Business Review* 13 (2001).

27. A. DeFelice, "Climbing to the Top," *Accounting Technology* 24, no. 1 (2008), pp. 12–18.

28. D. M. McCracken, "Winning the Talent War for Women: Sometimes It Takes a Revolution," *Harvard Business Review* (November–December 2000), pp. 159–67.

29. D. Bushey and M. Joll, "Social Network Analysis Comes to Raytheon," *The Monitor (Raytheon news magazine),* 2006; McGregor, "The Office Chart That Really Counts"; J. Reingold, "What's Your OQ?," *Fortune,* July 23, 2007, pp. 98–106; T. Cox, "Map Quest," *Quality Progress,* May 2008, p. 44.

30. D. Keltner, D. H. Gruenfeld, and C. Anderson, "Power, Approach, and Inhibition," *Psychological Review* 110, no. 2 (2003), pp. 265–84; B. Simpson and C. Borch, "Does Power Affect Perception in Social Networks? Two Arguments and an Experimental Test," *Social Psychology Quarterly* 68, no. 3 (2005), pp. 278–87; Galinsky et al., "Power and Perspectives Not Taken."

31. K. Atuahene-Gima and H. Li, "Marketing's Influence Tactics in New Product Development: A Study of High Technology Firms in China," *Journal of Product Innovation Management* 17 (2000), pp. 451–70; A. Somech and A. Drach-Zahavy, "Relative Power and Influence Strategy: The Effects of Agent/Target Organizational Power on Superiors' Choices of Influence Strategies," *Journal of Organizational Behavior* 23 (2002), pp. 167–79.

32. D. Kipnis, S. M. Schmidt, and I. Wilkinson, "Intraorganizational Influence Tactics: Explorations in Getting One's Way," *Journal of Applied Psychology* 65 (1980), pp. 440–52; A. Rao and K. Hashimoto, "Universal and Culturally Specific Aspects of Managerial Influence: A Study of Japanese Managers," *Leadership Quarterly* 8 (1997), pp. 295–312; L. A. McFarland, A. M. Ryan, and S. D. Kriska, "Field Study Investigation of Applicant Use of Influence Tactics in a Selection Interview," *Journal of Psychology* 136 (July 2002), pp. 383–98.

33. R. B. Cialdini and N. J. Goldstein, "Social Influence: Compliance and Conformity," *Annual Review of Psychology* 55 (2004), pp. 591–621.

34. Rao and Hashimoto, "Universal and Culturally Specific Aspects of Managerial Influence." Silent authority as an influence tactic in non-Western cultures is also discussed in S. F. Pasa, "Leadership Influence in a High Power Distance and Collectivist Culture," *Leadership & Organization Development Journal* 21 (2000), pp. 414–26.

35. C. De Gaulle, *The Edge of the Sword (Le Fil De L'epée),* trans. G. Hopkins (London: Faber, 1960), p. 59.

36. "Be Part of the Team If You Want to Catch the Eye," *Birmingham Post (UK),* August 31, 2000, p. 14; S. Maitlis, "Taking It from the Top: How CEOs Influence (and Fail to Influence) Their Boards," *Organization Studies* 25, no. 8 (2004), pp. 1275–1311.

37. A. T. Cobb, "Toward the Study of Organizational Coalitions: Participant Concerns and Activities in a Simulated Organizational Setting," *Human Relations* 44 (1991), pp. 1057–79; E. A. Mannix, "Organizations as Resource Dilemmas: The Effects of Power Balance on Coalition Formation in Small Groups," *Organizational Behavior and Human Decision Processes* 55 (1993), pp. 1–22; D. J. Terry, M. A. Hogg, and K. M. White, "The Theory of Planned Behavior: Self-Identity, Social Identity and Group Norms," *British Journal of Social Psychology* 38 (September 1999), pp. 225–44.

38. A. P. Brief, *Attitudes in and around Organizations* (Thousand Oaks, CA: Sage, 1998), pp. 69–84; D. J. O'Keefe, *Persuasion: Theory and Research* (Thousand Oaks, CA: Sage, 2002).

39. These and other features of message content in persuasion are detailed in R. Petty and J. Cacioppo, *Attitudes and Persuasion: Classic and Contemporary Approaches* (Dubuque, IA: W. C. Brown, 1981); M. Pfau, E. A. Szabo, and J. Anderson, "The Role and Impact of Affect in the Process of Resistance to Persuasion," *Human Communication Research* 27 (April 2001), pp. 216–52; O'Keefe, *Persuasion: Theory and Research,* Chap. 9; R. Buck et al., "Emotion and Reason in Persuasion: Applying the Ari Model and the Casc Scale," *Journal of Business Research* 57, no. 6 (2004), pp. 647–56; and W. D. Crano and R. Prislin, "Attitudes and Persuasion," *Annual Review of Psychology* 57 (2006), pp. 345–74.

40. N. Rhodes and W. Wood, "Self-Esteem and Intelligence Affect Influenceability: The Mediating Role of Message Reception," *Psychological Bulletin* 111, no. 1 (1992), pp. 156–71.

41. D. Strutton and L. E. Pelton, "Effects of Ingratiation on Lateral Relationship Quality within Sales Team Settings," *Journal of Business Research* 43 (1998), pp. 1–12; R. Vonk, "Self-Serving Interpretations of Flattery: Why Ingratiation Works," *Journal of Personality and Social Psychology* 82 (2002), pp. 515–26.

42. C. A. Higgins, T. A. Judge, and G. R. Ferris, "Influence Tactics and Work Outcomes: A Meta-Analysis," *Journal of Organizational Behavior* 24 (2003), pp. 90–106.

43. D. Strutton, L. E. Pelton, and J. Tanner, J. F., "Shall We Gather in the Garden: The Effect of Ingratiatory Behaviors on Buyer Trust in Salespeople," *Industrial Marketing Management* 25 (1996), pp. 151–62; J. O' Neil, "An Investigation of the Sources of Influence of Corporate Public Relations Practitioners," *Public Relations Review* 29 (June 2003), pp. 159–69.

44. M. C. Bolino and W. H. Tunley, "More Than One Way to Make an Impression: Exploring Profiles of Impression Management," *Journal of Management* 29 (2003), pp. 141–60.

45. T. Peters, "The Brand Called You," *Fast Company,* August 1997, http://www.fastcompany.com/magazine/10/brandyou.html; J. Sills, "Becoming Your Own Brand," *Psychology Today* 41, no. 1 (February 2008), pp. 62–63.

46. J. Foster, "Here Are Best Answers to Job Interview Questions," *The Herald (Rock Hill, S.C.),* April 4, 2010.

47. S. L. McShane, "Applicant Misrepresentations in Résumés and Interviews in Canada," *Labor Law Journal,* January 1994, pp. 15–24; S. Romero and M. Richtel, "Second Chance," *New York Times,* March 5, 2001, C1; P. Sabatini, "Fibs on Résumés Commonplace," *Pittsburgh Post-Gazette,* February 24, 2006.

48. J. Laucius, "Internet Guru's Credentials a True Work of Fiction," *Ottawa Citizen,* June 12, 2001.

49. A. W. Gouldner, "The Norm of Reciprocity: A Preliminary Statement," *American Sociological Review* 25 (1960), pp. 161–78.

50. Y. Fan, "Questioning Guanxi: Definition, Classification, and Implications," *International Business Review* 11 (2002), pp. 543–61; D. Tan and R. S. Snell, "The Third Eye: Exploring Guanxi and Relational Morality in the Workplace," *Journal of Business Ethics* 41 (December 2002), pp. 361–84; W. R. Vanhonacker, "When Good Guanxi Turns Bad," *Harvard Business Review* 82, no. 4 (April 2004), pp. 18–19.

51. C. M. Falbe and G. Yukl, "Consequences for Managers of Using Single Influence Tactics and Combinations of Tactics," *Academy of Management Journal* 35 (1992), pp. 638–52.

52. R. C. Ringer and R. W. Boss, "Hospital Professionals' Use of Upward Influence Tactics," *Journal of Managerial Issues* 12 (2000), pp. 92–108.

53. G. Blickle, "Do Work Values Predict the Use of Intraorganizational Influence Strategies?" *Journal of Applied Social Psychology* 30, no. 1 (January 2000), pp. 196–205; P. P. Fu et al., "The Impact of Societal Cultural Values and Individual Social Beliefs on the Perceived Effectiveness of Managerial Influence Strategies: A Meso Approach," *Journal of International Business Studies* 35, no. 4 (July 2004), pp. 284–305.

54. "The 2008 Wasting Time at Work Survey Reveals a Record Number of People Waste Time at Work," Salary.com news release (2008); "When It Comes to Red Tape, Many Canadian Employers Might Just Need to Cut It: RBC Study." CNW news release for RBC (Toronto: January 23, 2008); "Survey: More Than One-Quarter of Employees Have Had Ideas Stolen at Work," PR Newswire news release for OfficeTeam (October 8, 2009); "Survey: Majority of Employees Have Had Ideas Stolen at Work," Canada NewsWire news release for OfficeTeam (Toronto: November 10, 2009); J. Gifford et al., *The Management Agenda 2009* (Horsham, UK: Roffey Park Institute, January 13, 2009).

55. This definition of organizational politics has become the dominant perspective over the past 15 years. See G. R. Ferris and K. M. Kacmar, "Perceptions of Organizational Politics," *Journal of Management* 18 (1992), pp. 93–116; R. Cropanzano et al., "The Relationship of Organizational Politics and Support to Work Behaviors, Attitudes, and Stress," *Journal of Organizational Behavior* 18 (1997), pp. 159–80; and E. Vigoda, "Stress-Related Aftermaths to Workplace Politics: The Relationships among Politics, Job Distress, and Aggressive Behavior in Organizations," *Journal of Organizational Behavior* 23 (2002), pp. 571–91. However, organizational politics was previously viewed as influence tactics outside the formal role that could be either selfish or altruistic. This older definition is less common today, possibly because it is incongruent with popular views of politics and because it overlaps too much with the concept of influence. For the older perspective of organizational politics, see J. Pfeffer, *Power in Organizations* (Boston: Pitman, 1981); and Mintzberg, *Power in and around Organizations*.

56. K. M. Kacmar and R. A. Baron, "Organizational Politics: The State of the Field, Links to Related Processes, and an Agenda for Future Research," in *Research in Personnel and Human Resources Management,* ed. G. R. Ferris (Greenwich, CT: JAI Press, 1999), pp. 1–39; L. A. Witt, T. F. Hilton, and W. A. Hochwarter, "Addressing Politics in Matrix Teams," *Group & Organization Management* 26 (June 2001), pp. 230–47; Vigoda, "Stress-Related Aftermaths to Workplace Politics: The Relationships among Politics, Job Distress, and Aggressive Behavior in Organizations"; C.-H. Chang, C. C. Rosen, and P. E. Levy, "The Relationship between Perceptions of Organizational Politics and Employee Attitudes, Strain, and Behavior: A Meta-Analytic Examination," *Academy of Management Journal* 52, no. 4 (2009), pp. 779–801.

57. C. Hardy, *Strategies for Retrenchment and Turnaround: The Politics of Survival* (Berlin: Walter de Gruyter, 1990), Chap. 14; M. C. Andrews and K. M. Kacmar, "Discriminating among Organizational Politics, Justice, and Support," *Journal of Organizational Behavior* 22 (2001), pp. 347–66.

58. S. Blazejewski and W. Dorow, "Managing Organizational Politics for Radical Change: The Case of Beiersdorf-Lechia S.A., Poznan," *Journal of World Business* 38 (August 2003), pp. 204–23.

59. L. W. Porter, R. W. Allen, and H. L. Angle, "The Politics of Upward Influence in Organizations," *Research in Organizational Behavior* 3 (1981), pp. 120–22; R. J. House, "Power and Personality in Complex Organizations," *Research in Organizational Behavior* 10 (1988), pp. 305–57.

60. R. Christie and F. Geis, *Studies in Machiavellianism* (New York: Academic Press, 1970); S. M. Farmer et al., "Putting Upward Influence Strategies in Context," *Journal of Organizational Behavior* 18 (1997), pp. 17–42; K. S. Sauleya and A. G. Bedeian, "Equity Sensitivity: Construction of a Measure and Examination of Its Psychometric Properties," *Journal of Management* 26 (September 2000), pp. 885–910.

61. "Dark Theory of Alycia E-Mail," *New York Post,* June 5, 2008, p. 12; M. Klein, "Lane Suit Details Mendte Gossip," *Philadelphia Inquirer,* September 24, 2008, p. B01; M. Klein, "Alycia Lane Sues CBS3," *Philadelphia Inquirer,* June 20, 2008, p. B01; M. Klein, "Mendte Could Push Either Way," *Philadelphia Inquirer,* July 13, 2008, p. A01; P. Walters, "Fired Philly TV Anchor Charged in E-Mail Scandal," *Associated Press Newswires,* July 22, 2008.

62. G. R. Ferris et al., "Perceptions of Organizational Politics: Prediction, Stress-Related Implications, and Outcomes," *Human Relations* 49 (1996), pp. 233–63.

63. This famous quotation is attributed to both Niccolò Machiavelli and Sun Tzu. None of Machiavelli's five main books (translated) has any statement close to this quotation. Sun Tzu's *Art of War* book (translated) does not have this quotation, either, but he makes a similar statement about spies: "Hence it is that with none in the whole army are more intimate relations to be maintained than with spies." See Sun Tzu, *The Art of War,* trans. L. Giles (Mineola, NY: Dover, 2002), p. 98.

CHAPTER 10

1. L. Gravett and R. Throckmorton, *Bridging the Generation Gap* (Franklin Lakes, NJ: Career Press, 2007); P. Fogg, "When Generations Collide," *Chronicle of Higher Education* 54, no. 45 (2008), pp. B18–B20; N. Weil, "Welcome to the Generation Wars," *CIO,* February 1, 2008.

2. *Workplace Conflict and How Businesses Can Harness It to Thrive,* CPP Global Human Capital Report (Mountain View, CA: CPP, Inc., July 2008).

3. D. Tjosvold, *Working Together to Get Things Done* (Lexington, MA: Lexington, 1986), pp. 114–15; J. A. Wall and R. R. Callister, "Conflict and Its Management," *Journal of Management,* 21 (1995), pp. 515–58; M. A. Rahim, "Toward a Theory of Managing Organizational Conflict," *International Journal of Conflict Management* 13, no. 3 (2002), pp. 206–35; D. Tjosvold, "Defining Conflict and Making Choices about Its Management," *International Journal of Conflict Management* 17, no. 2 (2006), pp. 87–95.

4. For example, see L. Urwick, *The Elements of Administration,* 2nd ed. (London: Pitman, 1947); C. Argyris, "The Individual

and Organization: Some Problems of Mutual Adjustment," *Administrative Science Quarterly* 2, no. 1 (1957), pp. 1–24; K. E. Boulding, "Organization and Conflict," *Conflict Resolution* 1, no. 2 (June 1957), pp. 122–34; and R. R. Blake, H. A. Shepard, and J. S. Mouton, *Managing Intergroup Conflict in Industry* (Houston: Gulf Publishing, 1964).

5. C. K. W. De Dreu and L. R. Weingart, "A Contingency Theory of Task Conflict and Performance in Groups and Organizational Teams," in *International Handbook of Organizational Teamwork and Cooperative Working,* ed. M. A. West, D. Tjosvold, and K. G. Smith (Chicester, UK: John Wiley & Sons, 2003), pp. 151–66; K. A. Jehn and C. Bendersky, "Intragroup Conflict in Organizations: A Contingency Perspective on the Conflict–Outcome Relationship," *Research in Organizational Behavior* 25 (2003), pp. 187–242.

6. M. P. Follett, "Constructive Conflict," in *Dynamic Administration: The Collected Papers of Mary Parker Follett,* ed. H. C. Metcalf and L. Urwick (New York: Harper and Brothers, 1942), pp. 30–37.

7. Rahim, "Toward a Theory of Managing Organizational Conflict"; M. Duarte and G. Davies, "Testing the Conflict–Performance Assumption in Business-to-Business Relationships," *Industrial Marketing Management* 32 (2003), pp. 91–99. Although the 1970s marked a point when the benefits conflict became widely acknowledged, this view was expressed earlier by some writers. See L. A. Coser, *The Functions of Social Conflict* (New York: Free Press, 1956); J. A. Litterer, "Conflict in Organization: A Re-Examination," *Academy of Management Journal* 9 (1966), pp. 178–86; and H. Assael, "Constructive Role of Interorganizational Conflict," *Administrative Science Quarterly* 14, no. 4 (1969), pp. 573–82.

8. P. J. Carnevale, "Creativity in the Outcomes of Conflict," in *The Handbook of Conflict Resolution: Theory and Practice,* ed. M. Deutsch, P. T. Coleman, and E. C. Marcus, 2nd ed. (San Francisco: Jossey-Bass, 2006), pp. 414–35.

9. K. M. Eisenhardt, J. L. Kahwajy, and L. J. Bourgeois III, "How Management Teams Can Have a Good Fight," *Harvard Business Review* (July–August 1997), pp. 77–85; K. M. Eisenhardt, J. L. Kahwajy, and L. J. Bourgeois III, "Conflict and Strategic Choice: How Top Management Teams Disagree," *California Management Review* 39 (Winter 1997), pp. 42–62; T. Greitemeyer et al., "Information Sampling and Group Decision Making: The Effects of an Advocacy Decision Procedure and Task Experience," *Journal of Experimental Psychology-Applied* 12, no. 1 (March 2006), pp. 31–42; U. Klocke, "How to Improve Decision Making in Small Groups: Effects of Dissent and Training Interventions," *Small Group Research* 38, no. 3 (June 2007), pp. 437–68.

10. J. Dewey, *Human Nature and Conduct: An Introduction to Social Psychology* (New York: Holt, 1922), p. 300.

11. H. Guetzkow and J. Gyr, "An Analysis of Conflict in Decision-Making Groups," *Human Relations* 7, no. 3 (August 1954), pp. 367–82; L. H. Pelled, K. M. Eisenhardt, and K. R. Xin, "Exploring the Black Box: An Analysis of Work Group Diversity, Conflict, and Performance," *Administrative Science Quarterly* 44 (March 1999), pp. 1–28; Jehn and Bendersky, "Intragroup Conflict in Organizations". The notion of two types of conflict dates back to the 1950s but became the dominant perspective in the 1990s. We have avoided using the "cognitive" and "affective" conflict labels because each type of conflict includes both cognitive and emotional elements.

12. C. K. W. De Dreu, "When Too Little or Too Much Hurts: Evidence for a Curvilinear Relationship between Task Conflict and Innovation in Teams," *Journal of Management* 32, no. 1 (February 2006), pp. 83–107.

13. A. Grove, "How to Make Confrontation Work for You," in *The Book of Management Wisdom,* ed. P. Krass (New York: John Wiley & Sons, 2000), pp. 83–89; J. Detar, "Andy Grove, Intel's Inside Man," *Investor's Business Daily,* July 24, 2007; D. Senor and S. Singer, Start-up Nation: *The Story of Israel's Economic Miracle* (New York: Hachette Book Group, 2009).

14. C. K. W. De Dreu and L. R. Weingart, "Task versus Relationship Conflict, Team Performance, and Team Member Satisfaction: A Meta-Analysis," *Journal of Applied Psychology* 88 (August 2003), pp. 587–604; A. C. Mooney, P. J. Holahan, and A. C. Amason, "Don't Take It Personally: Exploring Cognitive Conflict as a Mediator of Affective Conflict," *Journal of Management Studies* 44, no. 5 (2007), pp. 733–58.

15. J. Yang and K. W. Mossholder, "Decoupling Task and Relationship Conflict: The Role of Intergroup Emotional Processing," *Journal of Organizational Behavior* 25 (2004), pp. 589–605.

16. A. C. Amason and H. J. Sapienza, "The Effects of Top Management Team Size and Interaction Norms on Cognitive and Affective Conflict," *Journal of Management* 23, no. 4 (1997), pp. 495–516.

17. L. Pondy, "Organizational Conflict: Concepts and Models," *Administrative Science Quarterly* 2 (1967), pp. 296–320; K. W. Thomas, "Conflict and Negotiation Processes in Organizations," in *Handbook of Industrial and Organizational Psychology,* ed. M. D. Dunnette and L. M. Hough, 2nd ed. (Palo Alto, CA: Consulting Psychologists Press, 1992), pp. 651–718.

18. H. Barki and J. Hartwick, "Conceptualizing the Construct of Interpersonal Conflict," *International Journal of Conflict Management* 15, no. 3 (2004), pp. 216–44.

19. M. A. Von Glinow, D. L. Shapiro, and J. M. Brett, "Can We Talk, and Should We? Managing Emotional Conflict in Multicultural Teams," *Academy of Management Review* 29, no. 4 (2004), pp. 578–92.

20. G. E. Martin and T. J. Bergman, "The Dynamics of Behavioral Response to Conflict in the Workplace," *Journal of Occupational & Organizational Psychology* 69 (December 1996), pp. 377–87; J. M. Brett, D. L. Shapiro, and A. L. Lytle, "Breaking the Bonds of Reciprocity in Negotiations," *Academy of Management Journal* 41 (August 1998), pp. 410–24.

21. R. E. Walton and J. M. Dutton, "The Management of Conflict: A Model and Review," *Administrative Science Quarterly* 14 (1969), pp. 73–84; S. M. Schmidt and T. A. Kochan, "Conflict: Toward Conceptual Clarity," *Administrative Science Quarterly* 17, no. 3 (September 1972), pp. 359–70.

22. B. Dudley, "Bring Back the Dazzle," *Seattle Times,* September 23, 2005; J. Greene, "Troubling Exits at Microsoft," *BusinessWeek,* September 26, 2005, p. 98; A. Linn, "Microsoft Reorganizes to Compete Better with Google, Yahoo," *Associated Press Newswires,* September 21, 2005; V. Murphy, "Microsoft's Midlife Crisis," *Forbes,* October 3, 2005, p. 88; L. Vaas, "Microsoft Expands Bureaucracy, Crowns MSN King," *eWeek,* September 20, 2005; J. L. Yang, "Microsoft's New Brain," *Fortune,* May 1, 2006, p. 56.

23. Although this quotation is widely attributed to Thomas Jefferson, scholars suggest that the third U.S. president and a founding father of the nation did not make this statement. However, Jefferson did write that young people should bring about change. According to one source, the popular quotation is a derivation of Jefferson's statement in a letter to Colonel William S. Smith on November 13, 1787: "God forbid we should ever be 20 years without such a rebellion." T. Jefferson, *Memoir, Correspondence, and Miscellanies, from the Papers of Thomas Jefferson,* 2nd ed. (Boston: Gray and Bowen,

1830), p. 267. For discussion of this quotation and its origins, see http://wiki.monticello.org.

24. J. A. McMullin, T. Duerden Comeau, and E. Jovic, "Generational Affinities and Discourses of Difference: A Case Study of Highly Skilled Information Technology Workers," *British Journal of Sociology* 58, no. 2 (2007), pp. 297–316.

25. Data are from the 2009 Kelly Global Workforce Index, based on information published in news releases in each country by Kelly Services in September 2009.

26. R. Wageman and G. Baker, "Incentives and Cooperation: The Joint Effects of Task and Reward Interdependence on Group Performance," *Journal of Organizational Behavior* 18, no. 2 (1997), pp. 139–58; G. S. van der Vegt, B. J. M. Emans, and E. van der Vliert, "Patterns of Interdependence in Work Teams: A Two-Level Investigation of the Relations with Job and Team Satisfaction," *Personnel Psychology* 54, no. 1 (2001), pp. 51–69.

27. P. C. Earley and G. B. Northcraft, "Goal Setting, Resource Interdependence, and Conflict Management," in *Managing Conflict: An Interdisciplinary Approach,* ed. M. A. Rahim (New York: Praeger, 1989), pp. 161–70; K. Jehn, "A Multi-method Examination of the Benefits and Detriments of Intragroup Conflict," *Administrative Science Quarterly* 40 (1995), pp. 245–82.

28. A. Risberg, "Employee Experiences of Acquisition Processes," *Journal of World Business* 36 (March 2001), pp. 58–84.

29. Jehn and Bendersky, "Intragroup Conflict in Organizations."

30. M. Hewstone, M. Rubin, and H. Willis, "Intergroup Bias," *Annual Review of Psychology* 53 (2002), pp. 575–604; J. Jetten, R. Spears, and T. Postmes, "Intergroup Distinctiveness and Differentiation: A Meta-Analytic Integration," *Journal of Personality and Social Psychology* 86, no. 6 (2004), pp. 862–79.

31. Follett, "Constructive Conflict"; Blake, Shepard, and Mouton, *Managing Intergroup Conflict in Industry;* T. Ruble and K. Thomas, "Support for a Two-Dimensional Model of Conflict Behavior," *Organizational Behavior and Human Performance* 16 (1976), pp. 143–55; C. K. W. De Dreu et al., "A Theory-Based Measure of Conflict Management Strategies in the Workplace," *Journal of Organizational Behavior* 22 (2001), pp. 645–68; Rahim, "Toward a Theory of Managing Organizational Conflict."

32. E. Knowles, *Little Oxford Dictionary of Proverbs* (Oxford, UK: Oxford University Press, 2009), p. 21.

33. Jehn, "A Multimethod Examination of the Benefits and Detriments of Intragroup Conflict."

34. D. W. Johnson et al., "Effects of Cooperative, Competitive, and Individualistic Goal Structures on Achievement: A Meta-Analysis," *Psychological Bulletin* 89 (1981), pp. 47–62; Rahim, "Toward a Theory of Managing Organizational Conflict"; G. A. Callanan, C. D. Benzing, and D. F. Perri, "Chcoie of Conflict-Handling Strategy: A Matter of Context," *Journal of Psychology* 140, no. 3 (2006), pp. 269–88.

35. R. A. Friedman et al., "What Goes Around Comes Around: The Impact of Personal Conflict Style on Work Conflict and Stress," *International Journal of Conflict Management* 11, no. 1 (2000), pp. 32–55; X. M. Song, J. Xile, and B. Dyer, "Antecedents and Consequences of Marketing Managers' Conflict-Handling Behaviors," *Journal of Marketing* 64 (January 2000), pp. 50–66; M. Song, B. Dyer, and R. J. Thieme, "Conflict Management and Innovation Performance: An Integrated Contingency Perspective," *Academy of Marketing Science* 34, no. 3 (2006), pp. 341–56; L. A. DeChurch, K. L. Hamilton, and C. Haas, "Effects of Conflict

Management Strategies on Perceptions of Intragroup Conflict," *Group Dynamics* 11, no. 1 (2007), pp. 66–78.

36. C. K. W. De Dreu and A. E. M. Van Vianen, "Managing Relationship Conflict and the Effectiveness of Organizational Teams," *Journal of Organizational Behavior* 22 (2001), pp. 309–28; R. J. Lewicki et al., *Negotiation,* 4th ed. (Burr Ridge, IL: McGraw-Hill/Irwin, 2003), pp. 35–36.

37. *Workplace Conflict and How Businesses Can Harness It to Thrive,* CPP Global Human Capital Report (Mountain View, CA: CPP, Inc., July 2008).

38. M. W. Morris and H.-Y. Fu, "How Does Culture Influence Conflict Resolution? Dynamic Constructivist Analysis," *Social Cognition* 19 (June 2001), pp. 324–49; C. H. Tinsley, "How Negotiators Get to Yes: Predicting the Constellation of Strategies Used across Cultures to Negotiate Conflict," *Journal of Applied Psychology* 86, no. 4 (2001), pp. 583–93; J. L. Holt and C. J. DeVore, "Culture, Gender, Organizational Role, and Styles of Conflict Resolution: A Meta-Analysis," *International Journal of Intercultural Relations* 29, no. 2 (2005), pp. 165–96.

39. D. A. Cai and E. L. Fink, "Conflict Style Differences between Individualists and Collectivists," *Communication Monographs* 69 (March 2002), pp. 67–87; C. H. Tinsley and E. Weldon, "Responses to a Normative Conflict among American and Chinese Managers," *International Journal of Conflict Management* 3, no. 2 (2003), pp. 183–94; F. P. Brew and D. R. Cairns, "Styles of Managing Interpersonal Workplace Conflict in Relation to Status and Face Concern: A Study with Anglos and Chinese," *International Journal of Conflict Management* 15, no. 1 (2004), pp. 27–57.

40. N. Brewer, P. Mitchell, and N. Weber, "Gender Role, Organizational Status, and Conflict Management Styles," *International Journal of Conflict Management* 13 (2002), pp. 78–95; N. B. Florea et al., "Negotiating from Mars to Venus: Gender in Simulated International Negotiations," *Simulation & Gaming* 34 (June 2003), pp. 226–48; Holt and DeVore, "Culture, Gender, Organizational Role, and Styles of Conflict Resolution."

41. K. Lewin, *Resolving Social Conflicts* (New York: Harper, 1948).

42. J. D. Hunger and L. W. Stern, "An Assessment of the Functionality of the Superordinate Goal in Reducing Conflict," *Academy of Management Journal* 19, no. 4 (1976), pp. 591–605; M. Sherif, "Superordinate Goals in the Reduction of Intergroup Conflict," *The American Journal of Sociology* 63, no. 4 (1958), pp. 349–56.

43. Sherif, "Superordinate Goals in the Reduction of Intergroup Conflict"; Eisenhardt, Kahwajy, and Bourgeois III, "How Management Teams Can Have a Good Fight"; Song, Xile, and Dyer, "Antecedents and Consequences of Marketing Managers' Conflict-Handling Behaviors."

44. H. C. Triandis, "The Future of Workforce Diversity in International Organisations: A Commentary," *Applied Psychology: An International Journal* 52, no. 3 (2003), pp. 486–95.

45. "Can the New CEO End a Culture Clash after a Merger?" *Financial Times,* September 10, 2008, p. 16.

46. T. F. Pettigrew, "Intergroup Contact Theory," *Annual Review of Psychology* 49 (1998), pp. 65–85; S. Brickson, "The Impact of Identity Orientation on Individual and Organizational Outcomes in Demographically Diverse Settings," *Academy of Management Review* 25 (January 2000), pp. 82–101; J. Dixon and K. Durrheim, "Contact and the Ecology of Racial Division: Some Varieties of Informal Segregation," *British Journal of Social Psychology* 42 (March 2003), pp. 1–23.

47. Triandis, "The Future of Workforce Diversity in International Organisations."

48. Von Glinow, Shapiro, and Brett, "Can We Talk, and Should We?"

49. Variations of this action plan are described in several sources, including A. Jay, P. Smith, and H. Barlcay, *From "No" to "Yes": The Constructive Route to Agreement* (London, Video Arts, 1988); D. Stone, B. Patton, and S. Heen, *Difficult Conversations: How to Discuss What Matters Most* (New York: Penguin, 1999); K. Patterson et al., *Crucial Conversations: Tools for Talking Whem Stakes Are High* (New York: McGraw-Hill, 2002).

50. E. Horwitt, "Knowledge, Knowledge, Who's Got the Knowledge," *Computerworld,* April 8, 1996, pp. 80, 81, 84.

51. L. L. Putnam, "Beyond Third Party Role: Disputes and Managerial Intervention," *Employee Responsibilities and Rights Journal* 7 (1994), pp. 23–36; A. R. Elangovan, "The Manager as the Third Party: Deciding How to Intervene in Employee Disputes," in *Negotiation: Readings, Exercises, and Cases,* ed. R. J. Lewicki, J. A. Litterer, and D. Saunders, 3rd ed. (New York: McGraw-Hill, 1999), pp. 458–69. For a somewhat different taxonomy of managerial conflict intervention, see P. G. Irving and J. P. Meyer, "A Multidimensional Scaling Analysis of Managerial Third-Party Conflict Intervention Strategies," *Canadian Journal of Behavioural Science* 29, no. 1 (January 1997), pp. 7–18. A recent review describes 10 species of third-party intervention, but these consist of variations of the three types described here. See D. E. Conlon et al., "Third Party Interventions across Cultures: No 'One Best Choice,'" in *Research in Personnel and Human Resources Management* (JAI, 2007), pp. 309–49.

52. B. H. Sheppard, "Managers as Inquisitors: Lessons from the Law," in *Bargaining inside Organizations,* ed. M. H. Bazerman and R. J. Lewicki (Beverly Hills, CA: Sage, 1983); N. H. Kim, D. W. Sohn, and J. A. Wall, "Korean Leaders' (and Subordinates') Conflict Management," *International Journal of Conflict Management* 10, no. 2 (April 1999), pp. 130–53; D. J. Moberg, "Managers as Judges in Employee Disputes: An Occasion for Moral Imagination," *Business Ethics Quarterly* 13, no. 4 (2003), pp. 453–77.

53. R. Karambayya and J. M. Brett, "Managers Handling Disputes: Third Party Roles and Perceptions of Fairness," *Academy of Management Journal* 32 (1989), pp. 687–704; R. Cropanzano et al., "Disputant Reactions to Managerial Conflict Resolution Tactics," *Group & Organization Management* 24 (June 1999), pp. 124–53.

54. A. R. Elangovan, "Managerial Intervention in Organizational Disputes: Testing a Prescriptive Model of Strategy Selection," *International Journal of Conflict Management* 4 (1998), pp. 301–35; P. S. Nugent, "Managing Conflict: Third-Party Interventions for Managers," *Academy of Management Executive* 16, no. 1 (February 2002), pp. 139–54.

55. J. P. Meyer, J. M. Gemmell, and P. G. Irving, "Evaluating the Management of Interpersonal Conflict in Organizations: A Factor-Analytic Study of Outcome Criteria," *Canadian Journal of Administrative Sciences* 14 (1997), pp. 1–13; L. B. Bingham, "Employment Dispute Resolution: The Case for Mediation," *Conflict Resolution Quarterly* 22, no. 1–2 (2004), pp. 145–74; M. Hyde et al., "Workplace Conflict Resolution and the Health of Employees in the Swedish and Finnish Units of an Industrial Company," *Social Science & Medicine* 63, no. 8 (2006), pp. 2218–27.

56. W. H. Ross and D. E. Conlon, "Hybrid Forms of Third-Party Dispute Resolution: Theoretical Implications of Combining Mediation and Arbitration," *Academy of Management Review* 25, no. 2 (2000), pp. 416–27; W. H. Ross, C. Brantmeier, and T. Ciriacks, "The Impact of Hybrid Dispute-Resolution Procedures on Constituent Fairness Judgments," *Journal of Applied Social Psychology* 32, no. 6 (June 2002), pp. 1151–88.

57. "AMC Uses Alternative Dispute Resolution to Solve Workplace Conflicts," Department of Defense, U.S. Air Force news release (Scott Air Force Base, IL: July 13, 2005).

58. S. L. Hayford, "Alternative Dispute Resolution," *Business Horizons* 43 (January–February 2000), pp. 2–4; O. Rabinovich-Einy, "Beyond IDR: Resolving Hospital Disputes and Healing Ailing Organizations through ITR," *St. John's Law Review* 81, no. 1 (January 2007), pp. 173–202; T. M. Marcum and E. A. Campbell, "Peer Review in Employment Disputes: An Employee Right or an Employee Wrong?" *Journal of Workplace Rights* 13, no. 1 (2008), pp. 41–58.

59. L. B. Bingham et al., "Mediating Employment Disputes at the United States Postal Service: A Comparison of In-House and Outside Neutral Mediator Models," *Review of Public Personnel Administration* 20, no. 1 (January 2000), pp. 5–19; T. Nabatchi, L. B. Bingham, and D. H. Good, "Organizational Justice and Workplace Mediation: A Six Factor Model," *International Journal of Conflict Management* 18, no. 2 (2007), pp. 148–74. Also see http://www.usps.com/redress/.

CHAPTER 11

1. "Driving the Engine," *Broadcasting & Cable* 133, no. 16 (April 21, 2003), p. 6A; S. Pappu, "The Queen of Tween," *Atlantic Monthly,* November 2004, pp. 118–25; A. Becker, "The Wonderful World of Sweeney," *Broadcasting & Cable,* February 25, 2008, p. 19; J. R. Littlejohn, "Distinguished Vanguard Award for Leadership," *Multichannel News,* May 19, 2008.

2. R. House, M. Javidan, and P. Dorfman, "Project GLOBE: An Introduction," *Applied Psychology: An International Review* 50 (2001), pp. 489–505; R. House et al., "Understanding Cultures and Implicit Leadership Theories across the Globe: An Introduction to Project GLOBE," *Journal of World Business* 37 (2002), pp. 3–10.

3. V. Garrow and E. Stirling, *The Management Agenda 2007: Overview of Findings* (West Sussex, UK: Roffey Park, 2007); S. Stern, "Lofty View from Davos Could Just Be a Mirage," *Finaicial Times,* January 28, 2008, p. 14; "Over Half of Employees Say Their Managers Are Ineffective." i4cp news release (Seattle: May 11, 2009).

4. R. G. Isaac, W. J. Zerbe, and D. C. Pitt, "Leadership and Motivation: The Effective Application of Expectancy Theory," *Journal of Managerial Issues* 13 (Summer 2001), pp. 212–26; C. L. Pearce and J. A. Conger, eds., *Shared Leadership: Reframing the Hows and Whys of Leadership* (Thousand Oaks, CA: Sage, 2003); J. S. Nielson, *The Myth of Leadership* (Palo Alto, CA: Davies-Black, 2004); J. A. Raelin, "We the Leaders: In Order to Form a Leaderful Organization," *Journal of Leadership & Organizational Studies* 12, no. 2 (2005), pp. 18–30.

5. J. A. Raelin, *Creating Leaderful Organizations: How to Bring Out Leadership in Everyone* (San Francisco: Berret-Koehler, 2003).

6. S. Marchionne, "Fiat's Extreme Makeover," *Harvard Business Review,* December 2008, pp. 45–48.

7. "Powered by Frontline People," *Employee Engagement Today,* September 2007; C. Hosford, "Flying High," *Incentive* 181, no. 12 (December 2007), pp. 14–20.

8. A. Deutschman, "The Fabric of Creativity," *Fast Company,* December 2004, p. 54; P. J. Kiger, "Power to the Individual," *Workforce Management,* February 27, 2006, pp. 1–7; G. Hamel,

The Future of Management (Boston: Harvard Business School Press, 2007), Chap. 5.

9. Many of these perspectives are summarized in R. N. Kanungo, "Leadership in Organizations: Looking Ahead to the 21st Century," *Canadian Psychology* 39 (Spring 1998), pp. 71–82; G. A. Yukl, *Leadership in Organizations,* 6th ed. (Upper Saddle River, NJ: Pearson Education, 2006).

10. The history of the trait perspective of leadership, as well as current research on this topic, is nicely summarized in S. J. Zaccaro, C. Kemp, and P. Bader, "Leader Traits and Attributes," in *The Nature of Leadership,* ed. J. Antonakis, A. T. Cianciolo, and R. J. Sternberg (Thousand Oaks, CA: Sage, 2004), pp. 101–24.

11. R. M. Stogdill, *Handbook of Leadership* (New York: The Free Press, 1974), Chap. 5.

12. J. Intagliata, D. Ulrich, and N. Smallwood, "Leveraging Leadership Competencies to Produce Leadership Brand: Creating Distinctiveness by Focusing on Strategy and Results," *Human Resources Planning* 23, no. 4 (2000), pp. 12–23; J. A. Conger and D. A. Ready, "Rethinking Leadership Competencies," *Leader to Leader* (Spring 2004), pp. 41–47; Zaccaro, Kemp, and Bader, "Leader Traits and Attributes."

13. This list is based on S. A. Kirkpatrick and E. A. Locke, "Leadership: Do Traits Matter?" *Academy of Management Executive* 5 (May 1991), pp. 48–60; R. M. Aditya, R. J. House, and S. Kerr, "Theory and Practice of Leadership: Into the New Millennium," in *Industrial and Organizational Psychology: Linking Theory with Practice,* ed. C. L. Cooper and E. A. Locke (Oxford, UK: Blackwell, 2000), pp. 130–65; D. Goleman, R. Boyatzis, and A. McKee, *Primal Leaders* (Boston: Harvard Business School Press, 2002); T. A. Judge et al., "Personality and Leadership: A Qualitative and Quantitative Review," *Journal Of Applied Psychology* 87, no. 4 (August 2002), pp. 765–80; T. A. Judge, A. E. Colbert, and R. Ilies, "Intelligence and Leadership: A Quantitative Review and Test of Theoretical Propositions," *Journal of Applied Psychology* 89, no. 3 (June 2004), pp. 542–52; Zaccaro, Kemp, and Bader, "Leader Traits and Attributes."

14. M. Popper et al., "The Capacity to Lead: Major Psychological Differences between Leaders and Nonleaders," *Military Psychology* 16, no. 4 (2004), pp. 245–63.

15. The large-scale studies are reported in C. Savoye, "Workers Say Honesty Is Best Company Policy," *Christian Science Monitor,* June 15, 2000; J. M. Kouzes and B. Z. Posner, *The Leadership Challenge,* 3rd ed. (San Francisco: Jossey-Bass, 2002), Chap. 2; J. Schettler, "Leadership in Corporate America," *Training & Development,* September 2002, pp. 66–73.

16. BlessingWhite, *The State of Employee Engagement 2008: Asia Pacific Overview* (Princeton, NJ: BlessingWhite, March 3, 2008).

17. R. Davidovitz et al., "Leaders as Attachment Figures: Leaders' Attachment Orientations Predict Leadership-Related Mental Representations and Followers' Performance and Mental Health," *Journal of Personality and Social Psychology* 93, no. 4 (2007), pp. 632–50.

18. J. B. Miner, "Twenty Years of Research on Role Motivation Theory of Managerial Effectiveness," *Personnel Psychology* 31 (1978), pp. 739–60; R. J. House and R. N. Aditya, "The Social Scientific Study of Leadership: Quo Vadis?" *Journal of Management* 23 (1997), pp. 409–73.

19. J. Hedlund et al., "Identifying and Assessing Tacit Knowledge: Understanding the Practical Intelligence of Military Leaders," *Leadership Quarterly* 14, no. 2 (2003), pp. 117–40; R. J. Sternberg, "A Systems Model of Leadership: WICS," *American Psychologist* 62, no. 1 (2007), pp. 34–42.

20. J. George, "Emotions and Leadership: The Role of Emotional Intelligence," *Human Relations* 53 (August 2000), pp. 1027–55; Goleman, Boyatzis, and McKee, *Primal Leaders;* R. G. Lord and R. J. Hall, "Identity, Deep Structure and the Development of Leadership Skill," *Leadership Quarterly* 16, no. 4 (August 2005), pp. 591–615; C. Skinner and P. Spurgeon, "Valuing Empathy and Emotional Intelligence in Health Leadership: A Study of Empathy, Leadership Behaviour and Outcome Effectiveness," *Health Services Management Research* 18, no. 1 (February 2005), pp. 1–12.

21. B. George, *Authentic Leadership* (San Francisco: Jossey-Bass, 2004); W. L. Gardner et al., "'Can You See the Real Me?' A Self-Based Model of Authentic Leader and Follower Development," *Leadership Quarterly* 16 (2005), pp. 343–72; B. George, True North (San Francisco: Jossey-Bass, 2007), Chap. 4; M. E. Palanski and F. J. Yammarino, "Integrity and Leadership: Clearing the Conceptual Confusion," *European Management Journal* 25, no. 3 (2007), pp. 171–84; F. O. Walumbwa et al., "Authentic Leadership: Development and Validation of a Theory-Based Measure{Dagger}," *Journal of Management* 34, no. 1 (February 2008), pp. 89–126.

22. R. Jacobs, "Using Human Resource Functions to Enhance Emotional Intelligence," in *The Emotionally Intelligent Workplace,* ed. C. Cherniss and D. Goleman (San Francisco: Jossey-Bass, 2001), pp. 161–63; Conger and Ready, "Rethinking Leadership Competencies."

23. R. G. Lord and D. J. Brown, *Leadership Processes and Self-Identity: A Follower-Centered Approach to Leadership* (Mahwah, NJ: Lawrence Erlbaum Associates, 2004); R. Bolden and J. Gosling, "Leadership Competencies: Time to Change the Tune?" *Leadership* 2, no. 2 (May 2006), pp. 147–63.

24. E. A. Fleishman, "The Description of Supervisory Behavior," *Journal of Applied Psychology* 37, no. 1 (1953), pp. 1–6. For discussion on methodological problems with the development of these people versus task-oriented leadership constructs, see C. A. Schriesheim, R. J. House, and S. Kerr, "Leader Initiating Structure: A Reconciliation of Discrepant Research Results and Some Empirical Tests," *Organizational Behavior and Human Performance* 15, no. 2 (1976), pp. 297–321; L. Tracy, "Consideration and Initiating Structure: Are They Basic Dimensions of Leader Behavior?" *Social Behavior and Personality* 15, no. 1 (1987), pp. 21–33.

25. A. K. Korman, "Consideration, Initiating Structure, and Organizational Criteria-A Review," *Personnel Psychology* 19 (1966), pp. 349–62; E. A. Fleishman, "Twenty Years of Consideration and Structure," in *Current Developments in the Study of Leadership,* ed. E. A. Fleishman and J. C. Hunt (Carbondale, IL: Southern Illinois University Press, 1973), pp. 1–40; T. A. Judge, R. F. Piccolo, and R. Ilies, "The Forgotten Ones? The Validity of Consideration and Initiating Structure in Leadership Research," *Journal of Applied Psychology* 89, no. 1 (2004), pp. 36–51; Yukl, *Leadership in Organizations,* pp. 62–75.

26. V. V. Baba, "Serendipity in Leadership: Initiating Structure and Consideration in the Classroom," *Human Relations* 42 (1989), pp. 509–25.

27. S. Kerr et al., "Towards a Contingency Theory of Leadership Based upon the Consideration and Initiating Structure Literature," *Organizational Behavior and Human Performance* 12 (1974), pp. 62–82; L. L. Larson, J. G. Hunt, and R. N. Osbom, "The Great Hi—Hi Leader Behavior Myth: A Lesson from Occam's Razor," *Academy of Management Journal* 19 (1976), pp. 628–41.

28. R. Tannenbaum and W. H. Schmidt, "How to Choose a Leadership Pattern," *Harvard Business Review* (May–June 1973), pp. 162–80.

29. R. P. Vecchio, J. E. Justin, and C. L. Pearce, "The Utility of Transactional and Transformational Leadership for Predicting Performance and Satisfaction within a Path-Goal Theory Framework," *Journal of Occupational and Organizational Psychology* 81 (2008), pp. 71–82.

30. For a thorough study of how expectancy theory of motivation relates to leadership, see Isaac, Zerbe, and Pitt, "Leadership and Motivation: The Effective Application of Expectancy Theory."

31. R. J. House, "A Path–Goal Theory of Leader Effectiveness," *Administrative Science Quarterly* 16 (1971), pp. 321–38; M. G. Evans, "Extensions of a Path–Goal Theory of Motivation," *Journal of Applied Psychology* 59 (1974), pp. 172–78; R. J. House and T. R. Mitchell, "Path–Goal Theory of Leadership," *Journal of Contemporary Business* (Autumn 1974), pp. 81–97; M. G. Evans, "Path–Goal Theory of Leadership," in *Leadership,* ed. L. L. Neider and C. A. Schriesheim (Greenwich, CT: Information Age Publishing, 2002), pp. 115–38.

32. Various thoughts on servant leadership are presented in L. C. Spears and M. Lawrence, eds., *Focus on Leadership: Servant-Leadership* (New York: John Wiley & Sons, 2002).

33. R. J. House, "Path–Goal Theory of Leadership: Lessons, Legacy, and a Reformulated Theory," *Leadership Quarterly* 7 (1996), pp. 323–52.

34. J. Indvik, "Path–Goal Theory of Leadership: A Meta-Analysis," *Academy of Management Proceedings* (1986), pp. 189–92; J. C. Wofford and L. Z. Liska, "Path–Goal Theories of Leadership: A Meta-Analysis," *Journal of Management* 19 (1993), pp. 857–76.

35. J. D. Houghton and S. K. Yoho, "Toward a Contingency Model of Leadership and Psychological Empowerment: When Should Self-Leadership Be Encouraged?" *Journal of Leadership & Organizational Studies* 11, no. 4 (2005), pp. 65–83.

36. R. T. Keller, "A Test of the Path–Goal Theory of Leadership with Need for Clarity as a Moderator in Research and Development Organizations," *Journal of Applied Psychology* 74 (1989), pp. 208–12.

37. C. A. Schriesheim and L. L. Neider, "Path–Goal Leadership Theory: The Long and Winding Road," *Leadership Quarterly* 7 (1996), pp. 317–21.

38. P. Hersey and K. H. Blanchard, *Management of Organizational Behavior: Utilizing Human Resources,* 5th ed. (Englewood Cliffs, NJ: Prentice Hall, 1988).

39. R. P. Vecchio, "Situational Leadership Theory: An Examination of a Prescriptive Theory," *Journal of Applied Psychology* 72 (1987), pp. 444–51; W. Blank, J. R. Weitzel, and S. G. Green, "A Test of the Situational Leadership Theory," *Personnel Psychology* 43 (1990), pp. 579–97; C. L. Graeff, "Evolution of Situational Leadership Theory: A Critical Review," *Leadership Quarterly* 8 (1997), pp. 153–70; G. Thompson and R. P. Vecchio, "Situational Leadership Theory: A Test of Three Versions," *The Leadership Quarterly* 20, no. 5 (2009), pp. 837–48.

40. Current information about situational leadership is from the company's Web site: http://www.situational.com. The 1997 figure is reported in K. Blanchard and B. Nelson, "Recognition and Reward," *Executive Excellence,* April 1997, p. 15.

41. F. E. Fiedler, *A Theory of Leadership Effectiveness* (New York: McGraw-Hill, 1967); F. E. Fiedler and M. M. Chemers, *Leadership and Effective Management* (Glenview, IL: Scott, Foresman, 1974).

42. F. E. Fiedler, "Engineer the Job to Fit the Manager," *Harvard Business Review* 43, no. 5 (1965), pp. 115–22.

43. For a summary of criticisms, see Yukl, *Leadership in Organizations,* pp. 217–18.

44. N. Nicholson, *Executive Instinct* (New York: Crown, 2000).

45. This observation has also been made by C. A. Schriesheim, "Substitutes-for-Leadership Theory: Development and Basic Concepts," *Leadership Quarterly* 8 (1997), pp. 103–8.

46. D. F. Elloy and A. Randolph, "The Effect of Superleader Behavior on Autonomous Work Groups in a Government Operated Railway Service," *Public Personnel Management* 26 (Summer 1997), pp. 257–72; C. C. Manz and H. Sims Jr., *The New SuperLeadership: Leading Others to Lead Themselves* (San Francisco: Berrett-Koehler, 2001).

47. M. L. Loughry, "Coworkers Are Watching: Performance Implications of Peer Monitoring," *Academy of Management Proceedings* (2002), pp. 01–06.

48. P. M. Podsakoff and S. B. MacKenzie, "Kerr and Jermier's Substitutes for Leadership Model: Background, Empirical Assessment, and Suggestions for Future Research," *Leadership Quarterly* 8 (1997), pp. 117–32; S. D. Dionne et al., "Neutralizing Substitutes for Leadership Theory: Leadership Effects and Common-Source Bias," *Journal of Applied Psychology* 87, no. 3 (June 2002), pp. 454–64; J. R. Villa et al., "Problems with Detecting Moderators in Leadership Research Using Moderated Multiple Regression," *Leadership Quarterly* 14, no. 1 (February 2003), pp. 3–23; S. D. Dionne et al., "Substitutes for Leadership, or Not," *The Leadership Quarterly* 16, no. 1 (2005), pp. 169–93.

49. J. M. Burns, *Leadership* (New York: Harper & Row, 1978); B. J. Avolio and F. J. Yammarino, eds., *Transformational and Charismatic Leadership: The Road Ahead* (Greenwich, CT: JAI Press, 2002); B. M. Bass and R. E. Riggio, *Transformational Leadership,* 2nd ed. (Mahwah, NJ: Lawrence Erlbaum Associates, 2006).

50. V. L. Goodwin, J. C. Wofford, and J. L. Whittington, "A Theoretical and Empirical Extension to the Transformational Leadership Construct," *Journal of Organizational Behavior* 22 (November 2001), pp. 759–74.

51. Burns, *Leadership,* pp. 19–20. Burns also describes transactional and "transforming leadership" in his more recent book: J. M. Burns, *Transforming Leadership* (New York: Grove Press, 2004). In both books, Burns describes both leadership concepts in complex and occasionally confounding ways.

52. For Burns's discussion of the ethics of transactional leadership, see Burns, *Transforming Leadership,* p. 28. Regarding transactional leadership and appealing to needs, justice, and morality, see Burns, *Leadership,* p. 258.

53. A. Zaleznik, "Managers and Leaders: Are They Different?" *Harvard Business Review* 55, no. 5 (1977), pp. 67–78; W. Bennis and B. Nanus, *Leaders: The Strategies for Taking Charge* (New York: Harper & Row, 1985). For a recent discussion regarding managing versus leading, see G. Yukl and R. Lepsinger, "Why Integrating the Leading and Managing Roles Is Essential for Organizational Effectiveness," *Organizational Dynamics* 34, no. 4 (2005), pp. 361–75.

54. Bennis and Nanus, Leaders, p. 20. Peter Drucker is also widely cited as the source of this quotation. The closest passage we could find, however, is in the first two pages of *The Effective Executive* (1966), where Drucker states that effective executives "get the right things done." On the next page, he states that manual workers only need efficiency—"that is, the ability to

do things right rather than the ability to get the right things done." See P. F. Drucker, *The Effective Executive* (New York: Harper Business, 1966), pp. 1–2.

55. B. M. Bass et al., "Predicting Unit Performance by Assessing Transformational and Transactional Leadership," *Journal of Applied Psychology* 88 (April 2003), pp. 207–18; Yukl and Lepsinger, "Why Integrating the Leading and Managing Roles Is Essential for Organizational Effectiveness."

56. For a discussion of the tendency to slide from transformational to transactional leadership, see W. Bennis, *An Invented Life: Reflections on Leadership and Change* (Reading, MA: Addison-Wesley, 1993).

57. R. J. House, "A 1976 Theory of Charismatic Leadership," in *Leadership: The Cutting Edge,* ed. J. G. Hunt and L. L. Larson (Carbondale, IL: Southern Illinois University Press, 1977), pp. 189–207; J. A. Conger, "Charismatic and Transformational Leadership in Organizations: An Insider's Perspective on These Developing Streams of Research," *Leadership Quarterly* 10 (Summer 1999), pp. 145–79.

58. J. E. Barbuto Jr., "Taking the Charisma out of Transformational Leadership," *Journal of Social Behavior & Personality* 12 (September 1997), pp. 689–97; Y. A. Nur, "Charisma and Managerial Leadership: The Gift That Never Was," *Business Horizons* 41 (July 1998), pp. 19–26; M. D. Mumford and J. R. Van Doorn, "The Leadership of Pragmatism—Reconsidering Franklin in the Age of Charisma," *Leadership Quarterly* 12, no. 3 (Fall 2001), pp. 279–309; A. Fanelli, "Bringing out Charisma: CEO Charisma and External Stakeholders," *The Academy of Management Review* 31, no. 4 (2006), pp. 1049–61; M. J. Platow et al., "A Special Gift We Bestow on You for Being Representative of Us: Considering Leader Charisma from a Self-Categorization Perspective," *British Journal of Social Psychology* 45, no. 2 (2006), pp. 303–20.

59. B. Shamir et al., "Correlates of Charismatic Leader Behavior in Military Units: Subordinates' Attitudes, Unit Characteristics, and Superiors' Appraisals of Leader Performance," *Academy of Management Journal* 41, no. 4 (1998), pp. 387–409; R. E. De Vries, R. A. Roe, and T. C. B. Taillieu, "On Charisma and Need for Leadership," *European Journal of Work and Organizational Psychology* 8 (1999), pp. 109–33; R. Khurana, *Searching for a Corporate Savior: The Irrational Quest for Charismatic CEOs* (Princeton, NJ: Princeton University Press, 2002).

60. N. Augustine, *Augustine's Laws,* 3rd ed. (New York: Viking, 1986), p. 32.

61. D. Olive, "The 7 Deadly Chief Executive Sins," *Toronto Star,* February 17, 2004, p. D01.

62. Y. Berson et al., "The Relationship between Vision Strength, Leadership Style, and Context," *The Leadership Quarterly* 12, no. 1 (2001), pp. 53–73.

63. Bennis and Nanus, *Leaders,* pp. 27–33, 89; I. M. Levin, "Vision Revisited," *Journal of Applied Behavioral Science* 36 (March 2000), pp. 91–107; R. E. Quinn, *Building the Bridge as You Walk on It: A Guide for Leading Change* (San Francisco: Jossey-Bass, 2004), Chap. 11; J. M. Strange and M. D. Mumford, "The Origins of Vision: Effects of Reflection, Models, and Analysis," *Leadership Quarterly* 16, no. 1 (2005), pp. 121–48.

64. J. R. Baum, E. A. Locke, and S. A. Kirkpatrick, "A Longitudinal Study of the Relation of Vision and Vision Communication to Venture Growth in Entrepreneurial Firms," *Journal of Applied Psychology* 83 (1998), pp. 43–54; S. L. Hoe and S. L. McShane, "Leadership Antecedents of Informal Knowledge Acquisition and Dissemination," *International Journal of Organisational Behaviour* 5 (2002), pp. 282–91.

65. "Canadian CEOs Give Themselves Top Marks for Leadership!" *Canada NewsWire,* September 9, 1999; L. Manfield, "Creating a Safety Culture from Top to Bottom," *WorkSafe Magazine,* February 2005, pp. 8–9.

66. J. A. Conger, "Inspiring Others: The Language of Leadership," *Academy of Management Executive* 5 (February 1991), pp. 31–45; G. T. Fairhurst and R. A. Sarr, *The Art of Framing: Managing the Language of Leadership* (San Francisco, CA: Jossey-Bass, 1996); A. E. Rafferty and M. A. Griffin, "Dimensions of Transformational Leadership: Conceptual and Empirical Extensions," *Leadership Quarterly* 15, no. 3 (2004), pp. 329–54.

67. Data from Towers Perrin and Towers Watson global workforce reports, talent reports, and news releases in selected years, such as Towers Perrin, *Working Today: Understanding What Drives Employee Engagement* (Stamford, CT: 2003); "Senior Leaders Improve Their Communication with Employees, Towers Perrin Consortium Finds," Business Wire news release for Towers Perrin (Stamford, CT: September 7, 2005).

68. D. E. Berlew, "Leadership and Organizational Excitement," *California Management Review* 17, no. 2 (Winter 1974), pp. 21–30; Bennis and Nanus, *Leaders,* pp. 43–55; T. Simons, "Behavioral Integrity: The Perceived Alignment between Managers' Words and Deeds as a Research Focus," *Organization Science* 13, no. 1 (January–February 2002), pp. 18–35.

69. J. Benson and A. Becker, "Synergy: Easy as ABC," *Broadcasting & Cable* 135, no. 41 (2005), pp. 10–12.

70. M. Webb, "Executive Profile: Peter C. Farrell," *San Diego Business Journal,* March 24, 2003, p. 32; P. Benesh, "He Likes Them Breathing Easy," *Investor's Business Daily,* September 13, 2005, p. A04. For a discussion of trust in leadership, see C. S. Burke et al., "Trust in Leadership: A Multi-Level Review and Integration," *Leadership Quarterly* 18, no. 6 (2007), pp. 606–32. The survey on leading by example is reported in J. C. Maxwell, "People Do What People See," *BusinessWeek,* November 19, 2007, p. 32.

71. C. Hymowitz, "Today's Bosses Find Mentoring Isn't Worth the Time and Risks," *The Wall Street Journal,* March 13, 2006, p. B1.

72. J. Barling, T. Weber, and E. K. Kelloway, "Effects of Transformational Leadership Training on Attitudinal and Financial Outcomes: A Field Experiment," *Journal of Applied Psychology* 81 (1996), pp. 827–32.

73. A. Bryman, "Leadership in Organizations," in *Handbook of Organization Studies,* ed. S. R. Clegg, C. Hardy, and W. R. Nord (Thousand Oaks, CA: Sage, 1996), pp. 276–92.

74. B. S. Pawar and K. K. Eastman, "The Nature and Implications of Contextual Influences on Transformational Leadership: A Conceptual Examination," *Academy of Management Review* 22 (1997), pp. 80–109; C. P. Egri and S. Herman, "Leadership in the North American Environmental Sector: Values, Leadership Styles, and Contexts of Environmental Leaders and Their Organizations," *Academy of Management Journal* 43, no. 4 (2000), pp. 571–604.

75. J. R. Meindl, "On Leadership: An Alternative to the Conventional Wisdom," *Research in Organizational Behavior* 12 (1990), pp. 159–203; L. R. Offermann, J. J. K. Kennedy, and P. W. Wirtz, "Implicit Leadership Theories: Content, Structure, and Generalizability," *Leadership Quarterly* 5, no. 1 (1994), pp. 43–58; R. J. Hall and R. G. Lord, "Multi-Level Information Processing Explanations of Followers' Leadership Perceptions," *Leadership Quarterly* 6 (1995), pp. 265–87; O. Epitropaki and R. Martin, "Implicit Leadership Theories in Applied Settings: Factor Structure, Generalizability, and Stability over Time," *Journal of Applied Psychology* 89, no. 2 (2004), pp. 293–310.

76. R. G. Lord et al., "Contextual Constraints on Prototype Generation and Their Multilevel Consequences for Leadership Perceptions," *Leadership Quarterly* 12, no. 3 (2001), pp. 311–38; T. Keller, "Parental Images as a Guide to Leadership Sensemaking: An Attachment Perspective on Implicit Leadership Theories," *Leadership Quarterly* 14 (2003), pp. 141–60; K. A. Scott and D. J. Brown, "Female First, Leader Second? Gender Bias in the Encoding of Leadership Behavior," *Organizational Behavior and Human Decision Processes* 101 (2006), pp. 230–42.

77. R. Ilies, M. W. Gerhardt, and H. Le, "Individual Differences in Leadership Emergence: Integrating Meta-Analytic Findings and Behavioral Genetics Estimates," *International Journal of Selection and Assessment* 12, no. 3 (September 2004), pp. 207–19.

78. S. F. Cronshaw and R. G. Lord, "Effects of Categorization, Attribution, and Encoding Processes on Leadership Perceptions," *Journal of Applied Psychology* 72 (1987), pp. 97–106; J. L. Nye and D. R. Forsyth, "The Effects of Prototype-Based Biases on Leadership Appraisals: A Test of Leadership Categorization Theory," *Small Group Research* 22 (1991), pp. 360–79.

79. Height statistics for *Fortune* 500 CEOs are from M. Gladwell, *Blink: The Power of Thinking without Thinking* (New York: Little, Brown, 2005), pp. 86–87. American adult male height statistics are from M. A. McDowell et al., *Anthropometric Reference Data for Children and Adults: United States, 2003–2006,* National Health Statistics Reports (Hyattsville, MD: National Center for Health Statistics, 2008).

80. L. M. Fisher, "Ricardo Semler Won't Take Control," *strategy+business,* no. 41 (Winter 2005), pp. 1–11.

81. Meindl, "On Leadership: An Alternative to the Conventional Wisdom"; J. Felfe and L.-E. Petersen, "Romance of Leadership and Management Decision Making," *European Journal of Work and Organizational Psychology* 16, no. 1 (2007), pp. 1–24; B. Schyns, J. R. Meindl, and M. A. Croon, "The Romance of Leadership Scale: Cross-Cultural Testing and Refinement," *Leadership* 3, no. 1 (February 2007), pp. 29–46.

82. J. Pfeffer, "The Ambiguity of Leadership," *Academy of Management Review* 2 (1977), pp. 102–12.

83. R. Weber et al., "The Illusion of Leadership: Misattribution of Cause in Coordination Games," *Organization Science* 12, no. 5 (2001), pp. 582–98; N. Ensari and S. E. Murphy, "Cross-Cultural Variations in Leadership Perceptions and Attribution of Charisma to the Leader," *Organizational Behavior and Human Decision Processes* 92 (2003), pp. 52–66; M. L. A. Hayward, V. P. Rindova, and T. G. Pollock, "Believing One's Own Press: The Causes and Consequences of CEO Celebrity," *Strategic Management Journal* 25, no. 7 (July 2004), pp. 637–53.

84. Six of the Project GLOBE clusters are described in a special issue of the *Journal of World Business,* 37 (2000). For an overview of Project GLOBE, see House, Javidan, and Dorfman, "Project GLOBE: An Introduction"; House et al., "Understanding Cultures and Implicit Leadership Theories across the Globe: An Introduction to Project GLOBE."

85. J. C. Jesiuno, "Latin Europe Cluster: From South to North," *Journal of World Business* 37 (2002), p. 88. Another GLOBE study, of Iranian managers, also reported that "charismatic visionary" stands out as a primary leadership dimension. See A. Dastmalchian, M. Javidan, and K. Alam, "Effective Leadership and Culture in Iran: An Empirical Study," *Applied Psychology: An International Review* 50 (2001), pp. 532–58.

86. D. N. Den Hartog et al., "Culture Specific and Cross-Cultural Generalizable Implicit Leadership Theories: Are Attributes of Charismatic/Transformational Leadership Universally Endorsed?" *Leadership Quarterly* 10 (1999), pp. 219–56; F. C. Brodbeck et al., "Cultural Variation of Leadership Prototypes across 22 European Countries," *Journal of Occupational and Organizational Psychology* 73 (2000), pp. 1–29; E. Szabo et al., "The Europe Cluster: Where Employees Have a Voice," *Journal of World Business* 37 (2002), pp. 55–68. The Mexican study is reported in C. E. Nicholls, H. W. Lane, and M. B. Brechu, "Taking Self-Managed Teams to Mexico," *Academy of Management Executive* 13 (August 1999), pp. 15–25.

87. G. N. Powell, "One More Time: Do Female and Male Managers Differ?" *Academy of Management Executive* 4 (1990), pp. 68–75; M. L. van Engen and T. M. Willemsen, "Sex and Leadership Styles: A Meta-Analysis of Research Published in the 1990s," *Psychological Reports* 94, no. 1 (February 2004), pp. 3–18.

88. R. Fend, "Wir Sind Die Firma (We Are the Company)," *Financial Times Deutschland,* October 2, 2008, p. 31; N. Klawitter et al., "Die Natur Der Macht (the Nature of Power)," *Der Spiegel,* September 22, 2008, p. 52; M. Schiessl, "Microsoft Reaps the Rewards of Female Managers," *Spiegel Online,* February 8, 2008, http://www.spiegel.de/international/business/0,1518,533852,00.html.

89. R. Sharpe, "As Leaders, Women Rule," *BusinessWeek,* November 20, 2000, p. 74; M. Sappenfield, "Women, It Seems, Are Better Bosses," *Christian Science Monitor,* January 16, 2001; A. H. Eagly and L. L. Carli, "The Female Leadership Advantage: An Evaluation of the Evidence," *The Leadership Quarterly* 14, no. 6 (December 2003), pp. 807–34; A. H. Eagly, M. C. Johannesen-Schmidt, and M. L. van Engen, "Transformational, Transactional, and Laissez-Faire Leadership Styles: A Meta-Analysis Comparing Women and Men," *Psychological Bulletin* 129 (July 2003), pp. 569–91.

90. A. H. Eagly, S. J. Karau, and M. G. Makhijani, "Gender and the Effectiveness of Leaders: A Meta-Analysis," *Psychological Bulletin* 117 (1995), pp. 125–45; J. G. Oakley, "Gender-Based Barriers to Senior Management Positions: Understanding the Scarcity of Female CEOs," *Journal of Business Ethics* 27 (2000), pp. 821–34; N. Z. Stelter, "Gender Differences in Leadership: Current Social Issues and Future Organizational Implications," *Journal of Leadership Studies* 8 (2002), pp. 88–99; M. E. Heilman et al., "Penalties for Success: Reactions to Women Who Succeed at Male Gender-Typed Tasks," *Journal of Applied Psychology* 89, no. 3 (2004), pp. 416–27; A. H. Eagly, "Achieving Relational Authenticity in Leadership: Does Gender Matter?," *The Leadership Quarterly* 16, no. 3 (June 2005), pp. 459–74.

CHAPTER 12

1. This description of Nokia's evolving organizational structures is based on information from its annual reports as well as "Nokia in Major Reorganization Plan," *Warren's Consumer Electronics Daily,* September 29, 2003; "Nokia Simplifies Its Organizational Structure to Accelerate Execution and Innovation," PR Newswire news release for Nokia Corporation (Espoo, Finland: May 11, 2010); and K. J. O'Brien, "Head of Nokia's Mobile Phone Unit Is Leaving," *The New York Times,* May 12, 2010, p. 5.

2. Nokia's new organizational structure is described at its Web site, including a less precise diagram than is shown here. See http://www.nokia.com/A4630650?category=company.

3. S. Ranson, R. Hinings, and R. Greenwood, "The Structuring of Organizational Structure," *Administrative Science Quarterly* 25 (1980), pp. 1–14; J.-E. Johanson, "Intraorganizational Influence," *Management Communication Quarterly* 13 (February 2000), pp. 393–435; K. Walsh, "Interpreting the Impact of Culture on Structure," *Journal of Applied Behavioral Science* 40, no. 3 (September 2004), pp. 302–22.

4. H. Mintzberg, *The Structuring of Organizations* (Englewood Cliffs, NJ: Prentice Hall, 1979), pp. 2–3.

5. E. E. Lawler III, *Motivation in Work Organizations* (Monterey, CA: Brooks/Cole, 1973); M. A. Campion, "Ability Requirement Implications of Job Design: An Interdisciplinary Perspective," *Personnel Psychology* 42 (1989), pp. 1–24.

6. Plato, *Republic* (Ware, UK: Wordsworth, 1997), p. 51.

7. G. S. Becker and K. M. Murphy, "The Division-of-Labor, Coordination Costs and Knowledge," *Quarterly Journal of Economics* 107, no. 4 (November 1992), pp. 1137–60; L. Borghans and B. Weel, "The Division of Labour, Worker Organisation, and Technological Change," *The Economic Journal* 116, no. 509 (2006), pp. F45–F72.

8. Mintzberg, *The Structuring of Organizations,* Chap. 1; D. A. Nadler and M. L. Tushman, *Competing by Design: The Power of Organizational Architecture* (New York: Oxford University Press, 1997), Chap. 6; J. R. Galbraith, *Designing Organizations: An Executive Guide to Strategy, Structure, and Process* (San Francisco: Jossey-Bass, 2002), Chap. 4.

9. J. Stephenson Jr., "Making Humanitarian Relief Networks More Effective: Operational Coordination, Trust and Sense Making," *Disasters* 29, no. 4 (2005), p. 337.

10. A. Willem, M. Buelens, and H. Scarbrough, "The Role of Inter-Unit Coordination Mechanisms in Knowledge Sharing: A Case Study of a British MNC," *Journal of Information Science* 32, no. 6 (2006), pp. 539–61; R. R. Gulati, "Silo Busting," *Harvard Business Review* 85, no. 5 (2007), pp. 98–108.

11. Borghans and Weel, "The Division of Labour, Worker Organisation, and Technological Change."

12. T. Van Alphen, "Magna in Overdrive," *Toronto Star,* July 24, 2006.

13. For a discussion of the role of brand manager at Proctor & Gamble, see C. Peale, "Branded for Success," *Cincinnati Enquirer,* May 20, 2001, p. A1. Details about how to design integrator roles in organizational structures are presented in Galbraith, *Designing Organizations,* pp. 66–72.

14. M. Hoque, M. Akter, and Y. Monden, "Concurrent Engineering: A Compromise Approach to Develop a Feasible and Customer-Pleasing Product," *International Journal of Production Research* 43, no. 8 (2005), pp. 1607–24; S. M. Sapuan, M. R. Osman, and Y. Nukman, "State of the Art of the Concurrent Engineering Technique in the Automotive Industry," *Journal of Engineering Design* 17, no. 2 (2006), pp. 143–57; D. H. Kincade, C. Regan, and F. Y. Gibson, "Concurrent Engineering for Product Development in Mass Customization for the Apparel Industry," *International Journal of Operations & Production Management* 27, no. 6 (2007), pp. 627–49.

15. A. H. Van De Ven, A. L. Delbecq, and R. J. Koenig Jr., "Determinants of Coordination Modes within Organizations," *American Sociological Review* 41, no. 2 (1976), pp. 322–38.

16. "One-Third of Employees Feel Micromanaged by Boss," BlessingWhite news release (Skillman, NJ: October 27, 2008).

17. Y.-M. Hsieh and A. Tien-Hsieh, "Enhancement of Service Quality with Job Standardisation," *Service Industries Journal* 21 (July 2001), pp. 147–66.

18. For recent discussion of span of control, see N. A. Theobald and S. Nicholson-Crotty, "The Many Faces of Span of Control: Organizational Structure across Multiple Goals," *Administration Society* 36, no. 6 (January 2005), pp. 648–60; R. M. Meyer, "Span of Management: Concept Analysis," *Journal of Advanced Nursing* 63, no. 1 (2008), pp. 104–12.

19. H. Fayol, *General and Industrial Management,* trans. C. Storrs (London: Pitman, 1949); D. D. Van Fleet and A. G. Bedeian, "A History of the Span of Management," *Academy of Management Review* 2 (1977), pp. 356–72; D. A. Wren, A. G. Bedeian, and J. D. Breeze, "The Foundations of Henri Fayol's Administrative Theory ", *Management Decision* 40, no. 9 (2002), pp. 906–18.

20. D. Drickhamer, "Lessons from the Leading Edge," *Industry Week,* February 21, 2000, pp. 23–26.

21. G. Anders, "Overseeing More Employees—with Fewer Managers—Consultants Are Urging Companies to Loosen Their Supervising Views," *The Wall Street Journal,* March 24, 2008, p. B6.

22. D. D. Van Fleet and A. G. Bedeian, "A History of the Span of Management," *Academy of Management Review* 2 (July 1977), pp. 356–72; B. Davison, "Management Span of Control: How Wide Is Too Wide?" *Journal of Business Strategy* 24, no. 4 (2003), pp. 22–29; S. Nix et al., *Span of Control in City Government Increases Overall* (Seattle, WA: Office of City Auditor, City of Seattle, September 19, 2005); "Fedex 2008 Shareowners Meeting," (Memphis, TN: Fedex, September 29, 2008), ; S. O. Iowa, "Results Iowa: Operational Scan," February 1, 2008 (accessed May 23, 2010); J. McLellan, *Administrative Review: An Agenda for Business Improvement* (Portland, OR: Multnomah County, May 19, 2009).

23. J. Greenwald, "Ward Compares the Best with the Rest," *Business Insurance,* August 26, 2002, p. 16.

24. J. H. Gittell, "Supervisory Span, Relational Coordination and Flight Departure Performance: A Reassessment of Post-bureaucracy Theory," *Organization Science* 12, no. 4 (July–August 2001), pp. 468–83.

25. P. Glader, "It's Not Easy Being Lean," *The Wall Street Journal,* June 19, 2006, p. B1; "About Us" (Charlotte, NC: Nucor Corporation, 2008), http://www.nucor.com/indexinner.aspx?finpage=aboutus (accessed September 2, 2008).

26. T. D. Wall, J. L. Cordery, and C. W. Clegg, "Empowerment, Performance, and Operational Uncertainty: A Theoretical Integration," *Applied Psychology: An International Review* 51 (2002), pp. 146–69.

27. J. Morris, J. Hassard, and L. McCann, "New Organizational Forms, Human Resource Management and Structural Convergence? A Study of Japanese Organizations," *Organization Studies* 27, no. 10 (2006), pp. 1485–511.

28. "BASF Culling Saves (GBP) 4M," *Personnel Today,* February 19, 2002, p. 3; A. Lashinsky, "The Hurt Way," *Fortune,* April 17, 2006, p. 92.

29. Q. N. Huy, "In Praise of Middle Managers," *Harvard Business Review* 79 (September 2001), pp. 72–79; C. R. Littler, R. Wiesner, and R. Dunford, "The Dynamics of Delayering: Changing Management Structures in Three Countries," *Journal of Management Studies* 40, no. 2 (2003), pp. 225–56; H. J. Leavitt, *Top Down: Why Hierarchies Are Here to Stay and How to Manage Them More Effectively* (Cambridge: Harvard Business School Press, 2005); L. McCann, J. Morris, and J. Hassard, "Normalized Intensity: The New Labour Process of Middle Management," *Journal of Management Studies* 45, no. 2 (2008), pp. 343–71.

30. Littler, Wiesner, and Dunford, "The Dynamics of Delayering: Changing Management Structures in Three Countries."

31. S. Wetlaufer, "The Business Case against Revolution: An Interview with Nestle's Peter Brabeck," *Harvard Business Review* 79, no. 2 (February 2001), pp. 112–19; H. A. Richardson et al., "Does Decentralization Make a Difference for the Organization? An Examination of the Boundary Conditions

Circumscribing Decentralized Decision-Making and Organizational Financial Performance," *Journal of Management* 28, no. 2 (2002), pp. 217–44; G. Masada, "To Centralize or Decentralize?" *Optimize,* May 2005, pp. 58–61.

32. J. G. Kelley, "Slurpees and Sausages: 7-Eleven Holds School," *Richmond (VA) Times-Dispatch,* March 12, 2004, p. C1; S. Marling, "The 24-Hour Supply Chain," *InformationWeek,* January 26, 2004, p. 43.

33. Mintzberg, *The Structuring of Organizations,* Chap. 5.

34. W. Dessein and T. Santos, "Adaptive Organizations," *Journal of Political Economy* 114, no. 5 (2006), pp. 956–95; A. A. M. Nasurdin et al., "Organizational Structure and Organizational Climate as Potential Predictors of Job Stress: Evidence from Malaysia," *International Journal of Commerce and Management* 16, no. 2 (2006), pp. 116–29; C.-J. Chen and J.-W. Huang, "How Organizational Climate and Structure Affect Knowledge Management—the Social Interaction Perspective," *International Journal of Information Management* 27, no. 2 (2007), pp. 104–18.

35. "Royal Bank Survey Finds Canadian Workplaces Buoyed by Optimism and High Level of Satisfaction," Canada NewsWire news release for R. B. O. Canada (Toronto: October 8, 1998); "When It Comes to Red Tape, Many Canadian Employers Might Just Need to Cut It: RBC Study." CNW news release for RBC (Toronto: January 23, 2008).

36. C. Holahan, "Bidding Yahoo Adieu," *BusinessWeek,* June 23, 2008, p. 23.

37. T. Burns and G. Stalker, *The Management of Innovation* (London Tavistock: 1961).

38. J. Tata, S. Prasad, and R. Thom, "The Influence of Organizational Structure on the Effectiveness of TQM Programs," *Journal of Managerial Issues* 11, no. 4 (Winter 1999), pp. 440–53; A. Lam, "Tacit Knowledge, Organizational Learning and Societal Institutions: An Integrated Framework," *Organization Studies* 21 (May 2000), pp. 487–513.

39. W. D. Sine, H. Mitsuhashi, and D. A. Kirsch, "Revisiting Burns and Stalker: Formal Structure and New Venture Performance in Emerging Economic Sectors," *Academy of Management Journal* 49, no. 1 (2006), pp. 121–32.

40. Mintzberg, *The Structuring of Organizations,* p. 106.

41. H. S. Geneen and A. Moscow, *Managing* (Garden City, NY: Doubleday Books, 1984), p. 81.

42. Mintzberg, *The Structuring of Organizations,* Chap. 17.

43. Galbraith, *Designing Organizations,* pp. 23–25.

44. E. E. Lawler III, *Rewarding Excellence: Pay Strategies for the New Economy* (San Francisco: Jossey-Bass, 2000), pp. 31–34.

45. These structures were identified from corporate Web sites and annual reports. These organizations typically rely on a mixture of other structures, so the charts shown have been adapted for learning purposes.

46. M. Goold and A. Campbell, "Do You Have a Well-Designed Organization?" *Harvard Business Review* 80 (March 2002), pp. 117–24.

47. J. R. Galbraith, "Structuring Global Organizations," in *Tomorrow's Organization,* ed. S. A. Mohrman et al. (San Francisco: Jossey-Bass, 1998), pp. 103–29; C. Homburg, J. P. Workman Jr., and O. Jensen, "Fundamental Changes in Marketing Organization: The Movement toward a Corganizational Structure," *Academy of Marketing Science. Journal* 28 (Fall 2000), pp. 459–78; T. H. Davenport, J. G. Harris, and A. K. Kohli, "How Do They Know Their Customers So Well?" *Sloan Management Review* 42 (Winter 2001), pp. 63–73; J. R.

Galbraith, "Organizing to Deliver Solutions," *Organizational Dynamics* 31 (2002), pp. 194–207.

48. "Google and Sony Are the World's Most Reputable Companies According to Consumers across 24 Countries," PR Newswire news release for Reputation Institute (New York: May 24, 2010).

49. S. J. Palmisano, "The Globally Integrated Enterprise," *Foreign Affairs* 85, no. 3 (May/June 2006), pp. 127–36; S. Palmisano, "The Globally Integrated Enterprise," *Vital Speeches of the Day* 73, no. 10 (2007), pp. 449–53.

50. Palmisano, "The Globally Integrated Enterprise."

51. "IBM Moves Engineering VP to China as Part of Global Focus," *Manufacturing Business Technology,* September 2007, p. 13; J. Bonasia, "Globalization: Learning to Close the Continental Divide," *Investor's Business Daily,* September 7, 2007.

52. J. R. Galbraith, E. E. Lawler III, and Associates, *Organizing for the Future: The New Logic for Managing Complex Organizations* (San Francisco, CA: Jossey-Bass, 1993); R. Bettis and M. Hitt, "The New Competitive Landscape," *Strategic Management Journal* 16 (1995), pp. 7–19.

53. P. C. Ensign, "Interdependence, Coordination, and Structure in Complex Organizations: Implications for Organization Design," *Mid-Atlantic Journal of Business* 34 (March 1998), pp. 5–22.

54. M. M. Fanning, "A Circular Organization Chart Promotes a Hospital-Wide Focus on Teams," *Hospital & Health Services Administration* 42 (June 1997), pp. 243–54; L. Y. Chan and B. E. Lynn, "Operating in Turbulent Times: How Ontario's Hospitals Are Meeting the Current Funding Crisis," *Health Care Management Review* 23 (June 1998), pp. 7–18.

55. R. Cross, "Looking before You Leap: Assessing the Jump to Teams in Knowledge-Based Work," *Business Horizons,* September 2000; M. Fenton-O'Creevy, "Employee Involvement and the Middle Manager: Saboteur or Scapegoat?" *Human Resource Management Journal* 11 (2001), pp. 24–40; G. Garda, K. Lindstrom, and M. Dallnera, "Towards a Learning Organization: The Introduction of a Client-Centered Team-Based Organization in Administrative Surveying Work," *Applied Ergonomics* 34 (2003), pp. 97–105; C. Douglas and W. L. Gardner, "Transition to Self-Directed Work Teams: Implications of Transition Time and Self-Monitoring for Managers' Use of Influence Tactics," *Journal of Organizational Behavior* 25 (2004), pp. 47–65.

56. R. Muzyka and G. Zeschuk, "Managing Multiple Projects," Game Developer, March 2003, pp. 34–42; M. Saltzman, "The Ex-Doctors Are In," *National Post,* March 24, 2004, p. AL4; R. McConnell, "For Edmonton's Bioware, Today's the Big Day," *Edmonton Journal,* April 14, 2005, p. C1; D. Gladstone and S. Molloy, "Doctors & Dragons," *Computer Gaming World,* December 2006.

57. R. C. Ford and W. A. Randolph, "Cross-Functional Structures: A Review and Integration of Matrix Organization and Project Management," *Journal of Management* 18 (1992), pp. 267–94.

58. N. Buckley, "P&G Shakes Up Its Global Units," *Financial Times (London),* May 19, 2004; "Merely Splitting Hairs," *Marketing Week,* February 17, 2005, pp. 26. Procter & Gamble's structure is more complex than we have described here. Its "four pillars" also include global business services and corporate functions. See P&G Corporate Info, Corporate Structure, Four Pillars, www.pg.com/jobs/corporate_structure/four_pillars.jhtml.

59. G. Calabrese, "Communication and Co-Operation in Product Development: A Case Study of a European Car Producer," *R & D Management* 27 (July 1997), pp. 239–52; T. Sy and L. S. D'Annunzio, "Challenges and Strategies of Matrix Organizations:

Top-Level and Mid-Level Managers' Perspectives," *Human Resource Planning* 28, no. 1 (2005), pp. 39–48.

60. D. Enrich, "Citigroup Will Revamp Capital-Markets Group," *The Wall Street Journal,* August 23, 2008, p. B7.

61. Nadler and Tushman, *Competing by Design,* Chap. 6; M. Goold and A. Campbell, "Structured Networks: Towards the Well-Designed Matrix," *Long Range Planning* 36, no. 5 (October 2003), pp. 427–39.

62. D. Ciampa and M. Watkins, "Rx for New CEOs," *Chief Executive,* January 2008.

63. K. Poynter, *Data Security at HMRC* (Progress Report to Chancellor of the Exchequer and HM Treasury, December 14, 2007); V. Houlder, "The Merger That Exposed a Taxing Problem for Managers," *Financial Times,* July 11, 2008, p. 12; K. Poynter, *Review of Information Security at HM Revenue and Customs* (London: HM Treasury, Government of the United Kingdom, June 2008).

64. P. Siekman, "This Is Not a BMW Plant," *Fortune,* April 18, 2005, p. 208; "Magna's Austria Plant to Lose Production of BMW X3," *Reuters,* May 16, 2007.

65. R. F. Miles and C. C. Snow, "The New Network Firm: A Spherical Structure Built on a Human Investment Philosophy," *Organizational Dynamics* 23, no. 4 (1995), pp. 5–18; C. Baldwin and K. Clark, "Managing in an Age of Modularity," *Harvard Business Review* 75 (September–October 1997), pp. 84–93.

66. J. Hagel III and M. Singer, "Unbundling the Corporation," *Harvard Business Review* 77 (March-April 1999), pp. 133–41; R. Hacki and J. Lighton, "The Future of the Networked Company," *McKinsey Quarterly* 3 (2001), pp. 26–39.

67. J. Dwyer, "Mind How You Go," *Facilities Management,* May 2008, pp. 22–25.

68. M. A. Schilling and H. K. Steensma, "The Use of Modular Organizational Forms: An Industry-Level Analysis," *Academy of Management Journal* 44 (December 2001), pp. 1149–68.

69. G. Morgan, *Images of Organization,* 2nd ed. (Newbury Park: Sage, 1996); G. Morgan, *Imagin-I-Zation: New Mindsets for Seeing, Organizing and Managing* (Thousand Oaks, CA: Sage, 1997).

70. H. Chesbrough and D. J. Teece, "When Is Virtual Virtuous? Organizing for Innovation," *Harvard Business Review* (January–February 1996), pp. 65–73; P. M. J. Christie and R. Levary, "Virtual Corporations: Recipe for Success," *Industrial Management* 40 (July 1998), pp. 7–11.

71. L. Donaldson, *The Contingency Theory of Organizations* (Thousand Oaks, CA: Sage, 2001); J. Birkenshaw, R. Nobel, and J. Ridderstråle, "Knowledge as a Contingency Variable: Do the Characteristics of Knowledge Predict Organizational Structure?" *Organization Science* 13, no. 3 (May-June 2002), pp. 274–89.

72. P. R. Lawrence and J. W. Lorsch, *Organization and Environment* (Homewood, IL: Irwin, 1967); Mintzberg, *The Structuring of Organizations,* Chap. 15.

73. Burns and Stalker, *The Management of Innovation;* Lawrence and Lorsch, *Organization and Environment.*

74. Mintzberg, *The Structuring of Organizations,* p. 282.

75. D. S. Pugh and C. R. Hinings, *Organizational Structure: Extensions and Replications* (Farnborough, England: Lexington Books, 1976); Mintzberg, *The Structuring of Organizations,* Chap. 13.

76. Galbraith, *Designing Organizations,* pp. 52–55; G. Hertel, S. Geister, and U. Konradt, "Managing Virtual Teams: A Review of Current Empirical Research," *Human Resource Management Review* 15 (2005), pp. 69–95.

77. C. Perrow, "A Framework for the Comparative Analysis of Organizations," *American Sociological Review* 32 (1967), pp. 194–208; D. Gerwin, "The Comparative Analysis of Structure and Technology: A Critical Appraisal," *Academy of Management Review* 4, no. 1 (1979), pp. 41–51; C. C. Miller et al., "Understanding Technology–Structure Relationships: Theory Development and Meta-Analytic Theory Testing," *Academy of Management Journal* 34, no. 2 (1991), pp. 370–99.

78. R. H. Kilmann, *Beyond the Quick Fix* (San Francisco: Jossey-Bass, 1984), p. 38.

79. A. D. Chandler, *Strategy and Structure* (Cambridge, MA: MIT Press, 1962).

80. D. Miller, "Configurations of Strategy and Structure," *Strategic Management Journal* 7 (1986), pp. 233–49.

CHAPTER 13

1. K. Linebaugh, D. Searcey, and N. Shirouzu, "Secretive Culture Led Toyota Astray," *The Wall Street Journal,* February 10, 2010.

2. "BP Culture Needs Closer Examination," *Altoona Mirror (Altoona, PA),* May 26, 2010.

3. R. Smith and D. Fitzpatrick, "Cultures Clash as Merrill Herd Meets 'Wal-Mart of Banking,'" *The Wall Street Journal,* November 14, 2008, p. C1.

4. F. Guerrera, H. Sender, and J. Patrick, "Damning Insight into Corporate Culture Sheds Light on Fall of a Wall Street Giant," *Financial Times (London),* March 13, 2010, p. 6.

5. A. Williams, P. Dobson, and M. Walters, *Changing Culture: New Organizational Approaches* (London: Institute of Personnel Management, 1989); E. H. Schein, "What Is Culture?" in *Reframing Organizational Culture,* ed. P. J. Frost et al. (Newbury Park, CA: Sage, 1991), pp. 243–53.

6. B. M. Meglino and E. C. Ravlin, "Individual Values in Organizations: Concepts, Controversies, and Research," *Journal of Management* 24, no. 3 (1998), pp. 351–89; B. R. Agle and C. B. Caldwell, "Understanding Research on Values in Business," *Business and Society* 38, no. 3 (September 1999), pp. 326–87; S. Hitlin and J. A. Pilavin, "Values: Reviving a Dormant Concept," *Annual Review of Sociology* 30 (2004), pp. 359–93.

7. N. M. Ashkanasy, "The Case for Culture," in *Debating Organization,* ed. R. Westwood and S. Clegg (Malden, MA: Blackwell, 2003), pp. 300–10.

8. M. Lagace, "Gerstner: Changing Culture at IBM," *HBS Working Knowledge,* September 12, 2002.

9. B. Kabanoff and J. Daly, "Espoused Values in Organisations," *Australian Journal of Management* 27, Special issue (2002), pp. 89–104.

10. "Norway Criticizes BP, Smedvig over Safety," *Energy Compass,* January 3, 2003; J. A. Lozano, "BP Refinery Had History of Dangerous Releases, Report Finds," *Associated Press,* October 28, 2005; S. McNulty, "A Corroded Culture?" *Financial Times (London),* December 18, 2006, p. 17; U.S. Chemical Safety and Hazard Inviestigation Board, *Investigation Report: Refinery Explosion and Fire (BP, Texas City, Texas, March 23, 2005),* (Washington, DC: U.S. Chemical Safety Board, March 2007); S. Greenhouse, "BP Faces Record Fine for '05 Refinery Explosion," *The New York Times,* October 30, 2009.

11. V. Garrow and G. Robertson-Smith, "Star Organisations Walk the Talk," *Developing People* (Roffey Park Newsletter), July 2006, pp. 6–7; M. Johnson and C. Roebuck, "Nurturing a New Kind of Capital," *Financial Executive,* July 2008, p. 32.

12. B. Darrow, "James Gooodnight, Founder and CEO, SAS Institute," *Computer Reseller News,* December 12, 2005, p. 23; "Doing

Well by Being Rather Nice," *Economist,* December 1, 2007, p. 84; "SAS Turned Down 'Numerous' Acquisition Inquiries This Year, Says CEO," *CMP TechWeb,* December 17, 2007.

13. C. Webb, "Argo Still Aims to Shake out the Golden Fleece," *The Age (Melbourne),* May 24. 2008, p. 4.

14. S. Shrinate, "Performance Appraisal: The 10% Rule," *Business Today (India),* December 5, 2004, p. 160; G. S. Alexander, "Expert Hand to Help Pick Kamath's Successor at ICICI," *Economic Times (India),* October 3, 2008; A. Dhall, "ICICI Bank: Measuring Success in Global Standards," *Economics Times (India),* September 14, 2008.

15. C. A. O'Reilly III, J. Chatman, and D. F. Caldwell, "People and Organizational Culture: A Profile Comparison Approach to Assessing Person–Organization Fit," *Academy of Management Journal* 34 (1991), pp. 487–516; J. J. van Muijen, "Organizational Culture," in *A Handbook of Work and Organizational Psychology: Organizational Psychology,* ed. P. J. D. Drenth, H. Thierry, and C. J. de Wolff, 2nd ed. (East Sussex, UK: Psychology Press, 1998), pp. 113–32; P. A. Balthazard, R. A. Cooke, and R. E. Potter, "Dysfunctional Culture, Dysfunctional Organization: Capturing the Behavioral Norms That Form Organizational Culture and Drive Performance," *Journal of Managerial Psychology* 21, no. 8 (2006), pp. 709–32; C. Helfrich et al., "Assessing an Organizational Culture Instrument Based on the Competing Values Framework: Exploratory and Confirmatory Factor Analyses," *Implementation Science* 2, no. 1 (2007), p. 13. For recent reviews of organizational culture survey instruments, see T. Scott et al., "The Quantitative Measurement of Organizational Culture in Health Care: A Review of the Available Instruments," *Health Services Research* 38, no. 3 (2003), pp. 923–45; D. E. Leidner and T. Kayworth, "A Review of Culture in Information Systems Research: Toward a Theory of Information Technology Culture Conflict," *MIS Quarterly* 30, no. 2 (2006), pp. 357–99; S. Scott-Findlay and C. A. Estabrooks, "Mapping the Organizational Culture Research in Nursing: A Literature Review," *Journal of Advanced Nursing* 56, no. 5 (2006), pp. 498–513.

16. J. Martin, P. J. Frost, and O. A. O'Neill, "Organizational Culture: Beyond Struggles for Intellectual Dominance," in *Handbook of Organization Studies,* ed. S. Clegg et al., 2nd ed. (London: Sage, 2006), pp. 725–53; N. E. Fenton and S. Inglis, "A Critical Perspective on Organizational Values," *Nonprofit Management and Leadership* 17, no. 3 (2007), pp. 335–47; K. Haukelid, "Theories of (Safety) Culture Revisited—An Anthropological Approach," *Safety Science* 46, no. 3 (2008), pp. 413–26.

17. J. A. Baker III et al., *The Report of the BP U.S. Refineries Independent Safety Review Panel* (Houston: The BP U.S. Refineries Independent Safety Review Panel, February 2007).

18. J. Martin and C. Siehl, "Organizational Culture and Counterculture: An Uneasy Symbiosis," *Organizational Dynamics* (Autumn 1983), pp. 52–64; G. Hofstede, "Identifying Organizational Subcultures: An Empirical Approach," *Journal of Management Studies* 35, no. 1 (1990), pp. 1–12; E. Ogbonna and L. C. Harris, "Organisational Culture in the Age of the Internet: An Exploratory Study," *New Technology, Work and Employment* 21, no. 2 (2006), pp. 162–75.

19. H. Silver, "Does a University Have a Culture?" *Studies in Higher Education* 28, no. 2 (2003), pp. 157–69.

20. A. Sinclair, "Approaches to Organizational Culture and Ethics," *Journal of Business Ethics* 12 (1993); A. Boisnier and J. Chatman, "The Role of Subcultures in Agile Organizations," in *Leading and Managing People in Dynamic Organizations,* ed. R. Petersen and E. Mannix (Mahwah, NJ: Lawrence Erlbaum Associates, 2003), pp. 87–112; C. Morrill, M. N. Zald, and H. Rao, "Covert Political

Conflict in Organizations: Challenges from Below," *Annual Review of Sociology* 29, no. 1 (2003), pp. 391–415.

21. J. S. Ott, *The Organizational Culture Perspective* (Pacific Grove, CA: Brooks/Cole, 1989), Chap. 2; J. S. Pederson and J. S. Sorensen, *Organizational Cultures in Theory and Practice* (Aldershot, England: Gower, 1989), pp. 27–29; M. O. Jones, *Studying Organizational Symbolism: What, How, Why?* (Thousand Oaks, CA: Sage, 1996).

22. E. H. Schein, "Organizational Culture," *American Psychologist* (February 1990), pp. 109–19; A. Furnham and B. Gunter, "Corporate Culture: Definition, Diagnosis, and Change," *International Review of Industrial and Organizational Psychology* 8 (1993), pp. 233–61; E. H. Schein, *The Corporate Culture Survival Guide* (San Francisco: Jossey-Bass, 1999), Chap. 4.

23. M. Doehrman, "Anthropologists—Deep in the Corporate Bush," *Daily Record (Kansas City, MO),* July 19, 2005, p. 1.

24. K. Roman, "The House That Ogilvy Built," *strategy+business,* April 29 2009, pp. 1–5.

25. C. J. Boudens, "The Story of Work: A Narrative Analysis of Workplace Emotion," *Organization Studies* 26, no. 9 (2005), pp. 1285–1306; S. Denning, *The Leader's Guide to Storytelling* (San Francisco: Jossey-Bass, 2005).

26. A. L. Wilkins, "Organizational Stories as Symbols Which Control the Organization," in *Organizational Symbolism,* ed. L. R. Pondy et al. (Greenwich, CT: JAI Press, 1984), pp. 81–92; R. Zemke, "Storytelling: Back to a Basic," *Training* 27 (March 1990), pp. 44–50; J. C. Meyer, "Tell Me a Story: Eliciting Organizational Values from Narratives," *Communication Quarterly* 43 (1995), pp. 210–24; W. Swap et al., "Using Mentoring and Storytelling to Transfer Knowledge in the Workplace," *Journal of Management Information Systems* 18 (Summer 2001), pp. 95–114.

27. "The Ultimate Chairman," *Business Times Singapore,* September 3, 2005.

28. D. Roth, "My Job at the Container Store," *Fortune,* January 10, 2000, pp. 74–78.

29. R. E. Quinn and N. T. Snyder, "Advance Change Theory: Culture Change at Whirlpool Corporation," in *The Leader's Change Handbook,* ed. J. A. Conger, G. M. Spreitzer, and E. E. Lawler III (San Francisco: Jossey-Bass, 1999), pp. 162–93.

30. G. Turner and J. Myerson, *New Workspace New Culture: Office Design as a Catalyst for Change* (Aldershot, UK: Gower, 1998).

31. K. D. Elsbach and B. A. Bechky, "It's More Than a Desk: Working Smarter through Leveraged Office Design," *California Management Review* 49, no. 2 (Winter 2007), pp. 80–101.

32. M. Burton, "Open Plan, Open Mind," *Director* (March 2005), pp. 68–72; B. Murray, "Agency Profile: Mother London," *Ihaveanidea,* January 28, 2007, www.ihaveanidea.org.

33. Churchill apparently made this statement on October 28, 1943, in the British House of Commons, when London, damaged by bombings in World War II, was about to be rebuilt.

34. J. C. Collins and J. I. Porras, *Built to Last: Successful Habits of Visionary Companies* (London: Century, 1994); T. E. Deal and A. A. Kennedy, *The New Corporate Cultures* (Cambridge, MA: Perseus Books, 1999); R. Barrett, *Building a Values-Driven Organization: A Whole System Approach to Cultural Transformation* (Burlington, MA: Butterworth-Heinemann, 2006); J. M. Kouzes and B. Z. Posner, *The Leadership Challenge,* 4th ed. (San Francisco: Jossey-Bass, 2007), Chap. 3.

35. C. Siehl and J. Martin, "Organizational Culture: A Key to Financial Performance?" in *Organizational Climate and Culture,* ed. B. Schneider (San Francisco, CA: Jossey-Bass, 1990),

pp. 241–81; G. G. Gordon and N. DiTomasco, "Predicting Corporate Performance from Organizational Culture," *Journal of Management Studies* 29 (1992), pp. 783–98; J. P. Kotter and J. L. Heskett, *Corporate Culture and Performance* (New York: Free Press, 1992); C. P. M. Wilderom, U. Glunk, and R. Maslowski, "Organizational Culture as a Predictor of Organizational Performance," in *Handbook of Organizational Culture and Climate,* ed. N. M. Ashkanasy, C. P. M. Wilderom, and M. F. Peterson (Thousand Oaks, CA: Sage, 2000), pp. 193–210; A. Carmeli and A. Tishler, "The Relationships between Intangible Organizational Elements and Organizational Performance," *Strategic Management Journal* 25 (2004), pp. 1257–78; S. Teerikangas and P. Very, "The Culture-Performance Relationship in M & A: From Yes/No to How," *British Journal of Management* 17, no. S1 (2006), pp. S31–S48.

36. L. Carapiet, "NAB's John Stewart Knows His ABCs," *Australian Banking & Finance,* December 2007, p. 6; J. H. Want, *Corporate Culture: Key Strategies of High-Performing Business Cultures* (New York: St. Martin's Press, 2007), p. 38.

37. J. C. Helms Mills and A. J. Mills, "Rules, Sensemaking, Formative Contexts, and Discourse in the Gendering of Organizational Culture," in *International Handbook of Organizational Climate and Culture,* ed. N. Ashkanasy, C. Wilderom, and M. Peterson (Thousand Oaks, CA: Sage, 2000), pp. 55–70; J. A. Chatman and S. E. Cha, "Leading by Leveraging Culture," *California Management Review* 45 (Summer 2003), pp. 20–34.

38. B. Ashforth and F. Mael, "Social Identity Theory and the Organization," *Academy of Management Review* 14 (1989), pp. 20–39.

39. M. R. Louis, "Surprise and Sensemaking: What Newcomers Experience in Entering Unfamiliar Organizational Settings," *Administrative Science Quarterly* 25 (1980), pp. 226–51; S. G. Harris, "Organizational Culture and Individual Sensemaking: A Schema-Based Perspective," *Organization Science* 5 (1994), pp. 309–21.

40. J. W. Barnes et al., "The Role of Culture Strength in Shaping Sales Force Outcomes," *Journal of Personal Selling & Sales Management* 26, no. 3 (Summer 2006), pp. 255–70.

41. Heidrick & Struggles, *Leadership Challenges Emerge as Asia Pacific Companies Go Global* (Melbourne: Heidrick & Struggles, August 2008).

42. N. Byrnes, P. Burrows, and L. Lee, "Dark Days at Dell," *BusinessWeek,* September 4, 2006, p. 26; S. Lohr, "Can Michael Dell Refocus His Namesake?" *The New York Times,* September 9, 2007, p. 1.

43. C. A. O'Reilly III and J. A. Chatman, "Culture as Social Control: Corporations, Cults, and Commitment," *Research in Organizational Behavior* 18 (1996), pp. 157–200; B. Spector and H. Lane, "Exploring the Distinctions between a High Performance Culture and a Cult," *Strategy & Leadership* 35, no. 3 (2007), pp. 18–24.

44. Kotter and Heskett, *Corporate Culture and Performance;* J. P. Kotter, "Cultures and Coalitions," *Executive Excellence* 15 (March 1998), pp. 14–15; B. M. Bass and R. E. Riggio, *Transformational Leadership,* 2nd ed. (New York: Routledge, 2006), Chap. 7. The term *adaptive culture* has a different meaning in organizational behavior than it has in cultural anthropology, where it refers to nonmaterial cultural conditions (such as ways of thinking) that lag the material culture (physical artifacts). For the anthropological perspective, see W. Griswold, *Cultures and Societies in a Changing World,* 3rd ed. (Thousand Oaks, CA: Pine Forge Press (Sage), 2008), p. 66.

45. W. E. Baker and J. M. Sinkula, "The Synergistic Effect of Market Orientation and Learning Orientation on Organizational Performance," *Academy of Marketing Science Journal* 27, no. 4 (Fall 1999), pp. 411–27; Z. Emden, A. Yaprak, and S. T. Cavusgil, "Learning from Experience in International Alliances: Antecedents and Firm Performance Implications," *Journal of Business Research* 58, no. 7 (2005), pp. 883–92.

46. D. Ho, "Michael Dell Says He Had No Role in Accounting Scandal," *Cox News Service,* September 6, 2007.

47. M. L. Marks, "Adding Cultural Fit to Your Diligence Checklist," *Mergers & Acquisitions* 34, no. 3 (November–December 1999), pp. 14–20; Schein, *The Corporate Culture Survival Guide,* Chap. 8; M. L. Marks, "Mixed Signals," *Across the Board,* May 2000, pp. 21–26; J. P. Daly, R. W. Pouder, and B. Kabanoff, "The Effects of Initial Differences in Firms' Espoused Values on Their Postmerger Performance," *Journal of Applied Behavioral Science* 40, no. 3 (September 2004), pp. 323–43.

48. Teerikangas and Very, "The Culture–Performance Relationship in M&A: From Yes/No to How"; G. K. Stahl and A. Voigt, "Do Cultural Differences Matter in Mergers and Acquisitions? A Tentative Model and Examination," *Organization Science* 19, no. 1 (January 2008), pp. 160–76.

49. M. L. Sirower, *The Synergy Trap: How Companies Lose the Acquisition Game* (New York: The Free Press, 1997); "KPMG Identifies Six Key Factors for Successful Mergers and Acquisitions," PR Newswire news release for KPMG (New York: November 29, 1999); C. Cook and D. Spitzer, *World Class Transactions* (London: KPMG, 2001); D. Henry, "Mergers: Why Most Big Deals Don't Pay Off," *BusinessWeek,* October 14, 2002; J. Krug, *Mergers and Acquisitions: Turmoil in Top Management Teams* (Williston, VT: Business Expert Press, 2009).

50. Smith and Fitzpatrick, "Cultures Clash as Merrill Herd Meets 'Wal-Mart of Banking'"; "Bank of America–Merrill Lynch: A $50 Billion Deal from Hell," *Deal Journal (Wall Street Journal Blog),* January 22, 2009; M. Read, "Wall Street's Entitlement Culture Hard to Shake," *Associated Press,* January 23, 2009; D. Sarch, "Merrill Lynch: Culture Change or Just the Latest Innovation? " *Investment News,* May 27, 2010.

51. C. A. Schorg, C. A. Raiborn, and M. F. Massoud, "Using a 'Cultural Audit' to Pick M & A Winners," *Journal of Corporate Accounting & Finance* (May/June 2004), pp. 47–55; W. Locke, "Higher Education Mergers: Integrating Organisational Cultures and Developing Appropriate Management Styles," *Higher Education Quarterly* 61, no. 1 (2007), pp. 83–102.

52. S. Greengard, "Due Diligence: The Devil in the Details," *Workforce,* October 1999, p. 68; Marks, "Adding Cultural Fit to Your Diligence Checklist."

53. A. B. Fisher and A. J. Michels, "How to Make a Merger Work," *Fortune* 1994, pp. 66–70.

54. A. R. Malekazedeh and A. Nahavandi, "Making Mergers Work by Managing Cultures," *Journal of Business Strategy,* May–June 1990, pp. 55–57; K. W. Smith, "A Brand-New Culture for the Merged Firm," *Mergers and Acquisitions* 35 (June 2000), pp. 45–50.

55. T. Hamilton, "RIM on a Roll," *Toronto Star,* February 22, 2004, p. C01.

56. "Sustaining High Performance," *CEOForum,* September 2006, ceoforum.com.au.

57. Hewitt Associates, "Mergers and Acquisitions May Be Driven by Business Strategy—but Often Stumble over People and Culture Issues," PR Newswire news release (Lincolnshire, IL: August 3, 1998).

58. J. Martin, "Can Organizational Culture Be Managed?" in *Organizational Culture,* ed. P. J. Frost et al. (Beverly Hills, CA: Sage, 1985), pp. 95–98.

59. E. H. Schein, "The Role of the Founder in Creating Organizational Culture," *Organizational Dynamics* 12, no. 1 (Summer 1983), pp. 13–28; R. House, M. Javidan, and P. Dorfman, "Project GLOBE: An Introduction," *Applied Psychology: An International Review* 50 (2001), pp. 489–505; R. House et al., "Understanding Cultures and Implicit Leadership Theories across the Globe: An Introduction to Project GLOBE," *Journal of World Business* 37 (2002), pp. 3–10.

60. A. S. Tsui et al., "Unpacking the Relationship between CEO Leadership Behavior and Organizational Culture," *Leadership Quarterly* 17 (2006), pp. 113–37; Y. Berson, S. Oreg, and T. Dvir, "CEO Values, Organizational Culture and Firm Outcomes," *Journal of Organizational Behavior* 29, no. 5 (July 2008), pp. 615–33.

61. M. De Pree, *Leadership Jazz: The Essential Elements of a Great Leader,* 2nd ed. (New York: Broadway Business, 2008).

62. M. De Pree, *Leadership Is an Art* (East Lansing, MI: Michigan State University Press, 1987).

63. J. Kerr and J. W. Slocum Jr., "Managing Corporate Culture through Reward Systems," *Academy of Management Executive* 1 (May 1987), pp. 99–107; J. M. Higgins et al., "Using Cultural Artifacts to Change and Perpetuate Strategy," *Journal of Change Management* 6, no. 4 (2006), pp. 397–415.

64. R. Charan, "Home Depot's Blueprint for Culture Change," *Harvard Business Review,* April 2006, pp. 61–70.

65. B. Schneider, "The People Make the Place," *Personnel Psychology* 40, no. 3 (1987), pp. 437–53; B. Schneider et al., "Personality and Organizations: A Test of the Homogeneity of Personality Hypothesis," *Journal of Applied Psychology* 83, no. 3 (June 1998), pp. 462–70; T. R. Giberson, C. J. Resick, and M. W. Dickson, "Embedding Leader Characteristics: An Examination of Homogeneity of Personality and Values in Organizations," *Journal of Applied Psychology* 90, no. 5 (2005), pp. 1002–10.

66. "WestJet, Tim Hortons and RBC Financial Group." CNW news release for Waterstone Human Capital and National Post (Toronto: October 13, 2005); Y. Lermusi, "The No. 1 Frustration of Your Job Candidates" (August 15, 2006), www.ere.net (accessed June 2, 2010); S. Singleton, "Starbucks, Goodlife Fitness among Most Admired Companies," *Money.Canoe.ca (Toronto),* November 12, 2009; Taleo Research, "Talent Management Processes" (Dublin, CA: Taleo, 2010), www.taleo.com (accessed June 2, 2010).

67. T. A. Judge and D. M. Cable, "Applicant Personality, Organizational Culture, and Organization Attraction," *Personnel Psychology* 50, no. 2 (1997), pp. 359–94; D. S. Chapman et al., "Applicant Attraction to Organizations and Job Choice: A Meta-Analytic Review of the Correlates of Recruiting Outcomes," *Journal of Applied Psychology* 90, no. 5 (2005), pp. 928–44; A. L. Kristof-Brown, R. D. Zimmerman, and E. C. Johnson, "Consequences of Individuals' Fit at Work: A Meta-Analysis of Person–Job, Person–Organization, Person–Group, and Person–Supervisor Fit," *Personnel Psychology* 58, no. 2 (2005), pp. 281–342; C. Hu, H.-C. Su, and C.-I. B. Chen, "The Effect of Person–Organization Fit Feedback via Recruitment Web Sites on Applicant Attraction," *Computers in Human Behavior* 23, no. 5 (2007), pp. 2509–23.

68. A. Kristof-Brown, "Perceived Applicant Fit: Distinguishing between Recruiters' Perceptions of Person–Job and Person–Organization Fit," *Personnel Psychology* 53, no. 3 (Autumn 2000), pp. 643–71; A. E. M. Van Vianen, "Person–Organization Fit: The Match between Newcomers' and Recruiters' Preferences for Organizational Cultures," *Personnel Psychology* 53 (Spring 2000), pp. 113–49.

69. S. Cruz, "Park Place Lexus Mission Viejo Seeing Improvements," *Orange County Business Journal,* May 12, 2008, p. 15; C. Hall, "'Emotional Intelligence' Counts in Job Hires," *Dallas Morning News,* August 20, 2008.

70. D. M. Cable and J. R. Edwards, "Complementary and Supplementary Fit: A Theoretical and Empirical Integration," *Journal of Applied Psychology* 89, no. 5 (2004), pp. 822–34.

71. J. Van Maanen, "Breaking In: Socialization to Work," in *Handbook of Work, Organization, and Society,* ed. R. Dubin (Chicago: Rand McNally, 1976).

72. D. G. Allen, "Do Organizational Socialization Tactics Influence Newcomer Embeddedness and Turnover?," *Journal of Management* 32, no. 2 (April 2006), pp. 237–56; A. M. Saks, K. L. Uggerslev, and N. E. Fassina, "Socialization Tactics and Newcomer Adjustment: A Meta-Analytic Review and Test of a Model," *Journal of Vocational Behavior* 70, no. 3 (2007), pp. 413–46.

73. G. T. Chao et al., "Organizational Socialization: Its Content and Consequences," *Journal of Applied Psychology* 79 (1994), pp. 450–63; H. D. Cooper-Thomas and N. Anderson, "Organizational Socialization: A Field Study into Socialization Success and Rate," *International Journal of Selection and Assessment* 13, no. 2 (2005), pp. 116–28.

74. N. Nicholson, "A Theory of Work Role Transitions," *Administrative Science Quarterly* 29 (1984), pp. 172–91; B. E. Ashforth, D. M. Sluss, and A. M. Saks, "Socialization Tactics, Proactive Behavior, and Newcomer Learning: Integrating Socialization Models," *Journal of Vocational Behavior* 70, no. 3 (2007), pp. 447–62; T. N. Bauer, "Newcomer Adjustment during Organizational Socialization: A Meta-Analytic Review of Antecedents, Outcomes, and Methods," *Journal of Applied Psychology* 92, no. 3 (2007), pp. 707–21; A. Elfering et al., "First Years in Job: A Three-Wave Analysis of Work Experiences," *Journal of Vocational Behavior* 70, no. 1 (2007), pp. 97–115.

75. J. M. Beyer and D. R. Hannah, "Building on the Past: Enacting Established Personal Identities in a New Work Setting," *Organization Science* 13 (November/December 2002), pp. 636–52; H. D. C. Thomas and N. Anderson, "Newcomer Adjustment: The Relationship between Organizational Socialization Tactics, Information Acquisition and Attitudes," *Journal of Occupational and Organizational Psychology* 75 (December 2002), pp. 423–37.

76. Towers Watson, *Capitalizing on Effective Communication* (New York: Towers Watson, February 4, 2010).

77. L. W. Porter, E. E. Lawler III, and J. R. Hackman, *Behavior in Organizations* (New York: McGraw-Hill, 1975), pp. 163–67; Van Maanen, "Breaking In: Socialization to Work"; D. C. Feldman, "The Multiple Socialization of Organization Members," *Academy of Management Review* 6 (1981), pp. 309–18.

78. B. E. Ashforth and A. M. Saks, "Socialization Tactics: Longitudinal Effects on Newcomer Adjustment," *Academy of Management Journal* 39 (1996), pp. 149–78; J. D. Kammeyer-Mueller and C. R. Wanberg, "Unwrapping the Organizational Entry Process: Disentangling Multiple Antecedents and Their Pathways to Adjustment," *Journal of Applied Psychology* 88, no. 5 (2003), pp. 779–94.

79. Porter, Lawler III, and Hackman, *Behavior in Organizations,* Chap. 5.

80. Louis, "Surprise and Sensemaking: What Newcomers Experience in Entering Unfamiliar Organizational Settings."

81. S. L. Robinson and D. M. Rousseau, "Violating the Psychological Contract: Not the Exception but the Norm," *Journal of Organizational Behavior* 15 (1994), pp. 245–59.

82. D. L. Nelson, "Organizational Socialization: A Stress Perspective," *Journal of Occupational Behavior* 8 (1987), pp. 311–24; Elfering et al., "First Years in Job."

83. "Culture Clash," PR Newswire news release for T. C. Group (Menlo Park, CA: April 30, 2008).

84. J. P. Wanous, *Organizational Entry* (Reading, MA: Addison-Wesley, 1992); J. A. Breaugh and M. Starke, "Research on Employee Recruitment: So Many Studies, So Many Remaining Questions," *Journal of Management* 26, no. 3 (2000), pp. 405–34.

85. E. Simon, "Employers Study Applicants' Personalities," *Associated Press,* November 5, 2007. Also see the Lindblad RJP video at www.expeditions.com/Theater17.asp?Media=475.

86. J. M. Phillips, "Effects of Realistic Job Previews on Multiple Organizational Outcomes: A Meta-Analysis," *Academy of Management Journal* 41 (December 1998), pp. 673–90.

87. Y. Ganzach et al., "Social Exchange and Organizational Commitment: Decision-Making Training for Job Choice as an Alternative to the Realistic Job Preview," *Personnel Psychology* 55 (Autumn 2002), pp. 613–37.

88. C. Ostroff and S. W. J. Koslowski, "Organizational Socialization as a Learning Process: The Role of Information Acquisition," *Personnel Psychology* 45 (1992), pp. 849–74; Cooper-Thomas and Anderson, "Organizational Socialization: A Field Study into Socialization Success and Rate"; A. Baber and L. Waymon, "Uncovering the Unconnected Employee," *T & D* (May 2008), pp. 60–66.

89. C. Fishman, "The Anarchist's Cookbook," *Fast Company,* July 2004, p. 70; "World's Finest Food Retailers: Whole Foods, Not Holy Food," *The Grocer,* November 12, 2005, p. 32.

90. L. Buchanan et al., "That's Chief Entertainment Officer," *Inc.* 29, no. 8 (August 2007), pp. 86–94; P. Burkes Erickson, "Welcoming Employees: Making That First Day a Great Experience," *Daily Oklahoman,* July 15, 2007.

CHAPTER 14

1. D. Blossom, "Lopez Foods Looks to Beef Up Profits, Take Bite into International Breakfasts," *The Daily Oklahoman,* April 9, 2008; A. Hanacek, "Star Power," *National Provisioner* 222, no. 2 (February 2008), pp. 22–29.

2. M. Vinson, C. Pung, and J. M. Gonzalez-Blanch, *Organizing for Successful Change Management: A Mckinsey Global Survey* (London, UK: McKinsey & Company, 2006).

3. D. Howes, "Future Hinges on Global Teams," *Detroit News,* December 21, 1998.

4. K. Lewin, *Field Theory in Social Science* (New York: Harper & Row, 1951).

5. D. Coghlan and T. Brannick, "Kurt Lewin: The 'Practical Theorist' for the 21st Century," *Irish Journal of Management* 24, no. 2 (2003), pp. 31–37; B. Burnes, "Kurt Lewin and the Planned Approach to Change: A Re-Appraisal," *Journal of Management Studies* 41, no. 6 (September 2004), pp. 977–1002.

6. D. Howell, "Nardelli Nears Five-Year Mark with Riveting Record," *DSN Retailing Today,* May 9, 2005, pp. 1, 38; R. Charan, "Home Depot's Blueprint for Culture Change," *Harvard Business Review* (April 2006), pp. 61–70; R. DeGross, "Five Years of Change: Home Depot's Results Mixed under Nardelli," *Atlanta Journal-Constitution,* January 1, 2006, p. F1; B. Grow, D. Brady, and M. Arndt, "Renovating Home Depot," *BusinessWeek,* March 6, 2006, pp. 50–57.

7. N. Machiavelli, *The Prince and Other Writings, trans.* W. A. Rebhorn, *Barnes & Noble Classics* (New York: Barnes & Noble, 2003), p. 25.

8. S. Chreim, "Postscript to Change: Survivors' Retrospective Views of Organizational Changes," *Personnel Review* 35, no. 3 (2006), pp. 315–35.

9. M. Haid et al., *Ready, Get Set . . . Change! The Impact of Change on Workforce Productivity and Engagement,* Leadership Insights (Philadelphia, PA: Right Management, 2009).

10. M. Johnson-Cramer, S. Parise, and R. Cross, "Managing Change through Networks and Values," *California Management Review* 49, no. 3 (Spring 2007), pp. 85–109.

11. G. L. Neilson, B. A. Pasternack, and K. E. Van Nuys, "The Passive–Aggressive Organization," *Harvard Business Review* 83, no. 10 (2005), pp. 82–92.

12. K. Shimizu, "Hoppy Enjoying Comeback after Radical Shift in Management," *Japan Times,* August 15, 2007.

13. B. J. Tepper et al., "Subordinates' Resistance and Managers' Evaluations of Subordinates' Performance," *Journal of Management* 32, no. 2 (April 2006), pp. 185–209; J. D. Ford, L. W. Ford, and A. D'Amelio, "Resistance to Change: The Rest of the Story," *Academy of Management Review* 33, no. 2 (2008), pp. 362–77.

14. E. B. Dent and S. G. Goldberg, "Challenging 'Resistance to Change,'" *Journal of Applied Behavioral Science* 35 (March 1999), pp. 25–41; D. B. Fedor, S. Caldwell, and D. M. Herold, "The Effects of Organizational Changes on Employee Commitment: A Multilevel Investigation," *Personnel Psychology* 59, no. 1 (2006), pp. 1–29.

15. J. K. Galbraith, *Economics, Peace, and Laughter* (Boston: Houghton Mifflin, 1971), p. 50.

16. C. O. Longenecker, D. J. Dwyer, and T. C. Stansfield, "Barriers and Gateways to Workforce Productivity," *Industrial Management,* March–April 1998, pp. 21–28; D. Miller, "Building Commitment to Major Change—What 1700 Change Agents Told Us Really Works," *Developing HR Strategy,* no. 22 (September 2008), pp. 5–8; W. Immen, "When Leaders Become Glory Hounds," *Globe & Mail (Toronto),* March 5, 2010, p. B15; Towers Watson, *Capitalizing on Effective Communication* (New York: Towers Watson, February 4, 2010).

17. For an excellent review of the resistance-to-change literature, see R. R. Sharma, *Change Management: Concepts and Applications* (New Delhi: Tata McGraw-Hill, 2007), Chap. 4.

18. D. A. Nadler, "The Effective Management of Organizational Change," in *Handbook of Organizational Behavior,* ed. J. W. Lorsch (Englewood Cliffs, NJ: Prentice Hall, 1987), pp. 358–69; R. Maurer, *Beyond the Wall of Resistance: Unconventional Strategies to Build Support for Change* (Austin, TX: Bard Books, 1996); P. Strebel, "Why Do Employees Resist Change?" *Harvard Business Review* (May–June 1996), pp. 86–92; D. A. Nadler, *Champions of Change* (San Francisco, CA: Jossey-Bass, 1998).

19. V. Newman, "The Psychology of Managing for Innovation," *KM Review* 9, no. 6 (2007), pp. 10–15.

20. *Bosses Want Change but Workers Want More of the Same!* (Sydney: Talent2, June 29, 2005).

21. R. Davis, *Leading for Growth: How Umpqua Bank Got Cool and Created a Culture of Greatness* (San Francisco, CA: Jossey-Bass, 2007), p. 40.

22. C. Ressler and J. Thompson, *Why Work Sucks and How to Fix It* (New York: Portfolio, 2008), Chap. 2.

23. T. G. Cummings, "The Role and Limits of Change Leadership," in *The Leader's Change Handbook,* ed. J. A. Conger, G. M. Spreitzer, and E. E. Lawler III (San Francisco: Jossey-Bass, 1999), pp. 301–20; J. P. Kotter and D. S. Cohen, *The Heart of Change* (Boston: Harvard Business School Press, 2002),

pp. 15–36; J. P. Kotter, *A Sense of Urgency* (Boston: Harvard Business School Press, 2008).

24. L. D. Goodstein and H. R. Butz, "Customer Value: The Linchpin of Organizational Change," *Organizational Dynamics* 27 (June 1998), pp. 21–35.

25. I. J. Bozon and P. N. Child, "Refining Shell's Position in Europe," *McKinsey Quarterly,* no. 2 (2003), pp. 42–51.

26. D. Darlin, "Growing Tomorrow," *Business 2.0,* May 2005, p. 126.

27. L. Grossman and S. Song, "Stevie's Little Wonder," *Time,* September 19, 2005, p. 63; S. Levy, "Honey, I Shrunk the iPod. A Lot," *Newsweek,* September 19, 2005, p. 58.

28. T. F. Cawsey and G. Deszca, *Toolkit for Organizational Change* (Los Angeles: Sage, 2007), p. 104.

29. J. P. Kotter and L. A. Schlesinger, "Choosing Strategies for Change," *Harvard Business Review* (March–April 1979), pp. 106–14.

30. B. Nanus and S. M. Dobbs, *Leaders Who Make a Difference* (San Francisco: Jossey-Bass, 1999); Kotter and Cohen, *The Heart of Change,* pp. 83–98. The recent survey is reported in M. Meaney and C. Pung, "Creating Organizational Trans-formations: McKinsey Global Survey Results," *McKinsey Quarterly,* July 2008, pp. 1–7.

31. J. J. Brazil, "Mission: Impossible?" *Fast Company,* April 2007, pp. 92–97, 108–9.

32. Towers Watson, *Capitalizing on Effective Communication.*

33. K. T. Dirks, L. L. Cummings, and J. L. Pierce, "Psychological Ownership in Organizations: Conditions under Which Individuals Promote and Resist Change," *Research in Organizational Change and Development* 9 (1996), pp. 1–23; A. Cox, S. Zagelmeyer, and M. Marchington, "Embedding Employee Involvement and Participation at Work," *Human Resource Management Journal* 16, no. 3 (2006), pp. 250–67.

34. N. T. Tan, "Maximising Human Resource Potential in the Midst of Organisational Change," *Singapore Management Review* 27, no. 2 (2005), pp. 25–35.

35. M. McHugh, "The Stress Factor: Another Item for the Change Management Agenda?" *Journal of Organizational Change Management* 10 (1997), pp. 345–62; D. Buchanan, T. Claydon, and M. Doyle, "Organisation Development and Change: The Legacy of the Nineties," *Human Resource Management Journal* 9 (1999), pp. 20–37.

36. G. Brennemann, "Right Away and All at Once: How We Saved Continental," *Harvard Business Review* (September–October 1998), pp. 162–79; Howell, "Nardelli Nears Five-Year Mark with Riveting Record"; Charan, "Home Depot's Blueprint for Culture Change."

37. D. Nicolini and M. B. Meznar, "The Social Construction of Organizational Learning: Conceptual and Practical Issues in the Field," *Human Relations* 48 (1995), pp. 727–46.

38. E. E. Lawler III, "Pay Can Be a Change Agent," *Compensation & Benefits Management* 16 (Summer 2000), pp. 23–26; Kotter and Cohen, *The Heart of Change,* pp. 161–77; M. A. Roberto and L. C. Levesque, "The Art of Making Change Initiatives Stick," *MIT Sloan Management Review* 46, no. 4 (Summer 2005), pp. 53–60.

39. Lawler III, "Pay Can Be a Change Agent."

40. Goodstein and Butz, "Customer Value: The Linchpin of Organizational Change"; R. H. Miles, "Leading Corporate Trans-formation: Are You up to the Task?" in *The Leader's Change Handbook,* ed. J. A. Conger, G. M. Spreitzer, and E. E. Lawler III (San Francisco: Jossey-Bass, 1999), pp. 221–67.

41. R. E. Quinn, *Building the Bridge as You Walk on It: A Guide for Leading Change* (San Francisco: Jossey-Bass, 2004), Chap. 11.

42. R. Caldwell, "Models of Change Agency: A Fourfold Classification," *British Journal of Management* 14 (June 2003), pp. 131–42.

43. C. Aitken and S. Keller, "The Irrational Side of Change Management," *McKinsey Quarterly,* no. 2 (2009), pp. 100–9.

44. Kotter and Cohen, *The Heart of Change,* pp. 61–82; D. S. Cohen and J. P. Kotter, *The Heart of Change Field Guide* (Boston: Harvard Business School Press, 2005).

45. J. Thottam, "Reworking Work," *Time,* July 25, 2005, p. 50; Ressler and Thompson, *Why Work Sucks and How to Fix It,* pp. 20, 45–48.

46. M. Beer, R. A. Eisenstat, and B. Spector, *The Critical Path to Corporate Renewal* (Boston, Mass.: Harvard Business School Press, 1990).

47. R. E. Walton, "Successful Strategies for Diffusing Work Innovations," *Journal of Contemporary Business* (Spring 1977), pp. 1–22; R. E. Walton, *Innovating to Compete: Lessons for Diffusing and Managing Change in the Workplace* (San Francisco: Jossey-Bass, 1987); Beer, Eisenstat, and Spector, *The Critical Path to Corporate Renewal,* Chap. 5.

48. E. M. Rogers, *Diffusion of Innovations,* 4th ed. (New York: Free Press, 1995).

49. P. Reason and H. Bradbury, *Handbook of Action Research* (London: Sage, 2001); Coghlan and Brannick, "Kurt Lewin: The 'Practical Theorist' for the 21st Century"; C. Huxham and S. Vangen, "Researching Organizational Practice through Action Research: Case Studies and Design Choices," *Organizational Research Methods* 6 (July 2003), pp. 383–403.

50. V. J. Marsick and M. A. Gephart, "Action Research: Building the Capacity for Learning and Change," *Human Resource Planning* 26 (2003), pp. 14–18.

51. L. Dickens and K. Watkins, "Action Research: Rethinking Lewin," *Management Learning* 30 (June 1999), pp. 127–40; J. Heron and P. Reason, "The Practice of Co-Operative Inquiry: Research 'with' Rather Than 'on' People," in *Handbook of Action Research,* ed. P. Reason and H. Bradbury (Thousand Oaks, CA: Sage, 2001), pp. 179–88.

52. D. A. Nadler, "Organizational Frame Bending: Types of Change in the Complex Organization," in *Corporate Transformation: Revitalizing Organizations for a Competitive World,* ed. R. H. Kilmann, T. J. Covin, and A. Associates (San Francisco: Jossey-Bass, 1988), pp. 66–83; K. E. Weick and R. E. Quinn, "Organizational Change and Development," *Annual Review of Psychology* 50 (1999), pp. 361–86.

53. T. M. Egan and C. M. Lancaster, "Comparing Appreciative Inquiry to Action Research: OD Practitioner Perspectives," *Organization Development Journal* 23, no. 2 (Summer 2005), pp. 29–49.

54. F. F. Luthans, "Positive Organizational Behavior: Developing and Managing Psychological Strengths," *The Academy of Management Executive* 16, no. 1 (2002), pp. 57–72; N. Turner, J. Barling, and A. Zacharatos, "Positive Psychology at Work," in *Handbook of Positive Psychology,* ed. C. R. Snyder and S. Lopez (Oxford, UK: Oxford University Press, 2002), pp. 715–30; K. Cameron, J. E. Dutton, and R. E. Quinn, eds., *Positive Organizational Scholarship: Foundation of a New Discipline* (San Francisco: Berrett Koehler Publishers, 2003); J. I. Krueger and D. C. Funder, "Towards a Balanced Social Psychology: Causes, Consequences, and Cures for the Problem-Seeking Approach to Social Behavior and Cognition," *Behavioral and Brain Sciences* 27, no. 3 (June

2004), pp. 313–27; S. L. Gable and J. Haidt, "What (and Why) Is Positive Psychology?" *Review of General Psychology* 9, no. 2 (2005), pp. 103–10; M. E. P. Seligman et al., "Positive Psychology Progress: Empirical Validation of Interventions," *American Psychologist* 60, no. 5 (2005), pp. 410–21.

55. D. Whitney and D. L. Cooperrider, "The Appreciative Inquiry Summit: Overview and Applications," *Employment Relations Today* 25 (Summer 1998), pp. 17–28; J. M. Watkins and B. J. Mohr, *Appreciative Inquiry: Change at the Speed of Imagination* (San Francisco: Jossey-Bass, 2001).

56. S. Berrisford, "Using Appreciative Inquiry to Drive Change at the BBC," *Strategic Communication Management* 9, no. 3 (2005), pp. 22–25; M.-Y. Cheung-Judge and E. H. Powley, "Innovation at the BBC," in *The Handbook of Large Group Methods,* ed. B. B. Bunker and B. T. Alban (New York: Wiley, 2006), pp. 45–61.

57. D. L. Cooperrider, *Appreciative Inquiry: A Positive Revolution in Change* (San Francisco: Berrett-Koehler, 2005); D. K. Whitney and A. Trosten-Bloom, *The Power of Appreciative Inquiry: A Practical Guide to Positive Change,* 2nd ed. (San Francisco: Berrett-Koehler Publishers, 2010).

58. F. J. Barrett and D. L. Cooperrider, "Generative Metaphor Intervention: A New Approach for Working with Systems Divided by Conflict and Caught in Defensive Perception," *Journal of Applied Behavioral Science* 26 (1990), pp. 219–39; Whitney and Cooperrider, "The Appreciative Inquiry Summit: Overview and Applications"; Watkins and Mohr, *Appreciative Inquiry: Change at the Speed of Imagination,* pp. 15–21.

59. M. Schiller, "Case Study: Avon Mexico," in *Appreciative Inquiry: Change at the Speed of Imagination,* ed. J. M. Watkins and B. J. Mohr (San Francisco: Jossey-Bass, 2001), pp. 123–26; P. Babcock, "Seeing a Brighter Future," *HRMagazine* 50, no. 9 (September 2005), p. 48; D. S. Bright, D. L. Cooperrider, and W. B. Galloway, "Appreciative Inquiry in the Office of Research and Development: Improving the Collaborative Capacity of Organization," *Public Performance & Management Review* 29, no. 3 (2006), p. 285; D. Gilmour and A. Radford, "Using OD to Enhance Shareholder Value: Delivering Business Results in BP Castrol Marine," *Organization Development Journal* 25, no. 3 (2007), pp. P97–P102; Whitney and Trosten-Bloom, *The Power of Appreciative Inquiry.*

60. T. F. Yaeger, P. F. Sorensen, and U. Bengtsson, "Assessment of the State of Appreciative Inquiry: Past, Present, and Future," *Research in Organizational Change and Development* 15 (2004), pp. 297–319; G. R. Bushe and A. F. Kassam, "When Is Appreciative Inquiry Transformational? A Meta-Case Analysis," *Journal of Applied Behavioral Science* 41, no. 2 (June 2005), pp. 161–81.

61. G. R. Bushe, "Five Theories of Change Embedded in Appreciative Inquiry," in *18th Annual World Congress of Organization Development* (Dublin, Ireland: July 14–18, 1998).

62. M. Weisbord and S. Janoff, *Future Search: An Action Guide to Finding Common Ground in Organizations and Communities* (San Francisco: Berrett-Koehler, 2000); R. M. Lent, M. T. McCormick, and D. S. Pearce, "Combining Future Search and Open Space to Address Special Situations," *Journal of Applied Behavioral Science* 41, no. 1 (March 2005), pp. 61–69; S. Janoff and M. Weisbord, "Future Search as 'Real-Time' Action Research," *Futures* 38, no. 6 (2006), pp. 716–22.

63. N. Aronson, E. Axelrod, and S. Crowther, "Lawrence Public Schools: Institutionalized Goals," in *Future Search in School*

District Change, ed. R. Schweitz, K. Martens, and N. Aronson (Lanham, Maryland: ScarecrowEducation, 2005), pp. 3–18; R. Lent, J. Van Patten, and T. Phair, "Creating a World-Class Manufacturer in Record Time," in *The Handbook of Large Group Methods,* ed. B. B. Bunker and B. T. Alban (New York: Wiley, 2006), pp. 112–24.

64. For a critique of future search conferences and similar whole-system events, see A. Oels, "Investigating the Emotional Roller-Coaster Ride: A Case Study–Based Assessment of the Future Search Conference Design," *Systems Research and Behavioral Science* 19 (July–August 2002), pp. 347–55; M. F. D. Polanyi, "Communicative Action in Practice: Future Search and the Pursuit of an Open, Critical and Non-Coercive Large-Group Process," *Systems Research and Behavioral Science* 19 (July 2002), pp. 357–66; A. De Grassi, "Envisioning Futures of African Agriculture: Representation, Power, and Socially Constituted Time," *Progress in Development Studies* 7, no. 2 (2007), pp. 79–98.

65. T. Shapley, "Trying to Fix What Everyone Else Has Broken," *Seattle Post-Intelligencer,* November 16, 2005, p. B8.

66. G. R. Bushe and A. B. Shani, *Parallel Learning Structures* (Reading, MA: Addison-Wesley, 1991); E. M. Van Aken, D. J. Monetta, and D. S. Sink, "Affinity Groups: The Missing Link in Employee Involvement," *Organization Dynamics* 22 (Spring 1994), pp. 38–54.

67. D. J. Knight, "Strategy in Practice: Making It Happen," *Strategy & Leadership* 26 (July–August 1998), pp. 29–33; R. T. Pascale, "Grassroots Leadership—Royal Dutch/Shell," *Fast Company,* no. 14 (April–May 1998), pp. 110–20; R. T. Pascale, "Leading from a Different Place," in *The Leader's Change Handbook,* ed. J. A. Conger, G. M. Spreitzer, and E. E. Lawler III (San Francisco: Jossey-Bass, 1999), pp. 301–20; R. Pascale, M. Millemann, and L. Gioja, *Surfing on the Edge of Chaos* (London: Texere, 2000).

68. T. C. Head and P. F. Sorenson, "Cultural Values and Organizational Development: A Seven-Country Study," *Leadership and Organization Development Journal* 14 (1993), pp. 3–7; R. J. Marshak, "Lewin Meets Confucius: A Review of the OD Model of Change," *Journal of Applied Behavioral Science* 29 (1993), pp. 395–415; C.-M. Lau, "A Culture-Based Perspective of Organization Development Implementation," *Research in Organizational Change and Development* 9 (1996), pp. 49–79; C. M. Lau and H. Y. Ngo, "Organization Development and Firm Performance: A Comparison of Multinational and Local Firms," *Journal of International Business Studies* 32, no. 1 (2001), pp. 95–114.

69. M. McKendall, "The Tyranny of Change: Organizational Development Revisited," *Journal of Business Ethics* 12 (February 1993), pp. 93–104; C. M. D. Deaner, "A Model of Organization Development Ethics," *Public Administration Quarterly* 17 (1994), pp. 435–46.

70. G. A. Walter, "Organization Development and Individual Rights," *Journal of Applied Behavioral Science* 20 (1984), pp. 423–39.

71. The source of this often-cited quotation was not found. It does not appear, even in rough form, in the books that Andrew Carnegie wrote (such as *Gospel of Wealth,* 1900; *Empire of Business,* 1902; and *Autobiography,* 1920). However, Carnegie may have stated these words (or similar ones) in other places. He gave a multitude of speeches and wrote many articles, and his words are reported by numerous other authors.

photo credits

Back cover: © John Cumming

CHAPTER 1
Page 2 Digital Vision/Getty Images
Page 4 Justin Sullivan/Getty Images
Page 6 Jim McIsaac/Getty Images
Page 9 Ingram Publishing/Alamy
Page 10 MIKE CLARKE/AFP/Getty Images
Page 11 Ingram Publishing/Alamy
Page 15 Courtesy of Aviva
Page 16 (t)Image Source/Corbis, (b)Comstock Images/Jupiterimages
Page 17 RubberBall Productions
Page 19 (t)Barros & Barros/Photographer's Choice/Getty Images, (b)Punchstock/Digital Vision

CHAPTER 2
Page 24–25 Colin Anderson/Brand X/Corbis
Page 26 Travel Ink/Gallo Images/Getty Images
Page 29 (l)GARY DOAK/Alamy, (r)Royalty-free/Corbis
Page 30 Hans Neleman/Stone/Getty Images
Page 31 Hugh Sitton/Photographer's Choice/Getty Images
Page 33 Creatas/PunchStock
Page 35 Library of Congress Prints and Photographs Division
Page 36 (t)C Squared Studios/Getty Images, (b)Ingram Publishing/Alamy
Page 37 Hamza Türkkol/iStockphoto
Page 38 2009 Jupiterimages
Page 42 Stockbyte/Getty Images
Page 44 Photodisc/Getty Images
Page 46 Burke/Triolo/Brand X Pictures/Jupiterimages

CHAPTER 3
Page 48 Jason Reed/Getty Images
Page 50 Royalty-free/Corbis
Page 51 Courtesy of Mary Ann Von Glinow
Page 52 PhotoLink/Getty Images
Page 53 Ingram Publishing/age Fotostock
Page 54 Royalty-free/Corbis
Page 55 Ingram Publishing/SuperStock
Page 56 (t)Royalty-Free/CORBIS, (b)Photodisc/Getty Images
Page 57 Royalty-free/Corbis
Page 60 ImageegamI/iStockphoto
Page 61 Digital Vision/Punchstock
Page 62 Roy McMahon/Corbis
Page 64 Courtesy of Mary Ann Von Glinow

CHAPTER 4
Page 68–69 Stockbyte/Punchstock Images
Page 70 (t)Photograph courtesy of the National Park Service, (b)Royalty-free/Corbis
Page 71 Richard Nelson/Cutcaster
Page 74 Brand X Pictures
Page 75 Getty Images/Tim Teebken
Page 76 (l)altrendo images/Getty Images; (r)Goh Seng Chong/Bloomberg via Getty Images
Page 77 Stockdisc/PunchStock
Page 78 Royalty-Free/CORBIS
Page 83 Creatas/PunchStock
Page 86 david pearson/Alamy
Page 87 Photo courtesy of Mark Wells

CHAPTER 5
Page 90 Duncan Smith/Getty Images
Page 92 Royalty-free/Corbis
Page 93 (t)C Squared Studios/Getty Images, (b)AP Photo/Matt York
Page 94 Digital Vision/Punchstock
Page 97 Royalty-free/Corbis
Page 98 (t)Ghislain & Marie David de Lossy/cultura/Corbis, (b)Brand X/Jupiterimages
Page 102 Stockbyte/Getty Images

Page 105 Ryan McVay/Getty Images
Page 107 Nick Servian/Alamy
Page 110 Courtesy of Rolls-Royce plc

CHAPTER 6
Page 114–115 Digital Vision/Getty Images
Page 118 Royalty-free/Corbis
Page 119 (l)Eric Audras/Photoalto/PIctureQuest, (r)Brand X Pictures
Page 122 Andrew Twort/Alamy
Page 124 diego cervo/iStockphoto
Page 125 (t)Steve & Ghy Sampson/Getty Images,(b)Comstock Images/Alamy
Page 126 Stockbyte/PunchStock
Page 129 M. Freeman/PhotoLink/Getty Images
Page 130 (t)Royalty-free/Corbis, (b)Brand X Pictures/PunchStock
Page 132 William Perlman/Star Ledger/Corbis
Page 133 (t)Royalty-free/Corbis, (b)Keith Eng 2007/The McGraw-Hill Companies

CHAPTER 7
Page 135–136 Dynamic Graphics/Jupiterimages
Page 139 Jay P. Morgan/Workbook Stock/Getty Images
Page 140 Dynamic Graphics/Jupiterimages
Page 142 Billy E. Barnes/PhotoEdit
Page 144 GENE J. PUSKAR/AFP/Getty Images
Page 146 Photo by staff sgt. Bennie J. Davis III/U.S. Air Force
Page 150 Royalty-free/Corbis
Page 152 (t)Courtesy of Whole Foods Market, (b)Colin Anderson/Getty Images
Page 154 John Lund/Digital Vision/Getty Images
Page 155 Johnson Space Center/NASA

CHAPTER 8
Page 158 Digital Vision
Page 162 Jeffrey Hamilton/Photodisc/Getty Images
Page 163 Photodisc
Page 164 Royalty-free/Corbis
Page 165 Brand X Pictures/PunchStock
Page 167 Stockbyte/PunchStock
Page 168 © Tim Fraser
Page 169 Comstock Images
Page 171 Susan LeVan/Artville
Page 174 Noah Berger/Bloomberg via Getty Images
Page 176 TRBfoto/Getty Images

CHAPTER 9
Page 178 J. Luke/PhotoLink/Getty Images
Page 180 Steve Allen/Brand X Pictures
Page 182 (t)Brand X Pictures, (b)AP Photo/Christophe Ena
Page 183 Roy McMahon/Corbis
Page 185 Danita Delimont/Alamy
Page 186 Robin Jareaux/Getty Images
Page 187 (t)Courtesy of Karl J. Arunski, Raytheon, (b)Joshua Ets-Hokin/Getty Images
Page 193 (t)Historicus, Inc., (b)Jon Schulte/iStockphoto
Page 194 Digital Vision/Getty Images

CHAPTER 10
Page 196–197 iStockphoto.com
Page 199 Big Cheese Photo/Jupiterimages
Page 200 Getty Images
Page 201 Comstock/PunchStock
Page 203 Creatas Images/Jupiterimages
Page 204 (t)Creatas/PunchStock, (b)Dynamic Graphics/PictureQuest
Page 205 Masterfile
Page 207 Mona Daly/Getty Images
Page 208 Image Source/PunchStock
Page 209 Stocktrek/Corbis
Page 210 Design Pics/PunchStock

CHAPTER 11
Page 212–213 Digital Vision/Getty Images
Page 216 (t)Comstock/PictureQuest, (b)Susan LeVan/Artville
Page 217 Getty Images
Page 218 Barbara Penoyar/Getty Images
Page 221 Brand X Pictures/PunchStock
Page 222 Glowimages/PunchStock
Page 225 (l)BananaStock/PictureQuest, (r)BananaStock/PictureQuest
Page 227 Royalty-free/Corbis
Page 230 (t)Getty Images, (b)© Mathias Woltmann

CHAPTER 12
Page 232 iStockphoto.com
Page 237 Digital Vision/Getty Images
Page 238 Ingram Publishing/Fotosearch
Page 239 AP Photo/Chuck Burton
Page 242 (tl)Adam Gault/OJO Images/Getty Images, (tr)Getty Images/MedicalRF.com, (c)Bildagentur-online/Alamy
Page 246 Yuri Arcurs/Cutcaster
Page 249 (t)Kevin Foy/Alamy, (b)Tom Sibley/Corbis
Page 252 Photo Resource Hawaii/Alamy

CHAPTER 13
Page 254–255 Atamu Rahi/Iconotec
Page 257 (l)Peter Bono/Getty Images, (r)U.S. Coast Guard Photo by Petty Officer 3rd Class Patrick Kelley

Page 260 (t)GOODSHOOT/Alamy, (b)Helen Sessions/Alamy
Page 261 Photodisc/Getty Images
Page 262 (l)Ronda Churchill/Bloomberg via Getty Images, (r)Royalty-free/Corbis; © Le Do/iStockphoto
Page 267 Steve Hamblin/Alamy Images
Page 269 © alxpin/iStockphoto
Page 271 The McGraw-Hill Companies, Inc./Jill Braaten, photographer
Page 272 Photos courtesy of Lindblad Expeditions

CHAPTER 14
Page 274–275 Royalty-free/Corbis
Page 278 Steve Mason/Getty Images
Page 279 (t)The Japan Times, (b)Dynamic Graphics/PictureQuest
Page 280 © Sergey Peterman/iStockphoto
Page 281 Design Pics/PunchStock
Page 284–286 Royalty-free/Corbis
Page 289 Yellow Dog Productions/Stone/Getty Images
Page 292 (t)Brand X Pictures/Jupiter Images, (b)Brand X Pictures/PunchStock
Page 293 © Bettmann/CORBIS

Index

Note: page numbers followed by *n* indicate material found in footnotes or source notes.

B

Baby boomers, 19, 73
Bachman, Greg, 142
Balsillie, Jim, 265
Bank of America (BofA), 256, 265
Bank of America New Jersey, 20
Barnard, Chester, 160
Barrett, F. J., 290n
Barrick Gold Corporation, 244
Barriers to communication
    information overload, 163, 170–171
    language differences, 169–170, 171
    noise, 160, 169–170
Barriers to entry, 187
BASF, 239
Bass, Carl, 228
"Bathroom effect," 174
BBC (British Broadcasting Corporation), 289, 291
Beersma, B., 205n
"Behave Safely Challenge," 65–66
Behavior, 15–18, 23
    attitudes and, 69–70
    changing jobs, 16, 17
    emotions and. *See* Emotion(s)
    ethics and, 45–47
    influence of emotions on, 74
    influence of past experiences on, 94, 95
    MARS model of. *See* MARS model of individual
        behavior
    organizational. *See* Organizational behavior
    "people problems," 25–26
    predictability of, 151
    preferred behaviors, 29
    regulation of, 219
    relation to drives and needs, 93–94
    role of emotional intelligence in, 100
    self-concept and, 36–39, 94, 95
    task performance, 16
    values and, 40–41
    in workplace. *See* Workplace behaviors
    Behavioral intentions, 72
Behavioral norms. *See* Norms
Behavioral perspective of leadership,
    219–220, 226
Behavior modeling, 66, 102
Behavior modification, 64–66
    ABCs of, 64
    contingencies of reinforcement, 64–65
    in practice, 65–66
    reinforcement schedules, 65
Beliefs, 72
Belongingness needs, 95, 96
Belz, Dorothee, 229
Bennett, Lucie, 138
Bennett, Steve, 282

Bennis, Warren, 226
Berg, Achim, 229
Berkshire Hathaway, 3
Berra, Yogi, 6
Best Buy, 87, 93, 281, 287
Best Practices Project, 19
Bethune, Gordon, 285
Biases. *See also* Stereotyping
    confirmation bias, 51, 125
    perceptual biases, 61
    in problem identification, 119–120
    self-enhancement, 37
    self-serving bias, 58
Bicultural audit, 266
Big Five personality dimensions,
    31–33, 216
Billing, Sean, 42–43
BioWare Corp., 247, 248
Bird, Brad, 79
Blake, R. R., 205n
Blanchard, Ken, 223
Blogs, 174
BMW, 245, 248–249, 249–250, 261
Boehnke, K., 41n
BofA (Bank of America), 256, 265
Bonaparte, Napoleon, 238, 238n
Bonding, 145, 153
Bonding drive, 99, 137, 166, 176–177
Bossidy, Larry, 125
"Bottom line," value of OB to, 6
Bounded rationality, 121
Boyatzis, R., 77n
BP (British Petroleum), 255,
    257–258, 259
Brainstorming, 156–157
Brand reputation, 15
Branson, Richard, 80
Brenneman, Greg, 285
British Broadcasting Corporation (BBC), 289, 291
British Petroleum (BP), 255,
    257–258, 259
Broadcast Australia, 143
Brooks's law, 139–140
"Brown paper" sessions, 275
Bryant, Elizabeth, 34
"Buddy system," 273
Buffering (buffers), 171, 208–209
Built to Last (Collins & Porras), 263
Bureau of Labor Statistics, U.S., 20n
Burning-platform strategy, 282
Burns, James McGregor, 225
Burton, Pierre, 104
Business ethics. *See* Ethics
Business knowledge, 217, 218
Business Objects, 208
"Bus rides," 282

C

Calcraft, Stef, 132
Calculative commitment, 82
Calculus-based trust, 151
Caldwell, D. F., 259*n*
Canadian Tire, 291
Capability building, 286
Capgemini, 15
Carnegie, Andrew, 293
Castrol Marine, 291
Categorical thinking, 53, 55, 56
Categorization, 54–55
Celestica, 249
Centrality, power and, 184, 186–187
Centralization, 240, 243, 251
CEOs (chief executive officers), 104, 228
Ceremonies, 261
Chain of command, 236, 242
Challenging goals, 105
Change, 40, 131, 184, 249, 292
Change agents, 279, 286–287
Changing jobs, 16, 17
Changing organizational culture, 267–269
    actions of founders and leaders, 268
    aligning artifacts, 268
    attraction–selection–attrition theory, 268–269
    culturally consistent rewards, 268
Charisma, 183, 226
Charismatic leadership, 226
Charismatic visionaries, 229–230
Chatman, J., 259*n*
Cheng, Albert, 214
Chief executive officers (CEOs), 104, 228
Child care support, 88
China National Petroleum, 5
Choices. *See also* Alternatives; Decision making
    choosing effectively, 124
    implementation of, 125
    intuition and, 123–124
    rational choice paradigm, 116–117
    role of emotions in, 117, 123
Choong, Lee Fong, 76
Chrysler Corporation, 170
Chrysler Group LLC, 115, 116
Churchill, Winston, 262
CIMB Group, 67
Circular logic, 228
Circumplex model of values, 40, 41
Cirque du Soleil, 263
Cisco, 73
Citigroup, Inc., 248
Clarity
    role clarity, 263, 280
    of self-concept, 36, 37
Client–consultant relationship, 288
Client divisional structure, 244, 245, 246
Client orientation, 265
Client relationships, 112
Closed systems, 7

Closing costs, 126
Clydesdale Bank, 69–70, 80–81
Coaching, 106–107, 230
Coalition formation, 188, 189
Coca-Cola Company, 3, 4, 244, 246
"Codebooks," 161
Coercion, 283, 285
Coercive power, 183
Cognition(s), 70, 73–74
Cognitive appraisal perspective, 83
Cognitive closure, 53
Cognitive dissonance, 74–75
Cognitive–emotional attitude
    process, 72–73
Cognitive intelligence, 130–131, 217, 218
Colgate-Palmolive, 138
Collaboration, 29, 205
Collective entities, 5
Collectivist cultures, 43–44, 207, 208
Collee, John, 133
Columbia disaster, 120
Comforting, 144, 145
Command-and-control approach, 13
Commitment
    decision commitment, 128, 129
    escalation of, 125–126
    goal commitment, 105, 208
    influence tactics and, 191
    organizational, 81–83
    to social issues, 14–15
    to strategic vision, 228
Communication, 158–177
    active listening and, 172–173
    among team members, 144, 145
    barriers to, 160, 163, 169–171
    computer-mediated, 162–164, 174
    conflict and, 198, 204, 208
    cross-cultural, 165, 171–172
    empathy in, 172, 173, 175
    face-to-face. *See* Face-to-face
        communication
    gender differences in, 172
    importance of, 160
    improving, 173–175, 208
    informal, 235, 236, 242, 251
    interpersonal, 142–143, 172–173
    knowledge sharing, 9, 247
    minimizing inequity through, 104
    model of, 160–161
    nonverbal. *See* Nonverbal communication
    oral, competency in, 29
    in organizational socialization, 269
    problems with, 20, 204
    in procedural justice, 104–105
    in reducing resistance to change, 282–284
    of strategic vision, 227
    in teams, 136, 142–143
    through "grapevine," 175–177
    with top management, 174–175
    written, 169

Emotional intelligence (EI), 77–78
  emotions as information, 123
  as leadership competency, 217, 218
  in reducing relationship conflict, 201
  role in motivation and behavior, 100
  virtual teams and, 153
Emotional labor, 75–76
Emotional markers, 50, 72, 123
Emotional meaning, 166
Emotional support, 58
Empathy
  in communication, 172, 173, 175
  cultural importance of, 171
  emotional intelligence and, 77
  meaningful interaction and, 63
Employee(s)
  age cohorts, 19–20, 20n, 73
  CEO/employee pay ratios, 104
  commitment to strategic vision, 228
  concerns about change, 280
  countervailing power of, 181
  high- or low-expectancy, 58
  influence of motivation on behavior, 89
  "managing," 225–226
  organizational socialization of, 269–272
  psychological characteristics of, 19–20
  resistance to change, 279–280
  retention of, 11
  as sensors of work environment, 128
  training. See Training and development
  well-being of, 12
Employee assistance programs (EAPs), 89
Employee dispute resolution, 211
Employee engagement, 92–93, 215
Employee-friendly organizational culture, 258
Employee involvement
  affective commitment and, 83
  communication and, 159
  in decision making, 127–129
  in HPWP, 12
  participative leadership style and, 221
  in reducing resistance to change, 283,
    284–285
Employee motivation. See Motivation
Employee turnover, 16, 17, 81, 272
Employee well-being, 12
Employment discrimination, 56, 57
Employment relationships, 20–21
Empowerment, 187, 215, 226, 230
Empowerment practices, 112–113
Enacted values, 257
Encoding, 160–161
Encounter stage, 270, 271
Enron Corporation, 46–47
Entitlement cultures, 265
Entrepreneurs, 97
Environmental responsibility, 7, 14, 255, 257–258
Epictetus, 173
Equal Employment Opportunity Commission, U.S. (EEOC), 57n
Equality principle, 103

Equity condition, 103
Equity principle, 103
Equity theory, 102–104
Ergon Energy, 138
Escalation of commitment, 125–126
Espoused–enacted values congruence, 42
Espoused values, 257, 258
Esteem needs, 96
Ethical principles, 45
Ethical sensitivity, 45–46
Ethics
  behavior and, 45–47
  of diversity, 20
  ethical reputation, 46
  job satisfaction and, 81
  organizational change and, 292
  organizational culture and, 265
  role of countercultures in, 259
  in stakeholder perspective, 13–14
  training in, 47
E-to-P expectancy, 100–102, 105
Eustress, 84, 87
Evaluation, 72–73, 107
  in action research approach, 289
  in active listening, 173
  of alternatives. See Alternatives
  of four-drive theory, 99–100
  of opportunities, 122
  of outcomes in decision making, 125–127
Evaluation apprehension, 154, 156, 157
Evaluation process, 123
Evers, A., 205n
Evidence-based management, 21–22
EVLN model of job satisfaction, 79–80
Exchange as influence tactic, 188, 190–191
Executive function of brain, 31
Exhaustion stage, 84
Exit, job satisfaction and, 79–80
Expectancy theory, 100–102
  components of, 100–101
    path–goal leadership theory and, 220
    in practice, 101–102
Expectations, 51–52, 58, 59, 271, 291
Experience(s), 208
  openness to, 31, 32, 33, 131
  past experiences, 94, 95, 206
  in path–goal leadership theory, 222
Experienced meaningfulness, 110
Experienced responsibility, 110
Experiential learning, 67
Experimentation, 9
Expert power, 183
Explicit knowledge, 63
External attributions, 57
External competition, 149–150
External environment(s)
  alignment with, 226, 264
  diversity in, 246
  divisional structure and, 244
  formalization and, 241

I

IAT (Implicit Association Test), 61
IBM, 14, 44, 62–63, 164, 174, 226, 246, 249, 257
ICICI Bank, 258
"Ideal worker norm," 85–86
Identification-based trust, 151
IKEA, 245
Imagination, 131
Impact, in empowerment, 112
Implicit Association Test (IAT), 61
Implicit-favorite comparison, 122
Implicit leadership theory, 228, 229
Impression management, 188, 190, 191, 271
Impuls Finanzmanagement, 73
Incompatible goals, 202
Incremental change, 289
Incubation, 129
Indianapolis, City of, 137
Indian State Railways, 5
Individual(s), 5–6, 16–17
Individual behavior. *See* Behavior
Individual differences
    job characteristics model and, 110
    in needs, 94–95
    needs hierarchy models and, 97
    in stress, 86–87
Individualistic cultures, 43–44
Individual-level analysis, 22, 23
Individual rights, 45, 292
Influence, 187. *See also* Power
    in leadership, 214–215
    situational influences, 46
Influence tactics, 187–192
    assertiveness, 188–189
    coalition formation, 188, 189
    consequences and contingencies of, 191–192
    exchange, 188, 190–191
    "hard" tactics, 188–189, 192, 205
    information control, 188, 189
    ingratiation/impression management, 188, 190, 191
    organizational politics and, 192–195
    persuasion, 188, 189–190
    in reducing resistance to change, 283, 285
    silent authority, 188
    "soft" tactics, 188, 189–191, 192
    upward appeal, 188, 189
Informal communication, 235, 236, 242, 251
Informal groups, 137
Informal roles, 147
Information
    for decision making, 162
    emotions as, 123
    knowledge contrasted, 11n
    manipulating access to, 189
    nonverbal cues, 165
    in preemployment socialization, 270–271
    sharing, 195
    as source of power, 183–184
Information control, 183–184, 188, 189, 239
Information explosion, 11, 11n
Information load, 171
Information overload, 163, 170–171
Information power, 183–184
Information processing, 121–122
Information processing capacity, 171
Ingram, Harry, 62
Ingratiation, 188, 190, 191
Inland Revenue and Customs/Excise (UK), 249
Inner purpose, 218–219
Innovative culture, 259
Innovative transformation, 8
Inoculation effect, 190
Inputs, 103
Inquisition, 210–211
Insight, 129–130
Instrumental values, 40
Integrated environments, 251
"Integration" perspective, 259
Integration strategy, 266, 267
Integrator roles, 236
Integrators, 209
Integrity, 29, 217, 218
Intel, 14, 201, 203–204
Intel Israel, 201
Intellectual capital, 10–11, 11–12, 185
Intel Technology India Pvt Ltd., 73
Intensity, 27–28
Intentional discrimination (prejudice), 56
Interdependence
    kinds of, 142, 143, 203
    power and, 180–181
    reducing, in conflict management, 208–209
    as source of conflict, 203, 239
    span of control and, 239
    in teams, 136
Intergenerational conflict, 203
Internal attributions, 57
Internal dispute resolution, 211
Internal Revenue Service, U.S., 244
Internal subsystems, 7–8
Internet-based businesses, 241
Internet-based communication, 174
Interpersonal communication
    active listening in, 172–173
    team structure and, 142–143
Interpersonal relations, 187
Interpersonal skills, 183, 230
Interpersonal skills training, 78, 247
Interventions, 289
Introversion, 32
Intuit, 282
Intuition, 123–124
Intuition orientation, 33
Ishiwatari, Mina, 279
Israeli Defense Force, 59

Mercedes, 249
Merck, 4
Mergers, 9, 203, 204, 208, 265–267
Merging Cultures Evaluation Index (MCEI), 265
Meridian Technology Centre, 273
Merrill Lynch, 255, 256, 265
Messages, 172, 173, 189–190
Metaphors, 227
Metropolitan Area Transit Authority (WMATA, Washington, DC), 25–26
Metropolitan Transit Authority (NYC), 184
M-form structure, 243
Micromanagement, 237
Microsoft Corporation, 4, 73, 202, 261
Microsoft Germany, 229
Milgram, Stanley, 182
Millennial employees, 20, 73
Mills, Deborah, 156
Mimicry, 165–166
Mintzberg, H., 236*n*
Misinterpretation, 163, 165
Mistakes, 67
Modeling strategic vision, 227–228
Models. *See also specific models*
   mental models. *See* Mental models
   of organizational culture, 258, 259
Mohr, B. J., 290*n*
Molson Coors, 47
Moods, 71
Moore, D. D., 145*n*
Moral intensity, 45, 46
Morphological analysis, 132
Mother, 132, 262–263
Motivation, 90–113
   absenteeism and, 17
   for diffusion of change, 287
   direction in, 27
   employee engagement and, 92–93
   empowerment and, 112–113
   expectancy theory of, 100–102
   feedback practices and, 106–107
   goal setting, 105–106
   influence on behavior, 89
   job design and, 108–112
   job satisfaction and, 80
   leadership motivation, 217, 218
   in MARS model, 27–28, 287
   needs and drives, 93–100
   organizational justice and, 102–105
   persistence and, 28
   perspectives of, 96–97
   in teams, 138–139, 140
   "telling" leadership style and, 223
   through job design, 109–110
Motivator–hygiene theory, 109
Motivators, 109
Motorola, 232
Moutin, J. S., 205*n*
MSN group (Microsoft), 202
Multicommunication, 168

Multiculturalism, 45
Multidisciplinary anchor of OB, 21, 22
Multidivisional structure, 243
Multiple levels of analysis, 22
Munificent environments, 251
Mutual understanding, 62
Muzyka, Ray, 247
MWH Global, 179
Myers-Briggs Type Indicator (MBTI), 33–34, 35, 123
MySpace, 137, 163
"Mythical man-month," 139–140

N

nAch (need for achievement), 97
Nadler, D. A., 236*n*
nAff (need for affiliation), 97, 131
Nahavandi, A., 266*n*
Nardelli, Robert, 170, 268, 277, 285
Nasser, Jacques, 276
National Aeronautics and Space Administration (NASA), 120, 155
National Australia Bank, 263
National Health Service (UK), 5, 185
Natural grouping, 111–112
Nature vs. nurture debate, 31
Nauta, A., 205*n*
Navteq, 234
Need for achievement (nAch), 97
Need for affiliation (nAff), 97, 131
Need for power (nPow), 97
Need principle, 103
Needs. *See also* Drive(s); *specific needs*
   individual differences in, 94–95
   kinds of, 95, 96, 98
   personal, teams and, 141
   relation to drives and behavior, 93–94
Needs theories
   four-drive theory, 98–100
   learned needs theory, 97–98
   needs hierarchy theory, 95–97
   problems with, 97
Negative feedback, 106–107
Negative reinforcement, 64–65
Neglect, 80
Negotiation, 191, 283, 285
Nestlé, 240, 244, 245
Nestlé UK, 148
Networking, 191
Network structure, 248–250
Neuroticism, 31, 32, 86
Newness, liability of, 242
New Zealand Post, 137
Nickelodeon, 214
Nilekani, Nandan, 264
Nin, Anaïs, 51
Nohria, Nitin, 98
Noise (barrier to communication), 160, 169–170
Nokia Corporation, 232–233, 235, 236–237
Nokia Siemens Networks, 234

Nominal group technique, 157
Nonprogrammed decisions, 117
Nonsocial sources of feedback, 107
Nontraditional workspaces, 132
Nonverbal communication, 164–166
    cross-cultural differences in, 165, 171–172
    emotional contagion and, 165–166
    persuasion and, 168
    verbal communication contrasted, 165
Nonverbal cues
    in communicating information, 165
    emotional meaning in, 166
    emotional support through, 58
    facial expressions, 163
    women more sensitive to, 172
Norming stage, 146, 147
Norm of reciprocity, 191
Norms
    cultural display rules, 75–76, 79, 201
    "divine discontent" norm, 120
    "ideal worker norm," 85–86
    management of group norms, 194
    organizational, 166
    performance-oriented, 223
    social norms, 94, 95
    team norms. See Team norms
Not-invented-here syndrome, 280–281
Nova Chemicals, 107
Novel situations, 163, 167–168, 237
nPow (need for power), 97
Nucor Corporation, 183, 239
Nugget Market, 73

O

OB. See Organizational behavior
Obeya, 142
Observational learning, 66
OCBs (organizational citizenship
    behaviors), 16–17
Occupational Safety and Health Administration
    (OSHA), 258
Office politics. See Organizational politics
Ogilvy, David, 260
Ohland, M. W., 145n
Oldham, G., 109n
OMD, 132
Omitting, 171
1-800-GOT-JUNK, 63, 174
Openness to change, 40, 131
Openness to experience, 31, 32, 33, 131
Open-space technology, 291
Open-systems perspective, 7–8, 264–265
Operant conditioning. See Behavior modification
Opportunities, 117, 122, 124
"Optimal conflict" perspective, 198–199
Optimism, 59
Oral communication competency, 29
O'Reilly, C. A., III, 259n
Organic structures, 241–242, 251

Organization(s), 5
    challenges to, 18–21
    conditions fostering creativity, 131–132
    large, decision making in, 251
    OCBs directed toward, 17
    project-based, 248
    stereotyping in, 55
Organizational behavior (OB), 3–23
    anchors of, 21–22
    challenges to organizations, 18–21
    ethics and, 45–47
    as field of study, 4–6
    individual behavior. See Behavior
    organizational citizenship, 16–17
    organizational effectiveness and. See Organizational
        effectiveness
    Project GLOBE, 19, 229–230
    self-concept and, 39
    self-fulfilling prophecy and, 59
Organizational change, 274–293
    action research approach to, 288–289
    appreciative inquiry approach to, 289–291
    change agents, 286–287
    cross-cultural and ethical issues, 292–293
    diffusion of, 287
    force field analysis model of, 277–281
    large group interventions, 291
    organizational politics and, 194
    parallel learning structure approach to, 291
    receptivity to, in adaptive cultures, 264–265
    strategic visions in, 282, 286–287, 298
    unfreezing, changing, and refreezing, 282–285
Organizational charts, 234, 242
Organizational citizenship behaviors
    (OCBs), 16–17
Organizational commitment, 81–83
Organizational comprehension, 83
Organizational culture, 254–273
    artifacts as symbols of, 260–263
    changing, 267–269
    content of, 258–259
    contingencies of, 264–265
    cultural fit, 268–269
    elements of, 256–258
    of ethical decision making, 47
    importance of, 263–264
    influence tactics in, 192
    learning orientation culture, 67, 112–113
    merging cultures, 265–267, 266–267
    relevance of transformational leadership in, 228
    role of countercultures, 259
    socialization to, 269–273
    subcultures, 259, 264
    values and. See Values
Organizational design, 250–253
    external environment and, 250–251
    organizational size and, 251
    organizational strategy and, 252–253
    technology and, 252
Organizational diagnosis, 288

Organizational effectiveness, 7–15
  culture strength and, 264–265
  HPWP perspective, 12
  open systems perspective, 7–8
  organizational learning perspective, 8–12
  role of strategic vision in, 227
  stakeholder perspective, 12–15
  teamwork and, 135–136
Organizational efficiency, 8, 226, 246, 250
Organizational environment, 141–142
Organizational goals, 5, 121, 129, 208, 221–222
Organizational justice, 102–105
  affective commitment and, 82–83
  equity theory, 102–104
  procedural justice, 104–105
Organizational learning
  absorptive capacity in, 10
  organic structures and, 241–242
  organizational "unlearning," 285
  strategies for, 9
  undermined by formalization, 241
  virtual teams and, 153
Organizational learning perspective, 8–12, 160
Organizational-level analysis, 22, 23
Organizational memory, 11–12
Organizational politics, 192–195
  ambiguous rules and, 204
  conditions supporting, 193–195
  extreme, example of, 194
  fueled by conflict, 198
  influence tactics perceived as, 193
  minimizing, 194–195
  opinions regarding, 193
  personal characteristics and, 194
Organizational size, 251
Organizational socialization, 269–273
  improving process, 272–273
  learning and adjustment, 269–270
  socialization agents in, 273
  stages of, 270–272
Organizational status, 162–163, 192
Organizational stories, 176
Organizational strategy, 252–253
Organizational structure, 232–253
  centralization and decentralization, 240
  contingencies of organizational design, 250–253
  coordination, 235–237
  departmentalization. *See* Departmentalization
  division of labor, 235
  formalization in, 241
  mechanistic vs. organic, 241–242
  nature of, 234
  span of control, 238–240
Organizational systems, 281
Organizational "unlearning," 285
Organizational values, 40, 255, 257–258
OSHA (Occupational Safety and Health Administration), 258
Outcome/input ratio, 103

Outcomes, 103, 137
Outcomes evaluation, 125–127
  escalation of commitment and, 125–126
  improving, 126–127
Outcome valences, 100, 101, 102
Output standardization, 237
Overreward inequity, 103
Overt acts, 17
Oyserman, D., 43*n*

P

Page, Kevin, 69, 80–81
Palmisano, Sam, 226, 245, 246
Parallel learning structure approach, 291
Park Place Dealerships, 269
Participative leadership style, 221, 222, 223, 230
Participative management. *See* Employee involvement
Past experiences, 94, 95, 206
Path–goal leadership theory, 220–223
  contingencies of, 222–223
  leadership styles, 220–222
  leadership substitutes compared, 224
Patterson, Robert, 258
Pay ratio, CEO/employee, 104
Peer arbitration, 211
Peer pressure, 183
People-oriented leadership, 219, 220, 221, 293
PepsiCo, 20
Perceiving orientation, 33, 34
Perception(s), 49–67
  attribution theory and, 56–58
  as barrier to communication, 169
  evidence and, 49–50
  improving perceptions, 61–63
  leadership and, 228
  learning and. *See* Learning; Organizational learning
  meaningful interaction and, 62–63
  perceptual bias, 61
  perceptual errors, 59–60
  process of. *See* Perceptual process
  reward inequity and, 104
  role perceptions, 27, 29, 287
  self-awareness, 61–62
  self-fulfilling prophecy, 58–59
  social identity and stereotyping, 54–56
  stress perceptions, 88
Perceptual biases, 61
Perceptual blindness, 52, 126
Perceptual defense, 120
Perceptual errors, 59–60
Perceptual grouping, 53
Perceptual misalignment, 52
Perceptual process, 37, 50–54
Performance
  benefits of teams to, 139
  contextual, 16–17
  job satisfaction and, 80
  key indicators of, 105

Prospect theory, 126
Prototypes, 120, 228
Proximity, 46
Psychological effects of stress, 84
Psychological harassment, 85
Psychological states, 110
Psychological support, 221
P-to-O expectancy, 100, 101, 102
Punishment, 64, 65
Purpose of teams, 136
PwC (PricewaterhouseCoopers), 34, 36, 138

Q

Quantum change, 289
Quid pro quo harassment, 85

R

Racial slurs, 56
Rackspace Hosting, Inc., 91–92, 100, 106, 137, 145
Rahim, M. A., 205*n*
"Rapport talk," 172
Rational choice paradigm, 116–117, 121, 122
Raytheon, 187
Razak, Datuk Nazir, 67
Razer, 73
Reactive drives, 99
Realistic job preview, 272–273
Reality shock, 271
Recency effect, 60
Reciprocal interdependence, 142, 143, 203
Reduced personal accomplishment, 85
Redundancy, 161
Referent power, 183, 186
Refreezing, 277, 285
Reinforcement, 66, 102, 286
    contingencies of, 64–65
    of team norms, 148–149
Reinforcement schedules, 64–65
Reinforcement theory, 64
Relational nature of leadership, 19
Relationship(s)
    building, 172, 269, 272
    client relationships, 112
    employment relationships, 20–21
    with stakeholders, 12–13
Relationship capital, 11
Relationship conflict, 200–201, 204
Relationship management, 77–78
Relevant goals, 105
Reliance Industries, 11
"Report talk," 172
Research in Motion (RIM), 234, 266
Research studies
    action research, 288–289
    on empowerment, 113
    first impression studies, 53
    on groupthink, 155

on Maslow's hierarchy of needs, 96
    in submission to authority, 182
    teamwork in, 135
Resilience, 86, 89
Resistance stage, 84
Resistance to change, 277–278
    reasons for, 280–281, 285
    as resource for change, 279–280
    restraining forces. *See* Restraining forces
    strategies for reducing, 282–285
    subtle vs. overt, 278–279
    unmet expectations and, 291
Resistance to influence tactics, 191
ResMed, 228
Resource(s)
    controlling access to, 184
    increasing, in conflict management, 209
    inefficient use of, 246
    job resources, 86
    scarcity as source of conflict, 203–204, 209
Resource allocation, 184, 193–194
Respectful culture, 259
Responding, 173
Responsibility, 257–258
Restraining forces, 277–281
    employee resistance as resource, 279–280
    reasons for resistance, 280–281
    reducing, 282–285
    weakening, 281–282
Restricted entry, 149
Results-driven orientation, 29
Results-only work environment (ROWE), 87, 287, 291
"Retail boot camps," 291
Reverse engineering, 11
Reward(s)
    in behavior modification, 65
    culturally consistent, 268
    differential, 258
    in directive leadership, 221
    in HPWP model, 12
    increasing P-to-O expectancy, 102
    performance linked to, 80, 224
Reward inequity, 103–104
"Reward inflation," 66
Reward power, 182–183
Reward systems, 224, 267, 268
Richard, Stephane, 83
RIM (Research in Motion), 234, 266
Risk of conflict, 128, 129
Rituals, 261
RMSI Private Limited, 73
Rogers Cable Communications Inc., 47
Rokeach, Milton, 40
Role(s)
    formal and informal, 147, 181
    separation of, 126–127
    team roles, 147
    in work coordination, 236
Role ambiguity, 247
Role clarity, 263, 280

in a nutshell

Organizational behavior, which is the study of what people think, feel, and do in and around organizations, is important for organizational effectiveness as well as individual career success. Organizational effectiveness is a multidimensional concept represented by open systems, organizational learning, high-performance work practices, and stakeholder perspectives. The five main types of individual behavior in organizations are task performance, organizational citizenship, counterproductive work behaviors, joining and staying with the organization, and work attendance. Three environmental shifts that are challenging organizations include globalization, increasing workforce diversity, and emerging employment relationships. Organizational behavior knowledge is based on the multidisciplinary anchor, systematic research anchor, contingency anchor, and multiple levels of analysis anchor.

The following questions will test your takeaway knowledge from this chapter. How well can you answer each of them?

LO.1. Define *organizational behavior* and *organizations,* and discuss the importance of this field of inquiry.

LO.2. Compare and contrast the four perspectives of organizational effectiveness.

LO.3. Summarize the five types of individual behavior in organizations.

LO.4. Debate the organizational opportunities and challenges of globalization, workforce diversity, and emerging employment relationships.

LO.5. Discuss the anchors on which organizational behavior knowledge is based.

Copyright © 2012 by The McGraw-Hill Companies. ISBN 0078029414 | McShane M 1e

Did your answers include the following important points?

LO.1. Define *organizational behavior* and *organizations,* and discuss the importance of this field of inquiry.

- Organizational behavior is the study of what people think, feel, and do in and around organizations.
- Organizations are groups of people who work interdependently toward some purpose.
- OB theories help people to (1) make sense of the workplace, (2) question and rebuild their personal mental models, and (3) get things done in organizations.

LO.2. Compare and contrast the four perspectives of organizational effectiveness.

- The open systems perspective views organizations as complex living organisms that receive resources and feedback from the external environment and return desirable and undesirable outputs to that environment. Organizations also consist of numerous subsystems, which transform inputs into various outputs.
- The organizational learning perspective states that organizational effectiveness increases with the organization's capacity to acquire, share, use, and store valuable knowledge.
- The high-performance work practices (HPWP) perspective identifies bundles of systems and structures that leverage workforce potential. The most widely identified HPWPs are employee involvement, job autonomy, developing employee competencies, and rewarding performance and skill development.
- The stakeholder perspective states that leaders manage the interests of diverse stakeholders by relying on their personal and organizational values for guidance. This perspective emphasizes ethics and corporate social responsibility.

LO.3. Summarize the five types of individual behavior in organizations.

- Task performance refers to goal-directed behaviors under the individual's control that support organizational objectives.

- Organizational citizenship behaviors (OCBs) are various forms of cooperation and helpfulness to others that support the organization's social and psychological context.
- Counterproductive work behaviors (CWBs) are voluntary behaviors that have the potential to directly or indirectly harm the organization.
- The other two types of individual behavior in organizations are joining and staying with the organization and work attendance.

LO.4. Debate the organizational opportunities and challenges of globalization, workforce diversity, and emerging employment relationships.

- Globalization offers larger markets, lower costs, and greater access to knowledge and innovation, but it may also be responsible for increasing work intensification, as well as reducing job security and work/life balance in developed countries.
- Diversity can become a competitive advantage by improving decision making and team performance on complex tasks, yet it brings numerous problems such as "fault lines" in informal group dynamics, slower team performance, and interpersonal conflict.
- Emerging employment relationships, including concerns about work-life balance and work flexibility through virtual work, potentially increase employee productivity and reduce employee stress.

LO.5. Discuss the anchors on which organizational behavior knowledge is based.

- The multidisciplinary anchor states that the field should develop from knowledge in other disciplines (e.g., psychology, sociology, economics), not just from its own isolated research base.
- The systematic research anchor states that OB knowledge should be based on systematic research, which is consistent with evidence-based management.
- The contingency anchor states that OB theories generally need to consider that there will be different consequences in different situations.
- The multiple levels of analysis anchor states that OB topics may be viewed from the individual, team, and organization levels of analysis.

Practical Application

LO.1.
- Organizations consist of people who interact with each other in a/an _____ way.
- OB knowledge is valuable because it helps people to _____ what is happening in the organization.

LO.2.
- Acme Corporation is very effective at transforming raw materials and labor (inputs) into final products and services (outputs). From the open systems perspective, Acme Corporation has a high degree of organizational _____.
- From the organizational learning perspective, organizational effectiveness depends on the organization's capacity to _____, share, use, and store valuable knowledge.
- Zap Electrical carefully selects job applicants for their skills and invests heavily in further training of its employees. Zap Electrical is practicing the high-performance work practice of strengthening employee _____.
- Satisfying stakeholder interests is challenging because stakeholders have _____ interests.

LO.3.
- Task performance refers to goal-directed _____ under the individual's control that support organizational objectives.
- Companies with high turnover suffer because vital _____ is often lost when people leave the organization.

LO.4.
- Organizations _____ when they actively participate in other countries and cultures.
- Jenny works in an organization that implicitly rewards people for their face time as much as their performance output. Given these conditions, Jenny should probably avoid participating in the emerging employment practice of _____.

LO.5.
- The field of organizational behavior encourages corporate leaders to make decisions based on _____.
- The contingency anchor states that the most appropriate action often depends on the _____.

in a nutshell

Individual behavior is influenced by motivation, ability, role perceptions, and situational factors (MARS). Most personality traits are represented within the five-factor model. Self-concept consists of complexity, consistency, and clarity, and people engage in self-enhancement, self-verification, self-evaluation, and social identity processes. People arrange their personal values into a hierarchy of preferences. Five values that differ across cultures are individualism, collectivism, power distance, uncertainty avoidance, and achievement–nurturing orientation. Three factors that influence ethical conduct are moral intensity, ethical sensitivity, and situational factors.

The following questions will test your takeaway knowledge from this chapter. How well can you answer each of them?

LO.1. Describe the four factors that directly influence voluntary individual behavior and performance.

LO.2. Describe personality, the "Big Five" personality traits, and the MBTI types.

LO.3. Describe self-concept and explain how social identity theory relates to a person's self-concept.

LO.4. Describe Schwartz's model of individual values as well as five values commonly studied across cultures, and identify the conditions under which values influence behavior.

LO.5. Discuss three factors that influence ethical behavior.

Copyright © 2012 by The McGraw-Hill Companies. ISBN 0078029414 | McShane M 1e

Did your answers include the following important points?

LO.1. Describe the four factors that directly influence voluntary individual behavior and performance.

- Four variables—motivation, ability, role perceptions, and situational factors, which are represented by the acronym MARS—direct influence individual behavior and performance.

- Motivation represents the forces within a person that affect his or her direction, intensity, and persistence of voluntary behavior; ability includes both the natural aptitudes and the learned capabilities required to successfully complete a task; role perceptions are the extent to which people understand the job duties (roles) assigned to them or expected of them; situational factors include conditions beyond the employee's immediate control that constrain or facilitate behavior and performance.

LO.2. Describe personality, the "Big Five" personality traits, and the MBTI types.

- Personality is the relatively enduring pattern of thoughts, emotions, and behaviors that characterize a person, along with the psychological processes behind those characteristics.

- The "Big Five" personality dimensions include conscientiousness, agreeableness, neuroticism, openness to experience, and extraversion.

- Based on Jungian personality theory, the Myers-Briggs Type Indicator (MBTI) identifies competing orientations for getting energy (extraversion vs. introversion), perceiving information (sensing vs. intuiting), making decisions (thinking vs. feeling), and orienting to the external world (judging vs. perceiving).

LO.3. Describe self-concept and explain how social identity theory relates to a person's self-concept.

- Self-concept, the individual's self-beliefs and self-evaluations, has degrees of complexity, consistency, and clarity.

- People inherently promote and protect a positive self-concept (self-enhancement), stabilize their self-concept through self-verification, engage in self-evaluation, and anchor their self-concept through social identity processes.

- Social identity theory states that people define themselves by the groups to which they belong or have an emotional attachment.

LO.4. Describe Schwartz's model of individual values as well as five values commonly studied across cultures, and identify the conditions under which values influence behavior.

- Schwartz's model organizes values—stable, evaluative beliefs that guide our preferences for outcomes or courses of action in a variety of situations—into a circumplex of ten dimensions along two bipolar dimensions: openness to change to conservation and self-enhancement to self-transcendence.

- Values influence behavior under three conditions: (1) we can think of specific reasons for doing so, (2) when the situation supports those values, and (3) when we actively think about them.

- Five values that are often studied across cultures are individualism (valuing independence and personal uniqueness); collectivism (valuing duty to in-groups and to group harmony); power distance (valuing unequal distribution of power); uncertainty avoidance (tolerating or feeling threatened by ambiguity and uncertainty); and achievement-nurturing orientation (valuing competition vs. cooperation).

LO.5. Discuss three factors that influence ethical behavior.

- Ethical behavior is influenced by the degree to which an issue demands the application of ethical principles (moral intensity), the individual's ability to recognize the presence and relative importance of an ethical issue (ethical sensitivity), and situational forces.

Practical Application

LO.1.

- The _____ model identifies the four direct predictors of individual behavior and performance.

- Motivation represents the forces within a person that affect his or her direction, intensity, and _____ of voluntary behavior.

LO.2.

- A basic premise of personality theory is that people have inherent _____ that can be identified by the consistency or stability of their behavior across time and situations.

- _____ are more inclined to direct their interests to ideas than to social events.

LO.3.

- Jack is reluctant to accept feedback that is inconsistent with his self-concept. Jack is engaging in _____.

- An individual's self-concept includes self-evaluation, which consists of self-esteem, self-efficacy, and _____.

- According to _____, people define themselves by the groups to which they belong or have an emotional attachment.

LO.4.

- People are more likely to apply values when they are _____ of them.

- Soo Lin defines herself by her group memberships, and she values harmonious relationships. Soo Lin likely has a high level of the _____ value.

LO.5.

- _____ is a personal characteristic that enables people to recognize the presence of an ethical issue and determine its relative importance.

- Pradeep faces a problem that he and other executives agree will have serious consequences for both customers and shareholders. From an ethical perspective, this issue has high _____.

in a nutshell

Perception involves selecting, organizing, and interpreting information to make sense of the world around us. There are several perceptual processes, including stereotyping, attribution, and self-fulfilling prophecy, which can operate or be minimized in beneficial ways. Four other perceptual errors are the halo effect, primacy effect, recency effect, and false consensus effect. Learning is a relatively permanent change in behavior (or behavior tendency) that occurs as a result of a person's interaction with the environment. Learning occurs through behavior modification, social learning, and experiential learning processes.

The following questions will test your takeaway knowledge from this chapter. How well can you answer each of them?

LO.1. Outline the perceptual process.

LO.2. Discuss the effects of stereotyping, attribution, self-fulfilling prophecy, halo, primacy, recency, and false-consensus effects on the perceptual process.

LO.3. Discuss three ways to improve social perception, with specific application to organizational situations.

LO.4. Describe and compare the three perspectives of learning in organizations.

Copyright © 2012 by The McGraw-Hill Companies. ISBN 0078029414 | McShane M 1e

Did your answers include the following important points?

LO.1. Outline the perceptual process.

- Perception—the process of receiving information about and making sense of the world around us—begins when environmental stimuli are received through our senses; the process of selective attention then applies to select and screen out stimuli.
- Perception also organizes and interprets the incoming information through categorical thinking, the emotional marker process, and mental models.
- Perception begins when environmental stimuli are received through our senses and screened through the process of selection attention. Stimuli are then organized and interpreted through categorical thinking, the emotional marker process, and mental models.

LO2. Discuss the effects of stereotyping, attribution, and self-fulfilling prophecy on the perceptual process.

- Stereotyping involves (1) developing categories of identifiable groups; (2) assigning people to one or more social categories based on easily observable information about them; and (3) assigning non-observable traits associated with the stereotype group to the individual identified with that group.
- The attribution process involves deciding whether an observed behavior or event is caused mainly by the person (internal factors) or by the environment (external factors). Two attribution errors are fundamental attribution error and self-serving bias.
- Self-fulfilling prophecy occurs when our expectations about another person cause that person to act in a way that is consistent with those expectations. This effect is stronger at the beginning of a relationship, when several people hold the same expectations of the individual, and among people with a history of low achievement.

LO3. Discuss three ways to improve social perception, with specific application to organizational situations.

- People can reduce perceptual biases by (1) knowing that they exist; (2) becoming more aware of biases in their own decisions and behavior (such as through the Johari Window process); and (3) interacting more with people with whom they tend to have biased perceptions. The third option, called meaningful interaction, is more powerful when people work toward a shared goal on a meaningful task in which they need to rely on each other in positions of relatively equal status.

LO4. Describe and compare the three perspectives of learning in organizations.

- The three perspectives of learning in organizations are behavior modification, social learning theory, and experiential learning.
- The central objective of behavior modification is to change behavior (B) by managing its antecedents (A) and consequences (C). This theory identifies four types of consequences—positive reinforcement, punishment, negative reinforcement, and extinction—as well as several schedules of reinforcement.
- Social learning theory states that much learning occurs by observing others and then modeling the behaviors that lead to favorable outcomes and avoiding behaviors that lead to punishing consequences. This theory emphasizes the role of logic and observation in the learning process, as well as the ability to engage in self-reinforcement.
- Experiential learning occurs through our interaction with the environment, but also includes reflection on that experience as well as forming and testing theories. Experiential learning benefits when the organization and its employees possess a strong learning orientation.

Practical Application

LO.1.

- When information is received through the senses, our brain quickly attaches _____ to information that is initially deemed to be relevant.
- _____ thinking refers to the mostly nonconscious process of organizing people and objects into preconceived categories that are stored in our long-term memory.
- Mental models consist of visual or relational _____ in our minds.

LO.2.

- Although people can learn to minimize the application of stereotypical information, it is difficult to prevent the _____ of stereotypes in our perceptual process.
- Josh has just made a fundamental attribution error regarding the reasons why a coworker has arrived late. Specifically, Josh has attributed the coworker's lateness to _____ factors.
- During the self-fulfilling prophecy process, supervisors tend to give high-expectancy employees more challenging _____.

LO.3.

- Comtech Corporation has introduced a team-building exercise that incorporates the Johari Window. Accordingly, this exercise attempts to improve perceptual awareness among coworkers by increasing each employee's _____ window to others on the team.
- Meaningful interaction is more likely to improve perceptions of others involved in the interaction when everyone has equal or similar _____.

LO.4.

- The _____ model explains how learning occurs through behavior modification.
- In most workplace situations, positive reinforcement should follow desired behaviors and _____ should follow undesirable behaviors.
- Liam continued working on his class assignment until he completed a previously set goal, then took a well-deserved break. According to social learning theory, Liam has engaged in _____.

in a nutshell

Emotions play a central role in employee attitudes, which consists of beliefs, feelings, and behavioral intentions. Emotional labor, which is often stressful, is most common in jobs requiring a variety of emotions, more intense emotions, and frequent or long interaction with others. Emotional intelligence includes four components arranged in a hierarchy: self-awareness, self-management, social awareness, and relationship management. Two of the most important workplace attitudes are job satisfaction and organizational commitment. Stress, an adaptive response to a situation that is perceived as challenging or threatening, is caused by stressors, but there are individual differences in the level of stress experienced.

The following questions will test your takeaway knowledge from this chapter. How well can you answer each of them?

LO.1. Explain how emotions and cognition (conscious reasoning) influence attitudes and behavior.

LO.2. Discuss the dynamics of emotional labor and the role of emotional intelligence in the workplace.

LO.3. Summarize the consequences of job dissatisfaction as well as strategies to increase organizational (affective) commitment.

LO.4. Describe the stress experience and review three major stressors.

LO.5. Identify five ways to manage workplace stress.

Copyright © 2012 by The McGraw-Hill Companies. ISBN 0078029414 | McShane M 1e

Did your answers include the following important points?

LO.1. Explain how emotions and cognition (conscious reasoning) influence attitudes and behavior.

- Emotions are physiological, behavioral, and psychological episodes experienced toward someone or something that create a state of readiness, whereas attitudes are beliefs, assessed feelings, and behavioral intentions.
- Emotions influence attitudes through emotional markers formed as soon as we receive information about the attitude object.
- Cognitive dissonance occurs when we perceive an inconsistency between our beliefs, feelings, and behavior, and the tension produced by this inconsistency motivates people to change their beliefs and feelings to reduce the inconsistency.

LO.2. Discuss the dynamics of emotional labor and the role of emotional intelligence in the workplace.

- Emotional labor refers to the effort, planning, and control needed to express organizationally desired emotions during interpersonal transactions.
- Conflict between required and true emotions is called emotional dissonance.
- Emotional intelligence (EI), the ability to recognize and regulate emotions in oneself and others, consists of four elements: self-awareness, self-management, social awareness, and relationships

LO.3. Summarize the consequences of job dissatisfaction as well as strategies to increase organizational (affective) commitment.

- Job satisfaction is a person's evaluation of his or her job and work context.
- The four ways that employees respond to job dissatisfaction is explained in the exit-voice-loyalty-neglect (EVLN) model.

- Job satisfaction has a moderately positive influence on job performance as well as on customer satisfaction.
- Organizational (affective) commitment is the employee's emotional attachment to, identification with, and involvement in a particular organization, whereas continuance commitment is a calculative attachment, whereby employees feel bound to remain because it would be too costly to quit.
- Five strategies for increasing organizational (affective) commitment are justice and support, shared values, trust, organizational comprehension, and employee involvement.

LO.4. Describe the stress experience and review three major stressors.

- Stress is an adaptive response to a situation that is perceived as challenging or threatening to the person's well-being.
- The stress experience, called the general adaptation syndrome, involves moving through three stages: alarm, resistance, and exhaustion.
- Stressors are the causes of stress and include any environmental conditions that place a physical or emotional demand on the person. Three significant stressors in the workplace are harassment/incivility, work overload, and low task control. People have different stress responses to the same stressor due to different thresholds to resistance, different coping strategies, and different levels of resilience.

LO.5. Identify five ways to manage workplace stress.

- Five types of strategies to minimize stress in the workplace are to remove the stressor, withdraw from the stressor, change stress perceptions, control stress consequences, and receive social support.

Practical Application

LO.1.
- The traditional attitude model consists of three components, including beliefs, _____, and behavioral intentions.
- Drew has just learned that a difficult manager from another department is about to become his new boss. According to the emerging model of work attitudes, Drew's attitude toward his new boss was partly formed by _____ before he logically thought through his beliefs and feelings about this manager.

LO.2.
- Unlike surface acting, deep acting involves _____ true emotions to match the required emotions.
- Yuki has an excellent ability to empathize with other people she meets. In the emotional intelligence model, Yuki would have a high degree of _____.

LO.3.
- The relationship between job satisfaction and performance is stronger where employees have more _____ over their job output.
- Employees with higher job satisfaction tend to provide better customer service because these employees are usually in a more _____ mood at work.

- Employees have high _____ commitment when they do not particularly identify with the organization but feel bound to remain there because it would be too costly to quit.
- NYC Widgets keeps employees up to date about organizational events, ensures that they understand functions of different parts of the organization, and teaches them about the organization's history. NYC Widgets is likely strengthening organizational commitment in its workers by improving their organizational _____.

LO.4.
- The general adaptation syndrome process has three stages, the last of which is _____.
- Even when he is under intense pressure, Carlos tries to ignore that stress and deny that he is feeling stressed. Amelia, one of his coworkers, has the same stressors but seeks social support from her friends when the stress becomes quite strong. Carlos suffers more than Amelia from the work stressors, most likely because Carlos relies on a less effective _____ strategy.

LO.5.
- One of the most important ways to _____ stressors is to assign employees to jobs that match their skills and preferences.
- Some forms of humor in the workplace can help employees to manage stress by reducing stress _____.

in a nutshell

Motivation is one of the four main influences on employee performance. Motivation originates with drives and emotions, which produce needs. Motivation is guided by expected performance and its outcomes, as well as distributive and procedural justice in the distribution of valued outcomes. Job characteristics also motivate employees.

The following questions will test your takeaway knowledge from this chapter. How well can you answer each of them?

LO.1. Explain how human drives result in employee motivation, and describe the three drive/need-based theories of motivation (needs hierarchy, learned needs, and four-drive theories).

LO.2. Explain employee motivation using expectancy, organizational justice, and goal setting/feedback theories.

LO.3. Compare and contrast job design approaches that increase work efficiency versus work motivation, and describe three strategies for improving employee motivation through job design.

LO.4. Define *empowerment* and identify strategies that support empowerment.

Copyright © 2012 by The McGraw-Hill Companies. ISBN 0078029414 | McShane M 1e

Did your answers include the following important points?

LO.1. Explain how human drives result in employee motivation, and describe the three drive/need-based theories of motivation (needs hierarchy, learned needs, and four-drive theories).

- Employee motivation originates with innate drives, which produce emotions that energize us to act on our environment. Needs are goal-directed forces that people experience as a result of emotions.
- Maslow's needs hierarchy theory, which identifies five needs categories as well as two needs not in the hierarchy, states that we are motivated mainly by the lowest unsatisfied need.
- McClelland studied how need strength can be altered through social influences, particularly with regard to the need for achievement, need for power, and need for affiliation.
- Four-drive theory states that everyone has four innate drives—the drive to acquire, bond, learn, and defend—which activate emotions regulated through a skill set that considers social norms, past experience, and personal values.

LO.2. Explain employee motivation using expectancy, organizational justice, and goal setting/feedback theories.

- Expectancy theory states that work effort is determined by the perception that effort will result in a particular level of performance (E-to-P expectancy), the perception that a specific behavior or performance level will lead to specific outcomes (P-to-O expectancy), and the valences that the person feels for those outcomes.
- Equity theory states that people are motivated to reduce the emotional tension by increasing or decreasing outcomes or inputs or oneself or the comparison other, by changing perceptions of the situation, or by changing the comparison other.
- Procedural justice increases by giving employees voice to the issue, and by ensuring that the decision maker is perceived as unbiased, relies on complete and accurate information, applies existing policies consistently, and has listened to all sides of the dispute.

- Goals are more effective when they are specific, relevant, and challenging; have employee commitment; are accompanied by meaningful feedback; and are usually participative. Effective feedback is specific, relevant, timely, credible, and sufficiently frequent.

LO.3. Compare and contrast job design approaches that increase work efficiency versus work motivation, and describe three strategies for improving employee motivation through job design.

- Job specialization increases work efficiency by speeding up task mastery, reducing time changing tasks, requiring less training, and allowing better matching of job duties with employee skills. However, high specialization tends to undermine employee motivation.
- The job characteristics model identifies five core job characteristics that motivate employees: skill variety, task identity, task significance, autonomy, and job feedback.
- The three strategies for improving employee motivation through job design are job rotation, whereby employees move to different workstations every few hours; job enlargement, in which tasks are added to an existing job; and job enrichment, which occurs when employees are given more responsibility for scheduling, coordinating, and planning their own work.

LO.4. Define *empowerment* and identify strategies that support empowerment.

- Empowerment—the psychological condition of self-determination, meaning, competence, and impact—increases when employees possess the necessary competencies, work in jobs with a high degree of autonomy and minimal bureaucratic control, have access to information and other resources, and work in companies with a learning orientation culture.

Practical Application

LO.1.

- _____, social norms, and past experience amplify or suppress drive-based emotions as well as regulate a person's motivated decisions and behavior.
- Maslow's needs hierarchy theory organizes primary needs into a hierarchy of five categories, with _____ at the top of the hierarchy.
- Four-drive theory states that the _____ generated by the four drives motivate us to act.

LO.2.

- Expectancy theory consists of three main elements: effort-to-performance expectancy, _____, and outcome valences.
- Yasmin recently discovered that she is paid more than a coworker whom she considers somewhat more experienced and capable at the job. A common response to this feeling of overreward inequity is that Yasmin will likely change her _____ to justify this situation.
- Goal setting improves performance by motivating employees and clarifying their _____.

LO.3.

- Very high levels of job specialization tend to reduce employee _____.
- Steve works on an assembly line that manufactures a complex aircraft engine component. His work on the line has a short two-minute cycle, representing a very small part of the entire assembly of the aircraft component, so he doesn't know quite how his work relates to the entire component. According to the job characteristics model, Steve likely has low task _____.
- Natural grouping of tasks and establishing client relationships are forms of job _____.

LO.4.

- Empowerment has four dimensions, including _____, meaning, competence, and impact.
- Employees are much more likely to experience empowerment (particularly the self-determination dimension) when working in jobs with a high degree of _____.

chapter SIX

in a nutshell

Decision making, the process of making choices among alternatives with the intention of moving toward some desired state of affairs, is a vital function for an organization's health. People usually strive for rational analysis, but they face several impediments to pure rationality, and this goal ignores the inherent role of emotions in decision making. Decision making also includes consideration of involving others in the process and engaging in creative thinking.

The following questions will test your takeaway knowledge from this chapter. How well can you answer each of them?

LO.1. Describe the rational choice paradigm.

LO.2. Explain why people differ from the rational choice paradigm when identifying problems/opportunities, evaluating/choosing alternatives, and evaluating decision outcomes.

LO.3. Discuss the roles of emotions and intuition in decision making.

LO.4. Describe the benefits of employee involvement and identify four contingencies that affect the optimal level of employee involvement.

Copyright © 2012 by The McGraw-Hill Companies. ISBN 0078029414 | McShane M 1e

Did your answers include the following important points?

LO.1. Describe the rational choice paradigm.

- The rational choice paradigm of decision making includes identifying problems and opportunities, choosing the best decision style, developing alternative solutions, choosing the best solution, implementing the selected alternative, and evaluating decision outcomes.

LO.2. Explain why people differ from the rational choice paradigm when identifying problems/opportunities, evaluating/choosing alternatives, and evaluating decision outcomes.

- Stakeholder framing, mental models, decisive leadership, and solution-oriented focus affect our ability to rationally identify problems and opportunities.
- People do not evaluate and choose alternatives rationally due to ambiguous or conflicting goals, limited information processing capabilities, perceptually distorted information, sequential evaluation of choices, and the tendency to satisfice.
- People differ from rational choice in evaluating decision outcomes due to confirmation bias and escalation of commitment. Escalation is caused by self-justification, prospect theory effect, perceptual blinders, and closing costs.

LO.3. Discuss the roles of emotions and intuition in decision making.

- Emotions influence our preferences through the emotional marker process (where incoming information is tagged with emotions).
- The decision maker's mood and current emotions influence attention and detail in evaluating alternatives.
- People deliberately listen in on their emotions to influence their choices.
- Intuition—the ability to know when a problem or opportunity exists and to select the best course of action without conscious reasoning—consists of emotional signals that signal problems or opportunities based on established mental models of the situation.

LO.4. Describe the benefits of employee involvement and identify four contingencies that affect the optimal level of employee involvement.

- Employee involvement tends to improve (1) problem recognition, (2) the number and quality of possible solutions, (3) the evaluation of alternatives, and (4) employee commitment to the decision.
- The optimal level of employee involvement depends on (1) whether the decision is programmed or nonprogrammed, (2) whether subordinates have additional information beyond the leader's knowledge to improve decision quality, (3) whether employees are unlikely to accept a decision made without their involvement, and (4) whether employees with have unresolvable conflict with each other or with organizational goals when choosing among alternatives.

LO.5. Describe employee characteristics, workplace conditions, and specific activities that support creativity.

- Four employee characteristics that improve creative potential are intelligence, persistence, knowledge and experience, and a cluster of personality traits and values representing independent imagination.
- Workplace conditions that support creativity include a learning orientation culture, motivation from the job itself (particularly task significance and autonomy), open communication, sufficient resources to perform the job, and support from leaders and coworkers.
- Three sets of activities that help employees think more creatively are: (a) redefining the problem, (b) associative play activities, and (c) cross-pollination.

Practical Application

LO.1.

- The decision-making step of identifying possible solutions usually begins by searching for _____ solutions.
- Alissa and her executive team are about to choose the best supplier of chemical materials for their company's production process. Several vendors have been carefully evaluated. According to the rational choice paradigm, Alissa's executive team should choose the supplier with the highest _____.

LO.2.

- A potentially useful opportunity is often dismissed when it differs from our existing _____.
- Decision makers typically evaluate alternatives _____ rather than all at the same time.
- Decision makers are more likely to engage in escalation of commitment when they have a strong need to _____ their decision.

LO.3.

- Neuroscientific evidence says that information produced from logical analysis is tagged with _____ that then motivate us to choose or avoid a particular alternative.
- When in a positive mood, we pay less attention to details and rely on a more _____ decision routine.

- Pedro has a gut feeling that one of his major clients will switch to a competitor's product. Whether or not Pedro's gut feeling in this situation represents intuition depends largely on his level of _____ with the client and similar situations.

LO.4.

- Employee involvement tends to strengthen employee _____ to the decision because employees feel personally responsible for the decision's success.
- _____ decisions are less likely to need employee involvement because the solutions are already worked out from past incidents.
- Only a low level of employee _____ is advisable when employee goals and norms conflict with the organization's goals.

LO.5.

- The _____ stage of creativity assists divergent thinking, which involves reframing the problem in a unique way and generating different approaches to the issue.
- Employees tend to be more creative where the job has high task significance and _____.

in a nutshell

Teams have become one of the main ingredients of contemporary organizations. Team effectiveness considers the team and organizational environment, team design, and team processes. Three team design elements are task characteristics, team size, and team composition. Team decisions are impeded by time constraints, evaluation apprehension, conformity to peer pressure, and groupthink; but specific team structures potentially improve team decision making.

The following questions will test your takeaway knowledge from this chapter. How well can you answer each of them?

LO.1. Discuss the benefits and limitations of teams, and explain why people are motivated to join informal groups.

LO.2. Outline the team effectiveness model and discuss how task characteristics, team size, and team composition influence team effectiveness.

LO.3. Discuss how the four team processes—team development, norms, cohesion, and trust—influence team effectiveness.

LO.4. Discuss the characteristics and factors required for success of self-directed teams and virtual teams.

LO.5. Identify four constraints on team decision making and discuss the advantages and disadvantages of four structures aimed at improving team decision making.

Copyright © 2012 by The McGraw-Hill Companies. ISBN 0078029414 | McShane M 1e

Did your answers include the following important points?

LO.1. Discuss the benefits and limitations of teams, and explain why people are motivated to join informal groups.

- Under the right conditions, teams tend to make better decisions, develop better products and services, and create a more engaged workforce than do employees working alone. However, teams have process losses and often suffer from social loafing.
- People are motivated to join informal groups because they help to fulfill the drive to bond, maintain a person's positive self-concept, accomplish goals that are difficult to achieve alone, and reduce stress through social support.

LO.2. Outline the team effectiveness model and discuss how task characteristics, team size, and team composition influence team effectiveness.

- The team effectiveness model considers the team and organizational environment, team design, and team processes.
- The best task characteristics for teams are complex work with high task interdependence.
- Teams should have as few members as possible, yet be large enough for the requisite competencies and resources.
- Effective teams are composed of people with the competencies and motivation to perform tasks in a team environment. Team diversity has advantages and disadvantages for team performance.

LO.3. Discuss how the four team processes—team development, norms, cohesion, and trust—influence team effectiveness.

- Teams development stages include forming, storming, norming, performing, and eventually adjourning. These activities include two processes: developing team identity and developing team competence.

- Teams develop norms to regulate and guide member behavior, and these norms typically develop through initial experiences, critical events, and the values brought to the group.
- Team cohesion increases with member similarity, smaller team size, higher degree of interaction, somewhat difficult entry, team success, and external challenges.
- Team members trust each other based on three foundations: calculus, knowledge, and identification.

LO.4. Discuss the characteristics and factors required for success of self-directed teams and virtual teams.

- Self-directed teams (SDTs) tend to be more successful when they are responsible for an entire work process, when they have sufficient autonomy to organize and coordinate their work, and when the work site and technology support coordination and communication among team members and increase job enrichment.
- Virtual teams tend to be more effective when their members have communication technology skills, strong self-leadership skills, and emotional intelligence; the team has the freedom to choose the preferred communication channels; and their members meet face-to-face fairly early in the team development process.

LO.5. Identify four constraints on team decision making and discuss the advantages and disadvantages of four structures aimed at improving team decision making.

- Team decisions are impeded by time constraints, evaluation apprehension, conformity to peer pressure, and groupthink (specifically overconfidence).
- Four strategies aimed at improving team decision making are constructive conflict, brainstorming, electronic brainstorming, and nominal group technique. Each has advantages and disadvantages.

Practical Application

LO.1.

- Karen is concerned that some members of her 20-person requisition team are not pulling their weight. To minimize the risk of social loafing, Karen can try to find ways to make each team member's contribution more _____.
- People join informal groups because everyone has a drive to _____.

LO.2.

- The highest level of interdependence among people is called _____ interdependence.
- Diverse teams are susceptible to _____, which may split a team into subgroups.

LO.3.

- Matt recently joined a newly formed legal research team. After the initial niceties, he could see that the team was experiencing interpersonal conflict as members became more proactive and competed for various team roles. Matt's team was likely going through the _____ stage of team development.
- Teams tend to have more cohesion when team members perform highly _____ tasks.

- _____ trust alone cannot sustain a team's relationship because it relies on deterrence.

LO.4.

- Self-directed teams tend to be more effective when they have sufficient _____ to organize and coordinate their work.
- Virtual teams tend to work better when they are given plenty of _____, such as clear operational objectives and documented work processes.

LO.5.

- _____ is a typical constraint in team decision making because in most team structures only one person can speak at a time.
- The main challenge with constructive conflict is that the discussion tends to slide into _____.
- _____ is less of a problem in brainstorming teams that embrace a learning orientation culture.

ANSWERS LO1•noticeable •bond LO2•reciprocal •fault lines LO3•storming •interdependent •Calculus-based LO4•autonomy •structure LO5•Production blocking •personal attacks •Evaluation apprehension

in a nutshell

Communication, which is the lifeblood of all organizations, is the process by which information is transmitted and *understood* between two or more people. The communication process involves forming, encoding, and transmitting the intended message to a receiver, and vice versa. The best communication medium depends on its social acceptance and media richness. Effective communication also minimizes sources of noise, includes active listening, and applies several organizational-level communication practices.

The following questions will test your takeaway knowledge from this chapter. How well can you answer each of them?

LO.1. Explain why communication is important in organizations and discuss four influences on effective communication encoding and decoding.

LO.2. Compare and contrast the advantages of and problems with electronic mail, other verbal communication media, and nonverbal communication.

LO.3. Discuss social acceptance and media richness as factors when selecting a communication channel.

LO.4. Identify various barriers (noise) to effective communication, and describe strategies for getting your message across and engaging in active listening.

LO.5. Summarize communication strategies in organizational hierarchies, including the role and relevance of the organizational grapevine.

Copyright © 2012 by The McGraw-Hill Companies. ISBN 0078029414 | McShane M 1e

Did your answers include the following important points?

LO.1. Explain why communication is important in organizations and discuss four influences on effective communication encoding and decoding.

- Communication supports work coordination, organizational learning, decision making, and employee well-being.
- The communication process involves forming, encoding, and transmitting the intended message to a receiver, who then decodes the message and provides feedback to the sender.
- Four ways to improve this process are that both sender and receiver are able and motivated to communicate through the communication channel, have common codebooks, share common mental models of the communication context, and are familiar with the message topic.

LO.2. Compare and contrast the advantages of and problems with electronic mail, other verbal communication media, and nonverbal communication.

- E-mail is relatively poor at communicating emotions; it tends to reduce politeness and respect; it is an inefficient medium for communicating in ambiguous, complex, and novel situations; and it contributes to information overload.
- Compared to verbal communication, nonverbal communication is less rule-bound and is mostly automatic and nonconscious.

LO.3. Discuss social acceptance and media richness as factors when selecting a communication channel.

- The most appropriate communication medium partly depends on social acceptance factors, including organization and team norms, individual preferences for specific communication channels, and the symbolic meaning of a channel.
- Communication channels with high media richness are better in nonroutine and ambiguous situations, but we also need to consider multi-communication, user proficiency, and social distractions of rich media.

LO.4. Identify various barriers (noise) to effective communication, and describe strategies for getting your message across and engaging in active listening.

- Communication noise (barriers) include misinterpretation due to perceptual biases, filtering of a message as it gets passed up the hierarchy, misinterpretation due to jargon and ambiguous language, and screened out or misinterpreted messages due to information overload.
- Communication noise also occurs in cross-cultural settings due to language barriers and codebook differences, as well as between genders due to differ expectations in communication (report vs. rapport talk).
- To get a message across, the sender must learn to empathize with the receiver, repeat the message, choose an appropriate time for the conversation, and be descriptive rather than evaluative.
- Active listeners engage in sensing, evaluating, and responding.

LO.5. Summarize communication strategies in organizational hierarchies, including the role and relevance of the organizational grapevine.

- Three communication strategies across the hierarchy include workspace design (such as open offices and team cloisters), Internet-based newsletters, and direct interaction between senior management and employees (such as through management by walking around and town hall meetings).
- The organizational grapevine is beneficial in communicating information not available through formal channels, is main conduit for communicating organizational stories, and provides a way for employees to fulfill the drive to bond. However, it tends to distort information.

Practical Application

LO.1.
- Communication is essential because people need to _____ with each other in organizations.
- During the communication process, the sender forms a message and _____ it into words and other symbols or signs.
- Communication participants are able to encode and decode more accurately when they have similar _____.

LO.2.
- E-mail is an ineffective medium for communicating _____.
- Nonverbal communication is less _____ than verbal communication.

LO.3.
- _____ refers to how well the communication medium is approved and supported by others.
- Lean media work well in _____ situations because the sender and receiver have common expectations through shared mental models.

LO.4.
- As a senior executive, Sandra often needs to describe ill-defined or complex ideas to employees. To achieve, this Sandra often uses metaphors and other _____ language.
- Compared to men, women engage in more _____ talk.
- Sensing, evaluating, and _____ represent the listener's three stages of communication in the communication model.

LO.5.
- SoftSilk Corporation moved head office staff to a new building where almost everyone works in an open office environment rather than closed offices. The objective of this arrangement is increase communication, but it has also resulted in higher _____ among employees due to increased noise and distractions.
- A communication strategy that gets executives out of their offices to communicate more often with employees is called

  _____.
- The grapevine often escalates rather than reduces employee anxiety because it _____ the original information.

ANSWERS LO1•coordinate •encodes •codebooks LO2•emotions •rule-bound LO3•Social acceptance •routine LO4•ambiguous •rapport •responding LO5•stress •management by walking around •distorts

in a nutshell

Power, the capacity to influence others, originates from legitimate, reward, coercive, expert, and referent sources and depends on nonsubstitutability, centrality, discretion, and visibility. Influence, or power in action, refers to any behavior that attempts to alter someone's attitudes or behavior. The main influence tactics are silent authority, assertiveness, information control, coalition formation, upward appeal, persuasion, ingratiation, and impression management, and exchange. Organizational politics refers to perceived self-serving influence tactics.

The following questions will test your takeaway knowledge from this chapter. How well can you answer each of them?

LO.1. Define power and describe the five sources of power in organizations as well as the two types of information-based power.

LO.2. Discuss the four contingencies of power and explain how social networking increases a person's power.

LO.3. Describe eight types of influence tactics, three consequences of influencing others, and three contingencies to consider when choosing an influence tactic.

LO.4. Identify the organizational conditions and personal characteristics that support organizational politics, as well as ways to minimize organizational politics.

Copyright © 2012 by The McGraw-Hill Companies. ISBN 0078029414 | McShane M 1e

Did your answers include the following important points?

LO.1. Define power and describe the five sources of power in organizations as well as the two types of information-based power.

- Power, the capacity to influence others, exists when one party perceives that he or she is dependent on the other for something of value.
- The five sources of power are legitimate (role-based right to request compliance), reward (ability to distribute rewards), coercive (ability to distribute punishment), expert (valued specialized knowledge), and referent (identification-based power).
- Employees gain power by controlling the flow of information that others need (based on legitimate power) and by being able to cope with uncertainties related to important organizational goals (based on expert power).

LO.2. Discuss the four contingencies of power and explain how social networking increases a person's power.

- People are more powerful when they are non-substitutable (such as by controlling tasks, knowledge, and labor, and by differentiating themselves), have high centrality (the number of people affected and how quickly they are affected), have high discretion (freedom to exercise judgment), and have high visibility (their sources of power are known to others).
- Social networking strengthens an individual's power by increasing his or her social capital (knowledge and other resources available through the social network), referent power by people in the network, and visibility and centrality due to connections with others.

LO.3. Describe eight types of influence tactics, three consequences of influencing others, and three contingencies to consider when choosing an influence tactic.

- Eight types of influence tactics include silent authority, assertiveness, information control, coalitions, upward appeal, persuasion, ingratiation, and exchange.
- The three consequences of influencing others are resistance, compliance, and commitment.
- The most appropriate influence tactic depends on which power source is strongest for the powerholder, the target person's relative position in the organization, and on personal, organizational, and cultural values.

LO.4. Identify the organizational conditions and personal characteristics that support organizational politics, as well as ways to minimize organizational politics.

- Organizational politics are behaviors perceived as self-serving tactics at the expense of others.
- Organizational politics is more likely to occur where there are scarce resources and where resource allocation decisions are ambiguous or lack formal rules (such as during organizational change).
- Individuals with a strong need for personal as opposed to socialized power and those with strong Machiavellian values are more likely to engage in organizational politics.
- Organizational politics can be minimized by introducing clear rules and regulations, applying effective organizational change practices, actively managing group norms, having leaders role model organizational citizenship, and giving employees more control over their work and keeping them informed of organizational events.

Practical Application

LO.1.
- The most basic prerequisite of power is that one person is _____ on another person or group for a resource of value.
- Legitimate, reward, and coercive power originate mainly from the _____ rather than the person.
- Ralph is a troubleshooter sent to branches where there have been sudden problems with theft, morale, or customer defections; within a few months he is usually able to improve the branch's performance. Ralph has power in the organization because he has the ability to help the organization cope with _____.

LO.2.
- Nonsubstitutability is strengthened by _____ access to the resource.
- People have high centrality when their actions affect many people and affect them _____.
- Social networks increase the flow of _____ among those within the network.

LO.3.
- A coalition can be a powerful influence tactic when others recognize that the existence of the coalition _____ the legitimacy of the issue.
- When persuading others, the _____ causes listeners to generate counterarguments to the anticipated persuasion attempts, which makes the opponent's subsequent persuasion attempts less effective.
- The most appropriate influence strategy depends on which source of power is _____.

LO.4.
- Organizational politics exists when people use _____ that are perceived by others as self-serving (i.e., for personal gain).
- Employees who engage in more organizational politics tend to have a strong need for _____ rather than socialized power.
- Organizational politics can be minimized by introducing clear _____ to specify the use of scarce resources.

in a nutshell

Conflict, which occurs when one party perceives that its interests are being opposed or negatively affected by another party, has both good and bad consequences for organizations and individuals. Conflict originates from incompatible goals, differentiation, interdependence, scarce resources, ambiguous rules, and communication problems. People approach conflict with one of the five conflict handling styles, the best of which depends on the situation. Conflict can be minimized through the structural practices of emphasizing superordinate goals, reducing differentiation, improving communication and understanding, reducing interdependence, increasing resources, and clarifying rules and procedures. Third-party interventions also help manage conflict.

The following questions will test your takeaway knowledge from this chapter. How well can you answer each of them?

LO.1. Debate the positive and negative consequences of conflict in the workplace.

LO.2. Distinguish constructive from relationship conflict and describe three strategies to minimize relationship conflict during constructive conflict episodes.

LO.3. Diagram the conflict process model and describe six structural sources of conflict in organizations.

LO.4. Outline the five conflict handling styles and discuss the circumstances in which each would be most appropriate.

LO.5. Compare and contrast six structural approaches to managing conflict and three types of third-party dispute resolution.

Copyright © 2012 by The McGraw-Hill Companies. ISBN 0078029414 | McShane M 1e

Did your answers include the following important points?

LO.1. Debate the positive and negative consequences of conflict in the workplace.

- Conflict potentially reduces job satisfaction, team cohesion, resource sharing, and productivity, while it tends to increase stress, turnover, and organizational politics.
- Moderate levels of conflict can improve decision making, organizational responsiveness to the environment, and team cohesion (when conflict is with sources outside the team).

LO.2. Distinguish constructive from relationship conflict and describe three strategies to minimize relationship conflict during constructive conflict episodes.

- Constructive conflict focuses on issues and a logical evaluation of ideas, whereas relationship conflict pays attention to interpersonal incompatibilities and flaws.
- Relationship conflict is less likely to dominate when the parties are emotionally intelligent, have a cohesive team, and have supportive team norms.

LO.3. Diagram the conflict process model and describe six structural sources of conflict in organizations.

- The conflict process model begins with the six structural sources of conflict, which cause conflict perceptions and emotions which, in turn, produce manifest conflict and conflict outcomes.
- The six structural sources of conflict include incompatible goals, differentiation (different values and beliefs), interdependence, scarce resources, ambiguous rules, and communication problems.

- The six structural sources of conflict include incompatible goals, differentiation (different values and beliefs), interdependence, scarce resources, ambiguous rules, and communication problems.

LO.4. Outline the five conflict handling styles and discuss the circumstances in which each would be most appropriate.

- The five conflict handling styles are problem solving, forcing, avoiding, yielding, and compromising.
- The problem solving style is best when interests are not completely opposing; forcing tends to be best when you have a strong conviction to your position; avoiding is best when conflict has become emotionally charged; yielding is best to situations where the other party has more power and clarity in their position; and compromising is best when there is time pressure and equal power.

LO.5. Compare and contrast six structural approaches to managing conflict and three types of third-party dispute resolution.

- The six structural approaches to managing conflict include emphasizing superordinate goals (focusing attention on higher-level common goals), reducing differentiation (developing shared experiences and beliefs), improving communication and understanding (applying the contact hypothesis), reducing interdependence, increasing resources (i.e. reducing scarcity), and clarifying rules and procedures
- Three types of third-party dispute resolution activities include arbitration (high decision control, low process control), inquisition (high decision control, high process control), and mediation (low decision control, high process control).

Practical Application

LO.1.

- When people experience conflict, they are less motivated to _____ resources with the other party.
- A moderate level of conflict encourages _____, which results in a closer examination of basic assumptions behind each party's preferences.

LO.2.

- Constructive conflict keeps the debate focused on the _____ rather than on the participants.
- Relationship conflict is less likely to occur or escalate when the parties have high levels of _____.
- Team members are motivated to avoid escalating relationship conflict when there is a high level of team _____.

LO.3.

- The conflict process model begins with the _____ of conflict.
- _____ potentially generates conflict where people have different backgrounds, values, and experiences.
- Conflict is more likely to occur where rules governing the distribution of resources are _____.

LO.4.

- _____ is the only conflict handling style with a purely win–win orientation.
- The _____ style of conflict resolution generates relationship conflict more quickly or intensely than other conflict handling styles.
- The compromising style may be best when there is _____ power between the parties.

LO.5.

- Senior management at a consumer products firm wants to reduce conflict incidents between engineering and marketing staff through an intervention that supposedly helps the two groups to understand each other better. However, the conflict management literature suggests that senior management should introduce this intervention only after _____ between the two sides has been reduced.
- Buffers and integrators represent two ways of managing conflict by reducing _____ between the conflicting parties.
- Mediators have high control over the intervention process but little or no control over the conflict resolution _____.

ANSWERS LO1•share •debate LO2•issue •emotional intelligence •cohesion LO3•sources LO3•Differentiation •ambiguous LO4•Problem solving •forcing •equal LO5 •differentiation •decision

in a nutshell

Leadership—the ability to influence, motivate, and enable others—can be understood from five perspectives: competency, behavioral, contingency, transformational, and implicit. Effective leaders have specific personality characteristics, positive self-concept, drive, integrity, leadership motivation, knowledge of the business, cognitive and practical intelligence, and emotional intelligence. Transformational leaders create a strategic vision, communicate that vision, model the vision, and build commitment toward the vision. Leaders adapt their style to the situation and need to be aware of implicit expectations followers have of leaders.

The following questions will test your takeaway knowledge from this chapter. How well can you answer each of them?

LO.1. Define *leadership* and *shared leadership*.

LO.2. Describe the competency and behavioral perspectives of leadership.

LO.3. Discuss the key elements of path-goal theory, Fiedler's contingency model, and leadership substitutes.

LO.4. Describe the four elements of transformational leadership and distinguish this theory from transactional and charismatic leadership.

LO.5. Describe the implicit leadership perspective.

LO.6. Discuss the similarities and differences in leadership across cultures and between genders.

Copyright © 2012 by The McGraw-Hill Companies. ISBN 0078029414 | McShane M 1e

Did your answers include the following important points?

LO.1. Define *leadership* and *shared leadership*.

- Leadership is defined as the ability to influence, motivate, and enable others to contribute toward the organization's effectiveness.
- Shared leadership means that leadership is broadly distributed rather than assigned to one person within the team and organization.

LO.2. Describe the competency and behavioral perspectives of leadership.

- Effective leaders have specific personality characteristics (particularly extraversion and conscientiousness), positive self-concept, drive, integrity, leadership motivation, knowledge of the business, cognitive and practical Intelligence, and emotional intelligence.
- Another leadership competency is authentic leadership, which refers to how well leaders are aware of, feel comfortable with, and act consistently with their self-concept.
- The behavioral perspective of leadership suggests that effective leaders have high levels of people-oriented and task-oriented leadership style.

LO.3. Discuss the key elements of path-goal theory, Fiedler's contingency model, and leadership substitutes.

- The path-goal theory of leadership identifies four leadership styles-directive, supportive, participative, and achievement-oriented—and states that the best leadership style depends on several contingencies relating to the characteristics of the employee and of the situation.
- According to Fiedler's contingency model, leader effectiveness depends on whether the person's natural leadership style is appropriately matched to the situation.

- Leadership substitutes theory identifies contingencies that either limit the leader's ability to influence subordinates or make that particular leadership style unnecessary.

LO.4. Describe the four elements of transformational leadership and distinguish this theory from transactional and charismatic leadership.

- Transformational leadership consists of a set of behaviors that include establishing a strategic vision, communicating that vision in an appealing way, enacting the vision (i.e. acting consistently with the vision), and building employee commitment to the strategic vision.
- Transactional leadership relies mainly on rewards, punishment, and negotiation; charismatic leadership relies on the leader's referent power over followers.

LO.5. Describe the implicit leadership perspective.

- The implicit leadership perspective states that people (a) evaluate the leader's effectiveness through prototypes, and (b) experience perceptual distortions to support their belief that leaders make a difference.

LO.6. Discuss the similarities and differences in leadership across cultures and between genders.

- Leadership varies to some degree across cultures because culture shapes the leader's values and norms, as well as the expectations that followers have of their leaders.
- Female leaders tend to be more participative style, but men and women do not vary in terms of people-oriented or task-oriented leadership.

Practical Application

LO.1.

- Leaders apply various forms of _____ to ensure that followers have the motivation and role clarity to achieve specified goals.
- Shared leadership requires a/an _____ rather than internally competitive culture.

LO.2.

- As a regional manager, Sophia engages in _____ leadership by receiving feedback from trusted people about her leadership performance and acting consistently with her values.
- Anders is a popular boss with his employees. He listens to employee suggestions, helps them out with work and personal problems, supports their interests, and treats them with respect. Anders exhibits a high degree of the _____ leadership style.

LO.3.

- According to path–goal theory research, leaders should use the _____ leadership style where employees work in teams with low team cohesion.
- Based on the leadership substitutes theory, performance-based reward systems might replace or reduce the need for _____ leadership.

LO.4.

- Transformational leadership views effective leaders as agents of _____.

- Charismatic leadership is based on a personal trait that provides _____ power over followers.
- When Jason Leung became president of Far East Widgets, he repeatedly stated that the company's success depended on a more customer-centric focus. Jason demonstrated this vision in many ways, including personally meeting with the major customers every month and holding quarterly roundtable sessions with a large group of employees each quarter where customer issues were discussed. As a transformational leader, Jason has been _____ his vision.

LO.5.

- The implicit leadership theory states that everyone has preconceived beliefs about the features and behaviors of effective leaders, called leadership _____.
- One element of the implicit leadership perspective states that people _____ their perceptions of the leader's influence over the environment.

LO.6.

- Field settings have generally found that male and female leaders engage in _____ levels of task-oriented or people-oriented leadership.
- There is some evidence that women are rated higher than men on the emerging leadership qualities of teamwork, empowering, and _____ employees.

in a nutshell

All organizational structures divide labor into distinct tasks and coordinate that labor to accomplish common goals. The four basic elements of organizational structure include span of control, centralization, formalization, and departmentalization. Various forms of departmentalization include simple, functional, divisional, team-based, matrix, and network. The best organizational structure depends on the firm's external environment, size, technology, and strategy.

The following questions will test your takeaway knowledge from this chapter. How well can you answer each of them?

LO.1. Describe three types of coordination in organizational structures.

LO.2. Discuss the advantages and disadvantages of span of control, centralization and formalization and relate these elements to organic and mechanistic organizational structures.

LO.3. Identify and evaluate six types of departmentalization.

LO.4. Explain how the external environment, organizational size, technology, and strategy are relevant when designing an organizational structure.

Copyright © 2012 by The McGraw-Hill Companies. ISBN 0078029414 | McShane M 1e

Did your answers include the following important points?

LO.1. Describe three types of coordination in organizational structures.

- All organizational structures divide labor into distinct tasks and coordinate that labor to accomplish common goals.
- The primary means of coordination are informal communication, formal hierarchy, and standardization, the latter of which includes standardization of skills, processes, and output. .

LO.2. Discuss the advantages and disadvantages of span of control, centralization and formalization and relate these elements to organic and mechanistic organizational structures.

- The optimal span of control (the number of people directly reporting to the next level in the hierarchy) depends on: (a) the presence of coordinating mechanisms other than formal hierarchy, (b) whether employees perform routine tasks, and (c) the degree of interdependence among employees within the department.
- Companies need to decentralize as they get larger and more complex, yet they also need to centralize some functions to realize cost efficiencies.
- Formalization potentially increases efficiency and compliance, but it may reduce organizational flexibility, organizational learning and creativity, and job satisfaction.
- A mechanistic organizational structure has a narrow span of control and high degree of formalization and centralization, whereas an organic structure has a wide span of control, decentralized decision making, and little formalization.

LO.3. Identify and evaluate six types of departmentalization.

- The six types of departmentalization are simple structure, functional structure, divisional structure (geographic, product,

client), team-based structure, matrix structure, and network structure.

- The functional structure offers economies of scale and easier supervision, but tends to focus employees on their expertise rather than the organization's objectives.
- The divisional organizational structure accommodates growth, but tends to duplicate resources and create silos of knowledge.
- A team-based organizational structure tends to be flexible and responsive, but may have higher employee development costs.
- The matrix structure usually makes very good use of resources and expertise and may improve communication and innovation, but it tends to produce conflict and stress among managers and employees.
- The network structure is more flexible and may produce higher efficiency, but exposes the core firm to market forces.

LO.4. Explain the relevance of external environment characteristics, organizational size, technology, and strategy when designing organizational structures.

- The four sets of external environments are dynamic/stable, complex/simple, diverse/integrated, and hostile/munificent.
- Organizations should be organic in dynamic and hostile environments, decentralize in complex environments, and rely on a corresponding divisional structure in diverse environments.
- Larger organizations require more elaborate coordinating mechanisms (typically standardization) and need to be more decentralized.
- An organic structure should be introduced where employees perform tasks with high variety and low analyzability, and where the organization's strategy is to compete through innovation.

Practical Application

LO.1.
- An organization's optimal level of division of labor partly depends on how well those people can _____ with each other.
- Soapy Brothers Inc., a major household goods company, relies on brand managers as integrators who coordinate product sales, marketing, manufacturing, purchasing, and so on. These brand managers represent a coordinating mechanism through _____.

LO.2.
- HyperComp Inc.'s large customer support center employs hundreds of employees, most of whom answer fairly well-structured issues with customers. Most problems are routine or are quickly addressed by call center staff if they use the online diagnostic "wizard" tool while talking to customers. HyperComp's customer support center should have a/an _____ span of control.
- Companies tend to have more _____ when they operate in environments with considerable government regulation and rules.
- Mechanistic structures operate better in _____ environments.

LO.3.
- Compared with other organizational structures, the functional structure usually produces more _____ and poorer coordination in serving clients.
- The divisional organizational structure is called a _____ structure because it accommodates growth relatively easily.
- Large global firms with a matrix organizational structure often design their matrix structure with _____ divisions on one axis and products/services or client divisions on the other.
- The best divisional structure to adopt is the one with the highest degree of uncertainty or _____.

LO.4.
- The more diversified its environment, the more a firm needs to use a/an _____ structure aligned with that diversity.
- As organizations get larger, they have greater division of labor and more specialized jobs, which require more elaborate forms of _____.
- A/an _____ structure is preferred where the technology has low variability and high analyzability, such as an assembly line.

in a nutshell

Organizational culture refers to the values and assumptions shared within an organization. Artifacts—including organizational stories and legends, rituals and ceremonies, language, physical structures and symbols—are the observable symbols and signs of an organization's culture. A strong organizational culture provides social control, social glue, and sense making, but strong cultures also have disadvantages. With difficulty, organizational culture may be changed or strengthened through the founder's or leader's actions; by aligning artifacts with the desired culture and introducing culturally consistent rewards; and by attracting, selecting, and socializing employees correctly.

The following questions will test your takeaway knowledge from this chapter. How well can you answer each of them?

LO.1. Describe the elements of organizational culture and discuss the importance of organizational subcultures.

LO.2. List four categories of artifacts through which corporate culture is deciphered.

LO.3. Discuss the importance of organizational culture and the conditions under which organizational culture strength improves organizational performance.

LO.4. Compare and contrast four strategies for merging organizational cultures.

LO.5. Identify four strategies for changing or strengthening an organization's culture, including the application of attraction-selection-attrition theory.

LO.6. Describe the organizational socialization process and identify strategies to improve that process.

Copyright © 2012 by The McGraw-Hill Companies. ISBN 0078029414 | McShane M 1e

Did your answers include the following important points?

LO.1. Describe the elements of organizational culture and discuss the importance of organizational subcultures.

- Organizational culture consists of shared values and assumptions.
- Subcultures maintain the organization's standards of performance and ethical behavior.

LO.2. List four categories of artifacts through which corporate culture is deciphered.

- Artifacts are the observable symbols and signs of an organization's culture.
- The four broad categories of artifacts include organizational stories and legends, rituals and ceremonies, language, and physical structures and symbols.

LO.3. Discuss the importance of organizational culture and the conditions under which organizational culture strength improves organizational performance.

- A strong organizational culture provides social control (influences employee decisions and behavior), social glue (bonds people together and makes them feel part of the organization), and sense making (understanding what goes on and why things happen in the company).
- Organizational culture strength improves organizational performance when the cultural content is appropriate for the organization's environment, when the culture is not so strong that it drives out dissenting values, and when it include an adaptive culture.

LO.4. Compare and contrast four strategies for merging organizational cultures.

- Organizational culture collisions during mergers can be minimized through a bicultural audit, which diagnoses cultural relations between the companies and identifies potential clashes.

LO.5. Identify four strategies for changing or strengthening an organization's culture, including the application of attraction-selection-attrition theory.

- An organization's culture can be changed or strengthened through the actions of founders and subsequent leaders; by creating artifacts that are consistent with the desired culture, introducing reward systems that are consistent with the desired culture; and by attracting, selecting, and socializing newcomers with values consistent with the desired culture.
- Attraction-selection-attrition theory explains how companies strengthen their culture by attracting people with compatible values, screening out applicants whose values are contrary to the company's culture, and removing (turnover, dismissal) employees whose values are significantly incongruent with the company's culture.

LO.6. Describe the organizational socialization process and identify strategies to improve that process.

- Organizational socialization is the process by which individuals learn the values, expected behaviors, and social knowledge necessary to assume their roles in the organization. It includes three stages: pre-employment socialization, encounter, and role management.
- The organizational socialization process can be improved through realistic job previews (giving applicants a balanced view about the job and work context) and through the support of socialization agents.

Practical Application

LO.1.

- A major grocery chain wants to examine its organizational culture and has hired a consulting firm to survey employees about the company's dominant shared values. A significant problem with this approach is that it fails to the recognize that organizational culture also consists of shared _____.
- Countercultures embrace values or assumptions that directly _____ the organization's dominant culture.

LO.2.

- Organizational stories and physical structures are types of _____ of an organizational culture.
- The four categories of artifacts are stories, rituals/ceremonies, physical structures, and _____.

LO.3.

- In strong cultures, values and assumptions are also institutionalized through well-established _____.
- Whether a strong organizational culture improves organizational effectiveness depends on whether the organization's culture content is _____ with the external environment.
- An _____ culture exists when employees are receptive to change and have a strong sense of ownership for the organization's performance.

LO.4.

- The _____ process begins by identifying cultural differences between merging companies.
- The _____ strategy for merging organizational cultures works best when the acquired company has a weak dysfunctional culture and the acquiring company's culture is strong and aligned with the external environment.

LO.5.

- As well as providing visible indicators of a company's culture, _____ are also mechanisms that keep the culture in place.
- Attraction–selection–attrition theory states that organizations have a natural tendency to attract, select, and retain people whose _____ are consistent with the organization's character.

LO.6.

- Organizational socialization is a process of both _____ and adjustment.
- Organizational socialization consists of three stages, including preemployment socialization, encounter, and _____.
- Realistic job previews help applicants develop more _____ preemployment expectations.

in a nutshell

With an increasingly turbulent environment, change has become the only constant in organizations. The dynamics of change can be understood using Lewin's force field analysis model, which considers both driving and restraining forces. The main reasons why people resist change are direct costs, saving face, fear of the unknown, breaking routines, incongruent team dynamics, and incongruent organizational systems. These can be minimized through communication, learning, involvement, stress management, negotiation, and coercion. Four approaches to leading change include action research, appreciative inquiry, large group interventions, and parallel learning structures.

The following questions will test your takeaway knowledge from this chapter. How well can you answer each of them?

LO.1. Describe the elements of Lewin's force field analysis model.

LO.2. Discuss the reasons why people resist organizational change and outline six strategies for minimizing this resistance.

LO.3. Debate the importance of leadership in organizational change and outline the conditions for effectively diffusing change from a pilot project.

LO.4. Describe and compare action research, appreciative inquiry, large group interventions, and parallel learning structures as formal approaches to organizational change.

LO.5. Discuss two cross-cultural and three ethical issues in organizational change.

Copyright © 2012 by The McGraw-Hill Companies. ISBN 0078029414 | McShane M 1e

Did your answers include the following important points?

LO.1. Describe the elements of Lewin's force field analysis model.

- Lewin's force field analysis model states that all systems have driving and restraining forces.
- Lewin's model states that change requires unfreezing, whereby the driving and restraining forces are in disequilibrium, then refreezing by realigning the organization's systems and structures with the desired behaviors.

LO.2. Discuss the reasons why people resist organizational change and outline six strategies for minimizing this resistance.

- The main reasons why people resist change are direct costs, saving face, fear of the unknown, breaking routines, incongruent team dynamics, and incongruent organizational systems.
- Resistance to change may be minimized by keeping employees informed about what to expect from the change effort (communicating); teaching employees valuable skills for the desired future (learning); involving them in the change process; helping them to manage stress; negotiating with those who lose from the change effort; and using coercion (sparingly and as a last resort).

LO.3. Debate the importance of leadership in organizational change and outline the conditions for effectively diffusing change from a pilot project.

- Transformational leaders are agents of change by developing a vision, which creates sense of direction and establishes the critical success factors for the change. Leaders also communicating that vision, modeling the vision, and building commitment to that vision.
- The diffusion of change is more effective when employees are motivated to do so (successful pilot project, recognition for involvement), when employees are able to adopt the pilot project's practices (training and role modeling from pilot project staff), when employees have clear role perceptions (sufficiently well defined transfer of the pilot project elsewhere), and when employees have a work environment that supports the changes.

LO.4. Describe and compare action research, appreciative inquiry, large group interventions, and parallel learning structures as formal approaches to organizational change.

- Action research is a highly participative, open systems approach to change management that combines an action orientation (changing attitudes and behavior) with a research orientation (testing theory).
- Appreciative inquiry consists of four stages—discovery, dreaming, designing, and delivering—and relies on five principles, including the positive principle, constructionist principle, simultaneity principle, poetic principle, and anticipatory principle.
- Large group interventions attempt to involve as many employees and other stakeholders as possible.
- Parallel learning structures rely on social structures developed alongside the formal hierarchy.

LO.5. Discuss two cross-cultural and three ethical issues in organizational change.

- Two characteristics of Western organizational change that might clashes with other cultures are the tendency to view change as (a) a logical linear sequence and (b) one that is necessarily punctuated by tension and overt conflict.
- Three ethical concerns with organizational change are (a) individual privacy rights, (b) potentially grater management power to induce compliance and conformity, and (c) the risk of undermining employee self-esteem.

Practical Application

LO.1.
- One side of Lewin's force field model represents the _____ that push organizations toward a new state of affairs.
- Lewin's force field model states that after unfreezing the current situation and moving to a desired condition, it is important to _____ the system so it remains in the desired state.

LO.2.
- SuperCorp's senior management chose new enterprise system software different from software recommended by the company's information technology (IT) group. When the software was installed, consultants complained that the IT staff actively looked for problems and allowed any issues to escalate. These actions were forms of resistance by the IT group due to _____.
- _____ is the highest priority and first strategy required for any organizational change.

LO.3.
- People more readily adopt ideas from pilot projects when they have an opportunity to _____ from people who worked in the pilot project.
- One challenge in diffusing change is to ensure that information about the pilot project's activities is not so _____ that it might seem irrelevant to other areas of the organization.

LO.4.
- In contrast to the action research approach to organizational change, appreciative inquiry focuses on the _____ aspects of the workplace to improve organizational success and individual well-being.
- In the Four-D model of appreciative inquiry, the _____ stage involves having participants listen to each other's models and assumptions and eventually form a collective model for thinking within the team.
- Parallel learning structures are social structures developed alongside the _____ with the purpose of increasing the organization's learning.

LO.5.
- Organizational change often involves collecting information from organizational members, which raises potential ethical concerns about violating individual _____ rights.
- The unfreezing process in some change interventions requires participants to disconfirm their existing beliefs and possibly their competence, which raises ethical concerns about undermining individuals' _____.

ANSWERS LO1•driving forces •refreeze LO2•saving face •Communication LO3•learn •specific LO4•positive •designing •formal hierarchy LO5•privacy •self-esteem